MW00995639

The Gilded Age

REVISED EDITION

EYEWITNESS HISTORY

The Gilded Age

REVISED EDITION

Judith Freeman Clark

Facts On File
An imprint of Infobase Publishing

NOTE ON PHOTOS

Many of the illustrations and photographs used in this book are old, historical images. The quality of the prints is not always up to modern standards, as in some cases the originals are damaged. The content of the illustrations, however, made their inclusion important despite problems in reproduction.

The Gilded Age, Revised Edition

Copyright © 2006, 1992 by Judith Freeman Clark
Maps and graphs © 2006 by Infobase Publishing

Facts On File, Inc.
An imprint of Infobase Publishing
132 West 31st Street
New York NY 10001

ISBN-10: 0-8160-5763-X
ISBN-13: 978-0-8160-5763-4

Library of Congress Cataloging-in-Publication Data
Clark, Judith Freeman.
    The Gilded Age / Judith Freeman Clark. — Rev. ed.
        p. cm. — (Eyewitness history)
    Rev. ed. of: America's Gilded Age.
    Includes bibliographical references and index.
    ISBN 0-8160-5763-X
    1. United States—History—1865–1921—Sources. I. Clark, Judith Freeman. America's Gilded Age. II. Title. III. Eyewitness history series.
    E661.C575 2006
    973.8—dc22   2005019438

Text design by Joan M. Toro
Cover design by Cathy Rincon
Maps and graphs by Sholto Ainslie

Printed in the United States of America

VB JT 10 9 8 7 6 5 4 3 2

This book is printed on acid-free paper.

For my mother, Lillian Elizabeth Bartlett,
and for my grand-girls,
Julia Fay Hawkins and Averie Marion Hawkins

CONTENTS

PREFACE

History often defines the details of a single life, a limited chronology, or a specific event. This approach can provide a convenient context within which a subject can be reviewed, interpreted, and described. But this "definitive" approach is at odds with the reality of human experience. Americans living in the second half of the 19th century may have struggled with immigration issues, labor disputes, the settlement of western regions, economic crises, political chicanery, and cultural pluralism, but citizens rarely thought in terms of a particular era. Critics and historians were the ones who would later use lively or eponymous terms, such as the McKinley years or the Progressive era, to label a historical period. Such terms frequently derived from assessments made years later, rather than from the views of the people living at the time.

To better understand the experiences of those living in the United States between 1865 and 1901, primary sources (firsthand descriptions of issues and events) present an authentic voice that aids in the understanding of an individual, or national, experience. Candid, unedited viewpoints, such as those found in letters and diaries or on-the-spot reporting in newspapers and magazines, make events and persons come alive in ways that no third-hand report can do. An eyewitness description invariably renders facts, statistics, and analyses more human, offering a freshness lacking in most retrospective accounts.

AN ERA KNOWN BY ITS EXCESSES

Inevitably, there must be a context within which these contemporary sources and vivid, if anecdotal, stories can be presented. For the period 1865 through 1901 in the United States, the context has become known as the "Gilded Age." Unlike other such nicknames, this was an era christened by someone who lived at the time: the writer Samuel Clemens (widely known by his pen name, "Mark Twain"). A master storyteller famous for his satire, Twain coauthored *The Gilded Age* with writer Charles Dudley Warner. In their book, Twain and Warner ridiculed and otherwise exposed the manners and morals of the years following the Civil War.

The "Gilded Age" became a catchphrase for the excesses of the post–Civil War decades, pointing to the reality that underneath the glitter was a base element. Corruption seemed to prevail among elected officials, and private citizens appeared more self-interested than altruistic. During the second half of the 19th century, accumulating wealth by whatever means possible (and enjoying that wealth, often at the expense of others) was a goal of so many that Mark Twain's book *The Gilded Age* seemed less like fiction than journalism. A handful of people made vast fortunes in the railroad industry, through iron and steel production, and in other corporate endeavors; countless others scraped together a livelihood, often risking physical and mental harm in menial labor on farms, in mines, or in factories, often working 16-hour days. Many Americans lost all their assets in the cyclical economic downturns that plagued the nation between 1865 and 1901.

A PERIOD OF INNOVATION AND REFORM

While this era was marked by the contrasts between crushing poverty and opulent excess, it was also an era of innovation, invention, and imagination. Some individuals exhibited heroic commitment to civic and social responsibility, devising ways to minimize immigrants' enormous disadvantages, to encourage the development of educational opportunities, and to enhance communication among the United States and its foreign allies. Prospects were numerous for the clever and ambitious, as well as for the selfless and tireless. Those willing to take reasonable risks amassed legitimate fortunes, enabling their philanthropic support of cultural institutions like libraries, museums, colleges, and orchestras. Others applied their creativity to inventions as diverse as the "safety" bicycle, the Pullman railroad car, electric lights, the internal combustion engine, the automobile, barbed wire, the telephone, motion pictures, the gramophone, and the X-ray machine.

Congressional action of the period is especially notable for its impact on the U.S. economy, as well as its culture. Constitutional amendments and legislative initiatives enacted after 1865 set the stage for empowerment of previously disenfranchised groups. The benefits of Reconstruction, antitrust legislation, and civil service reform irrevocably changed the lives of millions of Americans.

THE RISE OF BIG BUSINESS

The business climate underwent enormous changes after the Civil War. During the Gilded Age, government encouraged private-sector expansion at levels unheard of even a few decades later, thanks to the growth of regulatory legislation. But immediately after the war, most politicians seemed willing to permit any business activity whatsoever as a way to stimulate the nation's economic development. This despite the fact that some industrial and commercial enterprise was damaging to the environment, unhealthy for workers, questionable in terms of relations with other nations, and heedless of the rights and privileges of certain racial, ethnic, or minority groups.

Development of the domestic market was promoted through passage of high tariffs on foreign imports. Senators such as Orville H. Platt of Connecticut supported protective tariffs as a way of ensuring that U.S. goods would be favored in the marketplace. Platt, James G. Blaine (R-Maine), and Nelson W. Aldrich (R-Rhode Island) came from heavily industrialized states, and they believed that imposing any limits on business through legislative initiatives, such as the Sherman Anti-Trust Act of 1890, would lead only to economic chaos.

By looking at the growth of railroads in the United States, one can see that business expansion affected the entire nation in ways that were closely interconnected. Following the Civil War, railroads seemed to be progressive benefits

Two men lead a cattle drive from Texas. *(Library of Congress)*

to society, and soon, tracks crisscrossed the country. By the 1890s, a vast net-work of tracks stretched from one coast to the other. The United States claimed 33 percent of all the world's track mileage by 1890, and railroads enjoyed virtually limitless access to whatever territory proved most promising in terms of profits.

Nonetheless, such expansion was not beneficial to all. It pushed Native Americans out of their ancestral lands, leading to devastating conflict and ill-treatment at the hands of federal authorities. Too, farmers and ranchers were faced with rising shipping rates when they attempted to take crops or stock to market. Supposing themselves to be among the beneficiaries of railroad growth, farm owners challenged the prohibitive costs imposed by railroad owners who limited access to freight transport in the interest of their own pocketbooks. As a further response to this injustice, many facing discrimination by railroad owners formed alliances to oppose railroad monopolies.

Over time, these alliances became a significant force in the general demand for business and legislative reforms in the last third of the 19th century. One of many outcomes of the pressure brought to bear by agricultural alliances such as the Granger Movement was seen in 1887, when President Grover Cleveland established the Interstate Commerce Commission (ICC) to regulate railroads. The ICC was the first in a series of efforts to position the federal government in the role of watchdog over private business.

POLITICS TRANSFORMS SOCIETY

Social and political reform, which became more prevalent during the Gilded Age, was exemplified in the Pendleton Civil Service Act. Passed in 1883 during the administration of President Chester A. Arthur (and given more power under President Cleveland), the Pendleton Act established federal civil service examinations and attempted to eliminate patronage in filling government jobs.

In other areas, social reformers such as Chicago's Jane Addams and New York City's Lillian Wald introduced a new standard of commitment and selfless service to the immigrant and U.S.-born poor. Richard T. Ely, founder of the American Economic Association, educator John Dewey, and many other reformers helped articulate how to measure the relationship between prosperity and poverty, how to develop strategies to reduce the disparity between rich and poor, and how to encourage all U.S. citizens to improve the quality of life in both rural and urban America.

Politics in Gilded Age America was tainted with the bitterness of Reconstruction, the sophistry and apathy of dozens of millionaire congressmen, and the outright corruption of some political party bosses. In the later years of the century, a steadily growing controversy emerged, focusing on overseas expansion by the United States. Beginning in the 1880s, imperialists and anti-imperialists in Congress clashed over what role the United States was to play on the world stage. The thought of expanded trade opportunities for domestic products fueled the desire for a strengthened U.S. presence worldwide, but the appeal of increasing the territorial advantage of the United States was equally important to imperialists. Eventually, the imperialists would win the argument—but only after leading the nation into war with Spain on the strength of U.S. "assistance" for Cuban freedom fighters.

IMMIGRATION ENHANCES THE LANDSCAPE

Gilded Age immigration trends radically altered the national culture—perhaps more so even than industrial development or territorial expansion. Between the end of the Civil War and the turn of the century, roughly 10 million immigrants arrived from Europe, South America, Africa, and Asia. All hoped to find greater economic opportunity, pursue religious practices and beliefs, and enjoy the fruits of democracy with children and grandchildren. Their arrival during several decades had a sustained impact on the United States, providing a seemingly inexhaustible supply of cheap labor and creating instant markets for food, housing, and clothing. Some newcomers continued to the nation's interior, where they settled on prairie lands formerly uninhabited by anyone other than indigenous peoples of the region. The immigrants who chose life on the frontier cultivated the land, built communities, and developed what would later be termed the "breadbasket" region of the United States. Others flooded into existing urban areas like Boston, New York, Chicago, and San Francisco. There, they strained the municipal infrastructure and moved into overpopulated tenement slums. Native-born American citizens soon began to question the wisdom of encouraging—or even permitting—foreign-born immigrants' entry into the United States. These questions led, ultimately, to "protective" legislation, development of annual quotas, and limiting certain racial, ethnic, or national groups from making the United States their permanent home.

Yet others felt that these waves of foreign immigrants contained an untapped reservoir of energy, creativity, and commitment. Many saw that contributions from countless individuals, of every imaginable nationality or ethnicity, enabled the United States to grow and to develop its many strands of commerce and industry. The skills and abilities of transplanted citizens were, these optimists argued, key to strengthening the United States and making it more resilient—through farming, manufacturing, mining, banking, science, the arts, architecture, medicine, and myriad other attributes of a healthy culture.

Many who witnessed changes in the U.S. social fabric as a result of immigration—and were unafraid of such changes—agreed with Hull-House founder Jane Addams, of Chicago, Illinois. Throughout her career, Addams expressed a calm confidence in people's ability to "live quietly side by side with their neighbors, until they grow into a sense of relationship and mutual interests."[1]

ABOUT THE REVISED EDITION

Thanks to the proliferation of digital archives and Internet repositories of historical data, opportunities to research and incorporate previously inaccessible materials have grown significantly since the first edition of this volume appeared in the early 1990s. The simplicity of searching for, and the ease of online access to, sources such as U.S. Census records and geographical data, library archives and museum collections, and newspapers, magazines, and government documents, has contributed to an enhanced Eyewitness Testimony section, better and more detailed biographies, and expanded appendices in this revised edition of *The Gilded Age*.

Excerpts from letters, journals, and diary entries broaden the eyewitness commentary, providing readers with a greater number of intimate accounts and perspectives of events and issues than had previously been included. One letter in particular deserves mention with respect to its candor: the so-called de Lôme Letter, written to an associate in Spain by that nation's envoy, Enrique Dupuy de Lôme. The letter, which fell into the possession of a newspaper editor, was published in December 1897. Because of Enrique de Lôme's opinion of President McKinley and views about Spain's disposition of Cuba (which at that time was still a Spanish possession), candidly stated in the letter, a public outcry against Spain ensued. In the letter, the text of which appears in full in Appendix C, de Lôme notes that ". . . McKinley [is] weak and a bidder for the admiration of the crowd besides being a would-be politician [politicastro] who tries to leave a door open behind himself while keeping on good terms with the jingoes of his party." This letter assisted those in Washington, D.C., who favored war with Spain, and made the task of persuading others to support military action that much easier.

Public documents, no less than personal letters, also assist the reader to better grasp the story behind the historical record. In particular, a more generous inclusion of the full texts of Gilded Age legislation enhances the revised edition. Many of these acts of Congress underscore how reforms of, and revisions to, public policy were virtually mandated by some of the more sweeping technological innovations of the era. An example can be seen in Section 2 of the Interstate Commerce Act, which illustrates how railroad growth and expansion in the United States during the second half of the 19th century increased the likelihood that some groups or individuals would be favored at the expense of others in terms of rates, fees, and the like.

Accordingly, in passing the Interstate Commerce Act of 1887, Congress specifically noted:

That if any common carrier subject to the provisions of this act shall, directly or indirectly, by any special rate, rebate, drawback, or other device, charge, demand, collect, or receive from any person or persons a greater or less compensation for any service rendered, or to be rendered, in the transportation of passengers or property, subject to the provisions of this act, than it charges, demands, collects, or receives from any other person or persons for doing for him or them a like and contemporaneous service in the transportation of a like kind of traffic under substantially similar circumstances and conditions, *such common carrier shall be deemed guilty of unjust discrimination, which is hereby prohibited and declared to be unlawful.* [emphasis added]

An interestingly poignant combination of a public document with a personal letter to the U.S. House of Representatives appears in the appendix. In the text of the Joint Resolution to Provide for Annexing the Hawaiian Islands, of December 1898, is the official addendum of a statement of Queen Liliuokalani of Hawaii. In her statement, she appeals to Congress for return of her property:

I, Liliuokalani of Hawaii, named heir apparent on the 10th day of April, 1877, and proclaimed Queen of the Hawaiian Islands on the 29th day of January, 1891, do hereby earnestly and respectfully protest against the assertion of ownership by the United States of America of the so-called Hawaiian Crown Islands amounting to about one million acres and *which are my property.* [emphasis added]

In light of 21st-century debates concerning the exercise of imperial impulses and the respect (or lack thereof) of national sovereignty, one is invited to judge how the United States conducted its diplomacy with smaller, weaker, or less affluent nations during the Gilded Age. With the addition of key documents such as this one (above), the reader is afforded more and better information with which to enter such debates.

This revised edition includes a number of redrawn maps and charts. They have been assigned easy-to-read labels and more comprehensive keys to their use. The inclusion of charts showing all presidential election data for the years 1868–1904 gives readers the opportunity to form a broader understanding of the unique political forces at work during those years. The charts heighten awareness of Gilded Age geography and the significance of changes occurring politically as new states and territories became part of the United States.

In the biographies section of the revised edition, new and more comprehensive facts have been added to all biographical entries appearing in the first edition. Moreover, dozens of new entries have been added, and details have been provided concerning all candidates for president of the United States. In this way, the revised edition of *The Gilded Age* seeks to offer more complete and easily accessed information about those whose contributions to politics, education, industry, medicine, technology, commerce, and the arts transformed the United States between 1865 and 1901.

ACKNOWLEDGMENTS

Many people helped guide this book from idea to completed manuscript, and then on to this revised edition. Elizabeth Frost-Knappman, of New England Publishing Associates, provided encouragement whenever I needed it most. And I am deeply grateful to my daughter, Stephanie E. Hawkins for her enduring optimism, her wit, and her fresh perspective on publishing.

While I was preparing the original manuscript of *America's Gilded Age,* my professors in the History Department at the University of Massachusetts at Amherst gave me wise counsel. I thank Gerald McFarland for his cordial encouragement while I worked on the first edition of this book. My deep gratitude goes to Miriam U. Chrisman, emeritus professor of history, University of Massachusetts at Amherst, for her guidance, scholarly advice, and—most of all—her friendship.

My son Timothy S. Hawkins, my daughter-in-law Wendy S. Hawkins, and my grand-girls—Julia F. Hawkins and Averie M. Hawkins—made sure I had enough family time during which to recharge my batteries as I worked on this project. Finally, my husband, Robin E. Clark, deserves special mention. His understanding and support (and his courteous silence whenever I mentioned "book revision" or "deadline") makes it all possible.

1 Reconstruction, Reunion, Reconciliation
1865–1870

THE BACKGROUND

The Civil War began with an attack on Fort Sumter, South Carolina, on April 12, 1861.[1] The war lasted until April 1865, during which time the shattered nation's financial and human resources were devoted almost exclusively to the war effort. In early September 1864, Union general William Tecumseh Sherman's troops had occupied Atlanta, Georgia. Two months later his army began to move east, toward Savannah, in the now-infamous "March to the Sea." A month later, Sherman reached that coastal city, capturing it on December 22, 1864,[2] after a 10-day siege. With this triumph, the Confederacy's resolve was broken. A Northern victory was virtually ensured by January 1865 when, with the rebel resistance in tatters, federal troops prepared for a final assault on the Army of the Confederacy.

On January 15, 1865, North Carolina's Fort Fisher, home to 2,000 Southern soldiers, fell to Northern troops. This defeat meant that the Confederate port at Wilmington, North Carolina, was blockaded. Only the port at Galveston, Texas, was now open to Southern blockade-runners.

On January 31, 1865, the U.S. House of Representatives, confident that a Northern victory was on the horizon, passed the Thirteenth Amendment to the U.S. Constitution, abolishing slavery in all states.[3] On April 1, 1865, Union forces under the command of General Sheridan defeated Confederate troops, led by General Pickett, at Five Forks, Virginia. Federal soldiers took possession of Richmond, Virginia, on April 3.

As Confederate president Jefferson Davis retreated to Danville, Petersburg, Virginia, was evacuated pending occupation by Union forces. This retreat destroyed any hope of a Southern rally, and on April 9, 1865, at Appomattox Court House, General Robert E. Lee surrendered command of the Army of the Confederacy to Union General Ulysses S. Grant.[4]

The Union's military triumph in the South was moderated by several factors. Perhaps most significant was the task of reconciliation between former enemies. General Sherman's "March to the Sea" and Union soldiers' destruction of Southern property had made a rapid and seamless economic recovery impossible. Even more challenging was the deepening of the existing rift between Northerners and Southerners in the wake of this destruction.

The negative impact of the war cannot be underestimated. The cost in terms of human life was considerable, even by 21st-century standards: The combined death toll among the armies of the North and South, from battle injuries and from disease, was more than 1 million. And since civilian casualties added significantly to this number, it is obvious why the postwar period was, for so many, full of heartbreak, chaos, and desolation.

It would be decades before the former Confederate states began to regain even a semblance of stability, socially, culturally, and economically. It would take years for many in the South to overcome their intense hatred of all the North had done in the name of preserving the Union.

The President Is Assassinated

In mid-1865, war-weary Americans contemplated what the news of Lee's surrender to Grant might mean. However, this reverie was interrupted when national tragedy struck again. Just days after the announcement of the Confederacy's surrender came a shocking, almost unbelievable, news bulletin that President Abraham Lincoln had been assassinated. On April 14, the actor John Wilkes Booth, an ardent supporter of the now-defeated Confederacy, shot the president, who was attending a play at Ford's Theater, in Washington, D.C.

Early the next morning, the 56-year-old Lincoln, who had been so recently inaugurated into a second term of office, died of his wounds.[5] Immediately, Vice President Andrew Johnson was sworn in, becoming the 17th president of the United States. Grief-stricken Northerners struggled with private sorrows, and the tragic implications for the country, at the news about Lincoln. Many in the South celebrated his death. None, however, could claim with any certainty what the next several months might bring to a nation that had so recently rejoiced at the news about peace. It was unclear what President Johnson's approach to reunion would be, although he was known to be in sympathy with those Southern states who hoped for a quick and simple readmission process.

The Bumpy Road to Reconstruction

On December 4, 1865, President Andrew Johnson appointed the Joint Committee on Reconstruction.[6] This group, formed according to a plan put in place by President Lincoln before his death, would oversee the former Confederate states' readmission to the Union. Any hope that the committee would look kindly upon those who had participated in armed rebellion was quietly disposed of two weeks later.

On December 18, 1865, the Thirteenth Amendment (previously passed by the House of Representatives in January), abolishing slavery in all states, was ratified. The Fourteenth Amendment, ratified in 1868, granted full citizenship to male former slaves and guaranteed them the right to vote in federal elections.[7] The Fifteenth Amendment, ratified in 1870, protects individuals' voting rights against any actions by individual states.

President Johnson, eager to put the war in the past, announced in early 1866 that the insurrection was at an end. In June, the federal government's reconstruction initiatives, which included a proposed amnesty plan, were announced.

Attempts to reincorporate the former Confederate states into the Union were not enthusiastically embraced by everyone in the government, however. Reconstruction Acts proposed by a Radical Republican Congress placed restrictive conditions on readmission of former Confederate states. This series of legislative acts prompted President Johnson to fight congressional efforts at reunion, thereby revealing the deep rift that existed between Congress and the executive branch.

President Johnson Is Brought to Trial

Congressional dislike of President Johnson was of no small significance in the struggle to reconstruct the Union. Feelings against him were so great that the Senate began proceedings to remove him from office. His opposition to congressional reconstruction policies, and his vociferous criticism, were the chief reasons behind the attempts to impeach the president, but the official charge brought against him was violation of the Tenure of Office Act. (The president had removed Secretary of War Stanton from the cabinet because of Stanton's support of Reconstruction policies.)

During the Senate's impeachment trial, however, the president was found to be technically within his rights in removing the secretary of war, despite the opinion that he had been heavy-handed in his action. Johnson's supporters in the government and elsewhere vigorously argued against setting the precedent that would allow removal of a sitting president over disagreements with a majority in the Congress.

Thanks to a single-vote margin at the trial, President Johnson was able to finish his term in office.[8] Yet the ensuing stalemate between him and the Congress made speedy or simple reconciliation of the once-divided nation virtually impossible. Ultimately, the ideological split between the legislative and executive branches of government over how to repair the Union accomplished little except to deepen the divisiveness, add to the turmoil, and heighten the uncertainty in both the South and the North. On Christmas Day in 1868, in one of his final official acts as president, Andrew Johnson declared a general amnesty for all who had supported the Confederacy by fighting against the Union.

The Economic Effects of Reconstruction

The federal government faced an enormous set of obstacles as it set about rebuilding a political structure that had been fractured by civil strife. Reconstruction meant many things. The most far-reaching and controversial efforts were the Radical Republicans' Reconstruction policies. In the eyes of many Americans, reconstruction did not promote but, rather, delayed healing the nation's social, economic, and political wounds.

To rebuild meant to develop a new vision of what the United States could be as a nation, and how to make that vision a reality. Prior to the Confederate attack on Fort Sumter, most Americans cherished a frontier vision characteristic of the antebellum era. Growth was measured in acres, and personal success depended upon the extent of a farm or homestead. And although industrial innovations and technologies had begun to make changes in the economy of the early 1800s, it remained true that agriculture (and commerce related to land use) was the gauge of success and security.

After the war, this began to change rapidly. Opportunities abounded for various types of expansion, some agricultural, some variations of, or improvement on, existing manufacturing technologies. New prospects in all areas called for fresh skills, innovative thinking, and the courage and capacity for financial, political, and cultural risk-taking. In the aftermath of war, many were eager to explore—and exploit—every possible avenue.

The year 1865 marked a positive turning point for many Americans, despite the difficulty facing so many in the battle-scarred South. The decade following the war offered almost limitless possibilities for those willing, and able, to take advantage of them. During the years immediately after General Lee's surrender, federal legislation, economic policy, cultural shifts, scientific and technological advances, and social reforms would alter the nation's character and its physical qualities in complex, far-reaching ways.

Human Gains and Losses Resulting from Reconstruction

Of immediate concern to many in the federal government were issues pertaining to equality between the races. Supporters of Radical Reconstruction raised legitimate questions about how well the U.S. Constitution served the needs of all people. Their legacy of civil rights legislation remains in place today, however difficult it may have been for those in the former Confederate states to accommodate such changes right after the Civil War ended.

Too, federal land-use legislation changed the lives of millions of people, as it opened up the western regions of North America to development. Such expansion had the unfortunate effect of displacing many Native Americans, curtailing their access to their ancestral homelands and restricting their civil liberties. Among the tragedies of the immediate postwar period was the U.S. Army's increasing focus on control and restriction of many American Indian tribes.

As white settlement of the Great Plains and western regions grew, even the largest of the Native American nations encountered federal demands to relocate. These demands often were accompanied by the pressure of overwhelming military force, but the American Indians in large part rejected such demands, resulting in their virtual annihilation by U.S. Army troops.[9]

During the postwar period, immigration policies shaped and sought to control urban growth and development. Such policies also affected western regions and the frontier. Fiscal policies reexamined and redefined the nature and scope of business and industrial growth, giving rise to a new legal entity, the corporation, and creating a demand for new monetary strategies.

Education reform and the expansion of the public school system meant increased learning opportunities for immigrants, women, and black former slaves. The growth of colleges and universities, many of them founded for women, resulted in the entry of more women into the paid workforce. These colleges and universities, some private, some public, offered agricultural and

Homesteaders, such as Daniel Freeman in this photograph, moved out west and established homes on land that American Indians had often lived on for centuries. Freeman (in a 1904 photograph) settled in Beatrice, Nebraska, in 1863. *(Library of Congress)*

technological training and promoted development of such fields of study as astronomy, psychology, and agronomy, and growth in the newer professions of social work, library science, and domestic science.

Agricultural development, particularly in the regions opening up for white settlement west of the Mississippi River, meant new opportunities for native-born farmers, immigrants, and those displaced by war. In fact, these opportunities were unprecedented: More land was cultivated in the United States between 1860 and 1890 than in all years since 1789. In this 30-year period, the U.S. population more than doubled.[10]

Congress had encouraged this expansion and development by a legislative initiative known as the Morrill Land Grant Act, passed in 1862.[11] While virtually unused throughout the Civil War years, less than 12 months after the war many states used this law to help establish state agricultural colleges. Under the terms of this legislation, in 1865 the Maine State College of Agricultural and Mechanical Arts, Indiana Agricultural College and the Agricultural and Mechanical College of Kentucky were founded. Within two decades, additional state colleges and universities, many of them organized under the terms of the Morrill Act, would provide educational opportunities and promote technological developments needed by a nation that was expanding in both physical size and population.

The Changing Shape, Size, and Character of the Nation

As explorers and surveyors pushed farther west, the United States acquired more territory—some of it beyond the natural border of the Pacific. In 1867, plans were underway for a survey of Panama, so that a canal could be built to connect the Atlantic and Pacific oceans (and facilitate the U.S. Navy's access to coal at various Pacific stations).

Other areas of noncontiguous territorial expansion included acquisition of various Pacific islands and the purchase of Alaska. Bought from Russia at the urging of Secretary of State William Seward for a price of two cents per acre, the Alaska Territory became part of the United States on October 18, 1867.[12] It was popularly known as Seward's Folly, or Seward's Icebox.

The United States annexed the Midway Islands in August 1867, a move that was applauded by expansionists who saw this possession as key to preserving U.S. naval superiority.[13] (Imperialists later saw in it the opportunity for greater control of the Western Hemisphere's political network. Shortly before the turn of the 20th century, the expansionist impulse resulted, as well, in annexation of the Hawaiian Islands and Guam. In 1898, the United States was victorious in a war against Spain, leading ultimately to the addition of Puerto Rico and the Philippine Islands as U.S. territorial possessions.)

Along with increased territory, the United States experienced an increase in foreign immigration in the postwar years. Many immigrants came from Europe; others came from China. A growing nativism responded to this wave of immigration: native-born Americans imagined that their social and cultural traditions would be eroded by foreigners and demanded various protections under the law for those who had been born in the United States. Because many of the foreign-born flocked to cities, where factory work was readily available, the native-born feared for their job security.

In the immediate postwar years, native-born citizens established fraternal and labor organizations and secret societies designed to exclude "undesirable elements" and protect jobs. The Knights of Labor, founded in 1867, was one of the earliest labor unions. The Patrons of Husbandry, a secret society founded in 1867 by Oliver Kelley, advocated farmers' rights and promoted agricultural interests.[14] This group later joined forces with the Farmers' Alliance to become an important political force in the Midwest. The National Labor Union was founded in 1866 by Richard A. Trevellick and William Sylvis. Trevellick served as its chief executive officer until his death in 1869.

These organizations had multiple goals and concerns. Some feared the effects of immigration on the culture and society of the United States. Others were founded by those who had immigrated in search of financial stability, religious freedom, and greater personal opportunities. Still others—notably the Ku Klux Klan—were concerned with excluding, harassing, even persecuting, people on the basis of race, religion or ethnicity. However, virtually all the fraternal, labor, or secret societies founded in the decades following the Civil War grew out of concerns about regional and national economic instability, cultural norms, and employment conditions and opportunities.

Women's political activism became more evident after 1865, due in part to their involvement in the abolitionist movement during the war. Seeking greater personal equality during the ensuing decades, women sought access to higher education, entry into professions, and involvement in social reform activities outside the home. A growing number of women went to college after 1865, and women's political and reform organizations grew in number. The Young Women's Christian Association (YWCA), with its emphasis on religious and social responsibility, was established in 1866.

The Railroad Is King

Of all the technologically significant developments following the Civil War, the one with the most profound effect was growth and expansion of the nation's rail networks. The railroads were gradually combined, providing more efficient and effective ways to transport agricultural output and, later, facilitating travel between the East and West Coasts. This growth had led, by spring 1868, at

The Union Pacific Railroad would be part of the nation's first transcontinental railroad system. *(Library of Congress)*

The Great Union Stock Yards opened in Chicago in 1865. *(Library of Congress)*

Amboy, Illinois, to the formation of the first conductors' union, known as "Division Number 1 Conductors' Brotherhood." In November of that year, the organization held a convention in Columbus, Ohio. There, conductors from the United States and Canada adopted the name "Order of Railway Conductors of America."

Thanks to the railroads, the Union Stockyards in Chicago, Illinois, became the principal terminus for beef cattle and other livestock and produce that was shipped from the West and Southwest to markets in the East. All major rail lines in the United States connected with this center at Chicago.

After the Union Pacific and Central Pacific Railroads were joined together in 1867, the coast-to-coast railroad system in the United States was the most extensive, well-integrated means of transportation of goods and people in the world. A few years later, in August 1870, railroad switchmen working on Chicago-area railroads founded the Switchmen's Association in hopes of achieving some control over hours and conditions of labor. (By 1894, this group would become the Switchmen's Union of North America.)

Seeking Consensus

By the end of the 1860s, many Americans hoped that consensus—and, therefore, political, social, and fiscal stability—might result if a Republican president were elected. On May 21, 1868, at the Republican National Convention in Chicago, Illinois, former Union army general Ulysses S. Grant was nominated (unanimously, on the first ballot) for president of the United States.[15] He was elected in November, winning 214 Electoral College votes and 52.7 percent of the popular vote. (Grant's Democratic opponent, Horatio Seymour, of New York, carried 47.3 percent of the popular vote and 80 electoral votes.)

In 1868, symbolic of the nation's growing optimism and the potential that U.S. cities represented, New York City became the location for the first office building with an elevator. The physical urban development that was a hallmark of the post–Civil War era was accompanied by expanded municipal government structures. Political party bosses rightly saw in the larger cities new sources of support for machine politics. Some party leaders were honest; others became corrupt as their influence grew and they established constituent networks and coerced their backers to vote the party ticket at election time.

New York City's William Tweed—known as "Boss Tweed"—was one of many urban bosses whose villainy was concealed at first by his generosity and surface competence. Praised by newspaper editors for his largesse, especially among the immigrant population of the city, Tweed's true nature was, by the mid-1870s, revealed. His double-dealings transformed the previous goodwill among newspapers into lurid headlines exposing his dishonesty.

By 1870, the U.S. Congress convened with a full complement of states represented for the first time in 10 years. Readmission to the Union of all former Confederate states had been completed under the terms of Reconstruction legislation, and the federal government could now devote itself to peacetime

This cartoon in *Harper's Weekly* shows Thomas Nast's view of "Boss" Tweed. *(Library of Congress)*

concerns. Among its actions was passage, on February 3, 1870, of the Fifteenth Amendment to the U.S. Constitution, which guaranteed the right to vote for all male citizens of the United States. On February 23, Hiram R. Revels, (R-Mississippi), was sworn in as the first black U.S. Senator and the first African American to serve in the U.S. Congress.[16] In December 1870, Joseph H. Rainey (R–South Carolina) was the first African American to be sworn in as a member of the U.S. House of Representatives.

During peacetime, Americans began to indulge in a passion for sports old and new. Between 1868 and 1870, professional sports gained a wide following, and baseball rapidly became the nation's favorite sport. The Cincinnati Red Stockings were the first professional baseball team to wear official uniforms and began the first professional baseball tour in 1869. In 1870, pitcher Fred Goldsmith demonstrated his skill with the curveball in Brooklyn, New York.

Also in New York, the Athletic Club held its first indoor track meet. Nearby New Jersey claimed the first intercollegiate football team. The popularity of professional boxing skyrocketed; in St. Louis, the first international bare-knuckles boxing tourney was held, and in Louisiana, the first world heavyweight boxing championship took place.

People were inventive and energetic in other areas as well. In 1868, the first refrigerated railroad car was patented. George Westinghouse patented both the railroad airbrake and the vacuum cleaner. In 1870, a process for the manufacture of celluloid was patented, leading to a range of new products from men's shirt collars to explosives. In 1870, John D. Rockefeller incorporated Standard Oil of Ohio, a forerunner of one of the United States's earliest corporate monopolies. These and other efforts in manufacturing, business, and science placed U.S. industrial production ahead of that of all other nations by 1900.

Women found that, following the war, new avenues opened up for them for work and activity outside the home. Some energetically campaigned for women's voting rights, some sought equality in the workplace, and some combined the two. Journalist Jane Cunningham Croly, whose pen name was "Jennie June," was turned away from a New York Press Club event in 1868. In response, she organized a club for women only, naming it *Sorosis,* a Greek term meaning "an aggregation of many fruits." (In 1890, this club joined with others to become the General Federation of Women's Clubs.)

In New York City in 1868, women's rights crusader Susan B. Anthony published the first issue of *The Revolution,* and the sisters Victoria Woodhull and Tennessee Claflin began publication of a weekly newspaper promoting a range of topics from women's rights to legal prostitution. In Illinois that year, the *Chicago Legal News* was launched by lawyer Myra Colby Bradwell.

In January 1869, the American Equal Rights Association met in Washington, D.C.; in May, Elizabeth Cady Stanton was elected president of the National Woman Suffrage Association, which she had founded with Susan

Elizabeth Cady Stanton was president of the National Woman Suffrage Association. *(Library of Congress)*

B. Anthony. In November, the American Woman Suffrage Association was founded in Cleveland, Ohio, an effort led by Lucy Stone and Julia Ward Howe. (This group merged, in 1890 with the National Woman Suffrage Association. The new group was called the National American Woman Suffrage Association.) In 1869, the first woman was admitted to the Iowa bar to practice law. The following year, both the Utah and Wyoming territories granted women the right to vote.

CHRONICLE OF EVENTS

1865

Astronomer Maria Mitchell is appointed the first woman to the faculty of Vassar Female College and becomes a member of the American Philosophical Society.

Landscape architect Frederick Law Olmsted reports his findings on Yosemite Park to park commissioners. Andrew Carnegie founds Keystone Bridge Company.

January 15: Union forces take control of the Cape Fear River in North Carolina as Fort Fisher falls. This action blocks the last rebel port and spells disaster for the Confederacy.

February 3: President Lincoln meets with a Southern peace contingent at Hampton Roads, Virginia.

February 17: A fire in Columbia, South Carolina, nearly levels the city as General Sherman's troops draw closer.

February 22: Tennessee adopts a new state constitution abolishing slavery.

March 3: The Freedmen's Bureau bill is passed by Congress to protect the civil rights of former slaves. Existence of the bureau is authorized for 12 months after the end of the Civil War.

March 4: President Abraham Lincoln is inaugurated for his second term of office.

March 13: The Confederate States of America reluctantly incorporates African-American troops in its army.

March 18: The Congress of the Confederate States of America adjourns its final session.

March 29: In Virginia, the Battle of Appomattox Court House begins.

Passed in 1865, the Freedmen's Bureau bill protected the rights of former slaves. The bureau, which lasted until 1872, was charged with the education of slaves and resolving interracial disagreements. In this 1860s image, a man representing the Freedmen's Bureau separates two disagreeing groups. *(Library of Congress)*

April 1: Confederate Army General Robert E. Lee begins his last offensive, at Petersburg, Virginia.

April 2: Richmond, Virginia, is evacuated and Confederate President Jefferson Davis removes the rebel government to Danville, Virginia. Union troops enter Richmond the next day.

April 9: At Appomattox Court House, General Lee surrenders to General Grant.

April 14: President Lincoln is shot while attending the theater in Washington, D.C.

April 15: President Lincoln dies of gunshot wounds at age 56. Vice President Andrew Johnson is sworn in as the nation's 17th president.

April 15: New York theaters are closed for more than a week in observance of President Lincoln's death.

April 26: In Vicksburg, Mississippi, Confederate Memorial Day is celebrated for the first time.

April 26: John Wilkes Booth is shot and killed.

April 27: The Mississippi River is the site of a steamboat explosion. The *Sultana's* boilers explode, killing 1,547 people, the majority of whom are Union soldiers released from Confederate prisons.

April 29: By an executive order signed by President Johnson, commercial restrictions are lifted in the South. Texas is not included in this decree.

May 2: New York City forms the nation's first paid fire department.

May 5: In North Bend, Ohio, a railroad train is held up for the first time.

May 9: President Johnson recognizes the government of the state of Virginia.

May 10: Former Confederate president Jefferson Davis is captured by Union troops at Irwinville, Georgia.

May 23: In Washington, D.C., a parade down Pennsylvania Avenue celebrates the end of the Civil War.

May 25: Three hundred people are killed in Mobile, Alabama, when an ordnance depot explodes.

May 29: Building on a plan issued in 1863 by President Lincoln, President Andrew Johnson issues a Reconstruction agenda in which he outlines conditions for granting amnesty to Southerners. He appoints William W. Holden as provisional governor of the former Confederate state of North Carolina.

June 19: Texas announces that all slaves in this military district are now free.

July 21: Poet James Russell Lowell addresses Harvard College graduates and commemorates slain President Lincoln.

August 14: Mississippi votes to prohibit slavery in the state.

November 9: North Carolina votes to prohibit slavery in the state.

November 18: Mark Twain's story "The Celebrated Jumping Frog of Calaveras County" is published in the *New York Saturday Press.*

December 2: By ratifying an antislavery amendment to the U.S. Constitution, Alabama becomes the 27th state to approve the measure, ensuring its adoption by two-thirds of the states in the Union.

December 4: President Johnson appoints the Joint Committee on Reconstruction.

December 18: The Thirteenth Amendment to the U.S. Constitution is adopted. It abolishes slavery in all states and empowers Congress to enforce the constitutional article with appropriate legislation.

December 24: The Ku Klux Klan is founded in Pulaski, Tennessee, by ex-Confederate general Nathan Bedford Forrest.

December 25: Chicago's Union Stockyards open.

1866

January 1: As part of the Black Codes in force during the period known as Radical Reconstruction, all persons in Mississippi who are not employed are to be charged with vagrancy and fined $50.

February 12: In Washington, D.C., the first commemoration of President Lincoln's birthday is held.

February 19: An act of Congress increases the power and expands the tenure of the Bureau of Refugees, Freedmen, and Abandoned Lands. The Freedmen's Bureau, as it has been known, is to be given more extensive powers to protect the civil rights of blacks in the South. President Andrew Johnson vetoes the bill. He reasons that it is unconstitutional to give the federal government legal jurisdiction in states that have no representation in Congress.

February 22: In Washington, D.C., a group of politicians demonstrates support for President Johnson's February 19th veto. During a speech, the president exhibits behavior considered outrageous by some, calling his congressional opponents traitors. This incident causes the president to lose face among the general public.

March 2: The Joint Committee on Reconstruction passes a resolution stating that former Confederate states may not be admitted to Congress except by the express authority of that body.

April: As credit grows scarce and deflation increases, Congress passes a law to speed repayment of the nation's war debt.

April 1: The U.S. Telegraph Company is taken over by Western Union, forming a huge company providing communications services to the entire nation.

April 2: By presidential declaration, the Civil War is ended in the Confederate states of Alabama, Arkansas, Florida, Georgia, Louisiana, Mississippi, North Carolina, South Carolina, Tennessee, and Virginia.

April 6: In Decatur, Illinois, Benjamin F. Stephenson founds the Grand Army of the Republic (G.A.R.), a fraternal organization for veterans of the Union army who served in the Civil War. By 1890, the G.A.R. grows to 490,000 members.

April 10: After minimal debate in Congress, the Civil Rights Act is passed, granting full citizenship to all persons born in the United States, regardless of race or color. President Johnson does not support this constitutional amendment and vetoes it, only to be overridden by Congress, which passes the bill by a two-thirds majority on June 13. Most observers feel the debate and disagreement over this issue to be a critical negative turning point in President Johnson's ongoing struggle for executive power.

April 10: In New York City, the American Society for the Prevention of Cruelty to Animals is founded.

May 16: The U.S. Congress eliminates the half-dime coin, replacing it with a five-cent piece called the nickel.

May 16: Charles Elmer Hires develops a commercial version of root beer, a beverage made from various roots and barks, including sassafras, sarsaparilla, and dandelion.

June 8: The Canadian Parliament meets for the first time in Ottawa.

July 2: Tennessee is the first Southern state to be readmitted to the Union following the Civil War.

July 25: The U.S. Congress passes legislation authorizing the rank of General of the Army, designated by four silver stars. Lieutenant General Ulysses S. Grant is the first to hold this four-star rank.

July 27: The Atlantic Cable is successfully completed, allowing transatlantic telegraph communication for the first time.

July 28: The Metric Act of 1866 becomes law and legalizes the standardization of weights and measures in the United States.

August 20: The National Labor Congress meets for the first time, in Baltimore, Maryland.

August 29: The Mount Washington Cog Railroad in New Hampshire is opened for public inspection. The steepest of its type, the railway is not completed for another three years.

October 3: A steamer, the *Evening Star,* is lost at sea during a voyage from New York to New Orleans, Louisiana. The death toll is 250.

1867

The Belmont Stakes at Jerome Park Racecourse, in the Bronx, New York, is run for the first time. The winner is Ruthless, ridden by jockey Gilbert Patrick. The Belmont Stakes is named for financier August Belmont and will be held at Jerome Park until 1890, when it is moved briefly to Morris Park. In May 1905, it moves to its permanent home at Belmont Park in Elmont, New York.

A yellow fever epidemic kills more than 3,000 people in New Orleans, Louisiana.

The first dining car is introduced on Canada's Great Western Railway.

January 8: In the nation's capital, black male citizens are given the right to vote.

General Ulysses S. Grant led the North to victory over the Confederacy during the Civil War. *(Library of Congress)*

Andrew Johnson became president after Lincoln was assassinated. *(Library of Congress)*

January 23: In New York City, the East River freezes over.

February 14: In Hartford, Connecticut, the first boiler insurance company issues a policy.

February 25: Congress gives approval for a survey in Panama in order to make possible the construction of a canal connecting the Atlantic and Pacific Oceans.

March 1: Nebraska is admitted to the Union as the 37th state.

March 2: Over the president's veto, Congress passes the first Reconstruction Act, which divides former Confederate states (which already have had provisional governments established) into five military districts in order to ensure more efficient governing of these areas. These districts are to be under the jurisdiction of General of the Armies Ulysses S. Grant, not the president of the United States.

March 2: Congress passes the Tenure of Office Act. Among other things, this legislation prohibits the president from dismissing any members of his cabinet without prior Senate approval.

March 2: The U.S. Department of Education is authorized.

March 2: Howard Theological Seminary is founded at Washington, D.C. It is later known as Howard University.

March 7: Congress forms a committee to look into President Johnson's possible impeachment for "high crimes and misdemeanors." Johnson will be found in violation of the Tenure of Office Act for dismissing Secretary of War William Stanton.

March 7: Shoemakers in the United States form the Order of the Knights of St. Crispin to provide for wage stability.

March 15: In Michigan, the first state university in the nation is authorized to be supported by direct property taxes.

March 21: The New York Philatelic Society is organized in New York City.

March 23: Congress passes the second Reconstruction Act. It is a supplement to the legislation passed on March 2 and outlines specific details governing states' readmission to the Union. President Johnson vetoes this bill.

March 23: The first state forestry inquiry commission is established in Wisconsin.

African-American males vote during Reconstruction in the South. *(Library of Congress)*

The Patrons of Husbandry, or the "Grange," was founded in 1867. *(Library of Congress)*

March 25: In Chicago, Illinois, the first water supply conduit constructed for city use begins operations.

March 30: The United States purchases the Alaska territory from Russia for two cents per acre. The total cost is $7.2 million. Secretary of State Seward is responsible for the negotiations, which are carried out with great secrecy.

April 9: The Senate ratifies a treaty with Russia concerning purchase of Alaska Territory.

April 12: The United States Plate Glass Insurance Company is incorporated in Philadelphia, Pennsylvania.

April 23: W. E. Lincoln, of Providence, Rhode Island, patents the nation's first animated film machine, called the Zoetrope.

June 15: The nation's first gallstone operation is performed at Indianapolis, Indiana.

July 1: Canada Day, recognizing the establishment of the Dominion of Canada under the terms of the British North America Act, is celebrated for the first time.

July 2: The first elevated railroad opens in New York City.

July 16: In Newburg, Ohio, the first ready-mixed paint is patented.

July 17: The Harvard School of Dental Medicine is founded by Harvard University at Cambridge, Massachusetts.

July 19: Over another presidential veto, the third Reconstruction Act is passed by Congress.

August 20: The first cartridge belt is patented by Anson Mills.

August 27: The first railroad crossing gate is patented at Boston, Massachusetts.

August 28: The United States annexes the Midway Islands in the Pacific. This is the nation's first noncontiguous acquisition of territory.

October 9: Alaska Territory becomes a U.S. possession.

October 18: Transfer of Alaska Territory, known as Seward's Folly, occurs.

October 21: Near Medicine Lodge Creek, Kansas, a treaty is signed by U.S. government and leaders of the Kiowa and Comanche. The treaty obligates tribes to relocate to reservation lands in a region that is later to become western Oklahoma. A second treaty of this name is signed later by the Kiowa and the Apache.

October 25: Maimonides College opens in Philadelphia, Pennsylvania. It is the first rabbinical school in the nation.

October 28: The Medicine Lodge Treaty is signed by leaders of the Cheyenne and Arapaho.

November 2: Harper's Bazaar is published in New York City under the editorship of M. L. Booth. It is the nation's first fashion weekly.

December 2: Charles Dickens gives a reading in New York City for which people stood in a mile-long line to purchase tickets.

December 4: The Patrons of Husbandry, a secret agricultural society, is founded by Oliver Hudson Kelley. Soon known as the Granger movement, it becomes a strident and powerful voice in support of farmers' interests throughout the nation.

December 29: The nation's first telegraph ticker is installed by a New York brokerage house.

1868

January 13: The U.S. Senate refuses to support President Johnson's intended removal of Secretary of War Edwin Stanton.

January 14: Oscar James Dunn becomes the nation's first African American to be nominated as lieutenant governor of Louisiana.

January 16: A patent is granted to Detroit fish market owner William Davis for the first refrigerated railroad car, which Davis manufactures in 1869.

January 19: The first stamp collector's organization adopts its constitution as the New York Philatelic Society.

February 4: Congress passes an act that forbids cancellation of paper currency known as greenbacks which were not backed by gold and delays the federal debt-funding program.

February 16: The Benevolent Protective Order of Elks is founded in New York City.

February 21: President Johnson removes U.S. Secretary of War Edwin Stanton, who will barricade himself in his office for nearly two months. The U.S.

Senate charges the president with violating the Tenure of Office Act, and then the Senate begins impeachment proceedings.

February 24: Acting on behalf of Congress, Thaddeus Stevens charges President Andrew Johnson with violating the Tenure of Office Act because of his actions concerning Edwin Stanton. These are the first impeachment proceedings ever to begin against a U.S. president.

February 24: In Mobile, Alabama, the first parade to feature float tableaux is held.

March 1: The American Journal of Philately is published for the first time by the New York Philatelic Society.

March 2: The University of California is founded in Oakland, California.

March 4: The U.S. House of Representatives appoints seven managers to go to the U.S. Senate with 11 impeachment articles that will be brought against President Andrew Johnson. Eight of these

President Andrew Johnson was impeached but not convicted. *(Library of Congress)*

articles concern the Tenure of Office Act and the removal of Secretary of War Stanton.

March 5: The U.S. Senate convenes a court of impeachment to try President Andrew Johnson. Johnson is charged with violating terms of the Tenure of Office Act after he dismissed Secretary of War Stanton.

March 11: The fourth Reconstruction Act passes Congress, despite President Johnson's veto.

March 16: In casting the deciding veto of the Johnson impeachment trial, Senator Edmund G. Ross (R-Kansas) states "not guilty." With this, Congress fails to obtain the two-thirds majority it needs to impeach the president.

March 17: The first machine to cancel postage on letters is patented.

March 24: The Metropolitan Life Insurance Company is formed.

May: The *American Journal of Obstetrics,* the first such professional publication devoted to diseases of women and children, is published in New York City.

May 5: A national holiday is proclaimed in "General Order #11," by former Union general John Logan, a member of the Grand Army of the Republic. Logan wants to commemorate those who lost their lives in the Civil War.

May 20: The Republican Party's national convention opens in Chicago, Illinois. Ulysses S. Grant wins the nomination for president on the first ballot, with Schuyler Colfax as his vice presidential running mate.

May 26: The U.S. Senate acquits President Johnson on impeachment articles two and three. The Senate adjourns without voting on the eight remaining articles.

May 30: Because of "General Order #11," Memorial Day (known as "Decoration Day") is observed for the first time.

June 1: Former president James Buchanan dies.

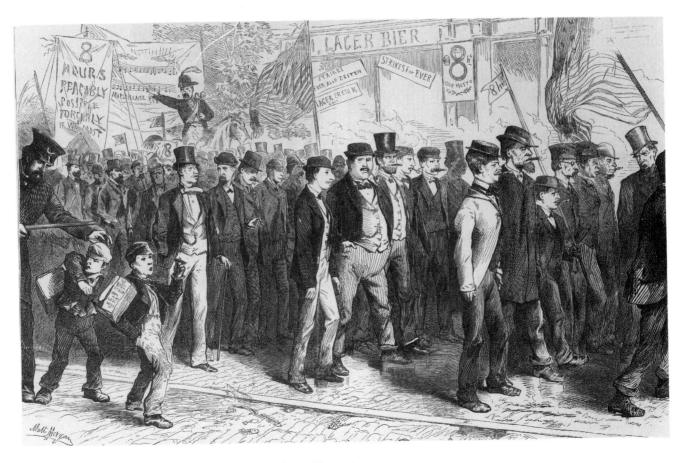

Workers strike in support of an eight-hour workday. *(Library of Congress)*

June 23: A workable typewriter is patented by C. L. Sholes.

June 25: Congress enacts a law providing for an eight-hour workday for government employees.

July: The nation's first cattle club, for owners of Jersey cattle, is formed in Newport, Rhode Island.

July: The Burlingame Treaty is signed in Washington, D.C. The treaty derives from a request made by the Chinese government a year earlier: The Chinese invited U.S. ambassador to China, Anson Burlingame, to join a Chinese diplomatic mission to the United States. He did so, which led to a revision of an earlier treaty with China.

July 4: In New York City, the Democrats hold the opening of their national convention. Horatio Seymour is nominated as president, with Francis P. Blair as the vice presidential nominee.

July 9: President Andrew Johnson submits the Burlingame Treaty between the United States and China to the U.S. Senate for approval.

July 14: The first tape measure is patented by A. J. Fellows at New Haven, Connecticut.

July 20: Congress passes legislation that imposes a cigarette tax.

July 25: The Wyoming Territory is created by an act of Congress.

July 28: The Fourteenth Amendment is ratified. It guarantees equal rights for all citizens in any state.

August: In Pittsburgh, Pennsylvania, the nation's first commercial high school is established.

September: In Georgia, African Americans are expelled from the state legislature, which causes martial law to be reestablished there. Georgia must now ratify the Fourteenth Amendment prior to its readmission to Congress.

September 8: The New York Athletic Club is organized.

October 6: A process for nickel plating is patented by W. H. Remington of Boston, Massachusetts.

October 7: A Cornell University in Ithaca, New York, the nation's first veterinary department offers courses.

October 21: In San Francisco, California, a strong earthquake causes more than $3 million in property damage.

October 31: The U.S. Postal Service authorizes that uniforms be issued to postal letter carriers.

November 3: In the presidential election, Republican Ulysses S. Grant receives 214 Electoral College votes.

He defeats a New York Democrat and the party chairman, Horatio Seymour, who receives only 80 Electoral College votes.

November 11: The New York Athletic Club holds the first indoor amateur track and field meet.

November 13: The American Philological Society is organized in New York City.

November 14: In Manhattan, Kansas, the first farmer's institute sponsored by a college is held.

November 27: At the Battle of the Washita River, General George Armstrong Custer attacks Cheyenne Indians who are led by a signer of the 1867 Medicine Lodge Treaty, Chief Black Kettle. Custer and his men kill about 100 Cheyenne.

December 3: At the federal circuit court in Richmond, Virginia, former Confederate president Jefferson Davis is brought to trial on charges of treason.

Ulysses S. Grant was elected U.S. president in 1868. *(Library of Congress)*

December 5: As an outgrowth of the new cycling craze sweeping the nation, the first bicycle school is opened in New York City.

December 25: President Andrew Johnson declares a general amnesty for all those who had fought against the Union in the Civil War.

1869

Fire burns down about 75 percent of the mostly wooden buildings in the city of Hancock, the northernmost community in Michigan.

James Gordon Bennet, owner of the *New York Herald,* sends journalist Henry Morton Stanley (real name John Rowlands) on a journey to locate a missionary, Dr. David Livingstone, who is known to be somewhere in Africa. Stanley locates Livingstone in November 1871 in what is now Tanzania. At the time of their first meeting, according to later reports, Stanley said, "Dr. Livingstone, I presume?" These same reports noted that the missionary's reply was a simple "yes."

January 19: The American Equal Rights Association meets in the nation's capital.

January 23: The first bureau of labor is established, in Massachusetts.

February 6: A whiskered cartoon drawing of Uncle Sam appears in *Harper's Weekly.* This figure becomes widely employed by satirists who see the character as synonymous with national interests and ambitions.

February 15: After President Johnson's announcement of a general amnesty, the treason charges against former Confederate president Jefferson Davis are dropped.

February 15: The University of Nebraska is chartered; classes will open in 1871.

March 4: The nation's 18th president, Ulysses S. Grant, is inaugurated. President Johnson does not attend the ceremony.

March 15: The Cincinnati Red Stockings become the nation's first professional baseball team as they begin an eight-month national tour.

April 10: The states of Georgia, Mississippi, Texas, and Virginia ratify the Fifteenth Amendment, which requires voting rights for all men, regardless of race, color, or previous condition of servitude.

May 10: The nation's first transcontinental railroad is completed as the Central Pacific and the Union Pacific lines are connected at Promontory Point, Utah.

May 15: The National Woman Suffrage Association is established, with Elizabeth Cady Stanton as its president.

June 8: A patent is awarded to a Chicago inventor for the first suction-principle vacuum cleaner.

June 15: Mike McCoole wins the first international bare-knuckle boxing championship, defeating British boxer Tom Allen, in St. Louis, Missouri.

September 6: In Avondale, Pennsylvania, 108 coal miners are suffocated in a mine collapse.

September 12: The Prohibition Party is formed in Chicago, Illinois, at the National Temperance Convention.

September 24: After President Grant belatedly approves the release of $4 million in federal gold reserves, the price of gold plummets. This situation contrasts sharply with a previous frenzy of gold purchasing among small and large investors, and many are left bankrupt as a result of "Black Friday" conditions.

October 8: Former president Franklin Pierce dies.

November 6: In New Brunswick, New Jersey, the first intercollegiate football game is played between Rutgers and Princeton. The final score is 6–4.

November 27: The case *Hepburn v. Griswold* is brought before the U.S. Supreme Court. A decision in the case will determine the legality of paper money issued by a government in lieu of hard currency.

December 6: The Colored National Labor Convention meets in Washington, D.C.

December 10: Wyoming Territory grants voting rights to women.

December 28: The Noble Order of the Knights of Labor is founded in Philadelphia, Pennsylvania, by Uriah S. Stephens. The secret organization is originally established by garment-cutters.

1870

January 2: Construction starts on the Brooklyn Bridge in New York.

January 4: The nation's telegraph operators go on strike.

January 6: The Knights of Labor meets again to elect its first officers.

January 10: In Cleveland, John D. Rockefeller incorporates the Standard Oil Company of Ohio.

The transcontinental railroad was completed at Promontory Point, Utah, on May 10, 1869. *(Library of Congress)*

This later will become the Standard Oil Trust, a virtual monopoly of the oil-refining industry.

January 11: President Grant vetoes the Private Relief Bill. During his two terms of office as president, he vetoes many additional relief bills.

January 15: A political drawing depicts the Democratic Party by showing a donkey. The drawing, done by cartoonist Thomas Nast, appears in *Harper's Weekly.*

January 26: Virginia is readmitted to the Union.

January 27: The first college sorority, Kappa Alpha Theta, is founded by Bettie Locke at DePauw University in Indiana. DePauw began admitting women in 1867, and Locke was among the first.

February 3: The Fifteenth Amendment to the U.S. Constitution is passed by Congress.

February 7: With reference to the Legal Tender Act, the U.S. Supreme Court, in *Hepburn v. Griswold,* declares that debts incurred before 1862, and

1863 (when provisions of the act were adopted) are not redeemable by the federal treasury in paper currency.

February 9: Congress establishes the National Weather Bureau, which in 1891 becomes part of the Department of Agriculture and, subsequently, in 1940, the Commerce Department.

February 10: Anaheim, California, is incorporated.

February 10: The Young Women's Christian Association (YWCA) is founded in New York City.

February 12: The Utah Territory grants full suffrage to women.

February 23: Mississippi is readmitted to the Union.

February 25: Having been appointed to the vacant Senate seat of Jefferson Davis, Hiram R. Revels of Mississippi becomes the first African American to sit in the U.S. Congress.

February 26: In New York City, the first pneumatically operated subway opens.

March 30: The Fifteenth Amendment is ratified and protects the male right to vote, despite race, color or previous condition of servitude.

April 20: The third of the Enforcement Acts, the Ku Klux Klan Act, is passed to support the Fourteenth Amendment. This legislation outlaws disguises, the intimidation of officials, and conspiracies. The act is designed to thwart the Ku Klux Klan, founded in 1865.

April 27: The floor of the state supreme courtroom in Richmond, Virginia, collapses, killing 61 and injuring more than 100.

May 10: Tom Allen fights Englishman Jem Mace for the world heavyweight boxing championship at Kennersville, Louisiana.

May 12: The Canadian province of Manitoba is established.

May 24: President Grant denounces Fenian Brotherhood attempts to damage U.S. relations with England by attacking Canada. The brotherhood, an Irish-American society, was founded in the United States by John O'Mahony in 1858. Its goal is to fight against British rule in Ireland. It is known that former President Andrew Johnson ignored some Fenian Brotherhood activities in America.

May 25: The Fenian Army of Vermont makes an unsuccessful attempt to invade Canada. The purpose of the raid was to take control of the Canadian transportation network, thereby forcing England to grant Irish independence.

June 22: Congress passes a bill that creates the Justice Department, under the direction of the attorney general of the United States. The Justice Department will have jurisdiction over the Federal Bureau of Investigation as well.

June 30: A tie vote in Congress disapproves a treaty of annexation with the Dominican Republic submitted to Congress by President Grant.

July 8: The U.S. Senate signs a joint treaty with Great Britain to stop the sale of African slaves.

July 12: The process for producing celluloid is patented by the Hyatt brothers of Albany, New York.

July 14: Congress enacts the Internal Revenue and Tariff Act, protecting industrial production by sustaining high tariffs on imported goods.

Oil magnate John D. Rockefeller, Sr., founded Standard Oil Trust, one of the largest monopolies in U.S. history. *(Library of Congress)*

July 15: Georgia is readmitted to the Union.

August 1: Women in Utah Territory vote for the first time.

August 14: Admiral David G. Farragut dies at Portsmouth, New Hampshire.

August 16: Pitcher Fred Goldsmith demonstrates the curveball in Brooklyn, New York.

October 3: Secretary of the Interior Jacob D. Cox resigns under pressure from industrial interests that seek freer access to the country's extensive natural resources.

October 4: Benjamin H. Bristow is appointed the first solicitor general of the United States.

October 8: A young schoolteacher in Canton, Massachusetts, Miss Etta Barstow, is stoned to death by unruly students.

October 12: General Robert E. Lee, the former commander in chief of the Confederate army, dies in Lexington, Virginia.

November 1: In the United States, the Weather Bureau (later the National Weather Service), makes its first forecast, predicting wind at Chicago and Milwaukee.

December 5: At the convening of Congress, each state is represented for the first time since 1860.

December 5: Governor William Woods Holden of North Carolina is impeached by the state legislature and replaced by Governor Tod R. Caldwell.

December 16: In Jackson, Tennessee, the Colored Methodist Episcopal Church is founded.

Eyewitness Testimony

I suppose you have learned even in the more secluded portions of the country that slavery is entirely abolished—a most unprecedented robbery, and most unwise policy. So it must appear even to the ignorant. I know it is only intended for a greater humiliation and loss to *us,* but I should think that even the powerful and unconscious conqueror would reap the ill effects of so unguarded a movement.

Eva B. Jones, of Augusta, Georgia, to her mother in Atlanta, letter of 1865, in Myers, The Children of Pride *(1972), p. 1,274.*

I am in distress and perplexity, and write to ask your help. The authorities here promised me transportation for the freedmen who wish to go from this to Savannah. Now, on the eve of leaving, they inform us that it can only be obtained through the bureau in Augusta. Will you be kind enough to obtain from General Tilson the necessary papers for me? These people are really in distressing circumstances. They are without means, and wish to return home where they can obtain an honest livelihood.

Mary Jones, of Atlanta, Georgia, to her daughter-in-law, letter of 1865, in Myers, The Children of Pride *(1972), p. 1,298.*

I am in favor of elevating the negro to the extent of his capacity and intelligence, and of our doing everything in our power to advance the race morally and mentally as well as physically, also socially. But I am opposed to making this advance by correspondingly debasing any portion of the white race.

General George Armstrong Custer, to a friend, letter of 1865, in Slotkin, The Fatal Environment *(1985), p. 388.*

If America is ever ruined, the Methodist Church will be to blame. For she is the strongest and most influential Church on the continent of America today.

Joseph Cook, Boston minister, decrying the evangelical nature of the Methodists, 1865, in Ahlstrom, A Religious History of the American People *(1972), p. 717.*

. . . seventy years of government, during which many and fierce conflicts over the rights of federal and state governments, and of resistance by large masses of men

General Robert E. Lee *(Library of Congress)*

to the authority of the former, show that all these differences may be adjusted without resort to arms. Nay further they convince me, after looking at the tariff agitation, and its result, nullification, that no question of less force and power than the slavery question ever could have produced armed rebellion against federal authority, of any serious extent.

Supreme Court justice Samuel Freeman Miller, to a friend, letter of 1865, in Fairman, Mr. Justice Miller and the Supreme Court *(1939), p. 126.*

After four years of arduous service, marked by unsurpassed courage and fortitude, the Army of Northern Virginia has been compelled to yield to overwhelming numbers and resources. I need not tell the brave survivors of so many hard fought battles, who have remained steadfast to the last, that I have consented to this result from no distrust of them. But feeling that valor and devotion could accomplish nothing that could compensate for the loss that must have attended the continuance of the contest, I determined to avoid the useless sacrifice of those whose past services have endeared them to their countrymen. By the terms of the agreement, officers and men can return to their homes and remain until exchanged. You will take with you the satisfaction that proceeds from the consciousness of duty faithfully performed; and I earnestly pray that a Merciful God will extend to you His blessings and protection. With an unceasing admiration of your constancy and devotion to your Country, and a grateful remembrance of your kind and generous consideration for myself, I bid you all an affectionate farewell.

General Robert E. Lee, to his troops following the surrender at Appomattox, Virginia, April 10, 1865. Available online at URL: http://www. virginiawestern.edu/vwhansd/HIS269/ Documents/LeeFarewell.html.

Sic semper tyrannus! [Thus be it ever to tyrants!]

John Wilkes Booth, to the audience, after shooting President Lincoln at Washington's Ford Theater, April 14, 1865, in Kelley, The Shaping of the American Past, *p. 369.*

Young men, this duty [of supporting Radical principles] devolves to you. Would to God, if only for that, that I were still in the prime of life, that I might aid you to fight through this last and greatest battle of Freedom.

. . . The whole fabric of southern society *must* be changed, and never can it be done if this opportunity is lost . . . How can republican institutions, free schools, free churches, free social intercourse exist in a mingled community of nabobs and serfs; of the owners of twenty-thousand acre manors with lordly palaces, and the occupants of narrow huts inhabited by "low white trash"? If the south is ever to be made a safe republic let her land be cultivated by the toil of the owners or the free labor of intelligent citizens. This must be done even though it drive her nobility into exile!

Representative and Radical Republican leader Thaddeus Stevens (R-Pennsylvania), in a speech at Lancaster, Pennsylvania, September 7, 1865, in Josephson, The Politicos, 1865–1893 *(1963), p. 20.*

In commenting a few weeks ago upon the course which the South is pursuing, we spoke of it as "a display of consummate political ability" and so we still consider it. At no time in its history have its leading men given stronger proofs of proficiency in the political art than during the last six months. A stupid, inexperienced, or clumsy-minded people would, after such a conflict as they have just gone through, have done what their admirers in England expected them to do—kept up an irregular warfare or displayed their passion and mortification in sullen passive resistance to Federal authority. But Lee had hardly laid down his arms when their leaders seemed to take the whole situation in at a glance, and decide upon their course with that swiftness, precision, and unanimity which won them so many Congressional victories in bygone days, and are, in our opinion, destined to win them many more. Northern fury was at once disarmed by loud protestations of submission and resignation. No pride, or sentiment, was allowed for one moment to stand in the way of any declarations which appeared to be necessary to appease the conqueror. And what has been more remarkable—and it furnishes a striking illustration of the extraordinary political discipline which is still maintained amongst the Southern population—whatever the leading men of each State decided upon was unhesitatingly supported by the whole people, without any preliminary agitation or discussion, without even meetings or newspapers.

E. L. Godkin, editor of The Nation, *in the October 26, 1865, issue of that magazine, p. 516.*

Every unregenerate rebel lately in arms against his government calls himself a Democrat.

Republican Thaddeus Stevens *(Library of Congress)*

The laws proposed by Mississippi, Alabama, South Carolina, etc. do but change the form of slavery. As it *was,* the individual slave belonged to, and laboured for the individual white man. As it is *proposed to be,* the whole body of the negro race in each state, must belong to and labour for the whole body of the white people of that state, under compulsion of law.

Supreme Court justice Samuel Freeman Miller, on Radical Reconstruction, 1866, in Fairman, Mr. Justice Miller and the Supreme Court *(1939), p. 129.*

. . . went by invitation to the Broker's Board . . . a full session, and much excitement. I had scarcely taken my seat when a member unknown to me rose and stated that they had present "one of the bravest and most gallant generals of the War," and proceeded to compliment your boy, by proposing three cheers for Major-General Custer.

General George A. Custer, to his wife, letter of 1866, in Slotkin, The Fatal Environment *(1985), p. 390.*

It seems to me that it ought to be an easy thing for the better elements of society to associate together and rescue politics from the degradation which in our large cities is becoming such an open scandal.

Henry C. Lea, scholar and publisher, of Philadelphia, Pennsylvania, to Charles Eliot Norton, letter of 1866, in Morgan, The Gilded Age *(1970), p. 63.*

MR. PRESIDENT: In consideration of a delicate sense of propriety as well as your own repeated intimations of indisposition to discuss or listen to a reply to the views and opinions you were pleased to express to us in your elaborate speech to-day, the undersigned would respectfully take this method of replying thereto. Believing as we do that the views and opinions you expressed in that address are entirely unsound and prejudicial to the highest interests of our race as well as our country at large, we cannot do other than expose the same, and, as far as may be in our power, arrest their dangerous influence. It is not necessary at this time to call attention to more than two or three features of your remarkable address:

The first point to which we feel especially bound to take exception, is your attempt to found a policy opposed to our enfranchisement, upon the alleged ground of an existing hostility on the part of the former slaves, toward the poor white people of the South. We admit the existence of this hostility, and

hold that it is entirely reciprocal. But you obviously commit an error by drawing an argument from an incident of slavery, and making it a basis for a policy adapted to a state of freedom. The hostility between the whites and blacks of the South is easily explained. It has its root and sap in the relation of slavery, and was incited on both sides by the cunning of the slave masters. These masters secured their ascendency over both the poor whites and blacks by putting enmity between them.

They divided both to conquer each. Them was no earthly reason why the blacks should not hate and dread the poor whites when in a state of slavery, for it was from this class that their masters received their slave catchers, slave drivers, and overseers. They were the men called in upon all occasions by the masters, whenever any fiendish outrage was to be committed upon the slave. Now, sir, you cannot but perceive, that the cause of this hatred removed, the effect must be removed also. Slavery is abolished. The cause of this antagonism is removed, and you must see, that it is altogether illogical (and "putting new wine into old bottles") to legislate from slaveholding and slave driving premises for a people whom you have repeatedly declared your purpose to maintain in freedom.

Frederick Douglass, in an excerpt from an address on Reconstruction delivered to President Andrew Johnson, February 1866, in Life and Times of Frederick Douglass, His Early Life as a Slave, His Escape from Bondage, and His Complete History to the Present Time *(1881), pp. 391–92.*

Most of the members of the Cabinet acquiesced or submitted to the usurpation. No appointments or nominations to office made by the Executive . . . were confirmed by the Senate, except the nominees first recommended or indorsed [sic] by Radical members of Congress. Some of the Cabinet under these circumstances surrendered and made terms.

Gideon Welles, secretary of the navy, in his personal journal, commenting on the power that the Republican Party had over President Johnson, 1866, in Josephson, The Politicos, 1865–1896 *(1963), p. 34.*

Every bounty jumper, every deserter, every sneak who ran away from the draft calls himself a Democrat. Bowles, Milligan, Walker, Dodd, Horsey and Humphreys call themselves Democrats. Every "Son of Liberty" who conspired to murder, burn, rob arsenals and release rebel prisoners calls himself a Democrat.

. . . In short, the Democratic party may be described as a common sewer and loathsome receptacle, into which is emptied every element of treason North and South, and every element of inhumanity and barbarism which has dishonored the age.

Republican governor Oliver P. Morton of Indiana, in his "Bloody Shirt" speech at Indianapolis, Indiana, June 1866, in Josephson, The Politicos, *p. 36.*

Before the rebellion there were 4,000,000 called colored persons held as slaves by about 340,000 people living in the South. That is, 340,000 slave owners paid expenses, bought land, and worked the negroes, and at the expiration of the year when cotton, tobacco, and rice were gathered and sold, after all paying expenses, these slave owners put the money in their pockets—[slight interruption]—your attention—they put the property in their pocket. In many instances there was no profit, and many came out in debt. Well that is the way things stood before the rebellion. The rebellion commenced and the slaves were turned loose. Then we come to the Freedmen's Bureau bill. And what did the bill propose? It proposed to appoint agents and sub-agents in all the cities, counties, school districts, and parishes, with power to make contracts for all the slaves, power to control, and power to hire them out-dispose of them, and in addition to that the whole military power of the government applied to carry it into execution.

President Andrew Johnson, in a speech at Cleveland, Ohio, September 3, 1866. Available online at URL: http://odur.let.rug.nl/~usa/D/18511875/ reconstruction/cleveland.htm.

My Dear Dodge:

I have read with intense interest your letter of the 14th, and though you wanted it kept to myself, I believe you will sanction my sending it to General Grant for his individual perusal, to be returned to me. It is almost a miracle to grasp your purpose to finish to Ft. Sanders (228 miles) this year, but you have done so much that I mistrust my own judgment and accept yours.

I regard this road of yours as the solution of the Indian affairs, and the Mormon question, and, therefore, give you all the aid I possibly can, but the demand for soldiers everywhere and the slowness of enlistment, especially among the blacks, limit our ability to respond. . . .

. . . the first step, of course, is to arrange for the accumulation of the necessary men and materials at the right points, for which your railroad is the very thing. So far as interest in your section is concerned, you may rest easy that both Grant and I feel deeply concerned in the safety of your great national enterprise.

General William T. Sherman, to Major General Granville M. Dodge, chief engineer of the Union Pacific Railroad, in a letter dated January 16, 1867, quoted in Maddow, A Sunday Between Wars *(1979), p. 51.*

Statesmen of America! beware what you do. The ploughshare of rebellion has gone through the land beam-deep. The soil is in readiness, and the seed-time has come. Nations, not less than individuals, reap as they sow. The dreadful calamities of the past few years came not by accident, nor unbidden, from the ground. You shudder to-day at the harvest of blood sown in the spring-time of the Republic by your patriot fathers. The principle of slavery, which they tolerated under the erroneous impression that it would soon die out, became at last the dominant principle and power at the South. It early mastered the Constitution, became superior to the Union, and enthroned itself above the law. Freedom of speech and of the press it slowly but successfully banished from the South, dictated its own code of honor and manners to the nation, brandished the bludgeon and the bowie-knife over Congressional debate, sapped the foundations of loyalty, dried up the springs of patriotism, blotted out the testimonies of the fathers against oppression, padlocked the pulpit, expelled liberty from its literature, invented nonsensical theories about master-races and slave-races of men, and in due season produced a Rebellion fierce, foul, and bloody. This evil principle again seeks admission into our body politic. It comes now in shape of a denial of political rights to four million loyal colored people. The South does not now ask for slavery. It only asks for a large degraded caste, which shall have no political rights. This ends the case. Statesmen, beware what you do. The destiny of unborn and unnumbered generations is in your hands. Will you repeat the mistake of your fathers, who sinned ignorantly? Or will you profit by the blood-bought wisdom all round you, and forever expel every vestige of the old abomination from our national borders? As you members of the Thirty-ninth Congress decide, will the country be peaceful, united, and happy, or troubled, divided, and miserable.

Frederick Douglass, in Appeal to Congress for Impartial Suffrage, *January, 1867. Available online at URL: http://www.law.ou.edu/hist/suff.html.*

... we have been wading knee deep in words, words, words, for a whole week, and we are but little more than half way across the turbid stream.

Representative James A. Garfield (R-Ohio), remarking on lengthy impeachment proceedings against President Johnson, 1867, in Josephson, The Politicos *(1963), p. 41.*

Engineering forces were started to their positions before cold weather was over, that they might be ready to begin their work as soon as the temperature would permit. I remember that the parties going to Salt Lake crossed the Wasatch Mountains on sledges and that the show covered the tops of the telegraph poles. . . . Spring found us with the track at Ogden, and by May 1st we had reached Promontory, five hundred and thirty-four miles west of our starting point twelve months before.

Grenville Dodge, excerpt of his description of the completion of the first transcontinental railroad in 1867, in "How We Built the Union Pacific Railway," Senate Document No. 447, 61st Congress, 2nd Session, quoted in Maddow, A Sunday Between Wars *(1979), p. 51.*

I have examined the bill "to provide for the more efficient government of the rebel States" with the care and the anxiety which its transcendent importance is calculated to awaken. I am unable to give it my assent for reasons so grave that I hope a statement of them may have some influence on the minds of the patriotic and enlightened men with whom the decision must ultimately rest.

The bill places all the people of the ten States therein named under the absolute domination of military rulers; and the preamble undertakes to give the reason upon which the measure is based and the ground upon which it is justified. It declares that there exists in those States no legal governments and no adequate protection for life or property, and asserts

the necessity of enforcing pcacc and good order within their limits . . .

. . . The purpose and object of the bill—the general intent which pervades it from beginning to end—is to change the entire structure and character of the State governments and to compel them by force to the adoption of organic laws and regulations which they are unwilling to accept if left to themselves. The negroes have not asked for the privilege of voting; the vast majority of them have no idea what it means. This bill not only thrusts it into their bands, but compels them, as well as the whites, to use it in a particular way . . .

. . . It is a part of our public history which can never be forgotten that both Houses of Congress, in July, 1861, declared in the form of a solemn resolution that the war was and should be carried on for no purpose of subjugation, but solely to enforce the Constitution and laws, and that when this was yielded by the parties in rebellion the contest should cease, with the constitutional rights of the States and of individuals unimpaired. This resolution was adopted and sent forth to the world unanimously by the Senate and with only two dissenting voices in the House. It was accepted by the friends of the Union in the South as well as in the North as expressing honestly and truly the object of the war. On the faith of it many thousands of persons in both sections gave their lives and their fortunes to the cause. To repudiate it now by refusing to the States and to the individuals within them the rights which the Constitution and laws of the Union would secure to them is a breach of our plighted honor for which I can imagine no excuse and to which I can not voluntarily become a party . . .

President Andrew Johnson, March 2, 1867, excerpts from a speech to the U.S. House of Representatives in which Johnson voiced his intention to veto the First Reconstruction Act. Available online at URL: http://odur.let.rug.nl/~usa/D/1851–1875/ reconstruction/veto.htm.

What bad news, sad news tonight. Pennsylvania and Ohio gone Democratic and the sad lessons of the war all forgotten. Well, God reigneth. His will and purposes will all be made known and enforced in good time.

Jay Cooke, financier and Republican Party supporter, commenting on the returns during the off-year elections, 1867, in Josephson, The Politicos *(1963), p. 57.*

I very much regret that the organization in the interest of the banks of which you spoke to me a year ago has not been quietly effected ready for action. The banks need to bestir themselves to avoid hostile legislation and yet any organization effected now would . . . perhaps do more harm than good. This universal suffrage country will never see the end of attempts of demagogues to excite the poor against the rich, labor against capital, and all who haven't money against the banks who have it.

William E. Chandler, assistant secretary of the Treasury,
to Republican financier Jay Cooke, letter of December
1867, in Josephson, The Politicos *(1963), p. 58.*

Tell Gen'l Grant from me that we'll all look to him to save to the country the legitimate results & fruits of the War.

Jay Cooke, Republican financier, to his brother Henry,
letter of 1867, in Josephson, The Politicos *(1963),*
p. 59.

After looking carefully over the field I know of but one man that in my humble judgement can beat this repudiation platform and that man is General Grant . . . If we run Grant, we can generally count upon the soldier's vote—they will vote for him to glorify themselves—feeling that to place him in the Presidential office will be an additional recognition of their own services . . . that is to say, they will prefer glory to repudiation. But with Chase or any of that school of politicians we will certainly be beaten . . . The people are uneasy . . . and inclined to try a change.

M. P. Brouns, to Elihu B. Washburne, December 1867,
in Josephson, The Politicos *(1963), p. 60.*

Mr. Boutwell who is perhaps the ablest member of the Judiciary Committee, declared last summer that the President must be removed, because what the radical majority wants to do cannot be accomplished while he remains. Now in all this I understand you to concur, and to be impatient at the delay of your representatives, in Congress, in putting it into execution.

Samuel Freeman Miller, Supreme Court associate justice,
to supporters of President Johnson's impeachment, 1867,
in Fairman, Mr. Justice Miller *(1939), p. 138.*

The condition of the civil service of the United States is deplorable. Even in the early days of the

Supreme Court associate justice Samuel Freeman Miller *(Library of Congress)*

Republic, although great care was taken to select for office only men of respectable character and qualifications, the need of a system of competitive examination was felt. But no such system was established, and, as far as the holders of office were concerned, a change for the worse took place in proportion to their increasing numbers and the vast increase of public business consequent to the rapid strides of our progress. Nothing was done to adapt the civil service to the exigencies of the new times.

Mr. Jenckes's bill deserves the warmest support, as much for the improvements which it actually proposes to enact by the introduction of open competitive examinations in the subordinate branches of the home civil service, and by the abolition of the system of irresponsibility and patronage, as for the way in which it prepares for the adoption of reforms in the foreign services and in all other administrative branches of the government.

Julius Bing, aide to Congressman Thomas A. Jenckes,
1867, in Hoogenboom and Hoogenboom,
The Gilded Age *(1967), p. 163.*

For a quarter of a century after the close of the Civil War the Trans-Missouri country was the scene of almost innumberable [sic] conflicts between the Caucasians and Indians. The latter stubbornly contested invasion of their hunting grounds by settlers. It is impossible to overestimate the importance of the services rendered by these Indian fighters. They opened the West to civilization and settlement. They battled with a brave, merciless and cunning foe. They usually faced fearful odds. This is just as much a state of war as existed before or after and there was nothing in any Indian campaign which exceeded their endurance and valor. It is absurd to speak of any special activities against the U.S. soldiers by the Indians as in formally declared wars as we see them among the civilized nations. But speaking of the war of 1867, it was just as much an Indian War as it could be. War was always or continually existing among all tribes west of the Mississippi river. It was in this way that the tribes united in war, and we must acknowledge that war with the Indians existed.

Report in 1867 to the U.S. Senate, "The Twenty-five Year Indian War," in William Thornton Parker, "A Soldier's Plea for Justice: An Indian War Veteran's Experience in Kansas and New Mexico During the Indian Wars of 1867–1868," quoted in Winners of the West, *Vol. XI, No. 3, St. Joseph, Missouri, February 28, 1934. Available online at URL: http://www.rootsweb.com/ ~nalakota/wotw/misc/soldier splea_ wotw022834.htm.*

. . . [the Republican party] totally abandoned all relations to the white race of the ten states. It resolved to make the black race the governing power in those states, and by means of them to bring into Congress twenty senators and fifty representatives—practically appointed by itself in Washington.

Samuel J. Tilden, chair of the New York State Democratic party, 1868, in Kelly, The Shaping of the American Past *(1978), pp. 385–386.*

Like all parties that have an undisturbed power for a long time, it has become corrupt, and I believe it is today the most corrupt and debauched political party that has ever existed.

Senator James Grimes (R-Iowa), concerning the Republican party, 1868, in Cashman, America in the Gilded Age *(1984), p. 187.*

You in Massachusetts are not in the Union. Butler is the only man who understands his countrymen and even he does not quite represent the dishonesty of our system.

Historian Henry Adams, to E. Atkinson, regarding election of Richard Henry Dana to the U.S. Senate in place of Ben Butler, 1868, in Morgan, The Gilded Age *(1970), p. 66.*

This whole question of Slavery, so-called, was but one relating to the proper *status* of the African races as an element of a society composed of the Caucasian and African races, and the *status* which was best, not for the one race or the other, but best, upon the whole, for both.

Over these questions, the Federal Government had no rightful control whatever. They were expressly excluded, in the Compact of Union, from its jurisdiction or authority. Any such assumed control was a palpable violation of the Compact, which released all the parties to the Compact, affected by such action, from their obligation under the Compact. On this point there can be no shadow of a doubt.

Alexander Stephens, "Colloquoy XII," A Constitutional View of the Late War Between the States; its Causes, Character, Conduct, and Results, Two Volumes, *Philadelphia, Chicago, St. Louis, and Atlanta: The National Publishing Company (1868), p. 522.*

To Hon. Edwin M. Stanton, Washington, D.C.
Sir: By virtue of the power and authority vested in me as President by the Constitution and laws of the United States, you are hereby removed from the office of Secretary of the Department of War, and your functions as such will terminate upon the receipt of this communication. You will transfer to Brevet Major-Gen. Lorenzo Thomas; Adjutant-General of the Army, who has this day been authorized and empowered to act as Secretary of War ad interim, all records, books, papers, and other public property now in your custody and charge.
Respectfully yours, Andrew Johnson

President Johnson, to Secretary of War Stanton, letter dated Washington, February 21, 1868. The letter provoked the U.S. Senate to begin impeachment proceedings against the president on the grounds that he had violated the Tenure of Office Act. Available online at URL: http://www.worldwideschool.org/library/books/ hst/northamerican/HistoryoftheImpeachmentof AndrewJohnsonPresidentoftheUnitedStates/chap6.html.

Most of the difficulties between whites and blacks resulted from the inevitable awkwardness of tyros in the mystery of free labor. Many of the planters seemed to be unable to understand that work could be other than a form of slavery, or that it could be accomplished without some prodigious binding and obligating of the hireling to the employer. Contracts which were brought to me for approval contained all sorts of ludicrous provisions . . . The idea seemed to be that if the laborer were not bound body and soul he would be of no use.

William DeForest, concerning his experience working for the Freedmen's Bureau, 1868, in Johanssen, Reconstruction, 1865–1877 *(1970), pp. 119–120.*

My dear Mother,
I start for Detroit tomorrow night . . . Charles Clement . . . has a good position in the Pennsylvania railroad—headquarters of the road being at Altoona—that is the Superintendent and machine shops are there. They employ 1500 men in the shops, which I examined in company with Charley. They disburse about $100,000 a month there—own the hotel and have large fine offices and houses . . .

. . . Eight miles on a branch road and we rode in the "cab" of the engine. Such a smokey country! As we came back in the dark we saw fires all around us on the ground where they were burning coal to make coke.

. . . Charley explained the way they did their business and although it reminded me by its magnitude of government undertakings . . . *economy* is the great controlling idea.

William R. Russell, letter to his mother, March 29, 1868, in Library of Congress, Manuscripts Division, quoted in: Maddow, A Sunday Between Wars *(1979), p. 47.*

Our Indian troubles commenced in 1864 and lasted until the tracks joined at Promontory. We lost most of our men and stock while building from Fort Kearney to Bitter Creek. At that time every mile of road had to be surveyed, graded, tied, and bridged under military protection. The order to every surveying corps, grading, bridging, and tie outfit was never to run when attacked. All were required to be armed, and I do not know that the order was disobeyed in a single instance, nor did I ever hear that the Indians had driven a party permanently from its work . . .

From the beginning to the completion of the road our success depended in great measure on the cordial and active support of the army, especially its commander in chief, General Grant, and the commander of the Military Division of the West, General Sherman.

Grenville M. Dodge, chief engineer of the Union Pacific Railroad, 1868, in Senate Document No. 447. 61st Cong. 2d. sess., "How We Built the Union Pacific Railway . . . ," (1910).

Our cause is a common one . . . Go ahead in the good work that you have undertaken, until the most glorious success crowns your efforts . . . monied power is fast eating up the substance of the people. We have made war upon it, and we mean to win it. If we can we will win through the ballot box; if not, we will resort to sterner means. A little bloodletting is sometimes necessary in desperate cases.

William Sylvis, National Labor Union founder, to Karl Marx, 1868, in Dubofsky, Industrialism and the American Worker, 1865–1920 *(1975), p. 53.*

There is a large class of persons in this country called *middlemen*, who operate in all communities, and who are of no benefit whatever. They are non-producers, deriving their sustenance from the labor of others, like a parasitic plant . . .

If the producers and consumers could be brought more directly together, so as to save the large profits of the middlemen, it would be greatly for the interests of both, and there would be less reason for bewailing the small profits of the one, and the high prices of products by the other.

George Brackett, about problems facing farmers, 1868, DeNovo, The Gilded Age and After *(1972), p. 110.*

I know no method to secure the repeal of bad or obnoxious laws so effectively as their stringent execution.

President Ulysses S. Grant, excerpt from his inaugural address, March 4, 1869, in Bartlett, Familiar Quotations, *12th Edition (1951), p. 549.*

Still a hue and cry was raised, through the influence of the Indian ring, in which some good and pious ecclesiastics took part, and became the aiders and abettors of savages who murdered without mercy, men, women and children.

Secretary of War Philip H. Sheridan, in an attempt to persuade against implementation of President Grant's peace policy with the Indians in his annual report, 1869, in Slotkin, The Fatal Environment *(1985), p. 401.*

Railroads encouraged western settlement. *(Library of Congress)*

[Colonel Adams] has industry, and is absolutely honest, he proposes to make what is called "rail-roading" his business for life. In addition to this, he is a man of general intelligence, and has a good style in writing on business matters. He is, also, a good age—thirty-four. Knowing him, as I do, very well, I will say that, if I were Governor, I should not appoint three commissioners like Colonel Adams. But if there are two such of sound practical judgment, and acquaintance with the subject, on the commission, I think they would find Col. Adams of great use, and that he would make a good third.

Francis E. Parker, urging the appointment of Charles Francis Adams to the Massachusetts state railroad commission, in a letter to Massachusetts governor Otis Norcross, June 24, 1869, in McCraw, Prophets of Regulation *(1984), p. 18.*

One can see all along the line of the now completed road the evidences of ingenious self-protection and defence which our men learned during the war. The same curious huts and underground dwellings which were a common sight along our army lines then, may now be seen burrowed into the sides of the hills, or built up with ready adaptability in sheltered spots. The whole organisation of the force engaged in the construction of the road is, in fact, semi-military . . .

William A. Bell, writing about the transcontinental railroad, in New Tracks in America, *London, 1869, II. p. 256, quoted in Maddow,* A Sunday Between Wars, *p. 51.*

While suppressing so rigorously all offences to the sight and smell, and punishing in general all disturbances of the peace, it would be only consistent to include in the proscription the still greater plague of noise.

Editorial in the Cleveland Leader, *on the problem of urban noise pollution, 1870, in Callow,* American Urban History *(1973), p. 131.*

. . . a member of this Assembly has the privilege to reveal his membership in this organization to those he desires to obtain for members; provided always, however, that he does not reveal the name or names of any other persons who are members of this organization, according to the terms of the obligation.

> *Robert McCauley, to the Knights of Labor, his member's motion at meeting in 1870, in Powderly,* Thirty Years of Labor, 1859–1889, *(1967), p. 77.*

I returned from Georgia yesterday. My visit to Montevideo was very pleasant but very sad. My beloved mother was not there, and my dear father—he too was gone! . . . Everything was in much better order than I expected to find it.

> *Charles Colcock Jones, son of Mary Jones of Montevideo, Georgia, in a letter describing his return to his family home, 1870, in Myers,* The Children of Pride *(1972), p. 83.*

Senator Tweed is in a fair way to distinguish himself as a reformer . . . From beginning to end the Tweed party has not manifested the slightest disposition to evade or prevaricate . . . As a whole, the appointments of the heads of the various departments of the City Government . . . are far above the average in point of personal fitness, and should be satisfactory.

> New York Times, *editorial published prior to widening scandal over "Boss" Tweed, 1870, in Callow,* American Urban History *(1973), pp. 231–232.*

I want to know what the ladies are doing in the way of taking stock for our company. We are getting started now. We have enough subscribed to begin with, and we are starting up with a good prospect of getting a quick sale for our goods as soon as we have got them ready for the market. Of course, we depend altogether on the working people of the country, and on the people who are able and willing to help working girls and wish to see them get along.

The stock is five dollars per share, and is only an investment, which will directly benefit working girls, not a charity . . . Any person wishing to subscribe for one share or more can address a note to [me].

> *Kate Mullany, president of the Laundry Union and Co-operative Collar Co., Troy, New York, 1870, in Baxandall,* America's Working Women *(1976), p. 98.*

Too much education of a certain sort, such as Greek, Latin, French, German, and especially bookkeeping, to a person of humble antecedents, is utterly demoralizing in nine cases out of ten, and is productive of an army of mean-spirited "gentlemen," who are above what is called "a trade," and who are only content to follow some such occupation as that of standing behind a counter, and selling silks, gloves, bobbins, or laces, or to "keep books."

Were the power lodged with me, no boy or girl should be educated at the public expense beyond what he or she could obtain at a grammar school, except for some useful occupation . . .

Were I in the position of General Eaton [U.S. Commissioner of Education], I would commence a crusade against the ignorance of our educators, and I would bring the people to a proper recognition of *"what knowledge is most worth,"* as Herbert Spencer has so well and truly sung, or these ignoramuses should have the satisfaction of lopping off my official head.

> *Henry Carey Baird, Philadelphia businessman, 1870, in DeNovo,* The Gilded Age and After *(1972), p. 23.*

2

Scandal, Economic Instability, and Expansion
1871–1875

CHANGING VIEWS CONCERNING NATIONAL FISCAL POLICY

During the 1870s, the economic activity of the United States grew at a faster rate than it had at any point before the Civil War. Industrial expansion and urban development were the chief characteristics of this growth. As a result, the nation was transformed from a primarily agricultural economy to one that was increasingly dependent on manufacturing and commerce. And while in view of many there were almost unlimited opportunities for personal financial success, a cycle of fiscal downturns tempered the optimism and resolve of all but the most wealthy.

Congress maintained an ambivalent, yet expedient, attitude toward federal monetary policies. Where the nation's citizenry was concerned, Congress was reluctant to act hastily. Where its personal interests were involved, Congress sought advantage where it could. The Salary Grab Act of 1873, passed on March 4, increased congressional salaries by 50 percent.[1] The bill also made provision for the pay increase to be retroactive for the past two years. At this same time, Congress doubled the salaries of the president and the U.S. Supreme Court justices. However, because of the public protest the legislation generated, Congress eventually repealed the act, but not before it damaged the reputation of those sitting in Congress at the time it was passed.

Debates over the pros and cons of protective import tariffs revealed the depth of the conflict Congress felt over financial policy. Farmers were especially hard hit during the 1870s, as the economy faltered repeatedly. Paradoxically, the difficulty rested in the farmers' success in the decades after the Civil War. Agricultural production grew at astronomical rates after 1865. As more and more farmers moved into the Great Plains area, they benefited from more and better machinery than had been available before the war. This allowed farmers to produce more. Thanks to the railroads, transportation-to-market costs decreased, which enabled farmers to take more crops to market. But as this happened, prices fell due to a surplus. Falling income meant inadequate capital to support the farm. Thousands of farmers went into debt, adding to the nation's financial woes, but Congress was reluctant to change its tariff policy.

Tariffs Affect Agriculture and Other Production

During the 1870s, this meant that farmers and others had to purchase the manufactured goods they needed in a market where prices were kept artificially high through tariff legislation. However, farmers had to sell crops at prices that were depressed due to oversupply and foreign competition. Protective tariffs were originally conceived to guarantee American manufacturers a profit when they sold their products. The federal government did this to encourage industrial production and to protect the nation's growing industrial economy. Import duties on manufactured goods coming into the United States made foreign items more expensive, encouraging consumers to buy American goods, which were cheaper than imports.[2]

Not surprisingly, U.S. manufacturers and their investors were strong supporters of this protectionist approach to trade. Opponents of federal tariff policies included consumers, farmers, entrepreneurs, and businesspeople, who pointed out that no one benefited but the banks and wealthy industrialists. Farmers were especially angry because tariffs were applied almost exclusively to industrial goods; agriculture received no such protection. To many, it seemed that manufacturing and commercial interests enjoyed unfair advantages. Farmers had no way to predict when or how they would be able to stabilize their segment of the economy. The anger and frustration felt by those who grew the nation's food and provided its livestock began to be expressed by liberal newspapers and periodicals that hoped to shake the hold that powerful and rich Republicans seemed to have on the entire nation.

The Demand for Reform

Newspapers were tireless in uncovering government dishonesty; some projects, like the completion in 1868 of the transcontinental railroad, became widely known as corrupt and riddled with betrayal; much of the blame for this corruption was aimed at elected authorities. And as U.S. cities grew, the ideological rift between them and rural areas grew, again due to dishonesty among those elected to serve. Many municipal governments were believed to be little more than dens of public thieves. The problem was clear to many: There was a lack of strong, reliable, and honest leadership at all levels of government.[3]

Some small improvements and reforms could be seen, however. Regulation and oversight of certain services and activities, such as federal elections, was imperative. In 1871, election supervision was federally mandated for cities with populations of 20,000 or more.[4] In 1872, those who favored even broader voting reforms included in the Republican Party platform a reference to support woman suffrage. This appeared to be more or less theoretical, however: On November 5, 1871, Susan B. Anthony and several other women attempted to cast their votes at polling places, and some, including Anthony, were arrested for their efforts. As the right to vote was extended legitimately to African-American former slaves, and as more immigrants sought citizenship, and as women continued to lobby for voting rights, the regulation of voting practices grew even more imperative.

An Expanding Consumer Economy

By 1873, the population had grown so much that the U.S. Postal Service now delivered mail to all communities of 20,000 or more. This enhanced service fueled an explosion in the mail-order market, which seemed tailor-made for a nation that spanned a 3,000-mile expanse from the Atlantic to the Pacific. Montgomery Ward, founded in 1872 in Chicago, and Sears, Roebuck & Co., founded a decade later, also in Chicago, helped provide farmers and city dwellers alike with virtually every type of consumer good imaginable. By the 1890s, the Montgomery Ward catalog contained more than 10,000 items. Despite the retail expansion reflected in the mail-order business, by mid-decade the nation's economy balanced on the edge of ruin. Get-rich-quick schemes threatened to tip the balance, and even as honest investors bought legitimate stocks, clever swindlers found ways to defraud the unsuspecting.

One of the more elaborate financial hoaxes led to the Crédit Mobilier scandal. When the hoax was uncovered, U.S. vice president Schuyler Colfax, U.S. congressman James A. Garfield (R-Ohio), U.S. representative Oakes Ames (R-Massachusetts), and others were implicated in a scheme of illegal business practices that had been conducted during the completion of the transcontinental railroad in the late 1860s.[5]

Connecting the Union Pacific and Central Pacific Railroads was, in the eyes of most Americans, an engineering marvel. But subsequent investigation into how that marvel was accomplished revealed a network of bribes, corruption, and personal treachery. The Crédit Mobilier of America construction company was held under the same ownership as the Union Pacific Railroad. Together, they exploited the government subsidies that paid for the transcontinental project. Crédit Mobilier charged unusually high fees to the Union Pacific—fees eventually paid for by the U.S. government.

Federal officials who cooperated in the scheme received underpriced stock options in Crédit Mobilier that provided them with huge dividends. The railroad investment scandal, which was widely publicized, caused many Americans to grow wary of the federal government's honesty. Reactions to the Crédit Mobilier swindle were reported in newspapers and periodicals nationwide, and some reformers seized this opportunity to make a change. A group of angry Republicans had broken away from the G.O.P., formed the Liberal Republican Party, and promoted a broad-minded candidate for election to the presidency in 1872: Horace Greeley, editor of the *New York Tribune*.

Greeley's backers were a bipartisan group that included Charles Francis Adams, Jr., of Massachusetts, a Massachusetts railroad commissioner and later president of the Union Pacific Railroad, and the journalist E. L. Godkin, founder of *The Nation* magazine in 1865. But despite support from both Democrats and Republicans, Greeley lost the election, and another decade would pass before a president with an aggressive reform agenda was elected.[6]

For many in the United States, the Crédit Mobilier scandal was proof that both elected and appointed officials were frequently dishonest and that the government needed to be reined in. Still, President Grant was popular with a majority of citizens, and was his party's only candidate at the Republican Convention in Philadelphia, in June 1872.

PRESIDENT GRANT'S SECOND TERM

By November, confidence in the federal government was as shaky as it had been during the 1868 Senate impeachment proceedings against President Andrew Johnson. Republicans faced repeated charges of corruption. In the face of particularly negative press attention, bad faith, and a generally contentious political climate, President Grant was reelected. He received an impressive 286 electoral votes to Greeley's 42. The popular vote reveals a slightly closer contest: 55.6 percent of the popular vote went to President Grant, 43.8 percent to Greeley, and .6 percent to other candidates.[7]

Greeley's unpopularity was a deciding factor in the Republican landslide victory: His critics labeled him a crank who supported spiritualism, vegetarianism, and socialism. Compared with the former Union army general and presidential incumbent, Greeley looked like nothing more than an outsider who was ill qualified to lead the nation.

TECHNOLOGY AND WEALTH CHANGE THE FACE OF U.S. CITIES

The rapid growth of cities was reflected in concerns about how to accommodate continuing expansion. Architects found a solution in steel-and-concrete construction, and by 1870, buildings were growing ever taller. In New York City, the first elevator-equipped building—the Equitable Life Assurance Society—was a seven-story marvel on lower Broadway.

Horace Greeley, founder of the *New York Tribune,* ran unsuccessfully for president against President Ulysses S. Grant in 1872. *(Library of Congress)*

Henry Hobson Richardson was an architect of this period whose influential designs are still visible in U.S. cities today. The libraries, churches, and other buildings he designed in and around Boston, Massachusetts, have a characteristic Richardson Romanesque style. Some of Richardson's buildings are Trinity Church in Copley Square, built in 1872, and Brattle Square Church in Cambridge, built in 1871. Other Gilded Age architects include Richard Morris Hunt, whose New York Tribune Building was completed in 1875, and Louis Sullivan, a Chicago architect who designed the Transportation Building for the World's Columbian Exposition in Chicago in 1893. Wealthy industrialists and philanthropists, who often wished to leave behind a monument to their own importance or to perpetuate a given institution, helped to fuel popularity for these ornate neo-Gothic and romanesque styles.

Accompanying the opulent designs of Richardson, Sullivan, and Richard Morris Hunt were the first generation of skyscrapers. Along with this was the development, in the United States, of a new field: landscape architecture. Prominent among them in the post–Civil War decades was Frederick Law Olmsted, who in May 1873 was asked by the U.S. Senate to plan and develop a 46-acre plot around the U.S. Capitol. Olmsted's influence can be seen in many cities throughout the United States, including New York, Chicago, Atlanta, Buffalo, and Boston, as well as in the design of Mont-Royal Park, in Montreal, Quebec, Canada. In 1888, Olmsted was invited to design the Stanford University campus in Palo Alto, California. (Stanford was founded under the terms of the Morrill Land Grant Act of 1862.) One of Frederick Law Olmsted's final projects was George Vanderbilt's 120,000-acre estate, Biltmore, in western North Carolina.

By the early 1870s, large numbers of Americans were crowding into what economist Thorstein Veblen would later define as the "middle class." People wanted more and better homes, furnishings, and clothing, and as manufacturing produced more consumer goods, people achieved a higher standard of living. Industrialization meant that many farmers and day laborers left the rural lifestyle behind, seeking work and opportunities that provided them and their families with more goods and services, more leisure time, and the tools with which to enjoy their leisure.

Many found that an increase in free time and a greater range of available sports provided the opportunity to be not simply spectators but participants. By 1871, the National Association of Professional Baseball Players had been organized and an ever-expanding roster of teams were touring the country. In 1873, four universities met in New York City to establish rules for varsity football.

Growing public interest in intercollegiate and professional sports could not divert public scrutiny of the increasingly troubled investment environment. A flurry of activity on Wall Street in late 1873 led to the collapse of a brokerage house headed by financier Jay Cooke. Soon after, 37 banks and investment houses failed, and the New York Stock Exchange closed for 10 days. According to most observers, the Panic of 1873 stemmed from a dozen or so years of excess speculation and inflated stock prices.

Whatever its cause, the crash affected some of the nation's largest and most prominent investors as well as destroying dreams of prosperity for tens of thousands of people. Plunging the United States into a financial depression that lasted for several years, the crash cast a shadow on Grover Cleveland's presidency, despite his administration's attempts to minimize the fallout from the Panic of 1873.[8]

It was only the first in a series of cyclical depressions and recessions that characterized the U.S. economy through the end of the century. Congressional debate over monetary policy became more intense as the depression grew, and as a result, in early 1874, Congress passed the Legal Tender Act.[9] This legislation promised to add nearly $20 million in greenbacks to the national economy, despite the fact that some economic forecasters were wary of the move. President Grant had repeatedly voiced his opposition to the bill, formally vetoing the Legal Tender Act on the grounds that it was inflationary. Congress, however, passed the measure on an override vote, one more example of the clash of executive and legislative views.

CURRENCY AND SCANDAL IN THE NEWS

Hard money supporters were incensed by passage of the Legal Tender Act, and although the issue of paper versus coin was debated continually, many agreed with the greenback measure. Farmers approved of any action that would alleviate the difficulties confronting American agriculture, even if the cure was short-lived. In November 1874, the Greenback Party held its convention in Indianapolis, Indiana. Greenbackers chose Peter Cooper, the former governor of New York, as their presidential nominee, hoping he would have the power to change federal monetary policy. (Popular support for Cooper was limited, however, and he received only about 80,000 votes in the 1876 election.)

In January 1875, in a move that acknowledged public pressure Congress passed the Resumption of Specie Payment Act. It called for gradual withdrawal of greenbacks from the economy and replacement of this paper currency with gold coin. Hard currency advocates were overjoyed; farmers and others hurt by the depression were dismayed. (These debates and disagreements continued for 20 years. In 1896, William Jennings Bryan would campaign for the presidency on a Democratic platform that featured free coinage of silver, as opposed to a single gold standard.)

The nation's problems extended beyond monetary policy. In addition to President Grant's unwillingness to support congressional monetary policies, scandal in the Republican administration fueled public criticism of the president and his associates. The Whiskey Ring scandal, which surfaced in may 1875, revealed that G.O.P. officials had accepted shakedown payments from midwestern distilleries. The chief clerk of the Treasury was named as one of those allegedly involved, as was Orville Babcock, President Grant's personal secretary. Following allegations in the Whiskey Ring scandal, the House of Representatives passed legislation in December 1875 limiting a U.S. president to two consecutive terms of office.[10]

These and other developments caused some observers to take a dim view of American culture and society. Among the more trenchant comments were those contained in a book coauthored by Mark Twain and Charles Dudley Warner, the novel *The Gilded Age*. The name of the book became synonymous with the era it so mercilessly described. Twain's insightful description of the fictional Colonel Beriah Sellers was a stereotype of the pompous, avaricious attitude so common in the post–Civil War era. Looking around him, Twain saw much to ridicule in the manners and morals of the newly rich. He and Warner underscored social problems by depicting them in a larger-than-life fashion in their book. This successful satire was similar in intent to Thomas Nast's caricatures which, when published in the newspapers, heightened readers' awareness of irresponsible civil servants, politicians, and others who sought private gain at public expense.

While the Grant administration attempted to polish its somewhat tarnished image, labor organizations gained more support. Labor had a strong foothold in America by the time the second session of the Industrial Congress of the United States met in Rochester, New York, in April 1874. Labor activity in this period increased, fueled by wage cuts in mining and manufacturing.[11] In the Hocking Valley of Ohio, for example, cuts in miners' pay led to a strike. By midsummer 1874, the Social Democratic Workingman's Party of the

The reputation of President Grant's administration was tarnished by his advisers' and associates' involvement in the Crédit Mobilier affair and the Whisky Ring scandal. *(Library of Congress)*

U.S.—later the Socialist Labor Party—was established. The proliferation of labor unions, secret societies, and similar groups that supported working persons' rights caused occasional ripples of concern among rich mine and factory owners. But in general, there was little real alarm on the part of owners, nor did they feel any responsibility to respond immediately to laborers' demands.

Overall, the nation grew more intolerant of publicly immoral or unethical behavior due to the scandals of the Grant administration as well as other scandals that had been widely reported in the newspapers. The subsequent disclosure of graft and corruption at high levels of New York City government and the breakup of the Tweed Ring outraged many Americans and prompted demands for reform.

An increased awareness of the need for change led to the formation of organizations seeking to impose higher public and personal standards. Groups like the Women's Christian Temperance Union (WCTU) attracted hundreds of members nationwide as the campaign to eliminate the consumption of alcoholic beverages increased.

As a means of controlling social behavior, or for the promotion of educational efforts, both the Chautauqua movement—rooted firmly in Christian tradition—and the Young Men's Hebrew Association exemplified the public desire for more upright behavior. In 1875, Mary Baker Eddy, founder of the Christian Science Church, published *Science and Health,* a volume that combined Christian theology with a growing popular awareness of the benefits of healthy lifestyles.

A breach of ethics was the focus of one of the nation's more titillating scandals. A well-known and respected Protestant minister was accused of adultery by a parishioner. Henry Ward Beecher (brother of novelist and abolitionist Harriet Beecher Stowe and writer Catherine Beecher) was publicly accused by Theodore Tilton of having an affair with Mrs. Tilton. While a church trial eventually found Beecher innocent of all charges, notoriety surrounding the allegations divided his New York City congregation and proved to be a frequent moral reference point in Sunday sermons for years to come.[12]

CHRONICLE OF EVENTS

1871

January 21: At a meeting of secret labor assembly The Knights of Labor, labor leader Uriah Stephens urges the adoption of more equitable work hours and wage conditions.

February 21: The District of Columbia establishes a territorial government.

February 28: Congress passes a law requiring federal election supervision in cities with populations greater than 20,000.

March 3: The Indian Appropriation Act is passed by Congress. This reverses earlier policy and now all Native Americans are considered wards of the state rather than members of independent political entities. Native American negotiating powers are severely curtailed with the passage of this act.

March 4: The Federal Civil Service Commission is established by President Grant. He appoints George W. Curtis to head the commission.

March 22: In North Carolina, William Holden is the first state governor to be removed from office by impeachment.

March 27: The Arkansas Industrial University is founded at Fayetteville. It is later to become the University of Arkansas.

May 1: The Legal Tender Act, passed in 1862, is declared constitutional by the U.S. Supreme Court decision in *Knox v. Lee.* The previous year, on February 7, the Court had declared the act unconstitutional in *Hepburn v. Griswold.*

July 8: The *New York Times* exposes the corruption of William Marcy ("Boss") Tweed. Tweed is later brought to trial and charged with a variety of fraudulent activities. Railroad baron Jay Gould helps post the $1 million bail bond required of Tweed.

July 12: Protestants and Roman Catholics in New York City riot; there are 52 deaths and substantial numbers injured.

July 12: North America's first public narrow gauge railway opens between Toronto and Uxbridge, in Canada.

July 20: British Columbia joins the Confederation of Canada. A condition of entry is construction of a railway connecting the Pacific coast with the railway system of Canada.

July 30: A boiler explodes aboard the *Westfield,* a ferry traveling between Staten Island and Manhattan, killing more than 100 people.

George William Curtis was the first head of the Civil Service Commission. *(Library of Congress)*

October 8: A fire in Chicago, Illinois, devastates 1,688 acres and destroys nearly $200 million in property, including 17,450 buildings. There are 250 known fatalities and 98,000 people made homeless as a result of the fire. Among the artifacts destroyed when the Chicago Historical Society burns is the original draft of President Abraham Lincoln's Emancipation Proclamation. In Peshtigo, Wisconsin, a fire consumes 1.2 million acres of land.

October 20: The Royal Regiment of Artillery creates two batteries of garrison artillery, later becoming the Royal Canadian Artillery.

October 24: Race riots aimed at Chinese immigrant labor erupt in Los Angeles, California.

November 17: New York state grants the National Rifle Association a charter.

December 16: William "Boss" Tweed is arrested for fraud and failure to conduct a proper audit of bills submitted to the city of New York.

December 25: Thomas Edison marries Mary Stilwell.

1872

January 2: Mormon leader Brigham Young is arrested for marrying 25 women.

February 2: Congress enacts legislation that provides for congressional elections to be held on the first Tuesday in November beginning in 1876.

February 20: In New York City, the Metropolitan Museum of Art opens.

February 22: The Prohibition Party holds its national convention in Columbus, Ohio. James Black is nominated for the presidency.

March 1: Yellowstone National Park is founded as the first national park in the United States.

March 5: George Westinghouse patents the air brake.

March 23: The *Indianapolis Sentinel* first used the term *Mugwump.* On this date, the term appears in the *New York Sun,* describing Republicans who do not support the policies of James G. Blaine. As the term gains broader usage, it grows to include any individual whose ideas are too lofty, too narrow, or too intellectual to fit mainstream political positions.

March 26: A light earthquake is recorded in San Francisco. While a majority of people do not feel it, the quake is later found to have struck at Owens Valley, in Inyo County, California, killing more than two dozen people.

April 10: Julius S. Morton proclaims this date as Arbor Day in Nebraska, a day on which trees should be planted to beautify and improve the landscape. Morton is named secretary of agriculture of the United States in 1885.

May 1: The Liberal Republican Party nominates Horace Greeley for president of the United States. He will later be selected to run as a Democrat, retaining Liberal Republican support.

May 10: Victoria Woodhull is the first woman nominated for president of the United States.

May 22: President Ulysses S. Grant signs the Amnesty Act, restoring civil rights to all but about 500 Confederate sympathizers.

May 23: Ulysses S. Grant is nominated for president at the Workingmen's National Convention in New York City.

June 5: The Republican National Convention opens in Philadelphia, Pennsylvania, and President Grant is endorsed on the first ballot. His vice presidential running mate is Henry Wilson. At this gathering, convention-goers hear speeches delivered by the first black Americans ever chosen as delegates to any major party convention. The three men are William E. Gray (Arkansas), B. B. Elliott (South Carolina), and John Roy Lynch (Mississippi).

June 14: In Canada, trade unions are legalized.

July 9: Democrats gather in Baltimore, Maryland, for the beginning of their party convention. Horace Greeley receives the nomination for president.

September 4: The Crédit Mobilier scandal is uncovered and made public in articles appearing in the *New York Sun.* The scandal involves high-level politicians who received substantial payments made by the federal government, funds dispersed during the building of the transcontinental railroad, which was completed in 1868. Massachusetts Representative Oakes Ames was chief among the organizers of Crédit Mobilier of America, a company receiving construction contracts estimated at $73 million. Shares in the company went to numerous congressmen, and even to the vice president of the United States, Schuyler Colfax.

November 5: President Ulysses S. Grant wins reelection with 286 electoral votes. Horace Greeley receives only 66 electoral votes.

November 5: Boss Tweed is convicted of defrauding the New York City government of $200,000.

November 9: In Boston, Massachusetts, a fire destroys 800 buildings, kills 13 people, and causes $75 million in damage.

1873

Adolph Coors and Jacob Schueler open the Golden Brewery, at Golden, Colorado. Thanks to their success, within seven years Coors purchases his partner's interest, taking ownership of the brewery.

Harvard Medical School professor Dr. Edward H. Clarke publishes *Sex in Education, or a Fair Chance for the Girls.* The book argues against higher education for women on the grounds that such experiences damage a woman's ability to bear children by causing the uterus to atrophy.

Montreal Golf Club is the first such club to be organized in North America. It is established in the city in an area of Mont-Royal Park. Later, in 1884, the club receives permission to add the adjective *Royal* to its name and is subsequently known as the Royal Montreal Club.

Henry Rose exhibits barbed wire at an Illinois fair. Joseph Glidden and Jacob Haish invent a machine to mass-produce barbed wire.

January 9: The *National Labor Tribune* begins publication in Pittsburgh, Pennsylvania. John M. Davis is the publisher, and circulation soon runs to 6,000. Readers are almost exclusively mine workers.

January 31: The Senate votes to abolish the congressional franking privilege in which members of Congress are permitted to use the U.S. Postal Service free of charge.

February 12: The Coinage Act is passed by Congress, removing silver coins from circulation and establishing a federal gold standard.

February 18: Despite being found guilty of bribery in the Crédit Mobilier scandal, Representative Oakes Ames (R-Massachusetts) is not expelled from Congress but is merely officially censured.

February 20: The University of California (UC) opens its first medical school in San Francisco, California. It is the only UC campus dedicated to the health sciences.

March 1: E. Remington and Sons of Ilion, New York, begin producing typewriters, adding to their production line of sewing machines and farm implements. By 1913, the name of the firm will be changed to Remington Typewriter Company.

March 3: Congress also enacts the "Act of the Suppression of Trade in, and Circulation of, Obscene Literature and Articles of Immoral Use," known as the Comstock Law (named for anti-obscenity crusader Anthony Comstock). This law makes it illegal to send "obscene, lewd, or lascivious" books through the mail. Any person convicted of a violation faces a possible five years imprisonment and a fine of up to $2,000.

March 3: Congress passes legislation known as the Salary Grab Act, in which it retroactively raises the salaries of most public officials, including the president and members of the Supreme Court, whose pay is doubled. Members of the House and Senate are to receive 50 percent increases. Due to widespread popular outrage at this measure, the act is later repealed.

March 3: Congress passes the Timber Culture Act, which awards 160 acres of land to any individual who will plant 25 percent of the land with trees.

March 3: Congress passes the Coal Lands Act.

March 4: President Grant is inaugurated for a second term of office, with Henry Wilson replacing Schuyler Colfax as vice president.

March 8: George W. Curtis, head of the Civil Service Commission, resigns.

April 14: The U.S. Supreme Court rules 5-4 that the state of Louisiana has acted unconstitutionally in enforcing a law permitting only one slaughterhouse in the city of New Orleans.

May 1: The first penny postcards are made available by the U.S. Postal Service.

May 7: Chief Justice Salmon P. Chase dies of paralysis from a stroke suffered in 1870.

May 23: The Canadian Parliament establishes the North West Mounted Police.

July: The Industrial Brotherhood is established to replace the National Labor Union, following the latter's fragmentation several years earlier.

July 1: Prince Edward Island joins the Canadian Confederation. A condition of its entry is completion of the Prince Edward Island Railway.

July 21: At Adair, Iowa, Jesse James and the James-Younger gang pull off the first successful train robbery, nabbing $3,000 from the Rock Island Express.

August 4: While protecting a railroad survey party in Montana, troops led by George Armstrong Custer clash for the first time with the Sioux.

August 18: The nation's highest peak, Mount Whitney, is conquered by three American climbers.

September: Educator Susan Elizabeth Blow opens the first public kindergarten, at the Des Peres in St. Louis, Missouri.

September 18: Jay Cooke and Co., a brokerage house in New York City, fails. This plunges the nation into an economic depression lasting five years. The Panic of 1873 was, according to most experts, the inevitable result of a dozen years of overspeculation and inflated prices. Cooke's firm had planned to underwrite the Northern Pacific Railroad, but due to its difficulties could not handle the financing required. The resulting crash also precipitates the closing of 37 other banking houses and brokerages.

September 20: The New York Stock Exchange closes for 10 days in the wake of the ruinous conditions among New York banks and other financial institutions caught up in the Panic. In response, the Treasury secretary issues greenbacks as a way of allaying the nationwide fiscal panic.

October 3–4: In Canada, between Stratford and Montreal, the Grand Trunk Railway converts to standard-gauge rail stock, completing the task in 24 hours with limited (16 hours) delay in service to trains. The use of standard-gauge stock enables uninterrupted service; by late October all Grand Trunk lines are standard gauge.

October 19: In New York City, four universities—Yale, Princeton, Columbia, and Rutgers—meet to draw up rules for playing football.

October 31: The steamer *Virginius* is captured by a Spanish gunboat in Cuban waters. Eight U.S. citizens are executed by authorities in Cuba.

November 7: Alexander Mackenzie becomes Canada's second prime minister.

November 19: William Marcy ("Boss") Tweed, former Democratic Party machine leader, is sentenced to 12 years' imprisonment.

November 27: The Hoosac Tunnel, begun in 1858, is completed in western Massachusetts.

December 24: In Hillsboro, Ohio, Eliza Trimble Thompson leads a group of temperance-minded women through the town, stopping at the doors of saloons to pray and sing hymns. This event is the beginning of a temperance effort known as the Women's Crusade.

1874

Educator Susan Elizabeth Blow establishes a training school for kindergarten teachers in St. Louis, Missouri.

January 1: New York City annexes the Bronx.

January 20: Congress repeals the Salary Grab Act.

February 21: The *Oakland Daily Tribune* publishes its first issue.

February 23: Walter Clopton Wingfield patents a game called "sphairistike," which is more commonly called lawn tennis.

March 8: Former President Millard Fillmore dies.

March 18: The Hawaiian Islands sign a treaty with the United States granting exclusive trading rights to the latter.

March 22: The Young Men's Hebrew Association is founded in New York City.

April 1: A wage cut for miners is announced in the Hocking Valley of Ohio. This leads to labor strikes in the area.

April 14: The Legal Tender Act passes Congress, adding nearly $20 million in greenbacks to the money circulating.

April 14: The second annual session of the Industrial Congress of the United States convenes in Rochester, New York. Robert Schilling is elected president.

April 15: In Arkansas, Joseph Brooks lays claim to the state capitol, despite his loss in recent gubernatorial elections to Elijah Baxter.

April 22: President Grant vetoes the Legal Tender Act. Despite his opposition to the bill, which he considers inflationary, Congress passes the legislation on an override vote.

May 15: President Grant proclaims Elijah Baxter to be the legal governor of Arkansas.

May 16: More than 100 people lose their lives as the Ashfield Reservoir Dam in Williamsburg, Massachusetts, collapses.

May 20: Levi Strauss and Jacob Davis take out a patent for blue trousers made with copper rivet reinforcements.

June 20: The governmental structure of the District of Columbia is changed from a territorial jurisdiction to one governed by a commission.

June 20: The Treasury Department is to award a Life-saving Medal, as enacted by Congress, to those who perform rescues "from the perils of the sea within the United States or upon any American vessel." This award precedes formation of the U.S. Coast Guard.

July 1: The first public zoo in the United States opens, at Philadelphia, Pennsylvania.

July 4: A steel bridge across the Mississippi River is completed at St. Louis, Missouri. It is the first such access across the nation's widest waterway.

July 4: The Social Democratic Workingmen's Party of the United States is founded. In 1877 it changes its name to the Socialist Labor Party.

July 24: Mathew Evans and Henry Woodward patent the first incandescent lamp that uses an electric lightbulb.

August 5: Edward Hammond Clarke delivers an address on the education of girls before the National Educational Association meeting in Detroit, Michigan.

August 21: Henry Ward Beecher, a well-known and respected Congregational minister and brother of novelist Harriet Beecher Stowe, is accused of adultery by parishioner Theodore Tilton. A church trial finds Beecher innocent.

November 7: The magazine *Harper's Weekly* is the first to use an elephant to symbolize the Republican Party. It appears in a cartoon drawn by Thomas Nast.

November 18: The Women's Christian Temperance Union (WCTU) is founded in Cleveland, Ohio. Annie Wittenmyer is elected the organization's first president, and the educator Frances Willard, corresponding secretary.

Completed on July 4, 1874, the St. Louis Bridge stretches across the Mississippi River at its namesake. *(Library of Congress)*

November 25: The Greenback Party is formed during a convention in Indianapolis, Indiana. Peter Cooper is named the party's presidential candidate.

1875

Professor Maria Mitchell of Vassar College is elected president of the American Association for the Advancement of Women.

In Boston, the Chinese Consolidated Benevolent Association (C.C.B.A.) is founded to help immigrants maintain cultural ties and to promote communication between Chinese immigrants and native-born Americans.

January: President Grant appoints a commission to arrange for negotiating purchase of the Black Hills from Indians in early summer.

January 4: The Prince Edward Island Railway opens a line between Charlottetown and Tignish.

January 7: The Specie Resumption Act is passed by Congress. Its purpose is to gradually withdraw greenback dollars from circulation and to replace them with hard currency.

January 30: The president of the United States signs a reciprocal trade agreement with the Hawaiian Islands. In it, the United States agrees to provide protection from third-party acquisition and receives duty-free import privileges in exchange.

February 1: A new lighthouse on Block Island, off the southern coast of New England, is lit for the first time. This is the island's fifth lighthouse and is visible for 35 miles. Its four large wicks are expected to burn as much as 1,000 pounds of lard oil annually.

March 1: The Civil Rights Act passes Congress.

March 3: Congress passes the Tariff Act.

March 18: A reciprocity treaty with the Hawaiian Islands is ratified by Congress, permitting duty-free imports.

May 1: The Whiskey Ring scandal is uncovered, further tarnishing President Grant's reputation. The scandal involves Republican officials, including the chief clerk of the Treasury, as well as President Grant's personal secretary, Orville Babcock. Allegations include acceptance of shakedown payments from at least 32 distillers in the Midwest, and use of blackmail and other threats.

May 17: The racehorse Aristides wins the first Kentucky Derby.

July 31: Former President Andrew Johnson dies at age 66.

September 1: A murder conviction forces the Molly Maguires—dissident Irish immigrant coal miners—to cease their anti-coal-mine-owner activities in northeastern Pennsylvania.

October 12: Rutherford B. Hayes is elected governor of Ohio.

November 3: President Grant meets with Generals Sherman and Sheridan to discuss Indian policy with respect to the Black Hills.

November 9: In Washington, D.C., Indian inspector E. C. Watkins issues a report that hundreds of Sioux and Cheyenne associated with Sitting Bull and Crazy Horse are hostile to the United States.

November 22: Vice President Henry Wilson dies.

November 29: The first high school on Block Island, off the coast of Rhode Island, is opened in the town hall. Sixteen students attend during the first term.

December 4: Notorious New York City political boss William "Boss" Tweed escapes from prison and flees to Cuba. From there, Tweed travels to Spain, hoping to elude U.S. authorities.

EYEWITNESS TESTIMONY

The system of corporate life and corporate power, as applied to industrial development, is yet in its infancy . . . It is a new power, for which our language contains no name. We know what aristocracy, autocracy, democracy are; but we have no word to express government by monied corporations . . . It remains to be seen what the next phase in this process of gradual development will be. History never quite repeats itself, and . . . the old familiar enemies may even now confront us, though arrayed in such a modern garb that no suspicion is excited.

Charles F. Adams and Henry Adams, 1871, in DeNovo,
The Gilded Age and After *(1972), p. 27.*

A dispatch from San Francisco states that the Apaches are committing many depredations—committing murders, running off large herds of cattle, etc. A freight train, fully armed, en route to Fort Goodwin, was attacked 30 miles east of Tucson by a large number of Indians, and after a sharp fight, in which one man was killed and two wounded, the Indians got away with some oxen.

*Article, January 6, 1871, Emporia News, Emporia,
Kansas. Available online at URL: http://www.
ausbcomp.com/%7Ebbott/cowley/Oldnews/
PAPERS/EMP4.HTM.*

I don't care a straw for your newspaper articles, my constituents don't know how to read, but they can't help seeing them damned pictures.

*Political boss William Marcy "Boss" Tweed, in the New
York Times, 1871, in Wingate, "Episode in Municipal
government," in Harper's Weekly,
July 1875, p. 150.*

The bill passed by the late Congress to incorporate a southern Pacific railroad, has been signed by the President. The title of the company is, The Texas Pacific Railroad. The main line is to run from El Paso, in Texas, to San Diego, California, with branches to New Orleans and San Francisco. There is no money subsidy, but land grants amounting to about 16,000,000 acres. The State of Texas also grants a liberal amount of land.

. . . The track is to be built of American iron. The time is not reported, or the names of the charter members, but there is no doubt but what the road will be speedily begun, and completed within a few years. The race will be between it and the Northern Pacific road, engineered by Jay Cooke & Co. By 1880 at farthest we may count upon three grand trunk railways from the Atlantic to the Pacific.

Excerpts from an editorial, March 10, 1871,
Emporia News, *Emporia, Kansas. Available online at
URL: http://www.ausbcomp.com/%7Ebbott/
cowley/Oldnews/PAPERS/EMP4.HTM.*

And while the toiler is thus engaged in creating the world's value, how fares his own interest and well-being? We answer, "Badly," for he has too little time, and his faculties become too much blunted by unremitting labor to analyze his condition or devise and perfect financial schemes or reformatory measures. The hours of labor are too long and should be shortened. I recommend a universal movement to cease work at five o'clock Saturday afternoon, as a beginning. There should be a greater participation in the profits of labor by the industrious and intelligent laborer. In the present arrangements of labor and capital, the condition of the employee is simply that of wage slavery—capital dictating, labor submitting; capital superior, labor inferior. This is an artificial and man-created condition, not God's arrangement and order; for it degrades man and ennobles mere pelf [money, riches]. It demeans those who live by useful labor, and, in proportion, exalts all those who eschew labor and live (no matter by what pretence or respectable cheat—for cheat it is) without productive work.

*Uriah Stevens of the fraternal order Knights of Labor
giving a speech at the organization's annual meeting,
January 12, 1871, in Powderly, Thirty Years of Labor.
Available online at URL:
http://www.geocities.com/doswind/myers/
am_fortune_305.html.*

Well, I don't think I'll do it. I made up my mind not long ago to put some of those fellows behind bars, and I'm going to put them there.

*Thomas Nast, cartoonist for the New York Tribune,
after being asked by Tweed Ring supporters to accept
$500,000 to leave the country to study art, 1871,
in Paine, Th. Nast: His Period and His Pictures
(1904), p. 182.*

The Times has been saying all the time I have no brains. Well, I'll show Jones that I have brains . . . I tell

Thomas Nast *(Library of Congress)*

It used to be a matter of pride with the better sort of our country people that they could raise on their own land or manufacture within their own households almost everything needed for domestic consumption. But if now you leave the rail, at whatever remote station, the very advertisements on its walls will manifest how greatly this is changed.

Frederick Law Olmsted, architect and landscape planner, 1871, in Hoogenboom and Hoogenboom, The Gilded Age *(1967), p. 113.*

There can hardly be a more serious act than a change of country. To emigrate is to take a step, of which neither the most hopeful nor the most thoughtful can correctly foresee the full consequences, for good or for evil. It means nothing less than to part for years, if not forever, with home, relations, and friends; to break up old and dear habits; to live among strangers in a strange land; to recommence, often from the very beginning, the struggle of life.

American Social Science Association, Handbook for Immigrants to the United States, *1871, in Hoogenboom and Hoogenboom,* The Gilded Age *(1967), p. 97.*

you, sir, if this man Jones had said the things he has said about me, twenty-five years ago, he wouldn't be alive now. But, you see, when a man has a wife and children, he can't do such a thing (clenching his fists). I would have killed him.

Political boss William "Boss" Tweed, in the New York Sun, *September 8, 1871, in Callow,* American Urban History *(1973), p. 240.*

Boston is the only place in America where wealth and knowledge of how to use it are apt to coincide.

E. L. Godkin, journalist and editor of The Nation, *1871, in Morgan,* The Gilded Age *(1970), p. 61.*

I was at Washington last week and found anarchy ruling our nation. I don't know who has power or is responsible, but whoever it is, I cannot find him, and no one confesses to more knowledge.

Henry Adams, to E. L. Godkin, 1871, in Morgan, The Gilded Age *(1970), p. 67.*

There is something in the country which repels men. In the city alone can they nourish the juices of life.

Mr. Steadman, who sought for an introduction to me, told me that during the war I had been to him, and, he believed, to most people, the beau ideal of the Chevalier Bayard, "knight sans peur et sans reproche" and that I stood unrivaled as the "young American hero." I repeat this *to you alone,* as I know it will please you. Another said no officer holding a commission was so popular with the retired men.

General George A. Custer, to his wife, letter of 1871, in Slotkin, The Fatal Environment *(1985), p. 406.*

. . . Soon after this my father sent for me. I saw he was dying. I took his hand in mine. He said, "My son, my body is returning to my mother earth, and my spirit is going very soon to see the Great Spirit Chief. When I am gone, think of your country. You are the chief of these people. They look to you to guide them. Always remember that your father never sold his country. You must stop ears whenever you are asked to sign a treaty selling your home. A few years more, and white men will be all around you. They have their eyes on this land. My son, never forget my dying words. This country holds your father's body. Never sell the bones of your father and your mother. I pressed my father's

William ("Boss") Tweed *(Library of Congress)*

woman to bring her daughter up without breaking her up in doing it. Our female idea of dress is all wrong. I have conversed with a good many physicians, who tell me that it is almost impossible to find a perfect female skeleton. It is a rare thing to see a woman perfectly well. But we can, if we choose, revolutionize this. Even the Bible says that maternity is a curse. Most women accept this doctrine as true; it is simply horrible, it is a monstrous lie. The Bible has been translated by men, and for men. *Will* in the original has been made *shall* in the translation. God never meant such a doctrine to be promulgated as His will. We must educate our daughters that motherhood is grand, and that God never cursed it, and the curse, if there be any, may be rolled off. My mission, among women is to preach the new gospel. If you suffer, it is not because you are cursed of God, but because you have violated His laws.

Elizabeth Cady Stanton, leader in women's rights. From an untitled address given at San Francisco, California, published in Woodhull & Claflin's Weekly, *September 30, 1871. Available online at URL: http://www.victoria-woodhull.com/ wcwarchive.htm.*

[Sheridan] has arranged with the genial and daring Buffalo Bill to be on hand and act as guide, and this renowned scout was promptly on hand in all his element. He was seated on a spanking charger, and with his long hair and spangled buckskin suit he appeared in his true character of the feared and beloved of all for miles around. White men and barbarous Indians are alike moved by his presence, and none of them dare do in word or deed contrary to the rules of law and civilization.

New York Herald, account of Buffalo Bill Cody's accompanying Russia's Grand Duke Alexis on a Great Plains buffalo hunt, 1871, in Slotkin, The Fatal Environment *(1985), p. 408.*

hand, and told him I would protect his grave with my life. My father smiled and passed away to the spirit land. I buried him in that beautiful valley of Winding Waters. I love that land more than all the rest of the world. A man who would not love his father's grave is worse than a wild animal.

Chief Joseph of the Nez Perce Indians, recalling his father's advice to him about the ancestral lands, 1871. Available online at URL: http://www. ourheritage.net/index_page_stuff/ Following_Trails/Chief_Joseph/1855_plus/ 1871_Old_Joseph_dies.html.

The idea that woman is weak inherently is a grand mistake. She is physically weak because she neglects her baths, because she violates every law of nature and of God, because she dresses in a way that would kill a man. I feel it to be my mission to arouse every

At 9:30 a small cow barn attached to a house on the corner of DeKoven and Jefferson streets, one block north of Twelfth street, emitted a bright light, followed by a blaze, and in a moment the building was hopelessly on fire. Before any aid could be extended the fire had communicated to a number of adjoining sheds, barns and dwellings, and was rapidly carried north and east, despite the efforts of the firemen. The fire seemed to leap over the engines, and commence far beyond them, and, working to the east and west, either surrounded the apparatus or compelled it to move away. . . . as far as the eye could reach, in an easterly direction—and that space was bounded by the river—a perfect sea of leaping flames covered the ground. The wind increased in fierceness as the flames rose, and the flames wailed more hungrily for their prey as the angry gusts impelled them onward. . . . people in the more southern localities bent all their energies to the recovery of such property as they could. With ample time to move all that was movable, and with a foreboding of what was coming, in their neighborhood at least, they were out and in safety long before the flames reached their dwellings. They were nearly all poor people, the savings of whose lifetime were represented in the little mass of furniture which blocked the streets, and impeded the firemen. They were principally laborers, most of them Germans or Scandinavians . . . it was evident by midnight that human ingenuity could not stem that fiery tide.

. . . The light from the burning remnants of these eighteen acres of ruins illuminated the heavens on Sunday evening. Precisely at half-past 9 o'clock the fire bells sounded an alarm, and a fresh light, distinct from the other only to those living west of the fire, sprung up. The wind at the time, as it had been for the preceding forty-eight hours, was strong from the southwest. This fire commenced on DeKoven street, at the corner of Jefferson, and one block north of Twelfth street. The wind carried this fire straight before it, through the block to the next block, and so on northward, until it reached Van Buren street, where it struck the south line of the district burnt the night before. Here this fire ought to have stopped . . . But the wind though fierce and direct, carried the flames before it, cutting as clean and well defined a swath as does the reaper in the fold . . . preceding [sic] the actual blaze was the shower of brands, falling upon roofs, breaking through windows, falling into yards, and each brand starting a new fire.

. . . No obstacle seemed to interrupt the progress of the fire. Stone walls crumbled before it. It reached the highest roofs, and swept the earth of everything combustible. The gale was intense in its severity. Having reached the lake, we on the west had high hopes that the destructive work would be confined to the distinct path thus mown through the very heart of the city . . . The hope . . . was an idle one. . . . The entire North Division, from the river to the lake, and as far north as North avenue [sic], was one seething mass of blaze. The roar of this fire was appalling. Just before daylight there was one continuous sheet of flame . . . making a semicircle the inner line of which was about seven miles long. All east of this was a perfect ocean of blaze.

News report, in the first issue of the Chicago Tribune *published after the fire, Wednesday, October 11, 1871. Available online at URL: http://www.chicagohs. org/fire/conflag/tribune.html.*

It can now be asked: What is the legitimate sequence of Social Freedom? To which I unhesitatingly reply: Free Love, or freedom of the affections. "And are you a Free Lover?" is the almost incredulous query.

I repeat a frequent reply: "I am; and I can honestly, in the fullness of my soul, raise on my voice to my Maker, and thank Him that *I am,* and that I have had the strength and the devotion to truth to stand before this traducing and vilifying community in a manner representative of that which shall come with healing

Victoria Woodhull *(New York Public Library Picture Collection)*

on its wings for the bruised hearts and crushed affections of humanity."

And to those who denounce me for this I reply: "Yes, I am a Free Lover. I have an *inalienable, constitutional* and *natural* right to love whom I may, to love *as long* or as *short* a period as I can; to *change* that love *every day* if I please, and with *that* right neither *you* nor any *law* you can frame have *any* right to interfere."

> *Victoria C. Woodhull, publisher and women's rights advocate, in a speech on the principles of social freedom, given in San Francisco, California, published in* Woodhull & Claflin's Weekly, *November 20, 1871. Available online at URL: http://www. victoria-woodhull.com/wcwarchive.htm.*

Equality in rights is not only the first of rights, it is an axiom of political truth. But an axiom, whether of science or philosophy, is universal, and without exception or limitation; and this is according to the very law of its nature. Therefore, it is not stating an axiom to announce grandly that only white men are equal in rights; nor is it stating an axiom to announce with the same grandeur that all persons are equal in rights, but that colored persons have no rights except to testify and vote. Nor is it a self-evident truth, as declared; for no truth is self-evident which is not universal. The asserted limitation destroys the original Declaration, making it a ridiculous sham, instead of that sublime Magna Carta before which kings, nobles, and all inequalities of birth must disappear as ghosts of night at the dawn.

> *Senator Charles Sumner, Radical Republican leader (Massachusetts), in a speech to the U.S. Senate, January 15, 1872, on supplementary civil rights bill as an amendment to the civil rights bill. Available online at URL: http://memory.loc.gov/ cgi-bin/query/r?ammem/murray:@field (DOCID+@lit(lcrbmrpt2415div6)).*

The Southern communities will be a desolation until there is a thorough change of affairs in all the departments of the government. There is now no responsibility—and we are fast losing all of our ancient notions of what is becoming & fit in administration. The public are tolerant of corruption, maladministration, partiality in courts, worthlessness in juries, & regard government as only a means of exploitation. Indifference to anything

Senator Charles Sumner *(Library of Congress)*

wrong is the common Sentiment. Hope is disappearing from the motives to exertion.

> *John A. Campbell, former Supreme Court associate justice, to Justice Clifford, letter of 1871, in Fairman,* Mr. Justice Miller and the Supreme Court *(1939), p. 180.*

There will be an informal meeting of the Presidents of the National and International Trade Organizations of America in Cleveland, Ohio on the 19th of November, 1872, for the purpose of taking the initiative steps looking to the formation of an Industrial Congress of North America, to be composed of bona fide representatives of bona fide labor organizations. It is to be hoped that there will be a representative from every National or International Trade Union in America present at the meeting . . .

> *M. A. Foran, in an 1872 advertisement in various trade society journals, in Powderly,* Thirty Years of Labor *(1967).*

The subject of female labor is one that demands our attention and most earnest consideration . . . If they received the same wages that men do for similar work, this objection would in a great measure disappear . . .

Woman was created and intended to be man's companion, not his slave.

> *William H. Sylvis, head of the National Labor Union, 1872, in Powderly,* Thirty Years of Labor *(1967), p. 57.*

Our country, right or wrong. When right, to be kept right; when wrong, to be put right.

> *Carl Schurz, address to the U.S. Congress, 1872, in Bartlett,* Familiar Quotations, 12th Edition *(1951), p. 580.*

The earthquake which occurred at half past 2 o'clock on the morning of Tuesday, March 26th, was the greatest convulsion of nature that has taken place in the United States since 1812.

. . . Although it was felt from Oregon to Central America and Mexico, it seems to have spent its force in the Owens river region, distant from this city hundreds of miles, and lying on the opposite side of the Sierra Nevada on the line of the state of Nevada . . . it was the fate of Lone Pine in Inyo County to be marked for destruction as the center of the earth's convulsive action.

. . . During the ensuing week it was computed that more than a thousand shocks were felt—in other words, the earth was almost constantly trembling.

> *Article in the* San Francisco Chronicle, *April 21, 1872. Available online at URL: http://www.sfmuseum.org/hist/1872eq.html.*

A home in the west more attractive than this in its location and offering a wider scope to the ambitious businessman and mechanic with a limited capital to commence a growth in business, remains as yet undiscovered.

. . . Winfield is most favorably located along the eastern skirt of the Walnut Valley (remarkable for its fertility of soil and the abundance of fine timber lining its shores and tributaries) and presents to the weary traveler in search of a place with which to anchor his hopes of a fortune in the west a most inviting prospect. The church and school advantages are superior to most towns of its size. The Baptist church is a handsome stone edifice, neatly furnished with all the necessaries calculated to adore the interior of the building to make it in keeping with the exterior.

. . . The house built by the Methodist fraternity is also a model of taste and an ornament though not yet completed. Services are held regularly every Sabbath.

. . . A thoroughly graded school, under the supervision of Rev. Parmelee and assistant, is being taught in the elegant two-story stone school-house. Citizens point with no small degree of pride to their facilities for giving the young a foundation on which to build a useful knowledge.

. . . Sections sixteen and thirty-six of every congressional township are set aside for school purposes and when sold to settlers, creates a fund to aid in the advancement of the school interests of the state.

. . . The manufacturing business is fast being developed in our midst, that will invite to our town the sturdy farmers of some of the western counties that are now unknown to us. A three and one-half story stone mill is rapidly approaching completion, built by Messrs. Bliss & Blandon, with an expenditure of twenty thousand dollars, and before it will be entirely completed will absorb at least five thousand more. This company are now introducing their superior machinery into the building and will have all in operation before the first of March. When the time arrives that will demand additions, they will be promptly made.

. . . Andrew Koehler, a miller of experience, has a frame structure underway to be used also for milling purposes. The design to secure power by tunneling through a neck of land to gain a fall of water without damaging the stream was an original idea and will prove a flattering success. These mills will both be run by waterpower, the economy of which in a country where fuel is an object, as it is here, will be realized when the profits of a year's business will be computed. The COURIER is read weekly by two hundred families to whom it is mailed regularly.

> *Editorial,* Winfield Courier, *Winfield, Kansas, Saturday, January 18, 1873. Available online at URL: http://www.ausbcomp.com/%7Ebbott/cowley/Oldnews/PAPERS/COURIERA.HTM.*

I can give you some striking examples of the profit of raising corn and wheat in this vicinity, if you desire . . .

I knew [another] man who took a ton of corn to market for the purpose of buying coal. It purchased just a ton, and he spent a day with his team in hauling . . .

Wheat is so uncertain a crop, it has so many enemies from the time it is sown until it is threshed, and it is so exacting of the farmer who must attend to it at a certain time, or he will lose it, that we can't afford to raise it for less than ninety cents a bushel.

Now something is wrong in all this. With our productive soil, and facilities for reaching market, the farmers of Illinois ought to be forehanded, comfortably housed and clothed, and able to save a little every year, instead of getting deeper and deeper into debt. We are an intelligent, hard-working, economical people, and every one of us who owns his farm is to that extent a capitalist; and we ought to be able to do as well as the journeyman mechanic, with less education than we and no capital.

. . . It is not worth eleven cents a bushel to take our corn from here to Chicago, and the railroad that is charging it is robbing us of a part of the fruits of our labor.

S. M. Smith, secretary of the Illinois State Farmers'
Association, 1873, in Hoogenboom and Hoogenboom,
The Gilded Age *(1967), p. 61.*

For many years it has not been the American fashion for the owners of railroads to put their own money into their construction. If it had been it would have insured a more conservative and businesslike use of that species of property. The favorite plan has been to get grants of land, and loans of credit from the General Government; guarantees of interest from the State governments; subscriptions and donations from counties, cities and individuals; and upon the credit of all this, issue all bonds that can be put upon the market; make a close estimate as to how much less the road can be built for than the sum of these assets; form a ring . . . for the purpose of constructing the road, dividing the bonds that are left, owning the lands, owning and operating the road until the first mortgage becomes due and graciously allowing the Government to pay principal and interest upon the loan of her credit, while "every tie in the road is the grave of a small stockholder." Under this plan the only men in the community who are absolutely certain not to contribute any money are those who own and control it when it is finished. The method requires a certain kind of genius, political influence, and power of manipulation, and furnished one clew to the reason why railroads "interfere in politics." The personal profit upon this enterprise is not a profit upon capital investment, but the result of brain work—administrative talent they call it—in a particular direction.

Jay Cooke, Republican financier, 1873, in Ginger,
People on the Move *(1975), p. 477.*

This act [creating the Union Pacific] was not passed to further the personal interests of the corporators, nor for the advancement of commercial interests, nor for the convenience of the general public alone; but in addition to these the interests, present and future, of the Government, as such, were to be subserved. A great highway was to be created, the use of which for postal, military, and other purposes was to be secured to the Government "at all times," but particularly in time of war . . . To make such a highway . . . required a strong solvent corporation . . .

Your committee find themselves constrained to report that the moneys borrowed by the corporation, under a power given them, only to meet the necessities of the construction and endowment of the road, have been distributed in dividends among the corporators; that the stock was issued, not to men who paid for it at par in money, but who paid for it at not more than 30 cents on the dollar . . .

. . . at least one of the commissioners appointed by the President has been directly bribed to betray his trust by the gift of $25,000; that the chief engineer of the road was largely interested in the contracts for its construction; and that there has been an attempt to prevent the exercise of the reserved power in Congress by inducing influential members of Congress to become interested in the profits of the transaction.

Congressman Jeremiah M. Wilson, chair, Select
Committee on the Crédit Mobilier, "Affairs of the
Union Pacific Railroad Company," House Report No.
78, 42nd Cong. 3d sess., 1873.

Today, I wholly surpassed my own expectation. I was in key all through and got hold of my audience—the strong wine of success filled my brain till I went to bed.

Charles Francis Adams, Jr., diary entry for February 14,
1873, in McCraw, Prophets of Regulation *(1984),*
p. 37.

We need all the Jay Cookes we have and a thousand more.

Writer in Baptist Quarterly, *remarking on the*
significance of wealth as a sign of piety, 1873, in
Baltzell, The Protestant Establishment *(1966),*
p. 101.

. . . A measure without any merit save to advance the interest of a patentee, or contractor, or railroad company, will become a law, while measures of interest to the whole people are suffered to slumber, and die at the close of the session from sheer neglect. It is known to Congressmen that these lobbyists are paid to influence legislation by the parties interested, and that dishonest and corrupt means are resorted to for the accomplishment of the object they have undertaken.

. . . Not one interest in the country nor all other interests combined are as powerful as the railroad interest. . . . With a network of roads throughout the country; with a large capital at command; with an organization perfect in all its parts, controlled by a few leading spirits like Scott, Vanderbilt, Jay Gould, Tracy and a dozen others, the whole strength and wealth of this corporate power can be put into operation at any moment, and Congressmen are bought and sold by it like any article of merchandise.

Conservative economist D. C. Cloud, 1873, in
Monopolies and the People, *pp. 155–156. Available
online at URL: http://www.hti.umich.edu/
cgi/t/text/pageviewer-idx?c=moa;cc=moa;sid=
8e2aa00d04458053731c9906b71dc434;rgn=
full%20text;idno=ABZ0161.0001.001;view=
image;seq=0161.*

Generally the proposition is true, that where you find the most religion there you find the most worldly parishioners.

*Henry Ward Beecher, congregational minister, sermon of
1873, in Baltzell,* The Protestant Establishment
(1966), p. 101.

The new Liberal Church has a consistent scheme of thought; it goes to the mind for its ideas; it admits the claim of spontaneity; its method of obtaining truth is rational; the harmony it demands is harmony of principles—the orderly sequence of laws.

*Octavius Brooks Frothingham, Unitarian minister and
first president of the Free Religious Association,
on a free religion for all Americans, 1873,
in Ahlstrom,* A Religious History of
the American People *(1972),
p. 765.*

Our modern frontiersman, who clings to the railroads out along the prairies, is a very different person. He insists on being followed up by all the modern conveniences. Not only must he have a

church and school, but he must have the newspapers and magazines, and his wife and daughters must have a piano and silk dresses, and the new novels, and their minds, instead of being intent on the homely joys of the forest and the prairie, are vexed by the social and religious discussions of the far East. They want to hear Froude lecture, wonder what Plymouth Church is going to do with Bowen, would like a chance of listening to Lucca, are eager to try the newest thing in stoves, and wonder what the Emperor of Austria will think of the Illinois school-house at the Vienna Exhibition.

The Nation, *editorial of 1873, in DeNovo,*
The Gilded Age and After *(1972), pp. 98–99.*

If we suppose the requirement of currency to increase from the growth of wealth and population faster than it decreases from improved communication and banking facilities, then a certain growing may be admitted, but, as it goes on, it exerts a slow, gradual, and pitiless contraction on prices, broken only, in Spring and Fall, by a succession of commercial crises. If then, there was backbone enough in the nation to endure this without having recourse to expansion, the growth might go on for ten or twenty years, by which time perhaps 750,000,000 of currency might be the specie requirement. No historical precedents exist to guide us in judging whether this process would indeed go on under such circumstances. As a matter of speculation, I am inclined to believe that the actual course of things would be that after every crisis, wages would fall, industry would be checked, and the country would be slowly and gradually arrested in its entire industrial life.

*Yale apologist for industrial economy William Graham
Sumner,* A History of American Currency, with
Chapters on the English Bank Restriction and
Austrian Paper Money *(1874), pp. 224–225.
Available online at URL:
http://www.hti.umich.edu/cgi/t/
text/pagevieweridx?sid=
d3a27df9f1b7d1a18d617cc86c456a27
&idno=aeu9382.0001.001&c=
moa&cc=moa&seq=227&size=s&view=text.*

The wealth producers of this nation are the men and women who dig, delve and spin. Upon their shoulders rests the burden of giving to all the people that which money merely represents—the wealth itself.

Without toil there can be no wealth. He who toils is a wealthmaker.

> *A delegate to the second annual convention of the*
> *Industrial Congress of the United States, 1874,*
> *in Powderly,* Thirty Years of Labor, 1859–1889
> *(1967), p. 63.*

[It is] neither right nor practicable for all the loss to be borne by the employers. Some of it must be shared by the workingmen . . . We must hereafter be contented with lower wages for our labor and be more thankful for the opportunity to labor at all.

> *James Swank, secretary, American Iron and Steel*
> *Association, 1874, in Annual Report of the Secretary of*
> *the American Iron and Steel Association*
> *for the Year 1874, n.p.*

I hope, however, that you will enlarge the sphere of your labors beyond this narrow field, and extend an invitation to the laborers and workers of all other cities and towns to form similar organizations, harmonizing in spirit and action with your own; more particularly with a view of joining hands with the farmers, the laborers of the country, your natural allies, in one common, united effort to free this country from the shackles of monopoly . . . extend a helping hand to the farmers, the laborers of the field. They are your vanguard . . . Aid them in their brave warfare with your common enemy, hydraheaded monopoly.

Workingmen, laborers, come in solid phalanx, unite with your brethren [*sic*] in the country . . .

> *Labor reformer Francis A. Hoffman, Jr., to the*
> *Workingmen's Party, Chicago, Illinois, address of January*
> *25, 1874, in Roche,* American Political Thought
> *from Jefferson to Progressivism (1967).*

Nature intended him for a savage state; every instinct, every impulse of his soul inclines him to it. The white race might fall into a barbarous state, and, afterwards, subjected to the influence of civilization, be reclaimed and prosper. Not so for the Indian. He cannot be himself and be civilized.

> *General Geroge A. Custer, writing in "My Life on the*
> *Plains," 1874, in Slotkin,* The Fatal Environment
> *(1985), p. 410.*

The simple fact is that a great many laboring men are out of work. It is not the fault of merchants and man-

Samuel Bowles was the editor of the *Springfield Republican. (Library of Congress)*

ufacturers that they refuse to employ four men when they can pay but one, and decline to pay four dollars for work which they can buy for two and a half.

> *New York Graphic, editorial of January 14, 1874, in*
> *Morgan,* The Gilded Age *(1970).*

We have got to go through hay-seed, possibly ignorance, most likely inexperience, to light. At any rate, the old must pass away and all things become new—through granges and young men's reform clubs and disgust, generally. Primary schools for political education are in order.

> *Samuel Bowles, editor of the* Springfield Republican,
> *to economist David A. Wells, letter of 1874, in Morgan,*
> The Gilded Age *(1970), p. 75.*

It is the center of all those trades which harden and brutalize the men who engage in them. Its gutters run with ordure and blood; its buildings reek with smells of slaughter and stenches abominable beyond description . . .

Narrow alleys, dark and filthy, bordered by sluggish black streams of stinking filth, traverse this quarter in every direction. Night-carts, which elsewhere leave far behind them a wake of stench suggestive of epidemics, here may pass through in broad daylight without betraying their presence. Amid these scenes and smells lives and labors a large and strangely healthy population of brawny butchers, sinewy coopers, muscular tanners—a foreign population, speaking a foreign tongue, and living the life of the Fatherland. The greater part of them labor in tanneries, slaughter-houses and soap factories, receiving small salaries upon which an American workman could not support his family, and doing work which Americans instinctively shrink from . . . The air they breathe is indeed foully odorous, but it is heavily rich with globules of fresh blood and tallow and reeking flesh—healthy for the lungs and veins of the breathers.

Lafcadio Hearn, reporter for the Cincinnati Enquirer, *describing an immigrant section of the city, 1874, in Hoogenboom and Hoogenboom,* The Gilded Age *(1967), p. 98.*

It should be our purpose to arrange a business system by which an exchange of products may be made direct between the producer and consumer without the intervention of an unnecessary number of middle men. It is of but little satisfaction to our brothers of the South to know that corn in Iowa is selling at thirty cents per bushel while they pay eighty, or that meat in Illinois is four cents per pound, while it costs them eight. It is a questionable consolation to the manufacturer of New England to know that in the valley of the Mississippi a yard of his cloth will buy three loaves of bread, when but one of them ever reaches his family.

Patrons of Husbandry, proceedings of their Seventh Session, St. Louis, Missouri, 1874, in DeNovo, The Gilded Age and After *(1972), p. 112.*

In our intercourse with the world we are barricaded, and the arrows let fly at our hearts are warded off; but not so with us at Home. Here our hearts wear no covering, no armor. Every arrow strikes them; every cold wind blows full upon them; every story bears

against them. What in the world we would pass by in sport, in our Homes will wound us to the quick.

Reverend G. S. Weaver, giving advice to women on a husband's emotional needs, in Aims and Aids for Girls and Young Women on the Various Duties of Life, *1875, p. 145, quoted in Matthaei,* An Economic History of Women in America, *p. 119.*

I think it is a great mistake to take from Joseph and his band of Nez Perce Indians that valley . . . possibly Congress can be induced to let these . . . peaceable Indians have this poor valley for their own.

General Oliver O. Howard, military commander of the Wallowa Valley area in Washington Territory, to the War Department, letter of 1875, in Lockwood and Harris, Reasoning with Democratic Values *(1985).*

If an Indian can be possessed of rights of country . . . this country [the Black Hills] belongs for occupation by the Sioux.

Commissioner of Indian Affairs E. P. Smith, in his Annual Report, 1875, in Slotkin, The Fatal Environment *(1985), p. 420.*

For years the ruling idea of the Western mind has been the bringing of remote acres . . . under cultivation. There was thought to be some occult virtue in expediting this process—a service to God and one's country. Every artificial appliance and inducement was thus set to work to force the population out in advance of the steady and healthy growth of civilization into regions beyond the reach of the world's centres and outside the pale of social influence . . .

The result brought about by the unnatural diffusion of population . . . was exactly what any thinking and observing man should have anticipated, overproduction at remote points. This difficulty no increased cheapness of transportation can alleviate; it can only transfer the locality of the difficulty to a point somewhat more remote. The darling vision of the Granger's dreams . . . is a double-track, steel-rail, government-built, exclusively freight railroad from every farmer's barn-door straight to the city of New York.

Charles Francis Adams, Jr., historian and railroad expert, in the North American Review, *1875, in DeNovo,* The Gilded Age and After *(1972), p. 108.*

Dear Miss Mabel,
I have just finished a long letter to Hon. George Brown concerning my telegraphic schemes—and

now I feel like writing a few lines to you to thank you for so promptly letting me know of your safe arrival home. I felt indeed more anxious than I care to tell you when I saw you drive off from the Station alone. The horse looked so spirited and you drove off so fast—that I felt I better lose my train—than let you run any danger. However when you stopped at the corner I knew you had control over the horse—and so stepped on board the cars with a lighter heart.

I found Dr. and Mrs. Marsh on board on their way to New York. Baby was there too looking well and comfortable. And an elderly lady whose name I forget. I hope you have obtained your drawing-book—and that you are making numerous sketches of Bethel and the neighborhood. Please remember me kindly to Miss True, and tell her how sorry I was not to see more of her. I hope she will come to Boston soon. Remember me also to my little friend—Helen I think her name is—but impress upon her memory the fact that I am not "Miss Bell". I was at Cambridge yesterday and your mother told me of a letter she had received from you on the subject of "Woman's Rights". I never suspected that you were one of these people who think women have rights. Do you actually suppose their wishes are to be considered with the same respect as those of men? That their opinions are entitled to the same weight? That—when forced by circumstances to gain their livelihood—they are to be permitted to choose their occupations as men are?

The wisdom of the world has decided that they are inferior beings doomed to exist within the narrow space called "Woman's Sphere". Why then should they seek to rebel against the decrees of fate?

Mrs. Mary Somerville was guilty of the most unladylike conduct in daring to write works on the Connection of the Physical Sciences. If Miss Herschel had only been banished to a Seminary for young ladies—she would have been taught very different things from photographing sun-spots! Nor would she have had the audacity to rob scientific men of the discovery of the connection between sun-spots and the Aurora Borealis! Why should any ambitious woman be allowed to invade man's sacred domains? And there is that Miss Susan Dimmock too—intended by nature to be a lady. Words are too weak to portray the enormity of her offences against society. Who would ever have thought of that pure womanly spirit willingly rebelling against the restraints that society had placed upon her sex—offending the feelings of her own kind—running the

gauntlet of the world's criticism—and all for what? To do what men are paid to do. It is true it was to benefit the sick and dying—But are there not men enough in the world to do the work? Men paid, and paid well too—for performing those very duties. If she was obliged to earn her own living why did she not go to dressmaking or to teaching. These subjects are included in "Woman's Sphere"! Medecine [sic] and Surgery belong to man. Astronomy and the Physical Sciences are ours. All the professions and businesses that are most lucrative and honorable belong to us.

Why cannot women be contented with the condition in which the condition in which nature has placed them? Why should they seek to make themselves the equals of men? Must they be allowed to take the law into their own hands and think and act for themselves? Why can't they let us think and act for them? Would they not be happier so? Were not the negroes happier as slaves than they are now as freemen? Then they had no cares—They were not then called upon to battle with the world alone. Not that women are considered as slaves!

Woman is free and we men guard her and protect her. We do everything for her. We attend her in sickness—we look after her law-affairs—we preach to her—we legislate for her—we do all her thinking for her—in fact we leave her nothing to do but to dress—make fancy-work—and read novels! And yet women are discontented! What ingratitude! They must have higher education!—they must be able to choose their own occupations!—they must vote!—in a word they must be free to do whatever they like! Do they not forget that they are different beings from ourselves? If slaveholders could look upon "Liberty" as the mottoe [sic] of their flag without a blush—because their negroes had not white skins—why should not we adopt our mottoe [sic] "No taxation without Representation"—with free consciences knowing that women are not men. Slaveholders asserted that the negroes ought to be slaves because they were unfitted for liberty.

Abolitionists said they were unfitted for liberty because they were slaves. We say that women cannot acquire a higher education because their mental attainments are inferior to ours. Women say their mental attainments are inferior to ours because they cannot acquire a higher education. If we won't admit them to Harvard or Yale—they straightway obtain endowments for the Boston University—or have a

College built for themselves—the selfish creatures—at Northampton.

Where is all this to end? Not content with serving on our School Committees—they are agitating for political rights. They are refusing to pay their taxes unless they are represented. I suppose it will not be long before we have a woman wanting to be President of the United States! Well it is not for me to say her "Nay"—seeing that I am a subject of Queen Victoria—a woman-sovereign—and one of the best the world has seen—so my best wishes go with her. If women want anything they are sure to get it in the long run—so we better give in gracefully at once.

I trust you will return to Cambridge soon. I have just five minutes to catch my train to Boston.
Please excuse haste.
Yours sincerely,
A. Graham Bell.

Alexander Graham Bell, letter to Mabel Hubbard Bell, October 5, 1875. Available online at URL: http://memory.loc.gov/cgi-bin/query/r?ammem/ magbell:@field(DOCID+@lit(magbell03400202)).

3
Compromise Politics and Fighting in the West
1876–1880

THE HISTORICAL CONTEXT

A curious mix of issues dominated the national scene in the mid-1870s. U.S. citizens were proud of their many industrial and technological accomplishments, a fact made clear during the Centennial Exhibition in Philadelphia, Pennsylvania, in 1876. Demonstrated at the exhibition was one of the most tantalizing of these advances, Alexander Graham Bell's telephone. More than 8 million admissions were tallied at the exhibition, which ran through November 10 of that year.

Public attention continued to be absorbed with concern over ethics and morality. The Prohibition Party met in spring 1876 and nominated as its presidential candidate General Green C. Smith, who ran on this single issue. Prohibition of alcohol was advocated by a small but vocal portion of the U.S. population; one representative from New Hampshire proposed a constitutional amendment banning the sale of liquor. It symbolized for many the inexorable changes overtaking American society—the influx of immigrants since the Civil War had forced the native-born to confront new ideas and new practices. For some, increased consumption of alcohol (and its concurrent problems) was a direct result of immigrant influence. For Prohibitionists it was a practice to be eliminated quickly and completely.

In June 1876, the Democrats held their convention and nominated Samuel J. Tilden. At the Republican Convention, Rutherford B. Hayes was nominated. President Grant was limited by tradition to two terms of office (he had served as president since 1868) so was out of the running. The race was a close one, and when the results were counted, Samuel J. Tilden had won the popular vote, garnering 250,000 votes out of a total of 8.5 million votes cast.

The Electoral College vote was a different situation, however. In three states, the results were contested. South Carolina, Florida, and Louisiana were strongly divided between the white vote and votes by newly enfranchised African Americans, and between critics of Reconstruction and its supporters. To determine how the disputed vote would be handled, Congress passed legislation establishing the Joint Electoral Commission. Under the terms of a compromise fashioned by the commission, Democrats agreed to accept Rutherford B. Hayes as the next U.S. president, as long as the Republican administration agreed to withdraw federal soldiers from the South, enact legislation that would support Southern industrialization, and appoint Democrats to key patronage positions and to a cabinet post.[1] The Compromise of 1877 meant the end of Reconstruction.[2] It also marked a clean break with the wartime era and seemed to symbolize the start of a new, more progressive and optimistic age.

Continued labor organization and growing unrest among the ranks of the nation's workers proved to be a serious political force, underscoring a need for social and economic reforms. For example, the Workingmen's Party, a socialist group, was formed in 1876, as was the secret fraternal society known as the Mystic Shrine. Boston-area women established the Women's Educational and Industrial Union to help provide a wider outlet for women's abilities. Some individuals also hoped to improve the condition of working people and did so by independent efforts; many of these were missionaries who served the thousands of immigrants flocking to urban areas.

Workers' power grew stronger through organizing efforts aimed at seizing control from the wealthy few. The Great Railroad Strike of 1877, which began in West Virginia after the Baltimore & Ohio Railroad cut wages for the second time in a year, was indicative of such labor power.[3] During the strike, protesting railroad workers vowed to prevent all trains from running again until the pay reduction was rescinded. Although the governor sent in the militia, soldiers were reluctant to use force against the strikers. (This prompted the governor to call for federal troops to break the strike.) Similarly, in Pittsburgh, Pennsylvania, local police refused to open fire on strikers. When the strike spread to Baltimore, Maryland, street fighting erupted between workers and militia, resulting in 10 deaths when the soldiers fired into the crowd.

Throughout the nation, railroad workers walked off the job, and soon workers in other industries were on strike, as well. The Chicago Workingmen's Party demonstrated in crowds of thousands, and in St. Louis, a general strike lasted almost seven days. Over the next 20 years, the Haymarket Riot, the Pullman strike, and others would focus public attention on the need for improved working conditions, better wages, and more realistic hours for laborers. Each time these riots or strikes occurred, they reminded onlookers of the real power behind the growth and expansion of the United States in the late 19th century—the power of the worker. As labor organizers planned campaigns for the future, politicians and corporate leadership moved to protect their interests. The strikes made clear that labor was powerful enough to shake the foundations of even the most stable corporate and industrial entities in the United States. The result was that some states passed legislation to prohibit conspiracy activities. In others, militia units were established in greater numbers, and construction of armories, from which National Guard troops could be deployed, became common in many cities.

Labor troubles were not the only difficulties facing the federal government at the midpoint of the decade. Congress continued to wrestle with conflicting demands over its monetary policy. Following the Panic of 1873, many citizens, especially farmers and those owing money to creditors, had demanded that the government print additional paper money, or "greenbacks," and provide for unlimited coinage of silver. By 1876, the National Greenback Party was pledging to fight on behalf of this voting bloc, campaigning on a pledge to overturn a fiscal-control bill passed in 1875, the Specie Resumption Act.[4] It was clear that the country would be back on a gold standard by the end of the decade, but while currency was now limited to gold coin, mining interests added their voices to the chorus of support for a return to silver coinage. Combined with tariff questions and discussion about trade regulation, this issue would become the most pressing question under debate in Congress into the new century.

The potential for white development of the American West provided for policy debate of a different order. Following the conclusion of the Civil War, several conflicts had erupted between Native Americans and government troops. These included, by the 1870s, the Red River War (1874–75) between Comanche and U.S. forces commanded by Generals William T. Sherman and Philip Sheridan, and the Black Hills War (1876–77), with the Lakota Sioux, and the Battle of Rosebud (1876). During the last-named, Lakota and Cheyenne fighters defeated U.S. Army troops that had been sent to reinforce the Seventh Cavalry, under the command of General George Armstrong Custer.[5] Because the federal government's interest in opening up western regions to settlement was continually thwarted by Native American resistance, Custer's outspoken views and flamboyant style put him in the spotlight. Canny federal officials saw in this vain, ambitious young man the answer to their dilemma over land use and Native American policy. Custer was given free rein to deal as he wished regarding removal of Native Americans from government land. His actions were enthusiastically reported in newspapers across the nation, and he was viewed as a hero, until he misjudged his adversary, in June 1876. Custer's death at the Little Bighorn River in South Dakota caused a national outcry.[6] When author Frederick Whittaker published the *Complete Life of George A. Custer,* shortly after the general's death, it became a best seller. Many later believed that because of Custer's broad popularity, the outcry over his death was hyperbolic, and fueled federal actions that were deliberately destructive to Native American life and culture.

There were strong arguments made, in Congress, for and against silver coinage, bimetallism, and paper currency. Most Americans were hard-pressed by an economy spiraling downward, particularly farmers and others dependent on agricultural production or on meager hourly wages. Various measures had been discussed and proposed by Congress as it sought ways to alleviate inflation and stimulate the economy. In February 1878, the Bland-Allison Act was passed, permitting coinage of silver and increasing the value of paper money.[7] This legislation had the support of midwestern congress whose constituents wanted relief from crushing debt loads on farm equipment and property. By the end of the year, paper currency would have a value equal to that of gold coin, but the debate over coinage and its effect on the economy continued to dominate politics through the end of the century.

In November, the Democrats again took control of the House and Senate although a Republican, President Rutherford B. Hayes, sat in the White House. In part because of this Democratic control of Congress, Hayes's record of achievement would be limited, and he was not nominated for reelection after his first term of office.

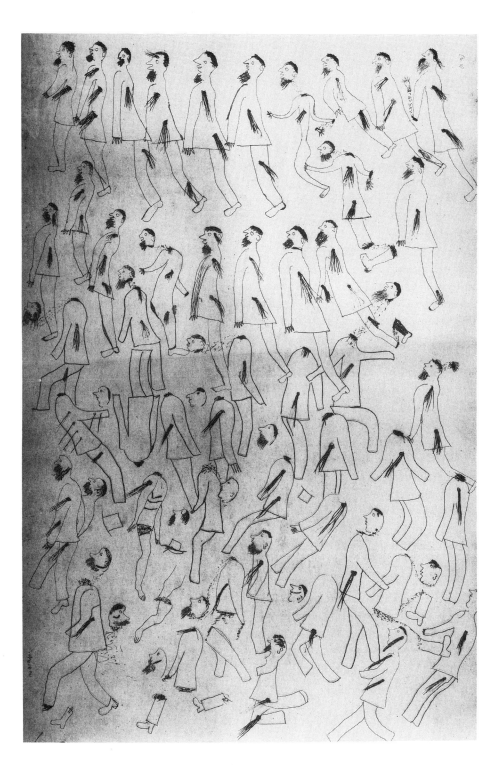

A Sioux artist depicted the Battle of Little Bighorn, in which General George A. Custer and many others lost their lives. *(National Anthropological Archives, Smithsonian Institution, from ms. 2367=A[031], neg. 47001)*

Women's rights continued to be promoted by advocates of gender equality, and in 1878, a woman suffrage amendment was proposed in Congress for the first time, although it would not be passed and ratified until 1920. In 1879, women achieved parity in the courtroom, when women lawyers were permitted to argue before the U.S. Supreme Court. Despite some gains, particularly in educational opportunity, U.S. women continued to struggle against social and cultural restrictions throughout the period.

Thomas A. Edison, who continued to amaze the nation with his technological abilities, developed and perfected the phonograph, and the lightbulb, and founded the first electric light company in New York City. Edison's inventions eased everyday life for thousands of Americans, and his ideas along with those of Alexander Graham Bell, were widely implemented by the end of the 1880s.[8]

Debate over the causes of the Great Railroad Strike, continued in Congress, and both railroad owners, public officials, and private citizens pressed for regulation of the growing railroad industry. In 1878, with the case *Hall v. Cuir,* the U.S. Supreme Court ruled that protection of an individual's civil rights did not extend to racial integration in railroad accommodations.[9]

Labor unions grew in number; in 1878, the Amalgamated Association in Iron, Steel, and Tin Workers was organized. It would later become one of the nation's most powerful union organizations. Labor leaders debated the best ways to bring about an eight-hour workday, and questioned whether union membership should be denied on the basis of certain occupations.

Control and review of immigration policy were priority issues for the federal government and also took precedence during discourse among labor unions and private reformers. The need for inexpensive labor encouraged large numbers of Chinese workers to immigrate to the United States beginning in the mid-19th century. These workers were employed primarily in railroad construction, and by 1867, the Chinese immigrant population in California alone was calculated to be close to 50,000. With the signing, in 1868, of the Burlingame Treaty (which guaranteed Chinese people immigration rights, but not citizenship rights), anti-Chinese sentiment began to increase sharply. This was due, in part, to unfounded prejudices against people whose culture, language, appearance, and religious heritage was radically different from that of native-born Americans.

In 1877, anti-Chinese riots broke out in San Francisco, prompting Congress in 1879 to pass anti–immigration legislation that President Hayes vetoed, believing it to be in violation of the Burlingame Treaty.[10] In 1880, a new treaty with China permitted the United States to regulate, limit, or suspend Chinese laborers' entry into the country (although not to prohibit Chinese immigration outright). Ultimately, in 1882, Congress passed the Chinese Exclusion Act, which banned Chinese immigrant labor for a decade.[11] Also, some labor leaders worried about the influence of the socialist ideas carried to this country by European immigrants. And there were increased investigations into the needs

Ellis Island, New York, was the point of entry for European immigrants. *(Library of Congress)*

of the immigrant population in large cities where immigrant health and housing problems had become a political issue as well as a moral one.

The cultural change, economic instability, and technological development that marked U.S. life in the 1880s resulted from the country's rapid transformation from a homogeneous, agrarian society to one characterized by industrial growth, international commerce, and a large increase in immigrant population. But for sheer drama, the election of James A. Garfield to the presidency in 1880—and his assassination only months later—overshadowed all else. Supreme Court decisions, debate over monetary policy, and western expansion continued, but were unable to command the public's attention. Shocked by Garfield's death, people focused their attention on the presidency and national politics. The singular technological innovations of the 1880s would be accepted as unremarkable just a few years later. Among them were the process for manufacturing rolls of camera film (patented by George Eastman of Rochester, New York), the completion of an elevated railway system in Manhattan, the development of the incandescent lamp by Thomas A. Edison and the manufacture of house paint by the Sherwin-Williams Company in Cleveland, Ohio.

The ever-growing popularity of sports such as baseball and lawn tennis, and more leisurely outdoor pursuits, like croquet and bicycling, proved that Americans continued to enjoy free time. This growing appreciation for recreation and pleasurable pastimes led to the greater regulation of some sports. The first U.S. Tennis Championships were played after the U.S. National Lawn Tennis Association (USNLTA) was founded by James Dwight, in 1881. New baseball rules were established, and the League of American Wheelmen was founded in Newport, Rhode Island, by bicycle enthusiasts hoping to gain national prominence for their sport.

Republican James A. Garfield was elected president in 1880. *(Library of Congress)*

As the executive branch carried out Congressional wishes, and avoided its own initiatives, the nation's two major parties kept busy. Maine's James G. Blaine and Connecticut's Orville H. Platt were two Republican senators who dominated their party and helped to promote and sustain high tariffs and government interest in business. The Democrats' ranks grew as immigration changed the urban electorate especially as xenophobia merged with prohibitionism and anti-labor-unionism, adding to the Democratic party ranks.

Because the desire among urban working people, and farmers, to organize had grown during the late 1870s, outspoken, sometimes visionary, leaders began to influence those Americans for whom conventional political and social approaches to problem-solving appeared ineffective. The National Farmers' Alliance was formed in 1880 by disgruntled farmers and other citizens committed to the needs and interests of agriculture. This group would later be transformed into one of the nation's most viable third parties, the Populists. At this same time, a somewhat obscure labor activist named Eugene V. Debs was named the national secretary-treasurer of the Brotherhood of Locomotive Firemen. Years later, Debs would become head of the Socialist Party and be jailed under the terms of the 1918 Sedition Act for his public statements against U.S. participation in World War I. The desire to congregate in groups defined by political ideology or cultural and ethnic lines continued into the 20th century. Even after it became apparent that Rutherford B. Hayes would not be reelected to a second presidential term, few people anticipated a great deal of change in the presidency. Garfield's election in 1880 carried with it no expectation of radical reform. Vice President Chester A. Arthur assumed leadership after Garfield's death in September 1881, and it seemed that the Republicans would continue to support industry and big business through high tariffs and that agriculture and labor would remain more or less on the economic periphery.

CHRONICLE OF EVENTS

1876

January 31: The United States orders all Native Americans to move onto reservations.

February: A contractor, Caleb P. Marsh, reports that he has been offered control of trading posts at Fort Sill, in Indian Territory, by Secretary of War Belknap, in exchange for a payment of $12,000.

February 2: The National League of Professional Baseball Clubs of Major League Baseball is formed.

February 14: Alexander Graham Bell applies for a patent for a new invention named the telephone, which is granted on March 7.

February 22: Johns Hopkins University is founded in Baltimore, Maryland.

March 2: Secretary of War William W. Belknap, found to have been selling trading post privileges in Indian Territory, has impeachment proceedings brought against him. He resigns, however, and Congress is unable to carry out the resolution for impeachment.

March 10: Alexander Graham Bell talks for the first time on the telephone with his assistant, Thomas Watson.

March 10: Ulysses S. Grant, president of the United States, together with the emperor of Brazil, opens the great International Exhibition at Fairmount Park in Philadelphia to launch the celebration of the U.S. centennial.

April 1: The first game of baseball in the National League is played—Boston beats Philadelphia, 6–5.

May 10: The Centennial Exhibition opens in Philadelphia, Pennsylvania. The exhibition is designed to display America's triumphs in areas of science and technology.

May 17: The Prohibition Party holds its national convention in Cleveland, Ohio, where General Green Clay Smith is nominated for the presidency of the United States; Gideon Stewart is nominated for vice president.

Above is a depiction of Custer's last charge at the Battle of Little Bighorn. *(Library of Congress)*

May 18: The Greenback Party has its convention in Indianapolis, Indiana. Peter Cooper and Samuel Cary are nominated for president and vice president, respectively.

June 4: The *Transcontinental Express* arrives in San Francisco, California, using the first transcontinental rail line, arriving 83 hours and 39 minutes after departing from New York City.

June 6: The Imperial Council of the Ancient Arabic Order of Nobles of the Mystic Shrine is organized in the United States. This group is connected to the Masonic Order.

June 14: Cincinnati, Ohio, is the site of the Republican National Convention, which opens today. Rutherford B. Hayes is nominated for president, and William A. Wheeler is selected as his running mate.

June 17: At the Battle of the Rosebud, 1,500 Sioux and Cheyenne Indians, led by Chief Crazy Horse, defeat General George Crook's troops at Rosebud Creek in Montana Territory.

June 23: The telephone is demonstrated at Massachusetts Institute of Technology. Two days later, Alexander Graham Bell demonstrates the invention at the Philadelphia Centennial Exhibition.

June 25: Lieutenant Colonel George Armstrong Custer of the U.S. Seventh Cavalry leads 300 men against a combined force of approximately 5,000 Lakota, Cheyenne, and Arapaho. Chief Sitting Bull and Chief Crazy Horse lead their combined forces into a battle in which they ultimately defeat and kill Custer and his troops.

June 28: The Democrats open their national convention at St. Louis, Missouri. Samuel J. Tilden and Thomas A. Hendricks are nominated for president and vice president, respectively.

July 4: The 100th anniversary of the Declaration of Independence is celebrated.

July 14: Despite widespread support for his candidacy, James G. Blaine is denied the Republican nomination for president, which goes instead to Rutherford B. Hayes.

July 25: Representative Richard P. Bland (D-Missouri) proposed legislation to issue unlimited silver coinage.

August 1: Colorado is the 38th state to enter the Union.

August 8: Thomas A. Edison receives a patent for the mimeograph machine.

September 7: Outlaw Jesse James and members of the James-Younger gang attempt to rob a bank in Northfield, Minnesota. A crowd of citizens drives them away.

November 7: Samuel J. Tilden wins the presidential election with a total of 4,284,020 popular votes. Hayes amasses 4,036,572 popular votes. But the votes in four states—Oregon, South Carolina, Florida, and Louisiana—are declared invalid.

November 10: The Centennial Exhibition at Philadelphia closes.

November 23: William "Boss" Tweed, former leader of the political machine known as Tammany Hall, is captured in Spain, after having eluded authorities who sought him on corruption charges. Tweed is released to police in New York City.

December 5: A fire in a Brooklyn, New York, theater kills more than 300 people.

December 6: Republican voters in the four disputed states cast all their votes for Rutherford B. Hayes, which gives him the majority with one electoral college vote. Democrats in these states cast their votes for Tilden. The returns are sent to Congress.

Rutherford B. Hayes served two terms as Ohio's governor before his nomination for U.S. president in 1876. *(Library of Congress)*

December 12: Henry W. Blair, a representative from New Hampshire, proposes a constitutional amendment prohibiting the production and sale of alcohol.

December 13: The House passes a bill permitting unlimited coinage of silver. The bill is sent to the Senate, where it languishes for over a year without action being taken on it.

1877

January 8: Crazy Horse and his warriors fight their last battle with the U.S. Cavalry in Montana.

January 9: Congress establishes the Joint Electoral Commission to clear up the dispute over the recent presidential election results.

January 30: Alexander Graham Bell obtains a second patent for an improved version of the telephone.

February 8: The Joint Electoral Commission, in ruling for Hayes, establishes the conditions necessary for federal troop withdrawal from the South.

March 1: The Supreme Court rules in favor of permitting individual states to regulate their own interstate and intrastate traffic as well as the charges for warehouse rates. The cases are *Peik v. Chicago & Northwestern Railroad Company* and *Munn v. Illinois.*

March 2: After President Hayes pledges to uphold certain compromise measures—chief among them is removal of federal troops from the three remaining Radical states (Louisiana, South Carolina, and Florida)—electoral votes are counted, and Hayes is named president of the United States.

March 3: The Desert Land Act passes Congress, offering 640 acres of land to anyone willing to irrigate a portion of the claim for a period of three years.

March 4: Emile Berliner invents the microphone.

March 5: Rutherford B. Hayes is inaugurated as the nation's 19th president.

April 10: By federal decree, troops are officially withdrawn from South Carolina, ending Reconstruction.

April 24: President Hayes orders the last of the federal troops removed from New Orleans, Louisiana.

May 6: Realizing that his people are weakened by cold and hunger, Chief Crazy Horse of the Oglala Sioux surrenders to U.S. troops in Nebraska.

May 8: At Gilmore's Gardens in New York City, the first Westminster Dog Show opens and runs for four days.

May 17: Former President Grant leaves for a round-the-world trip.

June 1: The Society of American Artists is established.

June 14: Flag Day is made a national holiday, commemorating the 100th anniversary of the United States flag.

June 15: Henry Ossian Flipper becomes the first African-American cadet to graduate from the U.S. Military Academy.

July 1: Workers at the Lackawanna Iron and Coal Company in Scranton, Pennsylvania, are notified that their wages are to be reduced. Within a month, they go on strike.

July 14: The Great Railroad Strike begins in response to pay cuts of 35 percent over a three-year period.

July 16: Activities surrounding the Great Railroad Strike are interrupted by federal troops, called out for the first time since before the Civil War.

July 20: Nine striking railroad workers are shot and others are wounded in Baltimore, Maryland, where militia have fired into a crowd of demonstrators.

July 21: A day after bloody rioting in Baltimore from Baltimore & Ohio Railroad workers and the deaths of nine rail workers at the hands of the Maryland militia, workers in Pittsburgh stage a sympathy strike that is met with an assault by the state militia. Pittsburgh then erupts into widespread rioting.

The Great Railroad Strike involved thousands of workers and resulted in extensive destruction of property. *(Library of Congress)*

July 26: Nineteen die in Chicago, Illinois, when police break up a gathering of strikers.

July 31: Despite the solidarity of thousands of striking railroad workers, the federal government is successful in bringing an end to the Great Railroad Strike. Few of the strikers' demands are met, but the labor movement has grown nationwide as a result of the summer's violent activities.

August 9: Near Big Hole River in Montana, a group of Nez Perce clash with U.S. Army troops.

August 12: Astronomer Asaph Hall discovers Deimos, the outermost moon of the planet Mars.

August 17: Arizona blacksmith F. P. Cahill is fatally wounded by notorious outlaw Billy the Kid.

August 18: Astronomer Asaph Hall discovers Phobos, the inner moon of Mars.

August 29: Mormon leader Brigham Young dies. His death will enable the Utah Territory to pass laws prohibiting polygamy and set the stage for Utah's entrance into the Union.

September 5: Oglala Sioux chief Crazy Horse is bayoneted by a U.S. soldier after resisting confinement in a guardhouse at Fort Robinson in Nebraska.

October 10: Following recovery of General George Armstrong Custer's body from the site of the Little Bighorn Battle the previous year, Custer is given a funeral with full military honors and is laid to rest at West Point, New York.

November 5: The Senate continues to avoid action on the proposed unlimited silver coinage bill.

November 21: Thomas Edison publicizes his new invention, the phonograph, a machine that can record sound.

November 23: The United States pays Great Britain $5.5 million for North Atlantic fishing privileges, under the terms of the Treaty of Washington.

November 29: Edison demonstrates the phonograph.

1878

January 10: Senator A. A. Sargent introduces a women's suffrage amendment into the Congress. It will not be adopted until 1920.

January 14: The Supreme Court rules, in *Hall v. Cuir,* that the railroads are under no obligation to provide equal accommodations to rail passengers regardless of race.

January 17: As part of a growing interest in expansion, the Congress ratifies a treaty between the United States and Samoa, giving the United States jurisdiction over the harbor at Pago Pago, where the United States can refuel its naval fleet.

January 28: The nation's first commercial telephone switchboard is installed in New Haven, Connecticut.

January 28: The Yale Daily News begins publication as the country's first college daily paper.

February 11: In Boston, Massachusetts, the nation's first bicycle club is formed.

February 12: F. W. Thayer patents the first baseball catcher's mask.

February 18: The Lincoln County War begins in Lincoln County, New Mexico.

February 19: Thomas A. Edison patents the first phonograph.

February 21: The first telephone directory is published in New Haven, Connecticut.

February 22: The Greenback Labor Party is formed in Toledo, Ohio.

February 28: The Bland-Allison Act is passed by Congress. It requires the government to mint silver coin in amounts between $2 million and $4 million per month.

February 28: The Agricultural and Mechanical College of the State of Mississippi (later known as Mississippi State University) is founded by the state legislature.

April 2: The Women's Hotel is opened, the first to be run exclusively for women, in New York City.

April 18: Thomas Edison reveals his newly developed phonograph to the National Academy of Sciences in Washington, D.C.

April 21: In New York City, the first firehouse pole is installed. This innovation quickly becomes a symbol of the efficiency and speed with which firefighters respond to alarms.

May 8: Paul Hines becomes the first professional baseball player to make an unassisted triple play.

June 3: Congress passes the Timber and Stone Act in order to make additional land available to farmers. The act permits the purchase of 160 acres of land at $2.50 per acre.

June 3: The American Laryngological Association is founded in Buffalo, New York, by physicians specializing in diseases of the throat.

June 11: The District of Columbia is permanently established as the nation's capital by act of Congress.

July 3: The first dirigible flight is scheduled.

July 9: Henry Tibbe patents the manufacture of corncob pipes.

July 11: President Hayes begins a series of much-needed civil service reforms by removing Chester A. Arthur from the post of customs collector for the Port of New York.

July 26: In California, an outlaw named "Black Bart" steals a safe box from a Wells Fargo stagecoach. The empty box is recovered later with nothing inside except a poem.

August 10: The nation's first home-study course is organized in Chautauqua, New York. Chautauqua will soon become synonymous with learning and the arts, and thousands will flock there during the summer months for institutes organized around a variety of subjects.

August 21: The American Bar Association is established in Saratoga, New York.

September 1: The first woman telephone operator is employed in Boston, Massachusetts.

October 4: The Chinese Embassy opens in Washington, D.C.

October 12: In Glasgow, Missouri, a contract for the construction of the first all-steel railroad bridge is signed.

October 15: Thomas Edison establishes the Edison Electric Light Company in New York City.

October 17: John A. Macdonald returns to office as Prime Minister of Canada. A yellow fever epidemic in Mississippi Valley leaves more than 13,000 people dead.

November 5: As an outcome of congressional elections nationwide, the Democratic party resumes control of both the House and the Senate.

November 14: The American Humane Association adopts its constitution in Baltimore, Maryland.

December 9: Today marks the first time, since the beginning of the Civil War, that greenbacks are equal to gold dollars and redeemable at face value on Wall Street.

December 26: The first retail store electric lighting is installed in Philadelphia, Pennsylvania.

1879

January 23: In Crawfordsville, Indiana, the first national archery association is established. Archery rapidly becomes a favorite pastime of many Americans, and the sport is among the first in which U.S. women will earn a medal in the 20th-century Olympic Games.

January 25: Congress passes the Arrears of Pension Act to authorize back-payment of military pensions.

February 12: At New York City's Gilmore's Gardens the first artificial ice rink in North America opens.

February 14: Blanche K. Bruce of Mississippi is the first African-American senator to preside over the U.S. Senate.

February 15: Women lawyers can now bring cases before the U.S. Supreme Court.

February 22: The first five-cent store opens in Utica, New York. Its proprietor is F. W. Woolworth.

March 1: President Hayes vetoes passage of a rider to the Army Appropriations Act designed to weaken the Enforcement Acts of 1865 and 1874. The latter provide the president with the authority to use federal troops during elections as a means of protecting civil rights. As Hayes is successful in these attempts to usurp executive powers, he begins to build once again the power of the presidency that has been eroding since the Reconstruction era.

Belva Lockwood was the first woman to practice law before the U.S. Supreme Court. *(Library of Congress)*

March 3: Belva Lockwood is the first woman to be admitted to practice law before the U.S. Supreme Court.

March 3: Congress authorizes issuance of the first postage-due stamps.

March 3: The U.S. Geological Survey is created.

March 11: Congress attempts to restrict Chinese immigration; President Hayes vetoes the proposed legislation.

April 2: Toll-line commercial service for telephone customers begins in Springfield, Massachusetts.

April 29: Electric lights are first used to illuminate city streets in Cleveland, Ohio.

April 30: The nation's first factory inspection law is enacted in Massachusetts.

May 8: An automobile patent is filed by George Selden in Rochester, New York. He is the first to perfect the internal combustion engine.

May 9: The first postage-due stamps are issued by the U.S. Postal Service.

May 10: The nation's first archaeological society is founded in Boston, Massachusetts.

May 23: The first state school of veterinary medicine opens in Ames, Iowa.

May 28: The Mississippi River Commission is formed by Congress to help make better use of the river for commercial and other purposes.

May 30: New York City's Gilmore's Garden is renamed Madison Square Garden by William Vanderbilt.

July 1: The Illinois legislature passes a law prohibiting employment of women.

July 4: The so-called Taughannock giant, a man's figure carved from stone and weighing 800 pounds, is unearthed on the shore of Lake Cayuga in Ithaca, New York. The seven-foot long statue is later deemed to be a hoax.

September 23: The first hearing aid is patented in River Park, Illinois. It is known as the audiophone.

September 27: The first amateur athletic competition is held in New York City.

October 21: Using a carbonized filament, Thomas Edison tests the first electric lightbulb. It lasts more than 13 hours before burning out.

November 1: An American Indian school opens in Carlisle, Pennsylvania.

November 4: A patent is taken out for the manufacture of a cash register in Dayton, Ohio.

November 17: Thomas Edison's incandescent lamp burns for an unprecedented 16 hours. This development ushers in the era of electric lighting.

December: The first photograph to be taken using incandescent lighting is shot in Menlo Park, New Jersey.

December 5: The first automatic telephone is patented.

December 10: The American Library Association is incorporated.

December 31: Thomas Edison demonstrates incandescent lighting to the public at Menlo Park, New Jersey.

1880

January 21: Memphis, Tennessee, becomes the first city in the nation to establish a separate system of sewage disposal.

January 27: Thomas A. Edison patents the incandescent lamp.

February 2: The first electric streetlight is installed in Wabash, Indiana.

February 12: President Hayes warns settlers on Indian lands west of the Mississippi that their illegal presence may further damage government relations with Native American tribes. Within a decade, however, the

Inventor Thomas Alva Edison helped to usher in a new technological age in the United States. *(Library of Congress)*

land will be taken from the Indians and made available to white settlers.

February 12: The first croquet league is founded.

February 16: The American Society of Mechanical Engineers is formed in New York City.

February 21: The first freight service on municipal railroads begins.

March: The U.S. branch of the Salvation Army is formed in Philadelphia, Pennsylvania. Commissioner George Railton and seven women are among these first U.S. members. Commander Evangeline Booth, daughter of Salvation Army founder William Booth, will later assume command of the American branch.

March 1: The U.S. Supreme Court rules that it is unconstitutional to deny black Americans participation in jury duty. The case is *Strauder v. West Virginia.*

March 4: The first halftone engraving is done at the *Daily Graphic,* a New York city newspaper.

March 10: Members of the charitable organization the Salvation Army arrive in the United States from Britain.

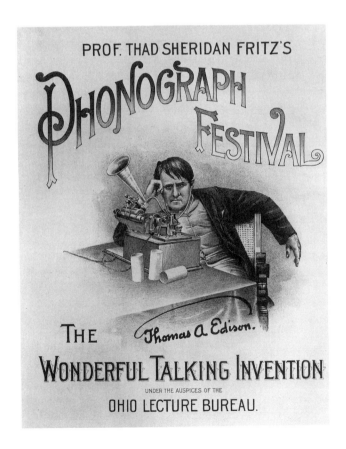

Among Edison's many inventions was the phonograph. *(Library of Congress)*

March 18: A House committee hears testimony from Ferdinand de Lesseps, builder of the Suez Canal. Congress is anxious to confirm U.S. authority over the canal being built across the isthmus of Panama by de Lesseps's company.

March 22: In Grand Rapids, Michigan, the nation's first hydroelectric commercial power plant is organized. It is named the Grand Rapids Electric Light and Power Company.

March 23: The first flour rolling mill is patented by John Stevens.

April: The National Farmers' Alliance is formed; it is later to become the Populist Party.

April: The first facility for occupational therapeutic treatment opens in Boston, Massachusetts. It is known as the Adams Nervine Asylum.

April 27: The first bone-conduction hearing aid device is patented.

May 13: In Menlo Park, New Jersey, Thomas Edison tests the first electric railway.

May 15: The Archeological Institute of America holds its annual meeting in Boston, Massachusetts.

June: The four-masted schooner *William J. White* is launched in Bath, Maine.

June 1: Paddy Ryan wins the world heavyweight bare-knuckle championship at Colliers, West Virginia.

June 1: The first pay telephone goes into service in New Haven, Connecticut.

June 2: Chicago, Illinois, is the site of the Republican National Convention, which opens today.

June 8: James A. Garfield wins the Republican nomination for president after 36 ballots, during which General Grant is also put forth as a candidate. Chester A. Arthur is nominated as the vice presidential candidate.

June 9: James B. Weaver is nominated for president of the United States by the Greenback Labor Party.

June 17: The Prohibition Party nominates Neal Dow for U.S. president.

June 23: Democrats open their national convention in Cincinnati, Ohio. General Winfield Scott Hancock receives the nomination for president; William H. English is his vice presidential running mate.

July 1: Dr. Emily Howard Stowe is the first woman licensed to practice medicine in Canada.

September: The nation's first Italian-language newspaper is published in New York City.

September 1: In Staten Island, New York, the first lawn tennis tournament of national importance is held.

James A. Garfield was nominated at the Republican National Convention in Chicago in 1880. *(Library of Congress)*

September 7: The clay pigeon target is patented for trapshooting enthusiasts by G. Ligowsky in Cincinnati, Ohio.

October: A severe winter storm, later termed the "Blizzard of 1880," causes hundreds of deaths in the United States.

October 1: In Menlo Park, New Jersey, the first incandescent lightbulb factory opens.

October 4: The University of Southern California is founded in Los Angeles.

November 2: James A. Garfield defeats the Democratic candidate for president, Winfield S. Hancock, by a 214–155 electoral college vote. This is the first time that a U.S. representative in office is elected president.

November 8: Actress Sarah Bernhardt makes her American stage debut.

November 17: A treaty with China allows the U.S. to regulate the number of, but not exclude, Chinese immigrants.

November 22: Actress Lillian Russell makes her stage debut at Tony Pastor's Theatre in New York City.

December 17: Edison Electric Illuminating Company of New York is organized. Thomas Edison intends to build electric generating stations throughout the city.

EYEWITNESS TESTIMONY

At a mighty interval and with unequal steps we are the followers of Copernicus and Galileo and Bacon and Newton and Adam Smith and Bentham. How does it concern us that the mass—the mighty majority—of our fellow voters are ignorant and stupid and selfish and short-sighted? That's the practical statesman's affair . . . Don't you talk to me of popular acceptance. The moment you and I begin on that we are lost.

> *Charles Francis Adams, Jr., writing about policies regarding trade regulation, 1876, in Morgan,* The Gilded Age *(1970), p. 68.*

Mr. Watson, come here. I want you.

> *Inventor Alexander Graham Bell, to his assistant Thomas A. Watson, via the first telephone, on March 10, 1876, in Schlesinger,* Almanac of American History *(1983), p. 330.*

The question to be determined in this case is whether the general assembly of Illinois can, under the limitations upon the legislative power of the States imposed by the Constitution of the United States, fix by law the maximum of charges for the storage of grain in warehouses at Chicago and other places in the State having not less than one hundred thousand inhabitants, 'in which grain is stored in bulk, and in which the grain of different owners is mixed together, or in which grain is stored in such a manner that the identity of different lots or parcels cannot be accurately preserved' . . .

When one becomes a member of society, he necessarily parts with some rights or privileges which, as an individual not affected by his relations to others, he might retain . . . It matters not in this case that these plaintiffs in error had built their warehouses and established their business before the regulations complained of were adopted. What they did was from the beginning subject to the power of the body politic to require them to conform to such regulations as might be established by the proper authorities for the common good. They entered upon their business and provided themselves with the means to carry it on subject to this condition. If they did not wish to submit themselves to such interference, they should not have clothed the public with an interest in their concerns.

The same principle applies to them that does to the proprietor of a hackney-carriage, and as to him it has never been supposed that he was exempt from regulating statutes or ordinances because he had purchased his horses and carriage and established his business before the statute or the ordinance was adopted.

It is insisted, however, that the owner of property is entitled to a reasonable compensation for its use, even though it be clothed with a public interest, and that what is reasonable is a judicial and not a legislative question.

> *U.S. Supreme Court chief justice Morrison R. Waite, issuing an opinion of the Court, in* Munn v. Illinois *94 U.S. 113, 1876. In this ruling (the case dealt with farmers' claims that they were being charged unfair rates by grain elevator operators) the U.S. Supreme Court determined that a state acts legitimately when it regulates private business because it does so to protect the public interest. Available online at URL: http://supct. law.cornell.edu/supct/html/historics/ USSC_CR_0094_0113_ZO.html.*

The earth was my mother . . . I could not consent to sever my affections from the land which bore me. I ask nothing of the President. I am able to take care of myself. I do not desire the Wallowa Valley as a reservation, for that would subject me to the will of another and make me dependent on him and subject to laws not of our own making. I am disposed to live peaceably.

> *Chief Joseph of the Nez Perce tribe, commenting on the U.S. Army order to move to a reservation, 1876, in Lockwood and Harris,* Reasoning with Democratic Values, *(1985), p. 60.*

It has been estimated that the government pays $1,000,000 for every Indian slain in battle, squaws and papooses not counted. This is hardly true of the estimates upon a fair basis, but if the dead Indians cost Uncle Sam so much it would be interesting, and perhaps more to the point, to know how much the self-sacrificing old gentleman is called upon to pay yearly for each live Indian.

> *General George A. Custer, 1876, in Slotkin,* The Fatal Environment *(1985), p. 447.*

The earth was created by the assistance of the sun, and it should be left as it was . . . The country was made without lines of demarcation, and it is no man's business to divide it. I see the whites all over the country gaining wealth, and see their desire to give us lands which are worthless. . . . The earth and myself are of one mind. The measure of the land and the measure of our bodies are the same. Say to us if you can say it, that you were sent by the Creative Power to talk to us. Perhaps you think the Creator sent you here to dispose of us as you see fit. If I thought you were sent by the Creator I might be induced to think you had a right to dispose of me. Do not misunderstand me, but understand me fully with reference to my affection for the land. I never said the land was mine to do with it as I chose. The one who has the right to dispose of it is the one who has created it. I claim a right to live on my land, and accord you the privilege to live on yours.

Chief Joseph of the Nez Perce Indians, statement to a U.S. Army commission investigating Indian claims to the Wallowa Valley in the Military Department of the Columbia, 1876. Available online at URL: http://www.nps.gov/nepe/greene/chap1b.htm.

It is really Custer's expedition, gotten up under his auspices and for his benefit, and that of his brother officer, if it be possible that any good can come of it . . . It is understood by many here that the object of the expedition is to succeed in driving the Indians from the Black Hills . . . so that white adventures may seize their lands . . . in the wild and crazy search for gold . . . It will also give Custer an opportunity to dis-

tinguish himself . . . gratify his restless and rash ambition, and secure his further promotion.

New York Herald article of 1876, in Slotkin, The Fatal Environment (1985), p. 437.

These heroes are dead. They died for liberty—they died for us. They are at rest. They sleep in the land they made free, under the flag they rendered stainless, under the solemn pines, the sad hemlocks, the tearful willows, the embracing vines. They sleep beneath the shadows of the clouds, careless alike of sunshine or storm, each in the windowless palace of rest. Earth may run red with other wars—they are at peace. In the midst of battles, in the roar of conflict, they found the serenity of death.

Robert Green Ingersoll, speech, "Vision of War," given at Indianapolis, Indiana, September 21, 1876, quoted in Bartlett, Familiar Quotations, 12th Edition (1951), p. 602.

Only a small part of the throng can get within a range of the orator's voice, but the rest seem none the less happy, for it is the holiday diversion, the crowds, the bravery of the procession, the music, the fun of the occasion they came chiefly to enjoy . . . The speaker, Gen. Harrison, is a man of medium height . . . In conversation his manner is quiet . . . He talks for an hour and a half about the war and the record of the Democratic party, and even goes way back to the Fugitive Slave law in hunting out the bad points in the record. There is almost nothing in his speech, except a brief reference to the Presidential candidates, that might not have been said just as well four years ago, or eight years ago; but the people are pleased with it. Evidently in their minds the memories of the Rebellion have but to be roused to supplant all later issues.

New York Tribune, description of a Republican meeting and a speech by Harrison, gubernatorial nominee, in Cambridge City, Indiana, September 1876, in Hoogenboom and Hoogenboom, The Gilded Age (1967), p. 157.

Would any gentleman stand up here and tell me that he is willing and ready to have his private correspondence scanned over and made public for the last eight or ten years? Does it imply guilt? Does it imply wrong-doing? Does it imply any sense of weakness that a man will protect his private correspondence?

General George Armstrong Custer died at the Battle of Little Bighorn. *(Library of Congress)*

No, sir: it is the first instinct to do it, and it is the last outrage upon any man to violate it.
Senator James G. Blaine (R-Maine), to a congressional committee investigating improper railroad investments, 1876, in Lockwood and Harris, Reasoning with Democratic Values *(1985), p. 27.*

The Corliss engine does not lend itself to description . . . It rises loftily in the centre of the huge structure, an athlete of steel and iron with not a superfluous ounce of metal on it; the mighty walking beams plunge their pistons downward, the enormous flywheel revolves with hoarded power that makes all tremble, the hundred life-like details do their office with unerring intelligence.
William Dean Howells, novelist and critic, on the 2,500-horsepower Corliss engine at the Centennial Exhibition in Philadelphia, 1876, in Schlesinger, Almanac of American History *(1983), p. 331.*

There is a sumptuous variety about the New England weather that compels the stranger's admiration—and regret. The weather is always doing something there; always attending strictly to business; always getting up new designs and trying them on people to see how they will go. But it gets through more business in Spring than in any other season. In the Spring I have counted one hundred and thirty-six different kinds of weather inside of twenty-four hours.
Samuel Clemens, speech given at the New England Society, December 22, 1876, in Bartlett, Familiar Quotations, 12th Edition *(1951), p. 549.*

No officers should be required or permitted to take part in the management of political organizations, caucuses, conventions, or electoral campaigns. Their right to vote or to express their views on public questions . . . is not denied, provided it does not interfere with the discharge of their official duties. No assessments for political purposes on officers . . . should be allowed. This rule is applicable to every department of the civil service. It should be understood by every officer of the general Government that he is expected to conform to its requirements.
President Rutherford B. Hayes, executive order, concerning reforms in the federal civil service, June 22, 1877, Josephson, The Politicos, *p. 240.*

I send you by today's mail a copy of my dissenting opinion in the Chicago Elevator case and in the so-called Granger cases. I think that the doctrine announced by the majority of the Court practically destroys the guarantees of the Constitution intended for the protection of the rights of private property.
Supreme Court associate justice Stephen J. Field, to David A. Wells, letter of June 25, 1877, in Roche, American Political Thought from Jefferson to Progressivism *(1967), p. 220.*

To violence of any kind Mr. Tilden was by nature strongly opposed . . . his intimate connection with many great industrial and corporate enterprises would naturally lead him to a conservative course of action.
Abram Hewitt, private journal entry, 1877, quoted in Josephson, The Politicos, *p. 235.*

When we come to inquire what part our own country has taken, and what contribution it has made in building up this science, we are struck at the outset by the fact that the growth of the United States has been a circumstance of prime importance in the economic history of the world during the century. It must be placed in the same rank with the brilliant succession of discoveries in the industrial arts, or with the extensive improvement of government and social organization, as one of the half-dozen great influences which have changed the face of the civilized world. Without entering into the details of a comparison, to which every reader is likely to have his attention sufficiently drawn during the present year, we may here note a review of the facts which have given to the development of this country so great an influence upon that of the rest of the world. Beginning with the statement of mere area, the organized States of the Union now occupy a territory larger than the whole of Europe, outside of the Russian Empire. The improved land of these States, measuring 295,000 square miles in 1870, cannot be much less than the total improved surface of England and Ireland, France and Prussia, together. Of this vast field of production, we may fairly say that the whole has been brought into the circle of international exchanges and added to the available resources of mankind within this century, so insignificant were its relations with the rest of the world a hundred years ago.
Charles F. Dunbar, "Economic Science in American, 1776–1876," in the North American Review, *1876, p. 125. Available online at URL: http://cdl.library.cornell.edu/cgi-bin/moa/moa-cgi?notisid=ABQ7578-0122&byte=977428 87.*

. . . these men have experience and command all the avenues to power, and every channel of communication with the heads of the government and the party is in their hands. All we want is a hearing.

H. A. Brown, to Carl Schurz, on the difficulty some Republican reformers face in becoming an effective influence on party decisions, 1877, in Morgan, The Gilded Age *(1970), p. 63.*

The overwhelming labor question has dwarfed all other questions into nothing. We have home questions enough to occupy attention now.

J. M. Dalzell, in a letter about the shift of federal attention from the South to urban centers of the North, to John Sherman, July 29, 1877, in Foner, Reconstruction *(1988), p. 586.*

We are taxed without representation. . . . We obey laws; others make them. We support state educational institutions, whose doors are virtually closed against us. We support asylums and hospitals, and our sick, deaf, dumb, or blind are met at the doors by invidious distinctions and unjust discriminations. . . . From these and many other oppressions. . . . our people long to be free.

Charles Harris to William Coppinger, describing the unwelcome attitude many in the South harbored toward African Americans, in a letter dated August 28, 1877, Foner, Reconstruction *(1988), p. 601.*

If I felt a perfect confidence that my history would be what I would like to make it, this part of life—from forty to fifty—would be all I want.

Henry Adams, 1877, letter to an unnamed correspondent, in which he explains that he is happy to be leaving Boston with his wife, Marian, for a new home in the nation's capital, quoted in Shepherd, The Adams Chronicles *(1976), p. 395.*

They [strikes] ought not to occur here. The great problem of the [nation's] future is the equal distribution of wealth out of the profits of labor . . . I believe myself that, in general, the laboring classes do not receive their fair share. Strikes are one of their means of getting more . . .

Reverend Charles Loring Brace, New York reformer, on the effects of the Great Railroad Strike, 1877, in Degler, The Age of the Economic Revolution, 1876–1900 *(1977), p. 170.*

I have just witnessed a terrible exhibition of the power of machinery. Friends had advised me to visit the huge cotton press at the Cotton Landing, and I spent several hours in watching its operation. Excepting, perhaps some of the monster cotton presses of India, it is said to be the most powerful in the world; but the East Indian presses box the cotton instead of baling it, with enormous loss of time. This "Champion" press at the New Orleans Levee weighs, with all its attachments, upwards of three thousand tons, and exerts the enormous pressure of four million pounds upon the bales placed in it . . . The spectacle of this colossal press in motion is really terrific. It is like a nightmare of iron and brass . . . It is not a press as we understand the term generally, but an enormous mouth of metal which seizes the bale and crushes it in its teeth.

Lafcadio Hearn, reporter for the Cincinnati Enquirer, *1877, in Hoogenboom and Hoogenboom,* The Gilded Age *(1967), p. 27.*

The Great Spirit made the world as it is and as He wanted it . . . I do not see where you get your authority to say that we shall not live here as He placed us.

A Nez Perce chief, to General Oliver O. Howard, 1877, in Lockwood and Harris, Reasoning with Democratic Values *(1985), p. 6.*

I stand here for the President, and there is no spirit good or bad that will hinder me. My orders are plain, and will be executed. I hoped that the Indians had good sense enough to make me their friend, and not their enemy.

General Oliver O. Howard, announcing the U.S. Army's intention of moving Nez Perce Indians to reservation lands, 1877, in Lockwood and Harris, Reasoning with Democratic Values *(1985), p. 6.*

That force of yours should pursue the Nez Perce to the death, lead where they may . . . If you are tired, give the command to some young energetic officer.

General William T. Sherman, commander of U.S. Army troops, to General Howard, 1877, in Lockwood and Harris, Reasoning with Democratic Values *(1985), p. 8.*

I am tired of fighting. The old men are all dead. [My brother] who led the young men is dead. It is cold and we have no blankets. The little children are freezing to death. My people, some of them, have run away to the hills. No one knows where they are. I want to have some time to look for my children and see how many I can find. Maybe I shall find them among the dead.

Hear me, my chiefs. From where the sun now stands, I will fight no more forever.

Chief Joseph of the Nez Perce tribe, after surrendering to troops under the command of General Oliver O. Howard, 1877, in Weinstein and Wilson, Freedom and Crisis *(1860), p. 509.*

You must not blame me. I have endeavored to keep my word, but the chief who is over me has given the order and I must obey it or resign. That would do you no good. Some officer would carry out the order.

Colonel Nelson Miles, to Nez Perce chief Joseph, at the surrender of Nez Perce Indians, 1877, in Lockwood and Harris, Reasoning with Democratic Values *(1985), p. 10.*

There is hardly a good thing in [the world] that is not the result of successful strife.

E. L. Godkin, The Nation'*s editor, on the superiority of the white race, 1877, in Slotkin,* The Fatal Environment *(1985), p. 49.*

Mr. President and gentlemen: I am obliged to my friend Dr. Clarke for the complimentary terms in which he has presented me to you. But I must appeal to your commiseration. Harvard and Yale! Can any undergraduate of either institution, can any recent graduate of either institution, imagine a man responding to that toast? . . .

We shall all agree that it is for the best interests of this country that it have sundry universities, of diverse tone, atmosphere, sphere, representing different opinions and different methods of study to some extent, and in different trainings, though with the same end.

Holding this view, I have been somewhat concerned to see of late that the original differences between Harvard and Yale seem to be rapidly disappearing. For example, a good many years ago, Harvard set out on what is called the "elective" system, and now I read in the Yale catalogue a long list of studies called "optional," which strikes me as bearing a strong resemblance to our elective courses. . . .

Now, it is unquestioned, that about the year 1700 a certain number of Congregationalist clergymen, who belonged to the Established Church (for we are too apt to forget that Congregationalism was the "Established Church" of that time, and none other was allowed), thought that Harvard was getting altogether too latitudinarian, and though they were every one of them graduates of Harvard, they went off and set up another college in Connecticut, where a stricter doctrine should be taught. Harvard men have rather nursed the hope that this distinction between Harvard and Yale might be permanent. But I regret to say that I have lately observed many strong indications that it is wholly likely to disappear.

For example, to come at once to the foundations, I read in the papers the other day, and I am credibly informed it is true, that the head of Yale College voted to install a minister whose opinions upon the vital, pivotal, fundamental doctrine of eternal damnation are unsound. Then, again, I look at the annual reports of the Bureau of Education on this department at Washington, and I read there for some years that Harvard College was unsectarian; and I knew that it was right, because I made the return myself.

I read also that Yale College was a Congregationalist College; and I had no doubt that that was right, because I supposed Dr. Porter had made the report. But now we read in that same report that Yale College is unsectarian. That is a great progress. The fact is, both these universities have found out that in a country which has no established church and no dominant sect you cannot build a university on a sect at all—you must build it upon the nation.

But, gentlemen, there are some other points, I think, of national education on which we shall find these two early founded universities to agree. For example, we have lately read, in the Message of the Chief Magistrate, that a national university would be a good thing. Harvard and Yale are of one mind upon that subject, but they want to have a national university defined. If it means a university of national resort, we say amen. If it means a university where the youth of this land are taught to love their country and to serve her, we say amen; and we point, both of us, to our past in proof that we are national in that sense. But if it means that the national university is to be a university administered and managed by the wise Congress of the United States, then we should agree in taking some slight exceptions.

We should not question for a moment the capacity of Congress to pick out and appoint the professors of Latin and Greek, and the ancient languages, because we find that there is an astonishing number of classical orators in Congress, and there is manifested there a singular acquaintance with the legislation of all the Latin races. But when it should come to some other humbler professorships we might perhaps entertain a doubt. For example, we have not entire faith in the trust that Congress has in the unchangeableness of the laws of arithmetic. We might think that their competency to select a professor of history might be doubted. They seem to have an impression that there is such a thing as "American" political economy, which can no more be than "American" chemistry or "American" physics. Finally, gentlemen, we should a little distrust the selection by Congress of a professor of ethics. Of course, we should feel no doubt in regard to the tenure of office of the professors being entirely suitable, it being the well-known practice of both branches of Congress to select men solely for fitness, without regard to locality, and to keep them in office as long as they are competent and faithful.

Dr. Charles W. Eliot, speech at the New England Society's annual dinner, December 22, 1877. Available online at URL: http://www.federalobserver.com/print.php?aid=1202.

The railway exercises political power, firstly, by reason of its being a great employer—as a matter of *esprit de corps* the employees will follow the unconcealed inclination of the employer towards one or the other of the political parties or nominees; secondly, by the expenditure of money in elections.

As for the press, the railway is among the largest of advertisers, and it is an interest, therefore, not to be criticized with impunity; and perhaps finding that the press is not wholly under the influence of its advertising columns, railway kings have become large proprietors of stock in newspapers—investments which are supposed not to be made in the expectation of large dividends on such stock, nor for philanthropical and educational purposes ...

Hence the railway is the real government—two removes behind a fluctuating, temporal government, as represented by our State and National officers. It has all the substantial elements of power, without the responsibility connected with the office.

Simon Sterne, a New York merchant, 1878, in Hoogenboom and Hoogenboom, The Gilded Age *(1967), p. 19.*

My friend Brandeis is a character in his way—one of the most brilliant legal minds they have ever had here ... Hails from Louisville, is not a college graduate, but has spent some years in Europe, has a rather foreign look and is currently believed to have some Jew blood in him, though you would not suppose it from his appearance—tall, well-made, dark, beardless, and with the brightest eyes I ever saw. Is supposed to know everything and to have it always in mind. The professors listen to his opinion with the greatest deference. And it is generally correct ...

William E. Cushing, Harvard Law School student, to his mother, letter of 1878, in Baltzell, The Protestant Establishment *(1966), p. 188.*

It does not appear that the friends of freedom should spend either time or talent in furtherance of this exodus [of former slaves out of the South] as a desirable measure, either for the North or the South. If the people of this country cannot be protected in every state of the Union, the government of the United States is shorn of its rightful dignity and power, the late rebellion has triumphed, the sovereignty of the nation is an empty name, and the power and authority in individual states is greater than the power and authority of the United States.

The colored people of the South, just beginning to accumulate a little property, and to lay the foundation of family, should not be in haste to sell that little and be off to the banks of the Mississippi. The habit of roaming from place to place in pursuit of better conditions of existence is never a good one. A man should never leave his home for a new one till he has earnestly endeavored to make his immediate surroundings accord with his wishes. The time and energy expended in wandering from place to place, if employed in making him a comfortable home where he is, will, in nine cases out of ten, prove the best investment. No people ever did much for themselves or for the world without the sense and inspiration of native land, of a fixed home, of familiar neighborhood, and common associations. The fact of being to the manor born has an elevating power upon the mind and heart of a man. It is a more cheerful thing to be able to say, I was born here and know all the people, than to say, I am a stranger here and know none of the people.

It cannot be doubted that, in so far as this exodus tends to promote restlessness in the colored people of the South, to unsettle their feeling of home, and to sacrifice positive advantages where they are or fancied ones in Kansas or elsewhere, it is an evil.

Frederick Douglass, black leader, 1879, "The Negro Exodus from the Gulf States," in Frank Leslie, Popular Monthly, *January 1880, Vol. 9, No. 1. p. 46.*

I wish to become known as a practicing lawyer. I wish to wait particularly for your letter giving the results of our examination of the prospects of a young law firm and more particularly your own prospects of securing business through your social and financial position.

Louis Brandeis to Samuel D. Warren, a Harvard Law School classmate, May 30, 1879, in McCraw, Prophets of Regulation *(1984), p. 18.*

The best things come, as a general thing, from the talents that are members of a group; every man works better when he has companions working in the same line, and yielding the stimulus of suggestion, comparison, emulation. Great things, of course, have been done by solitary workers; but they have been done with double the pains they would have cost if they had been produced in more genial circumstances.

Writer Henry James, 1879, in Schlesinger, Almanac of American History *(1983), p. 335.*

Here is the yard of No. 5 Jersey Street [New York City], on lines strung across, were thousands of rags hung up to dry; on the ground, piled against the board fences, rags mixed with bones, bottles, and papers; the middle of the yard covered with every imaginable variety of dirt . . . We then turned to go into the cellars, in which was a large and a small room (containing a cook-stove and sleeping-bunks). There was scarcely standing room for the heaps of bags and rags, and right opposite to them stood a large pile of bones, mostly having meat on them in various stages of decomposition . . . Notwithstanding the dense tobacco smoke, the smell could be likened only to that of an exhumed body.

Kate Holladay Claghorn, immigration specialist, in a report of 1878, in Hoogenboom and Hoogenboom, The Gilded Age *(1967), p. 103.*

Some misunderstanding exists as to the amount of rum a man has to sell to become a rum-seller. My idea is that no grander principle was ever ingrafted

Henry James explored the growth of American culture and its relationship with that of Europe in such works as *Daisy Miller* and *Washington Square. (Library of Congress)*

upon the laws of a labor organization than that law of ours which denies membership to the rum traffic. The two deadliest foes of labor are rum and ignorance. We should show no quarter to rum and its damning, blighting influence; but should rigidly prohibit membership to any one who sells *even a single glass.* Thus will this foe be conquered or made powerless.

Grand secretary Lichtman, Knights of Labor, 1879, in Powderly, Thirty Years of Labor, 1859–1889 *(1967), p. 305.*

. . . I deem it highly necessary to call your attention to the ominous frequency of the attempts being made all over the country to break down the ten-hour standard and enforce longer hours. Whether these movements are preconcerted and form a part of an organized effort to offset and obstruct the eight-hour movement, time will tell.

. . . a plain demand upon employees for an increase of hours of labor show that may be expected in this country; and they give us timely warning of the struggle and fierce opposition to be encountered before eight hours can be firmly established by statute law in the various States, backed as such laws will have to be by penal enactments for infringements in order to make them efficient.

. . . Active exertion and agitation will be necessary to bring public sentiment up to a point that will successfully carry the principle through the ballot-box. Until that is done absolutely nothing valuable has been gained.

Uriah Stephens, grand master of the Knights of Labor, 1879, in Powderly, Thirty Years of Labor *(1967), pp. 242–243.*

I detest the name of socialism on account of the actions of the men who profess to believe in it. They rush to every gathering and attempt to man or officer it. Having done that, and having driven all decent men away, they are supremely happy in the delusion that they have spread their ideas still further.

. . . They tear down and very seldom ever attempt to build up. They do nothing for the cause of labor, save to do it harm. If the socialists ever gain control . . . they will kill off the work of years.

Uriah Stephens, grand master of the Knights of Labor, 1879, in Powderly, Thirty Years of Labor *(1967), p. 275.*

Among the three or four million cradles now rocking in the land are some which this nation would preserve for ages as sacred things, if we could know which ones they are.

Samuel Clemens, speech at a banquet honoring General Ulysses S. Grant, Chicago, November 14, 1879, in Bartlett, Familiar Quotations, *12th Edition (1951), p. 617.*

There can be no complete . . . reform of the civil service until public opinion emancipates Congressmen from all control and influence over government patronage. Legislation is required to establish the reform. No proper legislation is to be expected as long as members of Congress are engaged in procuring offices for their constituents . . . I must do the best I can, unaided by public opinion, and opposed in and out of Congress by a large part of the most powerful men in my party.

President Rutherford B. Hayes, private communication, 1879, quoted in Josephson, The Politicos, *p. 274.*

To the Honorable Commissioner of Patents:

Your Petitioner Thomas A. Edison of Menlo Park in the State of New Jersey prays that Letters Patent may be granted to him for the invention of an Improvement in Electric Lamps and in the method of manufacturing the same set forth in the annexed specification. (Case no. 186). And further prays that you will recognize Lemuel W. Serrell, of the City of New York, N.Y., as his Attorney, with full power of substitution and revocation, to prosecute this application, to make alterations and amendments therein, to receive the Patent, and to transact all business in the Patent Office connected Therewith.

Thomas A. Edison, patent application letter, 1879. Available online at URL: http://www.ourdocuments.gov/ doc.php?doc=46&page=transcript.

The information furnished by the working girls shows that the wages earned by them constitute in many cases the chief, and sometimes the entire, support of the family; the parents looking to the earnings of one, two, three, and four daughters to pay household bills; the father often being reported not able to work much or always, on account of disability, from lack of steady work, or possibly, from disinclination to work while there is revenue from any other source. In large families, the earnings of the girls, together with the wages of the father, when all are working, do no more than cover living expenses.

Carroll Wright, excerpt of an 1880 Massachusetts Department of Labor Statistics study, in Working Girls of Boston *(1889), pp. 110–111.*

I do not allow myself to anticipate any very decided measure of success possibly because we live here so completely under the domination of a perfectly organized and vigorously managed machine that one grows hopeless of any permanent change for the better.

Henry C. Lea, scholar and publisher from Philadelphia, to Harvard professor Charles Eliot Norton, on the ability of reformers to effect change in the Republican party, 1880, in Morgan, The Gilded Age *(1970), p. 63.*

I believe in a country where every man has an equal chance. That's the reason why I work for the Republican party . . .

This is a Government of liberty regulated by law. This is a Government founded on reason. This is a Government where the people have honest thought on every subject. The man who has these privileges himself and is not willing to accord them to others is a barbarian . . . Is there a Democrat who denies the common right of free speech? He dare not say it! Is there a Democrat who denies the right to talk and breathe in one common air? He dare not say it.

Now, if that liberty is to be preserved, whom will you have preserve it? . . . I'm going further off, and the longer the lever the more I can lift! Maine is a good place in which to begin. Let a Republican try it in Alabama and see how soon he'll get Ku-Kluxed. Let a Greenbacker try it, and see how soon he'll get mobbed for attempting to draw voters away from the Democratic party!

. . . Are you going to have the South protect your ballot-box for you? In the South elections are a farce. It is there that Bulldozing holds the election, Dishonesty counts their votes, and Fraud declares the result! Now it is a fact, my friends, that since the Rebellion, the South has killed more men, in a time of profound peace, that our country lost in the two wars with Great Britain! Are they the men you will have protect your ballot-box? Do you want to leave it with the masked man who shoots fathers, mothers, and children? Oh, Mr. Honest Greenbacker and Democrat! 'Way down in your soul I know you say "No"! no matter what you say outside.

> *Robert G. Ingersoll, Radical Republican lawyer and orator, during a rally in Lewiston, Maine, 1880, in Garraty,* Labor and Capital in the Gilded Age *(1968).*

We must without delay begin to build a navy which will at least equal that of England when the canal shall have become a fact . . . That this will be done I don't for a moment hope but unless it is we may as well shut up about the Monroe Doctrine at once.

> *Alfred Thayer Mahan, naval historian, 1880, in Tuchman,* The Proud Tower *(1966).*

I knew the wild riders and the vacant land were about to vanish forever and the more I considered the subject, the bigger *forever* loomed . . . I began to record some facts around me.

> *Frederick Remington, sculptor and painter of the American West, recalling his view from a train crossing the prairie in 1880, in Schlesinger,* Almanac of American History, *p. 378.*

Organization once perfected, what must we do? In answer, study the best means of putting your organization to some practical use by embarking in a system of cooperation, which will eventually make every man his own master—every man his own employer; a system which will give the laborer a fair proportion of the products of his toils. It is too cooperation, then, as the lever of labor's emancipation that the eyes of the workingmen and women of the world are directed, upon cooperation their hopes are centered, and to it do I now direct your attention.

> *Terence V. Powderly, grand master workman, Knights of Labor, speech in Pittsburgh, Pennsylvania, September 1880, in Powderly,* Thirty Years of Labor, 1859–1889 *(1967), p. 235.*

4
Assassination, Reform Politics, and Immigration
1881–1885

Charles Julius Guiteau, a disgruntled lawyer, shot President James Abram Garfield in July 1881, only a few months into his administration.[1] Garfield died after his improperly tended wound became gangrenous. Few were more surprised than Garfield's vice president, Chester A. Arthur, the third chief executive to serve the nation in a 12-month period. A somewhat unimpressive man of few political accomplishments, President Arthur's main claim to prominence during his one term was establishment of a civil service system with competitive examinations and a merit system for promotions. The Pendleton Civil Service Act was a positive reflection on Arthur, and said much about his principles and his courage, particularly since few of his Republican Party cohorts wanted civil service reform to pass.[2]

Cornelius Vanderbilt was one of the several hundred prominent financiers whose extravagant lifestyle became a hallmark of the Gilded Age. *(Library of Congress)*

THE RICH ARE DIFFERENT

If there was little excitement in the White House in the early 1880s, there was a great deal of activity in the grand homes and estates of the very wealthy.

Materially, some Americans were beginning to see the effects of an expanding business sector. Shrewd, often ruthless men for whom the making of millions became a game grew more and more proficient at building up wealth and also were accomplished spenders. William Vanderbilt's mansion at Fifth Avenue and 52nd Street in New York City was completed in 1881, one of the nation's first opulent private homes in an urban setting. Vanderbilt set the style for the design and construction of hundreds of such homes for the rich and those with aspirations to wealth and social positions in various locations throughout the country. That same year, President Eliot of Harvard University built a summer home at Northeast Harbor, Maine, becoming one of the dozens of notable individuals whose leisure retreats made areas like Newport, Rhode Island, and the Adirondacks in upstate New York, both fashionable and inaccessible to all but the very wealthy.

A GROWING INTEREST IN LEISURE PASTIMES

The trend toward this rather conspicuous enjoyment of leisure time was specific to the Gilded Age.

Henry James's novel *The Portrait of a Lady*,[3] Mark Twain's *A Tramp Abroad*, and even Lew Wallace's *Ben Hur*, revealed a growing market for American prose. Magazines grew in popularity and circulation, and new ones appeared. *Century Magazine*, founded in 1881, formerly known as *Scribner's Monthly*, was recognized for its interest in social issues. *Century* published a range of material written by leaders such as Presidents McKinley and Roosevelt, as well as by professional journalists.[4]

In the 1880s, the public further refined its interest in art and architecture. The building of magnificent private homes continued as did the construction of commercial and municipal structures. Among H. H. Richardson's projects was the Metropolitan Museum of Art, which opened in New York City in 1880 housing the work of Mary Cassatt and John Singer Sargent, both of whom critics hailed in 1881 as original, innovative contributors to the American art scene.

Just as public appetites dictated architectural styles during the Gilded Age, public opinion shaped how journalists and publishers decided what to offer readers.

Entrepreneurs, publishers, and editors seized the opportunity to define what the public wanted and to determine how to make a profit at the same time. In 1882 the *New York Morning Journal*, published by Albert Pulitzer, was founded and quickly became notorious for its lurid headlines and sensational reporting.[5] The *Journal*'s circulation grew rapidly. In 1895 it would be renamed the *New York Journal*. To cater to and to cash in on the American woman's growing interest in improving herself and her family life, *Ladies' Home Journal* magazine was founded in 1883 by Cyrus H. K. Curtis, a publisher in Philadelphia, Pennsylvania. Many other publications appeared during the 1880s and by the end of the decade specialty journals and self-help or literary magazines were read nationwide.

EDUCATION OFFERS EXPANDED OPPORTUNITIES

The importance and availability of education grew in significance during the 1880s. Helen Hunt Jackson, a popular writer, published *The Training of Children* in 1882, in which she outlined various ways to help young children learn. Both public and private schools proliferated and public school populations changed as immigration brought more and more non-English-speaking children into urban areas. These children would need to learn the language and customs of their families' adopted nation in order to flourish there.

The wealthy sought exclusive educational opportunities for their children and founded numerous independent schools. In 1882, the Browne and Nichols School was founded in Cambridge, Massachusetts, for the children of rich, social prominent Bostonians. In nearby Groton, Massachusetts, the exclusive

By the 1880s, many found opportunity in homesteads on the western frontier, such as this one in South Dakota. *(Library of Congress)*

Groton School was established for young men by Endicott Peabody, the moving force behind this and several other schools. It was believed that educating young men according to the English public-school tradition would help prepare politically and socially adept leaders for the next century.

In higher education, there were similar patterns of growth and development. The Morrill Land Grant Act of 1862 continued to influence the growth of public higher education. In 1883, the University of North Dakota opened its doors, as did the University of Texas at Austin. In 1882, the University of Dakota was chartered under the terms of the Morrill Act. It would, in 1891, become the University of South Dakota. Cornell University offered the nation's first college-level electrical engineering course.

Education of women at separately established institutions also continued during the 1880s. In Massachusetts in 1883, Radcliffe College was chartered separately from Harvard University.[6] It joined Smith College (founded in 1872) and Wellesley College (founded in 1875), both also in Massachusetts, to become one of the country's top women's colleges. There and other schools would have a growing impact on the number of women entering society as social workers, educators, librarians, doctors, and other professionals.

Hostility toward immigrants, especially those from Asia, resulted in restrictive legislation and policies aimed at discouraging some new comers from feeling "at home" in the United States. In 1882 passage of the Chinese Exclusion Act ended Asian immigration.[7] In a reversal of this attitude, the Southern Immigration Association was founded in 1883, designed to encourage European settlement. The South continued to lag behind in economic development, thanks to the Civil War and the Reconstruction aftermath.[8]

Those immigrants who did come into the country raised concerns about health and welfare. Crowded city tenements meant living conditions so low that many municipalities established boards of inquiry or public health commissions to investigate ways in which the immigrant families could be helped. Some citizens who served on these commissions became leaders in the settlement-house movement, which grew in influence and strength throughout the 1880s and 1890s.

THE HISTORICAL CONTEXT

Helping immigrants to assimilate into U.S. society reflected the more general-ized and growing interest in popular culture. This interest was both fueled and reflected by newspapers and magazines, as well as in the growing market for works of fiction and nonfiction. In 1884, author Sarah Orne Jewett of Maine published *A Country Doctor,* the first of many well-received volumes about life in New England.[9] Historian Francis Parkman wrote about his research into the French and British generals so crucial to the settlement of North America, and published his study *Montcalm and Wolfe* in 1884.

One of the most popular novels of the time, however, was Mark Twain's *The Adventures of Huckleberry Finn.* This book enjoyed wide readership for decades, remaining the favorite among many of Twain's loyal fans. Twain's descriptions of an ideal world (or his satire of American culture, in the book *The Gilded Age,* coauthored with Charles Dudley Warner) were appreciated as fiction. In reality, reform of society, or at least the political structures that guid-ed society, was more challenging. Nonetheless, a radical initiative of the early 1880s attempted just that, when reform-minded Republicans left the G.O.P. These Republicans who would not, for ideological reasons, support the candi-dacy of James G. Blaine of Maine for president formed a third political party. They were known as the Liberal Republicans but referred to popularly as "Mugwumps." Frustrated with slavish adherence to conservative issues, they looked for a candidate with a broader viewpoint, one more responsive to the needs of the populace.

With the combined support of Democrats, they nominated the Democratic governor of New York, Grover Cleveland in June 1884. On November 4, Cleveland defeated Blaine. The race's outcome was determined by the Electoral College vote, with New York's vote providing what was needed for victory. Cleveland won with a plurality of 1,100 votes and became the first Democrat to be sent to the White House since the Civil War.

THE POWERFUL INFLUENCE OF ORGANIZED LABOR

While the politicians wrangled, the economy continued as a major concern. The desires for economic stability, improved salary and hours, and heightened productivity, all forced continued debate among government leaders, agrarian reformers, big business, and labor organizers. Differences of opinion had long since fragmented into

Samuel Clemens, known by his pen name of Mark Twain, was among the most popular writers of his day. *(Library of Congress)*

serious rifts, with the result that strikes, work stoppages and walk-outs increased in the mid-1880s as workers protested wage cuts. Union Pacific Railroad workers, hit with one such wage cut in 1885, promptly went on strike. A year earlier, Knights of Labor head Terence Powderly had made inflammatory statements about the need for a strong labor attitude against "the existing industrial system." And by the end of 1885, striking laborers at the McCormick Works threatened violence if their wage and hour demands went unmet.[10]

At the same time, reformers' concern over economic issues became more public, and brought greater attention to the needs of U.S. workers. The American Economic Association studied the nation's economy and sought ways of effecting change in the interdependent structures of commerce, manufacture and government.[11] The association's leaders, economist Richard T. Ely, of Johns Hopkins University, his colleagues Simon Patten, Washington Gladden and others hoped to apply economic theory to alleviate the nation's more pressing social ills.[12] Due to the growing unrest among workers and factory owners, and heightened concerns over pressure on the nation's economy members of the association sought a systematic, scientific analysis of fiscal problems.

The reformers knew that they needed a definition of key areas, so they lobbied to establish the Federal Bureau of Labor in 1884.[13] The bureau was to quantify the array of products, activities, and people contributing to the U.S. economy. Carroll D. Wright, formerly chief of the Massachusetts State Labor Statistics Bureau—the first of its kind in the country—was named the first commissioner of the new federal agency.

Cyrus Hall McCormick invented the reaping machine, which enabled farmers in the late 19th century to transform American agriculture. *(Library of Congress)*

CHRONICLE OF EVENTS

1881

January 24: The federal Income Tax Law of 1862 is declared constitutional by the U.S. Supreme Court in *Springer v. U.S.*

January 25: Thomas Edison and Alexander Graham Bell found the Oriental Telephone Company.

February 5: The city of Phoenix, Arizona, is incorporated.

February 19: Kansas is the first U.S. state to pass legislation prohibiting the sale of all alcoholic beverages.

February 22: According to President Hayes, no alcohol will be available for sale at U.S. military posts.

March 3: Congress establish a national registration agency to protect company trademarks.

March 4: President James A. Garfield is inaugurated.

March 5: Garfield appoints James G. Blaine secretary of state, which draws some G.O.P. criticism.

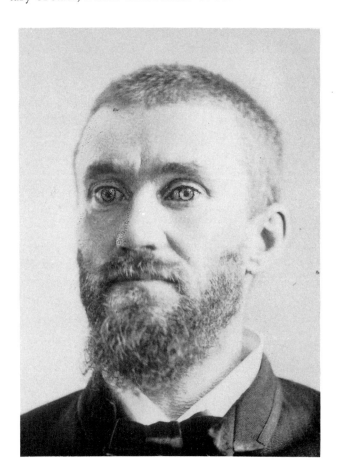

Charles J. Guiteau assassinated President Garfield. *(Library of Congress)*

May 16: Two New York senators, Roscoe Conkling and Thomas Platt, refuse to endorse James G. Blaine as secretary of state. They resign their seats, and are not reelected; Blaine's appointment is approved.

May 21: Clara Barton founds the American Red Cross in Washington, D.C.

May 21: The U.S. National Lawn Tennis Association (USNLTA) is founded by James Dwight. The organization later changes its name to the U.S. Tennis Association.

June 12: The USS *Jeannette* is crushed in an Arctic Ocean ice pack.

July 2: While waiting for a train in Washington, D.C., President Garfield is shot. His assassin, Charles J. Guiteau, a fanatic with a history of mental instability, had sought an appointment in the new Republican administration.

July 4: Booker T. Washington, founder of the Tuskegee Institute in Atlanta, Georgia, convenes his first class there.

July 20: Lakota Sioux chief Sitting Bull surrenders, with the last of his people, to U.S. Army troops at, Fort Buford, North Dakota.

August 8: The Brotherhood of Carpenters and Joiners of America is founded in Chicago, Illinois. In 1886 it will be combined with the American Federation of Labor.

August 24: A naval observatory is set up in Greenland by a group under the direction of Lieutenant Adolphus W. Greely. They remain there for two years preparing for an international scientific expedition.

September 6: The General Assembly of the Knights of Labor agree that after January 1, 1882, the name of their fraternal order should be used publicly on letterhead and other printed materials. They had operated as a secret organization until this time.

September 19: President Garfield succumbs to the wounds he received in July. His body is brought to the Capitol rotunda to lie in state, and two days later he is carried by train to Cleveland, Ohio, for burial.

September 20: Garfield's vice president, Chester A. Arthur, is sworn in as the nation's 21st President.

October 15: American Angler, the first U.S. fishing journal, is published in Philadelphia, Pennsylvania, by William C. Harris.

October 22: The Boston Symphony Orchestra performs its inaugural concert under the direction of Georg Henschel. The orchestra is founded by the

President James A. Garfield was shot on July 2, 1881. He died two months later. *(Library of Congress)*

philanthropist and Civil War veteran Henry Lee Higginson.

October 26: A gunfight breaks out at the O.K. Corral in Tombstone, Arizona.

November 17: Secretary of State James G. Blaine invites Latin American nations to a Pan-American meeting in Washington, D.C., in 1882. No meeting takes place, however, since Blaine will resign his cabinet position because of the death of President Garfield.

December 1: Secretary of State Blaine announces that the Hawaiian Islands are to be protected under the terms of the Monroe Doctrine.

1882

January 2: The Standard Oil Trust is formed under the leadership of John D. Rockefeller.

January 15: The U.S. Postal Service is charged with fraud in the Star Route scandal. During a two-year trial, it is revealed that bogus delivery routes generated hundreds of thousands of dollars in illegal budget requests. Several U.S. senators are indicted in the course of investigations, and Second Assistant Postmaster General Thomas J. Brady resigns under pressure.

February 7: In Mississippi City, Mississippi, the last heavyweight bare-knuckle boxing championship is held.

February 28: In Cambridge, Massachusetts, the first cooperative college store in the nation opens for business.

March 11: The U.S. Intercollegiate Lacrosse Association is organized in Princeton, New Jersey. The first member institutions are Harvard, Princeton, and Columbia Universities.

March 22: Congress enacts the Edmunds Law, aimed at further strengthening prohibitions against polygamy in the Utah Territory. Under this law, polygamists are denied voting privileges.

March 29: The Knights of Columbus, a Roman Catholic fraternal order, is chartered in Connecticut.

March 31: Congress passes a law that will provide an annual pension for the wives of U.S. presidents.

April 3: Outlaw Jesse James is shot and killed by Robert Ford, who seeks the reward, posted at $5,000.

James G. Blaine served as secretary of state under President Garfield. *(Library of Congress)*

April 4: President Arthur uses his power to veto the Chinese Exclusion Act, which seeks to limit Asian immigration. There is a strong labor lobby against permitting Asian workers to enter the country.

April 28: The country's first newspaper room in a public library is dedicated in Newburyport, Massachusetts.

May 6: Congress passes the Chinese Exclusion Act on an override. The act seeks to prevent Chinese laborers from entering the United States.

May 15: Congress establishes a tariff commission to protect U.S. business interests.

May 22: The United States recognizes Korea's independence and signs a commercial treaty with the Asian nation.

June 6: The electric iron is patented in New York City.

June 29: The American Forestry Congress merges with the American Forestry Association.

June 30: Congress authorizes establishment of the nation's first hospital for the military.

Assassin Charles Guiteau is hanged.

July 26: Congress votes to accept the Geneva Convention of 1864.

July 28: The country's first accounting society is established in New York City.

August 2: Congress votes to fund public works projects totaling $18 million under the terms of the Rivers and Harbors Bill.

August 5: The Standard Oil Company of New Jersey is founded.

August 7: The Senate Committee on Education and Labor adopts a resolution that will enable it to study and report on the causes and effects of the divisions existing between labor and capital.

August 16: Radcliffe College is chartered as a separate institution from Harvard University to educate young women.

September 4: By way of demonstrating its utility and potential for widespread business and industrial use, the electric light is turned on in several strategic buildings in New York City, including the Stock Exchange, the *New York Times* building and the *New York Herald* building.

September 5: The first Labor Day parade is held in New York City in honor of working people.

September 13: The Country Club is founded in Brookline, Massachusetts, the first of exclusive country clubs established by and for the wealthy.

November 6: Actress Lily Langtry appears in New York City in a production of *As You Like It.*

December 11: The Bijou Theater in Boston, Massachusetts, uses incandescent lighting for the first time at a Gilbert and Sullivan performance.

1883

January 10: The nation's most devastating hotel fire ever occurs in Milwaukee, Wisconsin, where 71 people die at the Newhall House.

January 16: Congress passes the Pendleton Act, which authorizes a bipartisan commission to administer civil service exams, eliminating a number of political appointment positions.

January 19: The first electric lighting system with overhead wires begins operations in Roselle, New Jersey. It was built by inventor Thomas Edison.

February 12: King Kalakaua and Queen Kapiolani are crowned in Honolulu in the Hawaiian Islands, a territory of the United States.

February 14: The first state to legalize labor unions is New Jersey.

February 16: The women's magazine *Ladies' Home Journal* publishes its first issue.

February 23: Alabama becomes the first state in the nation to pass antitrust legislation.

February 23: The Anti-Vivisection Society is organized in Philadelphia, Pennsylvania.

February 23: The University of North Dakota is founded.

February 27: The first cigar-rolling machine is patented by Oscar Hammerstein. His nephew and namesake will later become a famous songwriter.

February 28: A vaudeville theater opens in Boston, Massachusetts.

March 2: Illinois becomes the first state to provide funding to railroad lines.

March 3: Congress reduces the cost of first-class postage to one-half cent from two cents.

March 3: The U.S. Navy is authorized to contract for the construction of steel vessels.

March 16: In Philadelphia, Pennsylvania, Susan Hayhurst becomes the nation's first woman graduate of a pharmacy college.

March 24: New York and Chicago are connected for the first time by telephone lines.

March 28: In New York City, the nation's first cooperative apartment house is incorporated.

April 30: In Sunbury, Pennsylvania, the Edison Electric Illuminating Company incorporates the nation's first three-wire central-station lighting plant.

May 1: The first National League baseball game is played, with Philadelphia beating Providence, 4-3.

May 24: The Brooklyn Bridge, construction of which began in 1870, opens, connecting Manhattan to Brooklyn. The bridge spans 1,595 feet and has two stone towers.

May 30: A stampede crushes a dozen people in New York City after circulation of a false rumor concerning the imminent collapse of the Brooklyn Bridge.

June: The first intercollegiate lawn tennis match is held in Hartford, Connecticut.

In this image from *Harper's Weekly,* President Chester Arthur and his party cross the Brooklyn Bridge just after it has opened in May 1883. *(Library of Congress)*

June 2: In Fort Wayne, Indiana, the first baseball game is held under electric lights.

June 16: The first "Ladies' Day" is held by the New York Giants baseball team. Women are admitted to the park free of charge.

July 4: William F. "Buffalo Bill" Cody organizes his Wild West show along with E. Z. C. Judson. It has its premiere at the Omaha fairgrounds and draws an audience of 25,000.

September 6: T. E. Burns becomes the first baseball player to hit a home run and a double in one inning.

September 11: A mail chute is patented by J. G. Cutler in Rochester, New York.

September 15: The first classes are held at the University of Texas at Austin.

September 21: The United States is connected by telegraph to Brazil.

September 21: Cornell University in Ithaca, New York, establishes the first college electrical engineering course.

October 15: The U.S. Supreme Court states that the Civil Rights Act of 1875 is unconstitutional, except if it pertains to jury duty and interstate travel.

October 22: The first national horse show is held in New York City.

November 6: The New York Athletic Club hosts the nation's first cross-country championship meet.

November 18: Four time zones are established by Congress via the Interstate Commerce Commission. This action is taken as a way of helping to regularize railroad services nationwide.

November 28: Whitman College, a four-year institution, is chartered in Walla Walla, Washington.

December 4: The patriotic organization Sons of the American Revolution is organized in New York. Membership is limited to male descendants of those who participated in the War of Independence.

1884

January 8: The chrome process for tanning leather is patented by Augustus Schultz in New York City.

January 30: The Anti-Vivisection Society, which was founded the previous year, holds its annual meeting in Philadelphia, Pennsylvania.

February 7: The New York Cancer Hospital is organized in New York City.

February 9: Seven hundred people are killed by tornadoes in the South.

February 14: Flooding of the Ohio River causes widespread damage. The river crests at 71 feet, the highest flooding ever recorded.

March 3: The U.S. Supreme Court states that Congress is able to order Treasury notes printed for use as legal tender.

March 4: Iowa prohibits the sale of alcohol.

March 12: Mississippi Industrial Institute and College receives its charger at Columbus, Mississippi. The institute is the first among state-supported schools for women.

March 17: In Otay, California, the nation's first glider flight is completed.

April 22: The first bicycle rider to plan a round-the-world trip begins the first leg of his journey in San Francisco, California.

April 24: The Medico-Chirurgical Society is organized in Washington, D.C. It is the first medical society for African Americans.

May 1: The Federation of Organized Trades and Labor Unions in the United States proclaims the necessity of an eight-hour workday. May 1, which is known as May Day or Labor Day, is recognized in most industrialized nations.

May 1: Thomas Edison is elected vice president of the American Institute of Electrical Engineers (AIEE).

May 14: A political party, the Anti-Monopoly Organization of the United States, is founded by Benjamin F. Butler of Massachusetts. A former general in the Union army, Butler is nominated for the presidency at the Anti-Monopoly Party convention in Chicago.

May 16: The Tenth Annual Kentucky Derby is won by Buchanan in Churchill Downs, Kentucky. The purse is $3,990 and the winning jockey is an African American, Isaac Murphy, one of the finest American jockeys of his era.

May 28: The Greenback Party holds its national convention at Indianapolis, Indiana.

May 29: Congress establishes the Bureau of Animal Industry as a branch of the Department of Agriculture.

June 3: The Republican National Convention opens in Chicago, Illinois. James G. Blaine receives the nomination for president three days later; General John A. Logan is chosen as his running mate.

June 16: The Liberal Republicans—the Mugwumps—hold a convention in New York City.

During the 1884 presidential election, liberal Republicans broke with the G.O.P. and supported Democratic nominee Grover Cleveland, who was a strong proponent of civil service reform. *(Library of Congress)*

June 27: The U.S. Bureau of Labor is established by Congress; it will be part of the Department of the Interior.

July 11: In Chicago, Illinois, the Democrats hold their national party convention. The governor of New York, Grover Cleveland, is nominated for president, with Thomas A. Hendricks as his running mate.

July 23: The Prohibition Party convenes in Pittsburgh, Pennsylvania, where it nominates John P. St. John and William Daniel for president and vice president, respectively.

July 30: The Labor Party holds its national convention in Chicago, Illinois, and votes to support the Democratic ticket in the upcoming presidential election.

August 5: On Bedloe's Island in New York Harbor, the cornerstone of the Statute of Liberty is laid in place.

August 9: Thomas Edison's wife, Mary, dies at Menlo Park, New Jersey.

August 26: Ottmar Mergenthaler patents the linotype machine, which will revolutionize the publishing industry.

September 10: The American Historical Association is founded in Saratoga, New York.

October: At a meeting in Washington, D.C., the International Meridian Conference fixes the world's prime meridian at Greenwich, England.

October 6: The U.S. Naval War College is founded at Newport, Rhode Island.

November 4: Grover Cleveland, a Democrat, defeats Republican James G. Blaine in the presidential election, garnering 219 electoral votes to Blaine's 182 votes.

November 8: The first news syndicate is established by Samuel McClure.

December 6: Construction of the Washington Monument is completed.

December 16: The World's Industrial and Cotton Centennial Exposition opens in New Orleans, Louisiana.

1885

January 4: The first successful appendectomy is performed by Dr. William Grant on Mary Gartside in Davenport, Iowa.

January 20: L. A. Thompson patents the roller-coaster.

February: Rail workers on the Union Pacific Railroad strike after owner Jay Gould cuts wages by 10 percent. Through the efforts of the Knights of Labor, the wage cut is later rescinded.

February 1: The first modern tuberculosis sanatorium in the United States opens in Saranac Lake, New York.

February 18: Mark Twain publishes *Adventures of Huckleberry Finn.*

February 21: The newly completed Washington Monument, begun in 1848 and costing $1.3 million, is dedicated.

Pioneers pose near their covered wagons in Colorado, ca. 1885. *(New York Public Library Picture Collection)*

March: The North West Rebellion erupts in Canada. After the uprising is quelled by government troops, rebel leader Louis Riel is executed.

March 3: American Telephone and Telegraph (AT&T) is incorporated. It is a subsidiary of American Bell Telephone.

March 3: The first special delivery service is authorized by the U.S. Postal Service.

March 3: In California, the first state forest service is established.

March 4: Grover Cleveland is inaugurated as president of the United States, replacing Chester A. Arthur. Cleveland is the first Democrat to be elected to the White House in 24 years.

March 12: The University of Arizona is chartered.

March 26: The first commercial motion picture film is manufactured in Rochester, New York.

April 15: McCormick Harvester Works laborers go out on strike to protest a wage cut.

May 9: Canadian troops defeat the Métis rebels, who are under the leadership of Louis Riel, at the Battle of Batoche.

June 5: General William Tecumseh Sherman refuses to be considered for the Republican party's possible nomination as the next U.S. president.

June 17: The Statue of Liberty, a gift to the United States from France, arrives in New York Harbor.

June 24: S. D. Ferguson, the nation's first African-American bishop, is consecrated in the Protestant Episcopal Church.

July 1: The U.S. Navigation Bureau is organized.

The Economic Ornithology Division is established by the federal government as a bird protection agency.

July 23: Former President Ulysses S. Grant dies. He is buried in Riverside Park, New York, after lying in state at City Hall.

July 28: The first coin-operated scale is patented.

August 10: The first commercially operated electric streetcars appear in Baltimore, Maryland.

September 2: In Rock Springs, Wyoming, white miners attack Chinese mines. Twenty-eight people are killed and 15 are wounded.

September 3: The nation's first naval war college opens.

September 4: The first self-service restaurant in the nation opens in New York City.

September 9: The American Economic Association is founded in Saratoga, New York.

October 1: The first daily newspaper delivery by railroad is established by the *Daily News* out of Dallas, Texas.

October 23: Bryn Mawr College opens the nation's first graduate school for women.

November 7: The Canadian Pacific Railway is completed, the terminus being Craigellachie, British Columbia.

November 11: Stanford University is founded in Palo Alto, California.

November 16: Canadian Louis Riel, leader of the Métis in the North west Rebellion, is executed for treason.

November 24: The first nursing society in the country, the Philomena Society, is organized in New York City.

Frederick Law Olmsted, a writer before he began to design parks and public spaces, is probably most famous for codesigning Central Park in New York City with Calvert Vaux. *(Library of Congress)*

December 1: The U.S. Patent Office states that the beverage "Dr Pepper" was served for the first time on this date, although the specific date on which the drink was invented cannot be determined.

December 1: Chief Sitting Bull joins Buffalo Bill Cody's Wild West Show.

December 8: President Cleveland delivers his first annual message to the American people.

EYEWITNESS TESTIMONY

. . . the railroads do not make the discriminations or differences themselves and . . . The Creator instituted them when He determined not to make his creation a dead level of mud and water, and all other material elements stirred up together in uniform collusion, inhabited, perhaps, by a single variety of queer fish which would enjoy that sort of premises . . . He laid the foundation of every so-called discrimination in freight rates which exists in the United States to-day. *Every one of them is simply a railroad trying to complete with a water-route.* On the water the Creator gives free right-of-way, and maintains the road-bed and furnishes the motive power, if man is not too much hurried to wait on sailing vessels.

. . . So far as any discriminations exist simply against individuals . . . I condemn them utterly; and I am sure no railroad manager can attempt to justify them. But circumstances, I think, will often justify cases of apparent discrimination which would be pronounced unjust where the circumstances are not understood.

Edward Porter Alexander, vice president of the Louisville & Nashville Railroad, 1881, in Hoogenboom and Hoogenboom, The Gilded Age *(1967), p. 20.*

Kerosene has become, by its cheapness, the people's light the world over. In the United States we used 220,000,000 gallons of petroleum last year. It has come into such demand abroad that our exports of it increased from 79,458,888 gallons in 1868 to 417,648,544 in 1879. It goes all over Europe, and to the far East. The Oriental demand for it is increasing faster than any other . . . Very few of the forty millions of people in the United States who burn kerosene know that its production, manufacture, and export, its price at home and abroad, have been controlled for years by a single corporation, the Standard Oil Company. The company began in a partnership, in the early years of the civil war, between Samuel Andrews and John Rockefeller in Cleveland. Rockefeller had been a bookkeeper in some interior town in Ohio, and had afterwards made a few thousand dollars by keeping a flour store in Cleveland. Andrews had been a day laborer in refineries, and so poor that his wife took in sewing . . .

The contract is in print by which the Pennsylvania Railroad agreed with the Standard, under the name of the South Improvement Company, to double the freights on oil to everybody but to repay the Standard one dollar for every barrel of oil it shipped, and one dollar for every barrel of any its competitor's shipped . . . Ostensibly this contract was given up, in deference to the whirlwind of indignation it excited. But Rockefeller, the manager of the Standard, was a man who could learn from defeat. He made no more tell-tale contracts that could be printed . . .

Henry Demarest Lloyd, reformer and journalist, in "Story of a Great Monopoly," in the Atlantic Monthly, *Vol. 47, No. 281, pp. 317–320.*

It is a pity that instead of the Pilgrim Fathers landing on Plymouth Rock, Plymouth Rock had not landed on the Pilgrim Fathers.

Chauncey Depew, excerpt from speech, New England Society meeting, New York, December 22, 1881. Available online at URL: http://www.chiasmus.com/archive/msg00030.html.

I am a Connecticut Yankee by adoption. In me, you have Missouri morals, Connecticut culture; this, gentlemen, is the combination which makes the perfect man. But where are my ancestors? Whom shall I celebrate? Where shall I find the raw material?

My first American ancestor, gentlemen, was an Indian—an early Indian. Your ancestor skinned him alive, and I am an orphan. Not one drop of my blood flows in that Indian's veins today. I stand here, lone and forlorn, without an ancestor. They skinned him! I do not object to that, if they needed his fur; but alive, gentlemen—alive! They skinned him alive—and before company! That is what rankles.

Think how he must have felt; for he was a sensitive person and easily embarrassed. If he had been a bird, it would have been all right, and no violence done to his feelings, because he would have been considered "dressed."

But he was not a bird, gentlemen, he was a man, and probably one of the most undressed men that ever was. I ask you to put yourselves in his place. I ask it as a favor; I ask it as a tardy act of justice; I ask it in the interest of fidelity to the traditions of your ancestors; I ask it that the world may contemplate, with vision unobstructed by disguising swallow-tails and white cravats, the spectacle which the true New England Society ought to present.

Cease to come to these annual orgies in this hollow modern mockery—the surplusage [sic] of raiment. Come in character; come in the summer grace, come in the unadorned simplicity, come in the free and joyous costume which your sainted ancestors provided for mine.

Samuel Clemens, speech at Philadelphia, Pennsylvania, December 23, 1881, in Samuel Langhorne Clemens, ed., Plymouth Rock and the Pilgrims: Mark Twain's Speeches *(1910). Available online at URL: http://wyllie.lib.virginia.edu:8086/perl/ toccernew?id=TwaPlym.sgm&images=images/ modeng&data=/texts/english/modeng/ parsed&tag=public&part=teiHeader.*

Public officers are the servants and agents of the people, to execute the laws which the people have made.

Grover Cleveland, in his speech accepting the Democratic nomination for New York governor, 1882, in Bartlett, Familiar Quotations, 12th Edition *(1951), p. 527.*

Lincoln fell at the close of a mighty struggle, in which the passions of men had been deeply stirred . . . Garfield was slain in a day of peace, when brother had been reconciled to brother, and when anger and hate had been banished from the land.

Great in life, he was surpassingly great in death. For no cause, in the very frenzy of wantonness and wickedness, by the red hand of murder, he was thrust from the full tide of this world's interest, from its hopes, its aspirations, its victories, into the visible presence of death—and he did not quail. Not alone for one short moment in which, stunned and dazed, he could give up life, hardly aware of its relinquishment, but through days of deadly languor, through weeks of agony, that was not less agony because silently borne, with clear sight and calm courage he looked into his open grave . . .

. . . What blight and ruin met his anguished eyes, whose lips may tell—what brilliant, broken plans, what baffled, high ambitions, what sundering of strong, warm, manhood's friendship, what bitter rending of sweet house-hold ties!

. . . And his soul was not shaken. His countrymen were thrilled with instant, profound, and universal sympathy . . . he became the center of a nation's love, enshrined in the prayers of a world. But all the love and all the sympathy could not share with him his suffering. He trod the wine-press alone. With unfaltering front he faced death. With unfailing tenderness he took leave of life. Above the demoniac hiss of the assassin's bullet he heard the voice of God. With simple resignation he bowed to the Divine decree.

As the end drew near his early craving for the sea returned . . . he begged to be taken from his prison walls, from its oppressive, stifling air, from its homelessness and its hopelessness. Gently, silently, the love of a great people bore the pale sufferer to the longed-for healing of the sea, to live or to die, as God should will, within sight of the heaving billows . . . With a wan, fevered face . . . he looked out wistfully upon the ocean's changing wonders . . .

. . . Let us think that his dying eyes read a mystic meaning, which only the rapt and parting soul may know. Let us believe that in the silence of the receding world he heard the great waves breaking on a further shore and felt already upon his wasted brow the breath of the eternal morning.

Congressman James G. Blaine, excerpts from his speech to the U.S. House of Representatives, February 27, 1882. Available online at URL: http://www.federalobserver.com/ print.php?aid=1205.

No man in this country is so high that he is above the law. No officer of the law may set that law at defiance with impunity. All the officers of the government, from the highest to the lowest, are creatures of the law, and are bound to obey it.

It is the only supreme power in our system of government, and every man who by accepting office participates in its functions is only the more strongly bound to submit to that supremacy, and to observe the limitations which it imposes upon the exercise of the authority which it gives.

Samuel Freeman Miller, Supreme Court associate justice concerning United States v. Lee, *which dealt with sovereign immunity, 1882, in Fairman,* Mr. Justice Miller and the Supreme Court *(1939), p. 331.*

. . . if we ever expect to obtain commercial supremacy, if we ever expect to have our proper rank among the nations of the earth, we must have a navy.

Representative E. John Ellis (R-Louisiana), 1882, in Paterson, American Imperialism and Anti-Imperialism *(1973), p. 64.*

Sixteenth Street is a young Wall Street. Millions are talked of as lightly as nickels and all kinds of people are dabbling in steers. The chief justice of the Supreme Court has recently succumbed to the contagion and gone out to purchase a $40,000 herd. . . . A Cheyenne man who don't pretend to know a maverick from a mandamus has made a neat little margin of $15,000 this summer in small transactions and hasn't seen a cow yet that he has bought and sold.

A journalist's account of a men's club, 1882, in Cheyenne, Wyoming, quoted in Blum, The National Experience *(1968), p. 424.*

Mexico is now undergoing a physical conquest by our people. Our railroads and other enterprises are permeating her territory. Before long Mexico will wake up to the fact that she is gradually being subjugated by the United States; and then will come the recoil and the revolt, and the United States may be called upon to conserve the interests and property of her citizens there.

Representative E. John Ellis (R-Louisiana), 1882, in Paterson, American Imperialism and Anti-Imperialism *(1973), p. 65.*

The seventy-seventh annual dinner of the New-England Society of New-York was given at Delmonicos [sic] last evening, and about 250 gentlemen, members of the society and their friends, braved the inclement weather and celebrated the two hundred and sixty-second anniversary of the landing of the Pilgrims by attending the banquet. The banquet hall was decorated simply with American flags and steamers, and the shields of the 11 original States were scattered in convenient positions about the walls.

The raised table for the officers and distinguished guests extended along the entire western end of the room, and below this five lower tables stretched down the hall. These, however, were found insufficient to accommodate the large number of guests, and one of the parlors was transformed into a dining-room, in which covers were laid for about 25 of the guests. A string band enlivened the dinner with popular music . . .

. . . guests at the principal table were Senator Miller, of California; Gov. John D. Long, of Massachusetts; Gen. Horace Porter, Samuel L. Clemens, (Mark Twain), the Rev. J. R. Paxton, Commodore

Upshur, of the Brooklyn Navy Yard; Col. W. T. Villas, of Madison, Wis.; Gov. Hobart V. Bigelow, of Connecticut; Mayor Grace, Benjamin D. Stillman, President of the Brooklyn New-England Society; Judge Abram R. Lawrence, Chauncey M. Depew, F. W. Hurst, and the Rev. Arthur Brooks. . . .

Review, "On Plymouth Rock Again. The Pilgrims Sons Talking of Their Forefathers. New-England men in New-York Congratulating Themselves and the Country on Their Ancestors' Virtues and the Resultant Blessings," published in the New York Times, *December 23, 1882. Available online at URL: http://etext.lib.virginia.edu/railton/ onstage/woman82.html.*

I think that there is no disagreement between the great mass of the employees and their employers. These societies [labor unions] that are gotten up mag-

Jay Gould built a railroad empire in the 1860s and 1870s. *(Library of Congress)*

nify these things and create evils which do not exist—create trouble which ought not to exist.

Jay Gould, prominent New York financier and former head of the Erie Railroad, to the Senate, 1883, in Garraty, Labor and Capital in the Gilded Age *(1968).*

Registration laws, primarily intended for the protection of the profession, seem particularly liable to fall short of their intended objects, not so much because of defective construction, as of unfaithful interpretation; indeed, unless definite and comprehensive in expression, and fully sustained by public opinion, they may be made in practice to sanction and perpetuate the very evils they were intended to correct. It has been more than once asserted, by those fully qualified to judge, that in the neighboring State of New York the medical profession has really lost, by the Registration Act, more than it has gained. At the last meeting of the State Society of New York, it was mentioned as a fact, by one of its members, that an Indian medicine-man had driven into Rochester, in war-paint and feathers, though engaged in the peaceful art of selling patent medicine, and, having gone to the Prothonotary's office and paid the registration fee, he had obtained a certificate as a physician, with full authority to practice under the law . . .

Much disappointment has been expressed by physicians in Pennsylvania, as well as in New York, at the operation of the Registration act, it being claimed that the practical result is that, instead of elevating the profession above irregulars and charlatans, it has degraded the regular practitioner to the level of any one who can register under the act, however unworthy he may be to be in the ranks of the medical profession . . .

"Registration Laws and Their Operation," Philadelphia Medical Times, *XIII, July 14, 1883, quoted in Ronald Hamowy, "The Early Development of Medical Licensing Laws in the United States, 1875–1900,"* Journal of Libertarian Studies, *Vol. 3, No. 1, pp. 80–81. Available online at URL: http://www.mises.org/ jlsDisplay.asp?action=sort&volume= 3&number=1&submit=View.*

[The tenements of Manchester] are too small . . . they do not repair them at all for many years; and all around those tenements in the back streets all kinds of dirty things are allowed to stand. In many cases have seen that myself. When they have good houses they live well, and their health is good; but in many places they get sick on account of the bad condition of the houses.

I think that tenement houses ought to be kept in better condition.

Father Joseph A. Chevalier, Roman Catholic priest in Manchester, New Hampshire, testifying before a Senate committee, 1883, in National Archives Records of the Senate Committee on Labor and Public Welfare and Related Committees, 1869–1968, Record Group 46 (48A-H6.1).

I believe in general that the government is best which governs least, and that interference with trade or manufactures is very undesirable. Yet I recognize the fact that evils may and do exist which require correction by the force of law. I think government will reduce its function to the desired minimum best by diffusing information and spreading light, rather than by interfering positively by commands and prohibitions. Therefore I believe in governmental collection and diffusion of information in the highest degree, mainly because in that way I believe government may reduce to the lowest terms its own active interference with trade and industry.

Economist Francis A. Walker, superintendent of the U.S. Census of 1870 and 1880, and president of Massachusetts Institute of Technology, testifying before a Senate committee, 1883, in National Archives Records of the Senate Committee on Labor and Public Welfare and Related Committees, 1869–1968, Record Group 46 (48A-H6.1).

A department of health has two objects in view, one entirely of a public character, and another of a humanitarian character. The lives of laboring men are supposed to have a public or a business value . . . it is to the public interest that the lives of laboring men should be preserved, and also that their health be preserved, in order that they may settle their families and keep them from being subjects of charity.

Colonel Emmons Clark, secretary of the New York Board of Health, speaking before a Senate committee, 1883, in National Archives Records of the Senate Committee on Labor and Public Welfare and Related Committees, 1869–1968, Record Group 46 (48A-H6.1).

This is certainly a glorious country for opportunity. A man has no stone upon his head here unless he carries it voluntarily. He has a clear road if he wants to go up.

John W. Britton, president of a New York bank, testifying before the Senate Committee on Education and Labor, 1883, in National Archives Records of the Senate Committee on Labor and Public Welfare and Related Committees, 1869–1968, Record Group 46 (48A-H6.1).

That the rapid changes now going on are bringing up problems that demand the most earnest attention may be seen on every hand. Symptoms of danger, premonitions of violence, are appearing all over the civilized world. Creeds are dying, beliefs are changing, the old forces of conservatism are melting away. Political institutions are failing, as clearly in democratic America as in monarchical Europe. There is a growing unrest and bitterness among the masses, whatever be the form of government, a blind groping for escape from conditions becoming intolerable. To attribute all this to the teachings of demagogues is like attributing the fever to the quickened pulse. It is the new wine beginning to ferment in old bottles. To put into a sailing-ship the powerful engines of a first-class ocean steamer would be to tear her to pieces with their play. So the new powers rapidly changing all the relations of society must shatter social and political organizations not adapted to meet their strain.

Economic reformer Henry George, excerpt, Social Problems, *Chapter 1, 1883. Available online at URL: http://www.schalkenbach.org/library/george.henry/sp01.html.*

Those who devised the Fourteenth Amendment wrought to grave sincerity. They may have builded better than they knew.

They vitalized and energized a principle, as old and as everlasting as human rights. To some of them, the sunset of life may have given mystical lore.

They builded, not for a day, but for all time; not for a few, or for a race; but for man. They planted in the Constitution a monumental truth, to stand foursquare whatever wind might blow.

Roscoe Conkling, former Republican congressman from New York, 1883, in Fairman, Mr. Justice Miller and the Supreme Court *(1939), p. 297.*

Roscoe Conkling opposed Garfield's attempts at civil service reform. *(Library of Congress)*

The aggregation of large fortunes is not at all a thing to be regretted. On the contrary, it is a necessary condition of many forms of social advance. If we should set a limit to the accumulation of wealth, we should say to our most valuable producers, "We do not want you to do us the services which you best understand how to perform, beyond a certain point." It would be like killing off our generals in war. A great deal is said, in the cant of a certain school, about "ethical views of wealth," and we are told that some day men will be found of such public spirit that, after they have accumulated a few millions, they will be willing to go on and labor simply for the pleasure of paying the wages of their fellow-citizens.

Possibly this is true. It is a prophecy. It is as impossible to deny it as it is silly to affirm it. For if a time ever comes when there are men of this kind, the men of that age will arrange their affairs accordingly. There are no such men now, and those of us who live now cannot arrange our affairs by what men will be a hundred generations hence.

There is every indication that we are to see new developments of the power of aggregated capital to serve civilization, and that the new developments will be made right here in America. Joint-stock companies are yet in their infancy, and incorporated capital, instead of being a thing which can be overturned, is a thing which is becoming more and more indispensable. I shall have something to say in another chapter about the necessary checks and guarantees, in a political point of view, which must be established. Economically speaking, aggregated capital will be more and more essential to the performance of our social tasks. Furthermore, it seems to me certain that all aggregated capital will fall more and more under personal control.

Each great company will be known as controlled by one master mind. The reason for this lies in the great superiority of personal management over management by boards and committees. This tendency is in the public interest, for it is in the direction of more satisfactory responsibility. The great hindrance to the development of this continent has lain in the lack of capital.

William Graham Sumner, excerpts from his essay advocating compassion for and acceptance of the wealthy in America, in What Social Classes Owe to Each Other *(1883), pp. 43–57. Available online at URL: http://historymatters.gmu.edu/d/4998.*

People will have to marry by railroad time, and die by railroad time. Ministers will be required to preach by railroad time, banks will open and close by railroad time; in fact the Railroad Convention has taken charge of the time business, and the people may as well set about adjusting their affairs in accordance with its decree.

Article in the Indianapolis Sentinel, *quoted in Cashman,* America in the Gilded Age, *Third Edition (1984), p. 27.*

It is easy to break forth in joy and thanksgiving for Emancipation in the District of Columbia, to call up the noble sentiments and the starting events which made that measure possible. It is easy to trace the footsteps of the [N]egro in the past, marked as they are all the way along with blood. But the present occasion calls for something more. How stands the [N]egro to-day?

The Hon. Frederick Douglass, address on the 21st anniversary of emancipation in the District of Columbia, Congregational Church, Washington, D.C., April 16, 1883. Available online at URL: http://memory.loc.gov/ammem/aap/aapres.html.

A man's first duty is to his own conscience & honor—the party & the country come second to that, & never first . . . the only necessary thing to do, as I understand it, is that a man shall keep *himself* clean, (by withholding his vote for an improper man), even though the party & the country go to destruction in consequence.

Author Mark Twain, to William Dean Howells, letter of September 17, 1884. Available online at URL: http://mark-twain.classic-literature.co.uk/mark-twains-letters-1876-1885/ebook-page-81.asp.

According to Mr. Spencer, the divine energy which is mandated throughout the knowable universe is the same energy that wells up in us as consciousness. Speaking for myself, I can see no insuperable difficulty in the notion that at some period in the evolution of Humanity this divine spark may have acquired sufficient concentration and steadiness to survive the wreck of material forms and endure forever.

John Fiske, in The Destiny of Man *(1884), p. 87.*

[A ton of goods] can now be carried on the best managed railroads for a distance of a mile, for a sum so small that outside of China it would be difficult to find a coin of equivalent value to give a boy as a reward for carrying an ounce package across the street.

David A. Wells, economist, 1884, in Degler, The Age of the Economic Revolution, 1876–1900 *(1977), p. 21.*

Perhaps you would like to know what became of my presidential Boom. Well as I wrote you last spring I never permitted it to rise to the dignity of a boom. It was however the nicest and quietest little scheme and well arranged that you ever saw.

. . . I have thought ever since the reassembling of Congress last winter that Blaine would be nominated. I do not think this was very much due to active exertion of his own. But effort to elect Arthur and Edmunds necessarily brought Blaine's name to the front. The overthrow of the Cameron dynasty in Pennsylvania gave him that state. The northwest remained true to him and his nomination came spontaneously.

I had no reason to be dissatisfied with his course toward me. If he had failed he would have been for me and I should have been nominated, though my name was not put before the convention at all. This was my express instruction to many men who were there for that purpose. My name had but that one chance and it was not to be frittered away. No one can say now that I have ever sought the place or brought reproach or folly to the judicial ermine. I am fully content. I believe Blaine will be elected and I feel sure he ought to be. He is a friend and admirer of mine as I am of him.

Supreme Court associate justice Samuel Freeman Miller, to William Ballinger, letter of 1884, in Fairman, Mr. Justice Miller and the Supreme Court *(1939), p. 306.*

They love him most for the enemies he has made.

Governor Edward S. Bragg, in a speech seconding Grover Cleveland's nomination at the Democratic National Convention in Chicago, Illinois, July 9, 1884, in Bartlett, Familiar Quotations, *(1951), p. 569.*

In Jersey Street exist two courtyards . . . Six three-story houses are in each. These houses are old, and long ago worn out. They are packed with tenants, rotten with age and decay, and so constructed as to have made them very undesirable for dwelling purposes in their earliest infancy. The Italians who chiefly inhabit them are the scum of New York chiffoniers, and as such, saturated with the filth inseparable from their business . . . The courtyard swarms with, in daytime, females in the picturesque attire of Genoa and Piedmont, moving between the dirty children. The abundant rags, paper, sacks, barrows, barrels, wash-tubs, dogs, and cats, are all festooned overhead by clothes-lines weighted with such garments as are only known in Italy.

Kate Holladay Claghorn, immigration specialist, 1884, in Hoogenboom and Hoogenboom, The Gilded Age *(1967), p. 103.*

Our order contemplates a radical change in the existing industrial system, and labors to bring about that change. The attitude of our order to the existing industrial system is necessarily one of war.

Terence V. Powderly, leader of the Knights of Labor, to the group's 1884 general assembly in Dubofsky, Industrialism and the American Worker, 1865–1920 *(1975), p. 55.*

It is perhaps the highest distinction of the Greeks that they recognized the indissoluble connection of beauty and goodness.

Charles Eliot Norton, scholar and editor, in a report of the executive committee of the Archaeological Institute of America, 1884, in Bartlett, Familiar Quotations *(1951), p. 571.*

New England has a harsh climate, a barren soil, a rough and stormy coast, and yet we love it, even with a love passing that of dwellers of more favored regions.

Of "Americanism" of the right sort we cannot have too much. Mere vaporing and boasting become a nation as little as a man. But honest, outspoken pride and faith in our country are infinitely better and more to be respected than the cultivated reserve which sets it down as ill-bred and in bad taste ever to refer to our country except by way of deprecation, criticism, or general negation.

Henry Cabot Lodge, Massachusetts' opinion leader, to the New England Society of New York, address of 1884, in Bartlett, Familiar Quotations *(1951), p. 700.*

Mr. Clemens ran his hand through his hair, and with a few humorous remarks about the programme, calling for something he hadn't at hand, proceeded to ignore it. He read the story of a reporter's attempt to interview him, in which he solemnly stated that either her or his twin brother was drowned in the bathtub in infancy, which was never known, and also the account of his experience as temporary editor of an agricultural weekly. An old sea captain's story was well told, and in conclusion Mr. Clemens narrated a ghost story about the woman with the golden arm, a story similar to one of Uncle Remus's. It was like crooning a nursery tale to adults; but it was well told, and was so well received as to suggest that the Remus stories read by their author would find appreciative listeners.

. . . The hall was nearly filled by a select and cultured audience at the evening entertainment. . . . Mr. Clemens again took the liberty to change the selections which had been announced for him, for the double reason, as he stated in his characteristic manner, that he could not endure it to be always bound down to a fixed course of action, and he also knew that the audience would not endure to hear him read all that the programme had set out for him. It would take until after breakfast time next morning, and he was very particular about his breakfast . . . Mr. Clemens was very cordially applauded, both on his first appearance and at the end of each of his readings.

Review of "'Mark Twain' and Mr. Cable," Providence Daily Journal, *November 10, 1884. Available online at URL: http://etext.virginia.edu/etcbin/ twainrev2www?specfile=/lv6/workspace/railton/review/ twainreview.o2w&act=surround&offset=756979&tag= Twain-Cable+Providence+Revi ew&query=.*

It cannot be permitted that, when the Constitution of a State, the fundamental law of the land, has imposed upon its legislature the duty of guarding, by suitable laws, the health of its citizens, especially in crowded cities, and the protection of their person and property by suppressing and preventing crime, that the power which enables it to perform this duty can be sold, bargained away, under any circumstances, as if it were a mere privilege which the legislator could dispose of at his pleasure.

Supreme Court associate justice Samuel Freeman Miller, on upholding the principles set forth in the Slaughterhouse decision under the terms of the Fourteenth Amendment, 1884, in Fairman, Mr. Justice Miller *(1939), p. 186.*

. . . Mark Twain and George W. Cable entertained about 700 of their admirers in Mercantile Library Hall last night. They gave recitals of selections from their respective work, Mark Twain having four pieces on the programme and Mr. Cable the same number. Cable chose passages from his novel Dr. Sevier, in which he aimed to illustrate the character of Narcisse, the Creole, Kate Riley and Mary Richley. All his recitals were successful in pleasing the audience, and before the evening was at an end the author of Creole Days was a strong favorite with all present. Mark

President Grover Cleveland is inaugurated for his first term in 1885. *(Library of Congress)*

Twain did not fail, however, to hold his own. He kept the assemblage in excellent humor with his literary surprises . . .

Review in the St. Louis Daily Globe Democrat, *January 11, 1885. Available online at URL: http://etext.virginia.edu/etcbin/twainrev2www?specfile=/lv6/workspace/railton/reviews/twainrev iew.o2w&act= surround&offset=716316&tag= Twain-Cable+St.+Louis+Revie w&query=.*

I look upon the four years next to come as a dreadful self-inflicted penance for the good of my country. I can see no pleasure in it and no satisfaction, only a hope that I may be of service to my people.

President Grover Cleveland, in a private conversation prior to his inauguration, 1885, in Morgan, The Gilded Age *(1970), p. 134.*

Your every voter, as surely as your chief magistrate, exercises a public trust.

President Cleveland, to the nation, inaugural speech, 1885, in Bartlett, Familiar Quotations *(1951), p. 627.*

. . . The people demand reform in the administration of the Government and the application of business principles to public affairs.

President Cleveland, to the nation, inaugural speech, 1885, in Morgan, The Gilded Age *(1970), p. 134.*

[There is] a feeling here to-night stronger than I ever saw it before, that the war is over.

Atlanta Constitution, report on Inauguration Day, 1885, in Morgan, The Gilded Age *(1970), p. 129.*

This whole question of the farming interest is a very important one, and to show you another of the evils that grow out of these railroad grants and that are incident to them, I will refer to the fact that there is a very rapid change of ownership being made in the farming lands; that the small farmer as the owner of his farm is rapidly disappearing. Our whole northern country is filled with loan agents. In every considerable town and city you find often where they make a sole business of lending money upon farm lands and taking mortgages, and a large proportion of the money so loaned is foreign capital—a very large proportion.

William Godwin Moody, farm and labor supporter, 1885, in Hoogenboom and Hoogenboom, The Gilded Age *(1967), p. 56.*

A very deplorable fact is that the great body of literary criticism is mainly perfunctory. This is not due to a lack of ability or to a lack of knowledge. It is due to the fact that most of it is from the pens of newspaper writers who have no time to elaborate their ideas. They are in a hurry, and what they write is hurried. Under these circumstances it is not unnatural that they should take their cues from inadequate sources and give to the public opinions that are either conventional or that have no reasonable basis. . . .

All this is the outcome of the conditions and circumstances of American life. There is no demand for sound criticism any more than there is a demand for great poetry. We have a leisure class, but its tastes run towards horses, yachting and athletic sports, in imitation of the English young men who occasionally honor these shores with their presence. The imitation, after all, is a limping one. The young Englishman of leisure is not only fond of outdoor sports, but of books. He has culture and taste, and patronizes literature with as much enthusiasm as he does physical amusements. If our leisure class is to imitate the English, it would be better if the imitation extended somewhat in the direction of culture. . . .

The American leisure class—the class that might be expected to patronize good literature and to create a demand for sound, conservative criticism—is not only fond of horses, but is decidedly horsey. It is coarse and uncultivated. It has no taste in either literature or art. It reads few books and buys its pictures in Europe by the yard.

Unsigned review of an appearance onstage by Samuel Clemens, "'Huckleberry Finn' and His Critics," The Atlanta Constitution, *May 26, 1885. Available online at URL: http://etext.virginia.edu/etcbin/twainrev2www?specfile=/lv6/workspace/railton/reviews/twainrev iew.o2w&act=surround&offset= 184541&tag=The+Constitution+Review: +Huck&query=.*

The average wages of a farm laborer in the South is nearer fifty than seventy-five cents, out of which the laborer must feed and clothe his family. He seldom ever pays rent and he seldom ever sees a cent of currency. He is paid in "orders" on some storekeeper friendly to the planter. He cannot negotiate these precious "orders" to any other than the store indicated. Hence a system of fraud is connived at and practiced, to the utter demoralization and impoverishment of the ignorant, helpless laborer.

T. Thomas Fortune, editor of the New York Globe, *speaking before the Senate Committee on Education and Labor, 1885, in Hoogenboom and Hoogenboom,* The Gilded Age *(1967), p. 54.*

Your question, therefore, reduces itself to, What is the condition of the negroes? I should say good, as compared with a few years ago, and improving. You must recollect that it has only been 18 years since the negroes emerged from slavery without a dollar and with no education, and that for generations they had been taught to rely entirely upon others for guidance and support . . .

Where a laborer owns his own teams, gears, and implements necessary for making a crop, he gets two-thirds or three-fourths of the crop, according to the quality and location of the land.

Under the rental system proper, where a laborer is responsible and owns his team, &c., first-class land is rented to him for $8 or $10 per acre. With the land go certain privileges, such as those heretofore enumerated.

John C. Calhoun, grandson of the statesman, speaking before the Senate Committee on Education and Labor, 1885, in Hoogenboom and Hoogenboom, The Gilded Age *(1967), p. 52.*

Awakened at 5.15 a.m. My eyes were embarassed by the sunbeams—turned my back to them and tried to take another dip into oblivion—succeeded—awakened at 7 a.m. thought of Mina, Daisy, and Mamm G—put all 3 in my mental kaledescope to obtain a new combination a la Galton. Took Mina as a basis, tried to improve her beauty by discarding and adding certain features borrowed from Daisy and Mamma G. a sort of Raphaelized beauty, got into it too deep, mind flew away and I went to sleep again.

Awakened at 8:15 a.m. Powerful itching of my head, lots of white dry dandruff—what is this d-mnable material, Perhaps its the dust from the dry literary matter I've crowded into my noddle lately. Its nomadic. Gets all over my coat, must read about it in the Encyclopedia.

Smoking too much makes me nervous—must passo [sic] my natural tendency to acquire such habits—holding heavy cigar constantly in my mouth has deformed my upper lip, it has sort of Havanna curl.

Arose at 9 oclock came down stairs expecting twas too late for breakfast—twas'nt. Couldn't eat much, nerves of stomach too nicotinny. The roots of tobacco plants must go clear through to hell. Satans principal agent Dyspepsia.

Thomas A. Edison, excerpt from his personal diary, Menlo Park, New York, July 12, 1885. Special Collections Series: Thomas A. Edison Diary—Cat. 117 *(1885). Available online at URL: http://edison. rutgers.edu/taep.htm.*

By the war with Mexico, we had acquired, as we have seen, territory almost equal in extent to that we already possessed. It was seen that the volunteers of the Mexican war largely composed the pioneers to settle up the Pacific coast country. Their numbers, however, were scarcely sufficient to be a nucleus for the population of the important points of the territory acquired by that war. After our rebellion, when so many young men were at liberty to return to their homes, they found they were not satisfied with the farm, the store, or the work-shop of the villages, but wanted larger fields. The mines of the mountains first attracted them; but afterwards they found that rich valleys and productive grazing and farming lands were there. This territory, the geography of which was not known to us at the close of the rebellion, is now as well mapped as any portion of our country. Railroads traverse it in every direction, north, south, east, and west. The mines are worked. The high lands are used for grazing purposes, and rich agricultural lands are found in many of the valleys. This is the work of the volunteer. It is probable that the Indians would have had control of these lands for a century yet but for the war. We must conclude, therefore, that wars are not always evils unmixed with some good.

Ulysses S. Grant, Memoirs, *Vol. 6, Conclusion, 1885. Available online at URL: http://www.gutenberg. net/dirs/4/3/6/4367/4367-h/p6.htm#conclusion.*

All the work is done on horseback, and the quantity of ponies is thus of necessity very great, some of the large outfits numbering them by hundreds; on my own ranch there are eighty. Most of them are small, wiry beasts, not very speedy, but with good bottom, and able to pick up a living under the most adverse circumstances. There are usually a few large, fine horses kept for the special use of the ranchman or foremen. The best are those from Oregon; most of them come from Texas, and many are bought from the Indians. They are broken in a very rough manner, and many are in consequence vicious brutes, with the detestable habit of bucking. Of this habit I have a perfect dread, and, if I can help it, never get on a confirmed bucker. The horse puts his head down between his forefeet, arches his back, and with stiff legs gives a succession of jarring jumps, often "changing ends" as he does so. Even if a man can keep his seat, the performance gives him about as uncomfortable a shaking up as can be imagined.

Theodore Roosevelt, excerpt, Hunting Trips of a Ranchman; Sketches of Sport on the Northern Cattle Plains *(1885), p. 5.*

The whole question of these labor troubles is vast and important and throws more new light on a department of our manufacturing interests which we have not hitherto studied with a sufficient depth and understanding.

Cyrus McCormick, to his mother, Nettie Fowler McCormick, the summer before the Haymarket riot, letter of 1885, in Weinstein and Wilson, Freedom and Crisis *(1978), p. 520.*

We have had a week of trial and anxiety on the great subject of disturbances in our main factory—the serious labor troubles we have encountered—a great "strike," and all the resulting derangement of our relations—old and pleasant as they were—with our workmen.

Trouble has come to hundreds of families in consequence; hatred and fierce passions have been aroused; and an injury has resulted to our good name.

It began with a few molders and went on, one force operating on another, until 1,200 men went out, part of them by intimidation and part of them led by ignorant and blind passion. It ended by our conceding the terms demanded.

What sore heart I have carried these days!

Nettie Fowler McCormick, widow of the inventor of the reaping machine, to her daughter Virginia, letter of April 1885, in Weinstein and Wilson, Freedom and Crisis *(1978), p. 516.*

We find ourselves bound hand and foot, the majority delivering themselves over to the power of the minority that might oppose any particular measures, so that nothing could be done in the way of legislation except by unanimous consent or by a two-thirds vote . . .

During the last Congress a very important bill, that providing for the presidential succession . . . was reported from a committee of which I had the honor to be a member, and was placed on the calendar of the House on the 21st day of April, 1884 . . .

That bill, which was favored by nearly the entire House, was permitted to die on the calendar because there never was a moment, when under the rules as they then existed, the bill could be reached and passed by the House.

Owing to the fact that we could not transact business under the rules, all business was done under unanimous consent or under propositions to suspend the rules upon the two Mondays in each month on which suspensions were allowed.

Rep. William M. Springer, speech in the U.S. House of Representatives, December 10, 1885. Available online at URL: http://historicaltextarchive.com/ books.php?op=viewbook&bookid=42&cid=5.

We hold that the conflict of labor and capital has brought into prominence a vast number of social problems, whose solution requires the united efforts, each in its own sphere, of the church, of the state, and of science.

Economist Richard T. Ely, author of the original platform of the American Economic Association, 1885, in Baltzell, The Protestant Establishment *(1966), p. 162.*

If nominated, I will not accept. If elected, I will not serve.

General William T. Sherman, in reply to a request that he consider running for U.S. president, 1885, in Carruth, The Encyclopedia of American Facts and Dates *(1979), p. 337.*

5

Labor Unrest and Economic Instability
1886–1891

The selection of a reform-friendly president in 1884 was not sufficient to forestall some of the most violent labor agitation the nation would experience in the late 19th century. The Haymarket Square riot, in May of 1886, was the outcome of months of unsatisfactory dealings between labor leaders and management.[1] The McCormick Reaper Works, in Chicago, Illinois, employed workers who were out on strike over a wage dispute. At a planned rally, on May 4, 1886, a confrontation between police and demonstrators occurred at the rally's Haymarket Square location. A bomb exploded, and in the chaos that followed, police shot into the crowd. It is assumed that workers who were armed also fired, leaving one police officer dead at the scene, with six dying later. More than five dozen police were injured, although there was no official tally of civilian deaths or injuries.

Certain known anarchists were arrested following the riot, and 31 were indicted; eight men were tried and convicted. On November 11, 1887, four of the anarchists who had been found guilty were hanged.[2] One committed suicide in jail, two received sentences of life in prison, one took his own life, and another remained incarcerated despite the fact that there was no substantive case against him.

Several days prior to the riot, President Grover Cleveland sensed the mood in Chicago and tried to find an avenue of peaceful escape for angry negotiators in the labor dispute. The president made a national appeal to business and labor leaders to settle their differences peaceably and to seek assistance from federal officials. However, no means could be found to permit the government to act as arbitrator, and the violent event unfolded just as the president and others feared that it might.

In the aftermath of the Haymarket riot, humanitarian reformer and labor activist James Otis Sargent Huntington, an Episcopal priest, was prompted to establish the Church Association for the Advancement of the Interests of Labor (CAIL). This group was only one of many similar efforts that sought to determine ways to prevent future misunderstandings between labor and management.

Chicago's Haymarket Square riot of May 4, 1886, drew national attention to increasing demands by American laborers for better working conditions and adequate pay. *(Library of Congress)*

DIFFERENT APPROACHES TO THE ECONOMIC DILEMMA

But despite their fine intentions, these well-meaning attempts could do little to change the living and working conditions of the poor. And it had virtually no effect on labor activism, which continued to find a variety of aggressive ways to make itself heard. In 1886, for example, the American Federation of Labor (AFL) was founded, and Samuel Gompers was elected its president.[3] The AF of L would remain the leading labor organization throughout the 19th and 20th centuries.

Concurrent with James Huntington's work, in 1886, the first settlement in the United States, the Neighborhood Guild, was founded in New York City by Stanton Coit.[4] This simple effort was patterned after similar settlements in England—namely London's Toynbee Hall. It was among the first of many such attempts by a growing number of college-educated individuals to help the urban poor. Vida Scudder, a Smith College alumna, founded the College Settlement Association in 1887 along with several other young women who had also visited London to view Toynbee Hall. Among other well-known groups doing settlement work was that headed by Jane Addams at Hull-House in Chicago, Illinois. Addams had graduated from Rockford Female Seminary in Illinois after her father firmly discouraged her from attending her first choice, Smith College in Northampton, Massachusetts. While Rockford did not have the prestigious reputation of Smith, it permitted Addams the opportunity to do college work among young women similarly inclined to an academic life.

A college education was fast becoming the passport to a certain type of life—for young men as well as women—almost unimaginable earlier. During the post–Civil War years, hundreds of students entered the many institutions being founded by public mandate and through private efforts. In 1886, Bryn Mawr

College was founded in Pennsylvania and in 1887, Clark University was founded in Worcester, Massachusetts.

Those born into families of wealth and position could point to published evidence of their prominence when, in 1887 the *Social Register* was published. This book detailed for the first time an index of family associations among wealthy Americans. Inclusion in the *Social Register* was much sought after, sometimes discreetly, sometimes not, by hundreds.

While an individual's social status was determined by a variety of factors, and influenced but not determined absolutely by birth, the variables affecting the nation's monetary system were more fluid. The issue of silver coinage versus the minting of gold coin was vigorously debated, leading to an avalanche of advice and opinion on the subject of money flow, and its effect on the economy. Among the most enthusiastic supporters of free silver were the Populists, who believed the nation's future stability depended on silver coinage. A guide to bimetallism, *Seven Financial Conspiracies which have Enslaved the American People,* published in 1886 by Mrs. S. E. V. Emery, was one of many books on coinage read by thousands of Americans who sought an articulate explanation of the debate.

Samuel Gompers was head of the American Federation of Labor. *(Library of Congress)*

A REFORM-MINDED PRESIDENT TAKES ON THE RAILROADS

In 1887, President Cleveland signed the Interstate Commerce Act, which brought the railroads under the federal government's jurisdiction.[5] The legislation established a five-member panel, the Interstate Commerce Commission (ICC), which was responsible for ensuring compliance with the new law. Among the Interstate Commerce Act's more successful clauses was a requirement that railroads report yearly to the commission. This meant that the Interstate Commerce Commission could more effectively oppose laissez-faire government policies that favored big business.

The railroad industry was hit the hardest by passage of the Interstate Commerce Act. Because of the railroad's importance to the growth and development of the United States, the federal government had ignored the practice of individual railroad companies to maintain a monopoly in the specific areas they serviced. By so doing, however, these railroads were able to set their own shipping prices, which helped eliminate competitors and enabled them to control the market. Such control meant limited competition and punitive discrimination in rate-setting. Farmers, especially those with smaller holdings, could not provide the volume needed to get favorable shipping rates from the railroads. It was the agricultural sector that was involved, early, in lobbying federal officials for protective legislation.[6]

The Interstate Commerce Act addressed the problem of railroad monopolies. It set guidelines for how railroads were to conduct their business, obligating railroads to set "just and reasonable" rates, preventing the setting of special rates or rebates, and forbidding discrimination in rates on the basis of long- or short-haul shipping. The ICC revolutionized the way that the government treated private businesses that conducted transactions across state lines. Its existence was long a symbol of the power that various federal regulatory commissions wielded during the 1880s and 1890s.

NATIVE AMERICANS ARE GIVEN PROPERTY RIGHTS

At the same time that railroads came under federal regulation, the government also began to revise its American-Indian policies. While the federal government had previously stressed a range of negative approaches to Native Americans, attempts now deemphasized tribal reservations in favor of granting allotments of land to individuals.

Toward this end, on February 8, 1887, Congress passed the Dawes Act, named for Senator Henry Dawes (R–Massachusetts).[7] In order to receive an allotment, an Indian had to agree to a number of things, one of which was taking on a new "white" name. Culturally, the tribe not the individual was the most important. Acceptive allotment was in many was renouncing traditional beliefs. Under the terms of this legislation, a family of one who had met the conditions received 100 acres of land, with each dependent child receiving an additional 40 acres. The federal government held the land in trust for 25 years, and then a family (or an individual) would receive title to the parcel. The Dawes Act granted citizenship rights to Native Americans who received the land, but did not grant citizenship to those who would not agree to the terms of allotment.

By 1893, President Grover Cleveland had appointed the Dawes Commission, charged with negotiating with the Five Civilized Tribes. (Cherokee, Creek, Choctaw, Chickasaw, and Seminole). Subsequently, legislation was passed that gave property to the Five Civilized Tribes in exchange for an end to tribal government and under the condition that the Native American affected by the laws would recognize state and federal regulations governing their conduct. To receive an allotment, a member of a tribe was required to register with the Bureau of Indian Affairs, and the person's name was listed on the "Dawes rolls."

The Dawes Act, and those that followed, was supposedly aimed at protecting Indian property rights; however, the land they received was frequently less than desirable. And after allotments had been given out "excess" land, which formerly might have belonged to the tribe as a whole, was often sold to white settlers. In reality, allotment was a disaster for many tribes and Indians. Many lost land, tribal autonomy, and others were forced to abandon long held beliefs and traditions.

Railroad regulation, better land-development strategies, and increased awareness of labor's power were frequently discussed topics in the 1880s. Many Americans agreed that the nation's economy demanded regulation and oversight but no one was certain how best to relieve the monotonous cycle of recession and inflation. One man, however, had an answer to the widening gulf that separated the very rich and the very poor. Henry George, an economist, devised a simple strategy that he felt could solve the country's fiscal difficulties: the single tax.

A family poses in front of their sod house in Custer County, Nebraska, in 1886. *(Nebraska State Historical Society, Solomon D. Butcher Collection)*

The concept was simple—to eliminate all taxes except those on the value of land. George proposed that landowners be assessed for the value of their land as that value increased or decreased and that the tax be applied to the public good. In his book *Progress and Poverty,* George explained the nuances of his single-tax idea, and in numerous speaking engagements he was able to generate widespread support for its adoption. His ideas would perhaps have been better received if the era's most wealthy capitalists had not so vehemently opposed him.

By the late 1880s, America's industrial base was the focus of powerful, prominent, and persuasive citizens. Continued agitation by labor leaders could not convince the voters of the benefits of reform; indeed, the reverse was true. Noisier striking workers led to more entrenched, anti-reform voters.

Gradually, as the need for social and economic reform grew more apparent, people began to seek change. Education played a role in this, as did a greater number of publications dedicated to new reform approaches and unique ways of implementing change. In early 1888, Edward Bellamy's novel of socialist utopia, *Looking Backward,* was published.[8] This book was one of many that attempted to outline how social, economic or cultural reforms could improve human civilization. *Looking Backward* would sell more than 200,000 copies within a few years of its publication. It was widely read even outside the United States, as was the writing of social critic Henry George.

FRATERNAL AND CHARITABLE ORGANIZATIONS EXPAND THEIR INFLUENCE

Although they were not new, fraternal organizations continued to grow in popularity and broadened their membership base. Many were religious or political in connection, ideology, or form. The Southern Alliance was one of the more prominent political organizations of the late 1880s.[9] Formed when the National Farmers' Alliance (founded in 1880) joined with the Agricultural Wheel, it became one of the most powerful special interest groups in the nation. Aimed at improving the farmer's situation, it was particularly vehement in its opposition to railroad interests, which Alliance members claimed had taken precedence over the needs of agriculture in the United States.

Also in 1888, the Student Volunteer Movement was established. It sought to put to use the evangelistic, social-activist fervor affecting hundreds of young men and women, many of whom were among a new group of college-educated Americans. The movement encouraged missionary work and was led by John R. Mott. He would later become national secretary of the YMCA. This effort was closely allied with the settlement house movement, the flagship of which—Hull-House, in Chicago—opened in September 1889.[10]

While the reform impulse began to change people's response to society, changes in the way buildings were designed and constructed transformed the urban landscape. In 1888, architect Louis Sullivan designed the Schlesinger Building in Chicago. It later became the department store Carson, Pirie, Scott, and its elegant facade quickly made it a well-recognized Chicago landmark.[11] In Pittsburgh, Pennsylvania, the first Bessemer steel beams were produced, enabling construction of many skyscrapers nationwide. One of these, the 11-story Tower Building in New York City, was erected in 1888, the same year that the steel beams first became available. Among the first steel skeleton skyscrapers, the Tower Building was designed by architect Bradford Gilbert. Only three years later, Louis Sullivan—often referred to as the "father" of the skyscraper—completed the Wainwright Building in St. Louis, Missouri, another such steel-frame building.

Certain technological breakthroughs of the 1880s ushered in an entirely new world of leisure pursuits. Thomas A. Edison produced the first moving picture film in 1888, using technology developed by George Eastman of Rochester, New York. Within several decades, silent moving pictures would become popular wherever they were shown.

Bicycling grew more popular in 1889, especially with the advent of the safety bicycle, which had two equal-sized wheels. It replaced older-style bicycles with one large and one small wheel, which were much more difficult to maneuver. Also in 1889, the U.S. Lawn Tennis Association announced that its champion players were Henry Slocum and Bertha Townsend, indicating the public's growing interest in tennis as a spectator sport. That year, too, the first All-American football team was chosen and appeared in a feature in *Collier's Weekly*.

Some Americans found less active, though no less absorbing, ways to spend their leisure time. American theatergoers were entranced with David Belasco and Henry De Mille's play, *The Charity Ball,* which debuted in 1889.[12] In September, Bronson Howard's play about the Civil War, *Shenandoah,* was produced in New York City by Charles Frohman and became a theater classic. Elsewhere, in 1889, Henry James's short story "The Liar" was published. Mark Twain's popular novel *A Connecticut Yankee in King Arthur's Court* appeared that year and poet Emma Lazarus, who became famous for her verse inscribed at the base of the Statue of Liberty in New York Harbor, published *The Poems of Emma Lazarus.*

As part of the continuing trend of establishing separate postsecondary institutions for women, Barnard College was founded in 1889 as part of Columbia University. And another land-grant university, the University of New Mexico, was established in Albuquerque. Although initially founded as a way of promoting the most effective agricultural practices among those homesteading or farming previously unsettled areas, by the mid-1900s these schools would be among the most respected in the nation.

One of the most interesting phenomena of these years was the opening up of land in Oklahoma Territory, previously Indian Territory, to homesteading settlers. Within several hours of the starting gun at midday on April 22, thousands of settlers had staked claims and established themselves as "Sooners."[13] This land rush resulted in a population in the territory of more than 60,000 residents by the time the census was taken in 1890.

HOW AN ELECTION REFLECTED A SHIFT IN PUBLIC VIEWS

Relative confusion, decided ambivalence, and division in the electorate was reflected in the election of 1888. Prior to the 1880s, the nation's overriding concerns seemed to be domestic—railroad expansion, western settlement, civil

While the Gilded Age was a time of urban growth, westward expansion was also crucial to national economic expansion. Homesteading families like this one, traveling in a covered wagon, made such expansion possible. *(National Archives)*

service reform. The new decade, however, ushered in challenges of a new sort. Increasingly, the president and the U.S. Congress would be obliged to discern the emerging role of the United States on a world stage.

The responsibility for shaping this role would fall, initially, to Indiana's Benjamin Harrison, the Republican challenger of the Democratic incumbent, President Grover Cleveland. In November 1888, Cleveland won 48.6 percent of the popular vote, with Harrison receiving 47.8 percent of the popular vote. Although he won the popular election by a single percentage point, Cleveland carried neither Pennsylvania nor New York, his home state. He lost the Electoral College vote, 233-168, in part because of his failure to gain momentum within the party. This was directly due to Cleveland's support of civil service reform, which infuriated the Democrats. He also failed to win support from corporate leaders because of his request for a protective tariff reduction, and farmers were angry at Cleveland for favoring the gold standard.

Benjamin Harrison's election marked the start of two trends:[14] a gradual change in the federal government's position on social and economic issues, and the start of Republican control of the White House, control which (with a single exception) lasted until well into the 20th century.

In the beginning, President Harrison's administration gave only lip service to the needs of the poor in America—it was the friend of trusts, of big business, of the railroads. Nevertheless, there were individuals and groups in the United States whose concern was put into action on behalf of the silent millions who slept in overcrowded tenements, put in long hours in factories, mills, and mines and who were either too young—or too poorly educated—to vote.

As the plight of immigrants and the urban poor became more widely apparent, journalists actively promoted recognition of these problems. Among the more aggressive of these journalists was Jacob A. Riis. In 1890, he published *How the Other Half Lives,* a book that graphically depicted life in urban slums.[15] He added his voice to the growing choir of reform journalists, such

Expansion of the steel industry enriched a few, provided work for hundreds of thousands of laborers, and made the United States an industrial giant among the world's nations. Shown here is an Alabama blast furnace. *(Library of Congress)*

as Henry Demarest Lloyd, Edward Bellamy, and Robert Blatchford, who spoke for the poor.

URBAN PROBLEMS SPUR PUBLIC AND PRIVATE REFORM EFFORTS

Although the many problems facing laborers, immigrants, and the indigent were being publicized, there remained a complexity of issues crippling the nation's cities. Social workers tried their best to address these issues and to effect change by hands-on efforts and by promoting reform legislation. During this time, too, there was an upsurge in the formation of groups dedicated to changing urban conditions. In 1891, the Christian Social Union was founded in the United States, an organization that was the American branch of a British group. It was dedicated to reforming society for the general good. The young Johns Hopkins economist Richard T. Ely was among its first members.

Ely, and others who considered the effect of national economic development on individuals' problems, knew that the solution to poverty was not simple. Before the country could expect to change labor and living conditions among the poor, it needed to confront the stalemate in the nation's monetary policy. Lobbyists for the Sherman Silver Purchase Act were overjoyed when the act was passed in 1890, requiring the Treasury Department to buy 4.5 million ounces of silver each month. It was hoped that this would prevent a further decline in the value of money and shore up the flagging economy.

Fiscal issues and city slums were not the only targets of reform efforts. Education also became the focus of reform. Sometimes, the result was schooling for the privileged, as in the case of the Taft School. Founded in 1890, in Watertown, Connecticut, it was a private boarding school for wealthy young men. But educators also recognized the need to provide schooling for those who might otherwise never have the opportunity for advancement. The nation's first correspondence school was opened in 1891 by Thomas Jefferson Foster as a way of making education available to miners, many of whom were illiterate immigrant workers. The Committee of Ten on Secondary Schools was formed in 1891 to examine the preparation of students of public schools nationwide. And colleges and universities grew in number. The University of Chicago was chartered in 1891; Rice University and Throop Polytechnic (later the California Institute of Technology) were also founded that year. An interest in athletics was growing on college campuses, and several new sports were introduced. In 1890, a Canadian, Dr. James A. Naismith, invented the game of basketball at the YMCA Training College in Springfield, Massachusetts.[16]

As cultural interests and political affiliations of Americans became better articulated fraternal and social organizations flourished. The Daughters of the American Revolution was founded in 1891, as was the Colonial Dames. Both groups, with exclusive membership requirements, were the virtual opposites of the reform-oriented settlement organizations that attracted the attention of upper-middle-class women at the end of the 19th century. Within the next several years, more of these exclusive clubs would be founded. In 1893, the Daughters of the Cincinnati was founded for descendants of those who had

Benjamin Harrison served as president for one term. *(National Archives)*

fought in the Civil War, and the Society of Mayflower Descendants was also established. Membership in the latter was regarded as highly prestigious.

Big business continued to demand the attention and scrutiny of elected officials and of reform-minded private citizens. More companies' holdings included both the supply of raw materials and the manufacture of finished goods. Because these larger companies were so powerful, they edged out smaller, less profitable efforts and thereby reduced competition, particularly in the manufacturing areas such as steel production. A concerned U.S. Congress passed the Sherman Anti-Trust Act in 1890 to penalize companies that formed combinations "in restraint of trade."[17] The act's intention was to limit the financial power of giants such as Carnegie Steel, but however well-placed this intent, the government failed in its attempt to control big business. The Sherman Anti-Trust Act would later be rendered ineffective, in 1895, by a U.S. Supreme Court ruling, *U.S. v. Knight,* which stated that monopolies were not inherently illegal. This ruling set the stage for years of continuing profit for the nation's largest industries—at the expense of farmers and small business owners.

Because of the growing dissatisfaction that many felt toward Benjamin Harrison's administration, Democrats believed that Cleveland could be reelected in 1892. Too, an increasing number of Americans were disillusioned with the two-party system, and as a way of promoting reform these voters founded the People's party in 1891.

CHRONICLE OF EVENTS

1886

January 1: The Valley Hunt Club in Pasadena, California, holds its first Tournament of Roses.

January 19: The Presidential Succession Act passes Congress. It allows for the heads of executive departments of government to succeed to the presidency in the event of an emergency—such as death, removal, resignation—wherein the president and vice president are unable to serve.

January 19: In Red Wing, Minnesota, the nation's first local ski club is formed.

February 7: Rioting erupts in Seattle, Washington, where white residents protest the presence of Chinese immigrant workers. Federal troops are called in to restore order after more than 400 Chinese are driven from their homes.

February 9: Civil War hero General Winfield Scott Hancock dies.

February 14: The first railroad shipment of California oranges leaves the West Coast bound for markets in the eastern United States.

February 23: The process for manufacturing aluminum out of bauxite ore is perfected.

February 24: Thomas Alva Edison marries Mina Miller at Akron, Ohio.

March 4: The University of Wyoming receives its charter in Laramie.

March 6: In Great Barrington, Massachusetts, the nation's first alternating-current power plant begins operation.

March 6: More than 9,000 members of the Knights of Labor go on strike against the Missouri-Pacific Railroad.

March 6: In New York City, the first national nursing magazine—entitled *Nightingale*—is published.

April 8: Representative Richard P. Bland (D-Missouri) introduces a free coinage of silver bill into the House of Representatives.

April 22: President Cleveland, in a message to the nation concerning labor unrest, suggests that the federal government act as arbitrator between workers and management.

April 24: Augustus Tolton, the nation's first black Roman Catholic priest, is ordained.

May 1: Workers in Chicago, Illinois, begin a nationwide strike on behalf of an eight-hour workday. Between 40,000 and 60,000 strikers participate in the demonstration.

May 4: Strikers in Chicago's Haymarket Square riot as dynamite is thrown into the crowd. Police open fire on rioters; 10 people are killed and many—strikers, police, and some bystanders—are wounded. Months later, eight are jailed; four are convicted of murder and hanged for their alleged role in the rioting.

May 8: Pharmacist John Pemberton, of Atlanta, Georgia, devises a formula for a carbonated beverage, which he names Coca-Cola. In several weeks, he begins to advertise this new drink in the *Atlanta Journal* newspaper.

May 10: The U.S. Supreme Court rules that a corporation is protected under the Fourteenth Amendment in the same way that an individual is. Thus, a corporation cannot lawfully be deprived of profits or other rights without due process. The case is *Santa Clara County v. Southern Pacific Railroad.*

May 30: Specially scheduled trains carry hundreds of guests to Tuxedo Park, New York, where Pierre Lorillard unveils his exclusive residential community.

President Grover Cleveland and Frances Folsom were married at the White House on June 2, 1886. *(Library of Congress)*

June 1: In New York State the first State Board of Mediation and Arbitration is organized. The intention is that this body will help lessen the tension between management and labor during the numerous disputes cropping up between owners and workers.

June 2: President Grover Cleveland marries Frances Folsom at the White House in Washington, D.C. It is the first wedding of a U.S. president to take place in the executive mansion.

June 19: The trial of accused Haymarket riot assassins begins. The men—August Spies, Albert Parsons,

On May 4, 1886, approximately 15,000 workers gathered in Haymarket Square in Chicago to protest for shorter working days and against the killing of a laborer in a riot a few days earlier. During the demonstration, which became violent, nine people were killed and 130 were wounded. *(Library of Congress)*

Samuel Fielden, Michael Schwab, and four others—are charged with conspiracy to kill.

June 23: Thomas Edison announces that he will move his Edison Machine Works to Schenectady, New York.

June 29: In a move that illustrates the power of organized labor in pressing for demands from the federal government, Congress decrees that trade unions may be incorporated.

June 30: Congress forms the Division of Forestry, formerly part of the Department of Agriculture.

July 3: The *New York Daily Tribune* becomes the first newspaper in the country to be set by linotype machine.

July 7: Evangelist Dwight L. Moody organizes the first summer conference for Bible students in North-field, Massachusetts, on the site of what will become the Northfield Mount Hermon School.

August 3: Congress gives authorization for construction of several vessels that will help modernize the U.S. Navy. Two of the ships are ironclads and one is a torpedo boat.

August 4: The U.S. Postal Service announces that it will offer special delivery service, and issues stamps for this purpose.

August 10: An electric welding process is patented by Elihu Thompson in Lynn, Massachusetts.

August 20: Four anarchists are sentenced to be hanged for their activities during the Haymarket riot in Chicago in May.

September 4: Apache leader Geronimo is captured by General Nelson A. Miles and sent to a Florida reservation.

September 15: The first woman, Louise Betheme, is elected to membership in the American Institute of Architects.

September 16: The Anti-Saloon Republicans hold their national convention.

October: The Quarterly Journal of Economics begins publication in Boston, Massachusetts.

October 10: A type of formal evening wear for men is introduced at Tuxedo Park, New York, and soon becomes known as the "tuxedo."

October 12: A flood along Texas's Gulf Coast leaves 250 dead.

October 28: President Grover Cleveland dedicates *Liberty Enlightening the World* (better known as the Statue of Liberty), a gift from the people of France. It

President Cleveland dedicated the statue *Liberty Enlightening the World,* better known as the Statue of Liberty, on October 28, 1886. *(Library of Congress)*

is unveiled at Bedloe's Island (later known as Liberty Island) in New York Harbor.

November: Edison relocates his laboratory to the Edison Lamp Works at East Newark, New Jersey.

November 2: For the first time in the nation's history, two brothers, R. L. Taylor and A. A. Taylor of Tennessee, run against each other in a gubernatorial race.

November 2: An endless-chain-tread tractor design is patented by Charles Dinsmoor of Warren, Pennsylvania.

November 17: The American Newspaper Publishers Association is organized.

November 18: Former president Chester A. Arthur dies at age 56. He is buried in Albany, New York.

November 25: Following the defeat of U.S. Army troops at the Battle of the Little Bighorn, soldiers under the command of General Mackenzie attack a Cheyenne village, destroying all of the Indians' food and clothing and killing their horses.

December: The Hawaiian League forms, an organization of planters and businessmen dedicated to improving the island government and promoting the overthrow of the monarchy there.

December 8: The American Federation of Labor is organized in Columbus, Ohio. It is an outgrowth of the Federation of Organized Trades and Labor Unions established in 1881.

December 22: The American Association of Public Accountants is formed in New York City.

1887

January 20: The United States leases Pearl Harbor in the Hawaiian Islands as a naval station.

January 21: The Amateur Athletic Union (AAU) is formed.

February 2: In Punxsutawney, Pennsylvania, the first Groundhog Day is observed.

February 3: The Electoral Count Act is passed by Congress. It decrees that each state is to determine its own electoral returns and submit them to the federal government for acceptance by Congress.

February 4: The Interstate Commerce Act is passed by Congress, giving the federal government the right to regulate business that passes over state boundaries. The law provides also for the establishment of a regulatory body, the Interstate Commerce Commission, the first of such powerful federal commissions.

February 8: The Dawes Severalty Act passes Congress, providing for division of Native American lands among Indian families.

February 21: In Oregon, the state legislature declares Labor Day a legal holiday. It announces that the first Saturday in June will be the observance date. This is later changed to the first Monday in September.

March 2: The Hatch Act passes Congress. It provides for an agricultural experiment station to be part of each state's land-grant college.

March 3: The American Protective Association, a nativist, anti-immigrant society, is established in Clinton, Iowa.

April 4: Argonia, Kansas, elects Susanna Madora Salter as the first female mayor in the United States.

April 19: The Catholic University of America is founded in the nation's capital.

May 9: Buffalo Bill's Wild West Show opens in London.

June: The Hawaiian League demands governmental reform of King Kalakaua. It succeeds in forcing many of its demands to be met and the monarchy's powers are reduced.

June 23: The Rocky Mountains Park Act becomes law in Canada, creating the nation's first national park at Banff, Alberta.

June 28: Minot, North Dakota, is incorporated as a city.

July 17: The Great Railroad Strike begins in Martinsburg, West Virginia, when the Baltimore & Ohio Railroad reduces workers' pay for the second time in a 12-month period.

August 10: In Chatsworth, Illinois, a train derailment occurs when a bridge collapses. More than 100 people die in the accident.

September 5: The first Labor Day is celebrated as a legal holiday in New York State.

November 11: August Spies and four other anarchists are hanged for their role in the Haymarket riot of May 1886.

December 6: In his annual message to the country, President Cleveland announces his support of tariff reform. By lowering the tariff, Cleveland hopes to expand the power base of the Democrats and to appeal to those in favor of lower costs for raw materials and consumer goods. Most specifically, Cleveland anticipates that this position will provide his party with the unifying element, a common issue, it needs in order to face Republican opposition in the upcoming election year.

1888

The International Council for Women is founded; the organization holds its first meeting in Washington, D.C.

Ellen Eglui of Washington, D.C., receives $18 when she sells the patent rights for her clothes wringer for washing machines.

January 1: The nation's first municipally supported health laboratory is opened in Providence, Rhode Island.

January 3: Drinking straws are patented by M. C. Stone.

January 3: At the University of California's Lick Observatory, in the Diablo Mountains east of San Jose,

California, the world's first 91-centimeter telescope is put into use.

January 12: Blizzards in Dakota, Montana, Minnesota, Nebraska, and Texas leave 235 people dead. Many of those who die are children on their way home after school.

January 21: The Amateur Athletic Union of the United States is established.

January 24: The first typewriter ribbon is patented by J. L. Wortman in Philadelphia, Pennsylvania.

January 27: The National Geographic Society is founded at Washington, D.C.

February 19: A cyclone in Mount Vernon, Illinois, kills 35 people.

February 22: The Industrial Reform Party meets in Washington, D.C. Delegates to the convention nominate Albert E. Redstone for president.

February 24: In a change in the election laws in the state of Kentucky, the Australian ballot system is used for the first time in Louisville in local elections. This system requires a secret ballot; the last state to adopt it will be South Carolina in 1950.

March 2: In Richmond, Virginia, the nation's first bank owned and operated by and for black Americans is chartered.

March 11: A blizzard begins along the East Coast of the United States. The storm is so large that it shuts down virtually all business activity and results in the loss of more than 400 lives.

April: The first woman mayor and all-woman town council are elected in Oskaloosa, Kansas.

April 4: The first holding company laws in the nation are passed in New Jersey.

May: In New York City, actor DeWolf Hopper recites "Casey at the Bat" for the first time, at Wallacks Theater.

May 1: The first electric freight engine is built and tested in Pullman, Illinois.

May 15: The Equal Rights Party holds its second national convention in Des Moines, Iowa, and again nominates Belva P. Lockwood for president of the United States.

May 17: The Union Labor Party holds its first national convention in Cincinnati, Ohio. Robert H. Cowdrey is nominated for president.

May 21: In New York State, the nation's first authorized crematory is opened.

May 31: The Prohibition Party holds a national convention in Indianapolis, Indiana. General Clinton B. Fisk is nominated for the presidency.

June 1: The first seismograph is shown at the Lick Observatory at Mount Hamilton, California.

June 4: In New York State, Governor Hill signs legislation authorizing electrocution to be used in sentences of capital punishment. The law will take effect in 1889.

June 6: The Democrats hold their national convention in St. Louis, Missouri.

June 13: An act of Congress establishes the Department of Labor as separate from the Department of the Interior. It will not be given cabinet status until 1913.

June 19: Once again, Republicans gather in Chicago, Illinois, for their national party convention.

June 25: On the eighth ballot, the Republican Party nominates Benjamin Harrison and Levi P. Morton for president and vice president, respectively.

July 4: The nation's first rodeo competition is held in Prescott, Arizona.

July 27: Phillip Pratt demonstrates the first electric automobile, driven on storage batteries, in Boston, Massachusetts.

July 29: In Jacksonville, Florida, a yellow fever epidemic breaks out and lasts until December, killing more than 400 people.

August 7: The first revolving door is patented by T. Van Kannel of Philadelphia, Pennsylvania.

August 14: An electric meter is patented in Rochester, New York, by O. B. Shallenberger.

August 15: The American Party holds its convention in Philadelphia, Pennsylvania. The delegates nominate James L. Curtis for president.

August 21: A patent is taken out for the first adding machine.

September 1: In Worthington, Ohio, Pontifical College Josephinum is established

September 4: George Eastman, of Rochester, New York, registers the trademark Kodak, receiving a patent for a camera that uses roll film.

October 1: The Scott Act is passed, which prevents Chinese immigrants from returning to the United States if they leave, even for a brief visit to their ancestral homeland.

October 1: The nation's first interstate carrier arbitration law is enacted.

October 9: The Washington Monument is opened to the public.

October 14: Jane Addams, soon to be known for her social reform work in urban slums, is baptized at the age of 28 at the Presbyterian Church in Cedarville, Illinois. This acknowledgment of her personal faith acts as an initial public commitment in her lifetime of service and dedication to others.

October 17: The keel of the battleship *Maine* is laid in the first stage of its construction.

October 25: In Newburgh, New York, the first double-decker ferryboat is launched.

October 30: A patent is taken out for the first ball-point pen, by J. Loud of Weymouth, Massachusetts.

November 6: Republican Benjamin Harrison defeats Grover Cleveland in the presidential elections with an electoral vote of 233–168.

November 20: The first employee time clock is patented in Auburn, New York.

December 24: On the Mississippi River, fires on two steamboats cause 55 fatalities.

1889

January 19: The state of Georgia declares this date a legal holiday in observance of General Robert E. Lee's birthday.

January 28: Striking transit workers cause New York City's transportation system to come to a halt.

January 30: The University of Idaho is chartered.

February 9: With the increasing visibility and influence of farm interests in the United States, the Department of Agriculture is raised to a cabinet-level agency.

February 11: Norman J. Colman is named the first secretary of agriculture by President Cleveland.

February 20: Congress incorporates the Maritime Canal Company of Nicaragua. Its purpose is to construct a canal across the Central American isthmus, work on which is set to begin in October of this year.

February 22: President Cleveland signs an omnibus bill that grants North and South Dakota, Montana, and Washington statehood.

March 2: The state of Kansas passes an antitrust law.

March 4: Benjamin Harrison is inaugurated as the nation's 23rd president.

March 15: On Samoa, a civil war continues, with the United States backing the forces of King Malietoa. The Samoan Islands have provided a fueling

The Oklahoma land rush in 1889 provided land for over 50,000 settlers in the former Indian Territory. *(New York Public Library Picture Collection)*

station for American naval vessels since 1878. Germany supports the rebel cause on Samoa, and although Great Britain remains neutral it is prepared to aid U.S. interests at any time. Warships from the three nations cruise Samoan waters, but all except one are destroyed during a hurricane.

April 22: Despite a previous agreement that gives possession of large land areas in Oklahoma to Native Americans, the area opens to white settlement. More than 50,000 "Sooners" prepare to rush for the 2 million acres of land, and by the end of the day the entire area is claimed by white settlers.

April 29: Great Britain, Germany, and the United States meet and arrange to restore King Malietoa to his throne in Samoa. As a way of maintaining power over the island nation, however, the three countries hold the right to appoint the Supreme Court justice on the islands.

May 9: New Jersey permits holding companies to be chartered in that state.

May 13: Theodore Roosevelt is named to head the federal Civil Service Commission.

May 15: In Samoa, six ships—three from the United States and three from Germany—sink in a typhoon. Nearly 200 men are drowned. The British steamer *Calliope* escapes damage.

May 16: Helen Culver, owner of a large Chicago building, signs a rental agreement with Jane Addams. The building, known as Hull-House, is soon transformed into one of the nation's earliest settlement houses.

May 31: Nearly 5,000 people die in a flood in Johnstown, Pennsylvania, after a dam at Conemaugh Lake collapses. Although the lake was 18 miles away, the break allows a 40-foot-high wall of water to reach the city in eight minutes.

June 3: The nation's first long-distance electric transmission line is finished, stretching from a generator located at Willamette Falls to downtown Portland, Oregon, a distance of 14 miles.

June 5: Boxer James J. Corbett knocks out Joe Choyinski with a left hook.

June 10: The United Confederate Veterans meet in New Orleans and elect Governor John B. Gordon the first general of the organization.

June 14: The United States, Germany, and Great Britain agree to establish a three-nation protectorate on Samoa.

July 8: The final bare-knuckle boxing match is held at Richburg, Mississippi, between John L. Sullivan and Jake Kilrain. Following this match, all boxing is conducted with gloves under rules introduced by the marquess of Queensbury.

July 8: The first issue of the financial newspaper *The Wall Street Journal* is published.

July 12: A concert of music by American composers is given at the Paris Exhibition. It marks the first time that works from the United States are so acknowledged.

September 18: Jane Addams and Ellan Gates Starr move into the former Charles J. Hull mansion in Chicago, Illinois. It will soon become world famous as an urban settlement.

October 2: In Washington, D.C., the first International Conference of American States meets in an attempt to control trade issues in the Americas.

Farmers harvest wheat in Kansas. *(Library of Congress)*

Theodore Roosevelt, who rose quickly in public life, was appointed head of the Civil Service Commission in 1889. He was known for his passion for reform and his aggressive, take-charge approach to any task. *(Library of Congress)*

October 7: Columbia College announces that Seth Low is to be president of the institution. He later is elected mayor of New York City.

November 2: North and South Dakota are admitted to the Union as the 39th and 40th states, respectively.

November 8: Montana becomes the 41st state. Three days later, Washington is admitted as the nation's 42nd state.

November 11: The first Congress of Roman Catholic laypersons meets in Baltimore, Maryland.

November 14: Journalist Elizabeth Cochrane, known by her pen name of Nellie Bly, begins a trip around the world that takes 72 days. She does this to challenge French author Jules Verne, whose book, *Around the World in Eighty Days,* set a standard she was determined to beat.

December 6: Former Confederate president Jefferson Davis dies in New Orleans, Louisiana. He is buried there but is later reinterred in Richmond, Virginia.

December 14: The American Academy of Political and Social Science is founded in Philadelphia, Pennsylvania.

1890

January 1: The first Tournament of Roses parade is held in Pasadena, California.

January 2: Alice Sanger becomes the first female staff member for the U.S. White House.

January 3: The University of Wisconsin begins offering the nation's first collegiate course in dairy farming.

January 7: The naval vessel *Baltimore* is commissioned.

January 23: The Atchison, Topeka & Santa Fe railroad achieves the fastest speed ever recorded—78.1 miles per hour.

January 25: The United Mine Workers is formed.

Journalist Nellie Bly returns from her round-the-world tour, the first to be made by a woman traveling alone.

February 4: The U.S. Senate ratifies a treaty with Great Britain and Germany that sets up a Samoan protectorate.

February 10: The federal government releases 11 million acres of former Sioux territory to settlement by whites.

February 18: The National American Women's Suffrage Association is established when two formerly opposing groups—the American Woman Suffrage Association and the National Woman Suffrage Association—combine. Among the speakers at the convention is Carrie Chapman.

February 24: The U.S. House of Representatives selects Chicago, Illinois, as the location for the World's Columbian Exposition in commemoration of the 400th anniversary of the discovery of the New World in 1492.

March 18: In Massachusetts, the nation's first state naval militia is formed.

March 20: The General Federation of Women's Clubs meets for the first time in New York City.

March 24: The U.S. Supreme Court, reversing a decision made in 1877 in the Granger cases, rules that a state cannot set fees so as to deprive an individual of the right of "reasonable profit." In deciding the case, *Chicago, Milwaukee, & St. Paul Railroad v. Minnesota,* the Supreme Court offers unprecedented protection to railroad corporations under the Fourteenth Amendment.

April 4: New York State passes legislation aimed at stopping corrupt election practices.

April 14: The Pan-American Union is established with passage of a resolution at the Pan-American Conference, which has been meeting since October of the previous year.

April 22: The *Cushing,* a torpedo boat, is commissioned at Bristol, Pennsylvania.

April 28: In *Leisy v. Hardin,* the U.S. Supreme Court strikes down state laws prohibiting liquor from being transported across state lines. The court rules that such restriction would interfere with gainful profits.

April 28: In Ohio, the first state employment service in the nation opens.

May 1: Philadelphia's Bank of America fails, provoking the collapse of several other financial institutions.

May 1: Members of the American Federation of Labor have chosen this as the date on which an eight-hour day should be established.

May 2: The Oklahoma Territory is created by Congress, further reducing the size of Indian territory.

May 24: George Francis Train bests Nellie Bly's record of around-the-world travel, completing his journey in 67 days, 13 hours and three seconds.

May 30: Construction of the Washington Square Memorial Arch begins in New York City.

June 1: The U.S. Census Bureau begins using Herman Hollerith's tabulating machine to count census returns.

June 6: The U.S. Polo Association is formed in New York City.

June 9: The comic opera *Robin Hood* is performed in New York City. Author Reginald De Koven achieves lasting fame for two songs in this production, "Brown October Ale" and "Oh, Promise Me."

June 10: Feminist Carrie Chapman marries George Catt.

June 27: James Tanner is appointed commissioner of pensions by President Harrison. Under Tanner's direction, federal pensions increase from 676,000 to 970,000 between 1891 and 1895.

June 29: The Federal Elections Bill, or "Force Bill," of 1890 is introduced by Massachusetts Senator Henry Cabot Lodge to help guarantee federal super-

vision of elections. The Force Bill meets with House approval but fails to pass the Senate.

June 30: Congress passes legislation that authorizes three new steel-clad ships to replace those lost in the storm in Samoan waters in spring 1889.

July 2: The Sherman Anti-Trust Act, introduced to the Senate by John Sherman (D-Ohio), is passed. It renders illegal "every contract, combination in the form of trust or otherwise, or conspiracy, in restraint of trade or commerce among the several States, or with foreign nations."

July 3: Idaho becomes the nation's 43rd state.

July 10: Wyoming is admitted to statehood. It is the first state to grant women the right to vote, having approved women's suffrage in 1869 while it was still a territory.

July 14: Congress passes the Sherman Silver Purchase Act, which obligates the federal government to purchase 4 million ounces of silver each month and issue paper currency simultaneously.

August 6: At Auburn Prison in Auburn, New York, murderer William Kemmler is the first person to be executed by electrocution.

August 8: The Knights of Labor go out on strike against the New York Central and Hudson River Railroad.

August 30: Congress votes to permit the Department of Agriculture to inspect pork slated for foreign export.

September 1: New York City is the site of a conference on the single-tax issue.

September 3: The Single Tax League of the United States established by Henry George, meets at Cooper Union, New York, and adopts a single-tax platform.

September 22: The nation's first high school for business is opened in Washington, D.C.

September 25: Congress establishes Yosemite National park.

September 29: As a way to prompt railroads to continue expansion, Congress passes a bill requiring railroads to forfeit unused land.

October 1: The McKinley Tariff Act is passed, raising tariffs to their highest ever.

October 1: For the first time in U.S. history, federal regulations are passed dealing with narcotics.

October 1: The National Weather Bureau is made a part of the Department of Agriculture by Congress.

October 4: Ground is broken for a hydroelectric power facility to be built in Niagara Falls, New York.

October 6: The Mormon Church prohibits polygamy.

October 11: In Washington, D.C., the Daughters of the American Revolution is founded.

November 1: Mississippi accepts a new state constitution that limits voting rights of African Americans.

November 4: A working-class Democrat, Benjamin Tillman, is elected governor of South Carolina.

November 18: The battleship *Maine* is launched.

November 29: The first Army-Navy football game is played in West Point, New York, with a score of Navy 24, Army 0.

December 15: In South Dakota, Sioux chief Sitting Bull is killed in a clash with federal troops.

1891

Two new trade magazines are published—the first journal dealing with the phonograph industry, the *Phonogram,* and an optometry magazine, the *Optician.* Each points to greater professionalization of various fields, and a greater emphasis on the business aspects of each area.

January 20: Former Texas attorney general James Stephen Hogg is inaugurated as the first native-born Texan governor. Hogg was a conservative and a populist who serves until his attorney general, Charles Allen Culberson, became governor in 1895.

January 29: Liliuokalani is proclaimed queen of Hawaii, after the death of her brother, King David Kalakaua.

March 1: The U.S. Supreme Court invalidates the income tax, which it had imposed during the Civil War.

March 3: Congress establishes the Circuit Court of Appeals.

March 3: Congress passes the Forest Reserve Act, which will enable President Harrison to set aside 13 million acres of public land for national forests.

March 3: The Superintendent of Immigration Office is established by Congress.

March 4: The International Copyright Act is passed, initially protecting British, French, Belgian, and Swiss authors.

March 4: Kittel Halvorson, the first Prohibition candidate to be elected to the U.S. House of Representatives, begins his term of service.

March 14: In New Orleans, Louisiana, 14 Sicilian immigrants are lynched by an angry mob in retaliation for the death of a police officer there.

Liliuokalani became queen of the Hawaiian Islands after her brother's death. *(Library of Congress)*

March 30: The Shoshone National Forest is established in Wyoming, and Yellowstone Park Timberland Reserve is made a federal park.

April: The first pneumatic bicycle tire is manufactured in New York City.

April 1: Augustus Thomas produces his play *Alabama,* describing the newly united nation after the Civil War.

April 1: The Wrigley Company is founded in Chicago, Illinois, by William Wrigley, Jr. Originally established to manufacture soap and baking powder, the company shifts its production to chewing gum when the gum, offered as a premium with baking powder sales, becomes popular.

April 7: Nebraska passes a law establishing an eight-hour workday.

April 14: The president begins a tour of the southern states.

May 4: The nation's first integrated hospital, Provident Hospital, opens in Chicago, Illinois.

May 5: Carnegie Hall, built by philanthropic millionaire Andrew Carnegie, opens in New York City.

May 6: The Amateur Fencers League of America is organized in New York City.

May 13: The Kentucky Derby is won by Kingman. The jockey, Isaac Murphy, is the first in history to have ridden three Derby winners.

May 19: The Populist Party is formed in Cincinnati, Ohio, by farmers and others convinced that government ownership of railroads, among other things, is a way to guarantee economic stability.

May 20: At his laboratory in West Orange, New Jersey, Thomas Alva Edison gives a public demonstration of a prototype of his kinetoscope (an early movie camera).

June 16: John Abbott is elected prime minister of Canada. Abbott is Canada's third prime minister.

June 21: The Ames power plant, located outside of Telluride, Colorado, demonstrates the first long-distance transmission of alternating current (AC).

July 20: Miners who have walked off their jobs in Briceville, Tennessee, return to work as state troopers bring in convict labor to break the strike.

August 24: Thomas A. Edison patents the kinetoscope.

September 22: Another 900,000 acres of land owned by Indians in Oklahoma are taken by the federal government and opened up for white settlement.

October 1: Stanford University opens in California.

October 16: In Chile, American sailors from the USS *Baltimore* are attacked by a mob; two are killed.

October 18: The first international six-day bicycle race is held in Madison Square Garden, New York City.

November 3: William McKinley is elected governor of Ohio.

November 10: The Women's Christian Temperance Union (WCTU), holds its first worldwide convention.

November 21: Yale defeats Harvard to win the Intercollegiate Football Championship.

November 28: At the annual Army-Navy game, Army wins, 32-16.

December 29: Thomas A. Edison is granted a radio patent.

Eyewitness Testimony

The protectionists, in advocating their system, always spend a great deal of effort and eloquence on appeals to patriotism, and to international jealousies. These are all entirely aside from the point. The protective system is a domestic system, for domestic purposes, and it is sought by domestic means. The one who pays, and the one who gets, are both Americans. The victim and the beneficiary are amongst ourselves. It is just as unpatriotic to oppress one American as it is patriotic to favor another. If we make one American pay taxes to another American, it will neither vex nor please any foreign nation.

. . . Free trade means antagonism to this whole policy and theory at every point. The free trader regards it all as false, meretricious, and delusive. He considers it an invasion of private rights. In the best case, if all that the protectionist claims were true, he would be taking it upon himself to decide how his neighbor should spend his earnings, and—more than that—that his neighbor shall spend his earning for the advantage of the men who make the decision. This is plainly immoral and corrupting; nothing could be more so. The free trader also denies that the government either can, or ought to regulate the way in which a man shall employ his earnings. He sees that the government is nothing but a clique of the parties of interest.

. . . The free trader further holds that protection is all a mistake and a delusion to those who think that they win by it, in that it lessens their self-reliance and energy and exposes their business to vicissitudes which, not being incident to a natural order of things, cannot be foreseen and guarded against by business skill.

Economist and philosopher William Graham Sumner, speaking in 1886, in Hoogenboom and Hoogenboom, The Gilded Age *(1967), p. 169.*

The American . . . need not fear the unhealthy or abnormal growth of cities . . . The free play of economic laws is keeping all quite right . . . Oh, these grand, immutable, all-wise laws of natural forces, how perfectly they work if human legislators would only let them alone.

Industrialist Andrew Carnegie, in Triumphant Democracy *(1886), p. 378.*

It is evident that our members are not properly instructed, else we would not find them passing resolutions "approving of the action of our executive officers in fixing the 1st of May as the day to strike for eight hours." The executive officers of the Knights of Labor have never fixed upon the 1st of May for a strike of any kind, and they will not do so until the proper time arrives and the word goes forth from the General Assembly.

No Assembly of the Knights of Labor must strike for the eight-hour system on May 1 under the impression that they are obeying orders from headquarters, for such an order was not and will not be given. Neither employer nor employee are educated to the needs and necessities for the short-hour plan. If one branch of trade or one Assembly is in such a condition, remember that there are many who are in total ignorance of the movement. Out of the sixty millions of people in the United States and Canada, our Order has possibly three hundred thousand. Can we mould the sentiment of millions in favor of the short-hour plan before May 1? It is nonsense to think of it. Let us learn why our hours of labor should be reduced, and then teach others.

Terence V. Powderly, leader of the Knights of Labor, statement of 1886, in Powderly, Thirty Years of Labor, 1859–1889 *(1967), pp. 253–254.*

William Graham Sumner was an economist and philosopher. *(Library of Congress)*

Andrew Carnegie, a Scottish immigrant, became an American millionaire. *(Library of Congress)*

1. Labor, like flour or cotton cloth, should always be bought in the cheapest market and sold in the dearest.
2. The sole legitimate condition that regulates wages is the demand for service and the supply of workers. If the demand diminishes, wages decrease; if the supply diminishes, wages increase.
3. The wage ordinarily paid is not determined by the automatic division of the whole amount which a community is willing to pay for the specified sort of work, but the whole number of persons willing and able to do it.

> *William A. Croffut,* "What Rights Have Laborers?" *in* The Forum, I, *May 1886, pp. 294–296, in DeNovo,* The Gilded Age and After *(1972), p. 74.*

. . . On the labor question My position is:

1. The previous question always must be in any popular excitement the supremacy of law. All lawless violence must be suppressed instantly, with overwhelming force and at all hazards. To hesitate or tamper with it is a fatal mistake. Justice, humanity, and safety all require this.
2. I agree that Labor does not get its fair share of the wealth it creates. The Sermon on the Mount, the golden rule, the Declaration of Independence all require extensive reforms to the end that labor may be so rewarded that the working man can with temperance, industry & thrift own a home, educate his children, & lay up a support for old age.
3. The United States must begin to deal with the whole subject.

> *President Rutherford B. Hayes, to Guy M. Bryan, letter May 12, 1886, in DeNovo,* The Gilded Age and After *(1972), p. 72.*

Friends . . . I am told that a number of patrol wagons, carrying policeman . . . I understand that the militia have been called under arms. There seems to prevail the opinion in certain quarters that this meeting has been called for the purpose of inaugurating a riot, hence these warlike preparations on the part of the so-called "Law and Order." However, let me tell you at the beginning that . . . the object of this meeting is to explain the general situation of the Eight-Hour Movement, and to throw light upon various incidents in connection with it . . . For more than twenty years have the wage workers of this country begged and prayed their masters, the factory lords, to reduce their burdens. It has been in vain. They have pointed out the fact that over a million of willing and strong hands were in a state of enforced idleness and starvation, that to help them to obtain employment it would not only be advisable, nay, it was necessary to reduce the hours of daily toil of those who were fortunate enough in having found a buyer for their muscles, their bones, and their brain. The masters of this earth have treated them with contempt, have condemned them to vagabondage whenever they insisted. The legislatures have been called upon, one petition has succeeded the other, but with no avail . . .

All over the land we behold vast armies of producers, no longer begging, but demanding that eight hours shall henceforth constitute a normal working day. And what say the extortionists to this? They demand their pound of flesh, like Shylock. They will not yield one iota. They have grown rich and powerful on your labor. They amass stupendous fortunes, while you, who bring them into existence, are suffering from want. In answer to your pleadings they ask for the bodies of your little children, to utilize them in their gold mints, to make dollars out of them! Look at the slaves of McCormick! When they tried to remonstrate with their master he simply called upon "the protectors of these free and glorious institutions"—the police—to silence them . . . The capitalistic press, like the "respectable gentleman" McCormick, howls that the anarchists are responsible for the deeds of violence now committed all over this country . . . The attack upon McCormick's yesterday—Was it made by anarchists? . . . I had been invited by the Central Labor Union to address a meeting of lumberyard laborers on the Black road. I went out there yesterday at the appointed time, about three o'clock in the afternoon . . . When I was introduced to address them a few Poles or Bohemians in the crowd cried out: "He's a socialist." These cries were followed by a general commotion and derision—"We want no socialist; down with him . . ." Of course, I spoke anyway; the crowd became calm and quiet, and fifteen minutes later, elected me unanimously a delegate to see their bosses . . . you can see that these people are not socialists or anarchists, but "good, honest, law-abiding, church-going Christians and citizens." Such were the persons who left the meeting, as I afterwards learned, to "make the scabs at McCormick's quit work . . ." What does it mean when the police of this city, on this evening, rattle along in their patrol wagons? What does it mean when the militia stands warlike and ready for bloody work at our armories? What are the gatling guns and cannons for? Is this military display of barbarism arranged for your entertainment? All these preparations, my friends, ARE made in your behalf! . . . Your masters . . . do not like discontented slaves. They want to make you contented at all hazards . . . if you are stubborn they will force or kill you . . . Working men must arm themselves for defense, so that they may be able to cope with the government hirelings of their masters.

August Spies, excerpts from a speech delivered at the Haymarket Square riot, quoted in The Great Anarchist Trial. The Haymarket Speeches, as Delivered on the Evening of the Throwing of the Bomb, at Haymarket Square, Chicago, May 4, 1886, *Chicago: The Chicago Labor Press Association (1886), pp. 3–5.*

I am not here for the purpose of inciting anybody, but to spell out, to tell the facts as they exist, even though it shall cost me my life before morning. It behooves you, as you love your wife and children—if you don't want to see them perish with hunger, killed or cut down like dogs in the street—Americans, in the interest of your liberty and independence, to *arm*, to *arm* yourselves!

Albert Parsons, socialist agitator and journalist, at the Haymarket rally in May 1886, in Weinstein and Wilson, Freedom and Crisis: An American History *(1978), p. 525.*

When more of the people's sustenance is exacted through the form of taxation than is necessary to meet the just obligations of Government and expenses of its economical administration, such exaction becomes ruthless extortion and a violation of the fundamental principles of a free Government.

President Grover Cleveland, to the nation, his second Annual Message, December 1886, in Bartlett, Familiar Quotations, 12th Edition *(1951), p. 628.*

We will never try fill our works with new men . . . we could never get such good men as you are. It is the scalawags who are idle and looking for works when there is a strike . . . No one will ever have your places here. We like you too much.

Andrew Carnegie, to a group of striking workers, 1887, quoted in Davis and Woodman, Conflict and Consensus *(1987), p. 470.*

The American people are far in advance of Congress in respect to an American navy . . . We have no fear of any of the nations on this continent. Whenever the attack may come, it will come from across the seas. The American people almost unitedly are at the door of Congress today asking for something with which we may meet the foe away from our coast when he comes.

Representative Charles B. Lore (R-Delaware), 1887, in Campbell, Expansionism and Imperialism *(1970), p. 93.*

They are running their business at a loss; they are making articles to which this bill refers; and this bill says that if those eight men should combine to get a fair, living profit upon their manufacture, that contract, that agreement is against public policy, unlawful and void.

Senator Orville Platt (R-Connecticut), on the unconstitutionality of the Sherman Anti-Trust bill, 1887, in Ginger, Age of Excess *(1965), p. 119.*

As I approach the end, I am more than a little puzzled to account for the instances I have seen of business success—money-getting. It comes from a rather low instinct. Certainly, so far as my observation goes, it is rarely met with in combination with the finer or more interesting traits of character. I have known, and known tolerably well, a good many "successful" men—"big" financially—men famous during the last half-century; and a less interesting crowd I do not care to encounter. Not one that I have ever known would I care to meet again, either in this world or the next; nor is one of them associated in my mind with the idea of humor, thought or refinement. A set of mere money-getters and traders, they were essentially unattractive and uninteresting.

Charles Francis Adams, Jr., historian and railroad expert, 1887, in Josephson, The Robber Barons *(1962), p 338.*

There is something radically wrong in our industrial system. There is a screw loose. The wheels have dropped out of balance. The railroads have never been so prosperous, and yet agriculture languishes. The banks have never done a better or more profitable business, and yet agriculture languishes. Manufacturing enterprises never made more money or were in a more flourishing condition, and yet agriculture languishes. Towns and cities flourish and "boom" and grow and "boom" and yet agriculture languishes. Salaries and fees were never so temptingly high and desirable, and yet agriculture languishes.

Excerpt from a North Carolina agricultural journal, 1887, quoted in John D. Hicks, "The Farmers' Grievances," in Davis and Woodman, Conflict and Consensus in American History *(1987), p. 104.*

It has always been difficult for well-to-do people of the upper and middle classes to sympathize with and to understand the needs of their poorer neighbors.

Samuel Lane Loomis, Protestant minister, 1887, in Morgan, The Gilded Age *(1970), p. 34.*

The public land, the heritage of the people, [should] be reserved for actual settlers only—not other acre to railroads or speculators . . . That measures be taken to prevent aliens from acquiring title to lands in the United States . . . that Congress shall . . . prevent dealing in future of all agricultural and mechanical productions . . . a graduated income tax . . . the strict enforcement of laws prohibiting the importation of foreign labor under the contract system . . .

Excerpts from the stated goals of the farmers' movement known as the National Agricultural Wheel, at its meeting in McKenzie, Tennessee, 1887, in Smith, The Rise of Industrial America *(1984), p. 432.*

There will come a time when our silence will be more powerful than the voices you strangle today!

August Spies, a convicted anarchist who was executed, on November 11, 1887, for his role in the May 1887 Haymarket riot, in Chicago, Illinois, quoted in Smith, The Rise of Industrial America *(1984), p. 254.*

If those men were such idiots that when they received beer to drink they thought it was milk, we women knew by the smell as we passed the doors of the places that it was beer. The president of our Union was the wife of a grocer who was superintendent of the Sunday School and frequently had temperance afternoons. He obliged his wife to resign from the Union after that, and she did. The editor of the paper disavowed any responsibility for my work. My father said I was always too strong-minded for my own good, and my mother felt that her chicken had turned out to be a duckling.

Carrie Chapman Catt, feminist leader, in Charles City [Iowa] Intelligencer, December 13, 1887, in Van Voris, Carrie Chapman Catt *(1987), p. 17.*

Murder, insanity, suicide, divorce, drunkenness and all forms of immorality and crime have increased from that day [Panic of 1873] to this in the most appalling ratio.

Mrs. S. E. V. Emery, economics writer, observing that the nation's fiscal, social, and cultural problems have been fueled by federal monetary policies, 1887, in Davis and Woodman, Conflict and Consensus in American History *(1966), p. 127.*

These heroes are dead. They died for liberty—they died for us. They are at rest. They sleep in the land they made free, under the flag they rendered stainless, under the solemn pines, the sad hemlocks, the tearful willows, the embracing vines. They sleep beneath the shadows of the clouds, careless alike of sunshine or storm, each in the windowless palace of rest. Earth may run red with other wars—they are at peace. In the midst of battles, in the roar of conflict, they found the serenity of death.

> *Robert G. Ingersoll, lawyer and former Radical Republican well known for antisouthern oratory, repeating a speech he first gave in Indianapolis, Indiana, in 1876, in Bartlett,* Familiar Quotations, *12th Edition (1951), p. 602.*

I visited the Cheyenne School at the Caddo Spring, some two or three miles from the Agency. The location is a fine one, near a large and excellent spring. The natural drainage is good, and when the sewer and drainage pipes are put in, all refuse water will be thoroughly disposed of. The privies were the cleanest I have ever seen in connection with a public institution. The Superintendent, R. P. Collins, I believe to be well fitted for his place, and anxious to do his full duty. The school is in pretty good shape—the dormitories clean as could be expected, well-ventilated, but too much crowded; the bathing facilities very deficient; no place to care for the sick. Mr. Collins was drawing stone for the windmill with which to force the water from the spring into the school buildings, which will be a great improvement. Mrs. Collins and Mrs. Hoag, an excellent Quaker lady, were doing good, conscientious and intelligent work in the school room. The classes are much broken up by details of boys to work the garden and corn, and of girls for the laundry and other work. Mr. and Mrs. Collins were dropped from the roll of employees at the close of the year, and so are lost to the service. This is unfortunate, as they were about the only efficient members of the Agency force at that point.

I visited also the Arapahoe school, under the care of the third Superintendent appointed to it during the year, C. H. Steibolt, and, judging from appearances, it would be charitable to suppose each succeeding appointment had been worse than the preceding, for it would be difficult to believe there could have been a worse than the last. There had been four different industrial teachers during the year, four matrons, four assistant matrons, four seamstresses. Miss Lamond, the only teacher in the school who knew how to teach, had been twice teacher and once matron during the year. The larger children in the principal room were under the charge of Miss Lamond; the room was clean, the children prompt and in

good shape, the work done above the average of school work in Indian Reservation schools.

> *The Condition of Affairs in Indian Territory and California, A Report by Prof. C. C. Painter, Agent of the Indian Rights Association, Philadelphia, Indian Rights Association, 1888. Available online at URL: http://memory.loc.gov/cgi-bin/query/r?ammem/calbk:@field(DOCID+@lit(calbk052div1)).*

I am simply reminding our members of what the practical results of a strike are to our side of the house. A defeat is not the worst thing that can happen to men on strike; they lose hope, they abandon organization . . . What combination of hungry men could fight a battle against a combination of dollars? I believe that strikes are weakening the labor movement in America.

> *Terence V. Powderly, leader of the Knights of Labor, 1888, in Dubofsky,* Industrialism and the American Worker, 1865–1920. *(1975), p. 60.*

They are great prison-like structures of brick, with narrow doors and windows, cramped passages and steep rickety stairs. They are built through from one street to the other with a somewhat narrower building connecting them . . . The narrow court-yard . . . in the middle is a damp foul-smelling place, supposed to do duty as an airshaft; had the foul fiend designed these great barracks they could not have been more villainously arranged to avoid any chance of ventilation.

The drainage is horrible, and even the Croton as it flows from a tap in the noisome courtyard, seemed to be contaminated by its surroundings and have a fetid smell.

> *Allan Forman, reform journalist, in the* American Magazine, *describing "dumbbell" tenement apartments, November 1888, in Callow,* American Urban History *(1973), p. 329.*

Let every man honor and love the land of his birth and the race from which he springs and keep their memory green. It is a pious and honorable duty. But let us have done with British-Americans and Irish-Americans and German-Americans, and so on, and all be Americans . . . If a man is going to be an American at all let him be so without any qualifying adjectives;

and if he is going to be something else, let him drop the word American from his personal description.

Henry Cabot Lodge of Massachusetts, shortly before he won a congressional seat, speaking to the New England Society of Brooklyn, December 1888, in Bartlett Familiar Quotations *(1951), p. 700.*

The people admire old Grover's [Cleveland] strength so much, he is a positive man and an honest man, and when the people see these two exceptional virtues mixed happily in a candidate they grow to love and admire him out of the very idealism of their natures.

Franklin K. Lane, California journalist, to John H. Wigmore, in a letter dated February 27, 1888. Available online at URL: http://www.gutenberg.org/ dirs/etext03/ltrln10.txt.

. . . Is it reasonable to expect that Mr. Harrison, if elected, would oppose such a "clean sweep" with greater courage and firmness than was shown by Mr. Cleveland? Mr. Harrison is, in point of personal character, no doubt vastly preferable to Mr. Blaine. But neither his professions nor his antecedents stamp him

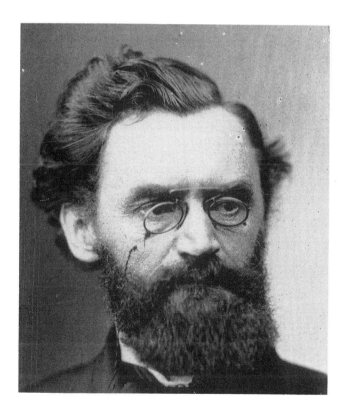

Carl Schurz, a civil service reform advocate, served as secretary of the interior under Rutherford B. Hayes. *(Library of Congress)*

as a man who would resist the demands of the influential politicians of his party. He would on the contrary, to the extent of his power, meet them, as he asked his demands to be met under a previous Republican Administration. The cause of civil service reform would, therefore, have to hope rather less from Mr. Harrison than from Mr. Cleveland.

Carl Schurz, liberal Republican and secretary of the interior under President Hayes, to Thaddeus C. Pound, letter of September 1888, in DeNovo, The Gilded Age and After *(1972), p. 137.*

. . . the work of creating new gigantic and dangerous "trusts" or combinations, seems to be increasing and going steadily on. The plain truth is that these gigantic corporations . . . are beyond and above the control of municipal ordinances or State laws. It is even doubted by many whether the vast powers of the General Government will prove to be sufficiently potential [*sic*] against such an aggregation of capital and brains. Exercising functions that are largely publicly in their character they nevertheless enjoy all the rights and all the advantages of private enterprises. As absolutely essential agencies for the transaction of business they are protected by the business interests of the country from the operation of laws enacted for the purpose of bringing them into subjection to authority.

There is nothing democratic about such vast monopolies for controlling those channels through which intelligence and traffic are effected. Competition is crushed by its very weight, holding business men by the throat, and forcing them to deliver. They are despotic in spirit, tyrannical in method, openly hostile to liberty and free institutions, and threatening menaces to the pursuit of happiness, and to equality and equal opportunities under the law. When the people of this country once get their eyes wide open they will hardly permit such dangerous excrescences to fasten their deathlike grip upon our liberties and our laws . . .

W. A. Rapsher, journalist, in an article in North American Review, *146, May 1888, pp. 509–514, in DeNovo,* The Gilded Age and After *(1972), pp. 51–52.*

We have lots of Republicans deeply dissatisfied with that rabid, unrepublican . . . plank but they have been kept from bolting from the strength of the old party ties . . . and the scarce cry of free trade against the

Democrats, and they have barely concluded the vote for Harrison on the assurance that the Republican Senate was framing a better reform bill than the Democratic House had done.

Joseph Medill, Chicago Tribune editor, letter to a friend concerning the tariff plank in the G.O.P. platform, 1888, in Smith, The Rise of Industrial America (1984), p. 463.

The tone of public life is lower than one expects to find in so great a nation. Just as we assume that an individual man will at any supreme moment in his own life rise to a higher level than that on which he usually moves, so we look to find those who conduct the affairs of a great state inspired by a sense of the magnitude of the interests entrusted to them. Their horizon ought to be expanded, their feeling of duty quickened, their dignity of attitude enhanced . . .

Such a sentiment is comparatively weak in America. A cabinet minister, or senator, or governor of a State, sometimes even a President, hardly feels himself more bound by it than the director of a railway company or the mayor of a town does in Europe. Not assuming himself to be individually wiser, stronger, or better than his fellow-citizens, he acts and speaks as though he were still simply one of them, and so far from magnifying his office and making it honourable, seems anxious to show that he is the mere creature of the popular vote, so filled by the sense that it is the people and not he who governs as to fear that he should be deemed to have forgotten his personal insignificance. There is in the United States abundance of patriotism, that is to say, or a passion for the greatness and happiness of the Republic, and a readiness to make sacrifices for it . . . But these sentiments do not bear their appropriate fruit in raising the conception of public office, or its worth and its dignity.

James Bryce, British diplomat, in The American Commonwealth II, 1888, pp. 453–454, in DeNovo, The Gilded Age and After (1972), p. 129.

It is a community for University men who live here, have their recreation and clubs and society all among the poor people, yet in the same style they would live in their own circle. It is so free from 'professional doing good,' so unaffectedly sincere and so productive

of good results in its classes and libraries so that it seems perfectly ideal.

Jane Addams, founder of Hull-House, to a friend, describing the English settlement Toynbee Hall, letter of 1888, in Davis, American Heroine (1973), p. 49.

I am experimenting upon an instrument which does for the eye what the phonograph does for the ear.

Thomas Alva Edison, letter, 1888, Josephson, Edison: A Biography (1959), p. 386.

A negro county alliance convention met at Monroe, in this state, on Saturday last and adopted resolutions in effect as follows: They pledge themselves not to pick or allow any of their family or any person they can control to pick a lock of cotton for any person, under any circumstances, for less than seventy-five cents per hundred. Second, that they will work for no person for less than $1 per day in the winter and $1.25 in the summer, and to work only eight hours per day. Third, that they recommend the grand jury to find true bills against every

Here photographed during World War I, Jane Addams was at the forefront of women's social activism and founded the first Chicago settlement house to help immigrants, called Hull-House. *(National Archives and Records Administration)*

"colored person" who loafs about town and send him to the county to farming. They also adopted a penalty for the violation of their pledges, but exactly what it was could not be learned. This movement has caused some agitation about Monroe, and it is feared that it will cause an unpleasant conflict between the white and colored alliance.

Excerpt from "A Colored Alliance at Work," in the Atlanta Constitution, *September 11, 1889. Available online at URL: http://www.historyteacher.net/ AHAP/Weblinks/AHAP_Weblinks15.htm.*

The "single tax will ruin the farmers" is shouted across the prairies and over the plains. If lifting a part of the burden from the back of the farmer, and placing it on the shoulders of the man who holds more acres than the farmer without the payment of a hundredth part of the taxes which the farmer is obliged to pay, is ruin, then indeed will the farmers be ruined . . . If there is a class of men on the soil of America who are directly interested in securing the passage of a single-tax law that class is to be found where farmers are numerous.

Previous to the birth of the land speculator in the West, the farmer was not troubled with such an encumbrance as a mortgage on his land, now he has an abundance of them. It was not to fight off the single tax that the farmers of the United States met in national convention in Georgetown, D.C. in January 1873, for the purpose of organizing the National Grange. They met because they were being gathered into the net of mortgage holder, because of excessive taxation, and because of discrimination in freights.

Terence V. Powderly, leader of the Knights of Labor, 1889, in Powderly, Thirty Years of Labor, 1859–1889 *(1967), p. 196.*

Frankly I don't know that I should be sorry to see a bit of a spar with Germany. The burning of New York and a few other sea coast cities would be a good object lesson in the need of an adequate system of coast defenses and I think it would have a good effect on our large German population to force them to an ostentatiously patriotic display of anger against Germany . . . It is very difficult for me not to wish a war with Spain, for such a war would result at once in getting a proper Navy.

Civil Service commissioner Theodore Roosevelt, to a friend, 1889, in Paterson, American Imperialism and Anti-Imperialism *(1973), p. 38.*

The artistic temperament is not a national trait of the English race. Our complex and exciting civilization has, indeed, developed, especially in America, a sensitiveness of nervous organization which often wears the semblance of the artistic temperament, and shows itself in manual dexterity and refined technical skill. And this tends to make mere workmanship, mere excellence of execution, the common test of merit in a work of the fine arts.

Charles Eliot Norton, scholar and editor in The Forum, *March 1889, in Bartlett,* Familiar Quotations *(1951), pp. 571–572.*

We have exchanged the Washingtonian dignity for the Jeffersonian simplicity, which was in truth only another name for the Jacksonian vulgarity.

Henry Codman Potter, Protestant Episcopal bishop of New York, Washington Centennial address at St. Paul's Chapel, New York City, April 30, 1889, in Bartlett, Familiar Quotations *(1951), p. 619.*

The state [South Dakota] contains thousands of women farmers, young women, spinsters, and widows who came here a few years ago, took up claims, improved them and are now full-fledged agriculturalists. In one county I found one hundred of these independent women farmers, yet it was not the county which contained the largest number by any means.

Carrie Chapman Catt, reformer, suffragist and temperance advocate, writing in 1890, in Van Voris, Carrie Chapman Catt: A Public Life *(1987), p. 24.*

The necessity of a navy, in the restricted sense of the word, springs . . . from the existence of a peaceful shipping, and disappears with it, except in the case of a nation which has aggressive tendencies, and keeping up a navy merely as a branch of the military establishment. As the United States has at present no aggressive purposes, and as its merchant service has disappeared, the dwindling of the armed fleet and general lack of interest in it are strictly logical consequences. When for any reason sea trade is again found to pay, a large enough shipping interest will reappear to compel the revival of the war fleet. It is possible that when a canal route through the Central-American Isthmus is seen to be a near certainty, the aggressive impulse may be strong enough to lead to the same result. This is doubtful, however, because a peaceful, gain-loving nation is not far-sighted, and far-sightedness is needed for adequate military preparation, especially in these days.

As a nation, with its unarmed and armed shipping, launched forth from its own shores, the need is soon felt of points upon which the ships can rely for peaceful trading, for refuge and supplies. In the present day friendly, through foreign, ports are to be found all over the world; and their shelter is enough while peace prevails. It was not always so, nor does peace always endure, though the United States have been favored by so long a continuing of it . . .

Alfred Thayer Mahan, in The Influence of Sea Power upon History, 1660–1783, *published in 1890. Avaiable online at URL: http://www. gutenberg.org/etext/13529.*

Is it not better . . . that the income of the government shall be secured by putting a tax or a duty upon foreign products, and at the same time carefully providing that such duties shall be on products of foreign growth and manufacture which compete with like products of home growth and manufacture, so that, while we are raising all the revenues needed by the government, we shall do it with a discriminating regard for our own people, their products, and their employments? . . .

The Free-Trader wants the world to enjoy with our own citizens equal benefits of trade in the United States. The Republican Protectionist would give the first chance to our people, and would so levy duties upon the products of other nations as to discriminate in favor of our own. The Democratic party would make no distinction; it would serve the alien and the stranger; the Republican party would serve the State and our own fellow-citizens.

Representative William McKinley (R-Ohio), 1890, in Hoogenboom and Hoogenboom, The Gilded Age *(1967), pp. 170–171.*

What you farmers need to do is raise less corn and more Hell!

Agrarian orator Mary Elizabeth Lease, to an early gathering of Populists at Topeka, Kansas, 1890, in The Almanac of American History *(1983), p. 372.*

. . . this bill proceeds upon the false assumption that all competition is beneficent to the country, and that every advance of price is an injury to the country. That is the assumption upon which this bill proceeds. There never was a greater fallacy in the world. Competition, which

Mary Elizabeth Lease was a Populist reformer. *(Kansas State Historical Society, Topeka, Kansas)*

this bill provides for as between any two persons, must be full and free. Unrestricted competition is brutal warfare, and injurious to the whole country, the great corporations of this country, the great monopolies of this country are every one of them built upon the graves of weaker competitors that have been forced to their death by remorseless competition. I am entirely sick of this idea that the lower the prices are the better for the country, and that any effort to advance prices, no matter how low they may be, and that any arrangement between persons engaged in business to advance prices, no matter how low they may be, is a wrong and ought to be repressed and punished.

Senator Orville H. Platt (R-Connecticut), to Congress, speech of March 27, 1890, in Ginger, People on the Move *(1975).*

I went around town and begged money to keep [her] working and then she went off and got married. The loss . . . is very discouraging.

Women's rights advocate Margaret Campbell, to friend and longtime feminist campaigner Lucy Stone, concerning the marriage of the feminist activist Carrie Chapman Catt, letter of July 30, 1890, in Van Voris, Carrie Chapman Catt *(1987), p. 19.*

. . . our greatest need is the need of a fighting-fleet. Forts alone could not prevent the occupation of any town or territory outside the range of their guns, or the general wasting of the seaboard; while a squadron of heavy battle-ships, able to sail out and attack the enemy's vessels as they approached, and possessing the great advantage of being near their own base of supplies, would effectually guard a thousand miles of coast. Passive defense, giving the assailant complete choice of the time and place for attack, is always the most dangerous expedient. Our ships should be the best of their kind,—this is the first desideratum; but, in addition, there should be plenty of them. We need a large navy, composed not merely of cruisers, but containing also a full proportion of powerful battle-ships, able to meet those of any other nation.

Anonymous review of Alfred Thayer Mahan's book on sea power, in Atlantic Monthly, *October 1890, p. 563.*

The Farmer's Alliance is in itself more the product of social hunger than political thought or action. The farm neighborhood has little social life, has none of the secret societies, nothing of clubs, scarcely a church sociable [sic]. We propose to put a Republican club into every farm neighborhood possible, as soon as we can, and make it a social and literary as well as political force.

James S. Clarkson, editor of the Des Moines Register, *to President Harrison, letter of May 5, 1891, in Morgan,* The Gilded Age *(1970), p. 150.*

I can still shut my eyes and see the stately procession of majestic vessels, freighted with the native products of the vast Mid-west, moving noiselessly along the pathway of beneficent exchanges. What a lesson is here against government interference! How wisely the well-instructed spirit of self-interest works in self-directed channels, and is developed by natural competition without fear of contact with malificient [sic] statutes.

Senator Thomas F. Bayard (D-Delaware), letter of July 11, 1891, in Morgan, The Gilded Age *(1970), p. 131.*

I came here a week ago. Ma left for Mt. Carroll two days afterwards. Today is her birthday and I have written her. She is very thin but I think quite well as she

has been for a long time. Twice I have been here there has been no outbreak which seems to me to indicate that she is better.

Jane Addams, letter to her sister Alice commenting on their stepmother's health, August 14, 1891, in Davis, American Heroine *(1973), p. 83.*

The biggest agricultural strike in the history of the world is imminent. If it takes place the matured cotton will rot in the fields. This is brought about by the Colored Farmers' Alliance of the United States. And the order goes into effect on Saturday next! . . .

This organization has been perfected through colored alliances, and numbers more than half a million with thousands being added every day throughout the southern states. Colonel R. M. Humphrey, general superintendent of the colored alliance, admitted the existence of this organization, saying it had been induced by the organization some time ago of planters and merchants in certain sections, notably Memphis and Charleston, to reduce the price for picking to a very low standard, and that the cotton pickers had combined to protect themselves from this dictation, and he thought they would be able to do so . . .

It is learned that a secret circular has been mailed at Houston to every sub-alliance throughout the cotton belt, fixing the date when the strike of cotton pickers will be simultaneously inaugurated, and how it shall be conducted . . .

The headquarters of the Colored National Alliance of the United States is in this city. Colonel R. M. Humphrey, general superintendent of the Colored Farmers' Alliance and Cotton Pickers' League, has been actively at work in organizing the colored men for a general strike all over the south. Today your correspondent obtained a copy of a secret circular which Humphrey is having distributed by thousands all through the cotton states . . .

The planters and speculators above mentioned are firm in their demand that you pick at starvation wages, as offered by them, and leave your families to suffer fearful consequences, placing to your account the present low price of their cotton . . .

Six hundred thousand pickers already have bound themselves together in covenant to pick no cotton for any one, except their own . . . now, therefore, I, R. H. Humphrey, by virtue of the authority in me vested, do issue this, my solemn proclamation, fixing the 12th day of September, 1891, it being Saturday, as the day upon which all our people shall cease from, and absolutely stop picking cotton, except their own . . .

Excerpts from article, "The Cotton Pickers,"
in the Atlanta Constitution, *September 7, 1891.*

Humanity demands that men should have sunlight, fresh air, the sight of grass and trees. It demands these things for the man himself, and it demands them still more urgently for his wife and children. No child has a fair chance in the world who is condemned to grow up in the dirt and confinement, the dreariness, ugliness and vice of the poorer quarters of a great city . . . There is, then a permanent conflict between the needs of industry and the needs of humanity. Industry says men must aggregate. Humanity says they must not, or if they must, let it be only during working hours and let the necessity not extend to their wives and children. It is the office of the city railways to reconcile these conflicting requirements.

Charles Horton Cooley, sociologist, 1891, in Callow,
American Urban History *(1973), p. 202.*

[The nation's alternatives are a] French Revolution . . . [or] an Anglo-Saxon revolution of peace, compromise and progress.

Henry Demarest Lloyd, reformer and writer, at a union
rally in Chicago, 1891, in Smith, The Rise of
Industrial America *(1984), p. 707.*

It was *great*. In logic & law it cannot be disputed. It made me feel that I am a hypocrite & a slave and added to my resolution to make my term of servitude short.

Clarence Darrow, lawyer, writing in his journal after
hearing Henry Demarest Lloyd speak at a union rally in
Chicago, 1891, in Smith, The Rise of Industrial
America *(1984), p. 707.*

The character of U.S. urbanization begins to develop, as shown here in Rockford, Illinois. *(Library of Congress)*

. . . national unity is the determining force in development of the modern constitutional states. The prime policy, therefore, of each of these states should be to attain proper physical boundaries and to render its population ethnically homogeneous. In other words, the policy in modern political organization should be to follow the indications of nature and aid the ethnical impulse to conscious development.

. . . The morality of a policy which insists upon the use of a common language and upon the establishment of homogeneous institutions and laws cannot be successfully disputed. Under certain circumstances the exercise of force to secure these ends is not only justifiable, but commendable, and not only commendable, but morally obligatory.

John W. Burgess, in Political Science and Comparative Constitutional Law *(1891), p. 94.*

6

Strikes, the World's Columbian Exposition, and Imperialism
1892–1896

THE HISTORICAL CONTEXT

Acting as the voice of the people, the Populist Party gathered political momentum—and voter support—as the presidential elections of 1892 grew near. Some of that force was weakened by the Democrats, who nominated Grover Cleveland as the answer to the problematic incumbent, President Benjamin Harrison. Cleveland's election by a wide electoral margin indicated the mood of the country. The United States hoped that a Democrat could do what the Republicans had been powerless to effect: bring balance to the industrial and business monopolies that threatened to eliminate opportunity for individual Americans and those working for hourly wages. Cleveland also promised civil service reform and did so convincingly. He was, however, to be the last Democrat in the White House until 1913, as his promised reforms were ineffectual.

Despite the attentive concern of many union leaders and intervention by federal officials, labor disputes continued to disrupt production in many areas of the nation right through the 1890s. Calls for an eight-hour workday and demands for safer, healthier working conditions, adequate housing and fairer pay resulted in a volatile environment at numerous worksites. Among the most desperate was the situation of workers at the Homestead Steel Mill in Pennsylvania. This enormous operation had made the immigrant Andrew Carnegie a millionaire. His wealth permitted him to live a life of ease and luxury away from the mill and he had hired Henry Clay Frick to manage the huge plant in his absence so as to continue to ensure its profitability—and Carnegie's wealth.

When their old contract expired, workers in the Homestead mill who belonged to the Amalgamated Association of Iron and Steel Workers demanded fairer contract terms. When Frick refused to deal with union members they went out on strike, in July 1892.[1] Frick's response was to hire several hundred Pinkerton police to protect strike-breakers brought in to maintain the steel operation. Infuriated workers attacked the incoming Pinkerton men as they arrived by barge on the Monongahela River.

In 1892, workers at Homestead Steel Mill, owned by Andrew Carnegie and located in Homestead, Pennsylvania, demanded better contract terms. In this photograph of the event, the strikers watch and wait. *(Library of Congress)*

The strikebreaking move was an enormous public relations error on Frick's part. President Cleveland had openly stated the fitness of meeting the needs of the steelworkers and Frick's action was an invitation to disaster. He was adamant, however, and Carnegie, who was vacationing in Scotland, allowed Frick to keep the plant closed. An angry worker attacked Frick, nearly killing him. The Homestead Steel Mill remained closed, but the strike was broken in November, when workers gave up the struggle and returned to their jobs.

The Homestead strike and the ill will and conflict it generated between labor and management was more publicized than many labor clashes. It illustrated clearly the need for federal intervention in assessing and responding to the changing balance of power between workers and their employers.

In addition to trying to meet the challenge of complex domestic issues, the United States wielded increasing influence in the political affairs of other nations. Interest in a strong U.S. Navy and sufficient bases from which to launch and maintain this fleet was generated by imperialists and expansionists such as Theodore Roosevelt, Henry Cabot Lodge, and Richard Olney who furthered their cause of making the United States a true world power by the turn of the 20th century.

The interest in U.S. expansion outside its continental limits was heightened as well in 1893 when historian Frederick Jackson Turner published his essay

"The Significance of the Frontier in American History."[2] This treatise described the positive effect on the development of the United States of sufficient land for settlement. In Turner's view, the nation required a frontier in order to thrive and prosper; expansionists seized on this position to advance their own interests.

America's enthusiasm for growth and innovation was perhaps most colorfully and completely reflected in what was seen by some as the most amazing event of the century: The World's Columbian Exposition of 1893.

The exposition, held in Chicago, Illinois, was for all who visited it (or even heard of it) a cultural and technological marvel of epic proportions. It is not hard to understand the appeal of this event, since it promised enormous returns on investment for anyone even remotely connected financially with the exposition. The commemoration of the 400th anniversary of Columbus's voyage to the New World ignited interest in many cities across the United States.[3] Municipal leaders and boosters cherished wild expectations about opportunities for wealth and growth that would go along with hosting the Columbian Exposition. In Chicago, the city council directed Mayor De Witt C. Cregier in July 1889 to appoint a committee to make a bid for Chicago as the best location.[4]

After months of consideration and conflict, the U.S. House of Representatives gave the honor to Chicago. The U.S. Congress decided that a board of oversight with representatives from every state and territory would ensure that the fair's planning and implementation process was judiciously managed. This body, known as the Commission, began its complex task in 1890: to facilitate every aspect of the exposition—before, during, and after the event.

Building construction and site selection and planning fell to the architectural firm of Burnham & Root, with Daniel H. Burnham as chief decision-maker (following the death of his partner). He and a well-known landscape architect, Frederick Law Olmsted, chose a location on Lake Michigan for the exhibition's many buildings.

By 1891, preparations for the fair at Jackson Park had created more than 40,000 jobs. The design and layout of the fairgrounds generated a great deal of interest, and spectators were permitted to observe construction progress if they paid a 25-cent fee. Ultimately, the site embraced 633 acres of land, used 75 million board feet of lumber, and an estimated 18,000 tons of iron and steel.[5] More than 100,000 electric lights were strung on 30,000 tons of wooden staff. Fourteen main buildings covered 63 million square feet. The size of the project meant inevitable delays, and opening day was moved from fall 1892 to spring of the following year. On May 1, 1893, the exposition officially opened, with President Grover Cleveland pushing a lever and activating the dynamos that generated electricity for the fair.[6]

Between May and October, it is estimated, more than 27 million people visited the exposition. This number is more than double the number of those who attended the 1876 Centennial Exhibition in Philadelphia, Pennsylvania, which attracted upward of 10 million people.

Despite the optimism reflected by the World's Columbian Exposition and the tens of thousands of men and women employed during the construction and run of the fair, employment concerns—especially labor conditions—continued to dominate public dialogue.

Deeply perplexing were situations in which perceived needs and best interests of one group clashed with the needs and interests of another group. Heated debate was sure to follow whenever groups concerned with promoting certain issues disagreed with those seeking other considerations for workers. In 1893, for example, Illinois enacted a law limiting women to an eight-hour workday. Reformers seeking better conditions applauded this law; but some women's rights activists decried protective legislation, saying it limited women's employment opportunities.

In 1892, Victor L. Berger founded the *Wisconsin Vorwarts,* a socialist newspaper. He later became a close associate of Eugene V. Debs, a leader of the American Railway Union strike in 1894 and a founder of the American Socialist Party.[7] Also in 1892, Terence V. Powderly, leader of the Noble Order of the Knights of Labor, resigned his office as Grand Master Workman, a post he had held for more than 15 years. The International Longshoremen's Association was founded in 1892, and owners of the mining project at Coeur d'Alene, Idaho, shut down operations and refused to reopen until striking miners there accepted a wage cut. Such developments indicate the

The World's Columbian Exposition, also known as the Chicago World's Fair, held in 1893, had almost 27 million visitors, equivalent to about half of the U.S. population. *(Library of Congress)*

Lillian Wald was a New York City social worker. *(Library of Congress)*

various ways in which labor activists sought fair treatment for workers and how workers themselves sought control over issues most affecting their lives, on and off the job.

While many in the late 19th century strove for workplace reforms, many recognized that local government was just as likely to bring about desired changes as the federal government. The Populist movement was an outgrowth of local efforts to make politics more responsive, a movement that would become most effective by 1896.

An example of this specialized approach to reform was an organization concerned with more effective local government—the National Municipal League. Founded in 1894 by urban mayors, its chief goal was to promote honest and responsive governments in cities and towns. Although the organization provided a forum in which community leaders could discuss common issues, it did little to alleviate the more serious problems facing those who made their homes in rapidly growing urban areas. Reformers like Jane Addams, Lillian Wald, Florence Kelley, and Lester Frank Ward tried to eliminate slum tenements and worked hard to seek solutions to unemployment, poor working conditions and low wages. But despite their intentions, corrupt city governments, along with foul air, dirty streets, illiteracy and other ills, presented seemingly insurmountable odds.

Chicago's history during this period particularly illustrates the problems facing U.S. cities in the late 19th century. In 1894, business and industry in this midwestern center were the targets of growing dissatisfaction among workers. This unrest and discontent was especially evident among laborers who belonged to the American Railway Union (ARU). These workers at the Pullman Palace Car Company, a manufacturer of railroad cars, demanded better conditions and higher pay. They threatened to strike if their demands were not met. They were not, and this labor stoppage in 1894 was one of the most disruptive—and effective—in U.S. history.[8] It involved some 60,000 workers and resulted in Attorney General Richard Olney deputizing nearly 4,000 men to maintain order in and around Chicago, largely to prevent disruption of mail delivery. Taking action even before the violent outbreaks that later occurred and obtaining a court injunction against the strikers, Olney indicated that the federal government had little tolerance for strikers.

Olney's action involved the federal government in Illinois's issues, despite the fact that the governor there had not requested help. This uninvited federal intervention caused more violence and resulted in President Cleveland's dispatch of federal troops to Illinois. Strikers caused a mail train derailment there, substantiating federal fears of problems with mail delivery. As troops arrived in the state on July 4, the leader of the ARU strike, Eugene V. Debs, was arrested and imprisoned.[9]

The ARU strike showed other labor groups that desperate measures were the best way to gain public sympathy. Even though the government moved swiftly to crush any strikes threatening the stability of the nation's industrial network, ARU strikers had been successful. Many people now recognized the high level of unhappiness among workers and were critical of the president for calling out federal troops to quell workers whose demands seemed to be reasonable.

In spite of dismal working conditions endured by many citizens, the mid-1890s offered some pleasures. A growing interest in sports (spectator and participant), and various other activities for men and women emphasized the health benefits of sports. This interest also reflected a greater availability of leisure time for those in the upper middle classes, and a slight relaxation of stereotyped attitudes about "proper behavior" for women.

Katherine Lee Bates drew on her strenuous, yet rewarding, experience of mountain climbing, turning sweat into poetry. In 1893, Bates climbed Pike's Peak, then wrote "America, the Beautiful," which was set to music. Two years later, Annie Smith Peck climbed the Matterhorn in Switzerland, wearing a pair of "knickerbocker" trousers and, although scandalizing some, helped women who enjoyed less extreme sports to do so in more sensible athletic clothing than was previously possible.

Bicycles, which became all the rage in the 1890s, prompted such a change in women's attire, as some women chose to wear "Bloomer" dresses for bicycle riding. With the invention of a "safety bicycle" that had two wheels (with rubber tires) of the same diameter and coaster brakes, men and women enjoyed cycling and formed clubs dedicated to this sport. In 1892, the popularity of bicycles even led Harry Dacre to write the lyrics to a song, "Daisy Bell," about a bicycle built for two.

Golf had, by 1894, become a game enjoyed by American women. A women's golf tournament was held that year at Morristown, New Jersey. Ice hockey was presumed, like golf, to be a mostly male sport, yet it grew in popularity with women in Canada. In 1893, a women's ice hockey team was established in Alberta, and a year later, in 1894, women students at Montreal's McGill University began holding regular weekly ice hockey games. Men's ice hockey became more systematized with the introduction of the Stanley Cup. This trophy, purchased in London by Sir Frederick Arthur Stanley, governor general of Canada, was a way to distinguish the top amateur ice hockey team in Canada each year. It was first awarded in 1893 to the Montreal AAA, then considered to be Canada's top hockey team.

Like enthusiasm for certain sports, there were fads devoted to various food and diet strategies in the mid-1890s. It would be 10 years before Upton Sinclair revealed the dangers, to consumers and laborers alike, of the meatpacking industry in his novel *The Jungle,* set in Chicago's Southwest side meatpacking district. However, in 1894, the U.S. Department of Agriculture (USDA) published its first-ever advisory on food and diet in the form of a farmer's bulletin. Men in America, the USDA said in this brochure, were encouraged to eat protein, carbohydrates, fat, and "mineral matter."

Eating crazes swept the nation during the last decade of the 19th century. Among such fads was Horace Fletcher's advice to chew each mouthful of food 100 times—a practice that by 1900 had earned him the nickname "the Great

Masticator." Fletcher's strategy was promoted by Dr. John Harvey Kellogg, himself a proponent of many unusual and awkward diet and health practices. Kellogg, best known for championing vegetarianism and for his sanitarium at Battle Creek, Michigan, withdrew his interest in Fletcher's approach to digestion. Kellogg taught, instead, the importance and value of dietary fiber.[10] He developed the breakfast cereal named granola in 1878, perfected mass production of corn flakes by 1894, and sold the cereal in grocery stores by the first decade of the 20th century.

Attitudes and approaches to food and leisure time may have raised skeptical eyebrows among some Americans. But other behaviors and situations caused actual alarm, and perhaps the most worrisome was the threat posed in 1894 by growing numbers of unemployed, homeless men. These were workers who may have participated in any of the approximately 1,400 strikes and walk-outs that took place during that year. Estimates suggest that 700,000 workers were involved in these actions.[11] In spring 1894, these unemployed, and in some cases, desperate, men came from cities and towns everywhere to march on Washington, D.C., hoping to promote action by Congress or the president on behalf of their plight. The most famous of these groups was known as "Coxey's Army," named for Jacob S. Coxey, a businessman from Ohio who spearheaded one of these grassroots efforts. Coxey's Army comprised over 500 despairing and desperate men who, upon arrival in Washington, D.C., demanded that the federal government set up relief programs to provide them with work and wages.[12] They were unsuccessful in achieving their goal of a federal work relief effort, but their protest further publicized the economic plight of many Americans.

Equally persuasive efforts to rally another oppressed group to advance its position were made by Booker T. Washington, head of the Tuskegee Institute. He emphasized the importance of self-help for the thousands of former slaves who eked out a living in rural and urban homes. At the 1895 Atlanta Exposition, Washington delivered a speech that made clear his dreams and desires for all African-American citizens.[13]

As the desire for more timely information created better markets for daily newspapers, considerable competition developed among established—and aspiring—publishers. In 1895, William Randolph Hearst purchased the *New York Morning Journal*. By doing so, he became a competitor of Joseph Pulitzer's

Coxey's army of unemployed workers leaves Massillon, Ohio, on March 25, 1894, for Washington, D.C. *(Library of Congress)*

World. He also launched a rivalry that would only grow more intense as the months passed.[14]

Hearst's correspondents grew infamous for their particularly lurid reporting and writing style, a style that was described by the term "yellow journalism." Their aggressive, inflammatory prose was popular, however. Some believed that these reporters were to blame for an increase in expansionism and war fever in Washington. It was certainly true that more and more stories appeared that encouraged a greater sense of nationalism. But these journalists generally reflected what was already being discussed in Congress: that the United States had a duty to act as the protector of the Western Hemisphere, and that it was obligatory that America fund military power sufficient to maintain that watchdog role.

This increasing interest in the rest of the world by Americans concerned about the future occurred at the same time that the domestic economy entered another period of depression. In 1893, the nation's gold reserve had dropped to less than $100 million and the Sherman Silver Purchase Act was repealed as a result.[15] But Cleveland's administration was doomed to failure, as evidenced by the fact that in the 1894 congressional elections the Republicans made a strong comeback. It would be only another two years before the executive branch of government, too, was controlled by the G.O.P.

In 1894, the desperation of Coxey's Army told one side of the U.S. economy's story. By 1896, another facet of that story was revealed in the excitement and drama of the national political arena. When the Republicans met in St. Louis, Missouri, at the 1896 convention, William McKinley, the governor of Ohio, was virtually assured of nomination. Some delegates declined to support the G.O.P. position favoring high protective tariffs and the gold standard and deserted the convention. Nonetheless, McKinley received his party's invitation to be their presidential nominee. Garret Augustus Hobart of New Jersey was named to run as the Republican vice presidential candidate.

The United States's economic picture was gloomy, due to the depression that had followed the Panic of 1893. President Grover Cleveland, a Democrat who favored continuation of the gold standard, faced a challenge. At the convention, the party platform committee was divided between gold and the free coinage of silver as a way of alleviating the financial strain that the country had endured for several years.

When William Jennings Bryan, a young two-term congressman from Nebraska, spoke at the Democratic convention, his appeal to all those who favored free silver was incontrovertible. Bryan received the nomination largely on the strength of his "cross of gold" speech, a diatribe criticizing those who supported the gold standard. The Democrats chose Arthur Sewall as Bryan's running mate.

Bryan's appeal was so strong that the Populist Party named him their nominee as well, although they believed Thomas E. Watson of Georgia was a better running mate. This meant that in November voters were given the choice of a single Democratic candidate with two choices for vice president.

The clash of ideologies between the nation's two principal parties had seldom been more clearly defined. The Republicans supported a high tariff and the gold standard. Conversely, the issue of free silver coinage was a major plank in the Democratic platform, along with a lower tariff and a national income tax. The Populists had long called for an end to the gold standard, and they supported Bryan because of his position on money. Some Democrats, unhappy with Bryan's demand for free silver coinage, withdrew their backing of the ex-congressman, and formed their own party, the National Democratic Party.

William McKinley chose not to travel during his campaign. Instead he remained in Canton, Ohio, where hundreds of thousands of supporters came to hear him speak.

William Jennings Bryan, on the other hand, traveled everywhere. By early fall 1886, it looked as if Bryan had the advantage and would win the election. Campaign contributions to support Bryan raised some $6 million, compared to about $300,000 raised for McKinley.

Finally, however, the Republicans' persistence in advertising, and the continuing corrosive effects of the fragile economy, undermined the Democrats' strength and derailed their quest for the White House. Many critics believed, as well, that Bryan's flamboyant, emotional style of public speaking, while effective in some areas of the West and the South, did little to help him garner support in Northern industrial states. McKinley prevailed, and his victory over Bryan represented one of the most definitive electoral margins in the nation's

Many debated the gold or silver standard, as illustrated in this 1896 *Washington Post* editorial cartoon. *(Library of Congress)*

history. The Electoral College vote was 217–176 in favor of McKinley; the popular vote stood at 7,104,779 to 6,502,925.[16]

Americans followed the campaigning, but it was not the only issue that people focused on in 1896. Foreign policy captured the attention of hundreds of thousands, as well. Congress, embroiled in debate over how—and if—the United States would take action with respect to Cuba, grew increasingly more assertive with respect to how the United States's interests were to be promoted internationally. Expansionists believed Spanish territory could be advantageous to U.S. interests. And since this island nation off the coast of Florida had rebelled against Spain and was now in the midst of civil war, those hoping to obtain control pushed for military intervention on the side of the freedom fighters in Cuba. Contributing to this conflict was the United States's passage of the Wilson-Gorman Tariff in 1894.[17] This ended Cuban sugar merchants' virtual monopoly on U.S. markets, and since these merchants were no longer guaranteed favored prices, an economic crisis in their homeland had preceded the Cuban move for independence.

After much debate, Congress decreed in 1896 that the United States would side with Cuba against Spain. Despite this, President Cleveland, nearing the end of his term, refused to send American troops to Cuba.[18] Not until late 1897, after McKinley's inauguration, would the U.S. military action become a reality.

William Jennings Bryan was the Democratic nominee for president in 1896. *(Library of Congress)*

CHRONICLE OF EVENTS

1892

The Wistar Institute of Anatomy and Biology is established in Philadelphia, Pennsylvania.

January 1: A facility at Ellis Island, in New York Harbor, opens to receive immigrants to the United States.

January 15: At Springfield, Massachusetts, Canadian James Naismith publishes rules for the game of basketball.

January 20: The first basketball game is played, officially, at the YMCA in Springfield, Massachusetts.

January 29: In Kansas, members of the Republican Party celebrate Kansas Day to commemorate the admission of their state to the Union in 1861.

February 12: President Abraham Lincoln's birthday is declared a national holiday.

May 5: Restrictive immigration legislation is passed that will affect Chinese immigrants who wish to come to the United States.

May 19: Rice Institute in Houston, Texas, is chartered.

May 28: The Sierra Club, an organization dedicated to conservation of natural resources, is founded in San Francisco, California, by John Muir.

June 7: The Republican National Convention opens in Minneapolis, Minnesota; Benjamin Harrison and Whitelaw Reid are nominated for president and vice president, respectively.

June 21: Chicago is once more the site of the Democratic National Convention. Grover Cleveland and Adlai Stevenson are named candidates for president and vice president, respectively.

June 29: The Prohibition Party opens its national convention in Cincinnati, Ohio, nominating John Bidwell and James Cranfill for president and vice president, respectively.

July 1: In Pennsylvania, Henry Clay Frick closes the Carnegie-owned Homestead Steel Mill, provoking a labor strike. Secretly, Frick hires Pinkerton guards to protect strikebreakers, although organized workers discover Frick's plan and rioting soon breaks out.

July 4: The Northern and Southern Alliances join in Omaha, Nebraska, to form the People's (Populist) Party. Their national convention immediately follows on the same day; James B. Weaver is named the party's presidential candidate, with James G. Field running as vice president.

July 6: Within several days of Pinkerton guards' arrival at the Homestead Steel Mill, at least nine striking workers and seven Pinkerton men are killed. Many others are shot during labor rioting there.

July 10: The governor of Pennsylvania sends in the state militia to the steelworks in Homestead, Pennsylvania, to break up the labor strike and restore order.

August 4: Lizzie Borden's family is discovered to have been murdered in their home at Fall River, Massachusetts.

August 9: Thomas Edison receives a patent for his two-way telegraph.

August 27: A fire nearly destroys New York City's Metropolitan Opera House.

August 28: In New York City, the Socialist Labor Party convenes and nominates Simon Wing as its presidential candidate and Charles H. Matchett as his running mate.

September: Charles and Frank Duryea, of Chicopee, Massachusetts, build a gasoline-powered automobile.

September: William Morrison, of Des Moines, Iowa, builds an electric automobile.

September 7: The first heavyweight boxing champ to win under marquess of Queensbury rules and wearing gloves, James J. Corbett, knocks out John L. Sullivan in New Orleans, Louisiana.

September 8: The Youth's Companion magazine publishes the Pledge of Allegiance to the flag. Its author is Francis Bellamy, of the magazine's editorial staff.

October 1: The University of Chicago opens.

October 3: The University of Idaho opens.

October 5: While attempting a robbery, the Dalton gang is all but eliminated in Coffeyville, Kansas.

October 12: The Pledge of Allegiance is recited for the first time, by public school students. It is read to commemorate the 400th anniversary of Columbus's arrival in the New World.

October 15: Land owned by the Crow Indians is opened to white settlers by the federal government.

October 20: The Columbian Exposition in Chicago is dedicated by Vice President Levi Morton. John Philip Sousa conducts the band at the ceremonies.

October 28: A fire in Milwaukee, Wisconsin, destroys more than $5 million in property.

November 8: Democrat Grover Cleveland is elected president by an electoral vote of 277-145, defeating Benjamin Harrison.

November 20: The Homestead Steel Mill strike ends when union workers decide to give up and return to their jobs. State militia had been at the site since July 9.

November 26: At their annual football game, Navy defeats Army, 12-4.

December: Thomas A. Edison builds the first motion picture studio at West Orange, New Jersey.

December 2: Railroad tycoon Jay Gould dies at age 56. His estate is estimated to be $72 million.

December 5: John Thompson becomes the fourth prime minister of Canada.

December 19: The University of Oklahoma opens in Norman.

December 27: Construction begins on the Cathedral of St. John the Divine in New York City.

1893

January 4: The federal government offers amnesty to all polygamists, hoping to appease the Mormon Church and lessen tensions in Utah.

January 14: The Annexation Club in Hawaii meets to draw up opposition strategy to Queen Liliuokalani's plans for a new constitution. As a response to these activities, U.S. marines once again arrive in the islands and land in Honolulu.

January 17: Members of the Annexation Club march to government headquarters in Honolulu and announce that the monarchy is overthrown and a provisional government is established.

January 17: Queen Liliuokalani steps down as the head of the Hawaiian government.

February 1: John Stevens, U.S. minister to Hawaii, declares that the islands are under the protection of the United States.

February 20: The Pennsylvania and Reading Railroads go into receivership as the first waves of economic disaster hit the nation, forerunners of the upcoming Panic of 1893.

February 21: Thomas Edison receives three U.S. patents. One is for a "Cut Out for Incandescent Electric Lamps" and another is for a "Stop Device" (No. 491,992-3). The third is No. 492,150 for "Process of Coating Conductors for Incandescent Lamps."

February 23: Rudolf Diesel receives a patent in Germany for the diesel engine.

March: President Grover Cleveland is inaugurated.

March: At the direction of President Cleveland, James Blount is sent to Hawaii as a special commissioner to investigate recent actions there. Blount issues a report critical of John Steven's call for mili-

tary backup and states that the Hawaiian people are not in favor of the overthrow of the monarchy on the island.

March: The General Manager's Association, a society comprising several dozen railroads in the Chicago area, establishes a pay scale for its switchmen.

March 1: Under the terms of the Diplomatic Appropriation Act, the rank of ambassador is created for U.S. citizens serving overseas. Thomas Bayard is named ambassador to Great Britain at this time, the first of all U.S. envoys to bear this title.

March 4: President Stephen Grover Cleveland is inaugurated.

March 9: President Cleveland withdraws the Hawaiian annexation treaty submitted by John Stevens.

April 13: Commissioner James Blount removes U.S. troops from the Hawaiian Islands.

Labor leader and Socialist Eugene V. Debs created the American Railway Union. *(Library of Congress)*

April 15: Gold certificates are no longer issued by the U.S. Treasury because gold reserves have fallen below the $100 million mark.

May: Labor leader "Big Bill" Haywood meets with others in Butte, Montana, to organize the Western Federation of Miners.

May 1: The president opens the World's Columbia Exposition in Chicago, Illinois.

May 5: A run on the New York Stock Exchange causes further economic panic.

May 9: Thomas Edison demonstrates his kinetoscope (movie camera) at the Brooklyn Institute.

June 20: Eugene V. Debs forms the American Railway Union.

June 26: Pardons are issued to the three remaining anarchists involved in the 1886 Haymarket riot.

June 27: The New York stock market crashes.

July 1: President Cleveland undergoes surgery for mouth cancer. The procedure is kept secret for fear of even more widespread national disruption on the economic scene.

July 12: Frederick Jackson Turner gives a lecture titled "The Significance of the Frontier in American History" to his colleagues at the American Historical Association's annual meeting in Chicago, Illinois.

August 7: Congress convenes in a special session, called by President Cleveland, to discuss repeal of the Sherman Silver Purchase Act.

August 13: A Minneapolis, Minnesota, fire leaves 1,500 homeless.

August 24: A cyclone kills 1,000 in Savannah, Georgia, and Charleston, South Carolina.

August 28: A hurricane strikes Savannah, Georgia, and Charleston and Seal Island in South Carolina, leaving 100 people dead.

September 11: A meeting of the World Parliament of Religions opens in Chicago, Illinois.

September 16: Land purchased by the federal government from the Cherokee nation is settled by more than 50,000 homesteaders.

October 2: A cyclone rips through the Gulf Coast region of Louisiana, killing more than 2,000.

October 31: The World's Columbian Exposition closes after having hosted more than 27 million visitors, a figure equal to almost one-quarter of the U.S. population.

November 1: President Cleveland signs a repeal of the Sherman Silver Purchase Act.

November 7: Women are granted the right to vote in Colorado.

December 18: President Cleveland announces that he will not support a Hawaiian annexation treaty.

1894

January 8: A fire causes $2 million in damage as it destroys nearly all the structures at the World's Columbian Exposition in Chicago.

January 9: New England Telephone and Telegraph installs the first battery-operated telephone switchboard at Lexington, Massachusetts.

January 17: The U.S. Treasury issues bonds as a means of building up gold reserves.

February 8: Congress repeals the Enforcement Act of 1871, leaving control of elections to the states.

February 13: Thirteen miners are killed in a Pennsylvania coal mine collapse.

March 1: Thomas McGreevy, a Canadian politician, is released from prison after serving his sentence for defrauding the government.

March 12: For the first time, the beverage Coca-Cola is sold in bottles.

March 25: Coxey's Army, the first significant American protest march, departs Massillon, Ohio, for Washington, D.C.

April 5: Rioting breaks out in Pennsylvania as striking miners clash over working conditions.

April 20: Nearly 150,000 coal miners are on strike in Columbus, Ohio, in protest of low wages.

April 30: Coxey's Army marches on the nation's capital to protest unemployment. Their leader, Jacob Coxey, will press for legislation that will favor the working classes over business interests.

May 11: Workers at the Pullman Palace Car Company in Chicago go out on strike over low wages and reduced working hours.

June: Under the leadership of organizer and president Eugene V. Debs, more than 20,000 American Railway Union (ARU) members go on strike in and around Chicago, Illinois. The ARU shows active support for other organized workers at the Pullman Palace Car Company, whose union has also gone out on strike to protest wage cuts and rent hikes.

June 21: William Jennings Bryan speaks out in favor of free silver at the Democratic National Convention in Omaha, Nebraska.

July 3: Rioting occurs on one of the striking railway lines going into Chicago. Strike leaders anticipate federal intervention to break up the work stoppage.

July 4: Two thousand federal troops arrive in Chicago to end the ARU strike. Outbreaks of severe violence result in more than 20 deaths and the destruction of several thousand railway cars.

July 4: The Republic of Hawaii is declared.

July 10: Under U.S. cavalry escort, the first stock train leaves the Chicago stockyards following the ARU strike.

September 1: A forest fire in Hinckley, Minnesota, kills more than 400 people.

September 4: In New York City, 12,000 tailors strike in protest against sweatshop working conditions.

December 21: Mackenzie Bowell becomes Canada's fifth prime minister.

1895

January 12: The Government Printing Office is established.

January 14: A trolley strike begins in Brooklyn, New York. State militia are eventually called in to quell ensuing riots.

January 22: In Cincinnati, Ohio, the National Association of Manufacturers gathers for its first meeting.

February 4: The nation's first rolling lift bridge is operational in Chicago, Illinois.

February 8: The U.S. Treasury purchases $62 million in gold from private banking houses.

February 17: Gratz College, the first Hebrew teacher's training school, is established in Philadelphia, Pennsylvania.

February 24: Cuban rebel José Martí, based in New York City, leads a revolt in Cuba against Spain.

February 26: M. J. Owens patents a glass blowing machine in Toledo, Ohio.

March 1: William L. Wilson is appointed U.S. postmaster general.

March 5: Democrats in the U.S. House of Representatives request free coinage of silver. Two of the most vociferous supporters of this fiscal move are Representatives Bland (Missouri) and Bryan (Nebraska).

March 13: The U.S. Navy awards its first submarine construction contract to J. P. Holland.

March 18: Several hundred former slaves emigrate to Liberia, Africa.

March 28: In Boston, Massachusetts, construction begins on the nation's first city subway system.

April 10: The first round-the-world bicycle trip begins in Chicago, Illinois.

April 17: The Hennepin Canal at Rock Island, Illinois, is opened. The locks in this canal are the nation's first to be constructed of concrete.

April 21: In New York City, a motion picture is shown on a projection screen for the first time.

April 29: The U.S. Postal Service issues its first watermarked stamp, depicting Benjamin Franklin.

May 8: The first cat show in the nation opens at Madison Square Garden in New York City.

May 15: In Chicago, Illinois, the first electric elevated railroad in the country is operational.

May 20: The U.S. Supreme Court declares the income-tax clause of the 1894 tariff act invalid.

May 25: Golf in America is published by J. P. Lee.

May 27: The U.S. Supreme Court upholds a federal injunction that prohibits strikers from interfering with interstate commerce.

August 19: The American frontier murderer and outlaw John Wesley Hardin is killed by an off-duty police officer in a saloon in El Paso, Texas.

September 3: The first professional football game is played, in Latrobe, Pennsylvania, between the Latrobe Y.M.C.A. and the Jeannette Athletic Club. Latrobe wins with a score of 12-0.

September 9: The American Bowling Congress is founded in Beethoven Hall, New York.

November 5: The Utah Territory adopts a constitution that permits women to vote.

November 5: George B. Selden is granted the first U.S. patent for an automobile.

December 21: President Cleveland is permitted by Congress to appoint a Venezuelan boundary commission.

1896

January 4: Utah becomes the nation's 45th state.

January 4: The Actor's National Protective Union is formed.

January 12: H. L. Smith takes the first X-ray photograph.

January 16: The first intercollegiate five-man basketball game is held in Iowa City, Iowa.

January 18: The nation's first X-ray machine is exhibited in New York City.

January 29: X-ray technology is used in the treatment of breast cancer for the first time in the United States.

February 28: Congress passes a resolution giving U.S. support to Cuban revolutionaries.

February 28: Spain subsequently rejects the president's offer to help arrange a peace settlement for the island nation.

March 11: The national command of the Military Order of Foreign Wars is established.

March 31: The hookless fastener—known also as the zipper—is patented in Chicago, Illinois.

April 2: The College of Notre Dame of Maryland, in Baltimore, is incorporated.

April 6: At the first Olympic Games held in modern times, U.S. athletes win nine out of the 12 events held.

April 23: The first successful showing of a motion picture takes place in New York City at Koster and Bial's Music Hall.

May 1: Charles Tupper becomes Canada's sixth prime minister.

May 12: In New York City, a health ordinance is enacted that prohibits spitting on public streets.

May 18: A Louisiana law, known as the Jim Crow Law, is declared constitutional by the U.S. Supreme Court. In its decision in *Plessy v. Ferguson,* the high court rules that segregated facilities are legal if they are offered equally to both races.

May 26: Charles Dow publishes the first edition of the Dow Jones Industrial Average.

May 27: A tornado in St. Louis, Missouri, kills more than 100 people and leaves thousands homeless.

May 28: At the Prohibition Party's national convention, Joshua Levering is nominated for president of the United States. Hale Johnson is selected as the vice presidential candidate.

May 30: The nation's first automobile accident occurs in New York City.

June 4: In Detroit, Michigan, the first automobile rolls off the assembly line at Henry Ford's factory.

June 16: Republicans convene in St. Louis, Missouri, to nominate their candidates for president and vice president. William McKinley receives the nomination, along with runningmate Garret A. Hobart.

June 22: Mary Stone becomes the first Chinese woman to receive an M.D. degree in the United States, in Ann Arbor, Michigan.

June 30: The first electric stove is patented by W. S. Hadaway in New York City.

July: Physical Education Magazine publishes the first rules for the game of volleyball.

July 4: The Socialist Labor Party convention opens in New York City. Charles H. Matchett and Matthew Maguire are nominated for president and vice president, respectively.

July 9: William Jennings Bryan delivers his "cross of gold" speech while campaigning for president.

July 11: The Democrats meet in Chicago, Illinois, for their national convention. William Jennings Bryan of Nebraska is nominated for president, and Arthur Sewall of Maine as vice president.

July 11: Wilfrid Laurier becomes Canada's seventh prime minister.

July 21: The National Association of Colored Women is founded, with Mary Church Terrell elected president.

July 22: The National Silver Party, known as "Silverites," holds its national convention in St. Louis, Missouri. It votes to uphold the Democratic candidates for president and vice president.

July 25: At the People's Party convention, the Democratic nomination of William Jennings Bryan is supported, and Thomas E. Watson is put forth as the Populist candidate for vice president.

August 11: Harvey Hubbell patents the first electric light socket with a pull chain.

August 12: In Yukon Territory, gold is discovered on Klondike Creek, provoking the second major gold rush in U.S. history.

William Jennings Bryan (far left) and his wife (right) greet supporters from the platform of his campaign train, 1896. *(Library of Congress)*

August 15: William Allen White, influential editor of the *Emporia Gazette,* publishes an editorial entitled "What's the Matter with Kansas?" It wins him instant notoriety and provokes intense interest in his newspaper's comments on national politics.

August 16: George Carmack discovers gold in the Klondike region of Canada.

September 2: The National Democratic Party holds a convention in Indianapolis, Indiana, and nominates John M. Palmer for president. This group represents the so-called sound money Democrats, who had no use for the free silver plank in Bryan's campaign platform.

September 7: In Cranston, Rhode Island, the first automobile race to be held on a track takes place.

September 15: A free hospital for the care of cancer patients opens in New York City.

October: Argosy, the nation's first all-fiction magazine, is published.

October 1: The U.S. Postal Service first offers free delivery for rural areas.

October 3: Noted western outlaws the Dalton brothers try to rob two banks, but only Emmet Dalton survives the shootout.

October 7: Beatrice Hoyt of Morristown, New Jersey, is the first winner of the U.S. Women's Amateur Golf Championship.

October 15: In Providence, Rhode Island, a cornerstone is laid for the State House, the first building with an all-marble dome.

November: McKinley defeats Bryan in the presidential election, becoming the nation's 25th chief executive.

November 15: A hydroelectric power plant at Niagara Falls provides electricity to Buffalo, New York.

November 24: Vermont enacts the nation's first absentee-voting law.

December 1: Frank Broaker becomes the nation's first certified public accountant.

December 10: The first intercollegiate basketball game is played in New Haven, Connecticut.

EYEWITNESS TESTIMONY

We are nearing a serious crisis. If the present strained relations between wealth owners and wealth producers continue much longer they will ripen into frightful disaster. This universal discontent must be quickly interpreted and its causes removed.

There is no power on earth that can defeat us. It is a fight between labor and capital, and labor is in the vast majority.

General James B. Weaver, Populist candidate for U.S. president, 1892, in Davis and Woodman, Conflict or Consensus in American History *(1966), p. 122.*

A vast conspiracy against mankind has been organized on two continents, and it is rapidly taking possession of the world. If not met and overthrown at once it forebodes terrible social convulsions, the destruction of civilization, or the establishment of an absolute despotism.

Ignatius Donnelly, in a preamble to the Populist platform, 1892, in Dubofsky, Industrialism and the American Worker, 1865–1920 *(1975), p. 125.*

Government control of railroads has not succeeded and never will succeed. So long as it is in the power of a board of directors to increase stocks, issue bonds, and give rebates in secret, the people will have to pay for all the water and the interest on the bonds. Favors are shown to trusts and combines; the trusts and combines are made up of the directors and stockholders of the railroads; they secretly allow rebates to their favorites, such as institutions as have railroad directors on the roll of stockholders having an undoubted advantage over their competitors. No systems of governmental control can reach the offenders. Public control is inconsistent with the idea of private ownership, and private ownership of public institutions is not consistent with well-founded principles of public policy and welfare. Public control without public ownership is an impossibility. What the government has a right to control it has a right to own and operate. Ownership must precede control, and the question must be solved in a very short time, or those who own the railroads will own the government.

Terence V. Powderly, leader of the Knights of Labor, 1892, in Dubofsky, Industrialism and the American Worker, 1865–1920 *(1975) p. 60.*

This won't do. This won't do at all. Find out who owns this paper and buy it.

Henry Clay Frick, manager of the Homestead Steel Mill, remarking on an offensive item in a Pittsburgh newspaper, 1892, in Tuchman, The Proud Tower *(1966), p. 82.*

Life is worth living again. First happy morning since July . . . congratulate all around—improve works—go ahead—clear track.

Andrew Carnegie, owner of the Homestead Steel Mill, cabling home from Italy after learning of the cessation of the strike, 1892, in Dubofsky, Industrialism and the American Worker, 1865–1920 *(1975), p. 45.*

Organized labor in America still occupies an aristocratic position and wherever possible leaves the ordinarily

James B. Weaver received more than a million votes as the Populist candidate in the 1892 presidential election. *(Library of Congress)*

Terence Powderly led the Knights of Labor from 1879 until 1893. In this illustration from *Frank Leslie's Illustrated Newspaper,* a delegate at the organization's 10th annual convention introduces Powderly. *(Library of Congress)*

badly paid occupations to the immigrants, only a small portion of whom enter the aristocratic trade unions.

Friedrich Engels, German socialist, 1892, in Dubofsky,
Industrialism and the American Worker, 1865–1920
(1975), p. 64.

I pledge allegiance to my Flag and the Republic for which it stands, one nation, indivisible, with liberty and justice for all.

Baptist minister and Christian Socialist Francis Bellamy
wrote the Pledge of Allegiance for a quadricentennial
celebration of Columbus Day, sponsored by the National
Education Association (NEA), for a flag-raising ceremony
in public schools nationwide, September 8, 1892,
in The Youth's Companion.

Habit is thus the enormous fly-wheel of society, its most precous conservative agent. It alone is what keeps us all within the bounds of ordinance.

William James, philosopher and psychologist, in
Psychology *(1892), p. 122.*

There is no place yet in America for a *third* party . . . The divergence of interests even in the *same* class group is so great . . . that wholly different groups and interests are represented in each of the two big parties . . . and almost each particular section of the possessing class has its representatives in each of the two parties . . . Only when there is a generation of native-born workers that cannot expect *anything* from speculation *any more [sic]* will we have a solid foothold in America.

Friedrich Engels, writing in 1892, in Dubofsky,
Industrialism and the American Worker, 1865–1920
(1975), p. 68.

Cultivate the society of men—particularly men of affairs. A lawyer who does not know men is handicapped . . . Every man that you know makes it to that extent easier to practice, to accomplish what you have in hand . . . Perhaps most important of all is the impressing of clients and satisfying them. Your law may be perfect, your ability to apply it great and yet you cannot be a successful advisor unless your advice is followed; it will not be followed unless you can satisfy your clients.

Louis Brandeis, letter to William Harrison Dunbar,
February 2, 1893, in McCraw, Prophets of
Regulation *(1984), p. 85.*

The "sweating system" is one of respectable antiquity and is a surviving remnant of the industrial system which preceded the factory system, when industry was chiefly conducted on the piece price plan in small shops or the homes of the workers. Machinery developed the modern factory and concentrated labor, but in the tailoring trades, the practice of sending out garments, ready-cut, to be made by journeymen at their homes and at a price per garment, has survived and is still maintained in custom work, in which the journeyman is still a skilled tailor who makes the whole garment. The modern demand for ready-made clothing in great quantities and of the cheaper grades, has, however, led to much subdivision of the labor on garments, and with it to the substitution of the contractor or sweater, with groups of employees in separate processes, for the individual tailor, skilled in all of them.

Florence Kelley, excerpts from "The Sweating System of
Chicago," Bureau of Statistics of Labor of Illinois,
Seventh Biennial Report, 1892 *(1893), p. 357.*
Available online at URL: http://womhist.
binghamton.edu/factory/doc1.htm.

I transmit herewith, with a view to its ratification, a treaty of annexation concluded on the 14th day of February, 1893 . . . The provisional treaty, it will be observed, does not attempt to deal in detail with the questions that grow out of annexation of the Hawaiian Islands to the United States. The commissioners representing the Hawaiian Government have consented to leave to the future and to the just and benevolent purposes of the United States the adjustment of all such questions.

President Harrison, to U.S. Congress, February 1893, in
Gianakos and Karson, American Diplomacy and the
Sense of Destiny *(1966), p. 47.*

The law of nations is founded upon reason and justice, and the rules of conduct governing individual relations between citizens or subjects of a civilized state are equally applicable as between enlightened nations. The considerations that international law is without a court for its enforcement, and that obedience to its commands practically depends upon good faith, instead of upon the mandate of a superior tribunal, only give additional sanction to the law itself and brand any deliberate infraction of it not merely as a wrong but as a disgrace.

A man of true horror protects the unwritten word which binds his conscience more scrupulously, if possible, than he does the bond a breach of which subjects him to legal liabilities; and the United States in aiming to maintain itself as one of the most enlightened of nations would do its citizens gross injustice if it applied to its international relations any other than a high standard of honor and morality . . .

These principles apply to the present case with irresistible force when the special conditions of the Queen's surrender of her sovereignty are recalled. She surrendered not to the provisional government, but to the United States. She surrendered not absolutely and permanently, but temporarily and conditionally until such time as the facts could be considered by the United States.

Furthermore, the provisional government acquiesced in her surrender in that manner and on those terms, not only by tacit consent, but through the positive acts of some members of that government who urged her peaceable submission, not merely to avoid bloodshed, but because she could place implicit reliance upon the justice of the United States, and that the whole subject would be finally considered at Washington.

I have not, however, overlooked an incident of this unfortunate affair which remains to be mentioned. The members of the provisional government and their supporters, though not entitled to extreme sympathy, have been led to their present predicament of revolt against the Government of the Queen by the indefensible encouragement and assistance of our diplomatic representative. This fact may entitle them to claim that in our effort to rectify the wrong committed some regard should be had for their safety. This sentiment is strongly seconded by my anxiety to do nothing which would invite either harsh retaliation on the part of the Queen or violence and bloodshed in any quarter.

In the belief that the Queen, as well as her enemies, would be willing to adopt such a course as would meet these conditions, and in view of the fact that both the Queen and the provisional government had at one time apparently acquiesced in a reference of the entire case to the United States Government, and considering the further fact that in any event the provisional government by its own declared limitation was only "to exist until terms of union with the United States of America have been negotiated and agreed upon," I hoped that after the assurance to the members of that government that such union could not be consummated I might compass a peaceful adjustment of the difficulty.

Actuated by these desires and purposes, and not unmindful of the inherent perplexities of the situation nor of the limitations upon my power, I instructed Minister Willis to advise the Queen and her supporters of my desires to aid in the restoration of the status existing before the lawless landing of the United States forces at Honolulu on the 16th of January last, if such restoration could be effected upon terms providing for clemency as well as justice to all parties concerned. The conditions suggested, as the instructions show, contemplate a general amnesty to those concerned in setting up the provisional government and a recognition of all its bonafide acts and obligations.

In short, they require that the past should be buried, and that the restored Government should reassume its authority as if its continuity had not been interrupted. These conditions have not proved acceptable to the Queen, and though she had been informed that they will be insisted upon, and that, unless acceded to, the efforts of the President to aid in the restoration of her Government will cease, I have not thus far learned that she is willing to yield them her acquiescence. The check which my plans have thus encountered has prevented their presentation to the members of the provisional government, while unfortunate public misrepresentations of the situation and exaggerated statements of the sentiments of our people have obviously injured the prospects of successful Executive mediation.

President Grover Cleveland, excerpts from a letter dated December 18, 1893, to the U.S. Congress withdrawing his support for the annexation of the Hawaiian Islands. Available online at URL: http://www. hawaii-nation.org/cleveland.html.

The chief underlying principle of all Populist financial schemes is fiat money. Free silver, a sub treasury, etc., are purely incidental. It is the cardinal faith of Populism, without which no man can be saved, that money can be created by the Government, in any desired quantity, out of any substance, with no basis but itself; and that such money will be good and legal tender, the Government stamp, only, being required . . .

The Government, say the Populists, which by Protection rolls wealth into the manufacturer's lap, which constructs great harbors, buildings and defences, which gave us free land, pensions bounties, railways, and created greebacks, can do anything to increase our money supply.

Frank B. Tracy, a newspaperman, 1893, in Hoogenboom and Hoogenboom, The Gilded Age (1967).

The best periodical in the world.

James Russell Lowell, poet and editor commenting on The Nation, *1893, in Tuchman,* The Proud Tower *(1966), p. 138.*

. . . the best paper printed in the English language.

James Bryce, author of The American Commonwealth, *describing E. L. Godkin's* Evening Post, *1893, in Tuchman,* The Proud Tower *(1966), p. 138.*

The trouble with the damned sheet is that every editor in New York State reads it.

New York Republican governor Hill, concerning the Evening Post, *1893, in Tuchman,* The Proud Tower *(1966), p. 138.*

Half a century ago women were at an infinite disadvantage in regard to their occupations. The idea that their sphere was at home, and only at home, was like a band of steel on society. But the spinning-wheel and the loom, which had given employment to women, had been superseded by machinery, and something else had to take their places. The taking care of the house and children, and the family sewing, and teaching the little summer school at a dollar per week, could not supply the needs nor fill the aspirations of women. But every departure from these conceded things was met with the cry, "You want to get out of your sphere," or, "To take women out of their sphere;" and that was to fly in the face of Providence, to unsex yourself in short, to be monstrous women, women who, while they orated in public, wanted men to rock the cradle and wash the dishes. We pleaded that whatever was fit to be done at all might with propriety be done by anybody who did it well; that the tools belonged to those who could use them; that the possession of a power presupposed a right to its use. This was urged from city to city, from state to state. Women were encouraged to try new occupations. We endeavored to create that wholesome discontent in women that would compel them to reach out after far better things. But every new step was a trial and a conflict. Men printers left when women took the type. They formed unions and pledged themselves not to work for men who employed women. But these tools belonged to women, and today a great army of women are printers unquestioned.

Lucy Stone, speech titled "The Progress of Fifty Years," delivered in 1893 at the Congress of Women held in the Woman's Pavilion at the World's Columbian Exposition. Available online at URL: http://womenhistory.about. com/liberty/etext/bl_1893_lucy_stone.htm.

What a fearful mental degeneracy results from reading [the *Evening Post*] or the *Nation* as a steady thing.

Theodore Roosevelt, U.S. Civil Service commissioner, to Alfred Thayer Mahan, letter of 1893, in Tuchman, The Proud Tower *(1966), p. 138.*

I need not remind you, comrades of the American Railway Union, that our order in the pursuit of the right was confronted with a storm of opposition such as never beat upon a labor organization in all time. Its brilliant victory on the Great Northern and its gallant championship of the unorganized employees of the Union Pacific had aroused the opposition of every railroad corporation in the land . . . To crush the American Railway Union was the one tie that united them all in the bonds of vengeance; it solidified the enemies of labor into one great association, one organization which, by its fabulous wealth, enabled it to bring into action resources aggregating billions of money and every appliance that money could purchase. But in this supreme hour the American Railway Union, undaunted, put forth its efforts to rescue Pullman's famine-cursed wage slaves from the grasp of an employer as heartless as a stone . . . The battle fought in the interest of starving men, women and children stands forth in the history of Labor's struggles as the great "Pullman Strike." It was a battle on the part of the American Railway Union fought for a cause as holy as ever aroused the courage of brave men; it was a battle in which upon one side were men thrice armed because their cause was just, but they fought against the combined power of corporations which by the use of money could debauch justice, and, by playing the part of incendiary, bring to their aid the military power of the government, and this solidified mass of venality, venom and vengeance constituted the foe against which the American Railway Union fought Labor's greatest battle for humanity.

Eugene V. Debs, excerpts from his Proclamation to American Railway Union, *after he was sentenced to prison following the American Railway Union strike of 1893. Available online at URL: http://www.marxists.org/archive/debs/works/1895/aru.htm.*

All my friends are going to Europe . . . The Hays, Camerons, Lodges, Blaines, all start before mid-summer.

Henry Adams, historian, 1893, in Smith, The Rise of Industrial America *(1984), p. 858.*

I am just now not reading but devouring Captain Mahan's book and am trying to learn it by heart.

Kaiser Wilhelm II of Germany, after reading Mahan's The Influence of Sea Power on History, *1894, in Tuchman,* The Proud Tower *(1966), p. 133.*

[Although] steam electricity, compressed air, are utilized to do the work of man, [they] have been made the monopoly of the few . . . In the face of the power exerted by the monopolists of these tremendous engines of industry and commerce the Republican and Democratic parties stand paralyzed—hypnotized, as it were, unable to control it or give direction and shape for common good . . . The failure to adapt the legislation of the country to the strange conditions which this new life has forced upon us is the cause in greater part of our industrial ills.

Frank Doster, Kansas leader of the Populist Party, in a Labor Day speech, 1894, in Davis and Woodman, Conflict or Consensus in American History *(1966), p. 125.*

A crisis is thought to be approaching in the circles of the unemployed in Stark county, due to the concentrating here of scores of disreputable-looking strangers, who announce that their visit is for the express purpose of joining the march to Washington of J. S. Coxey's army of peace. There are at least 4,000 unemployed in the county, and it is difficult to determine how they will act under the fiery and inflammatory harangues of Carl Brown, who acts as Organizer for Coxey.

Ray Stannard Baker, Chicago Daily Record, *March 14, 1894, in Maddow,* A Sunday Between Wars *(1979), p. 216.*

Coxey is a small man with round shoulders. His face is brown and oily. His mouth . . . is almost hidden by a scraggly straw-colored moustache . . . Coxey talks little and smiles a great deal . . .

Ray Stannard Baker, excerpt from an article, "Coxey and His Commonwealth," first published in The Tourney *(May 1894), quoted in Maddow,* A Sunday Between Wars *(1979), p. 214.*

I believe that every novel should have an intention. A man should mean something when he writes. Ah, this writing merely to amuse people—why, it seems to me altogether vulgar . . .

It is the business of the novel to picture the daily life in the most exact terms possible, with an absolute and clear sense of proportion. That is the important matter—the proportion. As a usual thing, I think, people have absolutely no sense of proportion . . .

[The novel] is a perspective made for the benefit of people who have no true use of their eyes. The novel, in its real meaning, adjusts the proportion. It preserves the balances. It is in this way that lessons are to be taught and reforms to be won. When people are introduced to each other they will see the resemblances, and won't want to fight so badly.

William Dean Howells, novelist and critic, in Ginger, People on the Move *(1975), p. 181.*

Along about the latter part of March or 1st of April, 1894, we began to organize, and in order to do so we had to go to Grand Crossing, as the Pullman company would not tolerate any union in their shops. If a man belonged to a union, if the company knew it, he was discharged; we had to go down to Grand Crossing for the purpose of organizing the first local union . . .

The conditions became worse; in April there was another cut, which made it impossible for us to maintain our families and pay our rent; we had to do something; times were hard and men could not get money enough to move away from Pullman; we did not really know what to do. I used my utmost endeavors to keep the men from striking . . . but it was utterly impossible for me to control those who wanted to strike; we then held meetings until we had about 35 percent of the men organized; and on the 10th of May . . . after they had used every effort with

Federal troops keep order during the Pullman strike of 1894. *(Library of Congress)*

the Pullman company to make some concessions . . . a strike was ordered.

> *Thomas W. Heathcoate, of the American Railway Union, 1894, in Hoogenboom and Hoogenboom,* The Gilded Age *(1967), p. 81.*

As soon as the firing began, of course the crowd scattered, but it was hemmed in on each side by long rows of box cars which they could not get between very well and so they had to run in the direction of the firing, and a number of men, women, and children were injured, or rather men and women, there were no children, and none of those who were injured were members of the mob that was trying to overturn the Pullman cars. I saw the man who was killed; he stood in the crowd not a great distance from me. He did not have hold of the ropes and he was apparently merely a spectator. The men who did have hold of the ropes were not strikers. I know that, because this big fellow who led the mob I looked up afterwards and found him to be a tough from Chicago . . .

In all that mob that had hold of the ropes I do not think there were many American Railway Union men. I think they were mostly roughs from Chicago who had been brought there by the excitement.

> *Ray Stannard Baker, journalist, on events following the ARU strike 1894, in Hoogenboom and Hoogenboom,* The Gilded Age *(1967), p. 86.*

Let the Populist party triumph in the approaching election, and capital will shun Colorado as people avoid a city stricken with plague. Our reviving mining interests will be stunted in their growth, and Colorado men will appeal in vain to Eastern and European capitalists from money with which to develop any of our natural resources or to embark in new industries.

> Denver Republican, *editorial of 1894, in Smith,* The Rise of Industrial America *(1984), p. 532.*

The rules of life which orthodox Hebrews so unflinchingly obey as laid down in the Mosaic code . . . are designed to maintain health. These rules are applied to the daily life of the individuals as no other sanitary laws can be . . . Food must be cooked properly, and hence the avenues through which the germs of disease may enter are destroyed. Meat must be 'kosher,' and this means that it must be perfectly healthy. Personal cleanliness is at times strictly compelled, and at least one day in the week the habitation must be thoroughly cleaned.

Dr. Anne Daniel, outlining health conditions in some urban tenements, 1894, in Callow, American Urban History *(1973), p. 332.*

There are two or three sides to the question of Americanism, and two or three senses in which the word "Americanism" can be used to express the antithesis of what is unwholesome and undesirable. In the first place we wish to be broadly American and national, as opposed to being local or sectional.

Theodore Roosevelt, Civil Service commissioner, in "What Americanism Means," in The Forum XVII *1894, in Callow,* American Urban History *(1973), p. 451.*

Chiefs! Our road is not built to last a thousand years, yet in a sense it is. When a road is once built, it is a strange thing how it collects traffic, how every year as it goes on, more and more people are found to walk thereon, and others are raised up to repair and perpetuate it, and keep it alive.

Robert Louis Stevenson, in an address given in October 1894, in Bartlett, Familiar Quotations, *12th Edition (1951), p. 549.*

When I first enjoyed this superb view, one glowing April day, from the summit of the Pacheco Pass, the Central Valley, but little trampled or plowed as yet, was one furred, rich sheet of golden composite, and the luminous wall of the mountains shone in all its glory. Then it seemed to me the Sierra should be called not the Nevada, or Snowy Range, but the Range of light . . .

After ten years spent in the heart of it, rejoicing and wondering, bathing in its glorious floods of light, seeing the sunbursts of morning among the icy peaks, the noonday radiance on the trees and rocks and snow, the flush of the alpenglow, and a thousand dashing waterfalls with their marvelous abundance of irised spray, it still seems to me above all others the Range of Light, the most divinely beautiful of all the mountain-chains I have ever seen.

John Muir, excerpt, The Mountains of California *(1894), n.p.*

Today the United States is practically sovereign on this continent, and its fiat is law upon the subjects to which it confines its interposition. Why? It is not because of the pure friendship or good will felt for it. It is not simply by reason of its high character as a civilized state, nor because wisdom, justice, and equity are the invariable characteristics of the dealings of the United States. It is because, in addition to all other grounds, its infinite resources combined with its isolated position render it master of the situation, and practically invulnerable as against any or all other powers.

Secretary of State Richard Olney, to the British prime minister, regarding a boundary dispute between Great Britain and Venezuela, 1895, in Ginger, Age of Excess *(1965), p. 189.*

It is sea power which is essential to every splendid people.

. . . We are a great people; we control this continent; we are dominant in this hemisphere; we have

Richard Olney served as attorney general during President Cleveland's second term. *(Library of Congress)*

too great an inheritance to be trifled with or parted with. It is ours to guard and extend.

> *Senator Henry Cabot Lodge (R-Massachusetts), 1895,*
> *in Ginger,* People on the Move *(1975).*

In the interests of our commerce . . . we should build the Nicaragua Canal and for the sake of our commercial supremacy in the Pacific we should control the Hawaiian Islands and maintain our influence in Samoa. England has studded the West Indies with strong places which are a standing menace to our Atlantic seaboard. We should have among those islands at least one strong naval station, and . . . the island of Cuba, still sparsely settled and of almost unbounded fertility, will become to us a necessity. Commerce follows the flag, and we should build up a navy strong enough to give protection to Americans in every quarter of the globe and sufficiently powerful to put our coasts beyond the possibility of successful attack.

> *Senator Henry Cabot Lodge (R-Massachusetts), in*
> the Forum, *March 1895, in Kelley,*
> The Shaping of the American Past *(1978), p. 465.*

Cuba should become an American colony.

> *Senator Morgan (D-Alabama), chair of the Senate*
> *Foreign Relations Committee, 1895, in Tuchman,*
> The Proud Tower *(1966), p. 136.*

. . . we certainly ought to have the island [Cuba] in order to round out our possessions. If we cannot buy it, I for one, should like an opportunity to acquire it by conquest.

> *Senator Frye (R-Maine), 1895, in Tuchman,*
> The Proud Tower *(1966), p. 136.*

The present assault upon capital is but the beginning. It will be but the stepping-stone to others, larger and more sweeping, 'til our political contests will become a war of the poor against the rich; a war constantly growing in intensity and bitterness.

> *Stephen J. Field, Supreme Court associate justice, on the*
> *recent income-tax law, 1895, in Degler,* The Age of the
> Economic Revolution, 1876–1900 *(1977), p. 124.*

It is time that some one woke up and realized the necessity of annexing some property. We want all this northern hemisphere, and when we begin to reach out to secure these advantages we will begin to have a

nation and our lawmakers will rise above the grade of politicians and become true statesmen.

> *Senator Shelby M. Cullom (R-Illinois), 1895, in*
> *Tuchman,* The Proud Tower *(1966), p. 136.*

The antics of the bankers, brokers and anglo-maniacs generally are humiliating to a degree . . . Personally I rather hope the fight will come soon. The clamor of the peace faction has convinced me that this country needs a war.

> *Theodore Roosevelt, U.S. Civil Service commissioner,*
> *1895, in* Selections from the Correspondence of
> Theodore Roosevelt and Henry Cabot Lodge,
> 1884–1918 *(1925), p. 204.*

[The United States] finds itself in possession of enormous power and is eager to use it in brutal fashion against anyone who comes along without knowing how to do so and is therefore constantly on the brink of some frightful catastrophe.

> *E. L. Godkin, editor of* The Nation, *to a friend, letter of*
> *1895, in Tuchman,* The Proud Tower *(1966), p. 138.*

Outspoken critic of U.S. imperialism Edwin Lawrence Godkin edited such publications as *The Nation* and *The New York Evening Post*. *(Library of Congress)*

Booker T. Washington ran Tuskegee Institute in Alabama. *(Library of Congress)*

The wisest among my race understand that the agitation of questions of social equality is the extremist folly, and that progress in the enjoyment of all the privileges that will come to us must be the result of severe and constant struggle, rather than artificial forcing. No race that has anything to contribute to the markets of the world is long in any degree ostracized. It is important and right that all privileges of the law be ours, but it is vastly more important that we be prepared for the exercises of these privileges. The opportunity to earn a dollar in a factory just now is worth infinitely more than the opportunity to spend a dollar in an opera house.

> *Booker T. Washington, African-American leader, to the Atlanta Exposition, 1895. Available online at URL: http://historymatters.gmu.edu/d/39.*

In the inside shops the sanitary conditions are fairly good; and power is frequently, though by no means uniformly, furnished for running machines . . . The sweating-system has affected disastrously the condition of the employees in the inside shops, since any demand of the inside hands for increased wages or shorter hours is promptly met by transfer of work from the inside shop to a sweater; and the cutters alone remain secure from this competition.

It is preposterous, on the face of it, that a trade employing from 25,000 to 30,000 persons in a single city, with an annual output of many millions of dollars, should be carried on with the same primitive machines which were used thirty years ago. In every other branch of manufacture the watchword of the present generation has been concentration. Everywhere steam, electricity, and human ingenuity have been pressed into service for the purpose of organization and centralization; but in the garment trades this process has been reversed, and the division of labor has been made a means of demoralization, disorganization, and degradation, carried to a point beyond which it is impossible to go.

> *Florence Kelley, state inspector of factories and worskhops for Illinois, 1895, in Hoogenboom and Hoogenboom,* The Gilded Age *(1967), p. 72.*

The Government of the United States is not entitled to affirm as a universal proposition, with reference to a number of independent States for whose conduct it assumes no responsibility, that its interests are necessarily concerned in whatever may befall those States simply because they are situated in the Western Hemisphere.

> *Lord Salisbury, letter to Sir Julian Pauncefote, voicing the former's opposition to U.S. secretary of state Richard Olney's interpretation of the Monroe Doctrine in Venezuela's boundary dispute with Great Britain, letter dated November 26, 1895, quoted in* U.S. Department of State, Papers Relating to the Foreign Relations of the United States . . . 1895, part 1, *p. 566.*

So far from New York children being duller at their play than those of other cities and lands, I believe the reverse to be true. They lack neither spirit nor inventiveness. I watched a crowd of them having a donkey party in the street one night, when those parties were all the rage. The donkey hung in the window of a notion store, and a knot of tenementhouse children with tails improvised from a newspaper and dragged in the gutter to make them stick, were staggering blindly across the sidewalk trying to fix them in place on the pane. They got a heap of fun out of the game, quite as much, it seemed to me, as any crowd of children could have got in a fine parlor, until the storekeeper came out with his club. Every cellar-door becomes a toboggan-slide when the children are around, unless it is hammered full of envious nails; every block a ball-ground when the policeman's back is turned, and every roof a kitefield; for that innocent amusement is also forbidden by city ordinance "below Fourteenth Street."

Jacob A. Riis, writer and photographer, 1895, in Hoogenboom and Hoogenboom, The Gilded Age *(1967), p. 118.*

Every few years our industrial system gets the jim-jams. Capital flies to cover, factories close and labor goes tramping across the country seeking honest employment and receiving a warm welcome—from militia companies with shotted guns. Cheerful idiots begins to prattle of "over-production," the economic M.D.'s to refurbish all the old remedies, from conjure-bags to communism. They all know exactly what caused the "crisis" and what to do for it; but despite the doctors the patient usually—survives. And the M.D. who succeeds in cramming his pet panacea down its throat claims all the credit for the recovery. We are slowly emerging from the crash of '93, and the cuckoos are cock-sure that a country fairly bursting with wealth was saved . . . by the blessed expedient of going into debt.

William Cowper Brann, controversial Texas newspaper publisher, in a speech titled "Slave or Sovereign," 1895, in Bartlett, Familiar Quotations, *12th Edition (1951), p. 715.*

For more than thirty years we have been so much absorbed with grave domestic questions that we have lost sight of these vast interests which lie just outside our borders. They ought to be neglected no longer. They are not only of material importance, but they are matters which concern our greatness as a nation and our future as a great people. They appeal to our national honor and dignity and to the pride of country and of race. If the humiliating foreign policy of the present Administration has served to call attention to these questions and to remind us that they are quite as important at least as tariffs and currency, it will perhaps prove to have been a blessing in disguise.

Senator Henry Cabot Lodge (R-Massachusetts), 1895, in Gianakos and Karson, American Diplomacy and the Sense of Destiny *(1966).*

Cleveland and Olney have relapsed into their normal hog-like attitudes of indifference, and Congress is disorganized, stupid and child-like as ever.

Historian Henry Adams, to his brother Brooks Adams, letter of 1895, in Smith, The Rise of Industrial America *(1984), p. 536.*

Our ancestors, when but three millions in number, had the courage to declare their political independence of every other nation; shall we, their descendants, when we have grown to seventy millions, declare that we are less independent than our fore-fathers? No my friends, that will never be the verdict of our people. Therefore, we care not upon what lines the battle is fought . . . If they dare to come out in the open field and defend the gold standard as a good thing, we will fight them to the uttermost. Having behind us the producing masses of this nation and the world, supported by the commercial interests, the laboring interests, and the toilers everywhere, we will answer their demand for a gold standard

Illinois governor John Peter Altgeld played a major role in the 1896 Democratic Convention. *(Library of Congress)*

by saying to them: You shall not press down upon the brow of labor this crown of thorns, you shall not crucify mankind upon a cross of gold.

William Jennings Bryan, "Cross of Gold" speech, given on July 9, 1896, at the Democratic National Convention, in Ronald F. Reid, Three Centuries of American Rhetorical Discourse *(1988), pp. 601–606.*

I have been thinking over Bryan's speech. What did he say, anyhow?

Illinois governor John P. Altgeld, at the Democratic National Convention, 1896, in Tuchman, The Proud Tower *(1966), p. 144.*

What's the matter with Kansas? We all know; yet here we are at it again. We have an old mossback Jacksonian who shouts and howls because there is a bathtub in the State house. We are running that old jay gain for governor . . . We have raked the ash heap of failure in the State and found an old human hoop-skirt who has failed as a business man, who has failed as an editor, who has failed as a preacher, and we are going to run him for congressman-at-large . . . Then for fear some hint that the State had become respectable might percolate through the civilized portions of the nation, we have decided to send three or four harpies out lecturing, telling the people that Kansas is raising hell and letting the corn go to weeds.

Progressive newspaper editor William Allen White, in the Emporia Gazette, *August 1896, in an editorial used by the McKinley campaign. Available online at URL: http://www.h-net.org/~shgape/internet/kansas.html.*

"[. . . possession of the Philippines would enable the United States] to take a large slice of the commerce of Asia. That is what we want. We are bound to share in the commerce of the Far East, and it is better to strike for it while the iron is hot."

Mark Hanna, campaign manager to William McKinley, in 1896, concerning the importance of acquiring the Philippines, in Carl Degler, The Age of the Economic Revolution, 1876–1900 *(1977), p. 162.*

I have traveled in this free country for twenty hours without anything to eat; not because I had no money to pay for it, but because I was colored. Other passengers of a lighter hue had breakfast, dinner and supper. In traveling we are thrown in "jim crow" cars, denied the

Senator Mark Hanna devoted many years to campaigning for William McKinley as president. *(Library of Congress)*

privilege of buying a berth in the sleeping coach. This foe of my race stands at the school house door and separates the children, by reason of 'color,' and denies to those who have a visible admixture of African blood in them the blessings of a graded school and equal privileges . . . We call upon all friends of 'Equal Rights' to assist in this struggle to secure the blessings of untrammeled liberty for ourselves and posterity.

Legislator Benjamin W. Arnett, speech delivered in the Ohio House of Representatives, 1886, describing life in segregated Ohio, "The Black Laws," March 10, 1886, African American Perspectives, 1818–1907. *Available online at URL: http://memory.loc. gov/ammem/today/today.html.*

The hatred of the East among many Westerners, and the crude ignorance of even elementary finance among such a multitude of well-meaning, but puzzle-headed, voters, give cause for serious alarm throughout this campaign.

Theodore Roosevelt, to Henry Cabot Lodge, letter of 1896, in Smith, The Rise of Industrial America *(1984), p. 823.*

. . . the position and power of the Rocky Mountain states . . . are certainly as foreign to democracy as anything can possibly be.

William Graham Sumner, economist and sociologist, 1896, in Smith, The Rise of Industrial America *(1984), p. 823.*

Few rich men own their own property. The property owns them.

Robert Ingersoll, lawyer and orator, to the McKinley League at Carnegie Hall, New York City, 1896, in Bartlett, Familiar Quotations, 12th Edition *(1951), p. 603.*

The white race deems itself to be the dominant race in this country. And so it is, in prestige, in achievement, in education, in wealth and in power . . . But in view of the Constitution, in the eye of the law, there is in this country no superior, ruling class of citizens. There is no caste here. Our Constitution is color blind, and neither knows nor tolerates classes among citizens.

Marshall Harlan, Supreme Court associate justice, on his dissenting vote in Plessy v. Ferguson, *1896, in Degler,* The Age of the Economic Revolution, 1876–1900 *(1977), p. 152.*

[The workers] have come to look upon the [Protestant] church and the ministry as the apologists and defenders of the wrongs committed against the interests of the people by employers and men of wealth.

Samuel Gompers, president of the American Federation of Labor, 1896, in Degler, The Age of the Economic Revolution, 1876–1900 *(1977), p. 169.*

We are bound to share in the commerce of the Far East, and it is better to strike for it while the iron is hot.

Senator Mark Hanna (R-Ohio), concerning a U.S. takeover of the Philippines, 1896, in Degler, The Age of the Economic Revolution, 1876–1900 *(1977), p. 162.*

There are far more human beings materially well off today than ever before in the history of the world. How interesting our times have been and still are!

Charles Eliot Norton, scholar and editor, 1896, in Tuchman, The Proud Tower *(1966), p. 140.*

7

Annexation and the Spanish-American War
1897–1901

In addition to congressional concerns over Cuba's desire for independence from Spain (and related debate on the economic impact of the Wilson-Gorman Tariff), there was growing interest in expanding U.S. influence in the Pacific. Among efforts to place the United States in a stronger position internationally was a move to annex the island nation of Hawaii. Although supporters of annexation argued its strategic importance, these same supporters were also aware (some privately, some not so privately) of Hawaii's economic value.

After President William McKinley was inaugurated in March 1897, he made clear his support of taking possession of Hawaii.[1] On June 16 of that year, he signed a treaty that would annex the Hawaiian Islands, sending this treaty to the U.S. Senate for ratification.

McKinley's action did not go unnoticed. It generated a native Hawaiian protest so profound that it culminated in a petition, signed by thousands of Hawaiians, rejecting annexation. Together with a personal appeal to the Senate by Queen Liliuokalani and a Hawaiian delegation, the petition was presented to the United States, which stopped congressional ratification of the treaty.

Not to be outdone, pro-annexation leaders then moved to achieve their goal through another mechanism: a joint resolution of the U.S. Congress. Unlike a treaty, which required a two-thirds majority to ratify, a joint resolution required only a simple majority. The House Joint Resolution, which was referred to as the Newlands Resolution, passed and Hawaii officially was now part of the United States.[2] The resolution was successful due partly to heightened U.S. sensitivity to Hawaii's strategic location in the Pacific. It was signed into law by President McKinley on July 7, 1898. In 1900, Sanford Dole, became the territory's first governor.

President William McKinley governed the United States during the Spanish-American War. *(Library of Congress)*

169

AMERICA'S IMPERIAL IMPULSE

In retrospect, this act of imperialism seemed predictable if not inevitable. Even as early as the antebellum period the United States had shown interest in Hawaii. Making clear its intention to block colonization of the Hawaiian Islands by any foreign power, the United States also opposed preferential trade options to foreign powers. Growing U.S. awareness of Hawaii's economic value, together with the fact that Hawaii was, by 1865, an important Pacific port-of-call for ships, fueled U.S. interest in the nation's future.

Because sugarcane interests in the United States had become a powerful voice in Washington, D.C., by 1875, they were successful in brokering with Hawaii an agreement that granted preferential U.S. treatment. Plantation owners integral to the island's sugarcane-based economy wished to increase control over this lucrative industry.

This struggle for control of the island nation appeared to have come to an end in 1887, when David Kalakaua was elected king. King Kalakaua signed a treaty with the United States that permitted the export of sugar, on a tax-free basis, to the United States. The struggle continued, however, when the king was coerced into signing a new constitution for his country that severely curtailed the powers of the monarchy. When Kalakaua died in 1891, he was succeeded by his sister, Queen Liliuokalani. She supported another, newer constitution, which would restore the power of the monarchy and the island nation's economic and political autonomy. However, she lacked the powerful support of certain U.S. business and agricultural leaders. They overthrew Queen Liliuokalani on January 17, 1893, and named an American planter and Hawaiian Supreme Court justice, Sanford Dole, as president of the new government.[3]

John Stevens, then the U.S. minister to Hawaii, recognized the revolutionary government of Hawaii and issued a proclamation terming the islands a U.S. protectorate. This was approved by President Benjamin Harrison, who soon dispatched a naval contingent to Hawaii to guard the Hawaiian royal palace and to support the provisional government.

When Grover Cleveland was elected president, he revealed that he was not in favor of Harrison's actions with respect to Hawaii. In 1894, President Cleveland ordered an investigation of the invasion of Hawaii, reversed Harrison's policy, and rejected annexation.[4] He then ordered restoration of Queen Liliuokalani to the monarchy.

In response, Sanford Dole and others declared Hawaiian independence in 1894, announcing the Republic of Hawaii and gaining official U.S. recognition. Native Hawaiian opposition to establishment of the republic prompted an armed revolt in January 1895, but this attempt failed. Revolutionary leaders, including Queen Liliuokalani, were jailed. By 1897, President McKinley threw his support behind the annexation of Hawaii, which, ultimately, could not be prevented—even by the queen.

The president was active in 1897 in other policy issues, as well. Fulfilling campaign promises, he supported passage of the Dingley Tariff, which raised foreign import rates to their highest level.[5] He worked to secure the gold standard, although this legislation would not pass for another three years.

Concerns over the world's supply of gold would eventually become less pressing, thanks to discovery of gold in both Alaska, a U.S. possession, and Canada's Klondike region in 1896. On August 16, gold was discovered in the Klondike River tributary.[6] The news spread and within two weeks, names like "Bonanza" and "Eldorado" were given to the locations with the greatest potential. By December 1896, as many as 3,000 miners had stampeded into the area. During the next several years, many more would pursue their dream of finding gold in the Klondike River or in one of the many creek beds that flowed from it. Few would ever come close to seeing those dreams become reality.

Although the Republicans had established control via the election, and many in America felt optimistic about the future, there were some who looked ahead more warily. Among them was a young African American, W. E. B. DuBois, newly appointed to the faculty at Atlanta University in 1897. Along with Booker T. Washington, DuBois advocated activism by—and for—American blacks. His ideas soon diverged from those of Washington, who favored cooperation, not separatism, but until the 20th century the two were perhaps the most powerful leaders in the nation's black community.

America had barely finished celebrating the new year of 1898 when it applauded yet another event: the sailing of the battleship *Maine* as it began a voyage to Havana harbor on a "friendly" visit, following a rebellion in Cuba. The voyage was meant as a show of force and indicated that the United States was serious about protecting its citizens living on the island nation. Pleased with this development, and with the recent election fresh on their minds, Republicans awaited the inauguration of William McKinley in March, feeling generally satisfied about the direction in which the nation was headed. Most hoped for a peaceful settlement in Cuba, although they realized the rebellion there had grown to proportions exceeding the ability of the United States to manage through diplomacy alone.

The hopeful atmosphere was destroyed by the revelation that, sometime in December 1897, the Spanish ambassador to the United States, Enrique Dupuy de Lôme, had written a letter in which he criticized President William McKinley.

The Spanish ambassador described the president as weak and as a person who worried mainly about his popularity. The letter (written to Spain's foreign minister, Don José Canelejas) revealed de Lôme's views about President McKinley's diplomatic abilities and personal character, as well as his perspective on Spain's plans for continued involvement in Cuba.[7]

Cuban revolutionaries intercepted the letter and released it to the press. It was published on February 9, 1898, in the *New York Journal*. The uncomplimentary references to McKinley did little to placate those in the

W. E. B. DuBois wrote a collection of essays titled *The Souls of Black Folk*. *(Library of Congress)*

government who wished to avoid war with Spain, and it hurt the president's reputation with the American public.

Two weeks into February, diplomats' hopes for a peaceful resolution of the Cuban problem came to an abrupt end with the sinking of the USS *Maine*.[8] This tragedy, which claimed more than 200 lives, horrified the nation. On April 11, President McKinley delivered his war message to Congress.[9] In his address, the president requested support for forcible intervention to aid Cuba's revolutionary forces in their quest to establish peace in their homeland.

There was a strong consensus, particularly among liberals, that Cuban rebels were justified in seeking independence from Spain. The voices of these liberals were joined by a large group of expansionists, who saw in the Cuban rebellion and subsequent Spanish-American conflict a perfect opportunity for

Theodore Roosevelt organized and led a U.S. Army regiment called the Rough Riders. This 1898 photograph features Roosevelt and two Rough Riders. *(Library of Congress)*

the United States to increase its influence over nations that were rich in resources but poor in the means by which such riches could be developed.

Following McKinley's appearance in Congress, the expansionists grew more vocal in presenting their case for a strong U.S. naval force. They also agitated for a stronger, more prominent U.S. profile worldwide. One of the people who supported the expansionist position was Theodore Roosevelt, then assistant secretary of the U.S. Navy. Roosevelt would later help organize a U.S. Army Regiment known as "Rough Riders," accompanying them into camp at Tampa, Florida and, later, to the front in Cuba.[10] His popularity and success as a soldier confirmed the foreshadowed success of his political career. In 1898, he was elected governor of New York; two years later, he was McKinley's vice presidential running mate.

Although it captured a lion's share of attention in the popular press, the war with Spain was not the sole concern of American citizens at the century's end. Innovative ideas in education, a rising tide of feminist protest and support for woman suffrage, and growing affluence in America were transforming the national character. This transformation, although gradual, was discussed and analyzed in books, magazines, and newspapers with greater frequency as the century drew to a close.

Interest in U.S. natural resources continued to grow, and people's interest in learning more about the environment led to the founding of Mount Rainier National Park in Washington. The U.S. Congress passed a resolution on March 2, 1899, that established the 235,625-acre park, which included an active volcano.[12] It was the fifth U.S. national park, following Yellowstone in 1872 and Yosemite, Sequoia, and General Grant National Parks in 1890.

Labor issues continued to cause problems for owners of factories, mines, and railroads, and these concerns generated a steady flow of federal legislation. In 1898, the Western Federation of Miners formed the Western Labor Union to increase its leverage in contract negotiations. In 1899, the Team Drivers International Union was founded. Later renamed the Teamsters' Union, it grew into the largest labor union in the nation.

In response to the growing strength of these groups, and because of lobbyists' demands, Congress enacted the Erdman Arbitration Act in 1898. This law arranged for government mediation in railroad labor disputes and prohibited the use of yellow-dog contracts by the railroads. As a condition of employment, a yellow-dog contract required a worker to agree not to join a union. Although it suggested an improvement in the government's attitude toward labor, the Erdman Act only softened the federal pro-business bias. Legislative and judicial actions remained slanted toward business interests until well into the 20th century.

While it would be several decades before women were granted federal voting rights, they had claimed a larger share of rights and responsibilities by the end of the century. They also had made an impression in many professions. In 1898, feminist theorist and writer Charlotte Perkins Gilman published her seminal work, *Women and Economics.* Thought by many to be an outrageous attack on traditional values and on conventional family structure, Gilman's work attracted much attention. While her ideas for releasing women from domestic drudgery never attained widespread acceptance, she nevertheless provoked much discussion about the role of women in society. The following year novelist Kate Chopin published *The Awakening*. Another feminist work, it was assailed by critics because it dealt openly with sexual feelings and with the question of individual freedom within marriage.

Another work published in 1899 that received much attention and publicity was by the educator John Dewey. He wrote *The School and Society* to explain his theory that learning could be accomplished only "by doing." It was an idea that would transform public education in America, making Dewey's name synonymous with educational reform.[11]

In 1899, economist Thorstein Veblen published *The Theory of the Leisure Class*. This incisive, controversial analysis of the buying and spending habits of Americans provoked instant response. According to Veblen, "conspicuous consumption" was a way for the dominant economic class to display its power. Veblen, a contemporary of Richard Ely and others in the college-trained crop of late 19th-century economists, was the most radical of those who applied economic theory to real-life situations.

Since the end of Reconstruction in the 1870s, the United States had forged a stronger federal system, built great cities, established a successful transportation network, and founded an empire of industry and commerce unrivaled elsewhere in the world.

These improvements provided campaign debate issues that enlivened during the months preceding the presidential election of 1900, which had much in common with the election in 1896. The major candidates had not changed, and many of the issues remained the same. As an incumbent, President McKinley had little to be concerned about, although he knew that a popular vice presidential nominee would give the Republicans added security in November. Garret Hobart's death had paved the way for the Republican convention to nominate someone who could provide that security. Theodore Roosevelt, governor of New York and Spanish-American War hero, seemed an inspired choice. At age 42, Roosevelt brought to his candidacy health, optimism, and a sense of vigor perfectly suited to a turn-of-the-century election.

Conservative Democrats were not certain that William Jennings Bryan could beat McKinley, and as a result, they tried to draft Commodore George Dewey, naval hero of Manila Bay, although he declined at first. After deciding that he would like to run as the conservatives' choice, he sent a message to supporters in which he said, "I am convinced that the office of the president is not such a very difficult one to fill."[13]

When this remark was publicized, Dewey's supporters became disillusioned and withdrew their offer. William Jennings Bryan then received the Democratic nomination at the convention. The Democrats' platform included a plank in support of an anti-imperialist approach to diplomacy. It also opposed the gold standard. (Due, however, to the discovery of gold in the Yukon, the Klondike, and elsewhere in the world, there was no longer a pressing concern about gold shortages. Bringing silver to the campaign debate was a strategic error. Public interest in gold had waned since it was now in greater supply.)

Republicans were confident that the strong economy would help McKinley in his reelection bid, a well-placed confidence. The Democrats lost again, this time by an even wider margin than in 1896. The Electoral College vote favored McKinley, 292–155; the popular vote was 7,207,923 for McKinley and 6,358,138 for Bryan.

President William McKinley died on September 14, 1901, in Buffalo, New York, from gunshot wounds sustained nine days earlier. *(Library of Congress)*

The G.O.P. celebration over McKinley's victory was to last only a few months. While paying an official visit to the Pan-American Exposition in Buffalo, New York, President McKinley was shot by an assassin, Leon Czolgosz. McKinley, who received what later was judged to be less-than-competent medical care for the gunshot wound to his stomach, died on September 14, 1901.[14] Vice President Theodore Roosevelt, at age 42 (he would be 43 in October, but was now the youngest man to become president) took the oath of office that same day at about 3:15 P.M., making him the nation's 26th president.

President McKinley's death, coming so violently and without warning, shocked the nation. Aware of his goodness and his personal integrity, the United States belatedly praised McKinley's devotion to the office of president. Then U.S. citizens turned with optimism (and no little curiosity) to their new chief executive—President Roosevelt.

And as the United States welcomed its new president, debate continued over the proper role of the federal government in regulating private business and industry. The glittering decades of financial excess could not be instantly erased by legions of reformers, although 1900 marked a delineation between the power of laissez-faire government policies and that of policy makers who favored an aggressive federal role. During the first two decades of the 1900s, social, political, and economic reforms would limit the previously untrammeled growth of private corporations.

A clearly defined sense of moral and civic duty was articulated in books and newspapers and from pulpits and speakers' platforms as Americans tried to make social and political structures more responsive. An example of this revived interest in responsibility toward one's tasks was perhaps most cogently stated in Elbert Hubbard's essay "A Message to Garcia."[15] While Hubbard merely voiced his personal philosophy in this short treatise on personal duty, he nonetheless struck a chord in the hearts and minds of his readers. Published in 1900, "A Message to Garcia" sold more than 80 million copies. A scant year later, when President Roosevelt told Congress of his desire to restrain government tendencies to lavish legislative and judicial approval on business interests, he appealed to his audience's sense of responsibility.

Roosevelt termed this new approach to federal action and decision making the principle of "public interest." And far from being an isolated Rooseveltian quirk, it was a principle that guided a whole new era of leaders, reformers, and civil servants. Their "progressive" approach to problem solving resulted in informed public policy and helped in setting federal, state, and local agendas until the outbreak of World War I.

CHRONICLE OF EVENTS

1897

January 7: The first amateur handball championship match is held in Jersey City, New Jersey.

January 12: The National Monetary Conference meets in Indianapolis, Indiana. Following this conference, a commission is established to set up a plan for a permanent gold standard in the United States.

January 25: The American Forestry Association is established.

February 2: In Harrisburg, Pennsylvania, fire destroys the state capitol building.

February 17: The National Congress of Mothers, a parent-teacher association, is formed in Washington, D.C.

February 25: Assistant Secretary of the Navy Theodore Roosevelt is left in charge of the Naval Department for several hours and nearly precipitates a series of confrontations in the Pacific by his take-charge attitude.

March 2: In one of the final acts of his presidency, Grover Cleveland vetoes an immigration law that, if passed, would require passage of a literacy test for those wishing to enter the United States.

March 4: William McKinley is inaugurated as president of the United States, succeeding Grover Cleveland.

March 17: E. G. Briggs is the first woman to graduate from a theological seminary—the Union Theological Seminary in New York City.

March 17: In a 14-round contest in Carson City, Nevada, "Gentleman Jim" Corbett defeats Bob Fitzsimmons in the first prizefight recorded on motion picture film.

March 30: The New York State Society of Certified Public Accountants is formed.

April 15: The nation's first indoor flycasting tournament opens in New York City.

April 19: The first annual marathon race in the nation is held with a course that goes from Hopkinton to Boston, Massachusetts.

April 20: The submarine *Argonaut* is fitted with an internal combustion engine, the first of its type, in Baltimore, Maryland.

April 27: Grant's Tomb is dedicated in New York.

May 1: C. G. Bothner is the first fencing champion to win three titles in one year in the United States.

May 24: Congress approves $50,000 to be sent to Cuba for relief of victims of the civil war there.

June 2: Mark Twain, hearing rumors that he has died, is quoted in the *New York Journal,* saying, "The report of my death was an exaggeration."

July 2: More than 75,000 coal miners strike in Pennsylvania, Ohio, and West Virginia.

July 7: Congress passes the Dingley Tariff, which means that imports will be tagged with a higher tariff prior to their sale in the United States.

July 17: A Klondike gold rush begins when prospectors arrive in Seattle, Washington, describing their experiences in the Alaska gold fields.

July 25: Writer Jack London joins the Klondike gold rush. He will later write of his experiences in stories including "All Gold Canyon," "The Law of Life," and "Love of Life."

September 1: The Boston subway opens, the first municipal underground transit system to operate in North America.

September 10: Deputies fire on striking coal miners in Pennsylvania, killing nearly two dozen men.

September 11: Striking coal miners settle their differences with owners, and are granted an eight-hour workday.

October 22: The United American Zionists is formed in New York City.

1898

Brooklyn, New York, merges with New York City.

January: John Mitchell is elected vice president of the United Mine Workers. He is soon elected president of this powerful labor group.

January 25: The U.S. battleship *Maine* arrives in the harbor at Havana, Cuba.

February 9: Hearst's *New York Journal* publishes a private letter written by the Spanish minister to the United States, Enrique Dupuy de Lôme. The letter angers U.S. readers, causes international embarrassment, and provokes the minister's resignation, since in the letter the Spanish minister maligns the character and abilities of U.S. President McKinley.

February 15: The U.S. battleship *Maine* blows up in the harbor at Havana; 260 lives are lost. Spanish saboteurs are blamed, and President McKinley is called upon to act in the nation's defense.

March 24: Robert Allison of Port Carbon, Pennsylvania, becomes the first person to buy an American-built automobile, a Winton.

In this group picture taken at the White House, shown from left to right are Andrew Carnegie, U.S. Steel Company; William Jennings Bryan, presidential nominee; J. J. Hill, railway president; and John Mitchell, president of the United Mine Workers of America. *(Library of Congress)*

March 31: Spain refuses to arbitrate with the United States over the *Maine* affair. President McKinley drafts a declaration of war.

April 5: President McKinley recalls American consuls from Cuba.

April 11: McKinley requests that Congress issue permission for the United States to use force in expelling Spain from Cuba.

April 19: Congress adopts resolutions that call for Cuban independence and for the president to use military force against Spanish authority there.

April 22: The United States initiates a blockade of Cuban ports.

April 22: Congress passes the Volunteer Army Act, which permits the First Regiment of U.S. Cavalry Volunteers to form. Commanded by Colonel Leonard Wood and Lieutenant Colonel Theodore Roosevelt, it is best known by its nickname, the "Rough Riders."

April 22: The U.S. gunboat *Nashville* captures a Spanish ship, the *Buena Ventura*.

April 23: President McKinley calls for 125,000 volunteers to fight against Spain.

April 24: Spain recognizes a state of war against the United States.

April 25: Congress passes a declaration of war against Spain. It dates the declaration to the 21st of the month, however, to ensure that naval action by

the United States on the 22nd would fall under the declaration's terms.

May 1: Commodore George Dewey sinks the Spanish Fleet at Manila Bay in the Philippines after a seven-hour battle. The United States sustains no casualties, while Spain loses nearly 400 men in the encounter.

May 15: Theodore Roosevelt resigns as assistant secretary of the U.S. Navy.

May 25: The president calls for an additional 75,000 military volunteers.

May 28: The U.S. Supreme Court rules that citizenship is a right of any person born in this country, regardless of the parents' nationality.

June 1: Congress passes the Erdman Arbitration Act, which permits federal mediation between interstate carriers and employees in cases of discrimination against union workers.

June 1: The Trans-Mississippi Exposition opens in Omaha, Nebraska.

June 10: Congress passes the War Revenue Bill, which authorizes issuance of government bonds up to $400 million as a means of supporting the war effort.

June 11: U.S. Marines land at Guantánamo Bay in Cuba.

June 12: American troops leave Key West, Florida, on a mission to Santiago, Cuba.

June 12: Emilio Aguinaldo declares independence for the Philippine Islands.

June 13: Canada establishes the Yukon Territory.

June 15: At Guantánamo Bay, Cuba, U.S. Marines engage Spanish forces and push them back.

June 15: Congress passes a law allowing for annexation of the Hawaiian Islands. President McKinley signs the law on July 7.

June 17: The Hospital Corps of the U.S. Navy is established.

June 20: The island of Guam surrenders to the United States.

June 24: In the first land battle of the Spanish-American war, the United States defeats opposing Spanish forces at Las Guásimas, Cuba. Troops leading the offensive include the Rough Riders, under the command of Theodore Roosevelt.

July 2: After two days of fighting at El Caney and San Juan, Cuba, U.S. troops defeat Spanish forces there.

July 3: U.S. ships destroy the Spanish fleet as they leave Santiago.

July 7: The Hawaiian Islands are annexed by the United States.

July 8: Commodore Dewey occupies Isla Granada in Subic Bay, near Manila in the Philippines.

July 17: Some 24,000 Spanish troops surrender to the United States at Santiago. There would be a total of 5,462 American deaths, most of them due to disease. More than 1,600 men were wounded.

July 21: In waters off the Cuban coast near Nipe, the last sea encounter of the war occurs. American ships seize the port there.

July 25: U.S. troops seize Guánica, Puerto Rico.

July 26: Spain requests terms of peace from the United States.

July 31: At Malate, near Manila, U.S. troops suffer significant casualties in an encounter with Spanish troops.

August 1: The death toll mounts in a yellow-fever epidemic in Cuba. More than 4,200 U.S. troops are sick.

August 9: American troops defeat Spanish military forces at Coamo, Puerto Rico.

August 9: Spain accepts peace terms proffered by the United States.

August 12: An armistice is signed with Spain as Cuba is freed and Puerto Rico and Guam are ceded to the United States.

September: John Hay, U.S. ambassador to Great Britain, is named by President McKinley to serve as secretary of state.

The USS *Maine* was blown up on February 15, 1898. *(National Archives)*

September 9: The U.S. Peace Commission, headed by Judge W. R. Day, prepares to sail for France to sign a peace treaty with Spain.

October 1: U.S. and Spanish peace commissioners meet to discuss the disposition of the Philippine Islands. The ensuing debate lasts for two years, during which time Philippine insurrectionists stage a revolt.

November 8: Theodore Roosevelt is elected governor of New York.

November 10: A race riot in Wilmington, North Carolina, leaves eight African Americans dead.

November 26: Off the shores of Cape Cod, Massachusetts, the vessel *City of Portland* is wrecked, with a resulting loss of 157 lives.

December 10: The United States and Spain sign a peace treaty in Paris. Under its terms, the United States gains control of Puerto Rico and Guam and pays $20 million for control of the Philippines, which remains under U.S. jurisdiction until 1949.

1899

January: Spain relinquishes its power over Cuba, and Emilio Aguinaldo becomes president of the Philippines.

January: The U.S. Senate debates ratification of the Treaty of Paris, which is later to be signed by the United States and Spain.

January 1: Queens and Staten Island officially become boroughs of New York City.

January 3: The word *automobile* is used for the first time in an editorial in the *New York Times*.

January 17: Wake Island in the Pacific Ocean becomes a U.S. possession.

January 20: The Commission on the Philippines is established by President McKinley. Its role is to map out strategies for how the islands will be ruled prior to instituting self-government there.

January 24: In Lowell, Massachusetts, a process for manufacturing the first rubber heel for shoes is patented.

January 28: The American Social Science Association is established.

February 4: War breaks out between Philippine and American forces in Manila.

February 6: The U.S. Senate ratifies the Treaty of Paris. During the debate, imperialists led by Senator Henry Cabot Lodge argue for the economic and political advantages the treaty represents. Opponents say the treaty embraces ideas in opposition to the Monroe Doctrine.

February 12: An international bicycle race is held in New York City.

February 14: Voting machines are authorized for use in federal elections in states where such machines are available.

March 1: The Union Reform Party adopts its platform at a convention in Cincinnati, Ohio.

March 2: Congress calls for additional volunteers for army duty in order to help suppress a rebellion in the Philippines led by Emilio Aguinaldo.

March 2: Commodore George Dewey, the hero of Manila Bay, is named Admiral of the Navy, only the third naval officer on whom this rank is conferred. Admirals Farragut and Porter held this rank before him.

March 2: In Washington, Mount Rainier National Park is founded.

March 3: The Isthmian Canal Commission is established by Congress, the third commission to propose such a waterway in the history of the United States.

March 20: At Sing Sing prison in Ossining, New York, the first woman is executed by electrocution.

April 21: An intercollegiate chess tournament is held via telephone cable between New York City and London.

April 24: In Wardner, Idaho, a miners' strike turns violent as demands are rejected by mine owners there.

April 27: The federal government opens a hospital for tuberculosis patients in Fort Stanton, New Mexico.

Missouri is struck by a tornado that kills several dozen people and leaves scores injured.

April 28: The Filipinos request peace terms, a request that is rejected by General Otis since the United States demands an unconditional surrender of insurrectionists.

May 18: The first Hague Peace Conference opens in Paris. At this conference, the United States requests—and obtains—the formation of a permanent court of international arbitration.

May 20: The first arrest for automobile speeding occurs in New York City.

The American Physics Society is established in New York City.

May 24: A public automobile garage is established in Boston, Massachusetts.

June 23: G. H. Wanton becomes the first black American to receive the Medal of Honor, for service in the Spanish-American War.

July 1: A juvenile court is opened in Chicago, Illinois.

July 1: The Christian Commercial Men's Association of America organizes the Gideons, which becomes famous for publishing Bibles that are placed in hotel rooms across the nation.

July 6: The nation's first automobile licensing board is established in Chicago, Illinois.

July 8: H. M. Harriman becomes the first American-born professional golf champion, in Lake Forest, Illinois.

July 18: Secretary of War Russell A. Alger resigns under heavy criticism after it is discovered that military commands were insufficiently prepared for service during the Spanish-American War.

July 29: A motorcycle-paced bicycle race is held in New York City at the Manhattan Beach Track. This marks the first time that gasoline-powered pacers are used in such an event.

August 8: A. T. Marshall of Brockton, Massachusetts, patents the first home refrigerator.

September 6: Secretary of State John Hay requests establishment of an "open door" policy in China, so as to ensure free access to all economic opportunities there. This request will be consented to in early 1900 by Britain, France, Germany, Italy, Japan, and Russia.

September 9: An automobile parade is held in Newport, Rhode Island.

September 13: In New York City, the first automobile-related death occurs.

October 4: Admiral Dewey sends additional troops to the Philippines.

October 14: President William McKinley rides in a Stanley Steamer, becoming the first U.S. president to ride in an automobile.

October 16: The first radio broadcast from a yacht takes place off Sandy Hook, New Jersey.

November 10: In a New Orleans, Louisiana, hospital, a spinal operation is performed using anesthesia, the first such procedure of its kind.

November 12: Vice President Garret A. Hobart dies in Paterson, New Jersey.

November 24: Reports from Central Luzon in the Philippines indicate that General Otis has taken three important prisoners: the Philippine president, secretary of state, and treasurer.

December 2: The Battle of Tirad Pass is fought in the Philippines. It is later referred to as the "Filipino Thermopylae," recalling an ancient Greek battle during which one army was destroyed by opposing forces.

December 4: The U.S. Supreme Court rules, in *Addyston Pipe & Steel Co. v. United States,* that companies cannot make noncompetition agreements without violating the Sherman Anti-Trust Law.

December 5: In his third address to Congress, President McKinley warns of the growing power of trusts in the United States, a statement that is seen as a bold move for the relatively conservative Republican president.

December 10: In Denver, Colorado, the National Jewish Hospital opens and offers free, nonsectarian service to tuberculosis patients.

December 12: The golf tee is patented in Boston, Massachusetts.

December 16: The nation's first children's museum is opened in Brooklyn, New York.

1900

January 2: An electric bus seating eight people begins service along Fifth Avenue in New York City.

January 2: U.S. Secretary of State John Hay announces an "open door" policy, designed to promote trade with China.

January 2: The Chicago Canal opens.

January 8: U.S. President William McKinley places Alaska under military rule.

January 25: Congress votes 268-50 to unseat Brigham H. Young, a Congressman elect from Utah, because he has three wives.

January 27: The Social Democratic Party of America holds its first convention in Rochester, New York.

January 27: Foreigners in Peking (Beijing), China, including the U.S. diplomatic delegation, request that the terms of the Burlingame Treaty be implemented as a way to quell Chinese rebels who wish to rid their country of Western influence.

January 29: In Philadelphia, Pennsylvania, the American League of Professional Baseball Clubs is organized with eight founding teams.

February 3: Gubernatorial candidate William Goebels is assassinated in Frankfort, Kentucky. Former secretary of state Caleb Powers was later found guilty in a conspiracy to kill Goebels.

February 6: Theodore Roosevelt, governor of New York, states flatly that he will not accept the nomination for vice president of the United States. Roosevelt's opponents are eager to see him in this essentially powerless position.

February 16: The nation's first Chinese daily newspaper, *Ching Sai Yat Po,* is published in San Francisco, California.

February 22: Hawaii officially becomes a territory of the United States.

March 5: At New York University, the first Hall of Fame is established by Mrs. Finley J. Shepard's gift of $250,000. Members are elected to the Hall of Fame every five years by a committee of 100 people.

March 6: A coal mine explosion in West Virginia traps 50 coal miners.

March 14: McKinley signs the Gold Standard Act, returning the nation to a single monetary standard, and establishing a gold dollar of 25.8 grains in weight.

March 24: In New Jersey, the new Carnegie Steel Company is incorporated. Formation of the company directly challenges the Sherman Anti-Trust Law.

March 24: New York City Mayor Robert Van Wyck breaks ground for the underground Rapid Transit Railroad, which would link Manhattan and Brooklyn.

March 25: The U.S. Socialist Party is founded in Indianapolis, Indiana.

March 31: The nation's first automobile advertisement appears in a magazine.

April 12: Puerto Rico is confirmed as a U.S. territory with passage of the Foraker Act, although Puerto Ricans will not become U.S. citizens until passage of the 1916 Jones Act.

April 12: The first couple to be married in a ceremony conducted by telegraph is held in Kansas City, Missouri.

April 14: A 50-mile cross-country automobile race is held between Springfield and Babylon, on Long Island, New York.

April 16: The U.S. Postal Service issues the first book of stamps.

April 30: Hawaii becomes a U.S. territory by an act of Congress.

May 1: In a coal mine in Scofield, Utah, a blasting powder explosion kills 200 people.

May 10: The Populist (Fusion) National Convention is held in Sioux Falls, South Dakota. William Jennings Bryan is nominated for president, with Charles A. Town his vice presidential running mate.

May 10: In Cincinnati, Ohio, the Populist Party breaks away from the main party group and holds a convention. It nominates Wharton Barker for president and chooses Ignatius Donnelly, a labor leader, as its nominee for vice president.

May 14: Sanford Dole becomes governor of the territory of Hawaii.

May 14: The U.S. Supreme Court rules in *Knowlton v. Moore* than an inheritance tax imposed under the War Revenue Act of 1898 is constitutional.

May 14: Women's Christian Temperance Union (WCTU) leader Carrie Nation begins her anti-saloon campaign in Kansas.

May 22: A pneumatic player piano is patented in Detroit, Michigan.

May 23: Sergeant William Harvey Carney becomes the first African American to be awarded the Congressional Medal of Honor. He is given the award for heroism in the Battle of Fort Wagner during the American Civil War.

May 26: Congress approves an appropriation to establish the Army War College.

June: The International Ladies' Garment Workers Union is established in New York City by delegates from seven unions, representing 2,000 members. The group does not wield any significant power until a strike in 1909.

June: The nation's first society of orthodontists is founded in St. Louis, Missouri.

June 1: Carry Nation demolishes 25 saloons in Medicine Lodge, Kansas.

June 2: The Socialist Labor Party holds a convention in New York City. The party nominees for president and vice president are Joseph P. Maloney and Valentine Remmel.

June 12: The nation's first trapshooting tournament is held in Interstate Park, New York.

June 14: Hawaii becomes a U.S. territory.

June 16: The first international revolver-shooting competition is held in Greenville, New Jersey.

June 19: The Republican National Convention opens in Philadelphia, Pennsylvania. Despite his previous protestations to the contrary, Theodore Roosevelt is nominated for vice president by acclamation and accepts the nomination to run alongside incumbent President William McKinley.

June 20: A wholesale uprising against foreign influence occurs in China, with a violent episode known as the Boxer Rebellion.

June 21: Filipino insurgents are granted amnesty.

June 27: The Prohibition Party convenes in Chicago, Illinois, and nominates John G. Woodley for president and Henry B. Metcalf for vice president.

June 30: At the piers of the North German Lloyd Steamship concern in Hoboken, New Jersey, a fire breaks out and kills 326 people.

July 1: In Camden, Maine, the nation's first six-masted schooner is launched.

July 3: Following events of the Boxer Rebellion in China, Secretary of State John Hay sends out a circular note to foreign nations, indicating that it is the United States' intention to "preserve Chinese territorial and administrative integrity." This communication with America's allies is a way of further establishing the nation's open door policy.

July 4: Kansas City, Missouri, is the site of the Democratic National Convention, which opens today. William Jennings Bryan is nominated for the presiden-

On September 8, 1900, a hurricane struck Galveston, Texas, killing more than 5,000 people and destroying much of the town. In this photograph of the disaster's aftermath, a man, woman, and children search the rubble for anything they can salvage. *(Library of Congress)*

cy, and Adlai E. Stevenson, of Illinois, receives the vice presidential nomination.

July 5: Elizabeth Cohn makes a second speech at the Democratic National Convention, becoming the first woman delegate in the nation to do so at a major political party convention.

July 18: The nation's first duckpin bowling match is held in Union Hill, New Jersey.

July 20: The first woman astronomer is employed at the U.S. Naval Observatory in Washington, D.C.

August 8: The Davis Cup lawn tennis match opens in Brookline, Massachusetts.

September: The nation's first industrial research laboratory is opened in Schenectady, New York.

September 3: The Union Reform party holds its first national convention in Baltimore, Maryland.

September 8: A hurricane in Galveston, Texas, kills at least 5,000 people. The winds are clocked at 120 miles per hour and Gulf waters flood inland, causing at least $20 million in damage.

September 17: A coal strike increases the cost of anthracite coal from $1 to $6.50 per ton.

September 18: In Minneapolis, Minnesota, the nation's first primary presidential election is held.

November 6: President McKinley is reelected, defeating William Jennings Bryan with an Electoral College vote of 292-155.

November 15: The Carnegie Institute of Technology, known as Carnegie Tech, is established by millionaire steel magnate Andrew Carnegie.

1901

January 1: In Providence, Rhode Island, the nation's first building with an all-marble dome, the Rhode Island State House, is occupied.

January 1: As a new century begins, "zero-ists" argue that a new century should be designated as beginning in 1900, but this suggestion is rejected.

January 8: The American Bowling Congress opens its first tournament in Chicago, Illinois.

January 10: In Beaumont, Texas, the Spindletop oil claim produces the first of what will be millions of gallons of "black gold."

February 2: Congress creates the U.S. Army Dental Corps and the Army Nurse Corps. The latter is formed as a branch of the U.S. Army.

February 5: Edwin Prescott patents the centrifugal railway.

After the initial strike at the Lucas Gusher well near Beaumont, Texas, in early 1901, the Spindletop oil field was dry within three years as a result of the many wells that were built there. However, it was the catalyst for the creation of the modern oil industry. *(Library of Congress)*

February 20: The Hawaiian territorial legislature convenes.

February 25: U.S. Steel Corporation is incorporated in New Jersey by J. P. Morgan, in defiance of the Sherman Anti-Trust Law.

March 2: Congress adopts the Platt Amendment as part of the Army Appropriations Act. The amendment establishes provisions under which the United States will withdraw military troops from the island of Cuba.

March 3: The U.S. Bureau of Standards is established.

March 4: President McKinley is inaugurated for his second term of office.

March 13: Former president Benjamin Harrison dies.

March 13: Filipino insurgent leader Emilio Aguinaldo is captured by an American patrol in the province of Luzon in the Philippines.

April 19: The Philippine Rebellion is ended by special proclamation.

April 25: New York is the first state to register automobiles and to issue license plates.

May 3: A fire in Jacksonville, Florida, destroys more than $11 million in property and leaves 10,000 people without shelter.

May 9: A struggle for control of the Great Northern and Northern Pacific railroads results in stock values increasing from $100 to $1,000 per share. Panic ensues as other stocks fall rapidly. Hill-Morgan and Kuhn and Loeb and Company, the two rival companies fighting for possession of the railroad lines, are obliged to come to an agreement in order to preserve national economic stability.

May 27: As a means of determining future tariff policy toward Puerto Rico and the Philippines, the Supreme Court determines that territories falling into U.S. hands during the Spanish-American War were not foreign nations at the time, nor were they part of the United States. The ruling, *De Lima v. Bidwell,* will be followed later this year by other high court decisions affecting trade with former foreign territories.

May 27: In New Jersey, the Edison Storage Battery Company is founded by Thomas A. Edison.

June 12: Cuba becomes a U.S. protectorate as a result of terms of the Treaty of Paris.

July 4: A 1,282-foot covered bridge opens, spanning the St. John River in Hartland, New Brunswick. Estimates are that this is the world's longest covered bridge.

July 24: The writer O. Henry, imprisoned for embezzlement, is released after serving a three-year term in Austin, Texas.

September 5: The National Association of Professional Baseball Leagues is established in Chicago, Illinois. The association is later known as Minor League Baseball.

September 6: An avowed anarchist, Leon F. Czolgosz, shoots President McKinley at close range as the chief executive attends a reception for the Pan-American Exhibition in Buffalo, New York.

September 14: At 2:15 A.M., President McKinley dies as a result of gunshot wounds received a week earlier. Vice President Theodore Roosevelt is sworn in that afternoon at 3:00 P.M. and becomes the nation's 26th—and youngest—president. Roosevelt is 42 years old.

October 16: Booker T. Washington is invited to be a guest at the White House by President Roosevelt.

October 29: In Amherst, Massachusetts, Jane Toppan, a nurse, is arrested for murder. She is charged with killing a Boston family by administering an overdose of morphine.

October 29: Leon Czolgosz, who shot President William McKinley, is executed by electrocution.

November 18: The U.S. signs the Hay-Pauncefote Treaty. This agreement will authorize construction of a U.S.-built and -operated canal across the isthmus of Panama.

December 3: President Roosevelt announces his intention to launch efforts to regulate trusts in the United States. Soon to be known as an aggressive champion of reform, Roosevelt determines such regulation of big business to be in "the public interest."

December 12: The first transatlantic radio signal, sent in Morse code, is received by Guglielmo Marconi in Newfoundland, Canada.

December 16: Congress ratifies the recently signed Hay-Pauncefote Treaty.

EYEWITNESS TESTIMONY

Do nothing unrighteous but take the [Hawaiian] islands first and solve afterward.

Alfred Thayer Mahan, naval historian, to Theodore
Roosevelt, 1897, in Tuchman, The Proud Tower
(1966), p. 148.

The depression of the past four years has fallen with especial severity upon the great body of toilers of the country, and upon none more than the holders of small farms. Agriculture has languished and labor suffered. The revival of manufacturing will be a relief to both. No portion of our population is more devoted to the institution of free government nor more loyal in their support, while none bears more cheerfully or fully its proper share in the maintenance of the Government or is better entitled to its wise and liberal care and protection. Legislation helpful to producers is beneficial to all. The depressed condition of industry on the farm and in the mine and factory has lessened the ability of the people to meet the demands upon them, and they rightfully expect that not only a system of revenue shall be established that will secure the largest income with the least burden, but that

Fashionable streets, like New York City's Fifth Avenue, were virtual parade grounds for the wealthy and well dressed in the Gilded Age. *(National Archives)*

every means will be taken to decrease, rather than increase, our public expenditures.

Business conditions are not the most promising. It will take time to restore the prosperity of former years. If we cannot promptly attain it, we can resolutely turn our faces in that direction and aid its return by friendly legislation. However troublesome the situation may appear, Congress will not, I am sure, be found lacking in disposition or ability to relieve it as far as legislation can do so. The restoration of confidence and the revival of business, which men of all parties so much desire, depend more largely upon the prompt, energetic, and intelligent action of Congress than upon any other single agency affecting the situation . . .

. . . Our naturalization and immigration laws should be further improved to the constant promotion of a safer, a better, and a higher citizenship. A grave peril to the Republic would be a citizenship too ignorant to understand or too vicious to appreciate the great value and beneficence of our institutions and laws, and against all who come here to make war upon them our gates must be promptly and tightly closed. Nor must we be unmindful of the need of improvement among our own citizens, but with the zeal of our forefathers encourage the spread of knowledge and free education. Illiteracy must be banished from the land if we shall attain that high destiny as the foremost of the enlightened nations of the world which, under Providence, we ought to achieve.

President William McKinley, March 4, 1897, excerpt,
First Inaugural Address, *Washington, D.C. Available*
online at URL: http://www.yale.edu/lawweb/
avalon/presiden/inaug/mckin1.htm.

No modern industry has gone with such leaps from primitive methods to the most highly developed mechanical perfection as that of oil; but these leaders of the trust did not invent nor introduce one of these improved processes—neither the pipe line nor the tank car nor the drill or still . . .

. . . the stock exchange value of the trust is in round numbers over $225,000,000.

The men who had "nothing" in the early sixties now have control of this fabulous sum in oil alone. The trust is a combination of corporations—a score or more. Hundreds of corporations all over the world have been condensed to make this score. Perhaps this lubrication of poverty into almost unaccountable millions is a triumph of co-operation.

. . . But the records show, on the sworn testimony of the organizers of the combination, that substantially the same men own the majority of this vast aggregation as began with nothing, and then formed the Standard Oil Company in 1870 with one million dollars capital.

Henry Demarest Lloyd, reformer and journalist,
1897, in Hoogenboom and Hoogenboom,
The Gilded Age *(1967).*

Everywhere [in America] the machine goes very rapidly, and it commands; the workman has to follow . . .

Even when the machine only plays a secondary role it is customary to go quickly and to lose no time, a necessary result of competition. The employer will not tolerate an idle or listless laborer, who causes him loss . . . The improvement of machinery and the growing power of industrial establishments, have diminished the price of a great number of goods, and this is one of the most laudable forward movements of industry whose object is to satisfy, as well as possible, the needs of man.

The laboring classes do not share this optimism. They reproach the machine with exhausting the physical powers of the laborer; but this can only apply to a very small number of cases to those where the workman is at the same time the motive power, as in certain sewing-machines. They reproach it with demanding such continued attention that it enervates, and of leaving no respite to the laborer, through the continuity of its movements.

. . . There is no social evolution which does not produce friction. That which urges industry toward machinery and large factories appears to me to-day irresistible, because it leads to cheapness, which the consumer seeks first of all, and which is one of the objects of economic civilization. It is Utopia to believe that the world could come back by some modification of the social order, or of mechanical motive powers to the system of the little family workshop. Such a workshop is far from being an ideal, as the sweating system proves.

E. Levasseur, French economist, 1897, in Hoogenboom and
Hoogenboom, The Gilded Age *(1967), pp. 67–71.*

If ever we come to nothing as a nation it will be because the teaching of Carl Schurz, President Eliot, the *Evening Post* and futile sentimentalists of the international arbitration type [will produce] a flabby timid type of character which eats away at the great fighting features of our race.

Theodore Roosevelt, assistant secretary of the navy, to
Henry Cabot Lodge, letter of 1897, in Tuchman,
The Proud Tower *(1966), p. 147.*

There is a depth of human feeling in the Jew that no other race ever possessed. We do no more than imitate and follow it. David, for instance, and his conduct about Uriah's wife and the child that died—and Absalom—and Jonathan. Compare the Greek—the Chinese, the Roman. These Jews are more human than any other men. It is the cause of the spread of their religion—for we are all adopted in Judah. The heart of the world is Jewish. There is the same spirit in the Old Testament as in the New. That monstrous perversion—that we should worship their God and despise themselves.

John Jay Chapman, essayist, 1897, in Baltzell,
The Protestant Establishment *(1966), p. 94.*

The West End Jews, who are a well-to-do class, did not differ much from Englishmen of the same class. Those from the East End, employed for the most part in sweat-shops upon the manufacture of cheap clothing, averaged more than three inches less in stature, and were inferior also in size of skull and in every particular covered by the measurements. The intellectual deterioration that goes with this cannot be measured, but that it must exist will hardly be doubted.

Charles H. Cooley, sociologist, 1897, in Baltzell,
The Protestant Establishment *(1966), p. 169.*

The family, rather than the individual, is the important social unit. If society as a whole is to gain by mobility and openness of structure, those who rise must stay up in successive generations, that the higher levels of society may be constantly enlarged, and that the proportion of pure, gentle, magnanimous, and refined persons may steadily be increased. New-risen talent should reinforce the upper ranks . . . The assured permanence of superior families is quite as important as the free starting of such families.

Charles W. Eliot, Harvard president, 1897, in Tuchman,
The Proud Tower *(1966), p. 146.*

In writing "progress and poverty," he dipped his pen into the tears of the human race, and with celestial clearness wrote down what he conceived to be eternal truths.

When he died, there was nowhere a soul that cried out: "There is one iron hand less to grind us, one wolf less to tear our flesh," but everywhere a feeling that a friend of the race had gone.

Judge John Peter Altgeld, former governor of Illinois, memorial address on the death of Henry George, 1897, in Bartlett, Familiar Quotations *(1951), p. 684.*

Order the squadron except Monoccay to Hong Kong. Keep full of coal. In the event of declaration war Spain, your duty will be to see that the Spanish squadron does not leave the Asiatic coast, and then offensive operations in Philippine Islands.

Theodore Roosevelt, as acting secretary of the navy, to Admiral Dewey, cable of 1897, in Tuchman, The Proud Tower *(1966), p. 150.*

He immediately began to launch peremptory orders: distributing ships; ordering ammunition, which there is no means to move, to places where there is no means to store it; sending for Captain Barker to come on about the guns of the *Vesuvius* . . . sending messages to Congress for immediate legislation, authorizing the enlistment of an unlimited number of seamen; and ordering guns from the Navy Yard at Washington to New York . . . He has gone at things like a bull in a china shop.

Secretary of the U.S. Navy John D. Long, remarking on Roosevelt's one afternoon as acting secretary of the navy, 1897, in Tuchman, The Proud Tower *(1966), p. 148.*

Every boy and man, many of the girls, and some of the women, regard an afternoon or an evening at the Dime now and then as an indispensable part of their lives. The Dime is to them that the theatre, the opera, and the symphony are to the more fortunate classes in the community. It is the only means by which they can obtain the enjoyment that is derived from the imagination. That the craving is strong is shown by the crowded houses always to be seen at this resort.

Longtime Boston resident Frederick Haynes, describing the most popular theater in South Boston, 1898, in Hoogenboom and Hoogenboom, The Gilded Age *(1967), p. 116.*

It is worse than folly, aye, it is a crime, to lull ourselves into the fancy that we shall escape the duties which we owe to our people by becoming a nation of conquerors, disregarding the lessons of nearly a century and a quarter of our national existence as an independent, progressive, humane and peace-loving nation. We cannot with safety to ourselves, or justice to others keep the workers and the lovers of reform and simple justice divided, or divert their attention, and thus render them powerless to expose abuses and remedy existing injustice.

. . . A "foreign war as a cure for domestic discontent" has been the device of tyrants and false counselors from time immemorial, but it has always lead to a Waterloo, a Sedan, to certain decadence and often utter ruin. In our country we are perhaps too powerful to incur outside disaster; but we shall certainly court worse evils at home if we try to benumb the nation's sense of justice and love of right, and prevent it from striving earnestly to correct all proved errors.

. . . If we attempt to force upon the natives of the Philippines our rule, and compel them to conform to our more or less rigid mold of government, how many lives shall we take? Of course, they will seem cheap, because they are poor laborers. They will be members of the majority in the Philippines, but they will be ruled and killed at the convenience of the very small minority there, backed up by our armed land and sea forces. The dominant class in the islands will ease its conscience because the victims will be poor, ignorant and weak.

. . . When innocent men can be shot down on the public highway as they were in Lattimer, Pennsylvania, and Virden, Illinois, men of our own flesh and blood, men who help to make this homogenous nation great, because they dare ask for humane conditions at the hands of the moneyed class of our country, how much more difficult will it be to arouse any sympathy, and secure relief for the poor semi-savages in the Philippines, much less indignation at any crime against their inherent and natural rights to life, liberty and the pursuit of happiness?

Samuel Gompers, founder, American Federation of Labor, excerpt of a speech delivered at the Chicago Peace Jubilee, October 18, 1898. Available online at URL: http://www.ashp.cuny.edu/video/gompers.html.

How much has happened since I last heard from you! To say nothing of the Zola trial, we now have the

Cuban war! A curious episode of history, showing how a nation's ideals can be changed in the twinkling of an eye, by a succession of outward events partly accidental. It is possible that, without the explosion of the Maine, we should still be at peace, though, since the basis of the whole American attitude is the persuasion on the part of the people that the cruelty and misrule of Spain in Cuba call for her expulsion . . . it is hardly possible that peace could have been maintained indefinitely longer, unless Spain had gone out—a consummation hardly to be expected by peaceful means.

. . . The self-conscious feeling of our people has been entirely based in a sense of philanthropic duty, without which not a step would have been taken . . . once the excitement of action gets loose, the taxes levied, the victories achieved, etc., the old human instincts will get into play with all their old strength,

and the ambition and sense of mastery which our nation has will set up new demands.

William James, philosopher and psychologist, to Francois Pilon, letter of 1898, in Hoogenboom and Hoogenboom, The Gilded Age *(1967), pp. 180–181.*

We shall have Hawaii, of course, if not in one way, in another, and there is nothing in the special pleas of lawyers or the public quirks of other public men, that will prevent our people from having their own way.

Murat Halstead, imperialist associate of Theodore Roosevelt, 1898, in Campbell, Expansionism and Imperialism *(1970).*

We need Hawaii just as much and a good deal more than we did California. It is Manifest Destiny.

President William A. McKinley, 1898, in Tuchman, The Proud Tower *(1966), p. 155.*

I think . . . possibly the President could have worked the business without a war, but the current was too strong, the demagogues too numerous, and the fall elections too near.

Senator John Spooner (R-Wisconsin), on the annexation of Hawaii, 1898, in Degler, The Age of the Economic Revolution, 1876–1900 *(1977), p. 159.*

We are the conquering race. We must obey our blood and occupy new markets and if necessary new lands. . . . In the Almighty's infinite plan . . . debased civilizations and decaying races [disappear] before the higher civilization of the nobler and more virile types of man.

Albert J. Beveridge, expansionist, 1898, in Tuchman, The Proud Tower *(1966), p. 153.*

I would give anything if President McKinley would order the fleet to Havana tomorrow . . . the *Maine* was sunk by an act of dirty treachery on the part of the Spaniards.

Theodore Roosevelt, assistant secretary of the navy, of the Maine *affair, 1898, in Kelley,* The Shaping of the American Past *(1978), p. 469.*

About three months.

Alfred Thayer Mahan, naval historian, responding to a question about how long the war with Spain might last, 1898, in Tuchman, The Proud Tower *(1966), p. 151.*

Brother of author Henry James, William James was a philosopher and psychologist. *(Library of Congress)*

There is no question that you stand head and shoulders above the rest of us. You have given us just the suggestions we want.

Theodore Roosevelt, a member of the U.S. Naval War Board, responding to suggestions for a campaign in the Philippines, 1898, in Tuchman, The Proud Tower *(1966), p. 151.*

More than Ordinary interest attaches to the struggle between "Johnny" Powers, the Democratic political king of Chicago, and the forces of reform, headed by Miss Jane Addams, of Hull House. Powers is seeking re-election to the City Council from the notorious Nineteenth Ward, of which he has been the undisputed political boss for many years. Somewhat to his astonishment and consternation, the better element of the community in which he lives, spurred onward by the women of the Settlement, have organized a formidable combination which is fighting him with his own black record of misrepresentation and corruption.

. . . but now that he feels his throne tottering under him he has come out openly, threatening Miss Addams and her helpers with expulsion from his domain. "Hull House," he declared angrily in a recent interview, "will be driven from the ward and its leaders will be forced to shut up shop."

. . . Powers has been more than ordinarily successful as a ward boss. He is cool-headed, cunning, and wholly unscrupulous, and yet he possesses that effective gift known, for lack of a better name, as "good-fellowship" or "good-heartedness." Among his constituents he appears in his kingly aspects of unlimited power and benevolence. He impresses them with the primitive generosity which has turkeys to give away by thousands at Christmas-time, which elevates a faithful follower to a position on the city pay-roll in a single day, or discharges him with equal ease . . . The Nineteenth Ward is fertile soil for growing a ward boss. Its population consists of Italians, Polish and Russian Jews, Irish of the poorest class, and the off-scourings of a dozen other nationalities . . . In this community Miss Addams quietly took up her residence more than ten years ago. She and a few helpers lived simply in an old brick mansion standing well back from the street, the remnant of a better day. Her first work was to make the acquaintance of the people around her, and to welcome them on terms of equality in her home. Presently she established a kindergarten, a gymnasium, evening classes, clubs for young people and clubs for old people, and a day nursery where working women might leave their children. . . .

The streets and alleys of the ward were notoriously filthy, and the contractors habitually neglected them, not failing, however, to draw their regular payments from the city treasury. Miss Addams herself applied for the position of garbage inspector, and, to the astonishment of Powers and his retainers, received the appointment. Within two months the Nineteenth Ward was one of the cleanest in the city—and the contractors were squirming and complaining. . . .

A few weeks ago Powers appeared before the Civil Service Commission and demanded the discharge of Miss Johnson as garbage inspector, on the ground that she had been finding fault with his record as an Alderman and advising people of the ward to vote against him. . . . Miss Addams felt that . . . she could exert enough influence to make a strong campaign against the corrupt reign of Powers, even if she could not beat him. . . . But the cunning "Johnny" Powers was not to be outdone. . . . Some of the business men of the ward who signed their names in support of Armstrong's candidacy dropped away suddenly and became Powers men . . . The fight is on. Powers controls all of the election machinery and the police, and he will stoop to any of the treacheries known to corrupt politics . . . Hull House still hopes to accomplish his defeat. If it does not succeed, at least the residents of the ward will have had a stirring lesson in political morality, which will clear a way for success at another time.

Ray Stannard Baker, journalist, "Hull House and the Ward Boss," in Outlook, *March 26, 1898, pp. 769–771.*

You may fire when ready, Gridley.

Commodore George Dewey, giving the command to begin attacking the Spanish fleet, in Manila Bay, April 30, 1898, in Tuchman, The Proud Tower *(1966), p. 151.*

We must on no account let the islands go . . . The American flag is up and it must stay.

Senator Henry Cabot Lodge (R-Massachusetts), 1898, in Tuchman, The Proud Tower *(1966), p. 151.*

Admiral George Dewey, who defeated the Spanish fleet at Manila Bay in the Philippines, is shown here with his faithful companion Bob Dewey. *(Library of Congress)*

It has been a splendid little war, carried on with magnificent intelligence and spirit, favored by that Fortune which loves the brave.

John Hay, letter to Theodore Roosevelt, concerning the July 3, 1898, battle in the harbor of Santiago, the Philippines, in Degler, The Age of the Economic Revolution, 1876–1900, *pp. 161–162.*

It was a most happy-go-lucky expedition, run with real American optimism and readiness to take big chances, and with the spirit of a people who recklessly trust that it will come out all right in the end, and that the barely possible may not happen . . . As one of the generals on board said, 'This is God Almighty's war, and we are only His agents.' "

Richard Harding Davis, journalist and war correspondent, 1898, in Degler, The Age of the Economic Revolution, 1867–1900 *(1977), p. 161.*

Tell the President for Heaven's sake to send us every regiment and above all every battery possible. We have won so far at a heavy cost, but the Spaniards fight very hard and charging these intrenchments against modern rifles is terrible . . . We *must* have help—thousands of men, batteries, and *food* and ammunition.

Theodore Roosevelt, leader of the volunteer Rough Riders, 1898, in Ginger, Age of Excess *(1965), p. 203.*

War is harsh; it is attended by hardship and suffering; it means a vast expenditure of men and money. We may well pray for the coming of the day, promised in Holy Writ, when the swords shall be beaten into plowshares and the spears into pruning hooks; but universal peace cannot come until Justice is enthroned throughout the world. Jehovah deals with nations as He deals with men, and for both decrees that the wages of sin is death. Until the right has triumphed in every land and love reigns in every heart government must, as a last resort, appeal to force. As long as the oppressor is deaf to the voice of reason, so long must the citizen accustom his shoulder to the musket and his hand to the saber. . . . Our nation exhausted diplomacy in its efforts to secure a peaceable solution of the Cuban question, and only took up arms when it was compelled to choose between war and servile acquiescence in cruelties which would have been a disgrace to barbarism. History will vindicate the position taken by the United States in the war with Spain.

William Jennings Bryan, excerpt of a speech given at the Trans-Mississippi Exposition, Omaha, Nebraska, June 14, 1898. Available online at URL: http:// www.omaha.lib.ne.us/transmiss/bee/june14.html.

American character will be still better understood when the whole world clearly perceives that the purpose of the war is only to remove from our very doors this cruel and inefficient piece of medievalism which is one of the . . . scandals of the closing years of the century; for it is not a want of conquest . . . Once free, let [Cuba] govern itself . . .

Walter Hines Page, editor of Atlantic Monthly, *June 1898, in Tuchman,* The Proud Tower *(1966), p. 130.*

As long as we remain free from distant possessions we are impregnable against serious attack; yet, it is true,

Roosevelt (center, with suspenders) and his troops at the top of the hill they captured in the Battle of San Juan. *(Library of Congress)*

we have to consider what obligations may fall upon us of an international character requiring us to send our forces to points beyond our own territory. Up to this time we have disclaimed all intention to interfere with affairs beyond our own continent, and only claimed the right to watch over American interests according to the Monroe Doctrine, which is now firmly established. This carries with it serious responsibilities, no doubt, which we cannot escape. European nations must consult us upon territorial questions pertaining to our continent, but this makes no tremendous demand upon our military or naval forces. We are at home, as it were, near our base, and sure of the support of the power in whose behalf and on whose request we may act. If it be found

essential to possess a coaling-station at Puerto Rico for future possible, though not probable, contingencies, there is no insuperable objection. Neither would the control of the West Indies be alarming if pressed upon us by Britain, since the islands are small and the populations must remain insignificant and without national aspirations. Besides, they are upon our own shores, American in every sense. Their defense by us would be easy. No protest need be entered against such legitimate and peaceful expansion in our own hemisphere, should events work in that direction. I am no "Little" American, afraid of growth, either in population or territory, provided always that the new territory be American, and that it will produce Americans, and not foreign races bound in time to be false to the Republic in order to be true to themselves.

Andrew Carnegie, excerpts from "Distant Possessions: The Parting of the Ways," in the North American Review, *August 1898, p. 242.*

. . . act vigorously for the protection of Americans.

John Hay, secretary of state, to the U.S. foreign minister in China, 1898, in Campbell, Expansionism and Imperialism *(1970), p. 153.*

. . . unless a vigorous policy is pursued on the part of the United States Government, these markets will be eventually closed to our trade, as has recently been the case in Madagascar . . . We earnestly call attention to the above facts, and ask that our representatives at St. Petersburgh [*sic*] be instructed to give special attention to the subject.

Fifty-three U.S. manufacturers and exporters of cotton textiles, to Congress, expressing joint concern over Russia's apparent interest in restricting or monopolizing trade with China, letter of 1899, in Campbell, Expansionism and Imperialism *(1970), p. 155.*

The cry suddenly raised that this great country has become too small for us is too ridiculous to demand an answer, in view of the fact that our present population may be tripled and still have ample elbow-room, with resources to support many more. But we are told that our industries are gasping for breath; that we are

Secretary of State John Hay, who was instrumental in encouraging China's "open door" policy, spoke strongly in support of U.S. commercial interests in Asia. *(Library of Congress)*

suffering from over production; that our products must have new outlets, and that we need colonies and dependencies the world over to give us more markets. More markets? Certainly. But do we, civilized beings, indulge in the absurd and barbarous notion that we must own the countries with which we wish to trade? . . .

"But the Pacific Ocean," we are mysteriously told, "will be the great commercial battlefield of the future, and we must quickly use the present opportunity to secure our position on it. The visible presence of great power is necessary for us to get our share of the trade of China. Therefore, we must have the Philippines." Well, the China trade is worth having, although for a time out of sight the Atlantic Ocean will be an infinitely more important battlefield of commerce. . . . But does the trade of China really require that we should have the Philippines and make a great display of power to get our share? . . .

"But we must have coaling stations for our navy!" Well, can we not get as many coaling stations as we need without owning populous countries behind them that would entangle us in dangerous political responsibilities and complications? Must Great Britain own the whole of Spain in order to hold Gibraltar?

"But we must civilize those poor people!" Are we not ingenious and charitable enough to do much of their civilization without subjugating and ruling them by criminal aggression?

The rest of the pleas for imperialism consist mostly of those high-sounding catch-words of which a free people when about to decide a great question should be especially suspicious. We are admonished that it is time for us to become a "world power." Well, we are a world power now, and have been for many years. What is a world power? A power strong enough to make its voice listened to with deference by the world whenever it chooses to speak. Is it necessary for a world power, in order to be such, to have its finger in every pie? Must we have the Philippines in order to become a world power?

Carl Schurz, excerpts from a convocation address delivered at the University of Chicago, January 4, 1899. Available online at URL: http://www.wadsworth.com/ history_d/special_features/ext/ap/ chapter19/19.4.antiimp.html.

We are, of course, opposed to the dismemberment of that Empire [China], and we do not think that the public opinion of the United States would justify this Government in taking part on the great game of spoliation now going on. At the same time we are keenly alive to the importance of safeguarding our great commercial interests in that Empire and representatives there have orders to watch closely everything that may seem calculated to injure us, and to prevent it by energetic and timely representations.

Secretary of State John Hay, to the editor of the New York Sun, *1899, in Campbell,* Expansionism and Imperialism *(1970). Available online at URL: http://www.opgc.org/books/tpemp10p46.htm.*

If they become states on an equal footing with the other states they will not only be permitted to govern themselves as to their home concerns, but will take part in governing the whole republic, in governing us, by sending senators and representatives into our Congress to help make our laws, and by voting for president and vice-president to give our national government its executive. The prospect of the consequences which would follow the admission of the Spanish creoles and the negroes of the West India islands and of the Malays and Tagals of the Philippines to participation in the conduct of our government is so alarming that you instinctively pause before taking the step.

Carl Schurz, liberal Republican and former secretary of the interior, 1899, in "American Imperialism: An address opposing annexation of the Philippines, January 4, 1899," American Imperialism in 1898 *(1955), p. 79.*

Neither the people nor the institutions of the United States can ever occupy the Philippines. The American home cannot endure there, the town-meeting cannot exist.

David Starr Jordan, president of Stanford University, 1899, in Lest We Forget: An Address Delivered before the Graduating Class of 1898, *Leland Stanford University on May 25, 1898, in* Leland Stanford University Publications, *published by John J. Valentine, Esq. (August 10, 1898), p. 9.*

Civilization is, as it were, suffocated in the tropics.

David Starr Jordan, president of Stanford University, 1899, in Degler, The Age of the Economic Revolution *(1977), p. 164.*

We want to send the products of our farms, our factories, and our mines into every market of the world; make the foreign peoples familiar with our products; and the way to do that is to make them familiar with our flag.

President McKinley, discussing the nation's economy following the Spanish-American conflict, 1899, in Ginger, People on the Move *(1975), p. 205.*

. . . our yellow journals have abundant time in which to raise new monuments of capitols to the victories of Old Glory, and in which to extol the unrestrained eagerness of our brave soldiers . . .

. . . It is horrible, simply horrible. Surely there cannot be many born and bred Americans who, when they look at the bare fact of what we are doing, the fact taken all by itself, do not feel this . . .

. . . But these are passions that interfere with the reasonable settlement of any affair, and in this affair we have to deal with a factor altogether peculiar with our belief, namely, in a national destiny which must be "big" at any cost . . . We are to be missionaries of civilization, and to bear the white man's burden, painful as it often is.

William James, philosopher and psychologist, to the Boston Evening Transcript, *letter of March 1, 1899. Available online at URL: http://www.des. emory.edu/mfp/james.html.*

Before you go I would like to say just a word about the Philippine business. I have been criticized a good deal about the Philippines, but don't deserve it. The truth is I didn't want the Philippines, and when they came to us, as a gift from the gods, I did not know what to do with them. When the Spanish war broke out Dewey was at Hongkong [sic], and I ordered him to go to Manila and capture or destroy the Spanish fleet, and he had to; because, if defeated, he had no place to refit on that side of the globe, and if the Dons were victorious they would likely cross the Pacific and ravage our Oregon and California coasts. And so he had to destroy the Spanish fleet, and did it! But that was as far as I thought then.

When next I realized that the Philippines had dropped into our laps I confess I did not know what to do with them. I sought counsel from all sides—

Democrats as well as Republicans—but, got little help.

President William McKinley, to a delegation from the General Missionary Committee of the Methodist Episcopal Church, November 21, 1899, in Rusling, "Interview with President William McKinley," The Christian Advocate *January 22, 1903, p. 17.*

From a nation of shopkeepers we become a nation of warriors. We escape the menace and peril of socialism and agrarianism, as England has escaped them, by a policy of colonization and conquest. From a provincial huddle of petty sovereignties held together by a rope and sand we rise to the dignity and prowess of an imperial republic incomparably greater than Rome. It is true that we exchange domestic dangers for foreign dangers; but in every direction we multiply the opportunities of the people. We risk Caesarism, certainly; but even Caesarism is preferable to anarchism. We risk wars; but a man has but one time to die, and either in peace or war, he is not likely to die until his time comes . . . In short, anything is better than the pace we were going before these present forces were started into life. Already the young manhood of the country is as a goodly brand snatched from the burning, and given a perspective replete with noble deeds and elevating ideas.

Henry Watterson, editor of the Louisville Courier-Journal, *promoting U.S. expansion, 1899, in Kelley,* The Shaping of the American Past *(1978), pp. 474–475.*

Some say that our duty to the foreign residents in the Philippines requires us to annex the islands. If we admit this argument we not only exalt the interests of foreigners above the interests of natives, but place a higher estimate upon the wishes of foreigners residing in Manila than upon the welfare of our own people.

. . . The fact that the subject of imperialism is being discussed through the newspapers and magazines, as well as in Congress, is evidence that the work of education is still going on. The advocates of a colonial policy must convince the conservative element of the country, by clear and satisfactory proof, they cannot rely upon catch-words.

The "Who will haul down the flag?" argument has already been discarded; "Destiny" is not as "manifest" as it was a few weeks ago, and the argument of "duty" is being analyzed. The people are face to face with a grave public problem. They have not acted upon it yet, and they will not be frightened away from the calm consideration of it by the repetition of unsupported prophesies.

The battle of Manila, which brought loss to us and disaster to the Filipinos, has not rendered "forcible annexation" less repugnant to our Nation's "code of morality." If it has any effect at all it ought to emphasize the dangers attendant upon (if I may be permitted to quote from the President again) "criminal aggression." The Filipinos were guilty of inexcusable ignorance if they thought that they could prevent the ratification of the treaty by an attack upon the American lines, but no act of theirs can determine the permanent policy of the United States. Imperialism has been described as "The White Man's Burden," but, since it crushes the wealth-producer beneath an increasing weight of taxes, it might with more propriety be called The Poor Man's Load.

. . . If the Peace Commissioners had demanded a harbor and coaling station in the Philippines and had required Spain to surrender the rest of the land to the Filipinos, as she surrendered Cuba to the Cubans, we would not now be considering how to let go of the islands. If the sum of twenty millions had been necessary to secure Spain's release, the payment of the amount by the Filipinos might have been guaranteed by the United States.

. . . But the failure of the Peace Commissioners to secure for the Filipinos the same rights that were obtained for the Cubans, could have been easily remedied by a resolution declaring the nation's purpose to establish a stable and independent government.

. . . It is still possible for the Senate alone, or for the Senate and House together, to adopt such a resolution.

William Jennings Bryan, excerpts from "What Next?" quoted in the New York Journal, *February 12, 1899. Available online at URL: http://www. boondocksnet.com/ai/ai/bryan.html.*

We cannot sit huddled within our own borders and avow ourselves merely an assemblage of well-to-do hucksters who care nothing for what happens beyond. Such a policy would defeat even its own end; for as the nations grow to have ever wider and wider interests, and are brought into closer and closer contact, if we are to hold our own in the struggle for naval and commercial supremacy, we must build up our power without our own borders. We must build the isthmian canal, and we must grasp the points of vantage which will enable us to have our say in deciding the destiny of the oceans of the East and the West.

Theodore Roosevelt, excerpt from a speech given at a meeting of the Hamilton Club, Chicago, Illinois, April 10, 1899, in The Strenuous Life; Essays and Addresses *(1904), p. 9.*

The great foe of democracy now and in the near future is plutocracy. Every year that passes brings out this antagonism more distinctly. It is to be the social war of the twentieth century. In that war militarism, expansion and imperialism will all favor plutocracy. In the first place, war and expansion will favor jobbery, both in the dependencies and at home. In the second place, they will take away the attention of the people from what the plutocrats are doing. In the third place they will cause large expenditures of the people's money, the return for which will not go into the treasury but into the hands of a few schemers. In the fourth place, they will call for a large public debt and taxes, and these things especially tend to make men unequal, because any social burdens bear more heavily on the weak than on the strong, and so make the weak weaker and the strong stronger. Therefore expansion and imperialism are a grand onslaught on democracy.

William Graham Sumner, Yale University economist, speech to Phi Beta Kappa Society of Yale University, College Street Hall, New Haven, January 16, 1899, in Albert Galloway Keller, ed., War and Other Essays by William Graham Sumner *(1919), pp. 297–334. Available online at URL: http://www.libertystory.net/ LSDOCSUMNERCONQUESTUS.htm.*

Imperialism Condemned

1. That the Declaration of Independence asserts as fundamental and inviolable three classes of rights—of the individual to life, liberty and the pursuit of happiness, of the citizen to equality before the law, of the people to self-government.
2. That forcible annexation violates all of these rights, as was recognized by Congress when it solemnly disclaimed the intent to conquer territory, and by President McKinley when he said that such conducts as to Cuba would be "criminal aggression."
3. That the people of the Philippines ought to be free and independent; that they have committed no wrong against us; they in no wise menace our

safety; they ask us only to leave them in peace to the establishment of such government as to them may seem desirable. Even to threaten them with violence is, by our code, without excuse. To kill them, or order them to be killed, for upholding rights that in their place we should jealously defend against a foreign aggressor would be wanton murder.

Brooklyn Single Tax League, excerpts from a declaration regarding the Philippines, in the Brooklyn Citizen, *March 5, 1899, n.p.*

. . . I felt certain that you must be opposed to the mad folly, not to say crime, of Imperialism. A man possessing such clear discernment as your public career has given rare evidence of could not fail to see that Imperialism is the new treason which now confronts our republic; treason to those high ideals that have given us all the greatness and glory which we can rightly claim to among the nations of history.

. . . We in Massachusetts who love the old ideals of our republic hang our heads with shame when we see only one of our senators at Washington contending for these ideals . . . Hoar, [Senator George F. Hoar, R-Mass.] whom I have never had any use for until now, is standing up nobly against the treaty which treats for war rather than peace, and I only hope that he will "stick," as Sumner advised Stanton to. We Anti-Imperialists in Massachusetts have done what we could to stem the tide of McKinley's cussedness . . .

A. W. Stevens, writer, to Representative George W. Julian, letter of 1899, in Hoogenboom and Hoogenboom, The Gilded Age *(1967), p. 183.*

We have beaten Spain in a military conflict, but we are submitting to be conquered by her on the field of ideas and policies. Expansionism and imperialism are nothing but the old philosophies of national prosperity which have brought Spain to where she is now . . . They would have no court and no pomp; nor orders, or ribbons, or decorations, or titles. They would have no public debt. There was to be no grand diplomacy, because they intended to mind their own business, and not be involved in any of the intrigues to which European statesmen were accustomed. There was to be no balance of power and no "reason of state" to cost the life and happiness of citizens . . . It is by virtue of this conception of a commonwealth that the United States has stood for something unique and grand in the history of mankind, and that its people have been happy.

William Graham Sumner, excerpt of an address, "The Conquest of the United States by Spain," delivered to the Yale Chapter of Phi Beta Kappa, January 16, 1899, quoted in Ralph Raico, American Foreign Policy: The Turning Point, 1898–1919, *February 1, 1995. Available online at URL: http://www.independent.org/ newsroom/article.asp?id=1345.*

. . . [a] class poet, blazoning an empty race prejudice.

John Jay Chapman, reformer and friend of Henry Adams, on Rudyard Kipling, 1899, in Baltzell, The Protestant Establishment *(1966), p. 94.*

The ordinary "horseless carriage" is at present a luxury for the wealthy; and although its price will probably fall in the future, it will never, of course, come into as common use as the bicycle.

Literary Digest, report of October 1899.

The walking-stick serves the purpose of an advertisement that the bearer's hands are employed otherwise than in useful effort, and it therefore has utility as an evidence of leisure . . . The adoption of the cap and gown is one of the striking atavistic features and modern college life . . . The classics have scarcely lost in absolute value as a voucher of scholastic respectability; since for this purpose it is only necessary that the scholar should be able to put in evidence some learning which is conventionally recognized as evidence of wasted time.

Thorstein Veblen, in The Theory of the Leisure Class, *1899.*

Whether the Spanish war shall be known in history as a war for liberty or a war of conquest; whether the principles of self-government shall be strengthened or abandoned; whether this nation shall remain a homogenous republic or become a heterogenous empire—these questions must be answered by the American people—when they speak, and not until then, will destiny be revealed.

Destiny is not a matter of chance, it is a matter of choice; it is not a thing to be waited for, it is a thing to be achieved.

. . . If we embark upon a career of conquest no one can tell how many islands we may be able to seize or how many races we may be able to subjugate; neither can anyone estimate the cost, immediate and remote, to the nation's purse and to the nation's character, but whether we shall enter upon such a career is a question which the people have a right to decide for themselves.

William Jennings Bryan, Populist Party leader, speech in Washington, D.C., 1899, at a banquet given by the Virginia Democratic Association, in Bryan on Imperialism *(1900). Available online at URL: http://www.boondocksnet.com/ai/ailtexts/ bryan990222.html.*

Briefly, if I were czar, I would make no dividends upon the common stock; save all surplus and spend it for a hoop and cotton-tie mill, for wire and nail mills, for tube mills, for lines of boats upon the Lakes.

Andrew Carnegie, steel magnate, to mill managers, letter of July 11, 1900, in Josephson, Robber Barons *(1962), p. 421.*

. . . We need the worker in the fields of social and civic reform; the man who is keenly interested in some university settlement, some civic club or citizens' association which is striving to elevate the standard of life. We need clean, healthy newspapers, with clean, healthy criticism which shall be fearless and truthful. We need upright politicians, who will take the time and trouble, and who possess the capacity, to manage caucuses, conventions, and public assemblies.

. . . We need men who try to be their poorer brothers' keepers . . . men who work in charitable associations, or, what is even better, strive to get into touch with the wage-workers, to understand them, and to champion their cause when it is just. We need the sound and healthy idealist; the theoretic writer, preacher, or teacher; the Emerson or Phillips Brooks, who helps to create the atmosphere of enthusiasm and practical endeavor.

. . . In public life we need not only men who are able to work in and through their parties, but also upright, fearless, rational independents, who will deal impartial justice to all men and all parties . . . We need scholarly men, too—men who study all the difficult question of our political life from the standpoint both of practice and of theory; men who thus study trusts, or municipal government, or finance, or taxation, or civil-service reform, as the authors of the "Federalist" studied the problems of federal government.

Theodore Roosevelt, excerpts from The Strenuous Life; Essays and Addresses *(1904), pp. 57–58.*

If a man lies under oath or procures the lie of another under oath, if he perjures himself or suborns perjury, he is guilty under the statute law. Under the higher law, under the great law of morality and righteousness, he is precisely as guilty if, instead of lying in a court, he lies in a newspaper or on the stump; and in all probability the evil effects of his conduct are infinitely more wide-spread and more pernicious. The difference between perjury and mendacity is not in the least one of morals or ethics. It is simply one of legal forms.

Theodore Roosevelt, excerpt from "Character and Success," appearing in The Outlook, *March 31, 1900, from* The Strenuous Life; Essays and Addresses *(1904), pp. 129–130.*

I want to start with the declaration that a monopoly in private hands is indefensible from any standpoint, and intolerable. I make no exceptions to the rule. I do not divide monopolies in private hands into good monopolies and bad monopolies. There is no good monopoly in private hands. There can be no good monopoly in private hands until the Almighty sends us angels to preside over the monopoly. There may be a despot who is better than another despot, but there is no good despotism. One trust may be less harmful than another. One trust magnate may be more benevolent than another, but there is no good monopoly in private hands . . .

. . . the government that created must retain control, and . . . the man-made man must be admonished: "Remember now thy Creator in the days of thy youth"—and throughout thy entire life.

What government gives, the government can take away. What the government creates, it can control; and I insist that both the state government and the federal government must protect the God-made man from the man-made man.

William Jennings Bryan, Populist Party leader, to the Chicago Conference on Trusts, 1900, in Hoogenboom and Hoogenboom, The Gilded Age *(1967), pp. 40–41.*

I am convinced that the office of the President is not such a very difficult one to fill, his duties being mainly to execute the laws of Congress.

Admiral George Dewey, in the New York World, *April 4, 1900, in Bartlett,* Familiar Quotations, *12th Edition (1951), p. 638.*

In all this Cuban business there is one man stands out on the horizon of my memory like Mars at perihelion. When war broke out between Spain and the United States, it was very necessary to communicate quickly with the leader of the Insurgents. Garcia was somewhere in the mountain fastnesses of Cuba—no one knew where. No mail or telegraph could reach him. The President must secure his co-operation, and quickly.

What to do!

Someone said to the President, "There's a fellow by the name of Rowan will find Garcia for you, if anybody can."

Rowan was sent for and given a letter to be delivered to Garcia . . .

The point I wish to make is this: McKinley gave Rowan a letter to be delivered to Garcia; Rowan took the letter and did not ask, "Where is he at?" By the Eternal! There is a man whose form should be cast in deathless bronze and the statue placed in every college in the land. It is not book-learning young men need, nor instruction about this or that, but a stiffening of the vertebrae which will cause them to be loyal to a trust, to act promptly, concentrate their energies; do the thing—"carry a message to Garcia!". . .

. . . this incapacity for independent action, this moral stupidity, this infirmity of the will, this unwillingness to cheerfully catch hold and lift, are the things that put pure socialism so far into the future. If men will not act for themselves, what will they do when the benefit of their effort is for all? . . . We have recently been hearing much maudlin sympathy expressed for the "downtrodden denizen of the sweat shop" and the "homeless wanderer searching for honest employment," and with it all often go many hard words for the men in power.

Nothing is said about the employer who grows old before his time in a vain attempt to get frowsy ne'er-do-wells to do intelligent work; and his long patient striving with "help" that does nothing but loaf when his back is turned. In every store and factory there is a constant weeding-out process goin on. The

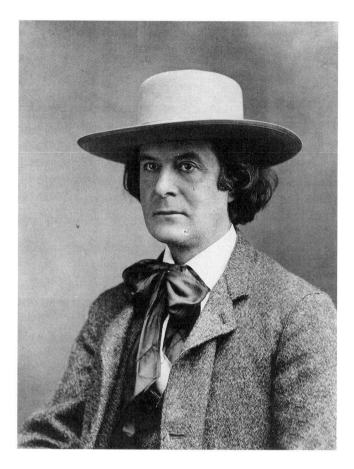

Elbert Hubbard's "A Message to García," based on an incident during the Spanish-American War, was published in the *Philistine* in March 1899. *(Library of Congress)*

employer is constantly sending away "help" that have shown their incapacity to further the interests of the business, and others are being taken on. No matter how good times are, this sorting continues, only if times are hard and work is scarce, this sorting is done finer—but out and forever out, the incompetent and unworthy go. It is the survival of the fittest. Self-interest prompts every employer to keep the best—those who can carry a message to Garcia . . .

Have I put the matter too strongly? Possibly I have; but when all the world has gone aslumming I wish to speak a word of sympathy for the man who succeeds—the man who, against great odds, has directed the efforts of others, and, having succeeded, finds there's nothing in it: nothing but bare board and clothes.

I have carried a dinner-pail and worked for a day's wages, and I have also been an employer of labor, and I know there is something to be said on both sides . . .

My heart goes out to the man who does his work when the "boss" is away, as well as when he is home. And the man who, when given a letter for Garcia, quietly takes the missive, without asking any idiotic questions, and with no lurking intention of chucking it into the nearest sewer, or of doing aught else but deliver it, never gets "laid off," nor has to go on strike for higher wages. Civilization is one long anxious search for just such individual . . . The world cries out for such; he is needed, and needed badly—the man who can carry a message to Garcia.

Elbert Hubbard, excerpts of his essay "A Message to García," originally published in the Philistine, *February, 1899. Available online at URL: http://www.roycrofter.com/garcia.htm.*

Beloved Comrades: We are met in our twenty-fourth annual convention in the historic city of Mankato . . .

. . . Today we are met to execute plans . . . to carry on our peaceful war for "God and Home and Native Land." There is an enemy in the land . . . the alcoholic liquor traffic. It is killing thousands annually and destroying hundreds of homes. We toil and sacrifice today to hasten the to-morrow when this enemy will be executed upon the gibbet of public opinion, and the liquor traffic be as dead as the Indians buried in yonder mound . . .

. . . My sisters, the King for whom we fight needs a standing army, ever ready for service. There is more hope in our own nation today than in any other. Yet we must strengthen our department of work among foreigners. We must meet the foreigners early and give them our customs before they have established theirs of the old world upon us.

Nothing must be too hard for us to do. Some of us must consecrate ourselves to learn a language and devote ourselves to a certain people. Nothing will so endear us to the homesick foreigner as to be able to speak to him in his mother tongue, understand the history of his nation and to teach him the language and history of the new. We have 6,000,000 Germans in our country today. We must have a regiment of American workers, who will learn the German language, love the German people, work among the German children and young people until we get them to love clear brains better than beer.

There must be others who for the love of country and dear humanity will learn the Scandinavian language and be real neighbors to the many people of this nationality who have come to make homes in America. Again others must learn the French and Italian and various dialects, even, that the truths of personal purity and total abstinence be taught to these who dwell among us.

We must feel it a duty to teach these people the English language to put them in sympathy with our purposes and our institutions. To the women who will do this will come great opportunities for service. Do not think I am discouraged in the warfare when I say these things. I came home feeling greater necessity to work in this cause than ever before and as determined as ever to give a life to this cause.

I firmly believe in the final triumph of total abstinence and the annihilation of the liquor business, but I also believe we shall work many years yet, must go deeper into science, lay still broader foundations, make greater sacrifices than we have yet made, must study to prepare ourselves for more effective service . . .

. . . Again and again has my blood boiled at the reports from missionaries and others of the hundreds of American saloons being established throughout our new possessions. According to the United States Bureau of Statistics dated July 20th, the export of malt liquors, brandy, whisky and other liquors for the Philippines altogether was three times greater in March than it was last November, although the government claims to have reduced the number of saloons.

And shame of shames, our military authorities in the Philippines have introduced that open and official sanction of prostitution which was prohibited in the British army through the protest and investigation of American women.

My sisters, our work for purity the coming year must engage our most earnest attention. The White Cross flag must follow the Red if our soldiers are to be protected from the most awful disease and death. The managing editor of one of the leading Manila daily papers, while riding past the national cemetery at Malate recently, said deliberately while pointing to the great number of fresh mounds: "Far more of our boys who are lying there met their death through bad women and drink than through the bullets of the Filipinos."

Bessie Laythe Scovell, excerpts from the President's Address, "Minutes of the Twenty-Fourth Annual Meeting of the W.C.T.U. of the State of Minnesota," 1900. Available online at URL: http://womhist. binghamton.edu/wctu/doc2.htm#D.

There is a homely adage which runs, 'Speak softly and carry a big stick, you will go far.'

Theodore Roosevelt, vice president–elect of the United States, speech at Minnesota State Fair, in Bartlett, Familiar Quotations, 12th Edition (1951), p. 734.

It receives and expends more money every year than any but the very greatest of the world's national governments; its debt is larger than that of many of the lesser nations of Europe; it absolutely controls the destinies of a population nearly as large as that of Maryland and Nebraska, and indirectly influences twice that number.

Ray Stannard Baker, journalist, in "What the United States Steel Corporation Really Is and How It Works," McClure's XVIII (November 1901), p. 10.

We face at this moment a most important question that of the future relations of the United States and Cuba. With our near neighbors we must remain close friends. The declaration of the purposes of this Government in the resolution of April 20, 1898, must be made good. Ever since the evacuation of the island by the army of Spain, the Executive, with all practicable speed, has been assisting its people in the successive steps necessary to the establishment of a free and independent government prepared to assume and perform the obligations of international law which now rest upon the United States under the treaty of Paris.

The convention elected by the people to frame a constitution is approaching the completion of its labors. The transfer of American control of the new government is of such great importance, involving an obligation resulting from our intervention and the treaty of peace, that I am glad to be advised by the recent act of Congress of the policy which the legislative branch of the Government deems essential to the best interests of Cuba and the United States. The principles which led to our intervention require that the fundamental law upon which the new government rests should be adapted to secure a government capable of performing the duties and discharging the functions of a separate nation, of observing its international obligations of protecting life and property, insuring order, safety, and liberty, and conforming to the established and historical policy of the United States in its relation to Cuba.

The peace which we are pledged to leave to the Cuban people must carry with it the guaranties of permanence. We became sponsors for the pacifica-tion of the island, and we remain accountable to the Cubans, no less than to our own country and peo-ple, for the reconstruction of Cuba as a free com-monwealth on abiding foundations of right, justice, liberty, and assured order. Our enfranchisement of the people will not be completed until free Cuba shall "be a reality, not a name; a perfect entity, not a hasty experiment bearing within itself the elements of failure."

President William McKinley, excerpt, Second Inaugural Address, Washington, D.C., March 4, 1901. Available online at URL: http://www.yale.edu/lawweb/ avalon/president/inaug/mckin2.htm.

Shall we? That is, shall we go on conferring our Civi-lizations upon the peoples that sit in darkness, or shall we give those poor things a rest? Shall we bang right ahead in our old-time, loud, pious way, and commit the new century to the game; or shall we sober up

and sit down and think it over first? Would it not be prudent to get our Civilization tools together, and see how much stock is left on hand in the way of Glass Beads and Theology, and Maxim Guns and Hymn Books, and Trade Gin and Torches of Progress and Enlightenment (patent adjustable ones, good to fire villages with, upon occasion), and balance the books, and arrive at the profit and loss, so that we may intel-ligently decide whether to continue the business or sell out the property and start a new Civilization Scheme on the proceedings?

Mark Twain, in the North American Review, *1901. Available online at URL: http://www. comw.org/qdr/1901twain.html.*

Good-bye, all. Good-bye. It is God's way. His will be done.

President William A. McKinley's dying words, September 14, 1901, in Kelley, The Shaping of the American Past *(1978), p. 476.*

APPENDIX A

Documents

1. The Constitution of the United States
2. Lincoln's proclamation of amnesty and reconstruction, December 8, 1863
3. Lincoln's second inaugural address, March 4, 1865
4. Johnson's proclamation of amnesty and reconstruction, May 29, 1865
5. Thirteenth Amendment to the U.S. Constitution, 1865
6. The Civil Rights Act, 1866
7. Fourteenth Amendment to the U.S. Constitution, 1868
8. The First Reconstruction Act, March 2, 1867
9. The Second Reconstruction Act, March 23, 1867
10. The Third Reconstruction Act, July 19, 1867
11. The Fourth Reconstruction Act, March 8, 1868
12. Letter on "The Great American Park of the Yosemite," written to the *New York Evening Post,* by Frederick Law Olmsted, 1868
13. Fifteenth Amendment to the U.S. Constitution, 1870
14. Act of Congress establishing Yellowstone National Park, March 1, 1872
15. National Woman Suffrage Association "People's Convention" platform, May 9, 1872
16. Excerpts from report of J. Q. Smith, commissioner of Indian Affairs, to the Department of the Interior, October 30, 1876
17. Bland-Allison Act (excerpt), February 28, 1878
18. An act to execute certain treaty stipulations relating to the Chinese, May 6, 1882
19. Pendleton Civil Service Reform Act, January 16, 1883
20. Dawes Act, February 8, 1887
21. Interstate Commerce Act, February 4, 1887
22. Sherman Anti-Trust Act, July 2, 1890
23. Sherman Silver Purchase Act, July 14, 1890
24. "The Solitude of Self" address to the House Judiciary Committee, by Elizabeth Cady Stanton, January 1892
25. The platform of the Populist Party, Omaha, Nebraska, 1892
26. The de Lôme Letter, ca. December 1897
27. Joint resolution to provide for annexing the Hawaiian Islands to the United States and letter of protest from Queen Liliuokalani of Hawaii to the House of Representatives, December 19, 1898
28. Treaty of peace between the United States and Spain, December 10, 1898
29. Platt Amendment, March 2, 1901

1. THE CONSTITUTION OF THE UNITED STATES

We the People of the United States, in Order to form a more perfect Union, establish Justice, insure domestic Tranquility, provide for the common defense, promote the general Welfare, and secure the Blessings of Liberty to ourselves and our Posterity, do ordain and establish this Constitution for the United States of America.

Article I.

SECTION 1. All legislative Powers herein granted shall be vested in a Congress of the United States, which shall consist of a Senate and House of Representatives.

SECTION 2. The House of Representatives shall be composed of Members chosen every second Year by the People of the several States, and the Electors in each State shall have the Qualifications requisite for Electors of the most numerous Branch of the State Legislature.

No Person shall be a Representative who shall not have attained to the Age of twenty five Years, and been seven Years a Citizen of the United States, and who shall not, when elected, be an Inhabitant of that State in which he shall be chosen.

Representatives and direct Taxes shall be apportioned among the several States which may be included within this Union, according to their respective Numbers, which shall be determined by adding to the whole Number of free Persons, including those bound to Service for a Term of Years, and excluding Indians not taxed, three fifths of all other Persons. The actual Enumeration shall be made within three Years after the first Meeting of the Congress of the United States, and within every subsequent Term of ten Years, in such Manner as they shall by Law direct. The Number of Representatives shall not exceed one for every thirty Thousand, but each State shall have at Least one Representative; and until such enumeration shall be made, the State of New Hampshire shall be entitled to chuse three, Massachusetts eight, Rhode-Island and Providence Plantations one, Connecticut five, New-York six, New Jersey four, Pennsylvania eight, Delaware one, Maryland six, Virginia ten, North Carolina five, South Carolina five, and Georgia three.

When vacancies happen in the Representation from any State, the Executive Authority thereof shall issue Writs of Election to fill such Vacancies.

The House of Representatives shall chuse their Speaker and other Officers; and shall have the sole Power of Impeachment.

SECTION 3. The Senate of the United States shall be composed of two Senators from each State, chosen by the Legislature thereof, for six Years; and each Senator shall have one Vote.

Immediately after they shall be assembled in Consequence of the first Election, they shall be divided as equally as may be into three Classes. The Seats of the Senators of the first Class shall be vacated at the Expiration of the second Year, of the second Class at the Expiration of the fourth Year, and of the third Class at the Expiration of the sixth Year, so that one third may be chosen every second Year; and if Vacancies happen by Resignation, or otherwise, during the Recess of the Legislature of any State, the Executive thereof may make temporary Appointments until the next Meeting of the Legislature, which shall then fill such Vacancies.

No Person shall be a Senator who shall not have attained to the Age of thirty Years, and been nine Years a Citizen of the United States, and who shall not, when elected, be an Inhabitant of that State for which he shall be chosen.

The Vice President of the United States shall be President of the Senate, but shall have no Vote, unless they be equally divided.

The Senate shall chuse their other Officers, and also a President pro tempore, in the Absence of the Vice President, or when he shall exercise the Office of President of the United States.

The Senate shall have the sole Power to try all Impeachments. When sitting for that Purpose, they shall be on Oath or Affirmation. When the President of the United States is tried, the Chief Justice shall preside: And no Person shall be convicted without the Concurrence of two thirds of the Members present.

Judgment in Cases of Impeachment shall not extend further than to removal from Office, and disqualification to hold and enjoy any Office of honor, Trust or Profit under the United States: but the Party convicted shall nevertheless be liable and subject to Indictment, Trial, Judgment and Punishment, according to Law.

SECTION 4. The Times, Places and Manner of holding Elections for Senators and Representatives, shall be prescribed in each State by the Legislature thereof; but the Congress may at any time by Law make or alter such Regulations, except as to the Place of chusing Senators.

The Congress shall assemble at least once in every Year, and such Meeting shall be on the first Monday in December, unless they shall by Law appoint a different Day.

Section 5. Each House shall be the Judge of the Elections, Returns and Qualifications of its own Members, and a Majority of each shall constitute a Quorum to do Business; but a smaller Number may adjourn from day to day, and may be authorized to compel the Attendance of absent Members, in such Manner, and under such Penalties as each House may provide.

Each House may determine the Rules of its Proceedings, punish its Members for disorderly Behaviour, and, with the Concurrence of two thirds, expel a Member.

Each House shall keep a Journal of its Proceedings, and from time to time publish the same, excepting such Parts as may in their Judgment require Secrecy; and the Yeas and Nays of the Members of either House on any question shall, at the Desire of one fifth of those Present, be entered on the Journal.

Neither House, during the Session of Congress, shall, without the Consent of the other, adjourn for more than three days, nor to any other Place than that in which the two Houses shall be sitting.

Section 6. The Senators and Representatives shall receive a Compensation for their Services, to be ascertained by Law, and paid out of the Treasury of the United States. They shall in all Cases, except Treason, Felony and Breach of Peace, be privileged from Arrest during their Attendance at the Session of their respective Houses, and in going to and returning from the same; and for any Speech or Debate in either House, they shall not be questioned in any other Place.

No Senator or Representative shall, during the Time for which he was elected, be appointed to any civil Office under the Authority of the United States, which shall have been created, or the Emoluments whereof shall have been increased during such time; and no Person holding any Office under the United States, shall be a Member of either House during his Continuance in Office.

Section 7. All Bills for raising Revenue shall originate in the House of Representatives; but the Senate may propose or concur with amendments as on other Bills.

Every Bill which shall have passed the House of Representatives and the Senate, shall, before it become a Law, be presented to the President of the United States; If he approve he shall sign it, but if not he shall return it, with his Objections to that House in which it shall have originated, who shall enter the Objections at large on their Journal, and proceed to reconsider it. If after such Reconsideration two thirds of that House shall agree to pass the Bill, it shall be sent, together with the Objections, to the other House, by which it shall likewise be reconsidered, and if approved by two thirds of that House, it shall become a Law. But in all such Cases the Votes of both Houses shall be determined by Yeas and Nays, and the Names of the Persons voting for and against the Bill shall be entered on the Journal of each House respectively. If any Bill shall not be returned by the President within ten Days (Sundays excepted) after it shall have been presented to him, the Same shall be a Law, in like Manner as if he had signed it, unless the Congress by their Adjournment prevent its Return, in which Case it shall not be a Law.

Every Order, Resolution, or Vote to which the Concurrence of the Senate and House of Representatives may be necessary (except on a question of Adjournment) shall be presented to the President of the United States; and before the Same shall take Effect, shall be approved by him, or being disapproved by him, shall be repassed by two thirds of the Senate and House of Representatives, according to the Rules and Limitations prescribed in the Case of a Bill.

Section 8. The Congress shall have Power To lay and collect Taxes, Duties, Imposts and Excises, to pay the Debts and provide for the common Defence and general Welfare of the United States; but all Duties, Imposts and Excises shall be uniform throughout the United States;

To Borrow Money on the credit of the United States;

To regulate Commerce with foreign Nations, and among the several States, and with the Indian Tribes;

To establish an uniform Rule of Naturalization, and uniform Laws on the subject of Bankruptcies throughout the United States;

To coin Money, regulate the Value thereof, and of foreign Coin, and fix the Standard of Weights and Measures;

To provide for the Punishment of counterfeiting the Securities and current Coin of the United States;

To establish Post Offices and post Roads;

To promote the Progress of Science and useful Arts, by securing for limited Times to Authors and Inventors the exclusive Right to their respective Writings and Discoveries;

To constitute Tribunals inferior to the supreme Court;

To define and punish Piracies and Felonies committed on the high Seas, and Offences against the Law of Nations;

To declare War, grant Letters of Marque and Reprisal, and make Rules concerning Captures on Land and Water;

To raise and support Armies, but no Appropriation of Money to that Use shall be for a longer Term than two Years;

To provide and maintain a Navy;

To make Rules for the Government and Regulations of the land and naval Forces;

To provide for calling forth the Militia to execute the Laws of the Union, suppress Insurrections and repel Invasions;

To provide for organizing, arming, and disciplining the Militia, and for governing such Part of them as may be employed in the Service of the United States, reserving to the States respectively, the Appointment of the Officers, and the Authority of training the Militia according to the discipline prescribed by Congress;

To exercise exclusive Legislation in all Cases whatsoever, over such District (not exceeding ten Miles square) as may, by Cession of Particular States, and the Acceptance of Congress, become the Seat of the Government of the United States, and to exercise like Authority over all Places purchased by the Consent of the Legislature of the State in which the Same shall be for the Erection of Forts, Magazines, Arsenals, dock-Yards, and other needful Buildings;—And

To make all Laws which shall be necessary and proper for carrying into Execution the foregoing Powers, and all other Powers vested by this Constitution in the Government of the United States, or in any Department or Officer thereof.

SECTION 9. The Migration or Importation of such Persons as any of the States now existing shall think proper to admit, shall not be prohibited by the Congress prior to the Year one thousand eight hundred and eight, but a Tax or duty may be imposed on such Importation, not exceeding ten dollars for each Person.

The Privilege of the Writ of Habeas Curpus shall not be suspended, unless when in Cases of Rebellion or Invasion the public Safety may require it.

No Bill of Attainder or ex post facto Law shall be passed.

No Capitation, or other direct, Tax shall be laid, unless in Proportion to the Census or Enumeration herein before directed to be taken.

No Tax or Duty shall be laid on Articles exported from any State.

No Preference shall be given by any Regulation of Commerce or Revenue to the Ports of one State over those of another; nor shall Vessels bound to, or from, one State, be obliged to enter, clear, or pay Duties in another.

No Money shall be drawn from the Treasury, but in Consequence of Appropriations made by Law; and a regular Statement and Account of the Receipts and Expenditures of all public Money shall be published from time to time.

No title of Nobility shall be granted by the United States: And no Person holding any Office of Profit or Trust under them, shall, without the Consent of Congress, accept any present, Emolument, Office, or Title, of any kind whatever, from any King, Prince, or foreign State.

SECTION 10. No State shall enter into any Treaty, Alliance, or Confederation; grant Letters of Marque and Reprisal; coin Money; emit Bills of Credit; make any Thing but gold and silver Coin a Tender in Payment of Debts; pass any Bill of Attainder, ex post facto Law, or Law impairing the Obligation of Contracts, or grant any Title of Nobility.

No State shall, without the Consent of the Congress, lay any Imposts or Duties on Imports or Exports, except what may be absolutely necessary for executing its inspection Laws: and the net Produce of all Duties and Imposts, laid by any State on Imports or Exports, shall be for the Use of the Treasury of the United States; and all such Laws shall be subjected to the Revision and Controul of the Congress.

No State shall, without the Consent of Congress, lay any Duty of Tonnage, keep Troops, or Ships of War in time of Peace, enter into any Agreement or Compact with another State, or with a foreign Power, or engage in War, unless actually invaded, or in such imminent Danger as will not admit of delay.

Article II.

SECTION 1. The executive Power shall be vested in a President of the United States of America. He shall hold his Office during the Term of four Years, and, together with the Vice President, chosen for the same term, be elected, as follows

Each State shall appoint, in such Manner as the Legislature thereof may direct, a Number of Electors, equal to the whole Number of Senators and Representatives to which the State may be entitled in the Congress: but no Senator or Representative, or Person holding an Office of Trust or Profit under the United States, shall be appointed an Elector.

The Electors shall meet in their respective States, and vote by Ballot for two Persons, of whom one at least shall not be an Inhabitant of the same State with themselves. And they shall make a List of all the Persons voted for, and of the Number of Votes for each; which List they shall sign and certify, and transmit sealed to the Seat of the Government of the United States, directed to the President of the Senate. The President of the Senate shall, in the Presence of the Senate and House of Representatives, open all the Certificates, and the Votes shall then be counted. The Person having the greatest Number of Votes shall be the President, if such Number be a Majority of the whole Number of Electors appointed, and if there be more than one who have such Majority, and have an equal Number of Votes, then the House of Representatives shall immediately chuse by Ballot one of them for President: and if no Person have a Majority, then from the five highest on the List the said House shall in like Manner chuse the President. But in chusing the President, the Votes shall be taken by States, the Representation from each State having one Vote; a quorum for this Purpose shall consist of a Member or Members from two thirds of the States, and a Majority of all the States shall be necessary to a Choice. In every Case, after the Choice of the President, the Person having the greatest Number of Votes of the Electors shall be the Vice President. But if there should remain two or more who have equal Votes, the Senate shall chuse from them by Ballot the Vice President.

The Congress may determine the Time of chusing the Electors, and the Day on which they shall give their Votes; which Day shall be the same throughout the United States.

No Person except a natural born Citizen, or a Citizen of the United States, at the time of Adoption of this Constitution, shall be eligible to the Office of President; neither shall any Person be eligible to that Office who shall not have attained to the Age of thirty five Years, and been fourteen Years a Resident within the United States.

In Case of the Removal of the President from Office, or of his Death, Resignation, or Inability to discharge the Powers and Duties of the said Inability to discharge the Powers and Duties of the said Office, the Same shall devolve on the Vice President, and the Congress may by Law provide for the Case of Removal, Death, Resignation or Inability, both of the President and Vice President, declaring what Officer shall then act as President, and such Officer shall act accordingly, until the Disability be removed, or a President shall be elected.

The President shall, at stated Times, receive for his Services, a Compensation, which shall neither be increased nor diminished during the Period for which he shall have been elected, and he shall not receive within that Period any other Emolument from the United States, or any of them.

Before he enter on the Execution of his Office, he shall take the following Oath or Affirmation:—"I do solemnly swear (or affirm) that I will faithfully execute the Office of President of the United States, and will to the best of my Ability, preserve, protect and defend the Constitution of the United States."

SECTION 2. The President shall be Commander in Chief of the Army and Navy of the United States, and of the Militia of the several States, when called into the actual Service of the United States; he may require the Opinion in writing, of the principal Officer in each of the executive Departments, upon any Subject relating to the Duties of their respective Offices, and he shall have Power to grant Reprieves and Pardons for Offences against the United States, except in Cases of Impeachment.

He shall have Power, by and with the Advice and Consent of the Senate, to make Treaties, provided two thirds of the Senators present concur; and he shall nominate, and by and with the Advice and Consent of the Senate; shall appoint Ambassadors, other public Ministers and Consuls, Judges of the supreme Court, and all other Offices of the United States, whose Appointments are not herein otherwise provided for, and which shall be established by Law: but the Congress may by Law vest the Appointment of such inferior Officers, as they think proper, in the President alone, in the Courts of Law, or in the Heads of Departments.

The President shall have Power to full up all Vacancies that may happen during the Recess of the Senate, by granting Commissions which shall expire at the End of their next Session.

SECTION 3. He shall from time to time give to the Congress Information of the State of the Union, and recommend to their Consideration such Measures as he shall judge necessary and expedient; he may, on extraordinary Occasions, convene both Houses, or either of them, and in Case of Disagreement between them, with Respect to the Time of Adjournment, he may adjourn them to such Time as he shall think proper; he shall receive Ambassadors and other public Ministers; he shall take care that the Laws be faithfully executed, and shall Commission all the Officers of the United States.

SECTION 4. The President, Vice President and all civil Officers of the United States, shall be removed from Office on Impeachment for, and Conviction of, Treason, Bribery, or other High Crimes and Misdemeanors.

Article III.

SECTION 1. The Judicial Power of the United States, shall be vested in one supreme Court, and in such inferior Courts as the Congress may from time to time ordain and establish. The Judges, both of the supreme and inferior Courts, shall hold their Offices during good Behaviour, and shall, at stated Times, receive for their Services a Compensation, which shall not be diminished during their Continuance in Office.

SECTION 2. The judicial Power shall extend to all Cases, in Law and Equity, arising under this Constitution, the Laws of the United States, and Treaties made, or which shall be made, under their Authority;—to all Cases affecting Ambassadors, other public Ministers and Consuls;—to all Cases of admiralty and maritime Jurisdiction;—to Controversies to which the United States shall be a Party;—to Controversies between two or more States;—between a State and Citizens of another State;—between Citizens of different States;—between Citizens of the same State claiming Lands under Grants of different States, and between a State, or the Citizens thereof, and foreign States, Citizens or Subjects.

In all Cases affecting Ambassadors, other public Ministers and Consuls, and those in which a State

shall be Party, the supreme Court shall have original Jurisdiction. In all the other Cases before mentioned, the supreme Court shall have appellate Jurisdiction, both as to Law and Fact, with such Exceptions, and under such Regulations as the Congress shall make.

The Trial of all Crimes, except in Cases of Impeachment, shall be by Jury; and such Trial shall be held in the State where the said Crimes shall have been committed; but when not committed within any State, the Trial shall be at such a Place or Places as the Congress may by Law have directed.

SECTION 3. Treason against the United States, shall consist only in levying War against them, or in adhering to their Enemies, giving them Aid and Comfort. No Person shall be convicted of Treason unless on the Testimony of two Witnesses to the same overt Act, or on Confession in open Court.

The Congress shall have Power to declare the Punishment of Treason, but no Attainder of Treason shall work Corruption of Blood, or Forfeiture except during the Life of the Person attained.

Article IV.

SECTION 1. Full Faith and Credit shall be given in each State to the public Acts, Records, and judicial Proceedings of every other State. And the Congress may by general Laws prescribe the Manner in which such Acts, Records and Proceedings shall be proved, and the Effect thereof.

SECTION 2. The Citizens of each State shall be entitled to all Privileges and Immunities of Citizens in the several States.

A Person charged in any State with Treason, Felony, or other Crime, who shall flee from Justice, and be found in another State, shall on Demand of the executive Authority of the State from which he fled, be delivered up, to be removed to the State having Jurisdiction of the Crime.

No Person held to Service or Labour in one State, under the Laws thereof, escaping into another, shall, in Consequence of any Law or Regulation therein, be discharged from such Service or Labour, but shall be delivered up on Claim of the Party to whom such Service or Labour may be due.

SECTION 3. New States may be admitted by the Congress into this Union; but no new State shall be formed or erected within the Jurisdiction of any other State; nor any State be formed by the Junction of two or more States, or Parts of States, without the

Consent of the Legislatures of the States concerned as well as of the Congress.

The Congress shall have Power to dispose of and make all needful Rules and Regulations respecting the Territory or other Property belonging to the United States; and nothing in this Constitution shall be so construed as to Prejudice any Claims of the United States, or of any particular State.

SECTION 4. The United States shall guarantee to every State in this Union a Republican Form of Government, and shall protect each of them against Invasion; and on Application of the Legislature, or of the Executive (when the Legislature cannot be convened) against domestic Violence.

Article V.

The Congress, whenever two thirds of both Houses shall deem it necessary, shall propose Amendments to this Constitution, or, on the Application of the Legislatures of two thirds of the several States, shall call a Convention for proposing Amendments, which, in either Case, shall be valid to all Intents and Purposes, as Part of this Constitution, when ratified by the Legislatures of three fourths of the several States, or by Conventions in three fourths thereof, as the one or the other Mode of Ratification may be proposed by the Congress; Provided that no Amendment which may be made prior to the Year One thousand eight hundred and eight shall in any Manner affect the first and fourth Clauses in the Ninth Section of the first Article; and that no State, without its Consent, shall be deprived of its equal Suffrage in the Senate.

Article VI.

All Debts contracted and Engagements entered into, before the Adoption of this Constitution shall be as valid against the United States under this Constitution, as under the Confederation.

This Constitution, and the Laws of the United States which shall be made in Pursuance thereof; and all Treaties made, or which shall be made, under the Authority of the United States, shall be the supreme Law of the Land; and the Judges in every State shall be bound thereby, any Thing in the Constitution or Laws of any State to the Contrary notwithstanding.

The Senators and Representatives before mentioned, and the Members of the several State Legislatures, and all executive and judicial Officers, both of the United States and of the several States, shall be bound by Oath or Affirmation, to support this Constitution; but no religious Test shall ever be required as a Qualification to any Office or public Trust under the United States.

Article VII.

The Ratification of the Conventions of nine States, shall be sufficient for the Establishment of this Constitution between the States so ratifying the Same. Done in Convention by the Unanimous Consent of the States present the Seventeenth Day of September in the Year of our Lord one thousand seven hundred and Eighty seven and the Independence of the United States of America the Twelfth IN WITNESS WHEREOF We have hereunto subscribed our Names,

New Hampshire	John Langdon
	Nicholas Gilman
Massachusetts	Nathaniel Gorham
	Rufus King
Connecticut	Wm. Saml. Johnson
	Roger Sherman
New York	Alexander Hamilton
New Jersey	Wil.: Livingston
	David Brearley.
	Wm. Paterson.
	Jona. Dayton
Pennsylvania	B Franklin
	Thomas Mifflin
	Robt Morris
	Geo. Clymer
	Thos. FitzSimons
	Jared Ingersoll
	James Wilson
	Gouv Morris
Delaware	Geo: Read
	Gunning Bedford jun
	John Dickinson
	Richard Bassett
	Jaco: Broom
Maryland	James McHenry
	Dan of St Thos. Jenifer
	Danl Carroll
Virginia	John Blair—
	James Madison Jr.
North Carolina	Wm. Blount
	Richd. Dobbs Spaight.
	Hu Williamson
South Carolina	J. Rutledge
	Charles Cotesworth Pinckney

Charles Pinckney
Pierce Butler.
Georgia   William Few
Abr Baldwin

In Convention Monday, September 17th 1787.
Present
The States of
New Hampshire, Massachusetts, Connecticut, Mr. Hamilton from New York, New Jersey, Pennsylvania, Delaware, Maryland, Virginia, North Carolina, South Carolina and Georgia.
Resolved,

That the preceeding Constitution be laid before the United States in Congress assembled, and that it is the Opinion of this Convention, that it should afterwards be submitted to a Convention of Delegates, chosen in each State by the People thereof, under the recommendation of its Legislature, for their Assent and Ratification; and that each Convention assenting to, and ratifying the Same, should give Notice thereof to the United States in Congress assembled. Resolved, That it is the Opinion of this Convention, that as soon as the Conventions of nine States shall have ratified this Constitution, the United States in Congress assembled should fix a Day on which the Electors should assemble to vote for the President, and the Time and Place for commencing Proceedings under this Constitution. That after such Publication the Electors should be appointed, and the Senators and Representatives elected: That the Electors should meet on the Day fixed for the Election of the President, and should transmit their Votes certified, signed, sealed and directed, as the Constitution requires, to the Secretary of the United States in Congress assembled, that the Senators and representatives should convene at the Time and Place assigned; that the Senators should appoint a President of the Senate, for the sole Purpose of receiving, opening and counting the Votes for President; and that after he shall be chosen, the Congress, together with the President, should, without Delay, proceed to execute this Constitution.

By the Unanimous Order of the Convention.
Go. Washington—Presidt.
W. Jackson Secretary.

Amendment I.

Congress shall make no law respecting an establishment of religion, or prohibiting the free exercise thereof; or abridging the freedom of speech, or of the press; or the right of the people peaceably to assemble, and to petition the Government for a redress of grievances.

Amendment II.

A well regulated Militia, being necessary to the security of a free State, the right of the people to keep and bear Arms, shall not be infringed.

Amendment III.

No Soldier shall, in time of peace, be quartered in any house, without the consent of the Owner, nor in time of war, but in a manner to be prescribed by law.

Amendment IV.

The right of the people to be secure in their persons, houses, papers, and effects, against unreasonable searches and seizures, shall not be violated, and no Warrants shall issue, but upon probable cause, supported by Oath or affirmation, and particularly describing the place to be searched, and the persons or things to be seized.

Amendment V.

No person shall be held to answer for a capital, or otherwise infamous crime, unless on a presentment or indictment of a Grand Jury, except in cases arising in the land or naval forces, or in the Militia, when in actual service in time of War or public danger; nor shal any person be subject for the same offence to be twice put in jeopardy of life or limb; nor shall be compelled in any criminal case to be a witness against himself, nor be deprived of life, liberty, or property, without due process of law; nor shall private property be taken for public use, without just compensation.

Amendment VI.

In all criminal prosecutions, the accused shall enjoy the right to a speedy and public trial, by an impartial jury of the State and district wherein the crime shall have been committed, which district shall have been previously ascertained by law, and to be informed of the nature and cause of the accusation; to be confronted with the witnesses against him; to have compulsory process for obtaining witnesses in his favor, and to have the Assistance of Counsel for his defence.

Amendment VII.

In Suits at common law, where the value in controversy shall exceed twenty dollars, the right of trial by jury shall be preserved, and no fact tried by a jury, shall be otherwise reexamined in any Court of the United States, than according to the rules of the common law.

Amendment VIII.

Excessive bail shall not be required, nor excessive fines imposed, nor cruel and unusual punishment inflicted.

Amendment IX.

The enumeration in the Constitution, of certain rights, shall not be construed to deny or disparage others retained by the people.

Amendment X.

The powers not delegated to the United States by the Constitution, nor prohibited by it to the States, are reserved to the States respectively, or to the people.

Amendment XI.

(Adopted January 8, 1798)

The Judicial power of the United States shall not be construed to extend to any suit in law or equity, commenced or prosecuted against one of the United States by Citizens of another State, or by Citizens or Subjects of any Foreign State.

Amendment XII.

(Adopted September 25, 1804)

The Electors shall meet in their respective states and vote by ballot for President and Vice-President, one of whom, at least, shall not be an inhabitant of the same state with themselves; they shall name in their ballots the person voted for as President, and in distinct ballots the person voted for as Vice-President, and they shall make distinct lists of all persons voted for as President, and of all persons voted for as Vice-President, and of the number of votes for each, which lists they shall sign and certify, and transmit sealed to the seat of the government of the United States, directed to the President of the Senate;—The President of the Senate shall, in presence of the Senate and House of Representatives, open all the certificates and the votes shall then be counted;—The person having the greatest number of votes for President, shall be the President, if such number be a majority of the whole number of Electors appointed; and if no person have such majority, then from the persons having the highest numbers not exceeding three on the list of those

voted for as President, the House of Representatives shall choose immediately, by ballot, the President. But in choosing the President, the votes shall be taken by states, the representation from each state having one vote; a quorum for this purpose shall consist of a member or members from two-thirds of the states, and a majority of all the states shall be necessary to a choice. And if the House of Representatives shall not choose a President whenever the right of choice shall devolve upon them, before the fourth day of March next following, then the Vice-President shall act as President, as in the case of the death or other constitutional disability of the President.—The person having the greatest number of votes as Vice-President, shall be the Vice-President, if such number be a majority of the whole number of Electors appointed, and if no person have a majority, then from the two highest numbers on the list, the Senate shall choose the Vice-President; a quorum for the purpose shall consist of two-thirds of the whole number of Senators, and a majority of the whole number shall be necessary to a choice. But no person constitutionally ineligible to the office of President shall be eligible to that of Vice-President of the United States.

Amendment XIII.

(Adopted December 18, 1865)

SECTION 1. Neither slavery nor involuntary servitude, except as a punishment for crime whereof the party shall have been duly convicted, shall exist within the United States, or any place subject to their jurisdiction.

SECTION 2. Congress shall have power to enforce this article by appropriate legislation.

Amendment XIV.

(Adopted July 28, 1868)

SECTION 1. All persons born or naturalized in the United States and subjects to the jurisdiction thereof, are citizens of the United States and of the State wherein they reside. No State shall make or enforce any law which shall abridge the privileges or immunities of citizens of the United States; nor shall any State deprive any person of life, liberty, or property, without due process of law; nor deny to any person within its jurisdiction the equal protection of the laws.

SECTION 2. Representatives shall be apportioned among the several States according to their respective numbers, counting the whole number of persons in each State, excluding Indians not taxed. But when the right to vote at any election for the choice of electors for President and Vice-President of the United States, Representatives in Congress, the Executive and Judicial officers of a State, or the members of the Legislature thereof, is denied to any of the male inhabitants of such State, being twenty-one years of age, and citizens of the United States, or in any way abridged, except for participation in rebellion, or other crime, the basis of representation therein shall be reduced in the proportion which the number of such male citizens shall bear to the whole number of male citizens twenty-one years of age in such State.

SECTION 3. No person shall be a Senator or Representative in Congress, or elector of President and Vice-President, or hold any office, civil or military, under the United States, or under any State, who, having previously taken an oath, as a member of Congress, or as an officer of the United States, or as a member of any State legislature, or as an executive or judicial officer of any State, to support the Constitution of the United States, shall have engaged in insurrection or rebellion against the same, or given aid or comfort to the enemies thereof. But Congress may by a vote of two-thirds of each House, remove such disability.

SECTION 4. The validity of the public debt of the United States, authorized by law, including debts incurred for payment of pensions and bounties for services in suppressing insurrection or rebellion, shall not be questioned. But neither the United States nor any State shall assume or pay any debt or obligation incurred in aid of insurrection or rebellion against the United States, or any claim for the loss or emancipation of any slave; but all such debts, obligations and claims shall be held illegal and void.

SECTION 5. The Congress shall have power to enforce, by appropriate legislation, the provisions of this article.

Amendment XV.
(Adopted March 30, 1870)

SECTION 1. The right of citizens of the United States to vote shall not be denied or abridged by the United States or by any State on account of race, color, or previous condition of servitude.

SECTION 2. The Congress shall have power to enforce this article by appropriate legislation.

Amendment XVI.
(Adopted February 25, 1913)

The Congress shall have power to lay and collect taxes on incomes, from whatever source derived, without apportionment among the several States, and without regard to any census or enumeration.

Amendment XVII.
(Adopted May 13, 1913)

SECTION 1. The Senate of the United States shall be composed of two Senators from each State, elected by the people thereof, for six years; and each Senator shall have one vote. The electors in each State shall have the qualifications requisite for electors of the most numerous branch of the State legislatures.

SECTION 2. When vacancies happen in the representation of any State in the Senate, the executive authority of such State shall issue writs of election to fill such vacancies: Provided, That the legislature of any State may empower the executive thereof to make temporary appointments until the people fill the vacancies by election as the legislature may direct.

SECTION 3. This amendment shall not be so construed as to affect the election or term of any Senator chosen before it becomes valid as part of the Constitution.

Amendment XVIII.
(Adopted January 29, 1919)

SECTION 1. After one year from ratification of this article the manufacture, sale, or transportation of intoxicating liquors within, the importation thereof into, or the exportation thereof from the United States and all territory subject to the jurisdiction thereof for beverage purposes is hereby prohibited.

SECTION 2. The Congress and the several States shall have concurrent power to enforce this article by appropriate legislation.

SECTION 3. This article shall be inoperative unless it shall have been ratified as an amendment to the Constitution by the legislatures of the several States, as provided in the Constitution, within seven years from the date of the submission hereof to the States by the Congress.

Amendment XIX.
(Adopted August 26, 1920)

The right of citizens of the United States to vote shall not be denied or abridged by the United States or by any State on account of sex.

Congress shall have power to enforce this article by appropriate legislation.

Amendment XX.

(Adopted February 6, 1933)

SECTION 1. The terms of the President and Vice President shall end at noon on the 20th day of January, and the terms of Senators and Representatives at noon at the 3d day of January, of the years in which such terms would have ended if this article had not been ratified; and the terms of their successors shall then begin.

SECTION 2. The Congress shall assemble at least once in every year, and such meeting shall begin at noon on the 3d day of January, unless they shall by law appoint a different day.

SECTION 3. If, at the time fixed for the beginning of the term of the President, the President elect shall have died, the Vice President elect shall become President. If a President shall not have been chosen before the time fixed for the beginning of his term, or if the President elect shall have failed to qualify, then the Vice President elect shall act as President until a President shall have qualified; and the Congress may by law provide for the case wherein neither a President elect nor a Vice President elect shall have qualified, declaring who shall then act as President, or the manner in which one who is to act shall be selected, and such person shall act accordingly until a President or Vice President shall have qualified.

SECTION 4. The Congress may by law provide for the case of the death of any of the persons from whom the House of Representatives may choose a President whenever the right of choice shall have devolved upon them, and for the case of the death of any of the persons from whom the Senate may choose a Vice President whenever the right of choice shall have devolved upon them.

SECTION 5. Sections 1 and 2 shall take effect on the 15th day of October following the ratification of this article.

SECTION 6. This article shall be inoperative unless it shall have been ratified as an amendment to the Constitution by the legislatures of three-fourths of the several States within seven years from the date of its submission.

Amendment XXI.

(Adopted December 5, 1933)

SECTION 1. The eighteenth article of amendment to the Constitution of the United States is hereby repealed.

SECTION 2. The transportation or importation into any State, Territory, or possession of the United States for delivery or use therein of intoxicating liquors, in violation of the laws thereof, is hereby prohibited.

SECTION 3. This article shall be inoperative unless it shall have been ratified as an amendment to the Constitution by conventions in the several States, as provided in the Constitution, within seven years from the date of the submission hereof to the States by the Congress.

Amendment XXII.

(Adopted February 27, 1951)

SECTION 1. No person shall be elected to the office of the President more than twice, and no person who has held the office of President, or acted as President, for more than two years of a term to which some other person was elected President shall be elected to the office of the President more than once. But this Article shall not apply to any person holding the office of President when this Article was proposed by the Congress, and shall not prevent any person who may be holding the office of President, or acting as President, during the term within which this Article becomes operative from holding the office of President or acting as President during the remainder of such term.

SECTION 2. This Article shall be inoperative unless it shall have been ratified as an amendment to the Constitution by the legislatures of three-fourths of the several States within seven years from the date of its submission to the States by the Congress.

Amendment XXIII.

(Adopted March 29, 1961)

SECTION 1. The District constituting the seat of Government of the United States shall appoint in such manner as the Congress may direct:

A number of electors of President and Vice President equal to the whole number of Senators and Representatives in Congress to which the District would be entitled if it were a State, but in no event more than the least populous State; they shall be in addition to those appointed by the States, but they shall be considered, for the purposes of the election of

President and Vice President, to be electors appointed by a State; and they shall meet in the District and perform such duties as provided by the twelfth article of amendment.

SECTION 2. The Congress shall have power to enforce this article by appropriate legislation.

Amendment XXIV.
(Adopted January 23, 1964)

SECTION 1. The right of citizens of the United States to vote in any primary or other election for President or Vice President, for electors for President or Vice President, or for Senator or Representative in Congress, shall not be denied or abridged by the United States or any State by reason of failure to pay any poll tax or other tax.

SECTION 2. The Congress shall have the power to enforce this article by appropriate legislation.

Amendment XXV.
(Adopted February 10, 1967)

SECTION 1. In case of the removal of the President from office or of his death or resignation, the Vice President shall become President.

SECTION 2. Whenever there is a vacancy in the office of the Vice President, the President shall nominate a Vice President who shall take the office upon confirmation by a majority vote of both houses of Congress.

SECTION 3. Whenever the President transmits to the President pro tempore of the Senate and the Speaker of the House of Representatives his written declaration that he is unable to discharge the powers and duties of his office, and until he transmits to them a written declaration to the contrary, such powers and duties shall be discharged by the Vice President as Acting President.

SECTION 4. Whenever the Vice President and a majority of either the principal officers of the executive departments or of such other body as Congress may by law provide, transmit to the President pro tempore of the Senate and the Speaker of the House of Representatives their written declaration that the President is unable to discharge the powers and duties of his office, the Vice President shall immediately assume the powers and duties of the office as Acting President.

Thereafter, when the President transmits to the President pro tempore of the Senate and the Speaker

of the House of Representatives his written declaration that no inability exists, he shall resume the powers and duties of his office unless the Vice President and a majority of either the principal officers of the executive departments or of such other body as Congress may by law provide, transmit within four days to the President pro tempore of the Senate and the Speaker of the House of Representatives their written declaration that the President is unable to discharge the powers and duties of his office. Thereupon Congress shall decide the issue, assembling within forty-eight hours for that purpose if not in session. If the Congress, within twenty-one days after receipt of the latter written declaration, or, if Congress is not in session, within twenty-one days after Congress is required to assemble, determines by two-thirds vote of both houses that the President is unable to discharge the powers and duties of his office, the Vice President shall continue to discharge the same as Acting President; otherwise, the President shall resume the powers and duties of his office.

Amendment XXVI.
(Adopted June 30, 1971)

SECTION 1. The right of citizens of the United States, who are 18 years of age or older, to vote shall not be denied or abridged by the United States or by any state on account of age.

SECTION 2. The Congress shall have power to enforce this article by appropriate legislation.

2. LINCOLN'S PROCLAMATION OF AMNESTY AND RECONSTRUCTION, DECEMBER 8, 1863

WHEREAS, in and by the Constitution of the United States, it is provided that the President "shall have power to grant reprieves and pardons for offences against the United States, except in cases of impeachment;" and

Whereas a rebellion now exists whereby the loyal State governments of several States have for a long time been subverted, and many persons have committed and are now guilty of treason against the United States; and

Whereas, with reference to said rebellion and treason, laws have been enacted by Congress declaring forfeitures and confiscation of property and liberation of slaves, all upon terms and conditions therein stated, and also declaring that the President was thereby authorized at any time thereafter, by proclamation, to extend to persons who may have participated in the existing rebellion, in any State or part thereof, pardon and amnesty, with such exceptions and at such times and on such conditions as he may deem expedient for the public welfare; and

Whereas the congressional declaration for limited and conditional pardon accords with well-established judicial exposition of the pardoning power; and

Whereas, with reference to said rebellion, the President of the United States has issued several proclamations, with provisions in regard to the liberation of slaves; and

Whereas it is now desired by some persons heretofore engaged in said rebellion to resume their allegiance to the United States, and to reinaugurate loyal State governments within and for their respective states; therefore,

I, Abraham Lincoln, President of the United States, do proclaim, declare, and make known to all persons who have, directly or by implication, participated in the existing rebellion, except as hereinafter excepted, that a full pardon is hereby granted to them and each of them, with restoration of all rights of property, except as to slaves, and in property cases where rights of third parties shall have intervened, and upon the condition that every such person shall take and subscribe an oath, and thenceforward keep and maintain said oath inviolate; and which oath shall be registered for permanent preservation, and shall be of the tenor and effect following, to wit:

"I, _____, do solemnly swear, in presence of Almighty God, that I will henceforth faithfully support, protect and defend the Constitution of the United States, and the union of the States thereunder; and that I will, in like manner, abide by and faithfully support all acts of Congress passed during the existing rebellion with reference to slaves, so long and so far as not repealed, modified or held void by Congress, or by decision of the Supreme Court; and that I will, in like manner, abide by and faithfully support all proclamations of the President made during the existing rebellion having reference to slaves, so long and so far as not modified or declared void by decision of the Supreme Court. So help me God."

The persons excepted from the benefits of the foregoing provisions are all who are, or shall have been, civil or diplomatic officers or agents of the so-called confederate government; all who have left judicial stations under the United States to aid the rebellion; all who are, or shall have been, military or naval officers of said so-called confederate government above the rank of colonel in the army, or of lieutenant in the navy; all who left seats in the United States Congress to aid the rebellion; all who resigned commissions in the army or navy of the United States, and afterwards aided the rebellion; and all who have engaged in any way in treating colored persons or white persons, in charge of such, otherwise than lawfully as prisoners of war, and which persons may have been found in the United States service, as soldiers, seamen, or in any other capacity.

And I do further proclaim, declare, and make known, that whenever, in any of the States of Arkansas, Texas, Louisiana, Mississippi, Tennessee, Alabama, Georgia, Florida, South Carolina, and North Carolina, a number of persons, not less than one-tenth in number of the votes cast in such State at the Presidential election of the year of our Lord One thousand eight hundred and sixty, each having taken the oath aforesaid and not having since violated it, and being a qualified voter by the election law of the State existing immediately before the so-called act of secession, and excluding all others, shall re-establish a State government which shall be republican, and in no wise contravening said oath, such shall be recognized as the true government of the State, and the State shall receive thereunder the benefits of the constitutional provision which declares that "The United States shall guaranty to every State in this union a republican form of government, and shall protect each of them against invasion; and, on application of the legislature, or the executive, (when the legislature cannot be convened,) against domestic violence."

And I do further proclaim, declare, and make known that any provision which may be adopted by such State government in relation to the freed people of such State, which shall recognize and declare their permanent freedom, provide for their education, and which may yet be consistent, as a temporary arrangement, with their present condition as a laboring, landless, and homeless class, will not be objected to by the national Executive. And it is suggested as not improper, that, in constructing a loyal State government in any State, the name of the State, the boundary, the subdivisions, the constitution, and the general code of laws, as before the rebellion, be maintained, subject only to the modifications made necessary by the conditions hereinbefore stated, and such others, if any, not contravening said conditions, and which may be deemed expedient by those framing the new State government.

To avoid misunderstanding, it may be proper to say that this proclamation, so far as it relates to State governments, has no reference to States wherein loyal State governments have all the while been maintained. And for the same reason, it may be proper to further say that whether members sent to Congress from any State shall be admitted to seats, constitutionally rests exclusively with the respective Houses, and not to any extent with the Executive. And still further, that this proclamation is intended to present the people of the States wherein the national authority has been suspended, and loyal State governments have been subverted, a mode in and by which the national authority and loyal State governments may be re-established within said States, or in any of them; and, while the mode presented is the best the Executive can suggest, with his present impressions, it must not be understood that no other possible mode would be acceptable.

Given under my hand at the city, of Washington, the 8th. day of December, A.D. *one thousand eight hundred and sixty-three, and of the independence of the United States of America the eighty-eighth.*

ABRAHAM LINCOLN

By the President:

WILLIAM H. SEWARD,
Secretary of State.

3. LINCOLN'S SECOND INAUGURAL ADDRESS, MARCH 4, 1865

At this second appearing to take the oath of the presidential office, there is less occasion for an extended address than there was at the first. Then a statement, somewhat in detail, of a course to be pursued, seemed fitting and proper. Now, at the expiration of four years, during which public declarations have been constantly called forth on every point and phase of the great contest which still absorbs the attention, and engrosses the energies [*sic*] of the nation, little that is new could be presented. The progress of our arms, upon which all else chiefly depends, is as well known to the public as to myself; and it is, I trust, reasonably satisfactory and encouraging to all. With high hope for the future, no prediction in regard to it is ventured.

On the occasion corresponding to this four years ago, all thoughts were anxiously directed to an impending civil-war. All dreaded it—all sought to avert it. While the inaugural address was being delivered from this place, devoted altogether to *saving* the Union without war, insurgent agents were in the city seeking to *destroy* it without war—seeking to dissol[v]e the Union, and divide effects, by negotiation. Both parties deprecated war; but one of them would *make* war rather than let the nation survive; and the other would *accept* war rather than let it perish. And the war came.

One eighth of the whole population were colored slaves, not distributed generally over the Union, but localized in the Southern part of it. These slaves constituted a peculiar and powerful interest. All knew that this interest was, somehow, the cause of the war. To strengthen, perpetuate, and extend this interest was the object for which the insurgents would rend the Union, even by war; while the government claimed no right to do more than to restrict the territorial enlargement of it. Neither party expected for the war, the magnitude, or the duration, which it has already attained. Neither anticipated that the *cause* of the conflict might cease with, or even before, the conflict itself should cease. Each looked for an easier triumph, and a result less fundamental and astounding. Both read the same Bible, and pray to the same God; and each invokes His aid against the other. It may seem strange that any men should dare to ask a just God's assistance in wringing their bread from the sweat of other men's faces; but let us judge not that we be not judged. The prayers of both could not be answered; that of neither has been answered fully. The Almighty has His own purposes. "Woe unto the world because of offences! for it must needs be that offences come; but woe to that man by whom the offence cometh!" If we shall suppose that American Slavery is one of those offences which, in the providence of God, must needs come, but which, having continued through His appointed time, He now wills to remove, and that He gives to both North and South, this terrible war, as the woe due to those by whom the offence came, shall we discern therein any departure from those divine attributes which the believers in a Living God always ascribe to Him? Fondly do we hope—fervently do we pray—that this mighty scourge of war may speedily pass away. Yet, if God wills that it continue, until all the wealth piled by the bond-man's two hundred and fifty years of unrequited toil shall be sunk, and until every drop of blood drawn with the lash, shall be paid by another drawn with the sword, as was said three thousand years ago, so still it must be said "the judgments of the Lord, are true and righteous altogether."

With malice toward none; with charity for all; with firmness in the right, as God gives us to see the right, let us strive on to finish the work we are in; to bind up the nation's wounds; to care for him who shall have borne the battle, and for his widow, and his orphan—to do all which may achieve and cherish a just, and a lasting peace, among ourselves, and with all nations.

4. JOHNSON'S PROCLAMATION OF AMNESTY AND RECONSTRUCTION, MAY 29, 1865

WHEREAS the President of the United States, on the 8th day of December, A.D. 1863, and on the 26th day of March, A.D. 1864, did, with the object to suppress the existing rebellion, to induce all persons to return to their loyalty, and to restore the authority of the United States, issue proclamations offering amnesty and pardon to certain persons who had, directly or by implication, participated in the said rebellion; and

Whereas many persons who had so engaged in said rebellion have, since the issuance of said proclamations, failed or neglected to take the benefits offered thereby; and

Whereas many persons who have been justly deprived of all claim to amnesty and pardon thereunder by reason of their participation, directly or by implication, in said rebellion and continued hostility to the Government of the United States since the date of said proclamations now desire to apply for and obtain amnesty and pardon.

To the end, therefore, that the authority of the Government of the United States may be restored and that peace, order, and freedom may be established, I, Andrew Johnson, President of the United States, do proclaim and declare that I hereby grant to all persons who have, directly or indirectly, participated in the existing rebellion, except as hereinafter excepted, amnesty and pardon, with restoration of all rights of property, except as to slaves and except in cases where legal proceedings under the laws of the United States providing for the confiscation of property of persons engaged in rebellion have been instituted; but upon the condition, nevertheless, that every such person shall take and subscribe the following oath (or affirmation) and thenceforward keep and maintain said oath inviolate, and which oath shall be registered for permanent preservation and shall be of the tenor and effect following, to wit:

I, _____, do solemnly swear (or affirm), in presence of Almighty God, that I will henceforth faithfully support, protect, and defend the Constitution of the United States and the Union of the States thereunder, and that I will in like manner abide by and faithfully support all laws and proclamations which have been made during the existing rebellion with reference to the emancipation of slaves. So help me God.

The following classes of persons are excepted from the benefits of this proclamation:

FIRST. All who are or shall have been pretended civil or diplomatic officers or otherwise domestic or foreign agents of the pretended Confederate government.

SECOND. All who left judicial stations under the United States to aid the rebellion.

THIRD. All who shall have been military or naval officers of said pretended Confederate government above the rank of colonel in the army or lieutenant in the navy.

FOURTH. All who left seats in the Congress of the United States to aid the rebellion.

FIFTH. All who resigned or tendered resignations of their commissions in the Army or Navy of the United States to evade duty in resisting the rebellion.

SIXTH. All who have engaged in any way in treating otherwise than lawfully as prisoners of war persons found in the United States service as officers, soldiers, seamen, or in other capacities.

SEVENTH. All persons who have been or are absentees from the United States for the purpose of aiding the rebellion.

EIGHTH. All military and naval officers in the rebel service who were educated by the Government in the Military Academy at West Point or the United States Naval Academy.

NINTH. All persons who held the pretended offices of governors of States in insurrection against the United States.

TENTH. All persons who left their homes within the jurisdiction and protection of the United States and passed beyond the Federal military lines into the pretended Confederate States for the purpose of aiding the rebellion.

ELEVENTH. All persons who have been engaged in the destruction of the commerce of the United States upon the high seas and all persons who have made raids into the United States from Canada or been engaged in destroying the commerce of the United States upon the lakes and rivers that separate the British Provinces from the United States.

TWELFTH. All persons who, at the time when they seek to obtain the benefits hereof by taking the oath herein prescribed, are in military, naval, or civil confinement or custody, or under bonds of the civil, military, or naval authorities or agents of the United States as prisoners of war, or persons detained for offenses of any kind, either before or after conviction.

THIRTEENTH. All persons who have voluntarily participated in said rebellion and the estimated value of whose taxable property is over $20,000.

FOURTEENTH. All persons who have taken the oath of amnesty as prescribed in the President's proclamation of December 8, A.D. 1863, or an oath of allegiance to the Government of the United States since the date of said proclamation and who have not thenceforward kept and maintained the same inviolate.

Provided, That special application may be made to the President for pardon by any person belonging to the excepted classes, and such clemency will be liberally extended as may be consistent with the facts of the case and the peace and dignity of the United States.

The Secretary of State will establish rules and regulations for administering and recording the said amnesty oath, so as to insure its benefit to the people and guard the Government against fraud.

In testimony whereof I have hereunto set my hand and caused the seal of the United States to be affixed.

Done at the city of Washington, the 29th day of May, A.D. *1865, and of the Independence of the United States the eighty-ninth.*

ANDREW JOHNSON

By the President:

WILLIAM H. SEWARD,
Secretary of State.

WHEREAS the fourth section of the fourth article of the Constitution of the United States declares that the United States shall guarantee to every State in the Union a republican form of government and shall protect each of them against invasion and domestic violence; and

Whereas the President of the United States is by the Constitution made Commander in Chief of the Army and Navy, as well as chief civil executive officer of the United States, and is bound by solemn oath faithfully to execute the office of President of the United States and to take care that the laws be faithfully executed; and

Whereas the rebellion which has been waged by a portion of the people of the United States against the properly constituted revolting form, but whose organized and armed forces have now been almost entirely overcome, has in its revolutionary progress deprived the people of the State of North Carolina of all civil government; and

Whereas it becomes necessary and proper to carry out and enforce the obligations of the United States to the people of North Carolina in securing them in the enjoyment of a republican form of government:

Now, therefore, in obedience to the high and solemn duties imposed upon me by the Constitution of the United States and for the purpose of enabling the loyal people of said State to organize a State government whereby justice may be established, domestic tranquillity insured, and loyal citizens protected in all their rights of life, liberty, and property, I, Andrew Johnson, President of the United States and Commander in Chief of the Army and Navy of the United States, do hereby appoint William W. Holden provisional governor of the State of North Carolina, whose duty it shall be, at the earliest practicable period, to prescribe such rules and regulations as may be necessary and proper for convening a convention composed of delegates to be chosen by that portion of the people of said State who are loyal to the United States, and no others, for the purpose of altering or amending the constitution thereof, and with authority to exercise within the limits of said State all the powers necessary and proper to enable such loyal people of the State of North Carolina to restore said State to its constitutional relations to the Federal Government and to present such a republican form of State government as will entitle the State to the guaranty of the United States therefor and its people to protection by the United States against invasion, insurrection, and domestic violence: *Provided,* That in any election that may be hereafter held for choosing delegates to any State convention as aforesaid no person shall be qualified as an elector or shall be eligible as a member of such convention unless he shall have previously taken and subscribed the oath of amnesty as set forth in the President's proclamation of May 29, A.D. 1865, and is a voter qualified as prescribed by the constitution and laws of the State of North Carolina in force immediately before the 20th day of May, A.D. 1861, the date of the so-called ordinance of secession; and the said convention, when convened, or the legislature that may be thereafter assembled, will prescribe the qualification of electors and the eligibility of persons to hold office under the constitution and laws of the State—a power the people of the several States composing the Federal Union have rightfully exercised from the origin of the Government to the present time.

And I do hereby direct—

FIRST. That the military commander of the department and all officers and persons in the military and naval service aid and assist the said provisional governor in carrying into effect this proclamation; and they are enjoined to abstain from in any way hindering, impeding, or discouraging the loyal people from the organization of a State government as herein authorized.

SECOND. That the Secretary of State proceed to put in force all laws of the United States the administration whereof belongs to the State Department applicable to the State Department applicable to the geographical limits aforesaid.

THIRD. That the Secretary of the Treasury proceed to nominate for appointment assessors of taxes and collectors of customs and internal revenue and such other officers of the Treasury Department as are authorized by law and put in execution the revenue laws of the United States within the geographical limits aforesaid. In making appointments the preference shall be given to qualified loyal persons residing within the districts where their respective duties are to be performed; but if suitable residents of the districts shall not be found, then persons residing in other States or districts shall be appointed.

FOURTH. That the Postmaster-General proceed to establish post-offices and post routes and put into execution the postal laws of the United States within the said State, giving to loyal residents the preference of appointment; but if suitable residents are not found, then to appoint agents, etc., from other States.

FIFTH. That the district judge for the judicial district in which North Carolina is included proceed to hold courts within said State in accordance with the provisions of the act of Congress. The Attorney-General will instruct the proper officers to libel and bring to judgment, confiscation, and sale property subject to confiscation and enforce the administration of justice within said State in all matters within the cognizance and jurisdiction of the Federal courts.

SIXTH. That the Secretary of the Navy take possession of all public property belonging to the Navy Department within said geographical limits and put in operation all acts of Congress in relation to naval affairs having application to the said State.

SEVENTH. That the Secretary of the Interior put in force the laws relating to the Interior Department applicable to the geographical limits aforesaid.

In testimony whereof I have hereunto set my hand and caused the seal of the United States to be affixed.

Done at the City of Washington, this 29th day of May, A.D. *1865, and of the Independence of the United States the eighty-ninth.*

ANDREW JOHNSON

By the President:

WILLIAM H. SEWARD,
Secretary of State.

5. THIRTEENTH AMENDMENT TO THE U.S. CONSTITUTION, 1865

SECTION 1. Neither slavery nor involuntary servitude, except as a punishment for crime whereof the party shall have been duly convicted, shall exist within the United States, or any place subject to their jurisdiction.

SECTION 2. Congress shall have power to enforce this article by appropriate legislation.

Proposal and Ratification

The amendment was proposed by the Thirty-eighth Congress, January 31, 1865. It was declared, by the Secretary of State, on December 18, 1865, to have been ratified by the legislatures of twenty-seven of the thirty-six states, as follows:

Illinois, February 1, 1865;
Rhode Island, February 2, 1865;
Michigan, February 2, 1865;
Maryland, February 3, 1865;
New York, February 3, 1865;
Pennsylvania, February 3, 1865;
West Virginia, February 3, 1865;
Missouri, February 6, 1865;
Maine, February 7, 1865;
Kansas, February 7, 1865;
Massachusetts, February 7, 1865;
Virginia, February 9, 1865;
Ohio, February 10, 1865;
Indiana, February 13, 1865;
Nevada, February 16, 1865;
Louisiana, February 17, 1865;
Minnesota, February 23, 1865;
Wisconsin, February 24, 1865;
Vermont, March 9, 1865;
Tennessee, April 7, 1865;
Arkansas, April 14, 1865;
Connecticut, May 4, 1865;
New Hampshire, July 1, 1865;
South Carolina, November 13, 1865;
Alabama, December 2, 1865;
North Carolina, December 4, 1865;
Georgia, December 6, 1865.

Ratification was completed on December 6, 1865.

The amendment was subsequently ratified by:

Oregon, December 8, 1865;
California, December 19, 1865;
Florida, December 28, 1865 (Florida reratified on June 9, 1868, upon its adoption of a new constitution);
Iowa, January 15, 1866;
New Jersey, January 23, 1866 (after having rejected the amendment on March 16, 1865);
Texas, February 18, 1870;

Delaware, February 12, 1901 (after rejecting the amendment on February 8, 1865);
Kentucky, March 18, 1976 (after rejecting it on February 24, 1865).

It was rejected (but not ratified thereafter) by Mississippi, December 4, 1865.

6. THE CIVIL RIGHTS ACT, 1866

Be it enacted by the Senate and House of Representatives of the United States of America in Congress assembled, That all persons born in the United States and not subject to any foreign power, excluding Indians not taxed, are hereby declared to be citizens of the United States; and such citizens, of every race and color, without regard to any previous condition of slavery or involuntary servitude, except as a punishment for crime whereof the party shall have been duly convicted, shall have the same right, in every State and Territory in the United States, to make and enforce contracts, to sue, be parties, and give evidence, to inherit, purchase, lease, sell, hold, and convey real and personal property, and to full and equal benefit of all laws and proceedings for the security of person and property, as is enjoyed by white citizens, and shall be subject to like punishment, pains, and penalties, and to none other, any law, statute, ordinance, regulation, or custom, to the contrary notwithstanding.

SECTION 2. *And be it further enacted,* That any person who, under color of any law, statute, ordinance, regulation, or custom, shall subject, or cause to be subjected, any inhabitant of any State or Territory to the deprivation of any right secured or protected by this act, or to different punishment, pains, or penalties on account of such person having at any time been held in a condition of slavery or involuntary servitude, except as a punishment for crime whereof the party shall have been duly convicted, or by reason of his color or race, than is prescribed for the punishment of white persons, shall be deemed guilty of a misdemeanor, and, on conviction, shall be punished by fine not exceeding one thousand dollars, or imprisonment not exceeding one year, or both, in the discretion of the court.

SECTION 3. *And be it further enacted,* That the district courts of the United States, within their respective districts, shall have, exclusively of the courts of the several States, cognizance of all crimes and offences committed against the provisions of this act, and also, concurrently with the circuit courts of the United States, of all causes, civil and criminal, affecting persons who are denied or cannot enforce in the courts or judicial tribunals of the State or locality where they may be any of the rights secured to them by the first section of this act; and if any suit or prosecution, civil or criminal, has been or shall be commenced in any State court, against any such person, for any cause whatsoever, or against any officer civil or military, or other person, for any arrest or imprisonment, trespasses, or wrongs done or committed by virtue or under color of authority derived from this act or the act establishing a Bureau for the relief of Freedmen and Refugees, and all acts amendatory thereof, or for refusing to do any act upon the ground that it would be inconsistent with this act, such defendant shall have the right to remove such cause for trial to the proper district or circuit court in the manner prescribed by the "Act relating to habeas corpus and regulating judicial proceedings in certain cases," approved March three, eighteen hundred and sixty-three, and all acts amendatory thereof. The jurisdiction in civil and criminal matters hereby conferred on the district and circuit courts of the United States shall be exercised and enforced in conformity with the laws of the United States, so far as such laws are suitable to carry the same into effect; but in all cases where such laws are not adapted to the object, or are deficient in the provisions necessary to furnish suitable remedies and punish offences against law, the common law, as modified and changed by the constitution and statutes of the State wherein the court having jurisdiction of the cause, civil or criminal, is held, so far as the same is not inconsistent with the Constitution and laws of the United States, shall be extended to and govern said courts in the trial and disposition of such cause, and, if of a criminal nature, in the infliction of punishment on the party found guilty.

SECTION 4. *And be it further enacted,* That the district attorneys, marshals, and deputy marshals of the United States, the commissioners appointed by the circuit and territorial courts of the United States, with powers of arresting, imprisoning, or bailing offenders against the laws of the United States, the officers and agents of the Freedmen's Bureau, and every other officer who may be specially empowered by the President of the United States, shall be, and they are hereby, specially authorized and required, at the expense of the United States, to institute proceedings against all and every person who shall violate the provisions of this act, and cause him or them to be arrested and imprisoned, or bailed, as the case may be, for trial before such court of the United States or territorial court as by this act has cognizance of the offence. And with a view to affording reasonable protection to all persons in their constitutional rights of equality before the law, without distinction of race or color, or previous condition of slavery or involuntary servitude, except as a punishment for crime, whereof the party shall have been duly convicted, and to the prompt discharge of the duties of this act, it shall be the duty of the circuit courts of the United States and the superior courts of the Territories of the United States, from time to time, to increase the number of commissioners, so as to afford a speedy and convenient means for the arrest and examination of persons charged with a violation of this act; and such commissioners are hereby authorized and required to exercise and discharge all the powers and duties conferred on them by this act, and the same duties with regard to offences created by this act, as they are authorized by law to exercise with regard to other offences against the laws of the United States.

SECTION 5. *And be it further enacted,* That it shall be the duty of all marshals and deputy marshals to obey and execute all warrants and precepts issued under the provisions of this act, when to them directed; and should any marshal or deputy marshal refuse to receive such warrant or other process when tendered, or to use all proper means diligently to execute the same, he shall, on conviction thereof, be fined in the sum of one thousand dollars, to the use of the person upon whom the accused is alleged to have committed the offence. And the better to enable the said commissioners to execute their duties faithfully and efficiently, in conformity with the Constitution of the United States and the requirements of this act, they are hereby authorized and empowered, within their counties respectively, to appoint, in writing, under their hands, any one or more suitable persons, from time to time, to execute all such warrants and other processes as may be issued by them in the lawful performance of their respective duties; and the persons so appointed to execute any warrant or process as aforesaid shall have authority to summon and call to their aid the bystanders or posse comitatus of the proper county, or such portion of the land or naval forces of the United States, or of the militia, as may be necessary to the performance of the duty with which they are charged, and to insure a faithful observance of the clause of the Constitution which prohibits slavery, in conformity with the provisions of this act; and said warrants shall run and be executed by said officers anywhere in the State or Territory within which they are issued.

SECTION 6. *And be it further enacted,* That any person who shall knowingly and wilfully obstruct, hinder, or prevent any officer, or other person charged with the execution of any warrant or process issued under the provisions of this act, or any person or persons lawfully assisting him or them, from arresting any person for whose apprehension such warrant or process may have been issued, or shall rescue or attempt to rescue such person from the custody of the officer, other person or persons, or those lawfully assisting as aforesaid, when so arrested pursuant to the authority herein given and declared, or shall aid, abet, or assist any person so arrested as aforesaid, directly or indirectly, to escape from the custody of the officer or other person legally authorized as aforesaid, or shall harbor or conceal any person for whose arrest a warrant or process shall have been issued as aforesaid, so as to prevent his discovery and arrest after notice or knowledge of the fact that a warrant has been issued for the apprehension of such person, shall, for either of said offences, be subject to a fine not exceeding one thousand dollars, and imprisonment not exceeding six months, by indictment and conviction before the district court of the United States for the district in which said offence may have been committed, or before the proper court of criminal jurisdiction, if committed within any one of the organized Territories of the United States.

SECTION 7. *And be it further enacted,* That the district attorneys, the marshals, their deputies, and the clerks of the said district and territorial courts shall be paid for their services the like fees as may be allowed to them for similar services in other cases; and in all cases where the proceedings are before a commissioner, he shall be entitled to a fee of ten dollars in full for his services in each case, inclusive of all services incident to such arrest and examination. The person or persons authorized to execute the process to be issued by such commissioners for the arrest of offenders against the provisions of this act shall be entitled to a fee of five dollars for each person he or they may

arrest and take before any such commissioner as aforesaid, with such other fees as may be deemed reasonable by such commissioner for such other additional services as may be necessarily performed by him or them, such as attending at the examination, keeping the prisoner in custody, and providing him with food and lodging during his detention, and until the final determination of such commissioner, and in general for performing such other duties as may be required in the premises; such fees to be made up in conformity with the fees usually charged by the officers of the courts of justice within the proper district or county, as near as may be practicable, and paid out of the Treasury of the United States on the certificate of the judge of the district within which the arrest is made, and to be recoverable from the defendant as part of the judgment in case of conviction.

SECTION 8. *And be it further enacted,* That whenever the President of the United States shall have reason to believe that offences have been or are likely to be committed against the provisions of this act within any judicial district, it shall be lawful for him, in his discretion, to direct the judge, marshal, and district attorney of such district to attend at such place within the district, and for such time as he may designate, for the purpose of the more speedy arrest and trial of persons charged with a violation of this act; and it shall be the duty of every judge or other officer, when any such requisition shall be received by him, to attend at the place and for the time therein designated.

SECTION 9. *And be it further enacted,* That it shall be lawful for the President of the United States, or such person as he may empower for that purpose, to employ such part of the land or naval forces of the United States, or of the militia, as shall be necessary to prevent the violation and enforce the due execution of this act.

SECTION 10. *And be it further enacted,* That upon all questions of law arising in any cause under the provisions of this act a final appeal may be taken to the Supreme Court of the United States.

7. FOURTEENTH AMENDMENT TO THE U.S. CONSTITUTION, 1866

Be it resolved by the Senate and House of Representatives of the United States of America in Congress assembled, (two thirds of both Houses concurring.) That the fol-

lowing article be proposed to the legislatures of the several States as an amendment to the Constitution of the United States, which, when ratified by three fourths of said legislatures, shall be valid as part of the Constitution, namely:—

Article XIV.

Section 1. All persons born or naturalized in the United States, and subject to the jurisdiction thereof, are citizens of the United States and of the State wherein they reside. No State shall make or enforce any law which shall abridge the privileges or immunities of citizens of the United States; nor shall any State deprive any person of life, liberty, or property, without due process of law, nor deny to any person within its jurisdiction the equal protection of the laws.

Section 2. Representatives shall be apportioned among the several States according to their respective numbers, counting the whole number of persons in each State, excluding Indians not taxed. But when the right to vote at any election for the choice of electors for President and Vice-President of the United States, representatives in Congress, the executive and judicial officers of a State, or the members of the legislature thereof, is denied to any of the male inhabitants of such State, being twenty-one years of age, and citizens of the United States, or in any way abridged, except for participation in rebellion or other crime, the basis of representation therein shall be reduced in the proportion which the number of such male citizens shall bear to the whole number of male citizens twenty-one years of age in such State.

Section 3. No person shall be a senator, or representative in Congress, or elector of President and Vice-President, or hold any office, civil or military under the United States, or under any State, who having previously taken an oath, as a member of Congress, or as an officer of the United States, or as a member of any State legislature, or as an executive or judicial officer of any State, to support the Constitution of the United States, shall have engaged in insurrection or rebellion against the same, or given aid or comfort to the enemies thereof. But Congress may by a vote of two thirds of each house remove such disability.

Section 4. The validity of the public debt of the United States, authorized by law, including debts incurred for payment of pensions and bounties for services in suppressing insurrection or rebellion, shall not be questioned. But neither the United States nor any State shall assume or pay any debt or obligation incurred in aid of insurrection or rebellion against the United States, or any claim for the loss or emancipation of any slave; but all such debts, obligations, and claims shall be held illegal and void.

Section 5. The Congress shall have power to enforce, by appropriate legislation, the provisions of this article.

8. The First Reconstruction Act, March 2, 1867

WHEREAS no legal State governments or adequate protection for life or property now exists in the rebel States of Virginia, North Carolina, South Carolina, Georgia, Mississippi, Alabama, Louisiana, Florida, Texas, and Arkansas; and whereas it is necessary that peace and good order should be enforced in said States until loyal and republican State governments can be legally established: Therefore,

Be it enacted . . . , That said rebel States shall be divided into military districts and made subject to the military authority of the United States as hereinafter prescribed, and for that purpose Virginia shall constitute the first district; North Carolina and South Carolina the second district; Georgia, Alabama, and Florida the third district; Mississippi and Arkansas the fourth district; and Louisiana and Texas the fifth district.

Section 2. And be it further enacted, That it shall be the duty of the President to assign to the command of each of said districts an officer of the army, not below the rank of brigadier-general, and to detail a sufficient military force to enable such officer to perform his duties and enforce his authority within the district to which he is assigned.

Section 3. And be it further enacted. That it shall be the duty of each officer assigned as aforesaid, to protect all persons in their rights of person and property, to suppress insurrection, disorder, and violence, and to punish, or cause to be punished, all disturbers of the public peace and criminals; and to this end he may allow local civil tribunals to take jurisdiction of and to try offenders, or, when in his judgment it may be necessary for the trial of offenders, he shall have power to organize military commissions or tribunals for that purpose, and all interference under color of

State authority with the exercise of military authority under this act, shall be null and void.

SECTION 4. *And be it further enacted,* That all persons put under military arrest by virtue of this act shall be tried without unnecessary delay, and no cruel or unusual punishment shall be inflicted, and no sentence of any military commission or tribunal hereby authorized, affecting the life or liberty of any person, shall be executed until it is approved by the officer in command of the district, and the laws and regulations for the government of the army shall not be affected by this act, except in so far as they conflict with its provisions: *Provided,* That no sentence of death under the provisions of this act shall be carried into effect without the approval of the President.

SECTION 5. *And be it further enacted,* That when the people of any one of said rebel States shall have formed a constitution of government in conformity with the Constitution of the United States in all respects, framed by a convention of delegates elected by the male citizens of said State, twenty-one years old and upward, of whatever race, color, or previous condition, who have been resident in said State for one year previous to the day of such election, except such as may be disfranchised for participation in the rebellion or for felony at common law, and when such constitution shall provide that the elective franchise shall be enjoyed by all such persons as have the qualifications herein stated for electors of delegates, and when such constitution shall be ratified by a majority of the persons voting on the question of ratification who are qualified as electors for delegates, and when such constitution shall have been submitted to Congress for examination and approval, and Congress shall have approved the same, and when said State, by a vote of its legislature elected under said constitution, shall have adopted the amendment to the Constitution of the United States, proposed by the Thirty-ninth Congress, and known as article fourteen and when said article shall have become a part of the Constitution of the United States said State shall be declared entitled to representation in Congress, and senators and representatives shall be admitted therefrom on their taking the oath prescribed by law, and then and thereafter the preceding sections of this act shall be inoperative in said State: *Provided,* That no person excluded from the privilege of holding office by said proposed amendment to the Constitution of the United States, shall be eligible to election as a

member of the convention to frame a constitution for any of said rebel States, nor shall any such person vote for members of such convention.

SECTION 6. *And be it further enacted,* That, until the people of said rebel States shall be by law admitted to representation in the Congress of the United States, any civil governments which may exist there in shall be deemed provisional only, and in all respects subject to the paramount authority of the United States at any time to abolish, modify, control, or supersede the same; and in all elections to any office under such provisional governments all persons shall be entitled to vote, and none others, who are entitled to vote, under the provisions of the fifth section of this act; and no persons shall be eligible to any office under any such provisional governments who would be disqualified from holding office under the provisions of the third article of said constitutional amendment.

9. THE SECOND RECONSTRUCTION ACT, MARCH 23, 1867

Be it enacted . . . , That the first day of September, eighteen hundred and sixty-seven, the commanding general in each district defined by an act entitled "An act to provide for the more efficient government of the rebel States," passed March second, eighteen hundred and sixty-seven, shall cause a registration to be made of the male citizens of the United States, twenty-one years of age and upwards, resident in each county or parish in the State or States included in his district, which registration shall include only those persons who are qualified to vote for delegates by the act aforesaid, and who shall have taken and subscribed the following oath or affirmation: "I, _____, do solemnly swear (or affirm), in the presence of Almighty God, that I am a citizen of the State of _____; that I have resided in said State for _____ months next preceding this day, and now reside in the county of _____, or the parish of _____, In said State (as the case may be); that I am twenty-one years old; that I have not been disfranchised for participation in any rebellion or civil war against the United States, or for felony committed against the laws of any State or of the United States; that I have never been a member of any State legislature, nor held any executive or judicial office in any State, and afterwards engaged in insurrection or rebellion against the United States, or given aid or comfort to the enemies thereof; that I have never taken an oath as a member of Congress of the United States, or as an officer of the United States, or as a member of any State legislature, or as an executive or judicial officer of any State, to support the Constitution of the United States, and afterwards engaged in insurrection or rebellion against the United States, or given aid or comfort to the enemies thereof; that I will faithfully support the Constitution and obey the laws of the United States, and will, to the best of my ability, encourage others so to do, so help me God"; which oath or affirmation may be administered by any registering officer.

SECTION 2. *And be it further enacted,* That after the completion of the registration hereby provided for in any State, at such time and places therein as the commanding general shall appoint and direct, of which at least thirty days' public notice shall be given, an election shall be held of delegates to a convention for the purpose of establishing a constitution and civil government for such State loyal to the Union, said convention in each State, except Virginia, to consist of the State legislature of such State in the year eighteen hundred and sixty, to be appointed among the several districts, counties, or parishes of such State by the commanding general, giving to each representation in the ratio of voters registered as aforesaid as nearly as may be. The convention in Virginia shall consist of the same number of members as represented the territory now constituting Virginia in the most numerous branch of the legislature of said State in the year eighteen hundred and sixty, to be apportioned as aforesaid.

SECTION 3. *And be it further enacted,* That at said election the registered voters of each State shall vote for or against a convention to form a constitution therefor under this act. . . . Those voting in favor of such a convention shall have written or printed on the ballots by which they vote for delegates, as aforesaid, the words "For a convention," and those voting against such a convention shall have written or printed on such ballots the words "Against a convention." The persons appointed to superintend said election, and to make return of the votes given thereat, as herein provided, shall count and make return of the votes given for and against a convention; and the commanding general to whom the same shall have been returned shall ascertain and declare the total vote in each State for and against a convention. If a majority

of the votes given on that question shall be for a convention, then such a convention shall be held as hereinafter provided; but if a majority of said votes shall be against a convention, then no such convention shall be held under this act: *Provided, That such convention shall not be held unless a majority of all such registered voters shall have voted on the question of holding such convention.*

SECTION 4. *And be it further enacted,* That the commanding general of each district shall appoint as many boards of registration as may be necessary, consisting of three loyal officers or persons, to make and complete the registration, superintend the election, and make return to him of the votes, lists of voters, and of the persons elected as delegates by a plurality of the votes cast at said election; and upon receiving said returns he shall open the same, ascertain the persons elected as delegates, according to the returns of the officers who conducted said election, and make proclamation thereof; and if a majority of the votes given on that question shall be for a convention, the commanding general, within sixty days from the date of election, shall notify the delegates to assemble in convention, at a time and place to be mentioned in the notification, and said convention, when organized, shall proceed to frame a constitution and civil government according to the provisions of this act, and the act to which it is supplementary; and when the same shall have been framed, said constitution shall be submitted by the convention for ratification to the persons registered under the provisions of this act at an election to be conducted by the officers or persons appointed or to be appointed by the commanding general, as hereinbefore provided, and to be held after the expiration of thirty days from the date of notice thereof, to be given by said convention; and the returns thereof shall be made to the commanding general of the district.

SECTION 5. *And be it further enacted,* That if, according to said returns, the constitution shall be ratified by a majority of the votes of the registered electors qualified as herein specified, cast at said election, at least one half of all the registered voters voting upon the question of such ratification, the president of the convention shall transmit a copy of the same, duly certified, to the President of the United States, who shall forthwith transmit the same to Congress, if then in session, and if not in session, then immediately upon its next assembling; and if it shall moreover appear to Congress that the election was one at which all the registered and qualified electors in the State had an opportunity to vote freely and without restraint, fear, or the influence of fraud, and if the Congress shall be satisfied that such constitution meets the approval of a majority of all the qualified electors in the State, and if the said constitution shall be declared by Congress to be in conformity with the provisions of the act to which this is supplementary, and the other provisions of said act shall have been complied with, and the said constitution shall be approved by Congress, the State shall be declared entitled to representation, and senators and representatives shall be admitted therefrom as therein provided.

SECTION 6. *And be it further enacted,* That all elections in the States mentioned in the said "Act to provided for the more efficient government of the rebel States," shall, during the operation of said act, be by ballot; and all officers making the said registration of voters and conducting said elections shall, before entering upon the discharge of their duties, take and subscribe the oath prescribed by the act approved July second, eighteen hundred and sixty two, entitled "An act to prescribe an oath of office": *Provided,* That if any person shall knowingly and falsely take and subscribe any oath in this act prescribed, such person so offending and being thereof duly convicted shall be subject to the pains, penalties, and disabilities which by law are provided for the punishment of the crime of wilful and corrupt perjury.

SECTION 7. *And be it further enacted,* That all expenses incurred by the several commanding generals, or by virtue of any orders issued, or appointments made, by then, under or by virtue of this act, shall be paid out of any moneys in the treasury not otherwise appropriated.

SECTION 8. *And be it further enacted.* That the convention for each State shall prescribe the fees, salary, and compensation to be paid to all delegates and other officers and agents herein authorized or necessary to carry into effect the purposes of this act not herein otherwise provided for, and shall provide for the levy and collection of such taxes on the property in such State as may be necessary to pay the same.

SECTION 9. *And be it further enacted,* That the word "article," in the sixth section of the act to which this is supplementary, shall be construed to mean "section."

10. THE THIRD RECONSTRUCTION ACT, JULY 19, 1867

Be it enacted . . . , That it is hereby declared to have been the true intent and meaning . . . [of the acts of March 2 and March 23, 1867] . . . , that the governments then existing in the rebel States of Virginia, North Carolina, South Carolina, Georgia, Mississippi, Alabama, Louisiana, Florida, Texas, and Arkansas were not legal State governments; and that thereafter said governments, if continued, were to be continued subject in all respects to the military commanders of the respective districts, and to the paramount authority of Congress.

SECTION 2. *And be it further enacted,* That the commander of any district named in said act shall have power, subject to the disapproval of the General of the army of the United States, and to have effect till disapproved, whenever in the opinion of such commander the proper administration of said act shall require it, to suspend or remove from office, or from the performance of official duties and the exercise of official powers, any officer or person holding or exercising, or professing to hold or exercise, any military office or duty in such district under any power, election, appointment or authority derived from, or granted by, or claimed under, any so-called State or the government thereof, or any municipal or other division thereof, and upon such suspension or removal such commander, subject to the disapproval of the General as aforesaid, shall have power to provide from time to time for the performance of the said duties of such officer or person so suspended or removed, by the detail of some competent officer or soldier of the army, or by the appointment of some other person, to perform the same, and to fill vacancies occasioned by death, resignation, or otherwise.

SECTION 3. *And be it further enacted,* That the General of the army of the United States shall be invested with all the powers of suspension, removal, appointment, and detail granted in the preceding section to district commanders.

SECTION 4. *And be it further enacted,* That the acts of the officers of the army already done in removing in said districts persons exercising the functions of civil officers, and appointing others in their stead, are hereby confirmed: *Provided,* That any person heretofore or hereafter appointed by any district commander to exercise the functions of any civil office, may be removed either by the military officer in command of the district, or by the General of the army. And it shall be the duty of such commander to remove from office as aforesaid all persons who are disloyal to the government of the United States, or who use their official influence in any manner to hinder, delay, prevent, or obstruct the due and proper administration of this act and the acts to which it is supplementary.

Section 5. *And be it further enacted,* That the boards of registration provided for in the act . . . [of March 23, 1867] . . . , shall have power, and it shall be their duty before allowing the registration of any person, to ascertain, upon such facts or information as they can obtain, whether such person is entitled to be registered under said act, and the oath required by said act shall not be conclusive on such question, and no person shall be registered unless such board shall decide that he is entitled thereto; and such board shall also have power to examine, under oath, (to be administered by any member of such board,) any one touching the qualification of any person claiming registration; but in every case of refusal by the board to register an applicant, and in every case of striking his name from the list as hereinafter provided, the board shall make a note or memorandum, which shall be returned with the registration list to the commanding general of the district, setting forth the grounds of such refusal or such striking from the list: *Provided,* That no person shall be disqualified as member of any board of registration by reason of race or color.

Section 6. *And be it further enacted,* That the true intent and meaning of the oath prescribed in said supplementary act is, (among other things,) that no person who has been a member of the legislature of any State, or who has held any executive or judicial office in any State, whether he has taken an oath to support the Constitution of the United States or not, and whether he was holding such office at the commencement of the rebellion, or had held it before, and who has afterwards engaged in insurrection or rebellion against the United States, or given aid or comfort to the enemies thereof, is entitled to be registered or to vote; and the words "executive or judicial office in any State" in said oath mentioned shall be construed to include all civil offices created by law for the administration of any general law of a State, or for the administration of justice.

Section 7. *And be it further enacted,* That the time for completing the original registration provided for in

said act may, in the discretion of the commander of any district, be extended to the first day of October, eighteen hundred and sixty-seven; and the boards of registration shall have power, and it shall be their duty, commencing fourteen days prior to any election under said act, and upon reasonable public notice of the time and place thereof, to revise, for a period of five days, the registration lists, and upon being satisfied that any person not entitled thereto has been registered, to strike the name of such person from the list, and such person shall not be allowed to vote. And such board shall also, during the same period, add to such registry the names of all persons who at that time possess the qualifications required by said act who have not been already registered; and no person shall, at any time, be entitled to be registered or to vote by reason of any executive pardon or amnesty for any act or thing which, without such pardon or amnesty, would disqualify him from registration or voting.

Section 8. *And be it further enacted,* That section four of said last-named act shall be construed to authorize the commanding general named herein, whenever he shall deem it needful, to remove any member of a board of registration and to appoint another in his stead, and to fill any vacancy in such board.

Section 9. *And be it further enacted,* That all members of said boards of registration and all persons hereafter elected or appointed to office in said military districts, under any so-called State or municipal authority, or by detail or appointment of the district commanders, shall be required to take and to subscribe the oath of office prescribed by law for officers of the United States.

Section 10. *And be it further enacted,* That no district commander or member of the board of registration, or any of the officers or appointees acting under them, shall be bound in his action by any opinion of any civil officer of the United States.

Section 11. *And be it further enacted,* That all the provisions of this act and of the acts to which this is supplementary shall be construed liberally, to the end that all the intents thereof may be fully and perfectly carried out.

11. THE FOURTH RECONSTRUCTION ACT, MARCH 8, 1868

Be it enacted . . . , That hereafter any election authorized by the act [of March 23, 1867] . . . , shall be decided by a majority of the votes actually cast; and at the election in which the question of the adoption or rejection of any constitution is submitted, any person duly registered in the State may vote in the election district where he offers to vote when he has resided therein for ten days next preceding such election, upon presentation of his certificate of registration, his affidavit, or other satisfactory evidence, under such regulations as the district commanders may prescribe.

SECTION 2. *And be it further enacted,* That the constitutional convention of any of the States mentioned in the acts to which this is amendatory may provide that at the time of voting upon the ratification of the constitution the registered voters may vote also for members of the House of Representatives of the United States, and for all elective officers provided for by the said constitution; and the same election officers who shall make the return of the votes cast on the ratification or rejection of the constitution, shall enumerate and certify the votes cast for members of Congress.

12. LETTER ON "THE GREAT AMERICAN PARK OF THE YOSEMITE," WRITTEN TO THE *NEW YORK EVENING POST,* BY FREDERICK LAW OLMSTED, 1868

To the Editors of the Evening Post:

With the early completion of the Pacific Railroad there can be no doubt that the Park established by act of Congress place of free recreation for the people of the United States and their guests forever, will be resorted to from all parts of the civilized world. Many intelligent men, nevertheless, have hardly yet heard of it, and hence an effort to give an account of the leading qualities of its scenery may be pardoned, however inadequate it is sure to be.

The main feature of the Yosemite is best indicated in one word as a chasm. It is a chasm nearly a mile in average width, however, and more than ten miles in length. The central and broader part of this chasm is occupied at the bottom by a series of groves of magnificent trees, and meadows of the most varied, luxuriant and exquisite herbiage, through which meanders a broad stream of the clearest water, rippling over a pebbly bottom, and eddying among banks of ferns and rushes; sometimes narrowed into sparkling rapids and sometimes expanding into placid pools which

reflect the wondrous heights on either side. The walls of the chasm are generally half a mile, sometimes nearly a mile in height above these meadows, and where most lofty and nearly perpendicular, sometimes over-jutting. At frequent intervals, however, they are cleft, broken, terraced and sloped, and in these places, as well as everywhere upon the summit, they are overgrown by thick clusters of trees.

There is nothing strange or exotic in the character of the vegetation most of the trees and plants, especially those of the meadows and waterside, are closely allied to and are not readily distinguished from those most common in the landscapes of the Eastern States or the midland counties of England. The stream is such a one as Shakespeare delighted in, and brings pleasing reminiscences to the traveler of the Avon or the upper Thames.

Banks of heartsease and beds of cowslips and daisies are frequent, and thickets of dogwood, alder and willow often fringe the shores. At several points streams of water flow into the chasm, descending at one leap from five hundred to fourteen hundred feet. One small stream falls, in three closely consecutive pitches, a distance of two thousand six hundred feet, which is more than fifteen times the height of the falls of Niagara. In the spray of these falls superb rainbows are seen.

At certain points the walls of rock are ploughed in polished horizontal furrows, at others moraines of boulders and pebbles are found; both evincing the terrific force with which in past ages of the earth's history a glacier has moved down the chasm from among the adjoining peaks of the Sierras. Beyond the lofty walls still loftier mountains rise, some crowned by forests, others in simple rounded cones of light, gray granite. The climate of the region is never dry like that of the lower parts of the state of California; even when, for several months, not a drop of rain has fallen twenty miles to the westward, and the country there is parched, and all vegetation withered, the Yosemite continues to receive frequent soft showers, and to be dressed throughout in living green.

After midsummer a light, transparent haze generally pervades the atmosphere, giving an indescribable softness and exquisite dreamy charm to the scenery, like that produced by the Indian summer in the East. Clouds gathering at this season upon the snowy peaks which rise within forty miles on each side of the chasm to a height of over twelve thousand feet, sometimes roll down over the cliffs in the afternoon, and, under the influence of the rays of the setting sun, form the most gorgeous and magnificent thunder heads. The average elevation of the ground is higher than that of the highest peak of the White Mountains, or the Alleghenies, and the air is bracing; yet, its temperature is never uncomfortably cool in summer, nor severe in winter.

Flowering shrubs of sweet fragrance and balmy herbs abound in the meadows, and there is everywhere a delicate odor of the prevailing foliage in the pines and cedars. The water of the streams is soft and limpid, as clear as crystal, abounds with trout and, except near its sources, is, during the heat of the summer, of an agreeable temperature for bathing. In the lower part of the valley there are copious mineral springs, the water of one of which is regarded by the aboriginal inhabitants as having remarkable curative properties. A basin still exists to which weak and sickly persons were brought for bathing. The water has not been analyzed, but that it possesses highly tonic as well as other medical qualities can be readily seen. In the neighboring mountains there are also springs strongly charged with carbonic acid gas, and said to resemble in taste the Empire Springs Saratoga.

The other district, associated with this by the act of Congress, consists of four sections of land, about thirty miles distant from it, on which stand in the midst of a forest composed of the usual trees and shrubs of the western slope of the Sierra Nevada, about six hundred mature trees of the giant Sequoia. Among them is one known through numerous paintings and photographs as the Grizzly Giant, which probably is the noblest tree in the world. Besides this, there are hundreds of such beauty and stateliness that, to one who moves among them in the reverent mood to which they so strongly incite the mind, it will not seem strange that intelligent travelers have declared that they would rather have passed by Niagara itself than have missed visiting this grove.

In the region intermediate between the two districts the scenery generally is of a grand character, consisting of granite mountains and a forest composed mainly of coniferous trees of great size, yet often more perfect, vigorous and luxuriant than trees of half the size are over found on the Atlantic side of the continent. It is not, however, in its grandeur or in its forest beauty that the attraction of this intermedi-

ate region consists, so much as in the more secluded charms of some of its glens, formed by mountain torrents fed from the snow banks of the higher Sierras.

These have worn deep and picturesque channels in the granite rocks, and in the moist shadows of their recesses grow tender plants of rare and peculiar loveliness. The broad parachute-like leaves of the peltate saxifrage, delicate ferns, soft mosses, and the most brilliant lichens abound, and in following up the ravines, cabinet pictures open at every turn, which, while composed of materials mainly new to the artist, constantly recall the most valued sketches of Calame in the Alps and Apennines.

The difference in the elevation of different parts of the district amounts to considerably more than a mile. Owing to this difference and the great variety of exposure and other circumstances there is a larger number of species of plants within the district than probably can be found within a similar space anywhere else on the continent. Professor Torrey, who has given the received botanical names to several hundred plants of California, states that on the space of a few acres of meadow land he found about three hundred species, and that within sight of the trail usually followed by visitors, at least six hundred may be observed, most of them being small and delicate flowering plants.

By no statement of the elements of the scenery can any idea of that scenery be given, any more than a true impression can be conveyed of a human face by a measured account of its features. It is conceivable that any one or all of the cliffs of the Yosemite might be changed in form and color, without lessening the enjoyment which is now obtained from the scenery. Nor is this enjoyment any more essentially derived from its meadows, its trees, its streams; least of all can it be attributed to the cascades. These, indeed, are scarcely to be named among the elements of the scenery. They are mere incidents, of far less consequence any day of the summer than the imperceptible humidity of the atmosphere and the soil. The chasm remains when they are dry, and the scenery may be, and often is, more effective, by reason of some temporary condition of the air, of clouds, of moonlight, or of sunlight through mist or smoke, in the season when the cascades attract the least attention, than when their volume of water is largest and their roar like constant thunder.

There are falls of water elsewhere finer, there are more stupendous rocks, more beetling cliffs, there are deeper and more awful chasms, there may be as beautiful streams, as lovely meadows, there are larger trees. It is in no scene or scenes the charm consists, but in the miles of scenery where cliffs of awful height and rocks of vast magnitude and of varied and exquisite coloring, and banked and fringed and draped and shadowed by the tender foliage of noble and lovely trees and bushes, reflected from the most placid pools, and associated with the most tranquil meadows, the most playful streams, and every variety of soft and peaceful pastoral beauty.

The union of the deepest sublimity with the deepest beauty of nature, not in one feature or another, not in one part or one scene or another, not any landscape that can be framed by itself, but all around and wherever the visitor goes, constitutes the Yosemite the greatest glory of nature. No photograph or series of photographs, no paintings ever prepare a visitor so that he is not taken by surprise, for could the scenes be faithfully represented the visitor is affected not only by that upon which his eye is at any moment fixed, but by all that with which on every side it is associated, and of which it is seen only as an inherent part. For the same reason no description, no measurements, no comparisons are of much value. Indeed, the attention called by these to points in some definite way remarkable, by fixing the mind on mere matters of wonder or curiosity, prevent the true and far more extraordinary character of the scenery from being appreciated.

F.L.O.

13. FIFTEENTH AMENDMENT TO THE U.S. CONSTITUTION, 1870

SECTION 1. The right of citizens of the United States to vote shall not be denied or abridged by the United States or by any State on account of race, color, or previous condition of servitude.

SECTION 2. The Congress shall have power to enforce this article by appropriate legislation.

Proposal and Ratification

The amendment was proposed by the Fortieth Congress, on February 26, 1869, and was declared by the Secretary of State, on March 30, 1870, to have been ratified by the legislatures of twenty-nine of the thirty-seven states:

Nevada, March 1, 1869;
West Virginia, March 3, 1869;
Illinois, March 5, 1869;
Louisiana, March 5, 1869;
North Carolina, March 5, 1869;
Michigan, March 8, 1869;
Wisconsin, March 9, 1869;
Maine, March 11, 1869;
Massachusetts, March 12, 1869;
Arkansas, March 15, 1869;
South Carolina, March 15, 1869;
Pennsylvania, March 25, 1869;
New York, April 14, 1869 (the N.Y. legislature passed a resolution January 5, 1870 to withdraw consent, but rescinded on March 30, 1970);
Indiana, May 14, 1869;
Connecticut, May 19, 1869;
Florida, June 14, 1869;
New Hampshire, July 1, 1869;
Virginia, October 8, 1869;
Vermont, October 20, 1869;
Missouri, January 7, 1870;
Minnesota, January 13, 1870;
Mississippi, January 17, 1870;
Rhode Island, January 18, 1870;
Kansas, January 19, 1870;
Ohio, January 27, 1870; (after having rejected it on April 30, 1869);
Georgia, February 2, 1870;
Iowa, February 3, 1870.

Ratification was completed on February 3, 1870, unless the withdrawal of ratification by New York was effective; in which event ratification was completed on February 17, 1870, when Nebraska ratified. The amendment was subsequently ratified by:

Texas, February 18, 1870;
New Jersey, February 15, 1871 (after having rejected it on February 7, 1870);
Delaware, February 12, 1901 (after having rejected it on March 18, 1869);
Oregon, February 24, 1959;
California, April 3, 1962 (after having rejected it on January 28, 1870);

Kentucky, March 18, 1976
(after having rejected it on
March 12, 1869).

The amendment was approved by the Governor of Maryland, May 7, 1973; Maryland having previously rejected it on February 26, 1870. The amendment was rejected, and never subsequently ratified, by Tennessee, November 16, 1869.

14. ACT OF CONGRESS ESTABLISHING YELLOWSTONE NATIONAL PARK, MARCH 1, 1872

AN ACT to set apart a certain tract of land lying near the headwaters of the Yellowstone River as a public park. Be it enacted by the Senate and House of Representatives of the United States of America in Congress assembled, That the tract of land in the Territories of Montana and Wyoming, lying near the headwaters of the Yellowstone River, and described as follows, to wit, commencing at the junction of Gardiner's river with the Yellowstone river, and running east to the meridian passing ten miles to the eastward of the most eastern point of Yellowstone lake; thence south along said meridian to the parallel of latitude passing ten miles south of the most southern point of Yellowstone lake; thence west along said parallel to the meridian passing fifteen miles west of the most western point of Madison lake; thence north along said meridian to the latitude of the junction of Yellowstone and Gardiner's river; thence east to the place of beginning, is hereby reserved and withdrawn from settlement, occupancy, or sale under the laws of the United States, and dedicated and set apart as a public park or pleasuring-ground for the benefit and enjoyment of the people; and all persons who shall locate or settle upon or occupy the same, or any part thereof, except as hereinafter provided, shall be considered trespassers and removed therefrom.

SECTION 2. That said public park shall be under the exclusive control of the Secretary of the Interior, whose duty it shall be, as soon as practicable, to make and publish such rules and regulations as he may deem necessary or proper for the care and management of the same. Such regulations shall provide for the preservation, from injury or spoliation, of all timber, mineral deposits, natural curiosities, or wonders within said park, and their retention in their natural condition. The Secretary may in his discretion, grant leases for building purposes for terms not exceeding ten years, of small parcels of ground, at such places in said park as shall require the erection of buildings for the accommodation of visitors; all of the proceeds of said leases, and all other revenues that may be derived from any source connected with said park, to be expended under his direction in the management of the same, and the construction of roads and bridle-paths therein. He shall provide against the wanton destruction of the fish and game found within said park, and against their capture or destruction for the purposes of merchandise or profit. He shall also cause all persons trespassing upon the same after the passage of this act to be removed therefrom, and generally shall be authorized to take all such measures as shall be necessary or proper to fully carry out the objects and purposes of this act.

15. NATIONAL WOMAN SUFFRAGE ASSOCIATION "PEOPLE'S CONVENTION" PLATFORM, MAY 9, 1872

We, women citizens of the United States, in national convention assembled at New York, proclaim the following principles as essential to just government.

1. We recognize the equality of all before the law, and hold that it is the duty of government in its dealings with the people to mete out equal and exact justice to all, of whatever nativity, race, color, sex or persuasion, religious or political.

2. We pledge ourselves to maintain the union of the States, and to oppose re-opening of the questions settled by the thirteenth, fourteenth and fifteenth amendments of the Constitution, which have emancipated and enfranchised the slaves and the women of the nation.

3. We demand the immediate and absolute removal of all disabilities now imposed on rebels and women, believing that universal suffrage and universal amnesty will result in complete purification in the family, and in all sections of the country.

4. We demand for the individual the largest liberty consistent with the public order, for the state self-government and for the national administration the methods of peace, and the constitutional limitations of power.

5. We demand a thorough civil service reform as one of the pressing necessities of the hour.

Honesty, capacity, and fidelity, without distinction of sex, should constitute the only valid claim to public employment. The first step in this reform is the one term principle, and the election of President, Vice President and United States Senators by the whole people.

6. We affirm that no form of taxation is just or wise which puts burdens upon the people by means of duties intended to increase the price of domestic products, and which are unnecessary for purposes of revenue. Taxes should not be laid upon the necessaries; but upon the luxuries of life, that the rich and not the poor may bear the burdens.

7. The highest consideration of commercial morality and honest government requires a thorough reform of the present financial system. The interests of the people demand a cheap, sound, uniform, abundant, and elastic currency, to be a permanent measure of value, based on the wealth of the nation. This will be found in the issue of currency, or certificates of value by the government for all duties, taxes, and imposts whatever, which shall be legal tender for all debts, public and private; such currency to be the lawful money of the United States, and convertible at the option of the holder into government bonds, bearing a rate of interest not exceeding 3 per cent, and to be reconvertible into currency at the will of the holder.

8. We remember with gratitude the heroism and sacrifices of the wives, sisters and mothers throughout this republic in the late war; the grand sanitary work they did in the hospital, on the battle-field, and in gathering in the harvest at home, have justly earned for the women of the country the generous recognition of all their political rights by every true American statesman.

9. We are opposed to all grants of lands to railroads or other corporations. The public domain should be held sacred to actual settlers, an inviolable homestead secured to every man and woman.

10. We believe in the principles of the referendum, minority representation, and a just system of graduation taxation.

11. It is the duty of government to regard children and criminals as wards of the State; to secure to the one the best advantages of education, and for the other more humane legislation and better methods of reform.

12. We hold it is the duty of the government in its intercourse with foreign countries to cultivate the friendships of peace, by treating will all on just and equal terms, and by insisting on the settlement of all differences by a congress of nations.

13. For the promotion of these vital principles and the establishment of a party based on them, we invite the co-operation of all "citizens," without distinction of race, color, sex, nationality or previous political affiliations.

16. EXCERPTS FROM REPORT OF J. Q. SMITH, COMMISSIONER OF INDIAN AFFAIRS, TO THE DEPARTMENT OF THE INTERIOR, OCTOBER 30, 1876

Sir: I have the honor to submit herewith, in accordance with law, the annual report of the Indian Office, accompanied by the reports of its superintendents and agents.

The management of Indian affairs is always attended with much of difficulty and embarrassment. In every other department of the public service, the officers of the Government conduct business mainly with civilized and intelligent men. The Indian Office, in representing the Government, has to deal mainly with an uncivilized and unintelligent people, whose ignorance superstition, and suspicion materially increase the difficulty both of controlling aud assisting them.

The traditionary [sic] belief, which largely prevails, that the Indian service, throughout its whole history, has been tainted with fraud, arises, I apprehend, not only from the fact that frauds have been committed, but also because, from the nature of the service itself, peculiar opportunities for fraud may be found. The agencies are usually located in distant and, in some cases, almost inaccessible places. They are, in many instances so far from the accustomed abodes of our people as to be rarely visited by any civilized men except the agent and his employees and persons furnishing supplies. It thus happens that the business of the agency is conducted without the restraints which generally surround public officers.

. . . No man, who is not possessed of talents of a high order and great variety, can be, completely successful as an Indian agent.

. . . In my judgment the welfare of the public service imperatively requires that the compensation offered an Indian agent should be somewhat in proportion to the capacity required in the office, and to the responsibility and labor of the duties to be performed. I respectfully recommend that this subject be brought to the attention of Congress, and that that body be requested to appropriate not less than $30,000, to be distributed as additional compensation to Indian agents having the most important and difficult agencies; the salary of no agent to amount to more than $3,000.

. . . In July last, through the failure of Congress to pass the annual appropriation bill, supplies at several Sioux agencies again became nearly exhausted, and though a temporary appropriation of $150,000 was made, many Indians, rendered excited and suspicious by the war in the north, abandoned their agencies to take part in hostilities. Congress still failing to pass the annual appropriation bill, a similar emergency existed in August, which was again met by a temporary relief bill, but produced a like effect on the Indians.

The above facts are not recited for the purpose of criticism or fault finding, but to vindicate this bureau from the charge made at the time, that the deficiency in supplies was owing to inefficiency and neglect on the part of the office. . . .

Annuity Purchases

The failure to pass the annual appropriation bill before the 15th of August last, has made the duty of purchasing supplies and transporting them to the agencies unusually arduous.

. . . Owing to the lateness of the season, transportation rates over several routes are higher than last year. Up the Missouri River, for instance, goods must be transported at a low stage of water, with a liability of the river closing with ice, thus increasing the distance over which they must be hauled by wagon over roads impeded with snow. The increase in the price of beef at some points is due in part to the lateness of the season, but more particularly to the greater stringency in terms of the contract as to the quality of the beef to be received.

The Policy to be Pursued

. . . From be first settlement of the country by white men until a comparatively recent period, the Indians have been constantly driven westward from the Atlantic. A zigzag, ever-varying line, more or less definitely marked, extending from Canada to the Gulf of Mexico, and always slowly moving west, has been known as the "frontier" or "border." Along this border has been an almost incessant struggle, the Indians to retain and the whites to get possession; the war being broken by periods of occasional and temporary peace, which usually followed treaties whereby the Indians agreed to surrender large tracts of their lands. This peace would continue until the lands surrendered had been occupied by whites, when the pressure of emigration would again break over the border, and the Indians, by force or treaty, be compelled to surrender another portion of these cherished hunting-grounds.

. . . Toward the close of the first half of this century the tide of emigration and adventure swept even the frontier away and rushed across the continent. Throughout the vast regions of the West the adventurous, grasping Anglo-Saxon race is dominant and in possession of the fairest and richest portions of the land. Except in the Indian Territory and perhaps Dakota, the white exceeds the Indian population. No new hunting-grounds remain, and the civilization or the utter destruction of the Indians is inevitable. The next twenty-five years are to determine the fate of a race. If they cannot be taught, and taught very soon, to accept the necessities of their situation and begin in earnest to provide for their own wants by labor in civilized pursuits, they are destined to speedy extinction. From the fact that for so long a period Indian civilization has been retarded, it must not be concluded that some inherent characteristic in the race disqualifies it for civilized life. It may well be doubted whether this be true of any race of men. Surely it cannot be true of a race, any portion of which has made the actual progress realized by some of our Indians. They can and do learn to labor; they can and do learn to read. Many thousands today are engaged in civilized occupations. But the road out of barbarism is a long and difficult one. Even in enlightened Europe there are millions of people whose ancestors a few generations ago were as ignorant and poor and degraded as our most advanced Indian tribes now are.

Civilization is a vague, indefinite, comparative term. Our children's grandchildren may look upon our civilization as very rude and imperfect. It is not my wish to give any rose-colored view of the present condition of our Indians. Many of them are as miserable and degraded as men can be; but it cannot be denied that others are making reasonably satisfactory progress.

Within a few years the Government has undertaken somewhat systematically to bring them into civilized life. The "peace policy" has sought to throw around them healthful associations; to place at the several agencies agents and employees of good moral and Christian character and of active sympathies; and an earnest effort has been made to teach Indians to labor and to read. It is too soon, perhaps, to assert that this effort has proved a success, but the accompanying reports of agents abundantly show that notwithstanding all surrounding difficulties, much has been accomplished toward establishing and maintaining peace, toward protecting Indians from evil influences, and toward awakening in them the desire for a better mode of life. The success of some of our agents, who have labored under reasonably favorable circumstances, deserves all praise, and has fully equaled the fondest hopes of the friends of the peace policy. Certainly enough improvement has been made to justify the continuance of the present benevolent efforts.

In considering whether modifications of existing methods may not be desirable, I have arrived at the conviction that the welfare and progress of the Indians require the adoption of three principles of policy:

First. Concentration of all Indians on a few reservations.

Second. Allotment to them of lands in severalty.

Third. Extension over them of United States law and the jurisdiction of United States courts.

Consolidation of Reservations

The reservations upon which, in my opinion, the Indians should be, consolidated, are the Indian Territory, the White Earth reservation in Northern Minnesota, and a reservation in the southern part of Washington Territory, probably the Yakama reservation. If it should be found impracticable to remove the Indians of Colorado, Utah, New Mexico, and Arizona, to the Indian Territory, they might be concentrated on some suitable reservation either in Colorado or Arizona.

Many of these Indians are now located on lands utterly unfit for cultivation, where starvation or perpetual support by the Government are the only alternatives. It is doubtful whether even white people could cultivate profitably the greater part of the Sioux reservation in Dakota. In the Indian Territory, on the other hand, are fertile land, a genial climate, and room for more Indians than there are in the whole Union.

That the Indian sentiment is opposed to such removal is true. Difficulties were experienced in bringing to the Territory its present inhabitants from east of the Mississippi; but the obstacles were over-come, and experience shows that there the race can thrive. With a fair degree of persistence the removal thither of other Indians can also be secured.

. . . The importance of reducing the number of reservations is shown by the following considerations:

Many of the present reserves are almost worthless for agricultural purposes; others are rich in soil, mineral wealth, and timber. Nearly all are too small to subsist the Indians by hunting, and too large for them to occupy in agricultural and civilized pursuits. Many are so remote and difficult of access, that needed supplies can be furnished only at great expense. Nearly all are surrounded by white settlers, more or less numerous. Wherever an Indian reservation has on it good land, or timber, or minerals, the cupidity of the white man is excited, and a constant struggle is inaugurated to dispossess the Indian, in which the avarice and determination of the white man usually prevails. The length of the boundary-line between the reservations and the contiguous white settlements amounts in the aggregate to thousands of miles, every mile being a point of contact and difficulty. This aggregate boundary is so extensive as to render almost impossible the prevention of illicit trade in arms and whisky. As now constituted, these reservations are a refuge to the most lawless and desperate white men in America. . . . Such men seriously obstruct, if they do not render nugatory, every effort to give assistance to the Indians.

By the concentration of Indians on a few reservations, it is obvious that much of the difficulty now surrounding the Indian question will vanish. Many agencies now conducted at large expense could be abolished. The aggregate boundary-lines between the reservations and country occupied by white people would be greatly reduced, and the danger of violence, bloodshed, and mutual wrong materially lessened. The sale of liquors and arms could be more effectually prevented; bad white men could more easily be kept out of the Indian country; necessary supplies could be more cheaply furnished; a far smaller military force would be required to keep the peace; and generally, the Indians, being more compact, could be more efficiently aided and controlled by the officers of the Government. Moreover, large bodies of land would be thrown open to settlement, proceeds of whose sale would be ample to defray all expense of the removals.

Allotments in Severalty

It is doubtful whether any high degree of civilization is possible without individual ownership of land. The records of the past and the experience of the present testify that the soil should be made secure to the individual by all the guarantees which law can devise, and that nothing less will induce men to put forth their best exertions. No general law exists which provides that Indians shall select allotments in severalty, and it seems to me a matter of great moment that provision should be made not only permitting, but requiring, the head of each Indian family, to accept the allotment of a reasonable amount of land, to be the property of himself and his lawful heirs, in lieu of any interest in any common tribal possession. Such allotments should be inalienable for at least twenty, perhaps fifty years, and if situated in a permanent Indian reservation, should be transferable only among Indians.

Law for Indians

My predecessors have frequently called attention to the startling fact that we have within our midst 275,000 people, the least intelligent portion of our population, for whom we provide no law, either for their protection or for the punishment of crime committed among themselves. Civilization even among white men could not long exist without the guarantees which law alone affords; yet our Indians are remitted by a great civilized government to the control, if control it can be called, of the rude regulations of petty, ignorant tribes. Year after year we expend millions of dollars for these people in the faint hope that, without law, we can civilize them. That hope has been, to a great degree, a long disappointment; and year after year we repeat the folly of the past.

. . . I believe it to be the duty of Congress at once to extend over Indian reservations the jurisdiction of United States courts, and to declare that each Indian in the United States shall occupy the same relation to law that a white man does. An Indian should be given to understand that no ancient custom, no tribal regulation, will shield him from just punishment for crime; and also that he will be effectually protected, by the authority and power of the Government, in his life, liberty, property, and character, as certainly as if he were a white man.

. . . I have little hope of any marked degree of success until the above suggestions are substantially adopted as a permanent Indian policy. If Congress concludes to act on these suggestions, laws should be passed at the coming session to extend the jurisdiction of the courts over all Indians, and to provide for the allotment of

lands in severalty in the Indian Territory, and on such other reservations as may be selected as permanent; and an appropriation should be made with which to begin the removal of Indians to their permanent homes.

I trust I may be pardoned for stating that it appears to me that the fundamental difficulty in our relations hitherto with Indians has been the want of a well-defined, clearly-understood, persistent purpose on the part of the Government... For a hundred years the United States has been wrestling with the "Indian question," but has never had an Indian policy.

. . . Surely it is time that a policy should be determined on, which shall be fully understood by the Government, the people, and the Indians. We cannot afford to allow this race to perish without making an honest effort to save it. We cannot afford to keep them in our midst as vagabonds and paupers.

I appeal to the statesmen of the country to give to this subject their earnest attention; the sooner it is settled on some wise and comprehensive principle the better for all concerned. We have despoiled the Indians of their rich hunting-grounds, thereby depriving them of their ancient means of support. Ought we not and shall we not give them at least a secure home, and the cheap but priceless benefit of just and equitable laws?

. . . I have the honor to be, sir, very respectfully, your obedient servant,

17. Bland-Allison Act (Excerpt), February 28, 1878

Be it enacted . . . , That there shall be coined, at the several mints of the United States, silver dollars of the weight of four hundred and twelve and a half grains Troy of standard silver, as provided in the act of . . . [January 18, 1837] . . . , on which shall be the devices and superscription provided by said act; which coins together with all silver dollars heretofore coined by the United States, of like weight and fineness, shall be a legal tender, at their nominal value, for all debts and dues public and private, except where otherwise expressly stipulated in the contract. And the Secretary of the Treasury is authorized and directed to purchase, from time to time, silver bullions at the market price thereof, not less than two million dollars worth per month, nor more than four million dollars worth per month, and cause the same to be coined monthly, as fast as so purchased into such dollars. . . . And any gain or seigniorage [sic] arising from this coinage shall be accounted for and paid into the Treasury, as provided under existing laws relative to the subsidiary coinage: Provided, That the amount of money at any one time invested in such silver bullion, exclusive of such resulting coin, shall not exceed five million dollars . . .

18. An Act to Execute Certain Treaty Stipulations Relating to the Chinese, May 6, 1882

Preamble. Whereas, in the opinion of the Government of the United States the coming of Chinese laborers to this country endangers the good order of certain localities within the territory thereof:

Therefore, Be it enacted by the Senate and House of Representatives of the United States of America in Congress assembled, That from and after the expiration of ninety days next after the passage of this act, and until the expiration of ten years next after the passage of this act, the coming of Chinese laborers to the United States be, and the same is hereby, suspended; and during such suspension it shall not be lawful for any Chinese laborer to come, or, having so come after the expiration of said ninety days, to remain within the United States.

SECTION 2. That the master of any vessel who shall knowingly bring within the United States on such vessel, and land or permit to be landed, and Chinese laborer, from any foreign port of place, shall be deemed guilty of a misdemeanor, and on conviction thereof shall be punished by a fine of not more than five hundred dollars for each and every such Chinese laborer so brought, and may be also imprisoned for a term not exceeding one year.

SECTION 3. That the two foregoing sections shall not apply to Chinese laborers who were in the United States on the seventeenth day of November, eighteen hundred and eighty, or who shall have come into the same before the expiration of ninety days next after the passage of this act, and who shall produce to such master before going on board such vessel, and shall produce to the collector of the port in the United States at which such vessel shall arrive, the evidence hereinafter in this act required of his being one of the laborers in this section mentioned; nor shall the two foregoing sections apply to the case of any master whose vessel, being bound to a port not within the United States by reason of being in distress or in stress of weather, or touching at any port of the United

States on its voyage to any foreign port of place; Provided, That all Chinese laborers brought on such vessel shall depart with the vessel on leaving port.

SECTION 4. That for the purpose of properly identifying Chinese laborers who were in the United States on the seventeenth day of November, eighteen hundred and eighty, or who shall have come into the same before the expiration of ninety days next after the passage of this act, and in order to furnish them with the proper evidence of their right to go from and come to the United States of their free will and accord, as provided by the treaty between the United States and China dated November seventeenth, eighteen hundred and eighty, the collector of customs of the district from which any such Chinese laborer shall depart from the United States shall, in person or by deputy, go on board each vessel having on board any such Chinese laborer and cleared or about to sail from his district for a foreign port, and on such vessel make a list of all such Chinese laborers, which shall be entered in registry-books to be kept for that purpose, in which shall be stated the name, age, occupation, last place of residence, physical marks or peculiarities, and all facts necessary for the identification of each of such Chinese laborers, which books shall be safely kept in the custom-house; and every such Chinese laborer so departing from the United States shall be entitled to, and shall receive, free of any charge or cost upon application therefore, from the collector or his deputy, at the time such list is taken, a certificate, signed by the collector or his deputy and attested by his seal of office, in such form as the Secretary of the Treasury shall prescribe, which certificate shall contain a statement of the name, age, occupation, last place of residence, personal description, and fact of identification of the Chinese laborer to whom the certificate is issued, corresponding with the said list and registry in all particulars. In case any Chinese laborer after having received such certificate shall leave such vessel before her departure he shall deliver his certificate to the master of the vessel, and if such Chinese laborer shall fail to return to such vessel before her departure from port the certificate shall be delivered by the master to the collector of customs for cancellation. The certificate herein provided for shall entitle the Chinese laborer to whom the same is issued to return to and re-enter the United States upon producing and delivering the same to the collector of customs of the district at which such Chinese laborer shall seek to re-enter; and upon delivery of such certificate by such Chinese laborer to the collector of customs at the time of re-entry in the United States, said collector shall cause the same to be filed in the custom house and duly canceled.

SECTION 5. That any Chinese laborer mentioned in section four of this act being in the United States, and desiring to depart from the United States by land, shall have the right to demand and receive, free of charge or cost, a certificate of identification similar to that provided for in section four of this act to be issued to such Chinese laborers as may desire to leave the United States by water; and it is hereby made the duty of the collector of customs of the district next adjoining the foreign country to which said Chinese laborer desires to go to issue such certificate, free of charge or cost, upon application by such Chinese laborer, and to enter the same upon registry-books to be kept by him for the purpose, as provided for in section four of this act.

SECTION 6. That in order to the faithful execution of articles one and two of the treaty in this act before mentioned, every Chinese person other than a laborer who may be entitled by said treaty and this act to come within the United States, and who shall be about to come to the United States, shall be identified as so entitled by the Chinese Government in each case, such identity to be evidenced by a certificate issued under the authority of said government, which certificate shall be in the English language or (if not in the English language) accompanied by a translation into English, stating such right to come, and which certificate shall state the name, title, or official rank, if any, the age, height, and all physical peculiarities, former and present occupation or profession, and place of residence in China of the person to whom the certificate is issued and that such person is entitled conformably to the treaty in this act mentioned to come within the United States. Such certificate shall be prima-facie evidence of the fact set forth therein, and shall be produced to the collector of customs, or his deputy, of the port in the district in the United States at which the person named therein shall arrive.

SECTION 7. That any person who shall knowingly and falsely alter or substitute any name for the name written in such certificate or forge any such certificate, or knowingly utter any forged or fraudulent certificate, or falsely personate any person named in any such certificate, shall be deemed guilty of a misde-

meanor; and upon conviction thereof shall be fined in a sum not exceeding one thousand dollars, an imprisoned in a penitentiary for a term of not more than five years.

SECTION 8. That the master of any vessel arriving in the United States from any foreign port or place shall, at the same time he delivers a manifest of the cargo, and if there be no cargo, then at the time of making a report of the entry of vessel pursuant to the law, in addition to the other matter required to be reported, and before landing, or permitting to land, and Chinese passengers, deliver and report to the collector of customs of the district in which such vessels shall have arrived a separate list of all Chinese passengers taken on board his vessel at any foreign port or place, and all such passengers on board the vessel at that time. Such list shall show the names of such passengers (and if accredited officers of the Chinese Government traveling on the business of that government, or their servants, with a note of such facts), and the name and other particulars, as shown by their respective certificates; and such list shall be sworn to by the master in the manner required by law in relation to the manifest of the cargo. Any willful refusal or neglect of any such master to comply with the provisions of this section shall incur the same penalties and forfeiture as are provided for a refusal or neglect to report and deliver a manifest of cargo.

SECTION 9. That before any Chinese passengers are landed from any such vessel, the collector, or his deputy, shall proceed to examine such passengers, comparing the certificates with the list and with the passengers; and no passenger shall be allowed to land in the United States from such vessel in violation of law.

SECTION 10. That every vessel whose master shall knowingly violate any of the provisions of this act shall be deemed forfeited to the United States, and shall be liable to seizure and condemnation on any district of the United States into which such vessel may enter or in which she may be found.

SECTION 11. That any person who shall knowingly bring into or cause to be brought into the United States by land, or who shall knowingly aid or abet the same, or aid or abet the landing in the United States from any vessel of any Chinese person not lawfully entitled to enter the United States, shall be deemed guilty of a misdemeanor, and shall, on conviction thereof, be fined in a sum not exceeding one thousand dollars, and imprisoned for a term not exceeding one year.

SECTION 12. That no Chinese person shall be permitted to enter the United States by land without producing to the proper officer of customs the certificate in this act required of Chinese persons seeking to land from a vessel. And any Chinese person found unlawfully within the United States shall be caused to be removed there from to the country from whence he came, by direction of the United States, after being brought before some justice, judge, or commissioner of a court of the United States and found to be one not lawfully entitled to be or remain in the United States.

SECTION 13. That this act shall not apply to diplomatic and other officers of the Chinese Government traveling upon the business of that government, whose credentials shall be taken as equivalent to the certificate in this act mentioned, and shall exempt them and their body and household servants from the provisions of this act as to other Chinese persons.

SECTION 14. That hereafter no State court or court of the United States shall admit Chinese to citizenship; and all laws in conflict with this act are hereby repealed.

SECTION 15. That the words "Chinese laborer", whenever used in this act, shall be construed to mean both skilled and unskilled laborers and Chinese employed in mining.

19. PENDLETON CIVIL SERVICE REFORM ACT, JANUARY 16, 1883

An act to regulate and improve the civil service of the United States.

Be it enacted by the Senate and House of Representatives of the United States of America in Congress assembled, That the President is authorized to appoint, by and with the advice and consent of the Senate, three persons, not more than two of whom shall be adherents of the same party, as Civil Service Commissioners, and said three commissioners shall constitute the United States Civil Service Commission. Said commissioners shall hold no other official place under the United States. The President may remove any commissioner; and any vacancy in the position of commissioner shall be so filled by the President, by and with the advice and consent of the Senate, as to conform to said conditions for the first selection of commissioners. The commissioners shall each receive a salary of three thousand five hundred dollars a year. And each of said commissioners shall be paid his necessary traveling expenses incurred in the discharge of his duty as a commissioner.

SECTION 2. That it shall be the duty of said commissioners:

FIRST. To aid the President, as he may request, in preparing suitable rules for carrying this act into effect, and when said rules shall have been promulgated it shall be the duty of all officers of the United States in the departments and offices to which any such rules may relate to aid, in all proper ways, in carrying said rules, and any modifications thereof, into effect.

SECOND. And, among other things, said rules shall provide and declare, as nearly as the conditions of good administration will warrant, as follows:

First, for open, competitive examinations for testing the fitness of applicants for the public service now classified or to be classified here-under. Such examinations shall be practical in their character, and so far as may be shall relate to those matters which will fairly test the relative capacity and fitness of the persons examined to discharge the duties of the service into which they seek to be appointed.

Second, that all the offices, places, and employments so arranged or to be arranged in classes shall be filled by selections according to grade from among those graded highest as the results of such competitive examinations.

Third, appointments to the public service aforesaid in the departments at Washington shall be apportioned among the several States and Territories and the District of Columbia upon the basis of population as ascertained at the last preceding census. Every application for an examination shall contain, among other things, a statement, under oath, setting forth his or her actual bona fide residence at the time of making the application, as well as how long he or she has been a resident of such place.

Fourth, that there shall be a period of probation before any absolute appointment or employment aforesaid.

Fifth, that no person in the public service is for the reason under any obligations to contribute to any political fund, or to render any political service, and that he will not be removed or otherwise prejudiced for refusing to do so.

Sixth, that no person in said service has any right to use his official authority or influence to coerce the political action of any person or body.

Seventh, there shall be non-competitive examinations in all proper cases before the commission, when competent persons do not compete, after notice has been given of the existence of the vacancy, under such rules as may be prescribed by the commissioners as to the manner of giving notice.

Eighth, that notice shall be given in writing by the appointing power to said commission of the persons selected for appointment or employment from among those who have been examined, of the place of residence of such persons, of the rejection of any such persons after probation, of transfers, resignations, and removals and of the date thereof, and a record of the same shall be kept by said commission. And any necessary exceptions from said eight fundamental provisions of the rules shall be set forth in connection with such rules, and the reasoned there-for shall be stated in the annual reports of the commission.

THIRD. Said commission shall, subject to the rules that may be made by the President, make regulations for, and have control of, such examinations, and, through its members or the examiners, it shall supervise and preserve the records of the same; and said commission shall keep minutes of its own proceedings.

FOURTH. Said commission may make investigations concerning the facts, and may report upon all matters touching the enforcement and effects of said rules and regulations, and concerning the action of any examiner or board of examiners hereinafter provided for, and its own subordinates, and those in the public service, in respect to the execution of this act.

FIFTH. Said commission shall make an annual report to the President for transmission to Congress, showing its own action, the rules and regulations and the exceptions thereto in force, the practical effects thereof, and any suggestions it may approve for the more effectual accomplishment of the purposes of this act.

SECTION 3. That said commission is authorized to employ a chief examiner, a part of whose duty it shall be, under its direction, to act with the examining boards, so far as practicable, whether at Washington or elsewhere, and to secure accuracy, uniformity, and justice in all their proceedings, which shall be at all times open to him. The chief examiner shall be entitled to receive a salary at the rate of three thousand dollars a year, and he shall be paid his necessary traveling expenses incurred in the discharge of his duty. The commission shall have a secretary, to be appointed by the President, who shall receive a salary of one thousand six hundred dollars per annum. It may, when necessary, employ a stenographer, and a messenger, who shall be paid, when employed, the former at the rate of one thousand six hundred dollars a year, and the latter at the rate of six hundred dollars a year. The commission shall, at Washington, and in one or more places in each State and Territory where examinations are to take place, designate and select a suitable number of persons, not less than three, in the official service of the United States, residing in said State or Territory, after consulting the head of the department or office in which such persons serve, to be members of boards of examiners, and may at any time substitute any other person in said service living in such State or Territory in the place of anyone so selected. Such boards of examiners shall be so located as to make it reasonably convenient and inexpensive for applicants to attend before them; and where there are persons to be examined in any State or Territory, examinations shall be held therein at least twice in each year. It shall be the duty of the collector, postmaster, and other officers of the United States at any place outside of the District of Columbia where examinations are directed by the President or by said board to be held, to allow the reasonable use of the public buildings for holding such examinations, and in all proper ways to facilitate the same.

SECTION 4. That it shall be the duty of the Secretary of the Interior to cause suitable and convenient rooms and accommodations to be assigned or provided, and to be furnished, heated, and lighted, at the city of Washington, for carrying on the work of said commission and said examinations, and to cause the necessary stationery and other articles to be supplied, and the necessary printing to be done for said commission.

SECTION 5. That any said commissioner, examiner, copyist, or messenger, or any person in the public service who shall willfully and corruptly, by himself or in co-operation with one or more other persons, defeat, deceive, or obstruct any person in respect of his or her right of examination according to any such rules or regulations, or who shall willfully, corruptly, and falsely mark, grade, estimate, or report upon the examination or proper standing of any person examined hereunder, or aid in so doing, or who shall willfully and corruptly make any false representations concerning the same or concerning the person examined, or who shall willfully and corruptly furnish to any person any special or secret information for the purpose of either improving or injuring the prospects or chances of any person so examined, or to be examined, being appointed, employed, or promoted, shall for each such offense be deemed guilty of a misdemeanor, and upon conviction thereof, shall be punished by a fine of not less than one hundred dollars, nor more than one thousand dollars, or by imprisonment not less than ten days, nor more than one year, or by both such fine and imprisonment.

SECTION 6. That within sixty days after the passage of this act it shall be the duty of the Secretary of the Treasury, in as near conformity as may be to the classification of certain clerks now existing under the one hundred and sixty-third section of the Revised Statutes to arrange in classes the several clerks and persons employed by the collector, naval officer, surveyor, and appraisers, or either of them, or being in the public service, at their respective offices in each customs district where the whole number of said clerks and persons shall be all together as many as fifty. And thereafter, from time to time, on the direction of the President, said Secretary shall make the like classification or arrangement of clerks and persons so employed, in connection with any said office or offices, in any other customs district. And, upon like request, and for the purposes of this act, said Secretary shall arrange in one or more of said classes, or of existing classes, any other clerks, agents, or persons employed under his department in any said district not now classified; and every such arrangement and classification upon being made shall be reported to the President.

Second. Within said sixty days it shall be the duty of the Postmaster-General, in general conformity to said one hundred and sixty-third section, to separately arrange in classes the several clerks and persons employed, or in the public service at each post-office, or under any post-master of the United States, where the whole number of said clerks and persons shall together amount to as many as fifty. And thereafter, from time to time, on the direction of the President, it shall be the duty of the Postmaster-General to arrange in like classes the clerks and persons so employed in the postal service in connection with any other post-office; and every such arrangement and classification upon being made shall be reported to the President.

Third. That from time to time said Secretary, the Postmaster-General, and each of the heads of departments mentioned in the one hundred and fifty-eight section of the Revised Statutes, and each head of an office, shall, on the direction of the President, and for facilitating the execution of this act, respectively revise any then existing classification or arrangement of those

in their respective departments and offices, and shall, for the purposes of the examination herein provided for, include in one or more of such classes, so far as practicable, subordinate places, clerks, and officers in the public service pertaining to their respective departments not before classified for examination.

SECTION 7. That after the expiration of six months from the passage of this act no officer or clerk shall be appointed, and no person shall be employed to enter or be promoted in either of the said classes now existing, or that may be arranged hereunder pursuant to said rules, until he has passed an examination, or is shown to be specially exempted from such examination in conformity herewith. But nothing herein contained shall be construed to take from those honorably discharged from the military or naval service any preference conferred by the seventeen hundred and fifty-fourth section of the Revised Statutes, nor to take from the President any authority not inconsistent with this act conferred by the seventeen hundred and fifty-third section of said statutes; nor shall any officer not in the executive branch of the government, or any person merely employed as a laborer or workman, be required to be classified hereunder; nor, unless by direction of the Senate, shall any person who has been nominated for confirmation by the Senate be required to be classified or to pass an examination.

SECTION 8. That no person habitually using intoxicating beverages to excess shall be appointed to, or retained in, any office, appointment, or employment to which the provisions of this act are applicable.

SECTION 9. That whenever there are already two or more members of a family in the public service in the grades covered by this act, no other member of such family shall be eligible to appointment to any of said grades.

SECTION 10. That no recommendation of any person who shall apply for office or place under the provisions of this act which may be given by any Senator or member of the House of Representatives, except as to the character or residence of the applicant, shall be received or considered by any person concerned in making any examination or appointment under this act.

SECTION 11. That no Senator, or Representative, or Territorial Delegate of the Congress, or Senator, Representative, or Delegate elect, or any officer or employee of either of said houses, and no executive, judicial, military, or naval officer of the United States, and no clerk or employee of any department, branch or bureau of the executive, judicial, or military or naval service of the United States, shall, directly or indirectly, solicit or receive, or be in any manner concerned ill soliciting or receiving, any assessment, subscription, or contribution for any political purpose whatever, from any officer, clerk, or employee of the United States, or any department, branch, or bureau thereof, or from any person receiving any salary or compensation from moneys derived from the Treasury of the United States.

SECTION 12. That no person shall, in any room or building occupied in the discharge of official duties by any officer or employee of the United States mentioned in this act, or in any navy-yard, fort, or arsenal, solicit in any manner whatever, or receive any contribution of money or any other thing of value for any political purpose whatever.

SECTION 13. No officer or employee of the United States mentioned in this act shall discharge, or promote, or degrade, or in manner change the official rank or compensation of any other officer or employee, or promise or threaten so to do, for giving or withholding or neglecting to make any contribution of money or other valuable thing for any political purpose.

SECTION 14. That no officer, clerk, or other person in the service of the United States shall, directly or indirectly, give or hand over to any other officer, clerk, or person in the service of the United States, or to any Senator or Member of the House of Representatives, or Territorial Delegate, any money or other valuable thing on account of or to be applied to the promotion of any political object whatever.

SECTION 15. That any person who shall be guilty of violating any provision of the four foregoing sections shall be deemed guilty of a misdemeanor, and shall, on conviction thereof, be punished by a fine not exceeding five thousand dollars, or by imprisonment for a term not exceeding three years, or by such fine and imprisonment both, in the discretion of the court.

20. DAWES ACT, FEBRUARY 8, 1887

An Act to provide for the allotment of lands in severalty to Indians on the various reservations, and to extend the protection of the laws of the United States and the Territories over the Indians, and for other purposes.

Be it enacted by the Senate and House of Representatives of the United States of America in Congress assembled, That in all cases where any tribe or band of Indians has been, or shall hereafter be, located upon any reservation created for their use, either by treaty stipulation or by virtue of an act of Congress or executive order setting apart the same for their use, the President of the United States be, and he hereby is, authorized, whenever in his opinion any reservation or any part thereof of such Indians is advantageous for agricultural and grazing purposes, to cause said reservation, or any part thereof, to be surveyed, or resurveyed if necessary, and to allot the lands in said reservation in severalty to any Indian located thereon in quantities as follows:

To each head of a family, one-quarter of a section;

To each single person over eighteen years of age, one-eighth of a section;

To each orphan child under eighteen years of age, one-eighth of a section; and

To each other single person under eighteen years now living, or who may be born prior to the date of the order of the President directing an allotment of the lands embraced in any reservation, one-sixteenth of a section:

Provided, That in case there is not sufficient land in any of said reservations to allot lands to each individual of the classes above named in quantities as above provided, the lands embraced in such reservation or reservations shall be allotted to each individual of each of said classes pro rata in accordance with the provisions of this act: And provided further, That where the treaty or act of Congress setting apart such reservation provides the allotment of lands in severalty in quantities in excess of those herein provided, the President, in making allotments upon such reservation, shall allot the lands to each individual Indian belonging thereon in quantity as specified in such treaty or act: And provided further, That when the lands allotted are only valuable for grazing purposes, an additional allotment of such grazing lands, quantities as above provided, shall be made to each individual.

SECTION 2. That all allotments set apart under the provisions of this act shall be selected by the Indians, heads of families selecting for their minor children, and the agents shall select for each orphan child, and in such manner as to embrace the improvements of the Indians making the selection, where the improvements of two or more Indians have been made on the same legal subdivision of land, unless they shall otherwise agree, a provisional line may be run dividing said lands between them, and the amount to which each is entitled shall be equalized in the assignment of the remainder of the land to which they are entitled under this act: Provided, That if any one entitled to an allotment shall fail to make a selection within four years after the President shall direct that allotments may be made on a particular reservation, the Secretary of the Interior may direct the agent of such tribe or band, if such there be, and if there be no agent, then a special agent appointed for that purpose, to make a selection for such Indian, which selection shall be allotted as in cases where selections are made by the Indians, and patents shall issue in like manner.

SECTION 3. That the allotments provided for in this act shall be made by special agents appointed by the President for such purpose, and the agents in charge of the respective reservations on which the allotments are directed to be made, under such rules and regulations as the Secretary of the Interior may from time to time prescribe, and shall be certified by such agents to the Commissioner of Indian Affairs, in duplicate, one copy to be retained in the Indian Office and the other to be transmitted to the Secretary of the Interior for his action, and to be deposited in the General Land Office.

SECTION 4. That where any Indian not residing upon a reservation, or for whose tribe no reservation has been provided by treaty, act of Congress, or executive order, shall make settlement upon any surveyed or unsurveyed lands of the United States not otherwise appropriated, he or she shall be entitled, upon application to the local land-office for the district in which the lands are located, to have the same allotted to him or her, and to his or her children, in quantities and manner as provided in this act for Indians residing upon reservations; and when such settlement is made upon unsurveyed lands, the grant to such Indians shall be adjusted upon the survey of the lands so as to conform thereto; and patents shall be issued to them for such lands in the manner and with the restrictions as herein provided. And the fees to which the officers of such local land-office would have been entitled had such lands been entered under the general laws for the disposition of the public lands shall be paid to them, from any moneys in the Treasury of the United States not otherwise appropriated, upon a statement of an account in their behalf for such fees by the Commissioner of the General Land Office, and a cer-

tification of such account to the Secretary of the Treasury by the Secretary of the Interior.

SECTION 5. That upon the approval of the allotments provided for in this act by the Secretary of the Interior, he shall cause patents to issue therefore in the name of the allottees, which patents shall be of the legal effect, and declare that the United States does and will hold the land thus allotted, for the period of twenty-five years, in trust for the sole use and benefit of the Indian to whom such allotment shall have been made, or, in case of his decease, of his heirs according to the laws of the State or Territory where such land is located, and that at the expiration of said period the United States will convey the same by patent to said Indian, or his heirs as aforesaid, in fee, discharged of said trust and free of all charge or incumbrance whatsoever. Provided, That the President of the United States may in any case in his discretion extend the period. And if any conveyance shall be made of the lands set apart and allotted as herein provided, or any contract made touching the same, before the expiration of the time above mentioned, such conveyance or contract shall be absolutely null and void: Provided, That the law of descent and partition in force in the State or Territory where such lands are situated shall apply thereto after patents therefore have been executed and delivered, except as herein otherwise provided; and the laws of the State of Kansas regulating the descent and partition of real estate shall, so far as practicable, apply to all lands in the Indian Territory which may be allotted in severalty under the provisions of this act: And provided further, That at any time after lands have been allotted to all the Indians of any tribe as herein provided, or sooner if in the opinion of the President it shall be for the best interests of said tribe, it shall be lawful for the Secretary of the Interior to negotiate with such Indian tribe for the purchase and release by said tribe, in conformity with the treaty or statute under which such reservation is held, of such portions of its reservation not allotted as such tribe shall, from time to time, consent to sell, on such terms and conditions as shall be considered just and equitable between the United States and said tribe of Indians, which purchase shall not be complete until ratified by Congress, and the form and manner of executing such release prescribed by Congress: Provided however, That all lands adapted to agriculture, with or without irrigation so sold or released to the United States by any Indian tribe shall be held by the United States for the sale purpose of securing homes to actual settlers and shall be disposed of by the United States to actual and bona fide settlers only tracts not exceeding one hundred and sixty acres to any one person, on such terms as Congress shall prescribe, subject to grants which Congress may make in aid of education: And provided further, That no patents shall issue therefore except to the person so taking the same as and homestead, or his heirs, and after the expiration of five years occupancy thereof as such homestead; and any conveyance of said lands taken as a homestead, or any contract touching the same, or lieu thereon, created prior to the date of such patent, shall be null and void. And the sums agreed to be paid by the United States as purchase money for any portion of any such reservation shall be held in the Treasury of the United States for the sole use of the tribe or tribes of Indians; to whom such reservations belonged; and the same, with interest thereon at three per cent per annum, shall be at all times subject to appropriation by Congress for the education and civilization of such tribe or tribes of Indians or the members thereof. The patents aforesaid shall be recorded in the General Land Office, and afterward delivered, free of charge, to the allottee entitled thereto. And if any religious society or other organization is now occupying any of the public lands to which this act is applicable, for religious or educational work among the Indians, the Secretary of the Interior is hereby authorized to confirm such occupation to such society or organization, in quantity not exceeding one hundred and sixty acres in any one tract, so long as the same shall be so occupied, on such terms as he shall deem just; but nothing herein contained shall change or alter any claim of such society for religious or educational purposes heretofore granted by law. And hereafter in the employment of Indian police, or any other employees in the public service among any of the Indian tribes or bands affected by this act, and where Indians can perform the duties required, those Indians who have availed themselves of the provisions of this act and become citizens of the United States shall be preferred.

SECTION 6. That upon the completion of said allotments and the patenting of the lands to said allottees, each and every number of the respective bands or tribes of Indians to whom allotments have been made shall have the benefit of and be subject to the laws, both civil and criminal, of the State or Territory in which they may reside; and no Territory shall pass or enforce any law denying any such Indian within its jurisdiction the equal protection of the law. And every Indian born within the territorial limits of the United States to whom allotments shall have been made under the provisions of this act, or under any law or treaty, and every Indian born within the territorial limits of the United States who has voluntarily taken up, within said limits, his residence separate and apart from any tribe of Indians therein, and has adopted the habits of civilized life, is hereby declared to be a citizen of the United States, and is entitled to all the rights, privileges, and immunities of such citizens, whether said Indian has been or not, by birth or otherwise, a member of any tribe of Indians within the territorial limits of the United States without in any manner affecting the right of any such Indian to tribal or other property.

SECTION 7. That in cases where the use of water for irrigation is necessary to render the lands within any Indian reservation available for agricultural purposes, the Secretary of the Interior be, and he is hereby, authorized to prescribe such rules and regulations as he may deem necessary to secure a just and equal distribution thereof among the Indians residing upon any such reservation; and no other appropriation or grant of water by any riparian proprietor shall be authorized or permitted to the damage of any other riparian proprietor.

SECTION 8. That the provisions of this act shall not extend to the territory occupied by the Cherokees, Creeks, Choctaws, Chickasaws, Seminoles, and Osage, Miamies and Peorias, and Sacs and Foxes, in the Indian Territory, nor to any of the reservations of the Seneca Nation of New York Indians in the State of New York, nor to that strip of territory in the State of Nebraska adjoining the Sioux Nation on the south added by executive order.

SECTION 9. That for the purpose of making the surveys and resurveys mentioned in section two of this act, there be, and hereby is, appropriated, out of any moneys in the Treasury not otherwise appropriated, the sum of one hundred thousand dollars, to be repaid proportionately out of the proceeds of the sales of such land as may be acquired from the Indians under the provisions of this act.

SECTION 10. That nothing in this act contained shall be so construed to affect the right and power of Congress to grant the right of way through any lands granted to an Indian, or a tribe of Indians, for railroads or other highways, or telegraph lines, for the public use, or condemn such lands to public uses, upon making just compensation.

SECTION 11. That nothing in this act shall be so construed as to prevent the removal of the Southern Ute Indians from their present reservation in Southwestern Colorado to a new reservation by and with consent of a majority of the adult male members of said tribe.

21. INTERSTATE COMMERCE ACT, FEBRUARY 4, 1887

An act to regulate Commerce.

Be it enacted by the Senate and House of Representatives of the United States of America in Congress assembled, That the provisions of this act shall apply to any common carrier or carriers engaged in the transportation of passengers or property wholly by railroad, or partly by railroad and partly by water when both are used, under a common control, management, or arrangement, for a continuous carriage or shipment, from one State or Territory of the United States, or the District of Columbia, to any other State or Territory of the United States, or the District of Columbia, or from any place in the United States to an adjacent foreign country, or from any place in the United States through a foreign country to any other place in the United States, and also to the transportation in like manner of property shipped from any place in the United States to a foreign country and carried from such place to a port of trans-shipment, or shipped from a foreign country to any place in the United States and carried to such place from a port of entry either in the United States or an adjacent foreign country: *Provided, however,* That the provisions of this act shall not apply to the transportation of passengers or property, or to the receiving, delivering, storage, or handling of property, wholly within one State, and not shipped to or from a foreign country from or to any State or Territory as aforesaid. The term "railroad" as used in this act shall include all bridges and ferries used or operated in connection with any railroad, and also all the road in use by any corporation operating a railroad, whether owned or operated under a contract, agreement, or lease; and the term "transportation" shall include all instrumentalities of shipment or carriage.

All charges made for any service rendered or to be rendered in the transportation of passengers or property as aforesaid, or in connection therewith, or for the receiving, delivering, storage, or handling of such property, shall be reasonable and just; and every unjust and unreasonable charge for such service is prohibited and declared to be unlawful.

SECTION 2. That if any common carrier subject to the provisions of this act shall, directly or indirectly, by any special rate, rebate, drawback, or other device, charge, demand, collect, or receive from any person or persons a greater or less compensation for any service rendered, or to be rendered, in the transportation of passengers or property, subject to the provisions of this act, than it charges, demands, collects, or receives from any other person or persons for doing for him or them a like and contemporaneous service in the transportation of a like kind of traffic under substantially similar circumstances and conditions, such common carrier shall be deemed guilty of unjust discrimination, which is hereby prohibited and declared to be unlawful.

SECTION 3. That it shall be unlawful for any common carrier subject to the provisions of this act to make or give any undue or unreasonable preference or advantage to any particular person, company, firm, corporation, or locality, or any particular description of traffic, in any respect whatsoever, or to subject any particular person, company, firm, corporation, or locality, or any particular description of traffic, to any undue or unreasonable prejudice or disadvantage in any respect whatsoever.

Every common carrier subject to the provisions of this act shall according to their respective powers, afford all reasonable, proper, and equal facilities for the interchange of traffic between their respective lines, and for the receiving, forwarding, and delivering of passengers and property to and from their several lines and those connection therewith, and shall not discriminate in their rates and charges between such connecting lines; but this shall not be construed as requiring any such common carrier to give the use of its tracks or terminal facilities to another carrier engaged in like business.

SECTION 4. That it shall be unlawful for any common carrier subject to the provisions of this act to charge or receive any greater compensation in the aggregate for the transportation of passengers or of like kind of property, under substantially similar circumstances and conditions, for a shorter than for a longer distance over the same line, in the same direction, the shorter being included within the longer distance; but this shall not be construed as authorizing any common carrier within the terms of this act to charge and receive as great compensation for a shorter as for a longer distance: *Provided, however,* That upon application to the Commission appointed under the provisions of this act, such common carrier may, in special cases, after investigation by the Commission, be authorized to charge less for longer than for shorter distances for the transportation of passengers or property; and the Commission may from time to time prescribe the extent to which such designated common carrier may be relieved from the operation of this section of this act.

SECTION 5. That it shall be unlawful for any common carrier subject to the provisions of this act to enter into any contract, agreement, or combination with any other common carrier or carriers for the pooling of freights of different and competing railroads, or to divide between them the aggregate or net proceeds of the earnings of such railroads, or any portion thereof; and in any case of an agreement for the pooling of freights as aforesaid, each day of its continuance shall be deemed a separate offense.

SECTION 6. That every common carrier subject to the provisions of this act shall print and keep for public inspection schedules showing the rates and fares and charges for the transportation of passengers and property which any such common carrier has established and which are in force at the time upon its railroad, as defined by the first section of this act. The schedules printed as aforesaid by any such common carrier shall plainly state the places upon its railroad between which property and passengers will be carried, and shall contain the classification of freight in force upon such railroad, and shall also state separately the terminal charges and any rules or regulations which in any wise change, affect, or determine any part of the aggregate of such aforesaid rates and fares and charges. Such schedules shall be plainly printed in large type, of at least the size of ordinary pica, and copies for the use of the public shall be kept in every depot or station upon any such railroad, in such places and in such form that they can be conveniently inspected.

Any common carrier subject to the provisions of this act receiving freight in the United States to be carried through a foreign country to any place in the United States shall also in like manner print and keep for public inspection, at every depot where such freight is received for shipment, schedules showing the through rates established and charged by such common carrier to all points in the United States beyond the foreign country to which it accepts freight for shipment; and any freight shipped from the United States through a foreign country into the United States, the through rate on which shall not have been made public as required by this act, shall, before it is admitted into the United States from said foreign country, be subject to customs duties as if said freight were of foreign production; and any law in conflict with this section is hereby repealed.

No advance shall be made in the rates, fares, and charges which have been established and published as aforesaid by any common carrier in compliance with the requirements of this section, except after ten days' public notice, which shall plainly state the changes proposed to be made in the schedule then in force, and the time when the increased rates, fares, or charges will go into effect; and the proposed changes shall be shown by printing new schedules, or shall be plainly indicated upon the schedules in force at the time and kept for public inspection. Reductions in such published rates, fares, or charges may be made without previous public notice; but whenever any such reduction is made, notice of the same shall immediately be publicly posted and the changes made shall immediately be made public by printing new schedules, or shall immediately be plainly indicated upon the schedules at the time in force and kept for public inspection.

And when any such common carrier shall have established and published its rates, fares, and charges in compliance with the provisions of this section, it shall be unlawful for such common carrier to charge, demand, collect, or receive from any person or persons a greater or less compensation for the transportation of passengers or property, or for any services in connection therewith, than is specified in such published schedule of rates, fares, and charges as may at the time be in force.

Every common carrier subject to the provisions of this act shall file with the Commission hereinafter provided for copies of its schedules of rates, fares, and charges which have been established and published in compliance with the requirements of this section, and shall promptly notify said Commission of all changes made in the same. Every such common carrier shall also file with said Commission copies of all contracts, agreements, or arrangements with other common carriers in relation to any traffic affected by the provisions of this act to which it may be a party. And in cases where passengers and freight pass over continuous lines or routes operated by more than one common carrier, and the several common carriers operating such lines or routes establish joint tariffs of rates or fares or charges for such continuous lines or routes, copies of such joint tariffs shall also, in like manner, be filed with said Commission. Such joint rates, fares, and charges on such continuous lines so filed as aforesaid shall be made public by such common carriers when directed by said Commission, in so far as may, in the judgment of the Commission, be deemed practicable; and said Commission shall from time to time prescribe the measure of publicity which shall be given to such rates, fares, and charges, or to such part of them as it may deem it practicable for such common carriers to publish, and the places in which they shall be published; but no common carrier party to any such joint tariff shall be liable for the failure of any other common carrier party thereto to observe and adhere to the rates, fares, or charges thus made and published.

If any such common carrier shall neglect or refuse to file or publish its schedules or tariffs of rates, fares, and charges as provided in this section, or any part of the same, such common carrier shall, in addition to other penalties herein prescribed, be subject to a writ of mandamus, to be issued by any circuit court of the United States in the judicial district wherein the principal office of said common carrier is situated or wherein such offense may be committed, and if such common carrier be a foreign corporation, in the judicial circuit wherein such common carrier accepts traffic and has an agent to perform such service, to compel compliance with the aforesaid provisions of this section; and such writ shall issue in the name of the people of the United States, at the relation of the Commissioners appointed under the provisions of this act; and failure to comply with its requirements shall be punishable as and for a contempt; and the said Commissioners, as complainants, may also apply, in any such circuit of the United States, for a writ of injunction against such common carrier, to restrain such common carrier from receiving or transporting property among the several States and Territories of the United States, or between the United States and adjacent foreign countries, or between ports of transshipment and of entry and the several States and Territories of the United States, as mentioned in the first section of this act, until such common carrier shall have complied with the aforesaid provisions of this section of this act.

SECTION 7. That it shall be unlawful for any common carrier subject to the provisions of this act to enter into any combination, contract, or agreement, expressed or implied, to prevent, by change of time schedule, carriage in different cars, or by other means or devices, the carriage of freights from being continuous from the place of shipment to the place of destination; and no break of bulk, stoppage, or interruption made by such common carrier shall prevent the carriage of freights from being and being treated as one continuous carriage from the place of shipment to the place of destination, unless such break, stoppage, or interruption was made in good faith for some necessary purpose, and without any intent to avoid or unnecessarily interrupt such continuous carriage or to evade any of the provisions of this act.

SECTION 8. That in case any common carrier subject to the provisions of this act shall do, cause to be done, or permit to be done any act, matter, or thing in this act prohibited or declared to be unlawful, or shall omit to do any act, matter, or thing in this act required to be done, such common carrier shall be liable to the person or persons injured thereby for the full amount of damages sustained in consequence of any such violation of the provisions of this act, together with a reasonable counsel or attorney's fee, to be fixed by the court in every case of recovery, which attorney's fee shall be taxed and collected as part of the costs in the case.

SECTION 9. That any person or persons claiming to be damaged by any common carrier subject to the provisions of this act may either make complaint to the Commission as hereinafter provided for, or may bring suit in his or their own behalf for the recovery of the damages for which such common carrier may be liable under the provisions of this act, in any district or circuit court of the United States of competent jurisdiction; but such person or persons shall not have the right to pursue both of said remedies, and must in each case elect which one of the two methods of procedure herein provided for he or they will adopt. In any such action brought for the recovery of damages the court before which the same shall be pending may compel any director, officer, receiver, trustee, or agent of the corporation or company defendant in such suit to attend, appear, and testify in such case, and may compel the production of the books and papers of such corporation or company party to any such suit; the claim that any such testimony or evidence may tend to criminate the person giving such evidence shall not excuse such witness from testifying, but such evidence or testimony shall not be used against such person on the trial of any criminal proceeding.

SECTION 10. That any common carrier subject to the provisions of this act, or, whenever such common carrier is a corporation, any director or officer thereof, or any receiver, trustee, lessee, agent, or person acting for or employed by such corporation, who, alone or with any other corporation, company, person, or party, shall willfully do or cause to be done, or shall willingly suffer or permit to be done, any act, matter, or thing in this act prohibited or declared to be unlawful, or who shall aid or abet therein, or shall willfully omit or fail to do any act, matter, or thing in this act required to be done, or shall cause or willingly suffer or permit any act, matter, or thing so directed or required by this act to be done not to be so done, or shall aid or abet any such omission or failure, or shall be guilty of any infraction of this act, or shall aid or abet therein, shall be deemed guilty of a misdemeanor, and shall, upon conviction thereof in any district court of the United States within the jurisdiction of which such offense was committed, be subject to a fine of not to exceed five thousand dollars for each offense.

SECTION 11. That a Commission is hereby created and established to be known as the Inter-State Commerce Commission, which shall be composed of five Commissioners, who shall be appointed by the President, by and with the advice and consent of the Senate. The Commissioners first appointed under this act shall continue in office for the term of two, three, four, five, and six years, respectively, from the first day of January, anno Domini eighteen hundred and eighty-seven, the term of each to be designated by the President; but their successors shall be appointed for terms of six years, except that any person chosen to fill a vacancy shall be appointed only for the unexpired term of the Commissioner whom he shall succeed. Any Commissioner may be removed by the President for inefficiency, neglect of duty, or malfea-

sance in office. Not more than three of the Commissioners shall be appointed from the same political party. No person in the employ of or holding any official relation to any common carrier subject to the provisions of this act, or owning stock or bonds thereof, or who is in any manner pecuniarily interested therein, shall enter upon the duties of or hold such office. Said Commissioners shall not engage in any other business, vocation, or employment. No vacancy in the Commission shall impair the right of the remaining Commissioners to exercise all the powers of the Commission.

SECTION 12. That the Commission hereby created shall have authority to inquire into the management of the business of all common carriers subject to the provisions of this act, and shall keep itself informed as to the manner and method in which the same is conducted, and shall have the right to obtain from such common carriers full and complete information necessary to enable the Commission to perform the duties and carry out the objects for which it was created; and for the purposes of this act the Commission shall have power to require the attendance and testimony of witnesses and the production of all books, papers, tariffs, contracts, agreements, and documents relating to any matter under investigation, and to that end may invoke the aid of any court of the United States in requiring the attendance and testimony of witnesses and the production of books, papers, and documents under the provisions of this section.

And any of the circuit courts of the United States within the jurisdiction of which such inquiry is carried on may, in case of contumacy or refusal to obey a subpoena issued to any common carrier subject to the provisions of this act, or other person, issue an order requiring such common carrier or other person to appear before said Commission (and produce books and papers if so ordered) and give evidence touching the matter in question; and any failure to obey such order of the court may be punished by such court as a contempt thereof. The claim that any such testimony or evidence may tend to criminate the person giving such evidence shall not excuse such witness from testifying; but such evidence or testimony shall not be used against such person on the trial of any criminal proceeding.

SECTION 13. That any person, firm, corporation, or association, or any mercantile, agricultural, or manufacturing society, or any body politic or municipal organization complaining of anything done or omitted to be done by any common carrier subject to the provisions of this act in contravention of the provisions thereof, may apply to said Commission by petition, which shall briefly state the facts; whereupon a statement of the charges thus made shall be forwarded by the Commission to such common carrier, who shall be called upon to satisfy the complaint or to answer the same in writing a reasonable time, to be specified by the Commission. If such common carrier, within the time specified, shall make reparation for the injury alleged to have been done, said carrier shall be relieved of liability to the complainant only for the particular violation of law thus complained of. If such carrier shall not satisfy the complaint within the time specified, or there shall appear to be any reasonable ground for investigating said complaint, it shall be the duty of the Commission to investigate the matters complained of in such manner and by such means as it shall deem proper.

Said Commission shall in like manner investigate any complaint forwarded by the railroad commissioner or railroad commission of any State or Territory, at the request of such commissioner or commission, and may institute any inquiry on its own motion in the same manner and to the same effect as though complaint had been made.

No complaint shall at any time be dismissed because of the absence of direct damage to the complainant.

SECTION 14. That whenever an investigation shall be made by said Commission, it shall be its duty to make a report in writing in respect thereto, which shall include the findings of fact upon which the conclusions of the Commission are based, together with its recommendation as to what reparation, if any, should be made by the common carrier to any party or parties who may be found to have been injured; and such findings so made shall thereafter, in all judicial proceedings, be deemed prima facie evidence as to each and every fact found.

All reports of investigations made by the Commission shall be entered of record, and a copy thereof shall be furnished to the party who may have complained, and to any common carrier that may have been complained of.

SECTION 15. That if in any case in which an investigation shall be made by said Commission it shall be made to appear to the satisfaction of the Commission, either by the testimony of witnesses or other evidence, that anything has been done or omitted to be done in violation of the provisions of this act, or of any law cognizable by said Commission, by any common carrier, or that any injury or damage has been sustained by the party or parties complaining, or by other parties aggrieved in consequence of any such violation, it shall be the duty of the Commission to forth with cause a copy of its report in respect thereto to be delivered to such common carrier, together with a notice to said common carrier to cease and desist from such violation, or to make reparation for the injury so found to have been done, or both, within a reasonable time, to be specified by the Commission; and if, within the time specified, it shall be made to appear to the Commission that such common carrier has ceased from such violation of law, and has made reparation for the injury found to have been done, in compliance with the report and notice of the Commission, or to the satisfaction of the party complaining, a statement to that effect shall be entered of record by the Commission, and the said common carrier shall thereupon be relieved from further liability or penalty for such particular violation of law.

SECTION 16. That whenever any common carrier, as defined in and subject to the provisions of this act, shall violate or refuse or neglect to obey and lawful order or requirement of the Commission in this act named, it shall be the duty of the Commission, and lawful for any company or person interested in such order or requirement, to apply, in a summary way, by petition, to the circuit court of the United States sitting in equity in the judicial district in which the common carrier complained of has its principal office, or in which the violation or disobedience of such order or requirement shall happen, alleging such violation or disobedience, as the case may be; and the said court shall have power to hear and determine the matter, on such short notice to the common carrier complained of as the court shall deem reasonable; and such notice may be served on such common carrier, his or its officers, agents, or servants, in such manner as the court shall direct; and said court shall proceed to hear and determine the matter speedily as a court of equity, and without the formal pleadings and proceedings applicable to ordinary suits in equity, but in such manner as to do justice in the premises; and to this end such court shall have power, if it think fit, to direct and prosecute, in such mode and by such persons as it may appoint, all such inquiries as the court may think needful to enable it to form a just judgment in the matter of such petition; and on such hearing the report of said Commission shall be prima facie evidence of the matters therein stated; and if it be made to appear to such court, on such hearing or on report of any such person or persons, that the lawful order or requirement of said Commission drawn in question has been violated or disobeyed, it shall be lawful for such court to issue a writ of injunction or other proper process, mandatory or otherwise, to restrain such common carrier from further continuing such violation or disobedience of such order or requirement of said Commission, and enjoining obedience to the same; and in case of any disobedience of any such writ of injunction or other proper process, mandatory or otherwise, it shall be lawful for such court to issue writs of attachment, or any other process of said court incident or applicable to writs of injunction or other proper process, mandatory or otherwise, against such common carrier, and if a corporation, against one or more of the directors, officers, or agents of the same, or against any owner, lessee, trustee, receiver, or other person failing to obey such writ of injunction or other proper process, mandatory or otherwise; and said court may, if it shall think fit, make an order directing such common carrier or other person so disobeying such writ of injunction or other proper process, mandatory or otherwise, to pay such sum of money not exceeding for each carrier or person in default the sum of five hundred dollars for every day after a day to be named in the order that such carrier or other person shall fail to obey such injunction or other proper process, mandatory or otherwise; and such moneys shall be payable as the court shall direct, either to the party complaining, or into court to abide the ultimate decision of the court, or into the Treasury; and payment thereof may, without prejudice to any other mode of recovering the same, be enforced by attachment or order in the nature of a writ of execution, in like manner as if the same had been recovered by a final decree in personam in such court. When the subject in dispute shall be of the value of two thousand dollars or more, either party to such proceeding before said court may appeal to the Supreme Court of the United States, under the same regulations now provided by law in respect of security for such appeal; but such appeal shall not operate to stay or supersede the order of the court or the execution of any writ or process thereon; and such court may, in every such matter, order the payment of such costs and counsel fees as shall be deemed reasonable. Whenever any such petition shall be filed or presented by the Commission it shall be the duty of the district attorney, under the direction of the Attorney-General of the United States, to prosecute the same; and the costs and expenses of such prosecution shall be paid out of the appropriation for the expenses of the courts of the United States. For the purposes of this act, excepting its penal provisions, the circuit courts of the United States shall be deemed to be always in session.

SECTION 17. That the Commission may conduct its proceedings in such manner as will best conduce to the proper dispatch of business and to the ends of justice. A majority of the Commission shall constitute a quorum for the transaction of business, but no Commissioner shall participate in any hearing or proceeding in which he has any pecuniary interest. Said Commission may, from time to time, make or amend such general rules or orders as may be requisite for the order and regulation of proceedings before it, including forms of notices and the service thereof, which shall conform, as nearly as may be, to those in use in the courts of the United States. Any party may appear before said Commission and be heard, in person or by attorney. Every vote and official act of the Commission shall be entered of record, and its proceedings shall be public upon the request of either party interested. Said Commission shall have an official seal, which shall be judicially noticed. Either of the members of the Commission may administer oaths and affirmations.

SECTION 18. That each Commissioner shall receive an annual salary of seven thousand five hundred dollars, payable in the same manner as the salaries of judges of the courts of the United States. The Commission shall appoint a secretary, who shall receive an annual salary of three thousand five hundred dollars, payable in like manner. The Commission shall have authority to employ and fix the compensation of such other employees as it may find necessary to the proper performance of its duties, subject to the approval of the Secretary of the Interior. The Commission shall be furnished by the Secretary of the Interior with suitable offices and all necessary office supplies. Witnesses summoned before the Commission shall be paid the same fees and mileage that are paid witnesses in the courts of the United States.

All of the expenses of the Commission, including all necessary expenses for transportation incurred by the Commissioners, or by their employees under their orders, in making any investigation in any other places than in the city of Washington, shall be allowed and paid, on the presentation of itemized vouchers therefor approved by the chairman of the Commission and the Secretary of the Interior.

SECTION 19. That the principal office of the Commission shall be in the city of Washington, where its general sessions shall be held; but whenever the convenience of the public or of the parties may be promoted or delay or expense prevented thereby, the Commission may hold special sessions in any part of the United States. It may, by one or more of the Commissioners, prosecute any inquiry necessary to its duties, in any part of the United States, into any matter or question of fact pertaining to the business of any common carrier subject to the provisions of this act.

SECTION 20. That the Commission is hereby authorized to require annual reports from all common carriers subject to the provisions of this act, to fix the time and prescribe the manner in which such reports shall be made, and to require from such carriers specific answers to all questions upon which the Commission may need information. Such annual reports shall show in detail the amount of capital stock issued, the amounts paid therefor, and the manner of payment for the same; the dividends paid, the surplus fund, if any, and the number of stockholders; the funded and floating debts and the interest paid thereon; the cost and value of the carrier's property, franchises, and equipment; the number of employees and the salaries paid each class; the amounts expended for improvements each year, how expended, and the character of such improvements; the earnings and receipts from each branch of business and from all sources; the operating and other expenses; the balances of profit and loss; and a complete exhibit of the financial operations of the carrier each year, including an annual balance sheet. Such reports shall also contain such information in relation to rates or regulations concerning fares or freights, or agreements, arrangements or contracts with other common carriers, as the Commission may require; and the said Commission may, within its discretion, for the purpose of enabling it the better to carry out the purposes of this act, prescribe (if in the opinion of the Commission it is practicable to prescribe such uniformity and methods of keeping accounts) a period of time within which all common carriers subject to the provisions of this act shall have, as near as may be, a uniform system of accounts, and the manner in which such accounts shall be kept.

SECTION 21. That the Commission shall, on or before the first day of December in each year, make a report to the Secretary of the Interior, which shall be by him transmitted to Congress, and copies of which shall be distributed as are the other reports issued from the Interior Department. This report shall contain such information and data collected by the Commission as may be considered of value in the determination of questions connected with the regulation of commerce, together with such recommendations as to additional legislation relating thereto as the Commission may deem necessary.

SECTION 22. That nothing in this act shall apply to the carriage, storage, or handling of property free or at reduced rates for the United States, State, or municipal governments, or for charitable purposes, or to or from fairs and expositions for exhibition threat, or the issuance of mileage, excursion, or commutation passenger tickets; nothing in this act shall be construed to prohibit any common carrier from giving reduced rates to ministers of religion; nothing in this act shall be construed to prevent railroads from giving free carriage to their own officers and employees, or to prevent the principal officers of any railroad company or companies from exchanging passes or tickets with other railroad companies for their officers and employees; and nothing in this act contained shall in any way abridge or alter the remedies now existing at common law or by statute, but the provisions of this act are in addition to such remedies; *Provided,* That no pending litigation shall in any way be affected by this act.

SECTION 23. That the sum of one hundred thousand dollars is hereby appropriated for the use and purposes of this act for the fiscal year ending June thirtieth, anno Domini eighteen hundred and eighty-eight, and the intervening time anterior thereto.

SECTION 24. That the provisions of sections eleven and eighteen of this act, relating to the appointment and organization of the Commission herein provided for, shall take effect immediately, and the remaining provisions of this act shall take effect sixty days after its passage.

22. SHERMAN ANTI-TRUST ACT, JULY 2, 1890

Be it enacted by the Senate and House of Representatives of the United States of America in Congress assembled,

SECTION 1. Every contract, combination in the form of trust or otherwise, or conspiracy, in restraint of trade or commerce among the several States, or with foreign nations, is hereby declared to be illegal. Every person who shall make any such contract or engage in any such combination or conspiracy, shall be deemed guilty of a misdemeanor, and, on conviction thereof, shall be punished by fine not exceeding five thousand dollars, or by imprisonment not exceeding one year, or by both said punishments, at the discretion of the court.

SECTION 2. Every person who shall monopolize, or attempt to monopolize, or combine or conspire with any other person or persons, to monopolize any part of the trade or commerce among the several States, or with foreign nations, shall be deemed guilty of a misdemeanor, and, on conviction thereof, shall be punished by fine not exceeding five thousand dollars, or by imprisonment not exceeding one year, or by both said punishments, in the discretion of the court.

SECTION 3. Every contract, combination in form of trust or otherwise, or conspiracy, in restraint of trade or commerce in any Territory of the United States or of the District of Columbia, or in restraint of trade or commerce between any such Territory and another, or between any such Territory or Territories and any State or States or the District of Columbia, or with foreign nations, or between the District of Columbia and any State or States or foreign nations, is hereby declared illegal. Every person who shall make any such contract or engage in any such combination or conspiracy, shall be deemed guilty of a misdemeanor, and, on conviction thereof, shall be punished by fine not exceeding five thousand dollars, or by imprisonment not exceeding one year, or by both said punishments, in the discretion of the court.

SECTION 4. The several circuit courts of the United States are hereby invested with jurisdiction to prevent and restrain violations of this act; and it shall be the duty of the several district attorneys of the United States, in their respective districts, under the direction of the Attorney-General, to institute proceedings in equity to prevent and restrain such violations. Such proceedings may be by way of petition setting forth the case and praying that such violation shall be enjoined or otherwise prohibited. When the parties complained of shall have been duly notified of such petition the court shall proceed, as soon as may be, to the hearing and determination of the case; and pending such petition and before final decree, the court may at any time make such temporary restraining order or prohibition as shall be deemed just in the premises.

SECTION 5. Whenever it shall appear to the court before which any proceeding under section four of this act may be pending, that the ends of justice require that other parties should be brought before the court, the court may cause them to be summoned, whether they reside in the district in which the court is held or not; and subpoenas to that end may be served in any district by the marshal thereof.

SECTION 6. Any property owned under any contract or by any combination, or pursuant to any conspiracy (and being the subject thereof) mentioned in section one of this act, and being in the course of transportation from one State to another, or to a foreign country, shall be forfeited to the United States, and may be seized and condemned by like proceedings as those provided by law for the forfeiture, seizure, and condemnation of property imported into the United States contrary to law.

SECTION 7. Any person who shall be injured in his business or property by any other person or corporation by reason of anything forbidden or declared to be unlawful by this act, may sue therefor in any circuit court of the United States in the district in which the defendant resides or is found, without respect to the amount in controversy, and shall recover three fold the damages by him sustained, and the costs of suit, including a reasonable attorney's fee.

SECTION 8. That the word "person," or "persons," wherever used in this act shall be deemed to include corporations and associations existing under or authorized by the laws of either the United States, the laws of any of the Territories, the laws of any State, or the laws of any foreign country.

23. SHERMAN SILVER PURCHASE ACT, JULY 14, 1890

Be it enacted. . . . That the Secretary of the Treasury is hereby directed to purchase, from time to time, silver bullion to the aggregate amount of four million five hundred thousand ounces, or so much thereof as may be offered in each month, at the market price thereof, not exceeding one dollar for three hundred and seventy-one and twenty-five hundredths grains of pure silver, and to issue in payment for such purchases of silver bullion Treasury notes of the United States to be prepared by the Secretary of the Treasury, in such form and of such denominations, not less than one dollar nor more than one thousand dollars, as he may prescribe.

SECTION 2. That the Treasury notes issued in accordance with the provisions of this act shall be redeemable on demand, in coin, at the Treasury of the United States, or at the office of any assistant treasurer of the United States, and when so redeemed may be reissued; but no greater or less amount of such notes shall be outstanding at any time than the cost of the silver bullion and the standard silver dollars coined therefrom, then held in the Treasury purchased by such notes; and such Treasury notes shall be a legal tender in payment of all debts, public and private, except where otherwise expressly stipulated in the contract, and shall be receivable for customs, taxes, and all public dues, and when so received may be reissued; and such notes, when held by any national banking association, may be counted as a part of its lawful reserve. That upon demand of the holder of any of the Treasury notes herein provided for the Secretary of the Treasury shall, under such regulations as he may prescribe, redeem such notes in gold or silver coin, at his discretion, it being the established policy of the United States to maintain the two metals on a parity with each other upon the present legal ratio, or such ratio as may be provided by law.

SECTION 3. That the Secretary of the Treasury shall each month coin two million ounces of the silver bullion purchased under the provisions of this act into standard silver dollars until . . . [July 1, 1891] . . . , and after that time he shall coin of the silver bullion purchased under the provisions of this act as much as may be necessary to provide for the redemption of the Treasury notes herein provided for, and any gain or seigniorage arising from such coinage shall be accounted for and paid into the Treasury . . .

SECTION 5. That so much of the act . . . [February 28, 1878] . . . , entitled "An act to authorize the coinage of the standard silver dollar and to restore its legal tender character," as requires the monthly purchase and coinage of the same into silver dollars of not less than two million dollars, nor more than four million dollars' worth of silver bullion, is hereby repealed.

24. "THE SOLITUDE OF SELF" ADDRESS TO THE HOUSE JUDICIARY COMMITTEE, BY ELIZABETH CADY STANTON, JANUARY 1892

Mr. Chairman and gentlemen of the committee:

We have been speaking before Committees of the Judiciary for the last twenty years, and we have gone over all the arguments in favor of a sixteenth amendment which are familiar to all you gentlemen; therefore, it will not be necessary that I should repeat them again.

The point I wish plainly to bring before you on this occasion is the individuality of each human soul; our Protestant idea, the right of individual conscience and judgment—our republican idea, individual citizenship. In discussing the rights of woman, we are to consider, first, what belongs to her as an individual, in a world of her own, the arbiter of her own destiny, an imaginary Robinson Crusoe with her woman Friday on a solitary island. Her rights under such circumstances are to use all her faculties for her own safety and happiness.

Secondly, if we consider her as a citizen, as a member of a great nation, she must have the same rights as all other members, according to the fundamental principles of our Government.

Thirdly, viewed as a woman, an equal factor in civilization, her rights and duties are still the same—individual happiness and development.

Fourthly, it is only the incidental relations of life, such as mother, wife, sister, daughter, that may involve some special duties and training. In the usual discussion in regard to woman's sphere, such as men as Herbert Spencer, Frederic Harrison, and Grant Allen uniformly subordinate her rights and duties as an individual, as a citizen, as a woman, to the necessities of these incidental relations, some of which a large class of woman may never assume. In discussing the sphere of man we do not decide his rights as an individual, as a citizen, as a man by his duties as a father, a husband, a brother, or a son, relations some of which he may never fill. Moreover he would be better fitted for these very relations and whatever special work he might choose to do to earn his bread by the complete development of all his faculties as an individual.

Just so with woman. The education that will fit her to discharge the duties in the largest sphere of human usefulness will best fit her for whatever special work she may be compelled to do.

The isolation of every human soul and the necessity of self-dependence must give each individual the right, to choose his own surroundings.

The strongest reason for giving woman all the opportunities for higher education, for the full development of her faculties, forces of mind and body; for giving her the most enlarged freedom of thought and action; a complete emancipation from all forms of bondage, of custom, dependence, superstition; from all the crippling influences of fear, is the solitude and personal responsibility of her own individual life. The strongest reason why we ask for woman a voice in the government under which she lives; in the religion she is asked to believe; equality in social life, where she is the chief factor; a place in the trades and professions, where she may earn her bread, is because of her birthright to self-sovereignty; because, as an individual, she must rely on herself. No matter how much women prefer to lean, to be protected and supported, nor how much men desire to have them do so, they must make the voyage of life alone, and for safety in an emergency they must know something of the laws of navigation. To guide our own craft, we must be captain, pilot, engineer; with chart and compass to stand at the wheel; to match the wind and waves and know when to take in the sail, and to read the signs in the firmament over all. It matters not whether the solitary voyager is man or woman.

Nature having endowed them equally, leaves them to their own skill and judgment in the hour of danger, and, if not equal to the occasion, alike they perish.

To appreciate the importance of fitting every human soul for independent action, think for a moment of the immeasurable solitude of self. We come into the world alone, unlike all who have gone before us; we leave it alone under circumstances peculiar to ourselves. No mortal ever has been, no mortal over will be like the soul just launched on the sea of life. There can never again be just such environments as make up the infancy, youth and manhood of this one. Nature never repeats herself, and the possibilities of one human soul will never be found in another. No one has ever found two blades of ribbon grass alike, and no one will ever find two human beings alike. Seeing, then, what must be the

infinite diversity in human, character, we can in a measure appreciate the loss to a nation when any large class of the people is uneducated and unrepresented in the government. We ask for the complete development of every individual, first, for his own benefit and happiness. In fitting out an army we give each soldier his own knapsack, arms, powder, his blanket, cup, knife, fork and spoon. We provide alike for all their individual necessities, then each man bears his own burden.

Again we ask complete individual development for the general good; for the consensus of the competent on the whole round of human interest; on all questions of national life, and here each man must bear his share of the general burden. It is sad to see how soon friendless children are left to bear their own burdens before they can analyze their feelings; before they can even tell their joys and sorrows, they are thrown on their own resources. The great lesson that nature seems to teach us at all ages is self-dependence, self-protection, self-support. What a touching instance of a child's solitude; of that hunger of heart for love and recognition, in the case of the little girl who helped to dress a Christmas tree for the children of the family in which she served. On finding there was no present for herself she slipped away in the darkness and spent the night in an open field sitting on a stone, and when found in the morning was weeping as if her heart would break. No mortal will ever know the thoughts that passed through the mind of that friendless child in the long hours of that cold night, with only the silent stars to keep her company. The mention of her case in the daily papers moved many generous hearts to send her presents, but in the hours of her keenest sufferings she was thrown wholly on herself for consolation.

In youth our most bitter disappointments, our brightest hopes and ambitions are known only to otherwise, even our friendship and love we never fully share with another; there is something of every passion in every situation we conceal. Even so in our triumphs and our defeats.

The successful candidate for Presidency and his opponent each have a solitude peculiarly his own, and good form forbid either in speak of his pleasure or regret. The solitude of the king on his throne and the prisoner in his cell differs in character and degree, but it is solitude nevertheless.

We ask no sympathy from others in the anxiety and agony of a broken friendship or shattered love. When death sunders our nearest ties, alone we sit in the shadows of our affliction. Alike mid the greatest triumphs and darkest tragedies of life we walk alone. On the divine heights of human attainments, eulogized land worshiped as a hero or saint, we stand alone. In ignorance, poverty, and vice, as a pauper or criminal, alone we starve or steal; alone we suffer the sneers and rebuffs of our fellows; alone we are hunted and hounded thro dark courts and alleys, in by-ways and highways; alone we stand in the judgment seat; alone in the prison cell we lament our crimes and misfortunes; alone we expiate them on the gallows. In hours like these we realize the awful solitude of individual life, its pains, its penalties, its responsibilities; hours in which the youngest and most helpless are thrown on their own resources for guidance and consolation. Seeing then that life must ever be a march and a battle, that each soldier must be equipped for his own protection, it is the height of cruelty to rob the individual of a single natural right.

To throw obstacle in the way of a complete education is like putting out the eyes; to deny the rights of property, like cutting off the hands. To deny political equality is to rob the ostracised of all self-respect; of credit in the market place; of recompense in the world of work; of a voice among those who make and administer the law; a choice in the jury before whom they are tried, and in the judge who decides their punishment. Shakespeare's play of Titus and Andronicus contains a terrible satire on woman's position in the nineteenth century—"Rude men" (the play tells us) "seized the king's daughter, cut out her tongue, cut off her hands, and then bade her go call for water and wash her hands." What a picture of woman's position. Robbed of her natural rights, handicapped by law and custom at every turn, yet compelled to fight her own battles, and in the emergencies of life to fall back on herself for protection.

The girl of sixteen, thrown on the world to support herself, to make her own place in society, to resist the temptations that surround her and maintain a spotless integrity, must do all this by native force or superior education. She does not acquire this power by being trained to trust others and distrust herself. If she wearies of the struggle, finding it hard work to swim upstream, and allow herself to drift with the current, she will find plenty of company, but not one

to share her misery in the hour of her deepest humiliation. If she tried to retrieve her position, to conceal the past, her life is hedged about with fears lest willing hands should tear the veil from what she fain would hide. Young and friendless, she knows the bitter solitude of self.

How the little courtesies of life on the surface of society, deemed so important from man towards woman, fade into utter insignificance in view of the deeper tragedies in which she must play her part alone, where no human aid is possible.

The young wife and mother, at the head of some establishment with a kind husband to shield her from the adverse winds of life, with wealth, fortune and position, has a certain harbor of safety, occurs against the ordinary ills of life. But to manage a household, have a desirable influence in society, keep her friends and the affections of her husband, train her children and servants well, she must have rare common sense, wisdom, diplomacy, and a knowledge of human nature. To do all this she needs the cardinal virtues and the strong points of character that the most successful statesman possesses.

An uneducated woman, trained to dependence, with no resources in herself must make a failure of any position in life. But society says women do not need a knowledge of the world, the liberal training that experience in public life must give, all the advantages of collegiate education; but when for the lock of all this, the woman's happiness is wrecked, alone she bears her humiliation; and the attitude of the weak and the ignorant in indeed pitiful in the wild chase for the price of life they are ground to powder.

In age, when the pleasures of youth are passed, children grown up, married and gone, the hurry and hustle of life in a measure over, when the hands are weary of active service, when the old armchair and the fireside are the chosen resorts, then men and women alike must fall back on their own resources. If they cannot find companionship in books, if they have no interest in the vital questions of the hour, no interest in watching the consummation of reforms, with which they might have been identified, they soon pass into their dotage. The more fully the faculties of the mind are developed and kept in use, the longer the period of vigor and active interest in all around us continues. If from a lifelong participation in public affairs a woman feels responsible for the laws regulating our system of education, the discipline of our jails and prisons, the sanitary conditions of our private homes, public buildings, and thoroughfares, an interest in commerce, finance, our foreign relations, in any or all of these questions, here solitude will at least be respectable, and she will not be driven to gossip or scandal for entertainment.

The chief reason for opening to every soul the doors to the whole round of human duties and pleasures is the individual development thus attained, the resources thus provided under all circumstances to mitigate the solitude that at times must come to everyone. I once asked Prince Krapotkin, the Russian nihilist, how he endured his long years in prison, deprived of books, pen, ink, and paper. "Ah," he said, "I thought out many questions in which I had a deep interest. In the pursuit of an idea I took no note of time. When tired of solving knotty problems I recited all the beautiful passages in prose or verse I have ever learned. I became acquainted with myself and my own resources. I had a world of my own, a vast empire, that no Russian jailor or Czar could invade." when shut off from all human companionship, bringing comfort and sunshine within even the four walls of a prison cell.

As women of times share a similar fate, should they not have all the consolation that the most liberal education can give? Their suffering in the prisons of St. Petersburg; in the long, weary marches to Siberia, and in the mines, working side by side with men, surely call for all the self-support that the most exalted sentiments of heroism can give. When suddenly roused at midnight, with the startling cry of "fire! fire!" to find the house over their heads in flames, do women wait for men to point the way to safety? And are the men, equally bewildered and half suffocated with smoke, in a position to more than try to save themselves?

At such times the most timid women have shown a courage and heroism in saving their husbands and children that has surprised everybody. Inasmuch, then, as woman shares equally the joys and sorrows of time and eternity, is it not the height of presumption in man to propose to represent her at the ballot box and the throne of grace, do her voting in the state, her praying in the church, and to assume the position of priest at the family alter.

Nothing strengthens the judgment and quickens the conscience like individual responsibility. Nothing

adds such dignity to character as the recognition of one's self-sovereignty; the right to an equal place, every where conceded; a place earned by personal merit, not an artificial attainment, by inheritance, wealth, family, and position. Seeing, then that the responsibilities of life rests equally on man and woman, that their destiny is the same, they need the same preparation for time and eternity. The talk of sheltering woman from the fierce sterns of life is the sheerest mockery, for they beat on her from every point of the compass, just as they do on man, and with more fatal results, for he has been trained to protect himself, to resist, to conquer. Such are the facts in human experience, the responsibilities of individual. Rich and poor, intelligent and ignorant, wise and foolish, virtuous and vicious, man and woman, it is ever the same, each soul must depend wholly on itself.

Whatever the theories may be of woman's dependence on man, in the supreme moments of her life he can not bear her burdens. Alone she goes to the gates of death to give life to every man that is born into the world. No one can share her fears, or one mitigate her pangs; and if her sorrow is greater than she can bear, alone she passes beyond the gates into the vast unknown.

From the mountain tops of Judea, long ago, a heavenly voice bade His disciples, "Bear ye one another's burdens," but humanity has not yet risen to that point of self-sacrifice, and if ever so willing, how few the burdens are that one soul can bear for another. In the highways of Palestine; in prayer and fasting on the solitary mountain top; in the Garden of Gethsemane; before the judgment seat of Pilate; betrayed by one of His trusted disciples at His last supper; in His agonies on the cross, even Jesus of Nazareth, in these last sad days on earth, felt the awful solitude of self. Deserted by man, in agony he cries, "My God! My God! Why hast Thou forsaken me?" And so it ever must be in the conflicting scenes of life, on the long weary march, each one walks alone. We may have many friends, love, kindness, sympathy and charity to smooth our pathway in everyday life, but in the tragedies and triumphs of human experience each moral stands alone.

But when all artificial trammels are removed, and women are recognized as individuals, responsible for their own environments, thoroughly educated for all the positions in life they may be called to fill; with all the resources in themselves that liberal thought and broad culture can give; guided by their own conscience and judgment; trained to self-protection by a healthy development of the muscular system and skill in the use of weapons of defense, and stimulated to self-support by the knowledge of the business world and the pleasure that pecuniary independence must ever give; when women are trained in this way they will, in a measure, be fitted for those hours of solitude that come alike to all, whether prepared or otherwise. As in our extremity we must depend on ourselves, the dictates of wisdom point of complete individual development.

In talking of education how shallow the argument that each class must be educated for the special work it proposed to do, and all those faculties not needed in this special walk must lie dormant and utterly wither for want of use, when, perhaps, these will be the very faculties needed in life's greatest emergencies. Some say, Where is the use of drilling girls in the languages, the Sciences, in law, medicine, theology? As wives, mothers, housekeepers, cooks, they need a different curriculum from boys who are to fill all positions. The chief cooks in our great hotels and ocean steamers are men. In large cities men run the bakeries; they make our bread, cake and pies. They manage the laundries; they are now considered our best milliners and dressmakers. Because some men fill these departments of usefulness, shall we regulate the curriculum in Harvard and Yale to their present necessities? If not why this talk in our best colleges of a curriculum for girls who are crowding into the trades and professions; teachers in all our public schools rapidly filling many lucrative and honorable positions in life? They are showing too, their calmness and courage in the most trying hours of human experience.

You have probably all read in the daily papers of the terrible storm in the Bay of Biscay when a tidal wave such havoc on the shore, wrecking vessels, unroofing houses and carrying destruction everywhere. Among other buildings the woman's prison was demolished. Those who escaped saw men struggling to reach the shore. They promptly by clasping hands made a chain of themselves and pushed out into the sea, again and again, at the risk of their lives until they had brought six men to shore, carried them to a shelter, and did all in their power for their comfort and protection.

What especial school of training could have prepared these women for this sublime moment of their lives. In times like this humanity rises above all college curriculums and recognises Nature as the greatest of all teachers in the hour of danger and death. Women are already the equals of men in the whole of ream of thought, in art, science, literature, and government. With telescope vision they explore the starry firmament, and bring back the history of the planetary world. With chart and compass they pilot ships across the mighty deep, and with skillful finger send electric messages around the globe. In galleries of art the beauties of nature and the virtues of humanity are immortalized by them on their canvas and by their inspired touch dull blocks of marble are transformed into angels of light.

In music they speak again the language of Mendelssohn, Beethoven, Chopin, Schumann, and are worthy interpreters of their great thoughts. The poetry and novels of the century are theirs, and they have touched the keynote of reform in religion, politics, and social life. They fill the editor's and professor's chair, and plead at the bar of justice, walk the wards of the hospital, and speak from the pulpit and the platform; such is the type of womanhood that an enlightened public sentiment welcomes today, and such the triumph of the facts of life over the false theories of the past.

Is it, then, consistent to hold the developed woman of this day within the same narrow political limits as the dame with the spinning wheel and knitting needle occupied in the past? No! no! Machinery has taken the labors of woman as well as man on its tireless shoulders; the loom and the spinning wheel are but dreams of the past; the pen, the brush, the easel, the chisel, have taken their places, while the hopes and ambitions of women are essentially changed.

We see reason sufficient in the outer conditions of human being for individual liberty and development, but when we consider the self dependence of every human soul we see the need of courage, judgment, and the exercise of every faculty of mind and body, strengthened and developed by use, in woman as well as man.

Whatever may be said of man's protecting power in ordinary conditions, mid all the terrible disasters by land and sea, in the supreme moments of danger, alone, woman must ever meet the horrors of the situation; the Angel of Death even makes no royal pathway for her. Man's love and sympathy enter only into the sunshine of our lives. In that solemn solitude of self, that links us with the immeasurable and the eternal, each soul lives alone forever. A recent writer says:

I remember once, in crossing the Atlantic, to have gone upon the deck of the ship at midnight, when a dense black cloud enveloped the sky, and the great deep was roaring madly under the lashes of demoniac winds. My feelings was [sic] not of danger or fear (which is a base surrender of the immortal soul), but of utter desolation and loneliness; a little speck of life shut in by a tremendous darkness. Again I remember to have climbed the slopes of the Swiss Alps, up beyond the point where vegetation ceases, and the stunted conifers no longer struggle against the unfeeling blasts. Around me lay a huge confusion of rocks, out of which the gigantic ice peaks shot into the measureless blue of the heavens, and again my only feeling was the awful solitude.

And yet, there is a solitude, which each and every one of us has always carried with him, more inaccessible than the ice-cold mountains, more profound than the midnight sea; the solitude of self. Our inner being, which we call our self, no eye nor touch of man or angel has ever pierced. It is more hidden than the caves of the gnome; the sacred adytum of the oracle; the hidden chamber of Eleusinian mystery, for to it only omniscience is permitted to enter.

Such is individual life. Who, I ask you, can take, dare take, on himself the rights, the duties, the responsibilities of another human soul?

25. THE PLATFORM OF THE POPULIST PARTY, OMAHA, NEBRASKA, 1892

Assembled upon the 116th anniversary of the Declaration of Independence, the People's Party of America, in their first national convention, invoking upon their action the blessing of Almighty God, put forth in the name and on behalf of the people of this country, the following preamble and declaration of principles:

Preamble

The conditions which surround us best justify our co-operation; we meet in the midst of a nation brought to the verge of moral, political, and material ruin. Corruption dominates the ballot-box, the Legislatures, the Congress, and touches even the ermine of the bench. The people are demoralized; most of the

States have been compelled to isolate the voters at the polling places to prevent universal intimidation and bribery. The newspapers are largely subsidized or muzzled, public opinion silenced, business prostrated, homes covered with mortgages, labor impoverished, and the land concentrating in the hands of capitalists. The urban workmen are denied the right to organize for self-protection, imported pauperized labor beats down their wages, a hireling standing army, unrecognized by our laws, is established to shoot them down, and they are rapidly degenerating into European conditions. The fruits of the toil of millions are boldly stolen to build up colossal fortunes for a few, unprecedented in the history of mankind; and the possessors of these, in turn, despise the Republic and endanger liberty. From the same prolific womb of governmental injustice we breed the two great classes—tramps and millionaires.

The national power to create money is appropriated to enrich bondholders; a vast public debt payable in legal-tender currency has been funded into gold-bearing bonds, thereby adding millions to the burdens of the people.

Silver, which has been accepted as coin since the dawn of history, has been demonetized to add to the purchasing power of gold by decreasing the value of all forms of property as well as human labor, and the supply of currency is purposely abridged to fatten usurers, bankrupt enterprise, and enslave industry. A vast conspiracy against mankind has been organized on two continents, and it is rapidly taking possession of the world. If not met and overthrown at once it forbodes terrible social convulsions, the destruction of civilization, or the establishment of an absolute despotism.

We have witnessed for more than a quarter of a century the struggles of the two great political parties for power and plunder, while grevious wrongs have been inflicted upon the suffering people. We charge that the controlling influences dominating both these parties have permitted the existing dreadful conditions to develop without serious effort to prevent or restrain them. Neither do they now promise us any substantial reform. They have agreed together to ignore, in the coming campaign, every issue but one. They propose to drown the outcries of a plundered people with the uproar of a sham battle over the tariff, so that capitalists, corporations, national banks, rings, trusts, watered stock, the demonetization of silver and the oppressions of the usurers may all be lost sight of. They propose to sacrifice our homes, lives, and children on the altar of mammon; to destroy the multitude in order to secure corruption funds from the millionaires.

Assembled on the anniversary of the birthday of the nation, and filled with the spirit of the grand general and chief who established our independence, we seek to restore the government of the Republic to the hands of the "plain people," with which class it originated. We assert our purposes to be identical with the purposes of the National Constitution; to form a more perfect union and establish justice, insure domestic tranquillity, provide for the common defence, promote the general welfare, and secure the blessings of liberty for ourselves and our posterity.

We declare that this Republic can only endure as a free government while built upon the love of the people for each other and for the nation; that it cannot be pinned together by bayonets; that the Civil War is over, and that every passion and resentment which grew out of it must die with it, and that we must be in fact, as we are in name, one united brotherhood of free men.

Our country finds itself confronted by conditions for which there is no precedent in the history of the world; our annual agricultural productions amount to billions of dollars in value, which must, within a few weeks or months, be exchanged for billions of dollars' worth of commodities consumed in their production; the existing currency supply is wholly inadequate to make this exchange; the results are falling prices, the formation of combines and rings, the impoverishment of the producing class. We pledge ourselves that if given power we will labor to correct these evils by wise and reasonable legislation, in accordance with the terms of our platform.

We believe that the power of government—in other words, of the people—should be expanded (as in the case of the postal service) as rapidly and as far as the good sense of an intelligent people and the teachings of experience shall justify, to the end that oppression, injustice, and poverty shall eventually cease in the land.

While our sympathies as a party of reform are naturally upon the side of every proposition which will tend to make men intelligent, virtuous, and temperate, we nevertheless regard these questions, important as they are, as secondary to the great issues now pressing for solution, and upon which not only our individual prosperity but the very existence of free institutions depend; and we ask all men to first help us to determine whether we are to have a republic to administer before we differ as to the conditions upon which it is to be administered, believing that the forces of reform this day organized will never cease to move forward until every wrong is righted and equal rights and equal privileges securely established for all the men and women of this country.

Platform

We declare, therefore—

First.—That the union of the labor forces of the United States this day consummated shall be permanent and perpetual; may its spirit enter into all hearts for the salvation of the Republic and the uplifting of mankind.

Second.—Wealth belongs to him who creates it, and every dollar taken from industry without an equivalent is robbery. "If any will not work, neither shall he eat." The interests of rural and civil labor are the same; their enemies are identical.

Third.—We believe that the time has come when the railroad corporations will either own the people or the people must own the railroads; and should the government enter upon the work of owning and managing all railroads, we should favor an amendment to the constitution by which all persons engaged in the government service shall be placed under a civil-service regulation of the most rigid character, so as to prevent the increase of the power of the national administration by the use of such additional government employees.

Finance.—We demand a national currency, safe, sound, and flexible issued by the general government only, a full legal tender for all debts, public and private, and that without the use of banking corporations; a just, equitable, and efficient means of distribution direct to the people, at a tax not to exceed 2 percent, per annum, to be provided, as set forth in the sub-treasury plan of the Farmers' Alliance, or a better system; also by payments in discharge of its obligations for public improvements.

1. We demand free and unlimited coinage of silver and gold at the present legal ratio of 16 to 1.
2. We demand that the amount of circulating medium be speedily increased to not less than $50 per capita.

3. We demand a graduated income tax.
4. We believe that the money of the country should be kept as much as possible in the hands of the people, and hence we demand that all State and national revenues shall be limited to the necessary expenses of the government, economically and honestly administered.
5. We demand that postal savings banks be established by the government for the safe deposit of the earnings of the people and to facilitate exchange.

Transportation.—Transportation being a means of exchange and a public necessity, the government should own and operate the railroads in the interest of the people. The telegraph and telephone, like the post-office system, being a necessity for the transmission of news, should be owned and operated by the government in the interest of the people.

Land.—The land, including all the natural sources of wealth, is the heritage of the people, and should not be monopolized for speculative purposes, and alien ownership of land should be prohibited. All land now held by railroads and other corporations in excess of their actual needs, and all lands now owned by aliens should be reclaimed by the government and held for actual settlers only.

Expression of Sentiments

Your Committee on Platform and Resolutions beg leave unanimously to report the following:

Whereas, Other questions have been presented for our consideration, we hereby submit the following, not as a part of the Platform of the People's Party, but as resolutions expressive of the sentiment of this Convention.

1. Resolved, That we demand a free ballot and a fair count in all elections, and pledge ourselves to secure it to every legal voter without Federal intervention, through the adoption by the States of the unperverted Australian or secret ballot system.
2. Resolved, That the revenue derived from a graduated income tax should be applied to the reduction of the burden of taxation now levied upon the domestic industries of this country.
3. Resolved, That we pledge our support to fair and liberal pensions to ex-Union soldiers and sailors.
4. Resolved, That we condemn the fallacy of protecting American labor under the present system, which opens our ports to the pauper and criminal classes of the world and crowds out our wage-earners; and we denounce the present ineffective laws against contract labor, and demand the further restriction of undesirable emigration.
5. Resolved, That we cordially sympathize with the efforts of organized workingmen to shorten the hours of labor, and demand a rigid enforcement of the existing eight-hour law on Government work, and ask that a penalty clause be added to the said law.
6. Resolved, That we regard the maintenance of a large standing army of mercenaries, known as the Pinkerton system, as a menace to our liberties, and we demand its abolition; and we condemn the recent invasion of the Territory of Wyoming by the hired assassins of plutocracy, assisted by Federal officers.
7. Resolved, That we commend to the favorable consideration of the people and the reform press the legislative system known as the initiative and referendum.
8. Resolved, That we favor a constitutional provision limiting the office of President and Vice-President to one term, and providing for the election of Senators of the United States by a direct vote of the people.
9. Resolved, That we oppose any subsidy or national aid to any private corporation for any purpose.
10. Resolved, That this convention sympathizes with the Knights of Labor and their righteous contest with the tyrannical combine of clothing manufacturers of Rochester, and declare it to be a duty of all who hate tyranny and oppression to refuse to purchase the goods made by the said manufacturers, or to patronize any merchants who sell such goods.

26. THE DE LÔME LETTER, CA. DECEMBER 1897

Legacion de España, Washington
His Excellency Don José Canalejas.
My distinguished and dear friend:
You have no reason to ask my excuses for not having written to me, I ought also to have written to you but I have put off doing so because overwhelmed with work and nous sommes quittes. The situation here remains the same. Everything depends on the political

and military outcome in Cuba. The prologue of all this, in this second stage [phase] of the war, will end the day when the colonial cabinet shall be appointed and we shall be relieved in the eyes of this country of a part of the responsibility for what is happening in Cuba while the Cubans, whom these people think so immaculate, will have to assume it. Until then, nothing can be clearly seen, and I regard it as a waste of time and progress, by a wrong road, to be sending emissaries to the rebel camp, or to negotiate with the autonomists who have as yet no legal standing, or to try to ascertain the intentions and plans of this government. The [Cuban] refugees will keep on returning one by one and as they do so will make their way into the sheep-fold, while the leaders in the field will gradually come back. Neither the one nor the other class had the courage to leave in a body and they will not be brave enough to return in a body.

The Message has been a disillusionment to the insurgents who expected something different; but I regard it as bad [for us]. Besides the ingrained and inevitable bluntness [grosería] with which is repeated all that the press and public opinion in Spain have said about Weyler, it once more shows what McKinley is, weak and a bidder for the admiration of the crowd besides being a would-be politician [politicastro] who tries to leave a door open behind himself while keeping on good terms with the jingoes of his party. Nevertheless, whether the practical results of it [the Message] are to be injurious and adverse depends only upon ourselves. I am entirely of your opinions; without a military end of the matter nothing will be accomplished in Cuba, and without a military and political settlement there will always be the danger of encouragement being give [sic] to the insurgents, by a part of the public opinion if not by the government. I do not think sufficient attention has been paid to the part England is playing. Nearly all the newspaper rabble that swarms in your hotels are Englishmen, and while writing for the Journal they are also correspondents of the most influential journals and reviews of London. It has been so ever since this thing began. As I look at it, England's only object is that the Americans should amuse themselves with us and leave her alone, and if there should be a war, that would the better stave off the conflict which she dreads but which will never come about. It would be very advantageous to take up, even if only for effect, the question of commercial relations and to have a man

of some prominence sent hither, in order that I may make use of him here to carry on a propaganda among the senators and others in opposition to the Junta and to try to win over the refugees. So, Amblard is coming. I think he devotes himself too much to petty politics, and we have got to do something very big or we shall fail. Adela returns your greeting, and we all trust that next year you may be a messenger of peace and take it as a Christmas gift to poor Spain.
Ever your attached friend and servant,
Enrique Dupuy de Lôme

27. JOINT RESOLUTION TO PROVIDE FOR ANNEXING THE HAWAIIAN ISLANDS TO THE UNITED STATES AND LETTER OF PROTEST FROM QUEEN LILIUOKALANI OF HAWAII TO THE HOUSE OF REPRESENTATIVES, DECEMBER 19, 1898

Joint Resolution To provide for annexing the Hawaiian Islands to the United States. Whereas, the Government of the Republic of Hawaii having, in due form, signified its consent, in the manner provided by its constitution, to cede absolutely and without reserve to the United States of America, all rights of sovereignty of whatsoever kind in and over the Hawaiian Islands and their dependencies, and also to cede and transfer to the United States, the absolute fee and ownership of all public, Government, or Crown lands, public buildings or edifices, ports, harbors, military equipment, and all other public property of every kind and description belonging to the Government of the Hawaiian Islands, together with every right and appurtenance thereunto appertaining: Therefore, *Resolved by the Senate and House of Representatives of the United States of America in Congress assembled,* That said cession is accepted, ratified, and confirmed, and that the said Hawaiian Islands and their dependencies be, and they are hereby, annexed as a part of the territory of the United States and are subject to the sovereign dominion thereof, and that all and singular the property and rights hereinbefore mentioned are vested in the United States of America.

The existing laws of the United States relative to public lands shall not apply to such lands in the Hawaiian Islands; but the Congress of the United States shall enact special laws for their management and disposition: *Provided,* That all revenue from or proceeds of the same, except as regards such part thereof as may be used or occupied for the civil, military, or naval purposes of the United States, or may be assigned for the use of the local government, shall be used solely for the benefit of the inhabitants of the Hawaiian Islands for educational and other public purposes. Until Congress shall provide for the government of such islands all the civil, judicial, and military powers exercised by the officers of the existing government in said islands shall be vested in such person or persons and shall be exercised in such manner as the President of the United States shall direct; and the President shall have power to remove said officers and fill the vacancies so occasioned.

The existing treaties of the Hawaiian Islands with foreign nations shall forthwith cease and determine, being replaced by such treaties as may exist, or as may be hereafter concluded, between the United States and such foreign nations. The municipal legislation of the Hawaiian Islands, not enacted for the fulfillment of the treaties so extinguished, and not inconsistent with this joint resolution nor contrary to the Constitution of the United States nor to any existing treaty of the United States, shall remain in force until the Congress of the United States shall otherwise determine. Until legislation shall be enacted extending the United States customs laws and regulations to the Hawaiian Islands the existing customs relations of the Hawaiian Islands with the United States and other countries shall remain unchanged.

The public debt of the Republic of Hawaii, lawfully existing at the date of the passage of this joint resolution, including the amounts due to depositors in the Hawaiian Postal Savings Bank, is hereby assumed by the Government of the United States; but the liability of the United States in this regard shall in no case exceed four million dollars. So long, however, as the existing Government and the present commercial relations of the Hawaiian Islands are continued as hereinbefore, provided said Government shall continue to pay the interest on said debt.

There shall be no further immigration of Chinese into the Hawaiian Islands, except upon such conditions as are now or may hereafter be allowed by the laws of the United States; and no Chinese, by reason of anything herein contained, shall be allowed to enter the United States from the Hawaiian Islands.

Sec. 1. The President shall appoint five commissioners, at least two of whom shall be residents of the Hawaiian Islands, who shall, as soon as reasonably practicable, recommend to Congress such legislation concerning the Hawaiian Islands as they shall deem necessary or proper.

Sec. 2. That the commissioners hereinbefore provided for shall be appointed by the President, by and with the advice and consent of the Senate.

Sec. 3. That the sum of one hundred thousand dollars, or so much thereof as may be necessary, is hereby appropriated, out of any money in the Treasury not otherwise appropriated, and to be immediately available, to be expended at the discretion of the President of the United States of America, for the purpose of carrying this joint resolution into effect.

Letter of Protest from Queen Liliuokalani of Hawaii to the House of Representatives

The House of Representatives of the United States:

I, Liliuokalani of Hawaii, named heir apparent on the 10th day of April, 1877, and proclaimed Queen of the Hawaiian Islands on the 29th day of January, 1891, do hereby earnestly and respectfully protest against the assertion of ownership by the United States of America of the so-called Hawaiian Crown Islands amounting to about one million acres and which are my property, and I especially protest against such assertion of ownership as a taking of property without due process of law and without just or other compensation. Therefore, supplementing my protest of June 17, 1897, I call upon the President and the National Legislature and the People of the United States to do justice in this matter and to restore to me this property, the enjoyment of which is being withheld from me by your Government under what must be a misapprehension of my right and title.

28. Treaty of Peace Between the United States and Spain, December 10, 1898

In conformity with the provisions of Articles I, II, and III of this treaty, Spain relinquishes in Cuba, and cedes in Porto Rico and other islands in the West Indies, in the island of Guam, and in the Philippine Archipelago, all the buildings, wharves, barracks, forts, structures, public highways and other immovable property which, in conformity with law, belong to the public domain, and as such belong to the Crown of Spain.

And it is hereby declared that the relinquishment or cession, as the case may be, to which the preceding paragraph refers, can not in any respect impair the property or rights which by law belong to the peaceful possession of property of all kinds, of provinces, municipalities, public or private establishments, ecclesiastical or civic bodies, or any other associations having legal capacity to acquire and possess property in the aforesaid territories renounced or ceded, or of private individuals, of whatsoever nationality such individuals may be.

The aforesaid relinquishment or cession, as the case may be, includes all documents exclusively referring to the sovereignty relinquished or ceded that may exist in the archives of the Peninsula. Where any document in such archives only in part relates to said sovereignty, a copy of such part will be furnished whenever it shall be requested. Like rules shall be reciprocally observed in favor of Spain in respect of documents in the archives of the islands above referred to.

In the aforesaid relinquishment or cession, as the case may be, are also included such rights as the Crown of Spain and its authorities possess in respect of the official archives and records, executive as well as judicial, in the islands above referred to, which relate to said islands or the rights and property of their inhabitants. Such archives and records shall be carefully preserved, and private persons shall without distinction have the right to require, in accordance with law, authenticated copies of the contracts, wills and other instruments forming part of notarial protocols or files, or which may be contained in the executive or judicial archives, be the latter in Spain or in the islands aforesaid.

Article IX.

Spanish subjects, natives of the Peninsula, residing in the territory over which Spain by the present treaty relinquishes or cedes her sovereignty, may remain in such territory or may remove therefrom, retaining in either event all their rights of property, including the right to sell or dispose of such property or of its proceeds; and they shall also have the right to carry on their industry, commerce and professions, being subject in respect thereof to such laws as are applicable to other foreigners. In case they remain in the territory they may preserve their allegiance to the Crown of Spain by making, before a court of record, within a

year from the date of the exchange of ratifications of this treaty, a declaration of their decision to preserve such allegiance; in default of which declaration they shall be held to have renounced it and to have adopted the nationality of the territory in which they may reside. The civil rights and political status of the native inhabitants of the territories hereby ceded to the United States shall be determined by the Congress.

Article X.

The inhabitants of the territories over which Spain relinquishes or cedes her sovereignty shall be secured in the free exercise of their religion.

Article XI.

The Spaniards residing in the territories over which Spain by this treaty cedes or relinquishes her sovereignty shall be subject in matters civil as well as criminal to the jurisdiction of the courts of the country wherein they reside, pursuant to the ordinary laws governing the same; and they shall have the right to appear before such courts, and to pursue the same course as citizens of the country to which the courts belong.

The present treaty shall be ratified by the President of the United States, by and with the advice and consent of the Senate thereof, and by Her Majesty the Queen Regent of Spain; and the ratifications shall be exchanged at Washington within six months from the date hereof, or earlier if possible.

In faith whereof, we, the respective Plenipotentiaries, have signed this treaty and have hereunto affixed our seals. Done in duplicate at Paris, the tenth day of December, in the year of Our Lord one thousand eight hundred and ninety-eight.

William R. Day
Cushman K. Davis
William P. Frye
Geo. Gray
Whitelaw Reid
Eugenio Montero Rios
B. de Abarzuza
J. de Garnica
W. R. de Villa Urrutia
Rafael Cerero

29. PLATT AMENDMENT, MARCH 2, 1901
(appropriations for support of the U.S. Army for fiscal year ending June 30, 1902)

Whereas the Congress of the United States of America, by an Act approved March 2, 1901, provided as follows: Provided further, That in fulfillment of the declaration contained in the joint resolution approved April twentieth, eighteen hundred and ninety-eight, entitled "For the recognition of the independence of the people of Cuba, demanding that the Government of Spain relinquish its authority and government in the island of Cuba, and withdraw its land and naval forces from Cuba and Cuban waters, and directing the President of the United States to use the land and naval forces of the United States to carry these resolutions into effect," the President is hereby authorized to "leave the government and control of the island of Cuba to its people" so soon as a government shall have been established in said island under a constitution which, either as a part thereof or in an ordinance appended thereto, shall define the future relations of the United States with Cuba, substantially as follows:

"I. That the government of Cuba shall never enter into any treaty or other compact with any foreign power or powers which will impair or tend to impair the independence of Cuba, nor in any manner authorize or permit any foreign power or powers to obtain by colonization or for military or naval purposes or otherwise, lodgement in or control over any portion of said island."

"II. That said government shall not assume or contract any public debt, to pay the interest upon which, and to make reasonable sinking fund provision for the ultimate discharge of which, the ordinary revenues of the island, after defraying the current expenses of government shall be inadequate."

"III. That the government of Cuba consents that the United States may exercise the right to intervene for the preservation of Cuban independence, the maintenance of a government adequate for the protection of life, property, and individual liberty, and for discharging the obligations with respect to Cuba imposed by the treaty of Paris on the United States, now to be assumed and undertaken by the government of Cuba."

"IV. That all Acts of the United States in Cuba during its military occupancy thereof are ratified and validated, and all lawful rights acquired thereunder shall be maintained and protected."

"V. That the government of Cuba will execute, and as far as necessary extend, the plans already devised or other plans to be mutually agreed upon, for the sanitation of the cities of the island, to the end that a recurrence of epidemic and infectious diseases may be prevented, thereby assuring protection to the people and commerce of Cuba, as well as to the commerce of the southern ports of the United States and the people residing therein."

"VI. That the Isle of Pines shall be omitted from the proposed constitutional boundaries of Cuba, the title thereto being left to future adjustment by treaty."

"VII. That to enable the United States to maintain the independence of Cuba, and to protect the people thereof, as well as for its own defense, the government of Cuba will sell or lease to the United States lands necessary for coaling or naval stations at certain specified points to be agreed upon with the President of the United States."

"VIII. That by way of further assurance the government of Cuba will embody the foregoing provisions in a permanent treaty with the United States."

APPENDIX B
Biographies of Major Personalities

Abbott, The Hon. Sir John Joseph Caldwell (March 12, 1821–October 30, 1893) *Canadian prime minister*
Sir John Abbott was prime minister of Canada for only 17 months. He became prime minister following the death in 1891 of John A. Macdonald. Abbott was the first Canadian prime minister to be a member of both the House of Commons and the Senate.

Adams, Charles Francis, Jr. (May 27, 1835–March 20, 1915) *president of the Union Pacific Railroad*
Charles Francis Adams, Jr., was born in Boston, Massachusetts, the son of the U.S. minister to the Court of St. James (England), grandson of the sixth U.S. president, John Quincy Adams, and great-grandson of John Adams, the second U.S. president. After attending Harvard, he joined the First Massachusetts Cavalry, where he commanded the Fifth Massachusetts, an African-American regiment. He fought in the Union army during the Civil War, at Antietam and Gettysburg, and was brevetted brigadier general on March 13, 1865. After discharge from military service, Adams devoted himself to establishing a railroad system in Massachusetts. He served as chair of the Massachusetts Board of Railroad Commissioners from 1872 to 1879 and was president of the Union Pacific Railroad for six years.

Adams, Henry (February 16, 1838–March 27, 1918) *editor of the* North American Review
Like his brother Charles Francis Adams, Jr., Henry Adams was born in Boston, Massachusetts. He married the talented Marian Hooper, a highly educated woman, also of Boston, whose salon was frequented by many intellectuals of the era. Adams, a professor of history at Harvard, was editor of the *North American Review* and a respected commentator on American culture. His autobiographical work, *The Education of Henry Adams,* reflected his reform ideals and his increasing discomfort with the urbanization of the United States in the latter half of the 19th century.

Adams, Brooks (June 24, 1848–February 13, 1927) *writer*
The brother of Charles Francis Adams, Jr., and Henry Adams, Brooks Adams graduated from Harvard University in 1870. Thereafter, he entered the law, but after a decade of practice, he concentrated on writing. His focus was primarily political economy, and his books included *The Law of Civilization and Decay* (1895) and *America's Economic Supremacy* (1900).

Addams, Jane (September 6, 1860–May 21, 1935) *reformer, peace activist*
Jane Addams was born in Cedarville, Illinois. Although eager to pursue a college education, Jane was discouraged as this path was not considered genteel for a woman. She attended Rockford Seminary in Illinois and then traveled to Europe. There, she visited a London settlement house, which prompted her, upon her return to the United States, to purchase a large house in Chicago. She established the settlement house, Hull-House, which was so successful that it was soon copied elsewhere by others interested in social reform. Adams fought for universal woman suffrage in the United States and was a member of several peace organizations, including the Women's Peace Party and the Women's International League for Peace and Freedom, which she helped found in 1919. In 1931, Jane Addams was named co-recipient, with Nicholas Murray Butler, of the Nobel Peace Prize.

Alcott, Louisa May (November 29, 1832–March 6, 1888) *writer*
Louisa May Alcott was born in Germantown, Pennsylvania, to philosopher and educator, Bronson Alcott,

and his wife Abigail May Alcott. She lived in Concord, Massachusetts, at Orchard House, from 1858 to 1877. While editing a children's magazine, Alcott wrote *Little Women,* a novel published in serial form between 1868 and 1870. This was followed by other novels, chiefly concerned with the triumph of poverty through strength of character. In 1879, Alcott became the first woman to register to vote in her hometown of Concord, when Massachusetts law gave women the right to vote on issues such as schools and taxes.

Aldrich, Nelson Wilmarth (November 6, 1841–April 16, 1915) *senator, financier*
Nelson Wilmarth Aldrich, a Rhode Island financier, was a political spokesman during the presidencies of McKinley and Roosevelt. He served in the military during the Civil War as a member of the Rhode Island National Guard. Later, Aldrich was elected to the Providence, Rhode Island, city council, and was elected to the Rhode Island State House of Representatives in 1875 and 1876, becoming House Speaker in 1876. He served as a Republican congressman and a U.S. Senator, for more than 30 years, urging banking reform and establishment of the Federal Reserve Bank.

Alger, Horatio (January 13, 1832–July 18, 1899) *writer*
Horatio Alger, a Unitarian minister from New England, is known best for his dime novels with the "rags-to-riches" theme that became synonymous with his name. Alger's popularity extended well into the 20th century. He wrote more than 118 novels and 500 short stories and had an additional 280 stories published serially in magazines.

Anthony, Susan Brownell (February 15, 1820–March 13, 1906) *equal rights activist*
Susan B. Anthony was born in Adams, Massachusetts, and learned to read at the age of three. After attending boarding school in Pennsylvania, she became a teacher, and in 1853, began her lifelong career as a reformer in the temperance, abolition, and women's rights movements. Following the Civil War, she devoted herself almost exclusively to women's rights. She worked on behalf of this cause with many other women, including Elizabeth Cady Stanton, Lucy Stone, and Carrie Chapman Catt.

Arthur, Chester Alan (October 5, 1829–November 18, 1886) *vice president and president of the United States*
Born in Fairfield, Vermont, Chester Arthur was appointed New York Port Authority collector by President Grant in 1871. By 1877, during the Hayes administration, Arthur's management of the authority was under federal investigation for alleged mismanagement, and he was suspended. Nonetheless, in 1880, Arthur was nominated as Republican James Garfield's vice presidential candidate. After Garfield's assassination in 1881, Arthur became known for support of civil service reform. Arthur lost his bid for nomination to a full term of office in 1884 when the Republican Party threw its support to James G. Blaine.

Barton, Clara (December 25, 1821–April 12, 1912) *humanitarian*
Born on a farm in Oxford, Massachusetts, in 1821, Clara Barton was first a schoolteacher and then a government worker, but later became widely known for her nursing skills during the Civil War. Under President Abraham Lincoln, Barton received funding from the U.S. Congress to establish a missing persons bureau. In 1870, she contributed to International Red Cross aid efforts in the war between France and Prussia. Upon her return to the United States, she founded a similar aid organization. In 1881, President James Garfield granted a charter to Barton's humanitarian agency, the American Red Cross. Barton served as its president until 1904.

Beaux, Cecilia (May 1, 1855–September 17, 1942) *artist*
Born in Philadelphia, Cecilia Beaux was privately educated. She trained at the Pennsylvania Academy of the Fine Arts. There she sharpened her skills in portraiture, which she further developed in her own studio in Philadelphia in 1883. She exhibited at the Pennsylvania Academy of Fine Arts in 1885 and benefited from studying the Académie Julian in Paris, France, in 1888. In 1894 she became an associate member of the National Academy of Design, and two years later, the Paris Salon hung six of Beaux's works in its annual exhibition. She became a full member of the academy in 1902, only the third woman admitted to this prestigious status.

Beecher, Henry Ward (June 24, 1813–March 8, 1887) *clergyman*

A Presbyterian minister, Beecher in 1844 wrote a book with an ethical theme, *Seven Lectures to Young Men.* In 1867, he published *Norwood,* a novel that emphasized the importance of moral living. Although he was wealthy, popular, and known for his good works, in 1872 allegations surfaced that Beecher had been romantically involved with Elizabeth Tilton, his parishioner at Plymouth Church in Brooklyn, New York. His accuser was Victoria Woodhull, who, with her sister Tennessee Claflin, was a free-love advocate. Despite the widely publicized scandal ensuing from the charges, Beecher was found innocent by a church board of inquiry. During the 1880s, Beecher spoke out on behalf of civil service reform. He became a Liberal Republican and supported Democratic Grover Cleveland in the latter's bid for the White House in 1885.

Bell, Alexander Graham (March 3, 1847–August 2, 1922) *inventor, educator*

Bell, an inventor, an educator, and supporter and advocate for educational rights for the deaf, was born in Edinburgh, Scotland. He emigrated with his family, first to Canada, and taught in Boston, Massachusetts, at a school for the deaf, later becoming an American citizen. His work as an educator led him to investigate the mechanics of sound, and his interest in this technology prompted his invention of the telephone. Bell lived in Nova Scotia, Canada, after his retirement and died of cardiac arrest shortly before transatlantic telephone service was introduced.

Bethune, Mary McLeod (July 10, 1875–May 18, 1955) *educator*

Mary McLeod Bethune, born in Maysville, South Carolina, the daughter of former slaves, believed African Americans who wished to improve their lives could do so best if they had the opportunity to receive an education. She attended Maysville Presbyterian Mission School, Scotia Seminary, and the Moody Bible Institute. In 1904, she founded the Daytona Normal and Industrial Institute for Negro Girls and was president from 1904 to 1942 and during the period 1946–47. Bethune was director of Negro affairs in the National Youth Administration, a Works Progress Administration program, between 1936 and 1944. The girls' school in Daytona later became Bethune-Cookman College.

Black Elk (ca. 1863–August 17, 1950) *Native American leader*

An Oglala Lakota Sioux spiritual leader, Black Elk fought at the Battle of Little Bighorn in 1876, when he was 13 years old. After the Sioux surrendered to federal troops and were removed to reservation land at Pine Ridge, South Dakota, Black Elk joined Buffalo Bill Cody's Wild West Show. Beginning in 1886, he performed with Cody's show in the United States and in Europe. After he returned from a European tour, he discovered his tribe living in poverty, which prompted him to join the Ghost Dance, a religion and reform movement. In 1890, he was a witness to the massacre of Native Americans at Wounded Knee, after which time he converted to Roman Catholicism. Black Elk remained active as a leader of his people until his death in South Dakota in 1950.

Blaine, James Gillespie (January 31, 1830–January 27, 1893) *congressman, presidential nominee*

Born in Pennsylvania, Blaine was educated in Ohio, then attended Washington and Jefferson College in Pennsylvania. After graduation he taught school and studied law. In 1854, he moved to Maine and was a founder of the Republican Party. He served in the state legislature from 1859 to 1862, then was elected to the U.S. House of Representatives, serving as Speaker for three terms (1863–1876). In 1876, he lost the presidential nomination to Rutherford B. Hayes. Following this defeat, Blaine resigned his seat in the U.S. House. Blaine supported Chinese exclusion because he believed these immigrants took jobs from U.S. laborers. In 1880, Blaine lost the presidential nomination to James Garfield, who later named Blaine secretary of state. Following Garfield's assassination, Blaine resigned his cabinet position and in 1884, he received the Republican presidential nomination. Independent Republicans (known as "Mugwumps"), however, preferred Democrat Grover Cleveland. Blaine was again secretary of state under President Harrison. In 1892, he tried unsuccessfully to unseat Harrison. Blaine died in Washington, D.C., in January 1893.

Blair, Francis Preston, Jr. (Frank Blair) (February 19, 1821–July 8, 1875) *congressman, vice presidential nominee*

Son of Francis Preston Blair, Sr., (of President Andrew Jackson's "kitchen cabinet" and editor of the *Congres-*

sional Globe) Frank Blair was a U.S. congressman from Missouri who backed Lincoln's proposed Reconstruction plan. In 1868, Democrats nominated Blair as the vice presidential running mate of Horatio Seymour, but they lost the election to General Ulysses S. Grant. Three years later, Blair won a special election to the U.S. Senate. In 1875, Blair suffered serious injuries in a fall and died at St. Louis, Missouri.

Booth, John Wilkes (May 10, 1838–
April 26, 1865) *presidential assassin*
John Wilkes Booth was born in Harford County, Maryland, the ninth of 10 children. He achieved some success as an actor but, consumed with Confederate pride, he was unable to contain his anger following the surrender of Robert E. Lee. Enraged, Booth shot President Abraham Lincoln while Lincoln attended a performance at Ford's Theater in Washington, D.C. During the chaotic chase that ensued after Booth fired his gun at the president, Booth was also shot, by Sergeant Boston Corbett. Booth died shortly thereafter, in Port Royal, Virginia. After an autopsy was performed, Secretary of War Edwin Stanton arranged for Booth's body to be buried in a hole in the ground at the Old Penitentiary in the Washington Arsenal. In 1867, Booth's remains were exhumed and then reinterred, this time in a pine box. In June 1869, his remains were again removed from the grave, and released to his family, who buried John Wilkes Booth in an unmarked plot in Green Mount Cemetery, in Baltimore, Maryland.

Bowell, The Hon. Sir Mackenzie (December 27, 1823–December 10, 1917) *Canadian prime minister*
Sir Mackenzie Bowell was widely known for his pro-English views. In 1870–78, he was the grandmaster of the Orange Order of British North America. In 1894, when Prime Minister Sir John Thompson died of a heart attack, Bowell became Conservative Party leader, then prime minister. In 1896, his cabinet demanded that he resign due to his refusal to support minority education rights. Bowell was opposition leader in the Canadian Senate from 1896 to 1906.

Bryan, William Jennings (March 19, 1860–
July 26, 1925) *congressman, presidential candidate*
William Jennings Bryan, born in Salem, Illinois, graduated from Illinois College in 1881. He practiced law before his election to the U.S. Congress in 1890. A progressive Democrat, he supported voting rights for women, an income tax, and labor regulation. In 1896, he was the Democratic candidate for the presidency, running against William McKinley, who easily defeated Bryan. The Electoral College vote was 271 to 176. Bryan ran two more times, losing in 1900 to William McKinley and in 1908 to William H. Taft.

Burlingame, Anson (November 14, 1820–
February 23, 1870) *diplomat*
Anson Burlingame was born in New Berlin, New York. Prior to the Civil War, he was elected to the Massachusetts state senate, and then to the U.S. House of Representatives. In 1860, President Lincoln appointed Burlingame to be the U.S. minister to China. In November 1867, he resigned his diplomatic post so that he could serve as the head of the first Chinese delegation, which visited the United States in March 1868. That year, on July 28, China and the United States signed the Burlingame Treaty, the terms of which included mutual agreement of respect for territorial sovereignty, protection of civilian rights and immunities, a guarantee of religious liberty, and recognition of U.S. immigration rights for all Chinese.

Carnegie, Andrew (November 25, 1835–
August 11, 1919) *steel magnate, philanthropist*
Andrew Carnegie was born in Dunfermline, Scotland, and immigrated to the United States in 1848, his family settling in Allegheny, Pennsylvania. At 12, he began working in a textile factory. Two years later he obtained a job as a messenger in a telegraph office. By 1859, after working as a secretary to the superintendent of the Pennsylvania Railroad, Carnegie had risen to the position of superintendent and had become closely acquainted with J. Edgar Thomson, president of the Pennsylvania Railroad. By this time, also, he had invested in several steel and iron mills and in an oilfield. He became manager of the Keystone Bridge Company in 1865. Within the next decade, he founded the J. Edgar Thomson Steel Works, later known as the Carnegie Steel Company (Thomson was an important financial backer). This new company was the first in the United States to use the Bessemer steelmaking process, imported from Britain. Among his associates were steel magnate Henry Clay Frick and his brother Thomas M. Carnegie. Thanks to

Carnegie's company, by 1890 U.S. steel output exceeded that of Great Britain. Carnegie married Louise Whitfield in 1887, and the couple lived in New York City, Scotland, and Lenox, Massachusetts. By 1900, Carnegie Steel had assets of $40 million. Carnegie sold the company to the U.S. Steel Corporation (owned by J. P. Morgan) in 1901 for $250 million, after which Carnegie retired. Thereafter, he devoted himself to philanthropy and to writing about business and social issues. His article "Wealth," published in the *North American Review* in June 1889, became a point of reference for those interested in a uniquely "Gilded Age" philosophy known as the "Gospel of Wealth."

Carver, George Washington (January 5, 1864–January 5, 1943) *scientist, educator*
George Washington Carver was born a slave in Missouri but pursued an education after the end of the Civil War. He was the first African-American student admitted to Simpson College in Indianola, Iowa. After graduating from Simpson, he worked as a custodian and attended what is now Iowa State University. Carver earned a degree in agricultural science in 1894, and two years later he received a master's degree. He became a member of the faculty at the Tuskegee Institute, in Alabama, where he stayed for nearly 40 years. Carver taught scientific agricultural methods and devoted himself to research. One of his many inventions was peanut butter.

Cassatt, Mary (May 22, 1844–June 14, 1926) *artist*
Born in Pennsylvania, Mary Cassatt attended the Philadelphia Academy of Art. She moved to Paris in 1874, and one of her paintings was accepted by the Paris Salon. Thereafter, she made her permanent home in France, where the painter Edgar Degas influenced her work. Degas encouraged Cassatt to develop her own impressionist style. She exhibited with other impressionists in the Paris exhibitions of 1879, 1880, 1881, and 1886 and was among the chief mentors of collectors, among them her brother Alexander, who imported impressionist works into the United States.

Catt, Carrie Chapman (January 9, 1859–March 9, 1947) *equal rights activist*
Carrie Chapman Catt, born in Ripon, Wisconsin, had the benefit of an education at a time when many young women of her age did not. After graduating from Iowa State College in 1880, she became a teacher and school superintendent. She married a newspaper editor, and after his death became heavily involved in the campaign for woman suffrage in Idaho and Colorado. She was leader of the National American Woman Suffrage Association, which worked to promote voting rights for women nationwide. Thanks to her efforts and those of her colleagues Susan Brownell Anthony and Lucy Stone, by 1920 the 19th Amendment to the U.S. Constitution was ratified, guaranteeing women in the United States the right to vote.

Clemens, Samuel Langhorne (Mark Twain) (November 30, 1835–April 21, 1910) *writer*
Widely known by the pen name "Mark Twain," Samuel L. Clemens was born in Florida, Missouri. As a young man, Clemens became an apprentice printer, working for his brother, a newspaper publisher. By 1856, Clemens was writing for the Keokuk (Iowa) *Saturday Post,* and later accompanied a riverboat pilot on the Mississippi River so that he could learn navigation. He spent three years working on the Mississippi, and after the outbreak of the Civil War he served as a Confederate army volunteer, although he deserted soon after enlisting. In 1862, he was again writing for a newspaper. Clemens was living in San Francisco when, in 1865, he published "The Celebrated Jumping Frog of Calaveras County." Shortly after this, he went east to enjoy New York City life, then in 1867 sailed for Europe. His book *Innocents Abroad* (1869) reflects his experiences during this period. In 1870, Samuel Clemens married Olivia Langdon, of Elmira, New York, and they settled in Hartford, Connecticut. Near the end of his life, Clemens experienced depression, initially because of the death of his beloved daughter, Susy, in 1896. When Clemens's wife, Olivia, died in 1904 and a second daughter died five years later, he continued to be troubled with depression. He died in Redding, Connecticut, in 1910.

Cleveland, Grover Stephen (March 18, 1837–June 24, 1908) *president of the United States*
Stephen Grover Cleveland, a Democrat, was the only U.S. president elected to two nonconsecutive terms. He was the first president to be married, and to become a father, while serving in the White House. In 1888, running for reelection, Cleveland won the popular vote, but lost the Electoral College vote to Benjamin Harrison. In 1892, Cleveland ran again and

was reelected, but faced the challenge of leading the country through a severe economic depression that began with the Panic of 1893. Cleveland's public service career ended when he declined to run in the 1896 election; he thereafter became a professor at Princeton University in New Jersey.

Cochrane, Elizabeth Jane (Nellie Bly, Nelly Bly) (ca. May 5, 1864–January 27, 1922) *journalist*

Elizabeth Jane Cochrane, born in Apollo, Pennsylvania, was best known for her record-breaking around-the-world trip between November 14, 1889, and January 25, 1890. Cochrane's interest in journalism began early; in 1885 she wrote under the pen name "Nellie Bly" (derived from a song by Stephen Foster). Cochrane's reports focused on real-life experiences and eyewitness descriptions. In 1887, Joseph Pulitzer hired her to write for the *New York World*. Jules Verne's novel *Around the World in Eighty Days* gave her the idea to challenge this 80-day travel record. Cochrane bested it by going around the world in 72 days, six hours, 11 minutes, and 14 seconds. Cochrane married Robert Seaman, a millionaire industrialist, in 1895. He died in 1904, leaving his wife to oversee his corporate holdings. During World War I, she served as a reporter for the *New York Evening Journal*. She died of pneumonia in January 1922.

Cody, William Frederick (Buffalo Bill Cody) (February 26, 1846–January 10, 1917) *hunter, army scout, entertainer*

Cody was born in Iowa but moved to Kansas when he was still a child. He rode for the Pony Express Company, carrying mail between California and Missouri, then, during the Civil War, served in the Union army. After the war was over, Cody became a buffalo hunter, providing meat to construction workers building the Transcontinental Railroad. He was also a civilian scout for the U.S. Army during the Indian campaigns, and in 1872, was a recipient of the Congressional Medal of Honor. Cody, known as "Buffalo Bill," founded his Wild West Show tour in 1873, and it remained immensely popular into the early 20th century.

Colfax, Schuyler (March 23, 1823–January 13, 1885) *congressman, vice president of the United States*

Schuyler Colfax, born in New York City, moved with his family to New Carlisle, Indiana, in 1836 and attended public schools there. He later became deputy auditor of Joseph County in 1841. He was a legislative correspondent for the *Indiana State Journal* and a member of the state constitutional convention in 1850. Colfax, a Republican, was elected to the 34th U.S. Congress and served terms between March 1855 and March 1869, although he was not up for renomination in 1868 because he had become his party's vice presidential nominee, and was elected, along with General Ulysses S. Grant. During Reconstruction, Colfax, a Radical Republican, supported suffrage for freed slaves. He was not renominated as vice president in 1872, due to his ties to the Crédit Mobilier scandal. Colfax died in Mankato, Minnesota, in January 1885.

Comstock, Anthony (March 7, 1844–September 21, 1915) *lobbyist*

Comstock was a crusader for anti–birth control statutes and the author of a New York state statute in 1868 that forbid the dissemination of "immoral works." In 1872, he traveled to Washington, D.C., seeking legislation to ban the sale and use of contraceptive devices. In March 1873, the U.S. Congress passed strict legislation that prohibited the sending of obscene matter via the U.S. Postal Service. This bill, later known as the Comstock Act, defined contraceptives as obscene and illicit. It thus became illegal to send birth control information or material through the mail or across state lines. Comstock organized the New York Society for the Suppression of Vice and served as its secretary until his death in 1915.

Conkling, Roscoe (October 30, 1829–April 18, 1888) *congressman, senator*

Roscoe Conkling was born in Albany, New York, and lived in Auburn, New York, where he studied law. He was admitted to the New York state bar in 1850. Conkling was a Republican who was elected mayor of Utica, New York, in 1858. He was elected to the U.S. House of Representatives in 1859, where he served in the 36th and 37th Congresses. He lost a reelection bid in 1862, but was returned to Congress for the 39th and 40th sessions. In 1867, he resigned his congressional seat after being elected to the U.S. Senate. In May 1881, Conkling resigned from the Senate after a dispute with President Garfield over federal appointments. Hoping for reelection, he was passed over in favor of other candidates. In 1882,

Conkling decided against accepting a nomination to the U.S. Supreme Court. He died in April 1888.

Cooke, Jay (August 10, 1821–February 18, 1905) *investment banker*

Jay Cooke, born in Sandusky, Ohio, learned about finance while working in a trading house in St. Louis, Missouri. At age 18, he joined E.W. Clark & Company, one of the nation's largest private banking institutions, and by age 30, he was a partner in several of the Clark Company's branches. He helped sell U.S. government bonds during the Civil War, and in 1870, he financed construction of the Northern Pacific Railway. He overinvested in this venture, and Cooke declared bankruptcy after he lost everything in the Panic of 1873, for which he was partially blamed. He later regained his financial position, thanks to shrewd mining investments, and died a wealthy man in 1905.

Custer, George Armstrong (December 5, 1839–June 25, 1876) *Union army general*

George Armstrong Custer graduated last in his class at West Point in 1861 and served in the Union army. He was promoted to brigadier general of volunteers shortly before the Battle of Gettysburg. After the war, Custer was appointed lieutenant colonel of the Seventh U.S. Cavalry. During his military career, he grew famous for his daring and infamous for his self-promotion. In June 1876, at the Battle of Little Bighorn, Custer and 300 members of his regiment were killed. It was widely understood that this disaster could have been averted had Custer heeded the advice of his more cautious military colleagues.

Czolgosz, Leon Frank (January 1, 1873–October 29, 1901) *presidential assassin*

Born in Detroit, Michigan, Leon Czolgosz went to work early, like many children who lived in poverty. He was employed at a steel mill at the age of 10, yet was subsequently unemployed, due to a series of strikes in factories where he and other workers had no labor union protection. By 1898, angry and broken in spirit, he had become reclusive. He developed an interest in both socialism and anarchism. On August 31, 1901, Czolgosz rented a room in Buffalo, New York. There, on September 6, he waited while President McKinley participated in a receiving line at the Pan-American Exposition. Seizing his opportunity, Czolgosz shot the president at close range, and

McKinley died of complications from the gunshot wounds he had received on September 14, 1901. Czolgosz was arrested, tried, and found guilty. He was electrocuted on October 29, 1901, at Auburn, New York.

Davis, Richard Harding (April 18, 1864–April 11, 1916) *journalist*

Richard Harding Davis was a reporter with the *Philadelphia Record*. Later, he wrote for the *New York Sun,* and in 1890 was named managing editor of *Harper's Weekly*. Davis was among the best-known war correspondents of his era. His reports of military action during the Spanish-American War were widely read throughout the United States. Davis was also a novelist and playwright.

Debs, Eugene Victor (November 5, 1855–October 20, 1926) *labor leader*

Debs attended public school in his hometown of Terre Haute, Indiana, but left school before graduating to work on the railroad. He attended night classes and, in 1874, found a job as a billing clerk in a grocery store. Debs was active in the Brotherhood of Locomotive Firemen, of which he became national secretary in 1881. He was also involved in a literary club. In 1879, Debs, a Democrat, was elected to the first of two terms as Terre Haute's city clerk. Five years later, he was elected to the Indiana General Assembly, representing Terre Haute and Vigo County. The following year, he married Kate Metzel. In June 1893, Debs organized the American Railway Union in Chicago, Illinois, and led the union's walkout of the Great Northern Railway. He supported the Pullman strike, which began on May 11, 1894. President Cleveland's attorney general, Richard Olney, advised calling in federal troops to break the strike. Due to Debs's participation in the labor action, he was jailed for contempt of court. Beginning in 1900, he ran for U.S. president. He had helped found the Social Democrat Party, which became the Socialist Party in 1901. Debs ran for president on the Socialist Party ticket, repeating this candidacy in 1904, 1908, and 1912. When Debs protested U.S. involvement in World War I, he was convicted on espionage charges. While serving time in prison in 1920 he ran for president again. President Warren G. Harding commuted Debs's sentence in 1921, and he was released. He died in 1926.

Dewey, George (December 26, 1837–January 16, 1917) *U.S. naval commander*
Although known chiefly for his skill during the Spanish-American War, George Dewey distinguished himself during several Civil War naval battles. In 1877, Dewey was appointed naval secretary to the Lighthouse Board in Washington, D.C., and in 1897, was appointed commander-in-chief of the Asiatic Fleet. At the outbreak of the Spanish-American War, he took his command to the Philippine Islands, arriving at Manila Bay on April 30, 1898. On May 1, U.S. forces destroyed the Spanish fleet—a victory that catapulted Dewey to fame as the "Hero of Manila." In 1899, he attracted a great deal of attention at one of New York City's first ticker tape parades. In March of that year, Congress promoted Dewey to rear admiral. Dewey declared his candidacy for U.S. president in 1900, but withdrew his name shortly thereafter. He served as president of the General Board of the Navy until 1916.

Dodge, Grenville Mellen (April 12, 1831–January 3, 1916) *railroad engineer*
Born in Danvers, Massachusetts, Grenville Dodge attended public school and, in 1851, graduated from Norwich University, Vermont, with a degree in civil engineering. In May 1854, Dodge married Ruth Anne Brown, and the couple moved to the Nebraska Territory to take up a homestead claim on the Elkhorn River. Indian attacks prompted them to relocate to Omaha. By 1860, they had moved to Iowa, where Dodge became a member of the Council Bluffs City Council in 1860, and where Dodge established himself in banking and real estate. He sold land and later was involved in land speculation and bribery, making his fortune as he surveyed land for railroads.

In 1861, Dodge joined the Union army, reaching the rank of major general prior to resigning in June 1866. Dodge became chief engineer of the Union Pacific Railroad and was elected to the U.S. Congress, serving from March 4, 1867, to March 3, 1869. He was a delegate to the Republican National Convention in 1868, and again in 1872 and 1876. He was appointed by President McKinley to serve as president of the commission that made inquiry into the War Department's conduct during the Spanish-American War. He died in Council Bluffs, Iowa, in 1916.

Douglass, Frederick (February 17, 1818–February 20, 1895) *former slave, civil rights activist*
Born into slavery, Douglass never knew his father, who was a white man. He was separated from his mother while an infant and lived with his grandmother on a Maryland plantation until he was eight. When he was sent to Baltimore, Maryland, to be a house slave, Douglass learned to read. Prior to the Civil War, he became active in the abolitionist movement. After the war ended, he remained active in civil rights activities, wrote, and was a sought-after public speaker.

DuBois, W. E. B. (W. E. Burghardt DuBois) (February 23, 1868–August 27, 1963) *civil rights activist*
DuBois was born in Great Barrington, Massachusetts, and graduated from Fisk University. He was the first African American to receive a Ph.D. from Harvard University. In 1905, DuBois helped found the Niagara Movement. Four years later, he was a founder of the National Association for the Advancement of Colored People (NAACP). A member of the faculty at Atlanta University, DuBois served for more than two decades as editor in chief of *The Crisis* magazine. He also was a newspaper columnist. He died in Accra, Ghana, in 1963.

Eastman, George (July 12, 1854–March 14, 1932) *inventor*
George Eastman was born in Waterville, New York. He quit school at age 15 to help support his family after his father's death in 1862. He worked as a bookkeeper and hoped to make a career in real estate. After obtaining photographic equipment and learning the rudiments of dry-plate photography, he decided in 1880 to launch a business selling photographic plates. By 1884, together with William Walker, he had begun to design a roller-holder for paper camera film. Eastman came up with the term *Kodak* as a name for this new, financially viable camera design. By the 1890s, the Eastman company, which had experienced some success, experienced some setbacks, but by 1900, Eastman introduced the Brownie camera and his company maintained a firm hold on its prominence as a supplier to amateur and professional photographers. Eastman, a widely traveled man who loved music, never married. He was a philanthropist committed to supporting a variety of causes. He died in March 1932.

Edison, Thomas Alva (February 11, 1847–
October 18, 1931) *inventor*
Edison was born in Milan, Ohio, and was educated at
home by his mother. At age 12, he convinced his parents to permit him to work as a newsboy, selling a
weekly paper, which he himself published, on a train
to Detroit. Soon, Edison learned to operate a telegraph so that he could earn more money. After several
years, Edison settled in New York City, working on
various inventions and experiments. He perfected
ideas for improving the telegraph and telephone,
which he worked on at a large shop at West Orange,
New Jersey. Edison invented the phonograph and the
electric light, and more than 1,000 other items and
processes, including a motion-picture machine, a storage battery, the mimeograph, and machinery used in
the production of iron and steel. Edison obtained his
last patent, number 1,093, when he was 83 years old.

Fish, Hamilton (August 3, 1808–September 7,
1893) *secretary of state*
Hamilton Fish was born in New York City and later
became a congressman and a senator. In 1869, he was
named secretary of state by President Ulysses S. Grant,
serving during both of Grant's terms of office. Among
Fish's accomplishments as secretary was to help craft a
treaty that ended a dispute of many years with Great
Britain, although this was not done without challenge, chiefly from the Senate foreign relations committee chair, Charles Sumner. In 1873, Fish handled
delicate diplomatic dealings with Spain, forestalling
war between the United States and that country over
Cuba's desire for independence.

Ford, Henry (July 30, 1863–April 7, 1947)
industrialist
Henry Ford was born in Dearborn, Michigan, to Irish
immigrant parents. By age 16, he had left school,
where he had been an indifferent student. He went to
live in Detroit, where he was employed by the Detroit
Edison Company. He married Clara Bryant on April
11, 1888. By 1893, Ford had constructed a gasoline
engine, and soon invented an automobile. In 1899, he
was working at the Detroit Automobile Company, but
in 1903, he set up the Ford Motor Company in
Highland Park, Michigan. In 1908, he developed the
Model T Ford, and in 1913 had inaugurated a moving
assembly line in his automobile manufacturing plant.
By 1927, when Ford stopped making the Model T, 15

million of these cars had been sold, making Henry
Ford the most successful car manufacturer in the
United States. Ford died at his home in April 1947.

Frick, Henry Clay (December 19, 1849–
December 2, 1919) *industrialist*
Frick made his fortune in the processing of coal into
coke. He built up the coke-making business and was
later known as the "Coke King." Frick merged his
coke interests with those of Andrew Carnegie, who
was known as the "Steel King," establishing a new
organization, the Carnegie Corporation (later named
U.S. Steel Corporation).

Garfield, James A. (November 19, 1831–
September 19, 1881) *congressman, president of the
United States*
Born in Cuyahoga County, Ohio, in 1831, James
Garfield graduated from Williams College in 1856.
Two years later, he married Lucretia Rudolph, on
November 11, 1858, in Hiram, Ohio, where he was
serving as president of Hiram College.

By 1880, Garfield, a Republican, was Speaker of
the U.S. House of Representatives and had received
his party's presidential nomination. Garfield was
considered a dark-horse candidate, as his nomination
was assured only after 36 convention ballots. Garfield
won the election, defeating his Democratic opponent,
Gen. Winfield Scott Hancock, by a slim margin of
10,000 popular votes. During his time in office,
Garfield became known for fighting political corruption and for challenging the control of powerful Senator Roscoe Conkling. In July 1881, less than a year
into his first term, President Garfield was shot by a
thwarted office-seeker, Charles Guiteau. Weeks passed
and the president continued to suffer from the
wounds he received. On September 19, 1881, President Garfield died as a result of internal bleeding and
infection.

Gilder, Richard Watson (February 8, 1844–
November 18, 1909) *editor*
For nearly 30 years, Richard Watson Gilder was editor
in chief of the *Century Monthly Magazine*. As the editor of the most widely read periodical in the United
States, Gilder's prestige and influence were virtually
boundless. He and his wife, the artist Helena de Kay,
lived in New York City, holding positions of considerable influence among New York's cultural elite. The

couple was famous for Friday evening salons attended by artists, writers, and musicians.

Glidden, Joseph (January 18, 1813–October 9, 1906) inventor

Glidden was born in Charlestown, New Hampshire, and later moved with his family to the state of New York. He studied to be a teacher, but after working as a teacher for a brief time, decided that he preferred farming. In 1837, he moved with his new wife, Clarissa Foster, to De Kalb, Illinois. After her death, Glidden married Lucinda Warne in 1851. Glidden went to a county fair in 1873 and noticed a display of wire fencing that appeared effective in keeping cattle out of fields of crops. After experimenting with improvements to this wire fencing, Glidden applied for and received a patent for a machine to make barbed wire. He and his partner, Isaac L. Ellwood, established the Barb Fence Company in De Kalb. Glidden became wealthy as the broad ranges of the West were gradually transformed into farmland, thanks to the use of barbed wire.

Godkin, Edwin Lawrence (October 2, 1831–May 21, 1902) journalist

Born in Ireland, Godkin attended in Queen's College, Belfast, and studied law in London. In 1856, he traveled to the United States. He was admitted to the New York bar in 1859, and in 1865, he founded the weekly publication *The Nation,* serving as its editor. In 1881, he became an associate editor of the *New York Post,* and succeeded Carl Schurz as editor in chief. An advocate of currency reform and civil service reform, Godkin attacked the political machine known as Tammany Hall and in 1894 was sued for libel for his outspoken and allegedly exaggerated claims against Tammany leaders. He opposed the war with Spain and retired from his editorial duties at the end of December 1899. Godkin suffered from a stroke in 1900 and died in England in May 1902.

Gompers, Samuel (January 27, 1850–December 13, 1924) labor leader

Gompers was born in London and immigrated to the United States with his parents in 1863. In 1864, he was working as a cigar maker and joined the local union. In 1881, he was a founder of the Federation of Organized Trades and Labor Unions, which, in 1886, became the American Federation of Labor. He was spokesman for the labor movement and was president of the American Federation of Labor until his death.

Gould, Jay (May 27, 1836–December 2, 1892) financier

Born on a farm in Roxbury, New York, Jay Gould was a good student. He left school at age 16 to pursue work as a surveyor and in banking. Early associated with the development of railroads, Jay Gould shrewdly applied his knowledge to the opportunities around him. By the time he was 21, he had amassed $5,000 in savings and began to speculate with his money. In 1859, Gould went to New York City and became a railway stock broker; in 1868, he was elected president of the Erie Railway. Working together with James Fisk, he and his partner were able to corner the gold market in 1869, leading to the Black Friday panic. Gould later bought a controlling interest in the Union Pacific Railroad, and by 1880 was known as a "robber baron" who owned one-ninth of all the railroad mileage in the United States. At his death, in 1892, his worth was estimated at $72 million.

Grant, Ulysses S. (April 27, 1822–July, 23, 1885) president of the United States

Grant was born in Point Pleasant, Ohio, and later attended West Point. During the Civil War, he was commander of all Union armies. Grant's skills enabled him to force Confederate general Robert E. Lee's Army of Northern Virginia to surrender on April 9, 1865. The next year, Congress made Grant the first full General of the Armies in U.S. history. Grant accepted the Republican nomination for president in 1868, won, and served two consecutive terms. After leaving the White House, Grant attempted to conduct business on Wall Street, but was unsuccessful. He then sought financial support through his writing. In summer 1884, Grant was diagnosed with throat cancer, and he retired to Mount McGregor, New York. There, he worked on a two-volume memoir. After his death, his body was laid to rest in a tomb in New York City, on April 27, 1897.

Greeley, Horace (February 3, 1811–November 29, 1872) editor, presidential candidate

Greeley, born in Amherst, New Hampshire, founded the *New York Tribune* in 1841. By the end of the Civil War, the newspaper had hundreds of thousands of subscribers. Greeley's eclectic interests included protesting slavery, capital punishment, and smoking, and supporting the prohibition of alcohol. He advocated equal rights for women, promoted the construction of a transcontinental railroad, and approved foreign trade protection. In 1864 and 1865, he published a two-volume work on the U.S. Civil War; in 1868, Greeley published his memoirs. In 1872, a group of Liberal Republicans persuaded him to accept nomination as a presidential candidate. The Democrats supported Greeley as well, but he had little chance against the incumbent, President Ulysses S. Grant. Because Greeley's reputation suffered after this defeat, he left his high-profile career at the *Tribune*.

Guiteau, Charles Julius (September 14, 1841–June 30, 1882) *presidential assassin*
Charles Guiteau was born in Freeport, Illinois, in 1841. He was severely abused as a child by his father. He inherited a small sum of money from his grandfather in 1859, which led Guiteau to enter law school, where he failed in his studies. He joined the utopian, religious Oneida Community, founded by John Humphrey Noyes, the following year, but left for good by 1865. He pursued the study of theology and wrote a book, *The Truth,* that was full of plagiarism. By 1869, he was married to a librarian named Annie Bunn, but the couple was divorced in 1874. On May 18, 1881, Guiteau allegedly had a vision that convinced him to kill President James A. Garfield. He carried out this deadly task on July 2, 1881, by shooting the president as the latter boarded a train in Washington, D.C. Garfield died in October, and in November, Guiteau went on trial for murder. A jury found him guilty in January 1882, and he was hanged in Washington, D.C., in June of that same year.

Hancock, Winfield Scott (February 14, 1824–February 9, 1886) *presidential candidate*
Named after a then well-known war hero (Winfield Scott had a major role in the War of 1812), Winfield Scott Hancock was born in Pennsylvania. He graduated from West Point in 1844 and served in the Union army during the Civil War. After this, Hancock remained in the army and served in the western theater. There, he experienced the military's persistent conflict with Native Americans. Nominated by the Democrats for the U.S. presidency in 1880, Hancock lost his election bid to Republican James Garfield. Hancock remained in the U.S. Army until his death in 1886.

Hanna, Mark (Marcus Alonzo Hanna)
(September 24, 1837–February 15, 1904)
politician
Mark Hanna was born in Lisbon, Ohio, and after attending college for a short time, joined his father in business. He became quite successful, and by 1880 began to pursue a career in the political area. He became a campaign manager, and in 1891 helped William McKinley win the election as Ohio governor. In 1896, Hanna again managed McKinley's campaign, again successfully, for the presidency. In 1897, Hanna was appointed to fill an open seat in the U.S. Senate, representing Ohio. In 1898, he was elected to that same seat. He worked closely with President McKinley until the assassination, and subsequently served as an adviser to President Theodore Roosevelt. Hanna died in 1904.

Harrison, Benjamin (August 20, 1833–March 13, 1901) *senator, president of the United States*
Benjamin Harrison was born in 1833 on a farm near Cincinnati, Ohio, the grandson of President William Henry Harrison. He attended Miami University in Oxford, Ohio, and later moved to Indianapolis, Indiana, to open a law practice there. In 1853, he married Caroline Lavinia Scott. In 1876, he ran for governor of Indiana but was defeated. He was appointed to the Mississippi River Commission in 1879 and to the U.S. Senate from Indiana, serving from 1881 to 1887. A year later, having received the Republican nomination for president, he won the election of 1888 against incumbent president Grover Cleveland. Although the president received more popular votes, Harrison received a majority of electoral votes (233-168). Among his accomplishments as president was passage of the Sherman Anti-Trust Act of 1890, the first law to offer protection against monopolies. Harrison was defeated in the election of 1892 by Grover Cleveland. His wife died that October of tuberculosis. When his term of office ended, Benjamin Harrison returned to practicing law in Indianapolis. There, in 1896, he married his former wife's niece, Mary Scott Lord Dimmick. Harrison died in 1901.

Harte, Bret (August 25, 1839–May 6, 1902) *writer*
Bret Harte was born in New York State but moved with his family to California. He wrote sketches of frontier life for a San Francisco magazine, the *Golden Era.* In the late 1860s, Harte published such short sto-

ries as "The Outcasts of Poker Flat" and "The Luck of Roaring Camp." He returned to the East Coast in 1871 and discovered that he was famous as a brilliant writer of western themes. In 1880, he became U.S. consul in Glasgow, Scotland. He traveled often to London, England, and settled there permanently in 1885.

Hay, John Milton (October 8, 1838–July 1, 1905) *secretary of state*

John Hay was born in Salem, Indiana, attended Brown University in Rhode Island, and later practiced law in Springfield, Illinois. There, Hay met Abraham Lincoln, becoming the president's assistant private secretary until Lincoln's death. He served in diplomatic posts and then worked as a journalist. Hay was named assistant secretary of state in 1878 by President Hayes. In 1897, his friend President McKinley appointed him ambassador to Great Britain, where Hay served throughout the Spanish-American War. From September 30, 1898, until his death in July 1905, Hay was secretary of state under both President McKinley and President Roosevelt. He helped negotiate the Treaty of Paris in 1898, and was chief author, in 1899, of a trade initiative known as the open door policy, which supported free trade between China and the United States. Hay was also a principal author, with Lord Julian Pauncefote of Great Britain, of the Hay-Pauncefote Treaty. The latter authorized the United States to build and maintain a Central American canal to join the Atlantic and Pacific Oceans. Beginning in 1891, Hay and his family spent summers at their retreat, "The Fells," in Newbury, New Hampshire.

Hayes, Rutherford Birchard (October 4, 1822–January 17, 1893) *president of the United States*

Born in Delaware, Ohio, Rutherford B. Hayes was the son of a farmer and distiller. In 1838, Hayes entered Kenyon College, where he excelled in academics. He graduated from Harvard Law School in 1845. In 1847, he married Lucy Webb, a confirmed temperance advocate with strong antislavery views. In 1859, Hayes was elected city solicitor for Cincinnati, Ohio, where he served for two years. He was in the 23rd Ohio Volunteer Infantry during the Civil War.

In 1865, Hayes, a Republican, was elected to fill an open seat representing Ohio in the U.S. Congress. He was reelected in 1866, supported President Andrew Johnson's impeachment, and then resigned from Congress in 1867, after which he was elected governor of Ohio. Hayes was reelected two years later, committing himself to civil service reform and to ratification of the Fifteenth Amendment. In 1872, he ran unsuccessfully for U.S. Congress, and in 1875 again accepted the gubernatorial nomination, winning the election. A year later, his name was placed on the ballot at the Republican National Convention. In November 1876, Democrat Samuel Tilden received the majority of popular votes, but due to an Electoral College contest the outcome was determined by a federal commission. In January 1877, Hayes had won the presidency by a single Electoral College vote.

Under Hayes, remaining federal troops were withdrawn from former Confederate states, and Reconstruction ended. In 1877, during the Great Railroad Strike, he advised use of federal troops to maintain peace. He supported civil service reform, signing the Pendleton Act in 1883. Hayes, who declined to run for reelection, died in 1893 in Fremont, Ohio.

Howe, Julia Ward (May 27, 1819–October 17, 1910) *equal rights activist, abolitionist*

Julia Ward Howe was born in New York City, but after her marriage to a reformer and transcendentalist, Samuel Gridley Howe, she lived in Boston, Massachusetts, where the couple was active in abolitionist circles. In the first year of the Civil War, Julia Ward Howe became widely known for her poem "The Battle Hymn of the Republic." It was set to music, using the tune of a battle song named "John Brown's Body." By 1865, "The Battle Hymn of the Republic" had become the unofficial wartime anthem for the Union cause.

James, Henry (April 15, 1843–February 28, 1916) *writer*

Henry James spent a large part of his childhood in Europe. After graduating from Harvard in 1865, James lived alternately in Europe and the United States for 10 years. He became a permanent resident of England in 1876, where he wrote a series of novels, including *Roderick Hudson, The Americans,* and *Daisy Miller.*

James, William (January 11, 1842–August 26, 1910) *philosopher, psychologist*

William James, brother of Henry James, earned a medical degree at Harvard in 1869. He was interested in philosophy and in what was, at the time, a new science: psychology. By the 1890s, James had become a leader in the philosophical discipline known as American pragmatism, concerned with the belief that truth, derived through experience, suggests that truth (like experience) is changeable.

Johnson, Andrew (December 29, 1808–July 31, 1875) *congressman, vice president, president of the United States*

Andrew Johnson, the 17th president of the United States, was born in Raleigh, North Carolina. Johnson helped found the Democratic Party in his region of Tennessee, was elected to the Greeneville, Tennessee, town council in 1829 then was elected mayor in 1831. He won elections to the state legislature in 1835, 1839, and 1841, and to the U.S. Congress in 1843. He lost his House seat in 1852 but was elected Tennessee governor in 1853. In 1857, Johnson was elected to the U.S. Senate. At the start of the Civil War, Johnson was the only Confederate senator who refused to leave Congress. He joined the Republicans and pro-war Democrats in the National Union Party. In 1862, Lincoln appointed Johnson as Tennessee's military governor, and in 1864, he selected Johnson as his vice presidential running mate on the National Union ticket. Johnson succeeded Lincoln after the latter's assassination six weeks later. Johnson's Reconstruction Plan, based on a draft of Lincoln's Reconstruction plans, would have permitted former Confederate states to return to the Union. Radical Republicans opposed him, however, and passed their own, more punitive, Reconstruction plan. In anger, Johnson fired Secretary of State Edwin Stanton, a removal which violated the Tenure of Office Act. The U.S. House sought his impeachment, but a U.S. Senate trial acquitted the president by a single vote. Johnson remained in office, made an unsuccessful bid in 1868 for the Democratic Party's presidential nomination, then returned to Tennessee. There, he lobbied for reelection to political office. In 1875, a coalition of Republicans and Democrats elected Johnson to the U.S. Senate, where he served for only five months before his death.

Laurier, The Right Hon. Sir Wilfrid (November 20, 1841–February 17, 1919) *Canadian prime minister*

Serving as prime minister of Canada for 15 years, Sir Wilfrid Laurier was fluent in French and English. He served the longest term of any prime minister up to that time. Before election, he had served for 45 years in the House of Commons. Throughout his public service career, he served both French-speaking and English-speaking Canadian citizens with equal commitment. During his term of office, in 1905, Alberta and Saskatchewan became provinces.

Lee, Robert E. (January 19, 1807–October 12, 1870) *Confederate general*

Robert E. Lee, a former superintendent of the U.S. Military Academy at West Point and a distinguished soldier during the U.S.-Mexican War, was highly regarded by President Abraham Lincoln. When hostilities between North and South appeared imminent in April 1861, Lincoln chose Lee as the Union's field commander. However, Lee, a Virginia native, rejected the president's offer and resigned his commission. On April 15, 1865, Lee surrendered to Union general Ulysses S. Grant at Appomattox Court House, Virginia, and returned to his home in Richmond to be with his family. He became president of what is now Washington and Lee University in Lexington, Virginia. He died in October 1870.

Lockwood, Belva Ann (October 24, 1830–May 19, 1917) *lawyer*

Belva Ann Lockwood was forbidden to teach physical education to female students in a rural New York school, but because of her protests she succeeded in changing the official policy in that school. She earned her law degree and successfully lobbied the U.S. Congress for the right to argue before the U.S. Supreme Court. In 1879, Lockwood became the first woman admitted to the federal bar. In 1884, she declared that she was a candidate for U.S. president. At a time when women still did not have voting rights, Lockwood received 4,149 votes—all from male voters.

Lodge, Henry Cabot (May 12, 1850–November 9, 1924) *senator*

Lodge, a graduate of Harvard, was a powerful U.S. Senator (R-Massachusetts), spokesperson for the G.O.P., and proponent of strengthening the United States's position as a world leader. He was appointed in 1903 by President Theodore Roosevelt to serve on the Alaskan Boundary Tribunal.

Low, Juliette Gordon (October 31, 1860– January 17, 1927) *founder of the Girl Scouts*
Born in Savannah, Georgia, Juliette Gordon enjoyed a pampered childhood. As an eligible young woman, she made her debut in society, and in 1886, she married William Mackay Low. He was the son of a wealthy family with ties to England and the United States. Juliette Gordon Low accompanied her husband to England, where they lived for nine years. In 1905, before their pending divorce became final, Juliette's husband died. However, William Mackay Low named his mistress as his sole heir, which left his widow virtually penniless. Seeking meaning for her life, Juliette Gordon Low became acquainted with Sir Robert Baden-Powell, who had founded the Boy Scouts. Enthused by the possibility of what such an organization might offer girls in the United States, Juliette Gordon Low returned to Savannah and organized the first group of Girl Scouts in the United States in 1912.

Macdonald, The Right Hon. Sir John Alexander (January 11, 1815–June 6, 1891) *Canadian prime minister*
Sir John A. Macdonald, the first prime minister of Canada, immigrated to Canada in 1819 from Glasgow, Scotland. Macdonald was responsible for drafting two-thirds of the provisions of the British North America Act, which created the Confederation. As prime minister, Macdonald established the North-West Mounted Police and gave his support to the movement for import tariff protection. During his tenure, the transcontinental Canadian Pacific Railway was completed. During his second term of office as prime minister, the North West Rebellion of 1885 occurred.

Mackenzie, The Hon. Alexander (January 28, 1822–April 17, 1892) *Canadian prime minister*
Alexander Mackenzie was born in Logierait, Perthshire, Scotland, and immigrated to Canada in 1842. He was the first Liberal Canadian prime minister. During his term of office, the Royal Military College of Canada was founded. He was also responsible for helping to guarantee passage of a bill in Parliament to establish the Supreme Court of Canada and the Department of Militia and Defence. Mackenzie supported election reform, and was a leading proponent of the Australian ballot.

McKinley, William (January 29, 1843– September 14, 1901) *congressman, governor, president of the United States*
Born in Niles, Ohio, William McKinley attended school there and also in Poland, Ohio. After a semester at Allegheny College, in Meadville, Pennsylvania, McKinley became a teacher. He enlisted in the U.S. Army at the outbreak of the Civil War. Later, he attended Albany Law School. In 1869, McKinley was elected prosecuting attorney for Stark County, Ohio. Two years later, he married Ida Saxton. By 1876, McKinley had been elected to Congress, where he served three consecutive terms in the House of Representatives. In 1891, he was elected governor of Ohio, and on June 16, 1896, he won the Republican presidential nomination on the first ballot. McKinley was elected in November, defeating William Jennings Bryan with 51 percent of the popular vote—the largest winning margin since 1872.

President McKinley, eager to reinstate protective tariffs, supported the Dingley Act, which passed in July 1897. The following year, under his orders, the battleship *Maine* sailed toward Havana, Cuba, in January—ostensibly to protect U.S. citizens there from possible retaliation by Spanish loyalists involved in the Cuban rebellion. When the *Maine* exploded and sank in Havana Harbor, killing 266 U.S. crewmembers in February, the president was under pressure to respond. In April, he requested that U.S. Congress approve intervention, and on April 25, a war resolution was passed. In May, U.S. admiral George Dewey destroyed the Spanish fleet in Manila Bay, the Philippines, and U.S. troops landed in what was then a Spanish colony. After Spain requested peace terms, the war ended, officially on August 12. In December, Spain and the United States signed a treaty transferring possession of the Philippines, Cuba, Guam, and Puerto Rico to the United States. On February 6, 1899, the U.S. Senate ratified the treaty by a vote of 57–27.

William Jennings Bryan again ran against McKinley in the election of 1900, but McKinley received 292 Electoral College votes to Bryan's 155. He became the first president elected to a second consecutive term since 1872. McKinley was shot by an assassin in September of that year while visiting the Pan-American Exposition in Buffalo, New York. He died on September 14.

Mitchell, Maria (August 1, 1818–June 28, 1889)
astronomer
Born in 1818, on Nantucket Island, Massachusetts, Maria Mitchell developed an early interest in astronomy. Her work as a librarian gave her many opportunities to observe the night sky. In 1847, she discovered the orbit of a comet. The next year she was named to the American Academy of Arts and Sciences. In 1850, she was elected to the American Association for the Advancement of Science. She traveled widely, and in 1861, moved to Lynn, Massachusetts, with her father. In 1864, she was invited to joined the faculty at Vassar College in Poughkeepsie, New York, as a professor of astronomy. She was elected to the American Philosophical Society in 1869. She helped found the Association for the Advancement of Women in 1873 and served as its president (1875–76). Mitchell retired from Vassar in failing health in 1888 and died in Lynn, Massachusetts, on June 28, 1889.

Muir, John (April 21, 1838–December 25, 1914)
conservationist
Muir, a geologist, explorer, and prolific writer, was born in Dunbar, Scotland. He came with his family to the United States as a child, and lived in Wisconsin, later attending the University of Wisconsin. After an extensive walking trip, he arrived in San Francisco in 1868. In 1880, he married Louise Strentzel. In 1889, he urged the formation of a national land reserve in Yosemite, and in 1890 this area became one of the first National Parks. He received many honorary academic degrees for his writing and advocacy of natural resource conservation. He lived in California, after completing his last trip, to South America, and died there, at his home in Martinez, in 1914.

Nast, Thomas (September 27, 1840–December 7, 1902) *political cartoonist*
Thomas Nast was born in Landau, Germany, and came to the United States in 1846. After developing his talent for illustrations and cartoon drawings, Nast sold a drawing to *Harper's Weekly* in 1859. He was well-known for his *Harper's* illustrations, completing more than 2,000 of them between 1859 and 1896. Nast helped shape U.S. political opinion for decades and was the creator of many political symbols, including the G.O.P. elephant and the Democratic Party donkey, and it was he who depicted Santa Claus as a rotund, genial figure. Nast's political cartoons were central in the electioneering efforts of both Republicans and Democrats, from Abraham Lincoln through Grover Cleveland. His series of incisive cartoons critiquing New York City's William Marcy "Boss" Tweed led to the arrest of Tweed in 1871. He championed the cause of Chinese immigrants into American society. In 1885, Nast went bankrupt, and in 1886, *Harper's* no longer carried his weekly cartoons. In 1902, Nast died in Ecuador.

Pendleton, George Hunt (July 29, 1825– November 24, 1889) *congressman, senator, vice presidential nominee*
Pendleton was born in Cincinnati, Ohio, the oldest child of Nathaniel Greene Pendleton and Jane Frances Hunt Pendleton. He was a U.S. congressman (D-Ohio) from 1856 to 1865 and a vice presidential nominee in the 1864 election. In the years after the Civil War, Pendleton supported the greenback position of paying government bonds in paper currency instead of gold coins (hard money). In 1868, he was the Democrats' pick for governor, but Pendleton lost to Rutherford B. Hayes. In 1878, he was elected to the U.S. Senate, where he took up civil service reform, becoming chair of a Senate committee on the subject. He championed the 1883 civil service reform legislation which, after its passage, was known as the Pendleton Act. In 1885, President Grover Cleveland named Pendleton minister to Germany. He died in Belgium in 1889.

Pullman, George (March 3, 1831–October 19, 1897) *inventor, industrialist*
Despite a limited education—he left school at 14—George Pullman achieved notable success in business and in society. Pullman went to Chicago in 1855 and became involved in construction and engineering projects, but his primary interest was in developing a railroad car that could comfortably accommodate its passengers.

His first attempt was completed in 1864. When the body of President Abraham Lincoln was transported to Springfield, Illinois, from the nation's capital, it was in a Pullman sleeper car. Soon, Pullman began receiving the attention—and the customers—he hoped to gain. He built a factory at Lake Calumet, a few miles away from Chicago. His business began to slow down in 1894, causing Pullman to eliminate jobs, reduce wages, and increase working hours, which resulted in a notorious strike. This walk-out was eventually dismantled by President Grover Cleveland, who sent in federal troops to ensure containment of the labor disturbance. When George Pullman died in 1897, his casket was a lead-lined box encased in asphalt, covered with steal rails, in an eight-foot-deep pit filled with concrete, all to prevent angry workers from desecrating the body.

Richardson, Henry Hobson (H. H. Richardson) (September 29, 1838–April 28, 1886) *architect*

Born in Louisiana, Henry Hobson Richardson attended Harvard, where he decided to become an architect. At that time, no schools in the United States taught architecture, so Richardson went to Paris in 1860 to train for this profession at the École des Beaux-Arts. After serving as an apprentice in France, he returned in 1865 to the United States, living in New York City. In 1874, he relocated to Boston and soon became one of the more highly respected architects of his era.

Rockefeller, John Davison (July 8 1839–May 23, 1937) *founder of Standard Oil*

Rockefeller, born in Richford, New York, moved with his family to Cleveland, Ohio. There he worked as a bookkeeper-clerk, and after oil was discovered in western Pennsylvania in 1859, he built a refinery in Cleveland in 1863. By 1870, Rockefeller and his business partners had formed the Standard Oil Company. In 1882, his legal advisers had invented the "trust" as a way of organizing a company, and Standard Oil became the first of many such corporate trusts. By 1897, Rockefeller, now an extremely wealthy man and a generous philanthropist, had retired. In 1889, he helped establish the University of Chicago, and later would give away hundreds of millions of dollars to various charitable organizations. He founded the Rockefeller Institute, the Rockefeller Foundation, and the Laura Spelman Rockefeller Memorial Foundation.

Roosevelt, Theodore (October 27, 1858–January 6, 1919) *governor, vice president, president of the United States*

Born in New York City, Theodore Roosevelt experienced ill health as a child. He became competitive and intellectually aggressive as a result. He graduated from Harvard University, and soon after married Alice Lee. In 1881, he was elected to the New York Assembly. He became governor of New York in 1898. He was McKinley's vice presidential running mate in the election of 1900, succeeding McKinley after the latter's assassination in September 1901. As a result, Theodore Roosevelt became the youngest president of the United States ever, at age 42.

Russell, Lillian (Helen Louise Leonard) (Dec. 4, 1861–June 6, 1922) *entertainer*

In 1879, Lillian Russell (born Helen Louise Leonard, in Clinton, Iowa), made her stage debut in New York, as part of a chorus in Gilbert and Sullivan's operetta *H.M.S. Pinafore.* Impresario Tony Pastor's influence helped establish her as "The American Beauty," and Russell appeared in many stage venues, including Weber and Fields's Music Hall. By the mid-1880s, she had become the premier star of the musical stage. Easily recognized by her statuesque appearance, she was known for her love of extravagant jewelry, and for her legendary affair with "Diamond Jim" Brady. Lillian Russell reigned for more than 20 years as the grande dame of American popular entertainment.

Sargent, John Singer (January 12, 1856–April 14, 1925) *artist*

John Singer Sargent, born in Florence, Italy, was reared by an expatriate American family originally from Philadelphia. He studied in Italy, Germany, and Paris. He is best known and admired for his portraits. His *Portrait of Madame X,* completed in 1884, is often regarded as among his finest, although it was highly controversial when it was first shown in Paris. Although Sargent spent less than one year in the United States, some of his finest work appears on exhibit there, particularly in Boston. Sargent abandoned portrait work in the later years of his career, preferring to work on landscapes.

Schurz, Carl (March 2, 1829–May 19, 1906) *secretary of the interior, senator, journalist*

Carl Schurz was born in Germany and educated in Cologne and at the University of Bonn. A journalist in England and France, he immigrated to the United States in 1852. As an abolitionist in Wisconsin, he found favor with the Republican Party, and in 1857 he received the party's nomination as lieutenant governor, although he lost the election. In 1861, President Lincoln appointed Schurz as minister to Spain. After the Civil War, he toured the South and submitted a report to Congress criticizing President

Johnson for his apparent indifference toward Reconstruction.

In 1868, Schurz delivered the keynote address at the Republican National Convention, and was elected, in 1869, to the U.S. Senate from Missouri. Schurz, a founder of the Liberal Republican movement, in 1872 presided over the party's convention in Cincinnati, Ohio. The Liberal Republicans nominated Horace Greeley, with Missouri Senator Gratz Brown, as his vice presidential nominee, but Grant was reelected. In 1881, Schurz joined E. L. Godkin and Horace White as coeditors of the *New York Evening Post,* but he left that publication in 1883 after a disagreement with Godkin. In 1892, Schurz became editor of *Harper's Weekly.* He died in 1906.

Seward, William H. (May 16, 1801–October 10, 1872) *secretary of state*

Seward was born in Florida, New York, in May 1801. He later graduated from Union College. He was named secretary of state by President Abraham Lincoln, and served also under President Johnson after Lincoln's assassination. While he was secretary of state, Seward successfully concluded negotiating a treaty with Russia for the purchase of Alaska. He died in Auburn, New York, in 1872.

Shaw, Anna Howard (February 14, 1847–July 2, 1919) *clergywoman, equal rights activist*

The Reverend Dr. Anna Howard Shaw began early in her life to help make life better for those around her. By age 12, she was a teacher, helping to support her mother, who was in ill health, and her siblings. Later, she attended high school while living with an older married sister and also began participating in the Methodist Church. She was licensed to preach in the church at age 24. She attended Albion College for two years and then entered Boston Theological Seminary (now Boston University School of Theology), graduating in 1878. Although a church in Massachusetts called her as their minister, the General Conference of the Methodist Episcopal Church would not ordain her. Shaw was finally ordained in 1880.

In addition to ministering at two churches, in 1886 she received a medical degree from Boston University, then became active in temperance work. She joined the campaign for woman suffrage, and in 1904 was elected president of the National American Woman Suffrage Association. While working toward establishment of the League of Nations, she died in July, 1919.

Sherman, William Tecumseh (February 8, 1820–February 14, 1891) *Union army general*

A pioneer of modern warfare, William Tecumseh Sherman graduated from the U.S. Military Academy at West Point in 1840. He began his Civil War career as a colonel and, under the command of Ulysses S. Grant, became a major general after the Battle of Shiloh. Their success in the Vicksburg and Chattanooga campaigns made them rising stars in the North. Sherman's capture of Atlanta in September 1864 was a major blow to the Confederacy and a significant factor in Lincoln's reelection in November. Sherman then implemented his philosophy of psychological warfare and property destruction by having his army march through Georgia to Savannah. When the war ended, he was promoted to general and became commander in chief, replacing General Ulysses S. Grant. After his retirement in 1884, he avoided involvement in politics, living the remaining years of his life in New York City. He died in 1891.

Stanton, Edwin (December 19, 1814–December 24, 1869) *secretary of war*

Born in Steubenville, Ohio, Edwin was a sickly child who was apprenticed at an early age to a bookseller. He attended school at night, and in 1830 he left Steubenville for Gambier, where he enrolled at Kenyon College and later studied law. In May 1836, Stanton married Mary Lamson. He was elected prosecuting attorney of Harrison County the following year. Ten years later, Stanton went to Pittsburgh, Pennsylvania, to practice law, joining in a partnership with Charles Shater. Now a widower, he married again in June 1856, and moved with his bride, Ellen Hutchison, to California, where he became a land commissioner. In 1860, he became attorney general under President Buchanan. When President Abraham Lincoln was elected, Stanton was named secretary of war. In 1865, after Lincoln's assassination, Stanton gave up his previous plan, which was to retire from government service. In April, he posted a $50,000 reward for John Wilkes Booth's capture; less than a week later, Booth was dead.

In 1868, Lincoln's successor Andrew Johnson called for Stanton's removal as secretary of war, prompting Radical Republicans in Congress to begin impeachment proceedings against Johnson.

Returning to private life, Stanton resumed his law practice. He tried to decline President Grant's invitation to serve on the U.S. Supreme Court, but Grant appointed him over his objections on the ground of ill health. On December 19, 1869, Stanton was confirmed as a justice, but he died four days later.

Stanton, Elizabeth Cady (November 12, 1815–October 26, 1902) *equal rights advocate*
Elizabeth Cady Stanton's genteel appearance belied her unswerving commitment as a leader of the United States's early feminist movement. To her mind, all issues of the day were subordinated or related to the inequities suffered by women. A prime mover behind America's first women's rights convention in 1848, she was the first to identify the vote for women as the key to winning all other rights for her sex. After the Civil War, she joined Susan B. Anthony in founding the National Woman Suffrage Association. Stanton's writings and speeches, however, extended well beyond the franchise question to include arguments for liberalizing divorce laws, reforming child-rearing practices, and correcting what she saw as the Bible's relegation of women to secondary status. When Stanton referred to God, she used the feminine pronouns.

Stowe, Harriet Beecher (June 14, 1811–July 1, 1896) *writer*
As the wife of an Ohio seminary professor, Harriet Beecher Stowe had no intention of becoming an international celebrity. But after passage of the Fugitive Slave Law in 1850, she began writing, and in 1851, produced *Uncle Tom's Cabin*. First published in serial form, it was issued as a book in 1852. This story, detailing the cruelties of Southern slavery, became one of the most widely read abolitionist tracts of its time. It was adapted as a play in 1853. In 1862, Harriet Beecher Stowe met President Abraham Lincoln at the White House. He is alleged to have said to the writer, "So you're the little woman who wrote the book that started this great war!"

Thompson, The Right Hon. Sir John Sparrow David (November 10, 1845–December 12, 1894) *Canadian prime minister*
Sir John Thompson is unique in having been the first Roman Catholic to be elected prime minister of Canada. Elected prime minister of Nova Scotia in 1882, he was the first head of a province subsequently elected Canadian prime minister. While at Windsor Castle, in England, shortly after having been sworn in as a member of Queen Victoria's Imperial Privy Council, he died suddenly after having served in office for only 24 months.

Tupper, The Right Hon. Sir Charles (July 2, 1821–October 30, 1915) *Canadian prime minister*
Sir Charles Tupper had earned an M.D. from the University of Edinburgh, Scotland, and was prime minister of Nova Scotia in 1867 when that province joined the Confederation. The Conservative Tupper served for only 10 weeks after his election as Prime Minister of Canada, the shortest term on record, when a new election was called due to internal upheaval between Conservatives and Liberals. The Liberals won, electing Wilfred Laurier to succeed Tupper.

Turner, Frederick Jackson (November 14, 1861–March 4, 1832) *historian*
Born in Portage, Wisconsin, Frederick Jackson Turner attended the University of Wisconsin, graduating in 1884. After working as a journalist, he went to graduate school to study history. In 1889, he joined the faculty at his alma mater in Wisconsin. In 1893, he wrote a scholarly paper, "The Significance of the Frontier in American History," and delivered it as a speech at the American Historical Association meeting that year in Chicago. Turner's "frontier thesis" would become the guiding theory explaining the importance and influence of westward expansion in the United States. Turner's work, which many believed stated a clarifying view of the beginnings of American democracy, included a book, *Rise of the New West, 1819–1829*, published in 1906.

Tweed, William Marcy (Boss Tweed) (April 3, 1823–April 12, 1878) *politician*
Born in New York City, William "Boss" Tweed led a New York City Democratic party machine known as the Tweed Ring. As an ambitious Democratic political operative of Tammany Hall, as the machine was also known, Tweed was given a post on New York City's Board of Supervisors in 1858, a position he maintained for 12 years. Tweed was elected, allegedly through bribery, to the New York state senate in 1867 and was reelected in 1869. In 1870, he helped revise New York City's charter, but gaining more personal control of municipal finances in the process. Between 1869 and

1871, New York City's debt is estimated to have tripled. Beginning in July 1871, several newspapers reported on Tweed's shady political dealings, and he was soon involved in a civil suit charging corruption. In December, Tweed resigned as Public Works Commissioner when he was arrested for fraud and faulty audit of municipal accounting records. By late 1872, he was convicted on a misdemeanor, fined, and sentenced to 13 years in jail. In December 1875, Tweed escaped and hid in New Jersey for a brief time, then fled the United States. He was arrested in Spain in September 1876 and was imprisoned in New York City. Tweed died in jail of heart failure on April 12, 1878.

Wald, Lillian (March 10, 1867–September 1, 1940) *reformer*

Like her contemporary Jane Addams, Lillian Wald wished to escape a life of relative affluence and devote herself to helping others. She decried the inadequate health services available for immigrants and soon organized nursing classes for immigrants living in New York's Lower East Side. By 1895, Wald had founded the Nurses' Settlement House on Henry Street. This organization soon became known for its devotion to improving conditions in the urban slums. Wald was a leading advocate of reform; she worked tirelessly to end child labor and to impose labor regulations on city factories.

Washington, Booker T. (April 5, 1856–November 14, 1915) *educator, African-American leader*

Born near Roanoke, Virginia, Booker T. Washington was a former slave who moved after emancipation, with his family, to West Virginia to work in the salt mines. He left mining and received an education at the Hampton Institute in the Tidewater area of Virginia, and then attended the Tuskegee Institute in Alabama. He became president of Tuskegee in 1881, and worked to bring it to prominence as one of the leading institutions for blacks in the United States. He authored the Atlanta Compromise, in which he shared his belief in the necessity of vocational training for African Americans. His autobiography, *Up from Slavery,* was published in 1901.

Wharton, Edith Newbold Jones (January 24, 1862–August 11, 1937) *writer*

Born into an affluent New York family, Wharton had written a novel by age 16 and learned to prefer Europe to her native United States. She was educated at home and had a career stretching across four decades. Wharton was a chronicler of American morals and manners, despite her choice to live as an expatriate. Her Pulitzer Prize–winning book, *Age of Innocence* (1920), showcased her talent for fiction, but her first book focused on the interiors of homes. Wharton coauthored *The Decoration of Houses,* with an architect colleague, Ogden Codman. She was married in 1885 to Edward ("Teddy") Robbins Wharton. She had homes in New York, in Newport, Rhode Island, and Lenox, Massachusetts, but preferred France, where she died in 1937.

Whistler, James Abbott McNeill (July 14, 1834–July 17, 1903) *painter*

James McNeill Whistler was one of a number of expatriates whose artistic achievements initially brought them greater respect in Europe than in the United States. Whistler studied at the École Impériale et Spéciale de Dessin in Paris, and then studied with the painter Charles Gabriel Gleyre. Whistler, a rebel, soon relied on his own perspectives and perceptions, and ceased to study formally with any single mentor.

Woolworth, Frank W. (April 13, 1852–April 8, 1919) *merchant*

Frank W. Woolworth's first five-cent store, in Utica, New York, opened in February 1879, but closed within weeks. His second attempt at retail was in Lancaster, Pennsylvania, where he further developed his "five-cent-store" idea to include items priced at 10 cents. By 1911, the F.W. Woolworth Company was incorporated. When Woolworth died in April 1919, he had more than 1,000 retail stores in the United States.

Wrigley, William, Jr. (September 30, 1861–January 26, 1932) *inventor*

William Wrigley, Jr., born in Philadelphia, Pennsylvania, started his career as a traveling soap salesman, working first for his father and then for a competitor. One of the soap products he represented was offered with a premium: chewing gum, which proved popular. Wrigley decided to sell only chewing gum. By 1893, he was selling two brands of gum, Lotta and Vassar. Later he added Juicy Fruit and Spearmint. Wrigley's advertising genius enabled his company to become one of the world's largest. Later in his life, he bought the Chicago Cubs baseball team.

Yerkes, Charles Tyson (June 25, 1837–
December 29, 1905) *financier*
Investment banker Charles Yerkes, born in Philadelphia, was a leading force behind the development of a
rapid-transit system in Chicago during the late 1880s,
and behind construction of the London Underground (known as the Tube). In October 1871, the
Great Chicago Fire resulted in a national economic
panic. This crash put Yerkes's investment company into
bankruptcy, and after being charged with misappro-
priation of funds, he was imprisoned. Pardoned after
serving only a partial sentence, Yerkes went to Chicago, where he purchased controlling interest in a
North Side streetcar company in 1886. By 1894,
Chicago boasted nearly 100 miles of cable tracks.
(Yerkes personally benefited from the business
arrangements connected with streetcars.) By the early
1890s, more than 50 percent of the private elevated
railway companies in Chicago, as well as most of the
streetcar system, belonged to him. In 1892, Yerkes
gave money to help build an observatory at the University of Chicago. Located at Lake Geneva, Wisconsin, the Yerkes Observatory boasts the world's largest
reflecting telescope.

Young, Brigham (June 1, 1801–August 29, 1877)
religious leader
Born in Vermont, Brigham Young was a Methodist
when he left home at age 16. He married for the first
time in 1824 and then moved to Mendon, New York.
Attracted to Joseph Smith's Church of Jesus Christ of
Latter-day Saints, (Mormons) in 1833 Young decided
to join with Smith. Along with other followers of
Smith, Young faced persecution for his religious con-
victions. By 1841, he had been named president of
the church's governing body. He arrived in Utah in
July 1847, and was named president of the church
after Smith's death. By 1851, Utah had been organized as a U.S. territory, and Young was appointed
governor of Utah Territory in 1851. Because of the
Mormons' influence there, the federal government
grew increasingly worried that Utah would become a
theocracy. When polygamy was pronounced legal for
church members in 1852, the public outcry against
Mormons grew louder. In 1871, Brigham Young was
brought to trial under an 1862 law forbidding plural
marriage in U.S. territories. Young, who by now had
more than 20 wives, was not convicted. Brigham
Young died six years later, in August 1877.

APPENDIX C
Maps, Graphs, and Tables

1. How the U.S. Constitution May Be Amended
2. Population in the U.S. Frontier, 1860
3. Indian Land Cessions in the United States by Region and Date, Pre-1784–1890
4. Comparison of Immigration Patterns by Region of Origin, 1860–1880 and 1880–1900
5. Agriculture in the United States, 1860–1890
6. Mining of Natural Resources in the United States, 1860–1890
7. States Admitted and Readmitted to the United States During the Gilded Age, 1865–1901
8. Early Pacific Railroad Lines, 1865–1884
9. End of Reconstruction, 1866–1877
10. Miles of Railroad Track Operating, 1866–1886
11. U.S. Possessions and Territories Acquired, 1867–1903
12. U.S. Presidential Elections: Electoral Vote, 1868
13. Growth in Foreign Imports and Exports, 1870–1900
14. U.S. School Enrollment Rates, All Races, 1870–1900
15. U.S. Presidential Elections: Electoral Vote, 1872
16. U.S. Presidential Elections: Electoral Vote, 1876
17. U.S. Presidential Elections: Electoral Vote, 1880
18. Population Growth Among Principal Midwestern Cities, 1880–1890
19. U.S. Presidential Elections: Electoral Vote, 1884
20. U.S. Presidential Elections: Electoral Vote, 1888
21. U.S. Population Density, 1890
22. Lakota Indian Reservations in the Dakotas, 1890
23. U.S. Presidential Elections: Electoral Vote, 1892
24. U.S. Presidential Elections: Electoral Vote, 1896
25. Spanish-American War, Pacific Campaign, 1898
26. Spanish-American War, Caribbean Campaign, 1898
27. Participation Rates of Men and Women in the U.S. Labor Force, 1900
28. U.S. Presidential Elections: Electoral Vote, 1900
29. U.S. Presidential Elections: Electoral Vote, 1904
30. Immigration by Region and Selected Country of Last Residence, Fiscal Years 1861–1900
31. U.S. Presidential Elections, 1868–1904
32. Chief Justices of the U.S. Supreme Court, 1865–1901
33. Canadian Prime Ministers, 1867–1911
34. Provinces and Territories Entered into Canadian Confederation, 1867–1905
35. Canadian Governors General, 1867–1911
36. Associate Justices of the U.S. Supreme Court, 1865–1901

HOW THE U.S. CONSTITUTION MAY BE AMENDED

	Methods of Ratification	
Methods of Proposal	Legislatures in three-fourths of the states	Ratifying conventions in three-fourths of the states
Two-thirds vote in both houses of Congress	Usual method used	Used only once— for Twenty-first Amendment
National constitutional convention called by Congress at the request of two-thirds of the state legislatures	Method still unused	Method still unused

POPULATION IN THE U.S. FRONTIER, 1860

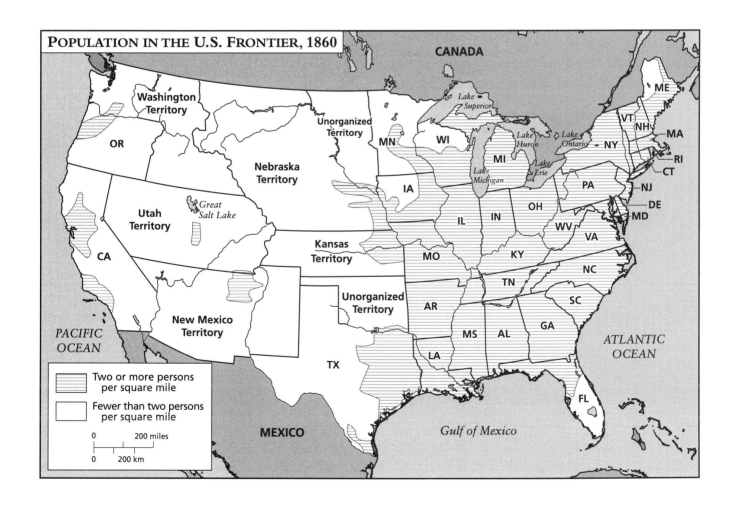

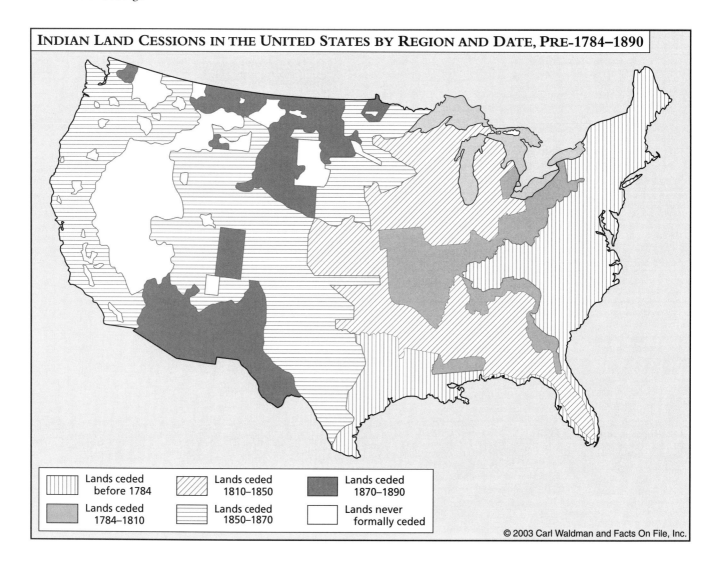

INDIAN LAND CESSIONS IN THE UNITED STATES BY REGION AND DATE, PRE-1784–1890

Lands ceded before 1784

Lands ceded 1784–1810

Lands ceded 1810–1850

Lands ceded 1850–1870

Lands ceded 1870–1890

Lands never formally ceded

© 2003 Carl Waldman and Facts On File, Inc.

COMPARISON OF IMMIGRATION PATTERNS BY REGION OF ORIGIN, 1860–1880 AND 1880–1900

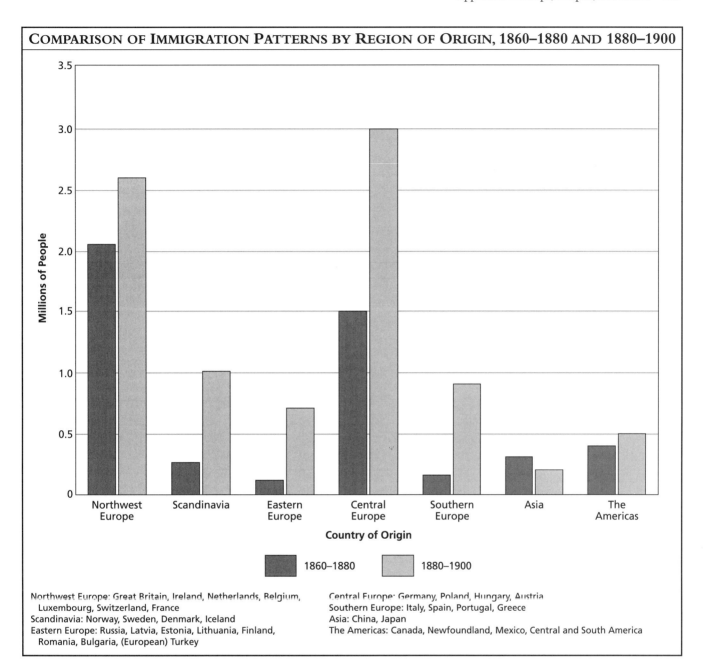

Northwest Europe: Great Britain, Ireland, Netherlands, Belgium, Luxembourg, Switzerland, France
Scandinavia: Norway, Sweden, Denmark, Iceland
Eastern Europe: Russia, Latvia, Estonia, Lithuania, Finland, Romania, Bulgaria, (European) Turkey

Central Europe: Germany, Poland, Hungary, Austria
Southern Europe: Italy, Spain, Portugal, Greece
Asia: China, Japan
The Americas: Canada, Newfoundland, Mexico, Central and South America

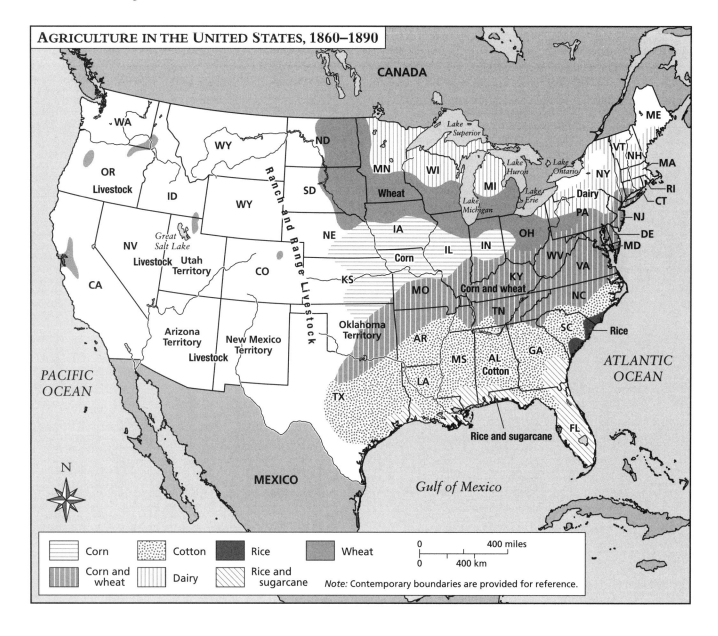

AGRICULTURE IN THE UNITED STATES, 1860–1890

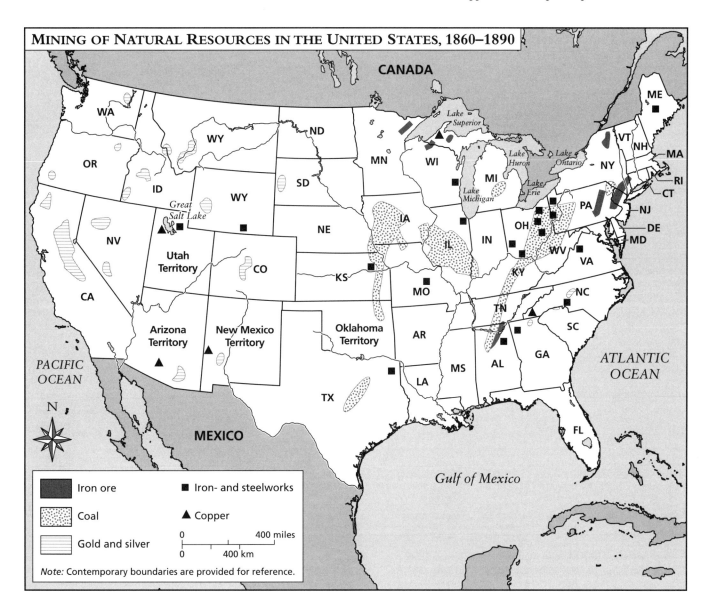

MINING OF NATURAL RESOURCES IN THE UNITED STATES, 1860–1890

Legend:
- Iron ore
- Coal
- Gold and silver
- Iron- and steelworks
- Copper

0 · 400 miles
0 · 400 km

Note: Contemporary boundaries are provided for reference.

STATES ADMITTED OR READMITTED TO THE UNITED STATES DURING THE GILDED AGE, 1865–1901

State	Admitted	Readmitted	
Tennessee	June 1, 1796	July 19, 1866	
Arkansas	June 15, 1836	April 6, 1868	
Nebraska	March 1, 1867		
Florida	March 3, 1845	June 9,1868	
North Carolina	November 21, 1789	July 4,1868*	*After having rejected the amendment on December 14, 1866
Louisiana	April 30, 1812	July 9, 1868*	*After having rejected the amendment on Febuary 6, 1867
South Carolina	May 23,1788	July 9, 1868*	*After having rejected the amendment on December 20, 1866
Alabama	December 14, 1819	July 13, 1868	
Georgia	January 2, 1788	July 21, 1868*	*After having rejected the amendment on November 9, 1866
Virginia	June 25, 1788	October 8, 1869*	*After having rejected the amendment on January 9, 1867
Mississippi	December 10, 1817	January 17,1870	
Texas	December 29, 1845	Febuary 18, 1870*	*After having rejected the amendment on October 27, 1866
Colorado	August 1,1876		
North Dakota	November 2, 1889		
South Dakota	November 2, 1889		
Montana	November 8, 1889		
Washington	November 11, 1889		
Idaho	July 3, 1890		
Wyoming	July 10, 1890		
Utah	January 4, 1896		

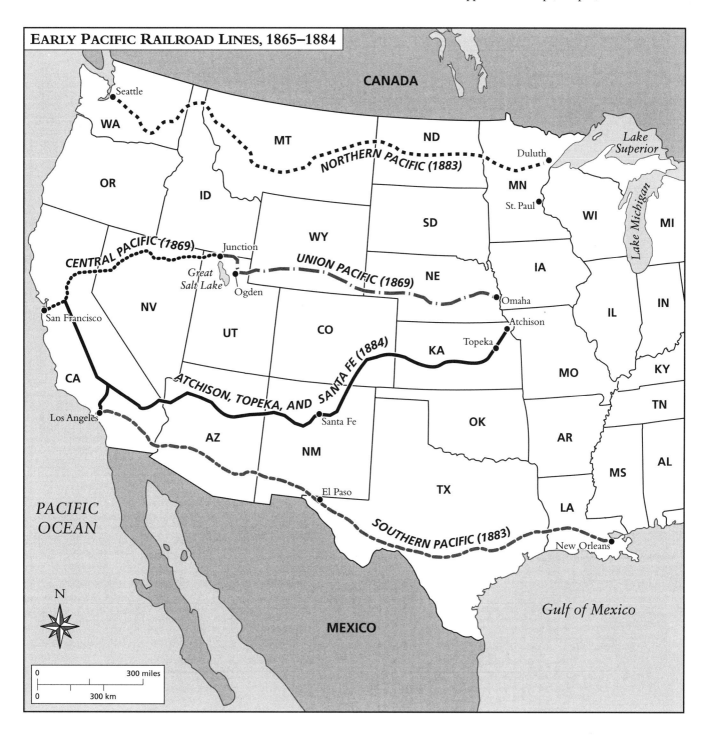

EARLY PACIFIC RAILROAD LINES, 1865–1884

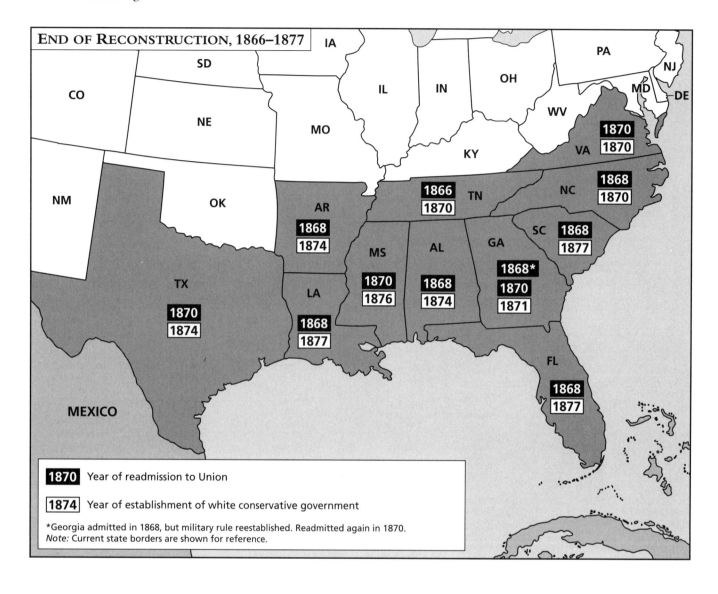

END OF RECONSTRUCTION, 1866–1877

1870 Year of readmission to Union

1874 Year of establishment of white conservative government

*Georgia admitted in 1868, but military rule reestablished. Readmitted again in 1870.
Note: Current state borders are shown for reference.

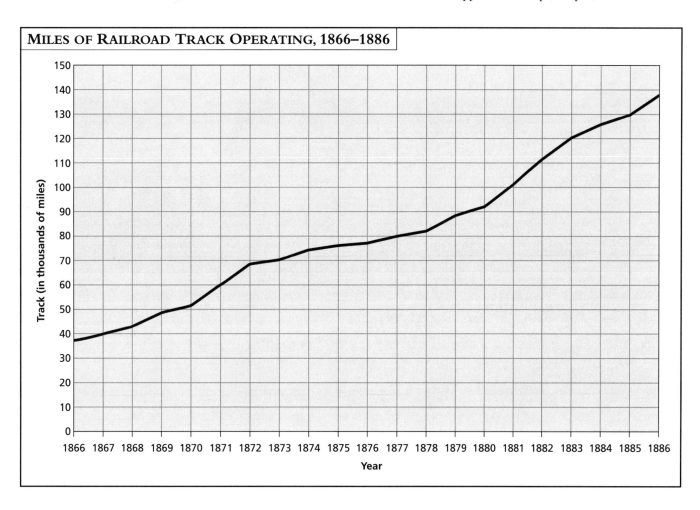

MILES OF RAILROAD TRACK OPERATING, 1866–1886

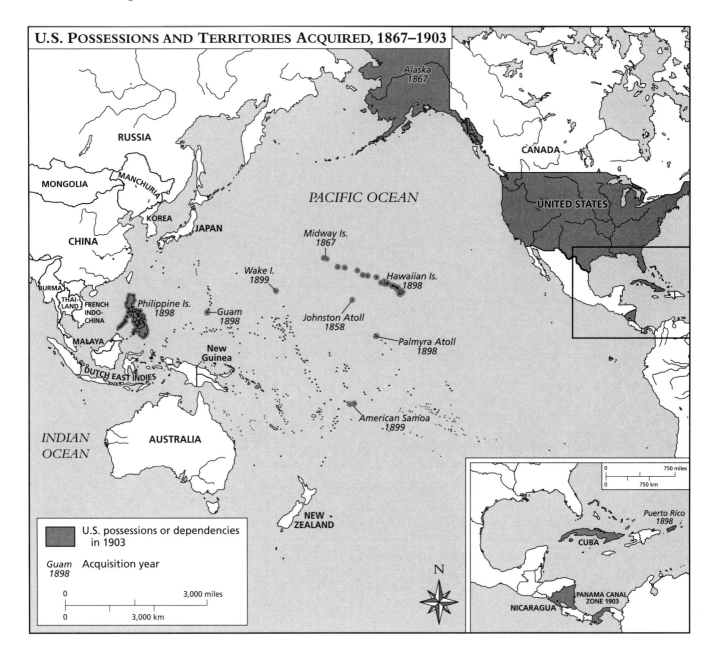

U.S. POSSESSIONS AND TERRITORIES ACQUIRED, 1867–1903

RUSSIA

MONGOLIA

MANCHURIA

KOREA

JAPAN

CHINA

BURMA

THAI-
LAND

FRENCH
INDO-
CHINA

MALAYA

Philippine Is.
1898

Wake I.
1899

Guam
1898

DUTCH EAST INDIES

New
Guinea

PACIFIC OCEAN

Midway Is.
1867

Hawaiian Is.
1898

Johnston Atoll
1858

Palmyra Atoll
1898

American Samoa
1899

INDIAN
OCEAN

AUSTRALIA

NEW
ZEALAND

Alaska
1867

CANADA

UNITED STATES

N

Legend

U.S. possessions or dependencies in 1903

Guam
1898   Acquisition year

0   3,000 miles

0   3,000 km

Inset

Puerto Rico
1898

CUBA

NICARAGUA

PANAMA CANAL
ZONE 1903

0   750 miles

0   750 km

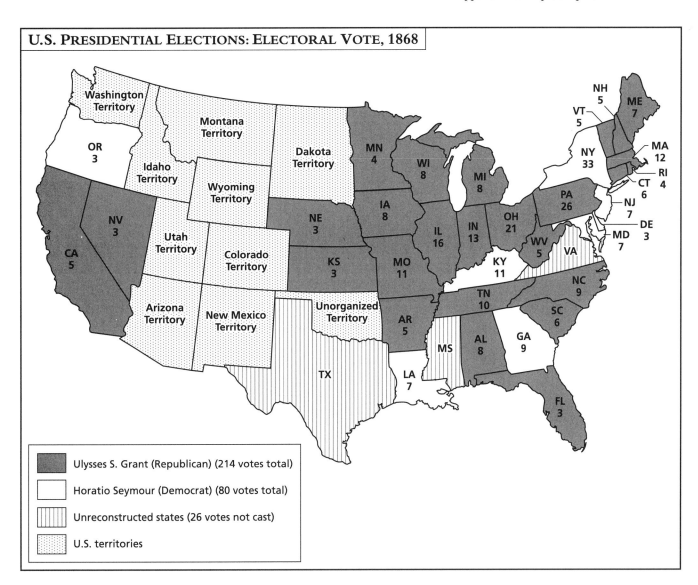

U.S. PRESIDENTIAL ELECTIONS: ELECTORAL VOTE, 1868

Washington Territory

OR
3

Montana Territory

Idaho Territory

Wyoming Territory

Dakota Territory

MN
4

WI
8

MI
8

NV
3

Utah Territory

Colorado Territory

NE
3

IA
8

IL
16

IN
13

OH
21

PA
26

NH
5

VT
5

ME
7

NY
33

MA
12

RI
4

CT
6

NJ
7

DE
3

MD
7

CA
5

Arizona Territory

New Mexico Territory

KS
3

MO
11

WV
5

VA

KY
11

NC
9

TN
10

SC
6

Unorganized Territory

AR
5

MS

AL
8

GA
9

TX

LA
7

FL
3

Ulysses S. Grant (Republican) (214 votes total)

Horatio Seymour (Democrat) (80 votes total)

Unreconstructed states (26 votes not cast)

U.S. territories

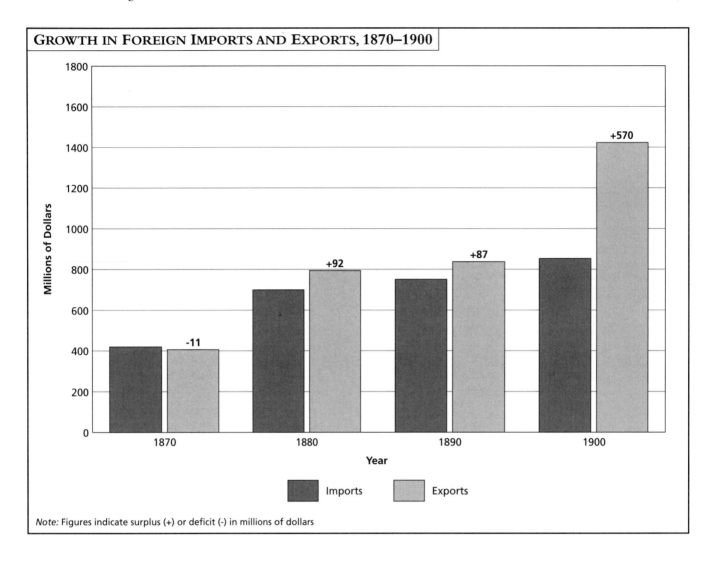

GROWTH IN FOREIGN IMPORTS AND EXPORTS, 1870–1900

Note: Figures indicate surplus (+) or deficit (-) in millions of dollars

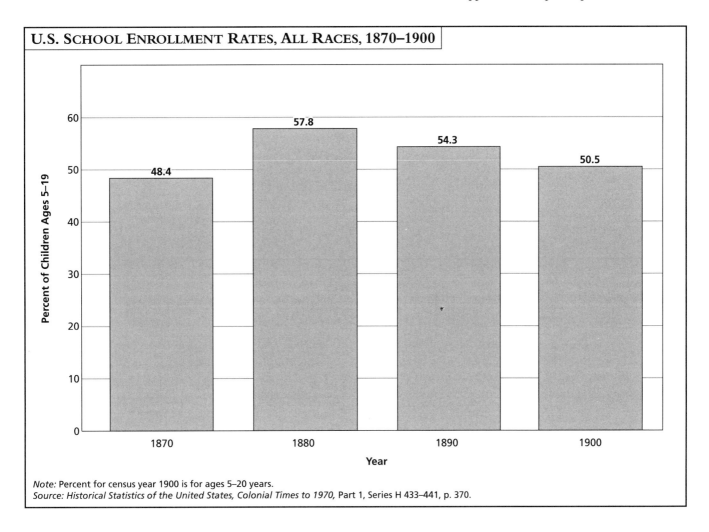

U.S. School Enrollment Rates, All Races, 1870–1900

Note: Percent for census year 1900 is for ages 5–20 years.
Source: Historical Statistics of the United States, Colonial Times to 1970, Part 1, Series H 433–441, p. 370.

U.S. PRESIDENTIAL ELECTIONS: ELECTORAL VOTE, 1872

Ulysses S. Grant (Republican)
(286 votes total)

Horace Greeley (Democrat)
(66 votes total)

When Horace Greeley dies on Nov. 29, his 66 electoral votes are counted for:

Thomas A. Hendricks (Independent Democrat) (42 votes total)

Charles Jenkins (2 votes total)

B. Gratz Brown (Democrat/Liberal Republican) (18 votes total)

David Davis (Labor Reform) (1 vote total)

Electoral vote not counted
† Electoral votes cast for Grant
* Electoral votes cast for Greeley

U.S. territories

Note: The coloring found in the states with a split electoral vote does not bear any geographic significance.

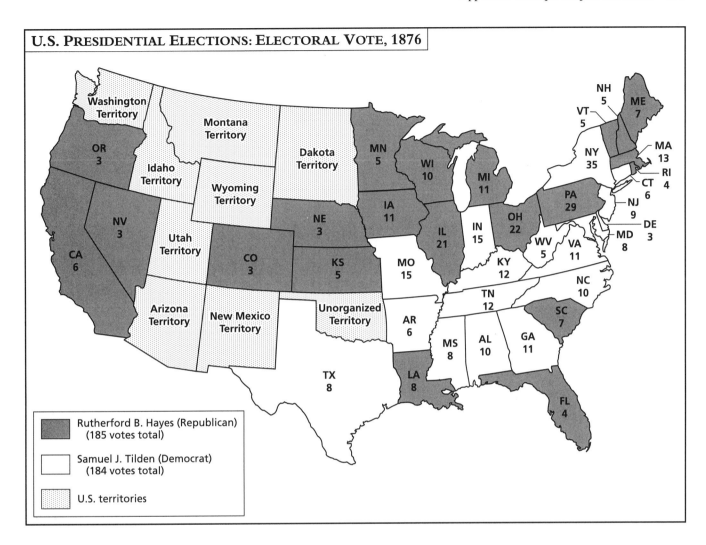

U.S. PRESIDENTIAL ELECTIONS: ELECTORAL VOTE, 1876

Washington Territory
Montana Territory
OR 3
Idaho Territory
Wyoming Territory
Dakota Territory
MN 5
WI 10
MI 11
NH 5
VT 5
ME 7
NY 35
MA 13
RI 4
CT 6
NV 3
Utah Territory
NE 3
IA 11
IL 21
IN 15
OH 22
PA 29
NJ 9
DE 3
MD 8
CA 6
CO 3
KS 5
MO 15
WV 5
VA 11
KY 12
NC 10
Arizona Territory
New Mexico Territory
Unorganized Territory
AR 6
TN 12
SC 7
MS 8
AL 10
GA 11
TX 8
LA 8
FL 4

Rutherford B. Hayes (Republican) (185 votes total)
Samuel J. Tilden (Democrat) (184 votes total)
U.S. territories

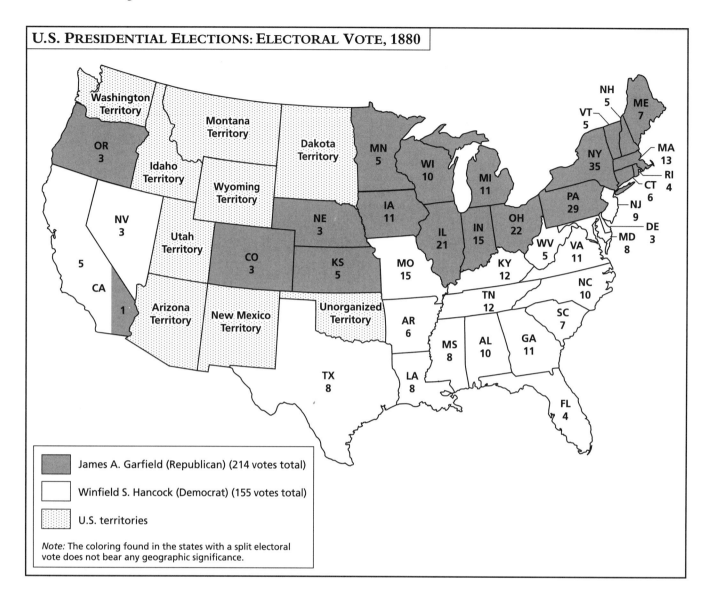

U.S. PRESIDENTIAL ELECTIONS: ELECTORAL VOTE, 1880

Washington Territory

Montana Territory

Dakota Territory

OR 3

Idaho Territory

Wyoming Territory

MN 5

WI 10

MI 11

NH 5

VT 5

ME 7

NY 35

MA 13

RI 4

CT 6

NV 3

Utah Territory

NE 3

IA 11

IL 21

IN 15

OH 22

PA 29

NJ 9

CA 5

1

CO 3

KS 5

MO 15

KY 12

WV 5

VA 11

DE 3

MD 8

NC 10

Arizona Territory

New Mexico Territory

Unorganized Territory

AR 6

TN 12

SC 7

MS 8

AL 10

GA 11

TX 8

LA 8

FL 4

James A. Garfield (Republican) (214 votes total)

Winfield S. Hancock (Democrat) (155 votes total)

U.S. territories

Note: The coloring found in the states with a split electoral
vote does not bear any geographic significance.

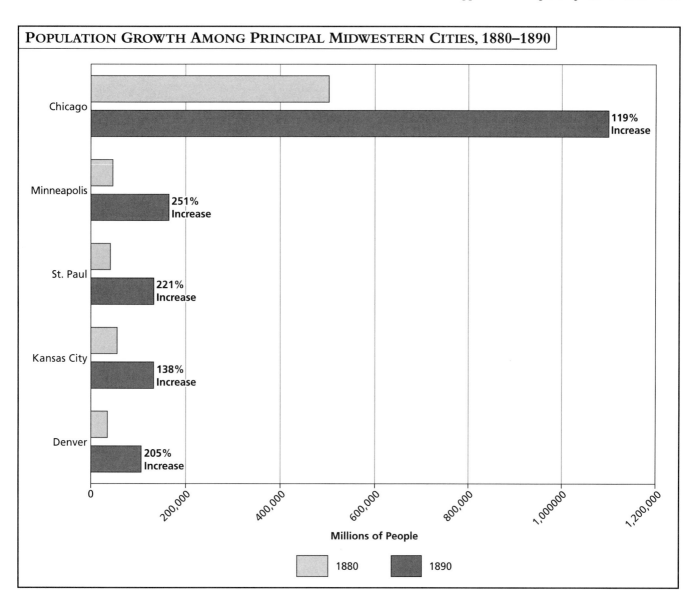

POPULATION GROWTH AMONG PRINCIPAL MIDWESTERN CITIES, 1880–1890

Chicago — **119% Increase**

Minneapolis — **251% Increase**

St. Paul — **221% Increase**

Kansas City — **138% Increase**

Denver — **205% Increase**

0   200,000   400,000   600,000   800,000   1,000,000   1,200,000

Millions of People

1880   1890

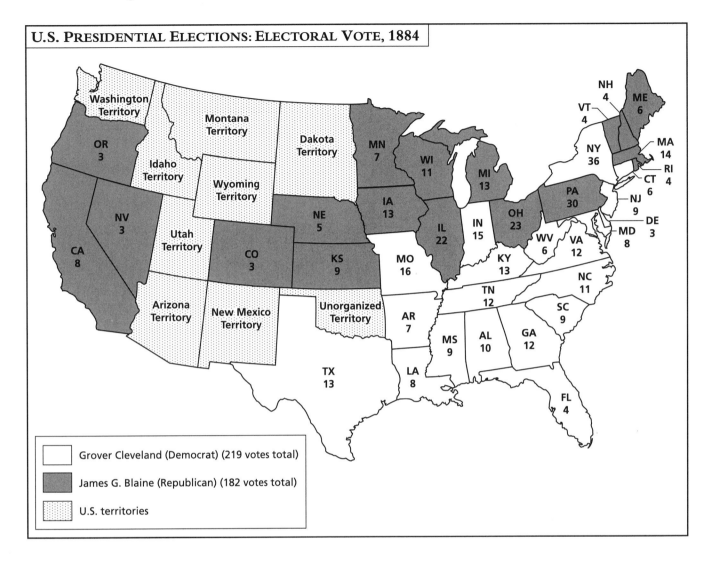

U.S. PRESIDENTIAL ELECTIONS: ELECTORAL VOTE, 1884

Washington Territory

OR 3

Montana Territory

Idaho Territory

Wyoming Territory

Dakota Territory

MN 7

NV 3

Utah Territory

CA 8

CO 3

NE 5

KS 9

IA 13

WI 11

MI 13

IL 22

IN 15

OH 23

PA 30

NH 4

ME 6

VT 4

NY 36

MA 14

RI 4

CT 6

NJ 9

DE 3

MD 8

WV 6

VA 12

KY 13

NC 11

Arizona Territory

New Mexico Territory

Unorganized Territory

AR 7

MO 16

TN 12

SC 9

MS 9

AL 10

GA 12

TX 13

LA 8

FL 4

Grover Cleveland (Democrat) (219 votes total)

James G. Blaine (Republican) (182 votes total)

U.S. territories

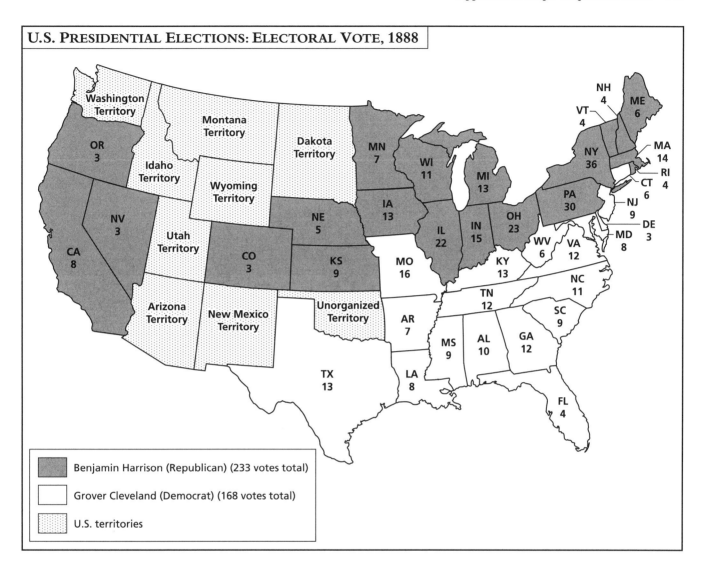

U.S. PRESIDENTIAL ELECTIONS: ELECTORAL VOTE, 1888

Washington Territory

Montana Territory

Dakota Territory

OR 3

Idaho Territory

Wyoming Territory

NV 3

Utah Territory

CA 8

Arizona Territory

New Mexico Territory

CO 3

NE 5

KS 9

Unorganized Territory

MN 7

IA 13

WI 11

IL 22

MI 13

IN 15

OH 23

MO 16

KY 13

AR 7

TN 12

MS 9

AL 10

GA 12

LA 8

TX 13

FL 4

NH 4

VT 4

ME 6

NY 36

MA 14

RI 4

CT 6

PA 30

NJ 9

DE 3

WV 6

VA 12

MD 8

NC 11

SC 9

Benjamin Harrison (Republican) (233 votes total)

Grover Cleveland (Democrat) (168 votes total)

U.S. territories

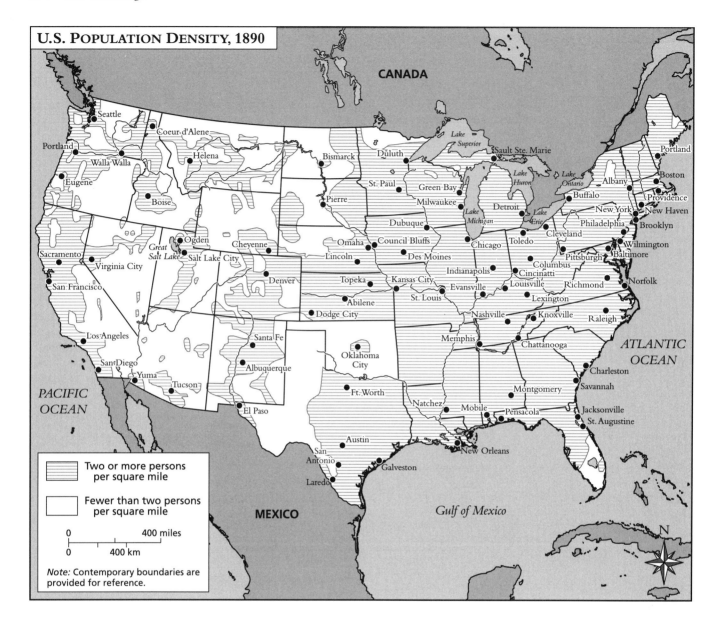

U.S. POPULATION DENSITY, 1890

CANADA

Seattle
Coeur d'Alene
Portland
Helena
Walla Walla
Eugene
Boise
Bismarck
Duluth
Sault Ste. Marie
Lake Superior
St. Paul
Green Bay
Milwaukee
Lake Huron
Lake Michigan
Detroit
Lake Ontario
Albany
Buffalo
Portland
Boston
Providence
New York
New Haven
Pierre
Dubuque
Philadelphia
Brooklyn
Lake Erie
Cleveland
Wilmington
Sacramento
Ogden
Cheyenne
Great Salt Lake
Salt Lake City
Omaha
Council Bluffs
Chicago
Toledo
Columbus
Pittsburgh
Baltimore
Virginia City
Lincoln
Des Moines
Indianapolis
Cincinatti
Richmond
Norfolk
San Francisco
Denver
Topeka
Kansas City
Evansville
Louisville
Lexington
Abilene
St. Louis
Nashville
Knoxville
Raleigh
Los Angeles
Dodge City
Memphis
Chattanooga
ATLANTIC OCEAN
Santa Fe
Oklahoma City
San Diego
Albuquerque
Charleston
Yuma
Montgomery
Savannah
Tucson
Ft. Worth
Natchez
Mobile
Pensacola
Jacksonville
El Paso
St. Augustine
PACIFIC OCEAN
Austin
San Antonio
New Orleans
Laredo
Galveston

MEXICO
Gulf of Mexico

Two or more persons per square mile

Fewer than two persons per square mile

0   400 miles
0   400 km

Note: Contemporary boundaries are provided for reference.

N

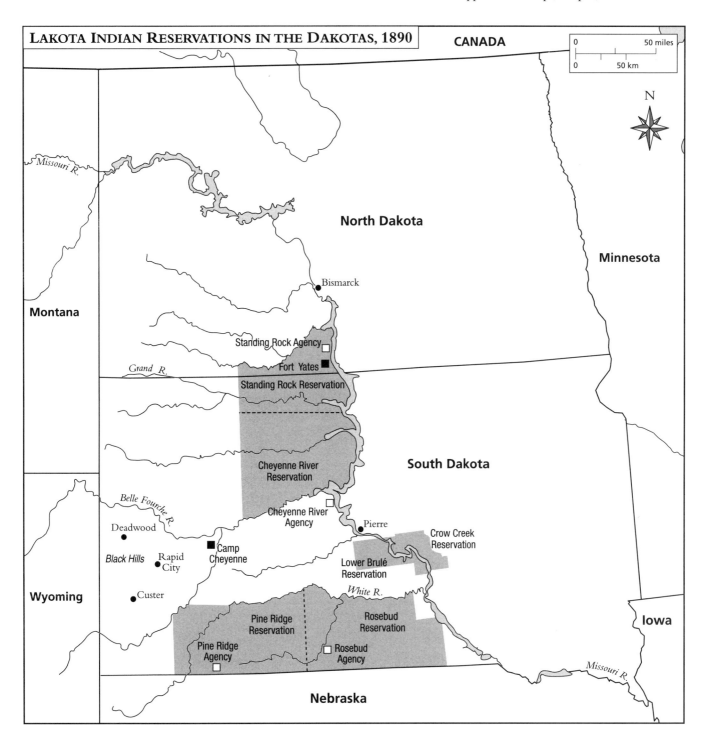

LAKOTA INDIAN RESERVATIONS IN THE DAKOTAS, 1890

CANADA

0   50 miles
0   50 km

N

Missouri R.

North Dakota

Minnesota

Montana

Bismarck

Standing Rock Agency
Grand R.
Fort Yates
Standing Rock Reservation

South Dakota

Cheyenne River
Reservation

Cheyenne River
Agency

Pierre

Crow Creek
Reservation

Belle Fourche R.

Deadwood

Black Hills   Rapid
City

Camp
Cheyenne

Lower Brulé
Reservation

White R.

Wyoming

Custer

Pine Ridge
Reservation

Rosebud
Reservation

Iowa

Pine Ridge
Agency

Rosebud
Agency

Missouri R.

Nebraska

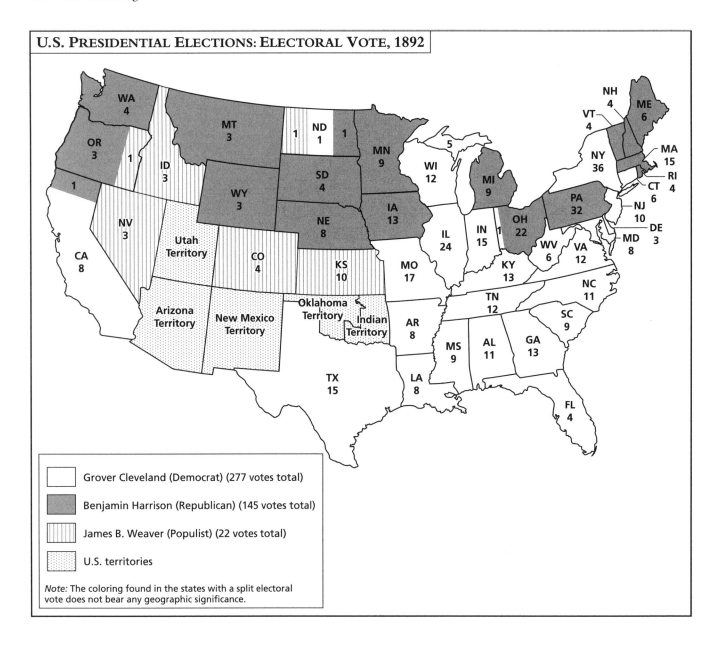

U.S. PRESIDENTIAL ELECTIONS: ELECTORAL VOTE, 1892

☐ Grover Cleveland (Democrat) (277 votes total)

▨ Benjamin Harrison (Republican) (145 votes total)

▥ James B. Weaver (Populist) (22 votes total)

▦ U.S. territories

Note: The coloring found in the states with a split electoral vote does not bear any geographic significance.

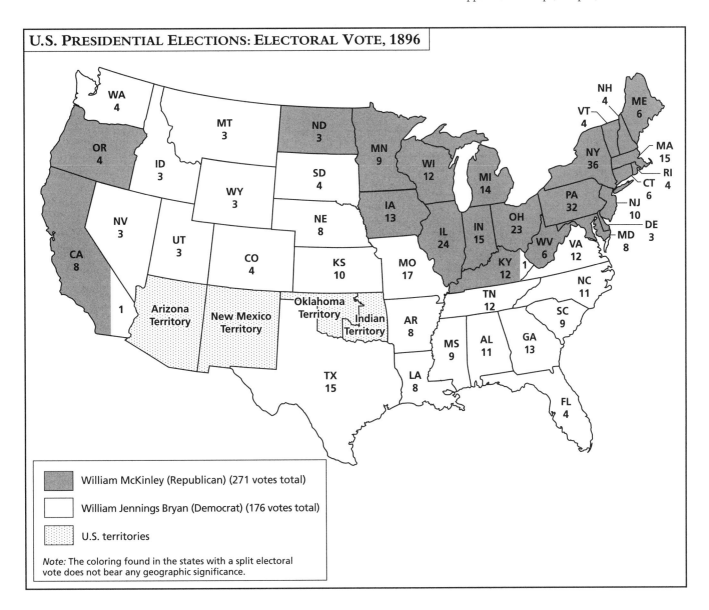

U.S. PRESIDENTIAL ELECTIONS: ELECTORAL VOTE, 1896

WA 4

OR 4

ID 3

NV 3

CA 8

1

MT 3

WY 3

UT 3

Arizona Territory

New Mexico Territory

ND 3

SD 4

NE 8

CO 4

KS 10

Oklahoma Territory

Indian Territory

TX 15

MN 9

IA 13

MO 17

AR 8

LA 8

WI 12

IL 24

MS 9

AL 11

MI 14

IN 15

KY 12   1

TN 12

GA 13

FL 4

OH 23

WV 6

VA 12

NC 11

SC 9

NH 4

VT 4

ME 6

NY 36

MA 15

RI 4

CT 6

PA 32

NJ 10

DE 3

MD 8

William McKinley (Republican) (271 votes total)

William Jennings Bryan (Democrat) (176 votes total)

U.S. territories

Note: The coloring found in the states with a split electoral vote does not bear any geographic significance.

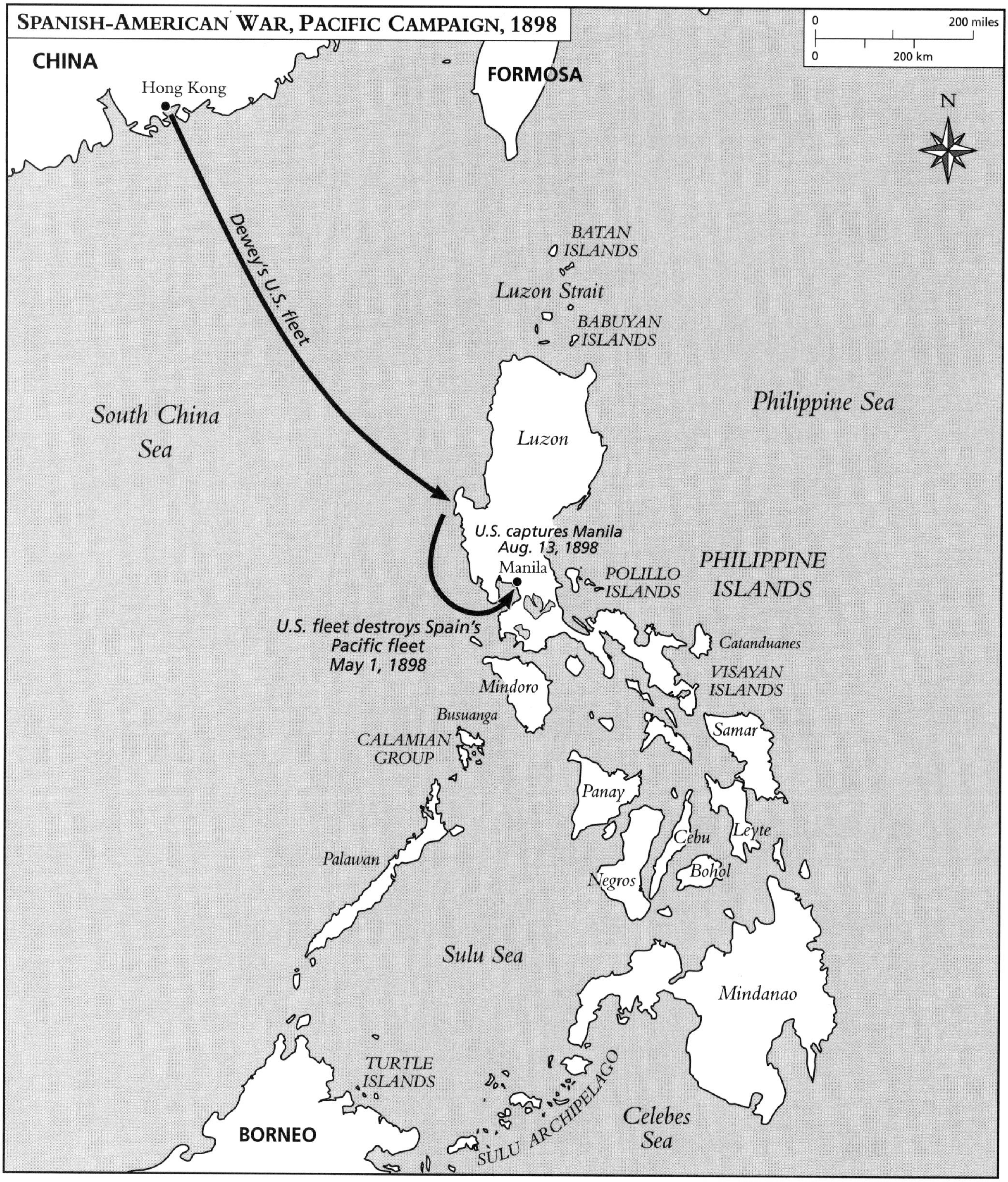

SPANISH-AMERICAN WAR, PACIFIC CAMPAIGN, 1898

CHINA

Hong Kong

FORMOSA

0   200 miles

0   200 km

N

Dewey's U.S. fleet

South China Sea

BATAN ISLANDS

Luzon Strait

BABUYAN ISLANDS

Philippine Sea

Luzon

U.S. captures Manila
Aug. 13, 1898

Manila

POLILLO ISLANDS

PHILIPPINE ISLANDS

U.S. fleet destroys Spain's
Pacific fleet
May 1, 1898

Catanduanes

Mindoro

VISAYAN ISLANDS

Busuanga

Samar

CALAMIAN GROUP

Panay

Palawan

Leyte

Cebu

Negros

Bohol

Sulu Sea

Mindanao

TURTLE ISLANDS

SULU ARCHIPELAGO

Celebes Sea

BORNEO

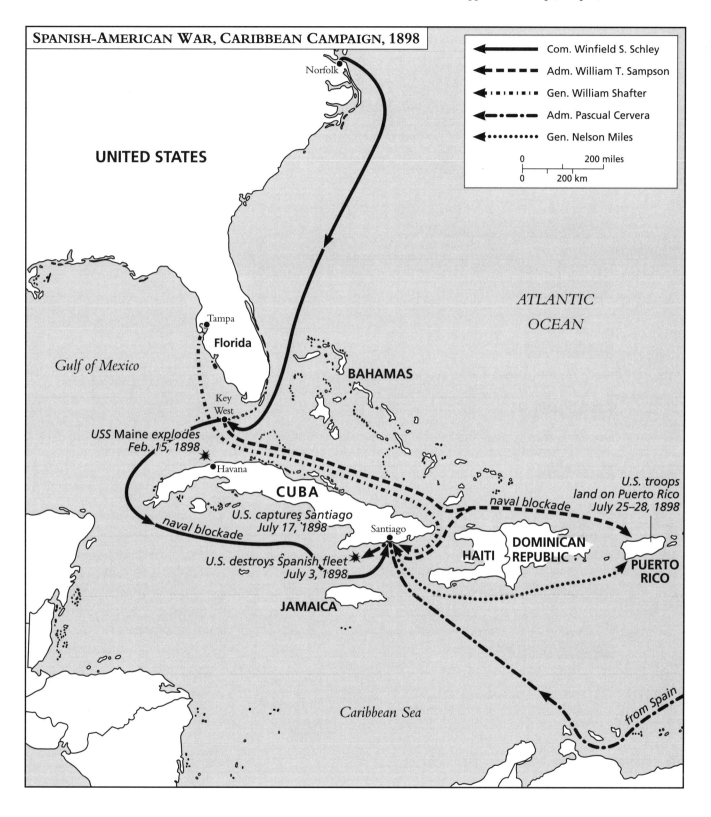

SPANISH-AMERICAN WAR, CARIBBEAN CAMPAIGN, 1898

Com. Winfield S. Schley
Adm. William T. Sampson
Gen. William Shafter
Adm. Pascual Cervera
Gen. Nelson Miles

0   200 miles
0   200 km

UNITED STATES

Norfolk

ATLANTIC

OCEAN

Tampa

Florida

Gulf of Mexico

BAHAMAS

Key West

USS Maine explodes
Feb. 15, 1898

Havana

naval blockade

CUBA

U.S. captures Santiago
July 17, 1898

Santiago

naval blockade

U.S. troops
land on Puerto Rico
July 25–28, 1898

DOMINICAN
REPUBLIC

HAITI

PUERTO
RICO

U.S. destroys Spanish fleet
July 3, 1898

JAMAICA

Caribbean Sea

from Spain

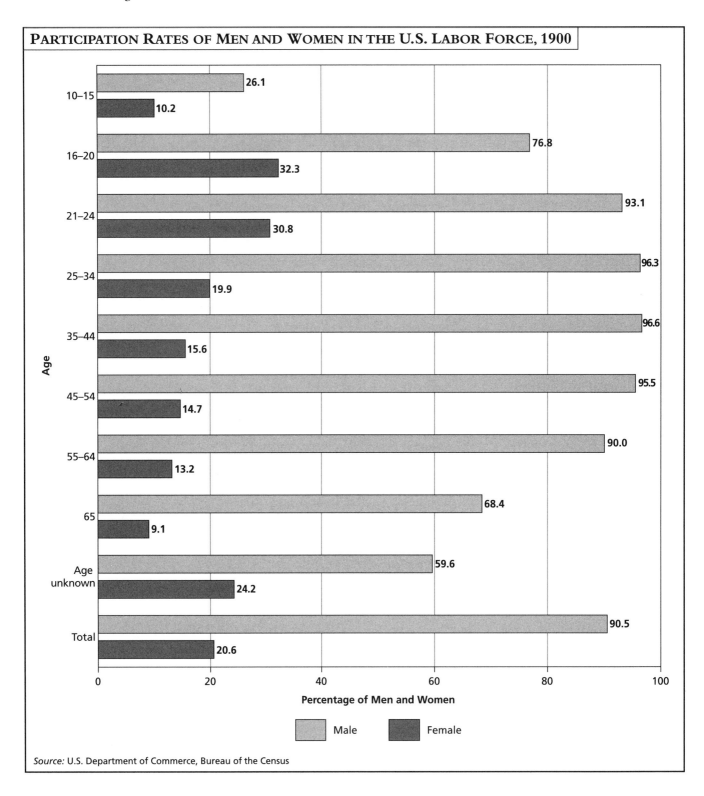

PARTICIPATION RATES OF MEN AND WOMEN IN THE U.S. LABOR FORCE, 1900

Source: U.S. Department of Commerce, Bureau of the Census

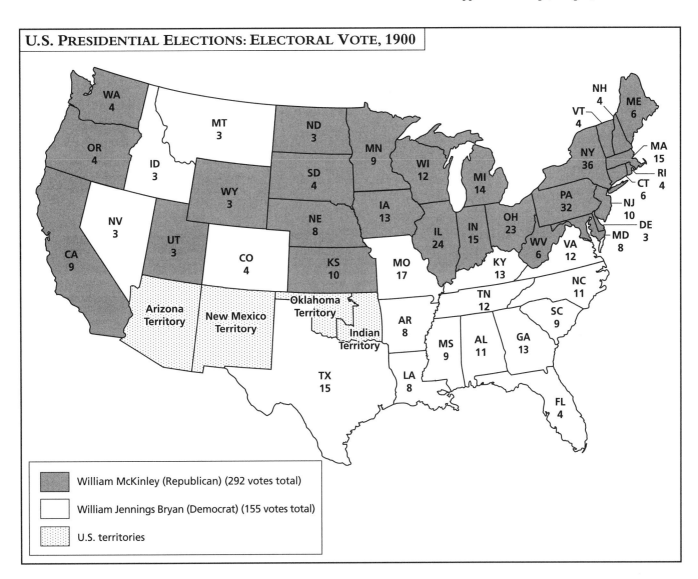

U.S. PRESIDENTIAL ELECTIONS: ELECTORAL VOTE, 1900

William McKinley (Republican) (292 votes total)

William Jennings Bryan (Democrat) (155 votes total)

U.S. territories

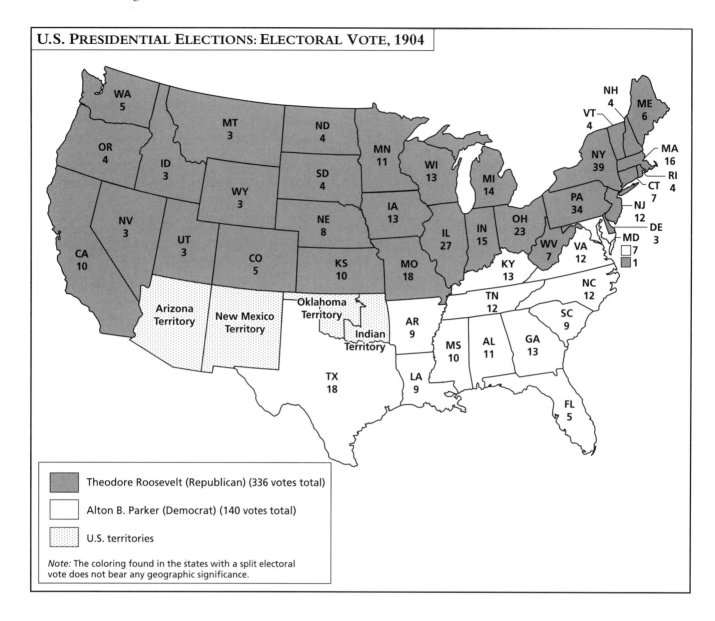

U.S. PRESIDENTIAL ELECTIONS: ELECTORAL VOTE, 1904

Theodore Roosevelt (Republican) (336 votes total)

Alton B. Parker (Democrat) (140 votes total)

U.S. territories

Note: The coloring found in the states with a split electoral vote does not bear any geographic significance.

Immigration by Region and Selected Country of Last Residence, Fiscal Years 1861–1900

Region and Country of Last Residence	1861–70	1871–80	1881–90	1891–1900
All countries	2,314,824	2,812,191	5,246,613	3,687,564
Europe	2,065,141	2,271,925	4,735,484	3,555,352
Austria-Hungary	7,800	72,969	353,719	592,707
Austria	7,124	63,009	226,038	234,081
Hungary	484	9,960	127,681	181,288
Belgium	6,734	7,221	20,177	18,167
Czechoslovakia				
Denmark	17,094	31,771	88,132	50,231
France	35,986	72,206	50,464	30,770
Germany	787,468	718,182	1,452,970	505,152
Greece	72	210	2,308	15,979
Ireland	435,778	436,871	655,482	388,416
Italy	11,725	55,759	307,309	651,893
Netherlands	9,102	16,541	53,701	26,758
Norway-Sweden	109,208	211,245	568,362	321,281
Norway	95,323	176,586	95,015	
Sweden	115,922	391,776	226,266	
Poland	2,027	12,970	51,806	96,720
Portugal	2,658	14,082	16,978	27,508
Romania		11	6,348	12,750
Soviet Union	2,512	39,284	213,282	505,290
Spain	6,697	5,266	4,419	8,731
Switzerland	23,286	28,293	81,988	31,179
United Kingdom	606,896	548,043	807,357	271,538
Yugoslavia				
Other Europe	8	1,001	682	282
Asia	64,759	124,160	69,942	74,862
China	64,301	123,201	61,711	14,799
Hong Kong				11
India	69	163	269	68
Iran				
Israel				
Japan	186	149	2,270	25,942
Korea	15	15		
Philippines	16	16		
Turkey	131	404	3,782	30,425
Vietnam				
Other Asia	72	243	1,910	3,628
North America	166,607	404,044	426,967	38,972
Canada & Newfoundland	153,878	383,640	393,304	3,311
Mexico	2,191	5,162	1,913	971
Caribbean	9,046	13,957	29,042	33,066
Cuba				
Dominican Republic				
Haiti				
Jamaica				
Other Caribbean	9046	13,957	29,042	33,066
Central America	95	157	404	549
El Salvador				
Other Central America	95	157	404	549
South America	1,397	1,128	2,304	1,075
Argentina				
Colombia				
Ecuador				
Other South America	1,397	1,128	2,304	1,075
Other America				
Africa	312	358	857	350
Oceania	214	10,914	12,574	3,965
Not specified	17,791	790	789	14,063

U.S. PRESIDENTIAL ELECTIONS, 1868–1904

Year	Names	Affiliation	Popular Vote	Electoral Vote
1868	ULYSSES S. GRANT	Republican	3,012,833	214
	Horatio Seymour	Democratic	2,703,249	80
1872	ULYSSES S. GRANT	Republican	3,596,745	286
	Horace Greeley	Democratic	2,843,446	66
1876	RUTHERFORD B. HAYES	Republican	4,036,572	185
	Samuel J. Tilden	Democratic	4,284,020	184
1880	JAMES A. GARFIELD	Republican	4,449,053	214
	Winfield S. Hancock	Democratic	4,442,032	155
	James B. Weaver	Greenback-Labor	308,578	
1884	GROVER CLEVELAND	Democratic	4,874,986	219
	James G. Blaine	Republican	4,851,981	182
	Benjamin F. Butler	Greenback-Labor	175,370	
1888	BENJAMIN HARRISON	Republican	5,444,337	233
	Grover Cleveland	Democratic	5,540,050	168
1892	GROVER CLEVELAND	Democratic	5,554,414	277
	Benjamin Harrison	Republican	5,190,802	145
	James B. Weaver	People's	1,027,329	22
1896	WILLIAM MCKINLEY	Republican	7,104,779	271
	William J. Bryan	Democratic; Populist	6,502,925	176
1900	WILLIAM MCKINLEY	Republican	7,219,530	292
	William J. Bryan	Democratic; Populist	6,356,734	155
1904	THEODORE ROOSEVELT	Republican	7,628,834	336
	Alton B. Parker	Democratic	5,084,401	140

CHIEF JUSTICES OF THE U.S. SUPREME COURT, 1865–1901

Name	Chase, Salmon Portland	Waite, Morrison Remick	Fuller, Melville Weston
Born	1/13/1808	11/29/1816	2/11/1833
Died	5/7/1873	3/23/1888	7/4/1910
Home	Ohio	Connecticut	Illinois
Graduated	Cincinnati College, Dartmouth	Yale	Bowdoin Harvard Law School
Appointed by	Lincoln	Grant	Cleveland
Confirmed	12/6/1864	1/1/1874	7/20/1888
Landmark decisions	*Ex parte Milligan* *Ex parte Garland* *Ex parte McCardle* *Texas v. White* *Hepburn v. Griswold* *Knox v. Lee* *Slaughterhouse Cases*	*Minor v. Happersett* *United States v. Reese* *United States v. Cruikshank* *Munn v. Illinois* *Peik v. Chicago & Northwestern Railroad Co.* *Stone v. Farmer's Loan & Trust Co.* *Hall v. DeCuir*	*United States v. Texas* *California v. Southern Pacific Co.* *United States v. E. C. Knight Co.* *Pollock v. Farmer's Land and Trust Co.* *United States v. Wong Kim Ark* *Loewe v. Lawlor*

CANADIAN PRIME MINISTERS, 1867–1911

Prime Minister	Birth	Death	Sworn In	Term
The Right Hon. Sir Wilfrid Laurier	November 20, 1841	February 17, 1919	July 11, 1896	1896–1911
The Right Hon. Sir Charles Tupper	July 2, 1821	October 30, 1915	May 1, 1896	1896
The Hon. Sir Mackenzie Bowell	December 27, 1823	December 10, 1917	Dec. 21, 1894	1894–1896
The Right Hon. Sir John Sparrow David Thompson	November 10, 1845	December 12, 1894	Dec. 5, 1892	1892–1894
The Hon. Sir John Joseph Caldwell Abbott	March 12, 1821	October 30, 1893	June 16, 1891	1891–1892
The Right Hon. Sir John Alexander Macdonald	January 11, 1815	June 6, 1891	Oct. 17, 1878	1878–1891
The Hon. Alexander Mackenzie	January 28, 1822	April 17, 1892	Nov. 7, 1873	1873–1878
The Right Hon. Sir John Alexander Macdonald	January 11, 1815	June 6, 1891	July 1, 1867	1867–1873

PROVINCES AND TERRITORIES ENTERED INTO CANADIAN CONFEDERATION, 1867–1905

Province/Territory	Date
Alberta	September 1, 1905
British Columbia	July 20, 1871
Manitoba	July 15, 1870
New Brunswick	July 1, 1867
Nova Scotia	July 1, 1867
Northwest Territories	July 15, 1870
Ontario	July 1, 1867
Prince Edward Island	July 1, 1873
Quebec	July 1, 1867
Saskatchewan	September 1, 1905
Yukon	June 13, 1898

Note: Newfoundland later entered on March 31, 1949; Nunavut later entered on April 1, 1999.

CANADIAN GOVERNORS GENERAL, 1867–1911

Name	Term of Office
Earl Grey	1904–1911
Earl of Minto	1898–1904
Earl of Aberdeen	1893–1898
Lord Stanley	1888–1893
Marquess of Lansdowne	1883–1888
Marquess of Lorne	1878–1883
Earl of Dufferin	1872–1878
Lord Lisgar	1869–1872
Viscount Monck	1867–1868

Note: The authority of a reigning sovereign, the head of state in Canada, is delegated to the Canadian governor general, whose role is largely ceremonial (the Canadian prime minister is the elected leader). A Canadian governor general's term of office is between five and seven years.

ASSOCIATE JUSTICES OF THE UNITED STATES SUPREME COURT, 1865–1901

Name	Born	Died	State	College	Law School
Wayne, James Moore	ca. 1790	7/5/1867	Georgia	Princeton	private study
Catron, John	ca. 1786	5/30/1865	Tennessee		private study
Nelson, Samuel	11/10/1792	12/13/1873	New York	Middlebury	private study
Grier, Robert Cooper	3/5/1794	9/26/1870	Penn.	Dickinson	private study
Clifford, Nathan	8/18/1803	7/25/1881	Maine	Haverhill	private study
Swayne, Noah Haynes	12/7/1804	6/8/1884	Ohio	Quaker Academy	private study
Miller, Samuel Freeman	4/5/1816	10/13/1890	Iowa	Transylvania University	private study
Davis, David	3/9/1815	6/26/1886	Illinois	Kenyon	Yale Law School
Field, Stephen Johnson	11/4/1816	4/9/1899	California	Williams	private study
Strong, William	5/6/1808	8/19/1895	Penn.	Yale	Yale Law School
Bradley, Joseph P.	3/14/1813	1/22/1892	New Jersey	Rutgers	private study
Hunt, Ward	6/14/1810	3/24/1886	New York	Union College	private study

| Appointed by | | Reason for Leaving | | | Landmark Decisions |
President	Date	Appointed as Chief Justice	Died	Resigned	
Jackson	1/9/1835		1867		*Scott v. Sandford* *Ex parte Milligan*
Jackson	3/8/1837		1865		*Scott v. Sandford*
Tyler	2/14/1845			1872	*Scott v. Sandford* *Ex parte Milligan* *Hepburn v. Griswold* *Knox v. Lee*
Polk	8/4/1846			1870	*Scott v. Sandford* *Ex parte McCardle*
Buchanan	1/12/1858		1881		*Ex parte Milligan* *Ex parte Garland* *Hepburn v. Griswold* *Ex parte Virginia*
Lincoln	1/24/1862			1881	*Ex parte Milligan* *Hepburn v. Griswold* *Knox v. Lee* *Slaughterhouse* Cases
Lincoln	7/16/1862	1890			*Ex parte Garland* *Hepburn v. Griswold* *Slaughterhouse* Cases
Lincoln	12/1/1862			1877	*Hepburn v. Griswold* *Slaughterhouse* Cases
Lincoln	3/10/1863			1897	*Ex parte Garland* *Paul v. Virginia* *Munn v. Illinois* *Bradley v. Fisher*
Grant	2/18/1870			1880	*Knox v. Lee* *Stauder v. West Virginia* *Ex parte Virginia*
Grant	3/21/1870		1892		*Knox v. Lee* *Slaughterhouse* Cases *Civil Rights* Cases
Grant	1/9/1873			1882	*Slaughterhouse* Cases *United States v. Reese* *Reading Railroad v. Pennsylvania*

(continues)

ASSOCIATE JUSTICES OF THE UNITED STATES SUPREME COURT, 1865–1901 *(continued)*

Name	Born	Died	State	College	Law School
Harlan, John Marshall	6/1/1833	10/14/1911	Kentucky	Centre College	Transylvania University
Woods, William Burnham	8/3/1824	5/14/1887	Georgia	West Reserve, Yale	private study
Matthews, Stanley	7/21/1824	3/22/1889	Ohio	Kenyon	private study
Gray, Horace	3/24/1828	9/15/1902	Mass.	Harvard	Harvard Law School
Blatchford, Samuel Milford	3/9/1820	7/7/1893	New York	Columbia	private study
Lamar, Lucius Quintus Cincinnatus	9/17/1825	1/23/1893	Mississippi	Emory	private study
Brewer, David Josiah	6/20/1837	3/28/1910	Kansas	Wesleyan, Yale	Albany Law School
Brown, Henry Billings	3/2/1836	9/4/1913	Michigan	Yale	Yale Law School, Harvard Law School
Shiras, George, Jr.	1/26/1832	8/2/1924	Pennsylvania	Ohio University, Yale	Yale Law School
Jackson, Howell Edmunds	4/8/1832	8/8/1895	Tennessee	W. Tenn. Col., University of Virginia, Cumberland	private study
White, Edward D.	11/3/1845	5/19/1921	Louisiana	Mount St. Mary's, Georgetown	private study
Peckham, Rufus Wheeler, Jr.	11/8/1838	10/24/1909	New York	Union	private study
McKenna, Joseph	8/10/1843	11/21/1926	California	St. Joseph's College	Benicia Collegiate Institut

| Appointed by | | Reason for Leaving | | | |
President	Date	Appointed as Chief Justice	Died	Resigned	Landmark Decisions
Hayes	10/29/1877		10/14/1911		*Plessy v. Ferguson* *Hennington v. Georgia* *Champion v. Ames* *United States v. Texas* *Northern Securities Co. v. United States*
Hayes	12/21/1880		5/14/1887		*United States v. Harris* *Presser v. Illinois* *United States v. Lee*
Garfield	5/12/1881		3/22/1889		*Bowman v. Chicago & N.W. Railway Co.* *Hurtado v. California* *Yick Wo v. Hopkins*
Arthur	12/20/1881		9/15/1902		*Mayre v. Parsons* *Poindexter v. Greenhow* *Bowman v. Chicago & N.W. Railway Co.* *Chicago, Milwaukee & St. Paul Railroad v. Minn.*
Arthur	3/27/1882		7/7/1882		*Chicago, Milwaukee & St. Paul Railroad v. Minn.* *Counselman v. Hitchcock* *In re Neagle*
Cleveland	1/16/1888		1/23/1893		*Chicago, Milwaukee & St. Paul Railroad v. Minn.* *In re Neagle* *United States v. Texas*
Harrison	12/18/1889		3/28/1910		*Reagan v. Farmers Loan & Trust Co.* *Kansas v. Colorado* *Muller v. Oregon* *In re Debs*
Harrison	12/29/1890			5/28/1906	*Pollock v. Farmers Loan & Trust Co.* *Plessy v. Ferguson* *Downes v. Bidwell* *Holden v. Hardy*
Harrison	7/26/1892			2/23/1903	*Pollock v. Farmers Loan & Trust Co.*
Harrison	2/18/1893		8/8/1895		*Pollock v. Farmers Loan & Trust Co.*
Cleveland	2/19/1894	12/18/1910			*United States v. E. C. Knight Co.* *Adair v. United States*
Cleveland	12/9/1895		10/24/1909		*Lochner v. New York* *Allgeyer v. Louisiana* *Maxwell v. Dow* *Ex parte Young*
McKinley	1/21/1898			1/5/1925	*Adair v. United States* *Adams v. Tanner* *Bunting v. Oregon* *Pettibone v. Nichols*

NOTES

PREFACE
1. Jane Addams. *Twenty Years at Hull-House with Autobiographical Notes,* 127.

1. RECONSTRUCTION, REUNION, RECONCILIATION: 1865–1870
1. Robert Kelley, *The Shaping of the American Past.* 2d ed. (Englewood Cliffs, N.J.: Prentice Hall, 1978), 340.
2. Allen Weinstein and R. Jackson Wilson, *Freedom and Crisis: An American History, Vol. 2, Since 1860* (New York: Random House, 1978), 429.
3. Gorton Carruth, *The Encyclopedia of American Facts and Dates.* 7th ed. (New York: Crowell, 1979), 276.
4. Kelley, *The Shaping of the American Past.* 2d ed., 367.
5. Carruth, *American Facts and Dates,* 278.
6. Carruth, *American Facts and Dates,* 278.
7. Carruth, *American Facts and Dates,* 278.
8. Arthur M. Schlesinger, ed., *Almanac of American History* (New York: Putnam's, 1983), 310.
9. Kelley, *The Shaping of the American Past.* 2d ed., 411.
10. Weinstein and Wilson, *Freedom and Crisis,* Vol. 2, 498.
11. Kelley, *The Shaping of the American Past,* 2d ed., 357.
12. Carruth, *American Facts and Dates,* 284.
13. Schlesinger, *Almanac of American History,* 308.
14. Schlesinger, *Almanac of American History,* 308.
15. Carruth, *American Facts and Dates,* 286.
16. Carruth, *American Facts and Dates,* 292.

2. SCANDAL, ECONOMIC INSTABILITY, AND EXPANSION: 1871–1875
1. Gorton Carruth, *The Encyclopedia of American Facts and Dates.* 7th ed. (New York: Crowell, 1979), 300.
2. Robert Kelley, *The Shaping of the American Past.* 2d ed. (Englewood Cliffs, N.J.: Prentice Hall, 1978), 407–09.
3. Kelley, *The Shaping of the American Past.* 2d ed., 399–403.
4. Carruth, *American Facts and Dates,* 294.
5. Allen Weinstein and R. Jackson Wilson, *Freedom and Crisis: An American History, Vol. 2, Since 1860* (New York: Random House, 1978), 472.
6. Arthur M. Schlesinger, ed., *Almanac of American History* (New York: Putnam's, 1983), 321.
7. Carruth, *American Facts and Dates,* 300.
8. Schlesinger, *Almanac of American History,* 324–25.
9. Carruth, *American Facts and Dates,* 297.
10. Schlesinger, *Almanac of American History,* 329.
11. Melvyn Dubofsky, *Industrialism and the American Worker, 1865–1920* (Arlington Heights, Ill.: AHM, 1975), 61.
12. Alan L. Lockwood and David E. Harris, *Reasoning with Democratic Values: Ethical Problems in United States History. Vol. 2, 1877 to the Present* (New York: Teachers' College Press, 1985), 19.

3. COMPROMISE POLITICS AND FIGHTING IN THE WEST: 1876–1880
1. Robert Kelley, *The Shaping of the American Past.* 2d ed. (Englewood Cliffs, N.J.: Prentice Hall, 1978), 393.
2. Robert Kelley, *The Shaping of the American Past.* 2d ed. (Englewood Cliffs, N.J.: Prentice Hall, 1978), 393.
3. Arthur M. Schlesinger, ed., *Almanac of American History* (New York: Putnam's, 1983), 336.
4. Gorton Carruth, *The Encyclopedia of American Facts and Dates.* 7th ed. (New York: Crowell, 1979), 306.

5. Allen Weinstein and R. Jackson Wilson, *Freedom and Crisis: An American History, Vol. 2, Since 1860* (New York: Random House, 1978), 511.
6. Schlesinger, *Almanac of American History*, 332–33.
7. Kelley, *The Shaping of the American Past.* 2d ed., 435.
8. Carruth, *American Facts and Dates*, 314.
9. Carruth, *American Facts and Dates*, 317.
10. Kelley, *The Shaping of the American Past.* 2d ed., 387.
11. Carruth, *American Facts and Dates*, 318.

4. ASSASSINATION, REFORM POLITICS, AND IMMIGRATION: 1881–1885

1. Allen Weinstein and R. Jackson Wilson, *Freedom and Crisis: An American History, Vol. 2, Since 1860* (New York: Random House, 1978), 461.
2. Weinstein and Wilson, *Freedom and Crisis, Vol. 2,* 474.
3. Gorton Carruth, *The Encyclopedia of American Facts and Dates.* 7th ed. (New York: Crowell, 1979), 320.
4. Robert Kelley, *The Shaping of the American Past.* 2d ed. (Englewood Cliffs, New Jersey: Prentice Hall, 1978), 499.
5. Carruth, *American Facts and Dates*, 326.
6. Kelley, *The Shaping of the American Past.* 2d ed., 485–87.
7. Carruth, *American Facts and Dates*, 326.
8. Carruth, *American Facts and Dates*, 328.
9. Carruth, *American Facts and Dates*, 316.
10. Weinstein and Wilson, *Freedom and Crisis, Vol. 2,* 518.
11. Arthur M. Schlesinger, ed., *Almanac of American History* (New York: Putnam's, 1983), 359.
12. Kelley, *The Shaping of the American Past.* 2d ed., 493.
13. Carruth, *American Facts and Dates*, 332.

5. LABOR UNREST AND ECONOMIC INSTABILITY: 1886–1891

1. Gorton Carruth, *The Encyclopedia of American Facts and Dates.* 7th ed. (New York: Crowell, 1979), 339.
2. Carruth, *American Facts and Dates*, 338.
3. Allen Weinstein and R. Jackson Wilson, *Freedom and Crisis: An American History, Vol. 2, Since 1860* (New York: Random House, 1978), 528–30.
4. Carruth, *American Facts and Dates*, 341.
5. Robert Kelley, *The Shaping of the American Past.* 2d ed. (Englewood Cliffs, N.J.: Prentice Hall, 1978), 399–400.
6. Kelley, *The Shaping of the American Past.* 2d ed., 432.
7. Weinstein and Wilson, *Freedom and Crisis, Vol. 2,* 511.
8. Carruth, *American Facts and Dates*, 342.
9. Weinstein and Wilson, *Freedom and Crisis, Vol. 2,* 568–70.
10. Carruth, *American Facts and Dates*, 347.
11. Carruth, *American Facts and Dates*, 348.
12. Carruth, *American Facts and Dates*, 350.
13. Schlesinger, *Almanac of American History*, 367.
14. Kelley, *The Shaping of the American Past.* 2d ed., 449.
15. Kelley, *The Shaping of the American Past.* 2d ed., 425–26.
16. Carruth, *American Facts and Dates*, 355.
17. Kelley, *The Shaping of the American Past.* 2d ed., 449.

6. STRIKES, THE WORLD'S COLUMBIAN EXPOSITION, AND IMPERIALISM: 1892–1896

1. Arthur M. Schlesinger, ed., *Almanac of American History* (New York: Putman's, 1983), 374.
2. Gorton Carruth, *The Encyclopedia of American Facts and Dates.* 7th ed. (New York: Crowell, 1979), 363.
3. Carruth, *American Facts and Dates*, 352.
4. Rose, "A History of the Fair." The World's Columbia Exposition. Available online: URL: http://xroads.virginia.edu/~MA96/WCE/history. html.
5. "The World's Columbian Exposition." Chicago Historical Society. Available online: URL: http://www.chicagohs.org/history/expo.html.
6. Rose, op cit.
7. Schlesinger, *Almanac of American History*, 376.
8. Robert Kelley, *The Shaping of the American Past.* 2d ed. (Englewood Cliffs, N.J.: Prentice Hall, 1978), 452.
9. Ibid.
10. Bob McCoy, "Dr. John Harvey Kellogg." Great American Quacks: the Museum of Questionable Medical Devices, URL: http://www.mtn.org/ quack/amquacks/kellogg.htm.

11. Kelley, *The Shaping of the American Past.* 2d ed., 452.
12. Weinstein and Wilson, *Freedom and Crisis, Vol. 2,* 557.
13. Weinstein and Wilson, *Freedom and Crisis, Vol. 2,* 604.
14. Kelley, *The Shaping of the American Past.* 2d ed., 468.
15. Schlesinger, *Almanac of American History,* 376.
16. Carruth, *American Facts and Dates,* 370.
17. Carruth, *American Facts and Dates,* 376.
18. Carruth, *American Facts and Dates,* 374.

7. ANNEXATION AND THE SPANISH-AMERICAN WAR: 1897–1901

1. Robert Kelley, *The Shaping of the American Past.* 2d ed. (Englewood Cliffs, N.J.: Prentice Hall, 1978), 463.
2. Kelley, *The Shaping of the American Past.* 2d ed., 475.
3. Gorton Carruth, *The Encyclopedia of American Facts and Dates.* 7th ed. (New York: Crowell, 1979), 362.
4. Carruth, *American Facts and Dates,* 368.
5. Arthur M. Schlesinger, ed., *Almanac of American History* (New York: Putnam's, 1983), 387.
6. Schlesinger, *Almanac of American History,* 382.
7. Schlesinger, *Almanac of American History,* 387.
8. Kelley, *The Shaping of the American Past.* 2d ed., 469.
9. Kelley, *The Shaping of the American Past.* 2d ed., 470.
10. Schlesinger, *Almanac of American History,* 391.
11. Alexander B. Callow, Jr., *American Urban History.* 2d ed. (New York: Oxford University Press, 1973), 422–24.
12. Interpretation and Education Division, "Mt. Rainier National Park," National Park Service. URL: http://www.nps.gov/mora/home.htm.
13. PBS, "Admiral George Dewey," *American 1900: People and Events.* URL: http://www.pbs.org/wgbh/amex/1900/peopleevents/pande1.html.
14. Carruth, *American Facts and Dates,* 392.
15. Carruth, *American Facts and Dates,* 372.

BIBLIOGRAPHY

Addams, Jane. *Twenty Years at Hull-House with Autobiographical Notes.* New York: Macmillan, 1912.

"Admiral George Dewey." America 1900: People and Events, Public Broadcasting Service. Available online. URL: http://www.pbs.org/wgbh/amex/ 1900/peopleevents/pande1.html. Downloaded on August 25, 2004.

Ahlstrom, Sydney E. *A Religious History of the American People.* New Haven, Conn.: Yale University Press, 2004.

Arnett, Benjamin W. Speech to Ohio State Legislature on the Black Laws, March 10, 1886. African American Perspectives: Pamphlets from the Daniel A. P. Murray Collection, 1818–1907. American Memory, Library of Congress. Available online. URL: http://memory.loc.gov/cgi-bin/query/r?ammem/ murray:@field(DOCID+@lit(lcrbmrpt0d06)). Downloaded on May 18, 2004.

Avrich, Paul. *The Haymarket Tragedy.* Princeton, N.J.: Princeton University Press, 1984.

Baker, Ray Stannard. "Hull House and the Ward Boss," *Outlook,* March 26, 1898.

Baltzell, E. Digby. *The Protestant Establishment.* New York: Vintage Books, 1966.

Barry, Kathleen. *Susan B. Anthony: A Biography.* New York: New York University Press, 1988.

Bartlett, John. *Familiar Quotations, 12th Edition.* Boston: Little, Brown, 1951.

Baxandall, Rosalyn, Linda Gordon, and Susan Reverby, eds. *America's Working Women: A Documentary History, 1600 to the Present.* New York: W. W. Norton & Co., 1995.

Bell, Alexander Graham. Letter to Mabel Hubbard Bell, October 5, 1875. *The Alexander Graham Bell Family Papers.* Available online. URL: http://memory.loc.gov/cgi-bin/query/r?ammem/magbell:@field (DOCID+@lit(magbell03400202)). Downloaded on August 9, 2004.

Blaine, James G. "Speech to the U.S. House of Representatives, February 27, 1882." The Federal Observer. Available online. URL: http://www.federalobserver.com/print.php?aid=1205. Downloaded on November 23, 2004.

Blum, John M., et al. *The National Experience: A History of the United States.* 2d ed. New York: Harcourt, Brace & World, 1968.

Boorstin, Daniel J. *The Americans: The Democratic Experience.* New York: Vintage Books, 1974.

Bryan, William Jennings. "America's Mission," *Bryan on Imperialism.* Chicago: Bentley & Co., 1900. Available online. URL: http://www.boondocksnet.com/ai/ailtexts/bryan990222.html. Downloaded on August 9, 2004.

————. "Excerpt from a Speech at Trans-Mississippi Exposition, Omaha, Nebraska, June 14, 1898." Trans-Mississippi and International Exposition, Omaha Public Library. Available online. URL: http://www.omaha.lib.ne.us/transmiss/bee/june14.html. Downloaded on August 9, 2004.

Buchler, Justus, et al. *Introduction to Contemporary Civilization in the West, A Source Book. Vol. II.* New York: Columbia University Press, 1946.

Burgess, John W. *The Foundation of Political Science.* Introduction by Nicholas Murray Butler. New York: Columbia University Press, 1933.

Burnett, Constance Buel. *Five for Freedom: Lucretia Mott, Elizabeth Cady Stanton, Lucy Stone, Susan B. Anthony, Carrie Chapman Catt.* New York: Greenwood Press, 1968.

Burns, James MacGregor, J. W. Pelatson, and Thomas E. Cronin. *Government by the People.* 13th ed. Englewood Cliffs, N.J.: Prentice Hall, 1987.

Callow, Alexander B., Jr. *American Urban History.* 2d ed. New York: Oxford University Press, 1973.

Campbell, A. E. *Expansionism and Imperialism.* New York: Harper & Row, 1970.

Carruth, Gorton. *The Encyclopedia of American Facts and Dates.* 7th ed. New York: Crowell, 1979.

Cashman, Sean Dennis: *America in the Gilded Age: From the Death of Lincoln to the Rise of Theodore Roosevelt.* New York: New York University Press, 1993.

Chidsey, Donald B. *The Gentleman from New York: A Life of Roscoe Conkling.* New Haven, Conn.: Yale University Press, 1935.

Chief Joseph. "The Flight of the Nez Perce—A Timeline." Our Heritage. Available online. URL: http://www.ourheritage.net/index_page_stuff/Following_Trails/Chief_Joseph/1855_plus/1871_Old_Joseph_dies.html. Downloaded on November 12, 2004.

———. "Statement to U.S. Army Commission, 1876." *Nez Perce, Summer 1877.* By Jerome A. Greene. Helena: Montana Historical Society Press, 2000. Available online. URL: http://www.nps.gov/nepe/greene/chap1b.htm. Downloaded on November 12, 2004.

Clemens, Samuel. "Speech at Philadelphia, Pennsylvania, December 23, 1881." In Samuel Langhorne Clemens, ed., *Plymouth Rock and the Pilgrims: Mark Twain's Speeches.* New York: Harper & Brothers, 1910. Available online. Electronic Text Center, University of Virginia Library. URL: http://wyllie.lib. virginia.edu:8086/perl/toccer-new?id=TwaPlym.sgm&images=images/ mo deng&data=/texts/english/modeng/parsed&tag=public&part=teiHeader. Downloaded on August 6, 2004.

Cleveland, Grover. "President Grover Cleveland's Message, December 18, 1893." Hawaiian Independence. Available online. URL: http://www.hawaii-nation. org/cleveland.html. Downloaded on November 16, 2004.

Cloud, D. C. *Monopolies and the People.* Davenport, Ia., Day, Egbert & Fidlar; Muscatine, Ia., A. Broomhall, 1873. Available online. URL: http://www.hti.umich. edu/cgi/t/text/pageviewer-idx?c=moa;cc=moa;sid=8e2aa00d0445805373 1c9906b71dc434;rgn=full%20text;idno=ABZ0161.0001.001;view=image; seq=0161. Downloaded on November 10, 2004.

Collier, Peter, and David Horowitz. *The Rockefellers: An American Dynasty.* New York: Henry Holt & Co., 1976.

Conway, Jill K., ed. *Written by Herself: Autobiographies of American Women: An Anthology.* New York: Vintage Books, 1992.

"The Cotton Pickers," *Atlanta Constitution,* September 7, 1891, n.p.

Current, Richard N., and John A. Garraty. *Words That Made American History, Colonial Times to the 1870's.* 2d ed. Boston: Little, Brown. 1965.

———. *Words That Made American History, Since the Civil War.* 2d ed. Boston: Little, Brown, 1965.

Davis, Allen F. *American Heroine.* 2d ed. Chicago, Ill.: Ivan R. Dee, 2000.

Davis, Allen F., and Harold D. Woodman. *Conflict or Consensus in American History.* Boston: D.C. Heath, 1966.

Debs, Eugene V. "Proclamation to American Railway Union." Eugene V. Debs Internet Archive, Marxists Internet Archive. Available online. URL: http:// www.marxists.org/archive/debs/works/1895/aru.htm. Downloaded on November 16, 2004.

Degler, Carl N. *The Age of the Economic Revolution, 1867–1900.* 2d ed. Glenview, Ill.: Scott, Foresman, 1977.

DeGregorio, William A. *The Complete Book of U.S. Presidents.* New York: Random House, 1993.

DeNovo, John A., ed. *The Gilded Age and After.* New York: Scribner's, 1972.

Depew, Chauncey. "Chiastic Quotes of the Week: July 29–August 4, 2001." Chiasmus.com. Available online. URL: http://www.chiasmus.com/archive/msg00030.html. Downloaded on November 18, 2004.

Donald, David. *Inside Lincoln's Cabinet, The Civil War Diaries of Salmon P. Chase.* New York: Longmans, Green and Co., 1954.

Douglass, Frederick. Address on the 21st Anniversary of Emancipation in the District of Columbia, Congregational Church, Washington, D.C., April 16, 1883. African American Perspectives: Pamphlets from the Daniel A. P. Murray Collection, 1818–1907. American Memory, Library of Congress. Available online: URL: http://memory.loc.gov/cgi-bin/query/r?ammem/murray:@field(DOCID+@lit(lcrbmrpt0a04)). Downloaded on April 16, 2004.

———. "Appeal to Congress for Impartial Suffrage, January, 1867." University of Oklahoma Law Center. Available online. URL: http://www.law.ou.edu/hist/suff.html. Downloaded on August 25, 2004.

———. *Life and Times of Frederick Douglass: His Early Life as a Slave, His Escape from Bondage, and His Complete History to the Present Time.* Hartford, Conn.: Park Publishing Co., 1881.

Dubofsky, Melvyn. *Industrialism and the American Worker, 1865–1920.* Arlington Heights, Ill.: AHM, 1975.

Dunbar, Charles F. "Economic Science in America, 1776–1876." In *North American Review, 1876,* p. 125. Making of America, Cornell University. Available online. URL: http://cdl.library.cornell.edu/cgi-bin/moa/moa-cgi?notisid=ABQ7578-0122&byte=97742887. Downloaded on November 12, 2005.

Dyal, Donald H. *Historical Dictionary of the Spanish American War.* Westport, Conn.: Greenwood Press, 1996.

Edison, Thomas A. *Thomas A. Edison Diary.* Special Collections Series: Thomas A. Edison Diary—Cat. 117 (1885). Thomas A. Edison Papers, Rutgers University. Available online. URL: http://edison.rutgers.edu/taep.htm. Downloaded on August 6, 2004.

———. "Transcription of Thomas Edison's Patent Application for the Light Bulb." Our Documents, National Archives. Available online. URL: http://www.ourdocuments.gov/doc.php?doc=46&page=transcript. Downloaded on July 7, 2004.

"Editorial," *Emporia News,* Emporia, Kansas. March 10, 1871. Available online. URL: http://www.ausbcomp.com/%7Ebbott/cowley/Oldnews/PAPERS/EMP4.HTM. Downloaded on May 18, 2004.

Elliott, Stephen P. *A Reference Guide to the United States Supreme Court.* New York: Facts On File, 1986.

Excerpt of item published in *Emporia News,* Emporia, Kansas, January 6, 1871. Cowley County History Resources. Available online. URL: http://www.ausbcomp.com/%7Ebbott/cowley/Oldnews/PAPERS/EMP4.HTM. Downloaded on May 18, 2004.

"Excerpts from *A Colored Alliance at Work,* September 11, 1889." *Atlanta Constitution.* American History A.P., Historyteacher.net. Available online. URL: http://www.historyteacher.net/AHAP/Weblinks/AHAP_Weblinks15.htm. Downloaded on November 16, 2004.

Fairman, Charles. *Mr. Justice Miller and the Supreme Court.* New York: Russell & Russell, 1939.

"Fire!" *Chicago Tribune.* Wednesday, October 11, 1871. Available online. URL: http://www.chicagohs.org/fire/conflag/tribune.html. Downloaded on August 6, 2004.

Foner, Eric. *Reconstruction: America's Unfinished Revolution, 1863–1877.* New York: Harper & Row, 1988.

Ford, Henry Jones. *The Cleveland Era: A Chronicle of the New Order in Politics.* New Haven, Conn.: Yale University Press, 1919. Historical Text Archive. Available online. URL: http://historicaltextarchive.com/books.php?op=viewbook&bookid=42&cid=5. Downloaded on November 16, 2004.

Garraty, John A., ed. *Labor and Capital in the Gilded Age.* Boston: Little, Brown, 1968.

Gianakos, Perry E., and Albert Karson. *American Diplomacy and the Sense of Destiny, Vol. I, The Initial Thrust, 1885–1900.* Belmont, Calif.: Wadsworth, 1966.

Gilbert, Paul Thomas, and Charles Lee Bryson. *Chicago and Its Makers.* Chicago: F. Mendelsohn, 1929.

Ginger, Ray. *Age of Excess: The United States from 1877 to 1914.* New York: Macmillan, 1965.

Gompers, Samuel. "Imperialism—Its Dangers and Wrongs." *Republic or Empire? The Philippine Question.* William Jennings Bryan, et al. Chicago: The Independence Co., 1899. Available online. URL: http://www.ashp.cuny.edu/video/gompers.html. Downloaded on August 9, 2004.

Gould, Lewis L. *The Presidency of William McKinley.* Lawrence: University Press of Kansas, 1980.

Grant, Ulysses S. *Memoirs, Vol. 6, Conclusion.* New York: Charles L. Webster Co., 1885. Project Gutenberg. Available online. URL: http://www.gutenberg.net/dirs/4/3/6/4367/4367-h/p6.htm#conclusion. Downloaded on August 4, 2004.

Grob, Gerald N., and George Athan Billias. *Interpretations of American History. Vol. II.* 2d ed. New York: Free Press, 1972.

Handlin, Oscar. *Strangers in the Land.* New York: Atheneum, 1975.

Harlan, Louis R., ed. *The Booker T. Washington Papers.* Vol. 3. Urbana: University of Illinois Press, 1974. Available online. URL: http://historymatters. gmu.edu/d/39.

Herringshaw, Thomas W., ed. *Prominent Men and Women of the Day.* Chicago: A. B. Gehman & Co., 1888.

Higham, John. *Strangers in the Land: Patterns of American Nativism, 1860–1925.* New Brunswick, N.J.: Rutgers University Press, 1983.

Hofstadter, Richard. *The American Political Tradition.* New York: Vintage Books, 1948.

Hoogenboom, Ari, and Olive Hoogenboom. *The Gilded Age.* Englewood Cliffs, N.J.: Prentice Hall, 1967.

Howe, Frederic C. *The Confessions of a Reformer.* New York: Quadrangle Books, 1967.

Hubbard, Elbert. "A Message to Garcia," *The Philistine,* February 1899. The Roycrofters. Available online. URL: http://www.roycrofter.com/garcia.htm. Downloaded on November 18, 2004.

"'*Huckleberry Finn*' and His Critics, May 26, 1885." *Atlanta Constitution.* Electronic Text Center, University of Virginia Library. Available online. URL: http://etext. virginia.edu/etcbin/twainrev2www?specfile=/lv6/workspace/railton/reviews/twainrev iew.o2w&act=surround&offset=184541&tag=The+Constitution+ Review:+Hu ck&query=. Downloaded on November 18, 2004.

Interpretation and Education Division, Mount Rainer National Park. "Welcome to Your National Park." National Park Service. Available online. URL: http://www.nps.gov/mora/home.htm. Downloaded on August 4, 2004.

"Inyo Earthquake of 1872." *San Francisco Chronicle,* April 21, 1872. The Virtual Museum of the City of San Francisco. Available online. URL: http://www. sfmuseum.org/hist/1872eq.html. Downloaded on July 28, 2004.

Johannsen, Robert W. *Reconstruction, 1865–1877.* New York: Free Press, 1970.

Johnson, Andrew. "Fellow Citizens of Cleveland." *Cleveland Plain Dealer,* September 4, 1866. Reprinted in *The Papers of Andrew Johnson,* edited by Paul H. Bergeron, vol. 11, Knoxville: University of Tennessee Press, 1994, pp. 174–180. Available online. URL: http://itw.sewanee.edu/reconstruction/html/docs/JohnsonClev.html. Downloaded on June 6, 2005.

———. "Speech to the U.S. House of Representatives, March 2, 1867." *From Revolution to Reconstruction.* Available online. URL: http://odur.let.rug.nl/~usa/D/1851-1875/reconstruction/veto.htm. Downloaded on April 12, 2004.

Jordan, David M. *Roscoe Conkling: Voice in the Senate.* Ithaca, N.Y.: Cornell University Press, 1971.

Jordan, David Starr. *Lest We Forget: An Address Delivered before the Graduating Class of 1898, Leland Stanford University on May 25, 1898.* Palo Alto, Calif.: Leland Stanford University Publications, 1898.

Josephson, Matthew. *The Politicos, 1865–1896.* New York: Harcourt, Brace and Co., 1938.

———. *The Robber Barons.* Orlando, Fla.: Harcourt Inc., 1962.

Kelley, Florence. "The Sweating System of Chicago." *Bureau of Statistics of Labor of Illinois, Seventh Biennial Report, 1892.* Springfield, Ill.: H.K. Rokker, 1893. Available online. URL: http://womhist.binghamton.edu/factory/doc1.htm. Downloaded on August 22, 2004.

Kelley, Robert. *The Shaping of the American Past.* 2d ed. Englewood Cliffs, N.J.: Prentice Hall, 1978.

Kennan, George F. *American Diplomacy, 1900–1950.* Chicago: University of Chicago Press, 1951.

Lane, Franklin K. "The Project Gutenberg Etext of The Letters of Franklin K. Lane." Project Gutenberg. Available online. URL: http://www.gutenberg.org/dirs/etext03/ltrln10.txt. Downloaded on November 16, 2004.

Lockwood, Alan L., and David E. Harris. *Reasoning with Democratic Values: Ethical Problems in United States History. Vol. 2, 1877 to the Present.* New York: Teachers College Press, 1985.

Lodge, Henry Cabot. *Early Memories.* New York: Scribner's, 1913.

Maddow, Ben. *A Sunday Between Wars. The Course of American Life from 1865 to 1917.* New York: W. W. Norton & Co., 1979.

"Mark Twain and George W. Cable," *St. Louis Daily Globe Democrat,* January 11, 1885. Electronic Text Center, University of Virginia Library. Available online. URL: http://etext.virginia.edu/etcbin/twainrev2www?specfile=/lv6/workspace/railton/reviews/twainrev iew.o2w&act=surround&offset=716316&tag=Twain-Cable+St.+Louis+Revie w&query=. Downloaded on November 18, 2004.

"'Mark Twain' and Mr. Cable," *Providence Daily Journal,* November 10, 1884. Electronic Text Center, University of Virginia Library. Available online. URL: http://etext.virginia.edu/etcbin/twainrev2www?specfile=/lv6/workspace/railton/reviews/twainrev iew.o2w&act=surround&offset=756979&tag=Twain-Cable+Providence+Revi ew&query=. Downloaded on November 18, 2004.

Mathews, Mary Mowll. *Mary Cassatt: A Life.* Reprint ed. New Haven, Conn.: Yale University Press, 1998.

Matthaei, Julie A. *An Economic History of Women in America.* New York: Schocken Books, 1982.

Mayer, Harold M., and Richard C. Wade. *Chicago: Growth of a Metropolis.* Chicago: University of Chicago Press, 1969.

McClain, Charles J. *In Search of Equality: The Chinese Struggle against Discrimination in Nineteenth-Century America.* Berkeley: University of California Press, 1994.

McCoy, Bob. "Dr. John Harvey Kellogg." Great American Quacks: The Museum of Questionable Medical Devices. Available online. URL: http://www.mtn.org/quack/amquacks/kellogg.htm. Downloaded on August 4, 2004.

McCraw, Thomas K. *Prophets of Regulation.* Cambridge, Mass.: The Belknap Press of Harvard University Press, 1984.

McKinley, William. "First Inaugural Address of William McKinley, Thursday, March 4, 1897." The Avalon Project at Yale Law School. Available online. URL: http://www.yale.edu/lawweb/avalon/presiden/inaug/mckin1.htm. Downloaded on August 25, 2004.

———. "Second Inaugural Address of William McKinley, Monday, March 4, 1901." The Avalon Project at Yale Law School. Available online. URL: http://www.yale.edu/lawweb/avalon/presiden/inaug/mckin2.htm. Downloaded on August 25, 2004.

McPherson, Stephanie Sammartino. *Peace and Bread: The Story of Jane Addams.* Minneapolis: Carolrhoda Books, 1993.

Morgan, H. Wayne, ed. *The Gilded Age.* Syracuse, N.Y.: Syracuse University Press, 1970.

Morris, Edmund. *Theodore Rex*. New York: Random House, 2001.

Munn v. Illinois 94 U.S. 113. Legal Information Institute. Available online. URL: http://supct.law.cornell.edu/supct/html/historics/ USSC_CR_0094_0113_ZO.html. Downloaded on August 9, 2004.

Muzzey, David Saville. *James G. Blaine: A Political Idol of Other Days*. New York: Dodd, Mead & Company, 1935.

Myers, Gustavus. *"Chapter V: History of the Great American Fortunes."* Chicago: C. H. Kerr and Company, 1910. URL: http://www.geocities.com/ doswind/myers/am_fortune_305.html. Downloaded on November 12, 2004.

Myers, Robert Manson, ed. *The Children of Pride. Vol. 3, The Night Season*. New Haven, Conn.: Yale University Press, 1972.

Neihardt, John G. (Flaming Rainbow). *Black Elk Speaks: Being the Life Story of a Holy Man of the Oglala Sioux*. Foreword by Vine Deloria, Jr. Illustrations by Standing Bear. Lincoln: University of Nebraska Press, 2000. Available online. URL: http://www.blackelkspeaks.unl.edu/toc.htm. Downloaded on November 9, 2004.

Nevins, Allan, and Milton Halse Thomas, eds. *The Diary of George Templeton Strong, 1835–1875, 4 Volumes*. New York: Macmillan, 1952.

Niven, John. *Salmon P. Chase: A Biography*. New York: Oxford University Press, 1995.

Olmsted, Frederick Law. "The Evolution of the Conservation Movement, 1850–1920, Letter to *New York Evening Post*, 1868. Frederick Law Olmsted papers, Library of Congress. American Memory: Historical Collections for the National Digital Library. Available online. URL: http://lcweb2.loc.gov/ cgi-bin/query/r?ammem/consrv:@field(DOCID+@lit(amrvmvm02di2)). Downloaded on July 27, 2005.

"On Plymouth Rock Again. The Pilgrims Sons Talking of Their Forefathers. New-England men in New-York Congratulating Themselves and the Country on Their Ancestors' Virtues and the Resultant Blessings," *New York Times*, December 23, 1882. Electronic Text Center, University of Virginia Library. Available online. URL: http://etext.lib.virginia.edu/railton/onstage/ woman82.html. Downloaded on November 18, 2004.

O'Toole, G. J. A. *The Spanish War: An American Epic, 1898*. New York: W. W. Norton & Company, 1984.

Paine, Albert Bigelow. *Th. Nast: His Period and His Pictures*. New York: Macmillan, 1904.

Painter, C. C. "Studying the Condition of Affairs in Indian Territory and California." Philadelphia, Pa.: Indian Rights Association, 1888. American Memory,

Library of Congress. Available online. URL: http://memory.loc.gov/cgi-bin/query/r?ammem/calbk:@field(DOCID+@lit(calbk052div1)). Downloaded on November 12, 2004.

Paradis, Adrian. *The Labor Reference Book.* New York: Chilton, 1972.

Parker, William Thornton. "A Soldier's Plea for Justice: An Indian War Veteran's Experience in Kansas and New Mexico during the Indian Wars of 1867–1868." In *Winners of the West,* vol. XI, no. 3, St. Joseph, Missouri, February 28, 1934. Available online. URL: http://www.rootsweb.com/~nalakota/wotw/misc/soldiersplea_wotw022834.htm. Downloaded on November 16, 2004.

Paterson, Thomas, ed. *American Imperialism and Anti-Imperialism.* New York: Crowell, 1973.

Pellauer, Mary D. *Toward a Tradition of Feminist Theology: The Religious Social Thought of Elizabeth Cady Stanton, Susan B. Anthony, and Anna Howard Shaw.* Brooklyn: Carlson, 1991.

Powderly, Terence V. *Thirty Years of Labor, 1859–1889.* New York: Augustus M. Kelley, 1967.

Read, Phyllis. *The Book of Women's Firsts.* New York: Random House, 1992.

Reid, Ronald F. *Three Centuries of American Rhetorical Discourse.* Prospect Heights, Ill.: Waveland Press, 1988.

"Registration Laws and Their Operation," XIII, *Philadelphia Medical Times,* July 14, 1883. Quoted in Ronald Hamowy, "The Early Development of Medical Licensing Laws in the United States, 1875–1900," *Journal of Libertarian Studies,* vol. 3, no. 1, pp. 80–81. Available online. URL: http://www.mises.org/jlsDisplay.asp?action=sort&volume=3&number=1&sub mit=View. Downloaded on November 9, 2004.

Roche, John P., ed. *American Political Thought from Jefferson to Progressivism.* New York: Harper & Row, 1967.

Roosevelt, Theodore. *Hunting Trips of a Ranchman; Sketches of Sport on the Northern Cattle Plains.* Illustrated by A. B. Frost, R. Swain Gifford, J. C. Beard, Fannie E. Gifford, and Henry Sandham. New York and London: G. P. Putnam's Sons, 1885.

———. "The Strenuous Life." *The Strenuous Life; Essays and Addresses.* New York: The Century Co., 1904.

———. "Character and Success," *The Outlook,* March 31, 1900. From *The Strenuous Life; Essays and Addresses.* New York: The Outlook Co., 1900. Bartleby.com. Available online. URL: http://www.bartleby.com/58/6.html. Downloaded on May 23, 2003.

Rose, Julie K. "A History of the Fair. The World's Columbia Exposition: Idea, Experience Aftermath." American Studies, University of Virginia. Available online: URL: http://xroads.virginia.edu/~MA96/WCE/ history.html. Downloaded on November 12, 2004.

Rusling, General James. "Interview with President William McKinley," *The Christian Advocate* (January 22, 1903), p. 17. Reprinted in *The Philippines Reader,* eds. Daniel Schirmer and Stephen Rosskamm Shalom, Boston: South End Press, 1987.

Salisbury, Lord. "Letter to Sir Julian Paunceforte," November 26, 1895. Quoted in *Papers Relating to the Foreign Relations of the United States . . . 1895,* part 1, U.S. Department of State.

Schlesinger, Arthur M., ed. *Almanac of American History.* New York: Putnam's, 1983.

Schurz, Carl. "American Imperialism: An Address opposing annexation of the Philippines, January 4, 1899." In *American Imperialism in 1898,* ed. Theodore P. Greene. Boston: D.C. Heath & Co., 1955.

———. "Carl Schurz against American Imperialism, 1899." Available online. URL: http://www.wadsworth.com/history_d/special_features/ ext/ap/chapter19/19.4.antiimp.html. Downloaded on November 16, 2004.

Scovell, Bessie Laythe. "President's Address." In *Minutes of the Twenty-Fourth Annual Meeting of the W.C.T.U. of the State of Minnesota, 1900.* St. Paul: W. J. Woodbury, 1900. Available online: URL: http://womhist.binghamton. edu/wctu/doc2.htm#D. Downloaded on August 22, 2004.

Shepherd, Jack. *The Adams Chronicles: Four Generations of Greatness.* Boston: Little, Brown, 1975.

Sicherman, Barbara, and Carol Hurd Green, eds. *Notable American Women: The Modern Period.* Cambridge, Mass.: Belknap Press, 1980.

Slotkin, Richard. *The Fatal Environment.* New York: Atheneum, 1985.

Smith, Carl S. *Urban Disorder and the Shape of Belief: The Great Chicago Fire, the Haymarket Bomb, and the Model Town of Pullman.* Chicago: University of Chicago Press, 1995.

Smith, J.Q. Letter from the commissioner of Indian Affairs to the U.S. secretary of the interior, October 30, 1876. *Report of the Secretary of the Interior,* 44th Cong., 2nd sess., 1876, H. Ex. Doc. 1, Part 5, Serial 1749, III–XXV, NADP Document R876001. In Office of Indian Affairs, *Letters Received by the Office of Indian Affairs, 1824–1880.* National Archives Microcopy 234, Roll 608 (excerpt). Native American Documents Project, NADP Document D1. Available online. URL: http://www.csusm.edu/nadp/r876001.htm. Downloaded on July 27, 2005.

Smith, Page. *The Rise of Industrial America.* New York: McGraw-Hill, 1984.

Sochen, June. *Herstory: A Woman's View of American History.* New York: Alfred, 1974.

Spies, August. "August Spies Defense of the Eight-Hour Movement, 1886." Quoted in *The Great Anarchist Trial. The Haymarket Speeches, as Delivered on the Evening of the Throwing of the Bomb, at Haymarket Square, Chicago, May 4, 1886.* Chicago: The Chicago Labor Press Association, 1886, pp. 3–5.

Stanton, Elizabeth Cady. "The Solitude of Self" address to the Committee of the Judiciary of the United States Congress, January 18, 1892. In *Votes for Women: Selections from the National American Woman Suffrage Association Collection, 1848–1921.* Library of Congress. American Memory: Historical Collections for the National Digital Library. Available online. URL: http://hdl.loc.gov/loc.rbc/rbnawsa.n9898. Downloaded on July 27, 2005.

———. "Untitled Address, published in *Woodhull & Claflin's Weekly,* September 30, 1871." Victoria Woodhull, the Spirit to Run the White House. Available online. URL: http://www.victoria-woodhull.com/wcwarchive.htm. Downloaded on October 6, 2003.

Stone, Lucy. "The Progress of Fifty Years." The Congress of Women Held in the Woman's Pavilion at the World's Columbian Exposition, 1893. About.com. Available online. URL: http://womenshistory.about.com/library/etext/bl_1893_lucy_stone.htm. Downloaded on November 16, 2004.

Sullivan, Mark. *Our Times: America at the Birth of the Twentieth Century.* New York: Scribner, 1996.

Sumner, William Graham. "A History of American Currency, with Chapters on the English Bank Restriction and Austrian Paper Money." New York: H. Holt and Company, 1874. Available online. URL: http://www.hti.umich.edu/cgi/t/text/pageviewer-idx?sid=d3a27df9f1b7d1a18d617cc86c456a27&idno=aeu9382.0001.001&c=moa&cc=moa&seq=227&size=s&view=text. Downloaded on November 12, 2004.

———. "The Conquest of the United States by Spain, January 16, 1899." In *War and Other Essays by William Graham Sumner, ed.* Albert Galloway Keller. New Haven, Conn.: Yale University Press, 1919. Libertystory.net. Available online. URL: http://www.libertystory.net/LSDOCSUMNERCONQUESTUS.htm. Downloaded on November 16, 2004.

———. "'The Rich Are Good-Natured': William Graham Sumner Defends the Wealthy." In *What Social Classes Owe to Each Other.* New York: Harper & Brothers, 1883, pp. 43–57. History Matters: A Project of the American Social History Project/Center for Media and Learning, City University of New York and Center for History and New Media, George Mason University. Available online. URL: http://historymatters.gmu.edu/d/4998. Downloaded on November 16, 2004.

Taylor, John M. *William Henry Seward: Lincoln's Right Hand.* New York: Harper-Collins, 1991.

Tsai, Shih-Shan Henry. *The Chinese Experience in America.* Bloomington: Indiana University Press, 1986.

Tuchman, Barbara. *The Proud Tower.* New York: Macmillan, 1966.

Van Voris, Jacqueline. *Carrie Chapman Catt: A Public Life.* New York: Feminist Press, 1987.

Warner, Sam Bass, Jr. *Streetcar Suburbs.* New York: Atheneum, 1976.

Weinstein, Allen, and Frank Otto Gatell. *Freedom and Crisis: An American History, Vol. 1, to 1877.* 3d ed. New York: Random House, 1981.

Weinstein, Allen, and R. Jackson Wilson. *Freedom and Crisis: An American History, Vol. 2, Since 1860.* New York: Random House, 1978.

Weisberg, Barbara. *Susan B. Anthony.* New York: Chelsea House, 1988.

Woodhull & Claflin's Weekly. Available online. URL: http://www.victoria-woodhull.com/wcarchive.htm. Downloaded on October 6, 2003.

"The World's Columbian Exposition." Chicago Historical Society. Available online. URL: http://www.chicagohs.org/history/expo.html. Downloaded on November 12, 2004.

Young, David. *Chicago Transit: An Illustrated History.* De Kalb: Northern Illinois University Press, 1998.

Zaitzevsky, Cynthia. *Frederick Law Olmsted and the Boston Park System.* Cambridge, Mass.: Belknap Press, 1982.

INDEX

Locators in *italic* indicate illustrations. Locators in **boldface** indicate main entries. Locators followed by *m* indicate maps. Locators followed by *g* indicate graphs. Locators followed by *t* indicate tables. Locators followed by *c* indicate chronology entries.